Boulton Paul

1917-1961

Boulton Paul

1917-1961
Aircraft, Projects and Studies

Les Whitehouse

www.crecy.co.uk

Crécy Publishing Ltd

www.crecy.co.uk

Published by Crécy Publishing Ltd 2021

Copyright © 2021 Les Whitehouse

A CIP record for this book is available from the British Library

ISBN 9781910809488

Printed in India by Thomson Press

Crécy Publishing Limited
1a Ringway Trading Estate, Shadowmoss Road, Manchester M22 5LH

www.crecy.co.uk

Front cover:
The first P.111 prototype being flown by RAE pilots.

The P.92-2 half scale model on the Wolverhampton compass base tried to accurately reproduce the wing and turret blister and the tailplane location, but with large compromises for the engine nacelles and pilot's position.

Rear cover from top:
Model of the Overstrand 1 made from a combination of the author's original production drawings and the drawings of the late Alan W. Hall. *Model and Photo by champion Greek modeller Aristidis Polyzos*

Tunnel model of the P.133 and P.133A.

Main: A rare view of the P.3 three-quarter starboard rear. The image has been digitally corrected since the glass plate was defaced, probably by a careless splash of chemicals immediately after development. Some of the weekly output of B&P Camels are in front of the hangars. Note the very wide rear end (6in) of the fuselage sternpost.

Bottom images from left:
Defiant serial L7012 was a production F. Mk.1 delivered in early 1940 with split colour undersides.

The P.111 at the Farnborough show after refit with a flat windscreen and coloured striping to hide the revised windscreen position. As well as the anti-glare panel, a thinner spray has been used to form three fuselage stripes. *Only known original colour of this finish courtesy T. Panopolis*

Competition Ships Sea Plane.

Front flap from top:
P.108B Sea Balliol T.21 serial WL723 of the Junior Officers Air Conversion course landing on.

B&P submitted this long-range bomber design based upon the P.15. It never received a project number but it had the new rudder system designed for the P.15 in January 1924.

Prior to the P.35 B&P were asked for their opinion of how a COW gun interceptor fighter should be laid out and responded with a side view of a two-seat biplane where the anti-bomber, anti-Zeppelin weapon was served by the crewman. This scheme had no design number allocated as it was simply a discussion piece but a fairing for the cannon was also developed.

Table of Contents

Introduction

WHEN JOHN DUDLEY NORTH was recruited from Austin to become manager of the Aeronautical and Research Department of Boulton & Paul in mid-1917 his first task was to set about the organisation of a system to control the in-house design and manufacture of new aeroplanes. The area known as the aircraft factory itself was already well organised and well respected for its output, but everything so far was orchestrated by War Department documentation and Royal Aircraft Factory drawings and amendments. Since 1915 the manufacture and assembly of the F.E.2b and F.E.2d machines had been ably controlled by Henry ffiske and Stanley Howes, now both directors of Boulton & Paul. They knew that they would remain subcontractors to the war's end, and only by employing someone who knew how to design new and advanced machines could the business continue and expand after the Armistice.

So it was that G. M. Chamberlain and ffiske sought and on 31 July 1917 formally obtained the services of John North from September 1917 'as designer and inventor of aircraft and parts thereof and to carry out experimental tests in connection with new types of aircraft'. His salary was £750 per annum payable monthly, with a yearly bonus of 0.5% on all sales exceeding £50,000 per year. The company itself was already a worldwide household name, having a pedigree stretching back to 1797, when William Moore left his deceased father's farm at Grove, Warham, in north Norfolk, to become an apprentice buyer in the metal fittings trade, returning five years later to set up his own shop in Norwich as a fully-fledged owner. That simple beginning had grown through various names and directors to the enormous four-division manufacturing conglomerate of Boulton & Paul Ltd, with numerous agents overseas including relatives of the ffiske family in Buenos Aires.

North himself was an aerospace prodigy at school age but was unable to attend university because of the sudden death of his father, despite being a promising pupil who excelled in maths and classics at Bedford School and setting up his own aviation group of school pupils. His family were forced to gain an early apprenticeship in marine engineering for him. Nevertheless, his heart remained in aeronautics and, after winning a yearly competition in *The Aeroplane* twice running, the editor was shocked to find his 'expert' was a mere youngster and lowly engineering apprentice. Under pressure from the editor, his apprenticeship was transferred to the Aeronautical Syndicate at Hendon under Horatio Barber and then to the Claude Grahame White concern at the same site. At the age of eighteen, North was both Chief Designer and Chief Engineer of the Grahame White Company after only one joint design with Barber. When he thought his skills were being under-utilised because Grahame White was sticking to government-based orders in small batches and pilot training contracts, he obtained a post at Austin Motors and was responsible for both establishing the company's quantity aircraft manufacture and turning it into a first-class subcontract production facility.

So North came with an impeccable pedigree of early design and manufacturing success. His lifelong friend, Harold Roxbee Cox (Lord Kings Norton), would record many years later that North was steered in his career by his own unerring logic and by a desire to learn, record, apply and re-utilise everything that would promote consistent and controlled safe flying. The result was a financially difficult and relatively modest output of prototype aircraft driven by the events of the time and, until 1937, but a single developed series of bombers outfitting one squadron and a production batch of nine P.9 civil two-seaters. What that hides, however, was a prolific output of proposals, experimental trials and inventions, many of which have been barely mentioned in literature and most of which have never before been accurately illustrated.

By 1934, with Boulton & Paul Ltd deciding to sell its Aeronautical and Research Department, North formed a consortium to purchase it from the agents and to create Boulton Paul Aircraft Ltd., moving the company to Wolverhampton two years later. The airframe design project series continued in sequence. From the initial night fighter, the N.F.I, to the P.148, a low-body height, air-transportable refueller, Boulton & Paul Aeronautical and Research Department and its successor company Boulton Paul Aircraft were always at the forefront of developments. North also devoted much of his time throughout to the various Society of Brits Aircraft Constructors (SBAC) and other committees, which forged better links between the aircraft industry and the Air Ministry on specifications and, post-Second World War, the formation of Cranfield as a centre for excellence in aerospace training. The company branched out into many other areas of aerospace products such as gun turrets, flight control systems and naval systems, and retained subcontract manufacture but always retained its core strength of airframe research and design capability.

This volume documents the projects N.F.I to P.148 and some of the developments that were necessary to improve the designs. It represents almost sixty years of research into the two companies and details many airframe engineering projects that have never before been clarified in any detail.

L. Whitehouse
November 2017

Acknowledgments

MOST OF THE PROJECTS that achieved manufacture are drawn in CAD and all other drawings have layouts that been developed for this volume by the author and remain his copyright. Unless noted illustration and photographic sources are either from the author's collection or courtesy of the Boulton Paul Association.

In a sojourn that has, on and off, taken sixty years it is impossible to acknowledge or even recall accurately to memory all who have assisted in helping the author obtain and collate the information for this record. If I have committed the sin of admission for anyone, then it is not deliberate. In particular, however, I would mention the following dedicated researchers and friends, whose aim was always to seek original sources and document proven information. Their guidance has confirmed and honed my quest for accuracy on many research subjects:

Greg Baughen, Jack Bruce, John Burgess, Tony Buttler, Phil Butler, Joe Cherrie, Peter N. Dent, Ken Ellis, Dave Forster, J. A. Jackson, Alan W. Hall, R C. (Bob) Jones, Paul Lucas, Ralph Pegram, Bruce Robertson, Richard Leask (Dick) Ward.

M. C. Young and H. Monument (Castle Museum and Brideswell Museum, Norwich circa 1971).

Boulton Paul/Dowty staff in particular:

Joyce Bloom (former secretary to J. D. North and secretary to then Technical Director), R. C. (Bobby) Briggs, F. F. (Fred) Crocombe (Technical Director). H.H. (Bert) Dixon, Colin Evans, John Goodier (Managing Director), Dennis Griggs, Dennis Gwilliam, Derek Hammond, Terry Herrington, Raymond Hilton (Technical Director), Jim Hitchcock (Head of Technical Publications), Jack Holmes, Brian Holmes, Charles Vivian Kenmir, Terry & Anne Latewood, Richard (Dickie) Mancus, Colin Morris, Walter (Wally) Prosser, Cyril Plimmer, Ted Reading, Cecil (Ross) Rossington, Peter. E. N. Smith. D. J. (John) Steed, Paul Strothers, Charles Taylor, Joyce Tooby, Ivan E. Utting, John Williams, Leonard (Len) Williams, Don Wilson and G. A. Woolsey.

Mrs D. J. Dunworth, wife of late test pilot Geoff (Loopy) Dunworth David Gunn, son of late chief test pilot Alexander Ewen (Ben) Gunn.

The family of the late chief test pilot Robert (Robin) Lindsay Neale.

The family of the late Robert Fincher.

The family of the late George Marshall (Engine Fitter).

The members and former members of the Boulton Paul Association not already mentioned, particularly the late Jack Chambers and Alec Brew.

The Defiant 'as-built' drawings in particular would not be to such a high standard were it not for the assistance of the staff at Airfix Products and RAF Museum staff at Cosford and Hendon. Similarly for the P.108A Balliol and P.108B Sea Balliol at Cosford.

Finally my long-suffering wife Maureen, who alone committed the photographic log notebooks to a database over a period of ten long months and, together with my daughter Debi, assisted with the packing of the BP Association Archive for safe storage in 2012–13.

CHAPTER ONE

Early Interest in Fighters and Engines – Projects up to P.5 and HN.3

B Y SEPTEMBER 1917, when John North joined as the management head of the newly declared Aeronautical and Research Department, his main interest was in fighter aircraft, which were generally being ordered in large quantities. That month an O/400 bomber order was cancelled in favour of existing Camel contracts. North was faced with reorganising an aircraft department to co-ordinate and develop new designs.

North gathered around him qualified people whom he trusted to support the enterprise: M. Edouard Boudot, formerly of F. G. Nestler, whose HN.1 scout he had admired and seen flying at Hendon; M. A. S. Riach, a mathematician and engineer responsible for designing the propellers at the Grahame White company, who had provided North with a solution for the Austin AFB.1 by modifying a six-unit, thin blade design of his own into two two-blade sections that outperformed all other types tried on the AFB.1 and dramatically increased the climb rate of the machine; and Otto Glauert, a schoolmaster in Norwich and a mathematician, who assisted North on optimum span and wing section transforms, became the chief stressman for a period. Otto was the older brother of Hermann Glauert, one of the most promising experimental engineers at Farnborough at the time with major contributions to aerofoils, autogyros and helicopters. North also inherited the thriving aircraft contract manufacture side run efficiently by W. H. ffiske and Stanley S. Howes.

The internal combustion engine (marine) business, while producing useful war output in small batches for military river craft, was failing because of the lack of trained engineers and machinists,

who were being drawn off into the B&P aircraft factory or taken into government military service. It seemed logical for the board to close the marine engine business as a separate unit and absorb it into the Aeronautical and Research Department.

The N.F.I and M.I

One of the specific problems facing the War Department was dealing adequately with Zeppelins and Gotha bombers over England. They needed a suitable airframe with a means of attacking upwards. The latter was the Eiman mount, which adapted three staggered and angled Lewis guns into a mount set at 45° upwards or more to fire into the enemy at height. They also required more powerful engines capable of operating at and reaching the enemy height quickly, or some form of supercharging to enable the engine to maintain performance in the rarer air. The first project tackled by North's team

This partly covered aircraft trial is the P.3 Hawk airframe test assembled at the Norwich works for government inspectors. It was around this time that the name Hawk was rejected and revised to Boblink.

was therefore an Eiman-carrying aircraft designated the N.F.I. The N.F.I was an aircraft for night fighting aimed at taking out the high-flying enemy. During October/November 1917 the first ideas for the shape of the aircraft came together in early drawings D3 and D4 issued on 17 November.

In parallel with the work on the N.F.I, there was also an idea for supercharging an engine to increase its height performance, so work also commenced on a two-stroke model engine and adaption of the design for supercharging. This test model engine was finally designated M.I. North patented his idea for increasing the height possible with interceptor aircraft as 120480 in November 1918. This was to increase the pressure and flow rate of air fed into the engine by using a separate cylinder to the force air and fuel into the power cylinder(s) supercharging the mixture. He also wanted a two-stroke engine so it produced power on every downward stroke, doubling the power output per minute. North's new engine team were set to work on this 'two-stroke' engine concept, which later became designated M.I.

Within a couple of months the N.F.I fighter, with an initial Hispano-Suiza 200hp inline, was abandoned. There was little interest in North's N.F.I design and the War Department were probably stringing him along to back up possible failure of the Vickers FB.26, which had already flown prior to North even joining B&P, and had then been re-ordered on 19 September 1917 as six redesigned new prototypes instead of the N.F.I. Work continued on the M.I and in 1918 a multiple-cylinder F.S.E.1. The degree to which anything useful was achieved on these is unknown but probably at the end of the war this research faded along with many wartime projects as rotary engines became slowly replaced with better radial and inline. It is not clear if the N.F.I was to be single or two seat (Specifications A.1c or A.2c) as the original drawings have been lost, but also being drawn up parallel with the N.F.I and M.I there was a 'single-seat fighter' allocated the reference P.3 – there was no P.1 or P.2 – and the working name 'Hawk'. It seems unlikely that this curt description would have been used if the N.F.I was already single seat. Many of the components of the N.F.I and the P.3 were identical, in particular the tailplane and fin/rudder. All three projects: N.F.I, M.I and P.3, were started together during October/November 1917, suggesting that the N.F.I and P.3 were likely to be very similar in everything other than power plants and wing area/length. By the end of November 1917, large numbers of components already drawn were absorbed into the P.3 programme or scrapped.

The P.3 Hawk and P.3 Boblink

The P.3 design first drawing views in November 1917 were numbered D9 through to D14 and two plan views were drawn indicating two engine types requiring differing wingspan. The specification sequence was A. 1c and then the all-embracing specification A.1, later revised to the A.1(a) high-altitude fighter. The P.3 was expected to be ordered in a six prototype sequence. Of interest as a day, night or naval fighter, three machines had a projected ABC engine, the Wasp, and three machines the alternative BR(a) – probably an experimental prototype of the BR.1 or 2. Many P.3 components were drawn in detail only to be scrapped and redrawn again as the design progressed. What finally emerged was a rather neat and simple-looking biplane fighter. The company referred to the design as the 'Hawk' on the drawing title blocks. The prototypes were intended to conform to Specification A.1 under AS 37485 in December 1917. The first group was allocated C8652 to C8654 and the second group C8655 to 8657. There has been historical speculation that the first group were project numbered P.5, but no formal P.5 designation was ever drawn and logged by B&P and no drawing records used the number P.5; all were recorded as P.3. From a study of formal government contract records and early drawing

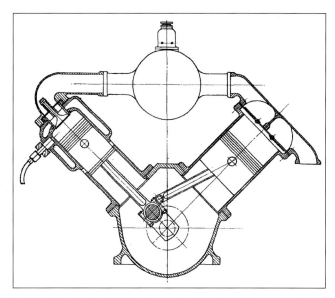

North's design for the M.1 development test engine, which occupied the space of the second project in development. This is part of the drawings by his team for the patent application. The left cylinder is the two-stroke power and the right is the compressor with flap valves to allow air in. A reservoir at the top stores the compressed intake air and feeds it to the power cylinder.

allocations, what appears to have happened was that a handwritten straight-topped 'P.3' was interpreted wrongly as 'P.5'. The aircraft ordered were therefore written in War Department contract records as P.5 when the B&P allocations would not even reach P.4 for another three months. Development of the ABC Wasp engine was protracted, and insufficient prototypes were around to supply all the manufacturers, which could indicate the reason for reallocation of the first three serials to other aeroplanes. Similarly the first P.3 completed, C8655, eventually received not a BR(a) as expected but instead a BR.2; the fourth built.

Well into the design programme, the North/Boudot-inspired name Hawk was suddenly rejected by the War Department around February 1918 to introduce a naming system of birds for fighters but with the first two letters specific to the design company. The first letters now allocated to Boulton & Paul were a very difficult BO. The P.3 had to be renamed Boblink. Between early January and 18 February 1918 therefore the mnemonic title on some drawings changed from Hawk to Boblink and the engine changed from BR(a) to the BR.2 under new spec A.1(a). The manufacturer's installation drawing of the BR.2 engine had been booked into the drawing register on 22 February 1918, having been used to complete installation sketches on receipt of the physical BR.2 example, which arrived late in January. North's team confirmed a 'ready for flight' date around the end of February 1918. The aircraft then moved to Martlesham Heath on 21 February 1918, but the as-built drawing revisions would take time to catch up.

The airframe was similar to the Sopwith designs like the Pup and Camel. Lightness of the wing structure was one of the worries, but it met the requirements for safety factors of eight times the load on the front spar and six times on the rear spar. North also specified jettisonable fuel tanks, so that the main tank and feeder tank, behind the pilot in a fire-treated plywood bay, could be dropped out of the bottom of the airframe if they caught fire – indeed the rounded bottom of the tank system protruded below the fuselage to carry the eventually specified quantity of fuel on the first prototype. The wings were two bay on C8655, the only prototype completed, and used North's 'N' strut jointing, as used on the Grahame White Thirteen seaplane.

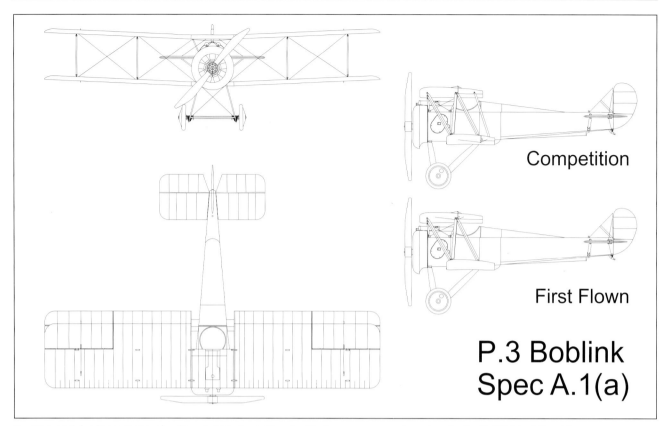

Competition

First Flown

P.3 Boblink
Spec A.1(a)

The P.3 Boblink (earlier name Hawk) as flown in trials. Inset: Aircraft with ailerons on upper wing only as for the first flights at Norwich.

The lower wings fitted to small stub spar sockets with streamlined fairings so that the lower wing halves left large viewing 'windows' downwards between and forward/aft of the spar joints; only centre spar sections themselves passed under the fuselage. Both strut and wing joint fittings were through-bolted vertically into bushed holes on the spars. The upper wing halves were similar in shape but of larger chord compared to the lower and sat level with the pilot's eyes so that he could look both above and below the wing. A gravity tank was fitted in the centre section of the upper plane, which ceased at the wing rear spar, allegedly giving the pilot a very good view from the cockpit in flight. The drawing D127 (dated 20 February 1918), by which time the aircraft was given the mnemonic title Boblink, shows the specified but unfitted Aldis-type sight. The size of ailerons shown by Boudot on this drawing were short chord, not matching any ever fitted to the sole airframe. In the same week the department personnel were drawing wings for two prototype stages: The now BR(a)-engined Hawk to spec A.1 and the BR.2-engined Boblink to spec A.1(a). The former drawing was marked 'for first machine only' and the only difference between the two was the lower wing spar spacing, which was to be 26.5in on the first and 3in more on the later Boblink machines. The difference reduced the lower wing aileron area possible on planned machines 2 and 3. Upper spar spacing on both was 30.5in.

As initially assembled the aircraft had large-chord ailerons on the upper wings only. It seems likely that plain lower wings may have been in more advanced completion and it was deemed expedient to erect the airframe with them to test fly before trials at Mousehold Heath and to keep Air Board visitors happy that progress was being made. The aileron-equipped lower wings with strutted links were fitted after pilots had carried out the first flights and criticised the lateral control. In reality however, the details of the airframe were constantly changing from October 1917 through into February/March 1918 and many drawings that might be termed 'as-built' or new plans were only drawn around its Martlesham tenure. The spar spacing increased by 3in during

the design process and may have indicated the change of fuel capacity between BR(a) Spec A.1 and BR.2 Spec A1(a). This probably explains why the tank stuck out of the bottom of the first prototype tank bay – because it was essentially an A.1 P.3 Hawk fuselage converted to take the diameter of the BR.2 to A.1(a) with a bulged cowling. The span of the P.3 was published at 29ft. A study of the few remaining drawings suggests that this was a stressed span of 28ft 11.5in, ie measured along and in contact with the top of the spars but without covering on prototype No 1. Note that all straight-wing military designs up to P.25 quoted stressed rather than projected span (see Appendix). Unusually, the wings were at zero incidence and trim was provided by the entire tailplane being varied in incidence by a screw jack, which also allowed for the change in trim if the main tanks with frangible links were dropped from the fuselage. This also allowed for variation in engine weights without having to change the fuselage.

In initial formal testing there was little to choose between the Boblink, the Sopwith Snipe and others. The Boblink was heavier and more robust in the fuselage, because the main longerons were less tapered nose to tail as on the Camel. Some reviewers felt each type tried had merit and one report thought the weight of the P.3 lower wing design at only 29lb was much too flimsy. There was criticism of both designs on the ground handling, and the Snipe was chosen as being more suitable for mass production out of the four products compared. This is difficult to fathom when the two key designs are compared since the Boblink is much simpler, suggesting the real reason was the government officers' desire to stick with the previous success of the many Sopwith designs. In hindsight at least two key reports suggest that the Boblink was eventually placed fourth of the four flying contenders. None of the designs met the specified 135mph minimum speed.

Some of the drawings after the first aircraft had been passed over for the Snipe were in anticipation of production orders for a naval variant. Although airframes 2 and 3 were virtually complete, their completion had been cancelled. The sole prototype was modified

P.3 Boblink as first flown at Mousehold Heath with ailerons on the upper wing only. Only well after testing at Martlesham, probably late First World War, was the name spelling revised as Bobolink when the press were publishing details.

A rare view of three-quarter starboard rear. The image has been digitally corrected since the glass plate was defaced, probably by a careless splash of chemicals immediately after development. Some of the weekly output of B&P Camels are in front of the hangars. Note the very wide rear end (6in) of the fuselage sternpost.

partly to the company's original plan for airframes 2 and 3 by replacing the upper centre section with one incorporating tubular steel spars and cast end fittings instead of wooden spars. This scheme was drawn as early as 8 March 1918, leaving an open upper centre section and wing gravity tank offset to port. Modified to this state, it was passed back and forth between RNAS Hendon and Mousehold Heath 18 June to 22 July 1918 having modifications in between. A rounded spinner or 'propeller dome' was also drawn for the machine in June 1918, but there is no confirmation that it was ever fitted.

Throughout its testing life until rejected, the aircraft on trials was known as the Boblink; the change to the spelling Bobolink was only made later in providing information to the press. Drawing D140 for the tailplane layout was stencilled 'BO BO LINK' instead of

'BOBLINK', by mistake. The standard nomenclature report for the month the machine was returned to the makers on 15 March 1918 finally stated: 'On account of the decision that the design represented should not go into production the registration of the name Boblink has been cancelled.' The other two prototypes remained as part-assembled, near-finished components since their completion had been cancelled on 9 April 2018, and they stood in the workshop as sub-assemblies into 1919.

Horn-balanced rudder at Martlesham. The machine is now unarmed and has a straight angled upper cowl aft of the bulged BR2 ring cowl. The centre section of the upper wing is open steel tube with an aerofoil section-profiled tank offset to port.

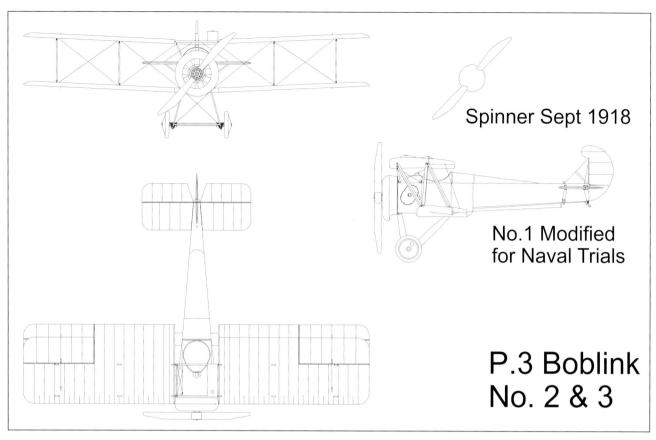

Spinner Sept 1918

No.1 Modified
for Naval Trials

P.3 Boblink
No. 2 & 3

The Boblink following the addition of a horn balance rudder and cable-linked ailerons. The centre section of the aircraft has been replaced with an uncovered steel tube frame to leave the entire upper centre plane open other than a header tank, which has now been moved to the port side. The configuration is as tested by the Admiralty. Shown without weapons, the bulged cowl for the BR.2 is clearly seen in the side profile.

P.8 'Atlantic' being built, with fuselage mock-up behind. However, of particular interest is the second or third prototype rear fuselage of the P.3 Boblink standing on a box and without a fuselage serial. Behind and to the rear above is an experimental tubular tail boom and tailplane test piece, probably for the two-seat boom tail aircraft of September 1918, which was not allocated an official project number.

P.4

A parallel project, P.4, existed only as a provisional GA, drawing D144, dated 11 March 1918 and may actually represent the naval version of the P.3 (Spec N.1a). As with some of the later projects up to P.30, details were not retained by the company and a copy of this general arrangement drawing (GA) has not been found. The potential alternative is that it was possibly a redraw of the HN.3 (see below).

P.5

The P.5 has always been something of an enigma. As stated in the section on the P.3, not one drawing designated P.5 was ever logged or produced, so like the P.1 and P.2 the designation appears at first sight not to have existed other than to complete some internal or external researcher's need for a full sequenced list produced years later. With the Admiralty list and contract list appearing to wrongly allocate P.5 Hawk to the P.3 Hawk design and with any other formal correspondence potentially copying this, the company decided to simply skip the use of the designation P.5 on a new project to avoid further confusion. The problem with conflicting designations between B&P and the War Department was not uncommon (see later P.7 series). Other than in government contract records therefore the designation P.5 never existed.

HN.3 Fighter

Around the time that the P.5 designation was being withheld, another potential design was being looked at, probably unofficially. When North employed Edouard Boudot as draftsman/designer he brought with him the ideas and a drawing of the Nestler HN.3 fighter, which he had been working on. (The only two known Nestler designs in the 1960s were HN.1 and HN.2, according to historian Jack Bruce, the latter only being known in correspondence). A side profile of his 'HN.3 Biplane Scout' was booked into the received drawing register on 25 June 1918, probably after he had left the company (The B&P allocation was 'received drawing' reference number 71, the original drawing had Nestler reference 3043). A wind tunnel model seems to have already been made to scale because it was photographed stored under the wind tunnel and therefore there was perhaps no need for a formal and registered B&P drawing for the machine at that stage. The model had a BR.2-size engine cowling and the upper wing sat on the fuselage, giving the pilot a 360° view of the upper hemisphere. As originally designed it had a single interplane strut at mid-spar position. The model suggests a very small lightweight fighter was intended when Boudot was designing for Nestler and he had a tunnel model made from this drawing for testing in the B&P tunnel.

Nothing more seems to have happened with this project because suddenly Boudot was either sacked or headhunted by the Grahame White factory. Boudot left B&P and moved to work with Claude Grahame White after the P.3 was rejected by the Air Board, producing the GW Ganymede at Hendon from around July/August 1918. The HN.3 design and ideas taken with him morphed again post-war into the Boudot-designed Grahame White GWE-6/6A 'Gentleman's Sporting Aeroplane' with smaller cowling diameter and a less powerful engine. The visual difference between the Boulton & Paul wind tunnel model and the GWE-6/6A was that Boudot employed North's pre-First World War 'N'-style interplane struts on the GWE-6A and the smaller less powerful engine diameter produced a visual gap between the upper wing and the fuselage on GWE-6 K150, which was not there on the B&P wind tunnel model. The GWE-6A K153 and a second 6A shipped abroad had this area filled in. So Boudot appears to have got his basic HN.3 design built in the end, but at Hendon with North's old mentor.

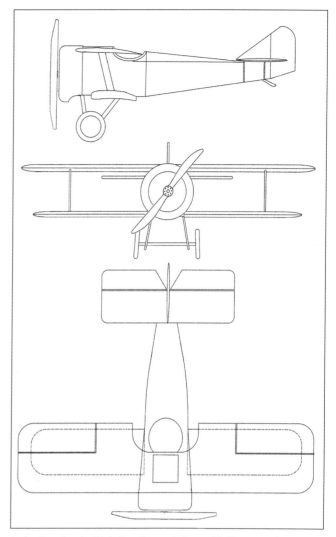

At the time that the P.5 designation was being avoided because of government error, another design was Boudot's small HN3 fighter scout, which he had already drawn up before joining the company. No drawing numbers for the P.5 were ever allocated and the scout was abandoned when Boudot left so that work could concentrate on the more promising P.7.

The NPL 4ft 'Wind Channel' completed during 1918. Note the models under the trestles. The glass plate for this one was snapped in two and a print has been digitally repaired.

CHAPTER TWO

P.7 Bourges Fighter-Bomber

A DEPARTURE FROM the B&P range of single-engine machines occurred with the P.7 project. Here North set about designing a twin-engine, multi-role machine that would fit easily into any of three new government specifications being planned, when they were formally issued. RAF specifications Type IVa, VI and VIII called for a photo-reconnaissance machine, a short-distance day bomber and a long-distance day bomber respectively. Testing of the RAF 15 aerofoil cross section for the P.7 started in April 1918. The machine was intended to have the new ABC Dragonfly I radial engine, which was being ordered in large quantities but consisted at that time only of a limited number of production units. In the pressure to have a new war-winning engine, the untested design had no prototypes. North's team referred to the P.7 design as a fighter and believed that it could be made as manoeuvrable as a fighter. That belief was noted by the Air Board Technical Department, who also referred to it variously at first as a fighter or fighter-bomber. All known detail drawings of the P.7 stated 'Fighter' in the 'Type' box on the drawing outline and data boxes. For the fighter attack or defensive role it had an armament of four Lewis guns as pairs in two standard ring mounts, one in the nose and the second in a rear dorsal location.

Technically, the initial design was for a stressed 54ft span (53ft 11in projected span uncovered), 37ft-long aircraft with the engines mounted just above mid-gap in tractor mode. The upper wing was larger than the lower, having an 8ft chord upper with 6ft 6in chord lower. The rear fuselage cranked upwards aft of the wing trailing edge so the machine sat at a wing incidence of 17.5° when static. This gave the rear gunner better sighting conditions under the tailplane. It was to fly at an upper wing incidence of 2°, plus an engine nacelle with Dragonfly engine down thrust of 1°. Stagger to the wings was 3.6in. The three design cases could be met with the minimum of changes since the only differences at that stage were in the amount of fuel required to be carried and the provision of either camera or bomb load, or both in each case. The company employed RAF 15 section and stressed for the maximum loading.

With the Dragonfly engines initially unavailable, North was forced to revise the planned nacelles to take other engines. The American Liberty and the Bentley BR.2 were two known contenders schemed. The 45° vee inline Liberty was moved down within the interplane gap to where it was supported by four angled struts like the Dragonfly, but set in a vee up to the top plane. The simplest change was if the 230hp BR.2 was employed and the Bentley BR.2 rotary engine in circular cowlings forward of the nacelles was chosen. The nacelle diameter and mounting plate was selected to transfer flow from the engine body and lower cylinders with the upper

Because of the lack of engines the P.7 first prototype was completed as the P.7A Bourges IIA with the same rear engine nacelle design but Bentley BR.2 engines in larger First World War-style cowlings. The performance was impressive on F2903 partly because of the choice of open back cowling.

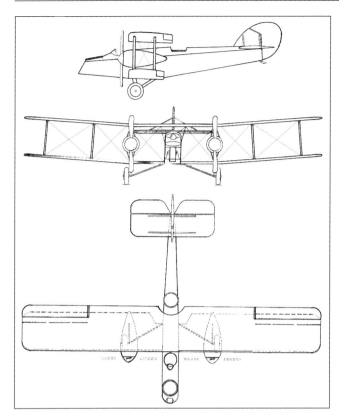

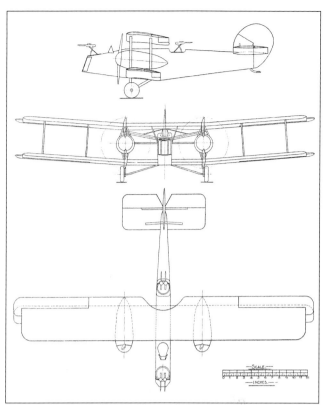

The initial study of the P.7 twin-engine fighter being developed to RAF specifications IV, VI and VIII for reconnaissance, short- and long-range bombing. This is likely to be drawing C.45 dated 15 May 1918 rather than the later C.45X dated 8 October 1918.

For an omnibus testing regime of various constructor's models by the government B&P submitted a wind tunnel model of the P.7. This was a hybrid, consisting of an IA wing and a IB 10° vee tailplane with the original mid-gap Dragonfly engine nacelles. Because the report authors were not familiar with the steep rear fuselage angle of the P.7, the drawing has a false assumption of horizontal that gives the impression of high wing incidence and up thrust on the engine nacelles.

cylinder cooling air exhausting straight from the cowling annulus and expanding over the nacelle surface, the cowling was therefore thought to add an amount of thrust to cater for the lower-power Bentley engines and represented North's first investigation into what would eventually be known at B&P as anti-turbulence cowls and finally by the later pure marketing description Boulton Paul Townend Rings. A crew of three with front and rear gun positions was envisaged. A camera hatch in the rear fuselage and an internal bomb load were employed. North patented a design for loading the internal bombs into 'cells' or loading pre-filled 'cells', then winched and carried in the lower fuselage, plus a second design for a fabric 'shutter' that could be used to close off the underside of the bay while in flight to maintain clean airflow. The bomb cell design and the shutter received patents 125270 and 129161 respectively.

What was also significant but not generally known even today was that all the fuel tanks on the P.7 Bourges design were self-sealing for protection of the crew and airframe in the event of combat damage. By late May 1918, at 54ft stressed span the wing areas of the design were estimated to be 416sq ft upper wing and 322sq ft lower wing. For weight calculation, however, the company hedged its bets and worked all weights on a 57ft-span aircraft. The stressing for the basic aircraft was approved for flight in June 1918 but further work was added when the firm were required to restress for cases where the flying wires were cut (eg: by bullets or flak). As early as May 1918 a Lion-engined machine was also being investigated. Initially this had a very odd wing revision with an increased wing area on the upper wing and a reduced one on the lower (450 + 315) for a total of 765sq ft, suggesting a 57ft span upper wing and perhaps some miscalculation from the person using the plan-o-meter on the lower.

Three machine serials were allocated as prototypes to test out variations to the three specifications. Spec IVa was a reconnaissance

machine with maximum fuel and a camera but no bombs. Spec VIII had no camera and a reduced fuel load but maximum bombs as a day bomber. Spec VI had no camera, a reduced bomb and fuel load as a short-range day bomber. Completion of the three had been staggered when it became obvious that planned engines would be slow in appearing and others would have to be substituted. Serials F2903 to 2905 were issued against contract 35A/909/C.730 ITP dated 24/25 April 1918, with F2903 being the first completion with Bentley rotaries because of the lack of Dragonfly units and therefore redesignated P.7A Bourges Mk.II. The three prototypes were not completed in the planned form for the three RAF specifications as time went on. Several variations had been investigated on paper while F2903 was being worked on. Because a new design of cowling was possible with the Dragonfly, figures were optimistic with this engine nacelle. Then the model Dragonfly nacelle was tested with the addition of interference flow from the wings above and below in the B&P tunnel. The team found that the wing slot effect above and below the engine was adverse to the value of drag of the nacelle tested alone, a complete surprise compared with the BR2 version, which had not been tested that way. North wrote to the War Office on 6 June: 'At 100ft/sec the drag from the nacelle alone was a 28.7lbs, but with the slot effect of the wings this has increased by 75% to 50.2lbs in accepting the turbulent flow from the exposed engine cylinders passing through the slot … the result, of course, has a detrimental effect on performance predictions'. It was found, however, that it was possible to improve the situation in the future if the planned 40in diameter dragonfly nacelle was moved into contact with the lower wing and faired to reduce the interference drag, with the top wing influence now too far away.

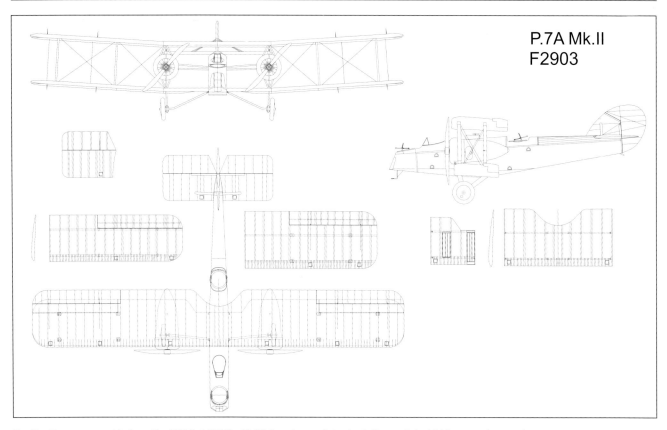

P.7A Mk.II
F2903

The first Bourges assembled was the P.7 Mk.II F2903 with BR.2 engines and standard ailerons. It had 54 ft stressed-span wings.

Conversion of F2903 to Dragonfly – the original Mk.1A design. The machine also has the first of the balanced ailerons fitted, which B&P called 'flapped ailerons'.

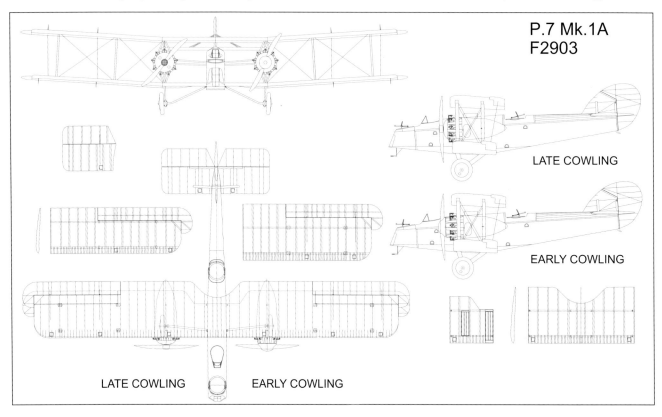

P.7 Mk.1A
F2903

LATE COWLING

EARLY COWLING

LATE COWLING   EARLY COWLING

In the meantime, the design was utilised in another North idea to improve the field of fire for both of the upper gun rings on his fighter by drooping the centre sections of the upper wing to mate with the fuselage, and also to give the tailplane 10° of dihedral. The tailplane dihedral allowed the rear gunner an even better field of fire under the tailplane. As there was now less official interest in the mid-gap layout, the drawing for a Liberty version was released from its secret status and part traced as the patent drawing for North's drooped wing

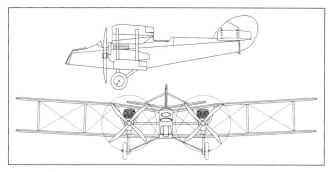

Two specific engine types were studied as temporary replacements, the BR2 rotary and the American V-12 Liberty. This is a sketch of the direct-drive 400hp Liberty variant, which was initially shelved but used as a model to submit drawings patenting North's drooped centre section and vee tail. The 10° vee tail was retained but the wing droop was correctly 14° on the second Bourges Dragonfly prototype. Here the droop angle appears to match that of the tailplane because of the design having a larger span.

Loan engine for study by B&P clearly shows the narrow vee of the Liberty and a Liberty 1 data plate. Note, however, that the War Department could only supply an engine on a temporary basis for measurements and the unit loaned is in an exhaust configuration for a pusher aircraft. This is the rear end of the engine. From this scale models were made for wind tunnel testing.

patent 125864. The engines in this patent still showed the now defunct mid gap installation and an approximate 10° tailplane and upper centre section angle, although the small drawing was eventually distorted by the patent tracers. This Liberty version also seems to have an extended wingspan and may have been the first of the designers approximately 62ft 6in 'optimum span' project designs.

It was decided in September 1918 to complete F2904 with the engines on the lower wing upper surface and a drooped centre section – the top plane centre section being removed and the upper wing inner halves drooping at 14° to the fuselage in line with North's idea. The structure was also restressed entirely for the use of Grade B spruce in production as Grade A was now unavailable in such quantities. This time the machine was to fulfil the RAF Specification VI for a short-range day bomber but with photographic capability, so it retained the bomb bay shutter and camera port, but also seems to have had a second smaller tactical camera installation at the bottom longeron on the port side of the nose. This improved airframe layout was allocated the designation Bourges Mk.II in correspondence by the Air Board. The company had preferred to define each wing layout depending on if it had a normal wing (design A) or a drooped centre section (design B). Hence the second prototype, the P.7A Bourges II F2904 was strictly a Bourges IIB according to the Air Board once the drooped centre section was decided upon, while the first prototype F2903 was a Bourges 1A. The company itself objected

strongly to the incorrect designation Bourges II internally because they had already used the designation for the BR.2 engines. To avoid design designation errors internally, the company therefore religiously avoided the designation Bourges II and called F2904 the Bourges Mk.IB. Annoyed with the Air Board choice, each original correspondence received from official (Air Board or War Department) sources about their Bourges II had the numeral II struck out in pencil and Mk.IB substituted upon letter or document receipt before it was circulated internally. As far as B&P were concerned, F2903 was a IA design once fitted with the Dragonfly and F2904 with the same engine would remain a IB. The conflict between Air Board and Company designations for project number/letter and Mk. number results in confusion by historians even now. As with the P.3, the company avoided the incorrect government designations by simply ignoring them, while deliberately reducing in detail how they described the machines to outside officials.

The first prototype when refitted with Dragonfly engines as the P.7 Bourges 1A. The horn-balanced ailerons were converted in the cheapest way – by a triangular addition to the tip at the rear and by revision/recovering of the aileron and tip.

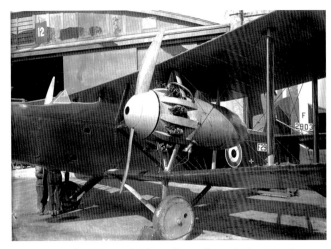

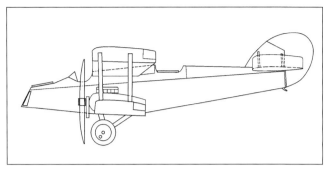

Sketch of the Puma engine machine allocated Mk IV by the company but never built.

Close picture of P.7 Bourges 1A shows the cowling and spinner for the Dragonfly. Although it performed well when the engines worked, the team had already discovered disadvantages of the uncowled cylinder design flow when fitted at mid-gap. The spinner was also unsatisfactory for cooling.

Changes to prototypes to improve aileron action involved the introduction of horn-balanced ailerons on the Dragonfly models, and although mooted, a decision was taken not to apply the V-tail idea to the first IA prototype at that stage. These changes increased the overall span to 57ft 3.36in stressed and 57ft 2.4in projected at the aileron tip. While B&P were continuing with the detailing of the first and second prototype Dragonfly fit, they were also working on the P.7B Bourges Mk.IIIA and IIIB, which was the redesign of the structure to take the Napier Lion engine above the lower wing.

Into the mix the Air Board Technical Department asked them to look also at the Siddeley Deasy Puma engine, which ABTD referred to in stressing documents and correspondence as 'Bourges IIIA & B with Puma'. This machine was assumed to be the answer to a combat aircraft to meet both Specifications IVa and VIII, ie for photo-reconnaissance and long-range bombing, if the redesigned Dragonfly IA engine failed. The Puma, which was originally to be replaced by the Dragonfly, seems to have been well favoured because of the large manufactured quantities immediately available.

Government pressure was applied for B&P to get all the stressing for this machine approved as soon as possible 'so that all is ready to start should the design be ordered into production'. Even ten days after the Armistice it was expected by both B&P and the Air Board that the currently unbuilt Puma-engine machine was close to a large production order. Sadly, that order failed to be signed. Instructions to complete even a Bourges prototype with Puma engines failed to appear. Since the Lion engine was the Bourges Mk.III, the company again ignored the Air Board designation 'Bourges III with Puma' and

applied the name Bourges Mk.IV. In addition, with the receipt of Liberty engine drawings, in September 1918 they retrospectively allocated their crude Liberty Bourges sketch the designation Mk.V. Development work on the use of metal for spars for the Bourges went ahead right at the end of the war, development for what was known as the 'V' type wing being ordered under 35A/1747/C.1857 allocated Job No 330 and the basic Bourges under 35A/1748/C.1858 allocated Job No 329.

Finally, B&P were instructed to bring the IIIA and IIIB series work up to date based upon the Lion engine, and with this engine fit as the Bourges Mk.IIIA or Mk.IIIB the now defunct Air Board Puma version was theoretically shelved during 1919. However, internally, small details and improvements were still being allocated as Bourges IV as late as July 1922 in the hope of resurrecting the type for sale elsewhere and conversion of one of the prototypes. Work on the P.7B Lion-engine Bourges Mk.III was allocated the Bourges F2905 airframe, which was to be revised as Mk.IIIA format with normal upper wing centre section to new specification D of R Type III. In fitting the P.7B with the Lion the design of as many parts as possible from the P.7 Bourges Mk.I were retained but the fuselage had to be lengthened and the engine area/centre span redesigned.

The P.7A Bourges Mk.II (BR.2) F2903 had been erected in skeleton form for Air Board inspection early in August 1918 and approved, but flights were delayed by the insistence in September that it be restressed and approved for the use of Grade B spruce. It first flew officially in early 1919 in the hands of the eminently capable Frank Courtney and proved that even with its low-power engines it was an exceptional machine, capable of being rolled and spun with ease even with one engine shut down. As stated, the P.7 aileron shape had been changed almost immediately with the introduction of horn balance ailerons to improve roll control, increasing the stressed span by 3ft 3.36in to 57ft 3.36in. The original projected span of 53ft 11in became 57ft 2.4in. The P.7 Bourges Mk.IA (Dragonfly at mid-gap) also reconverted from F2903 first flew in May 1919, proving itself

P.7 Bourges 1B had the Dragonfly moved to the bottom wing and Type B drooped centre section, which is explained well by this view. The outer wings are identical to the Bourges 1A.

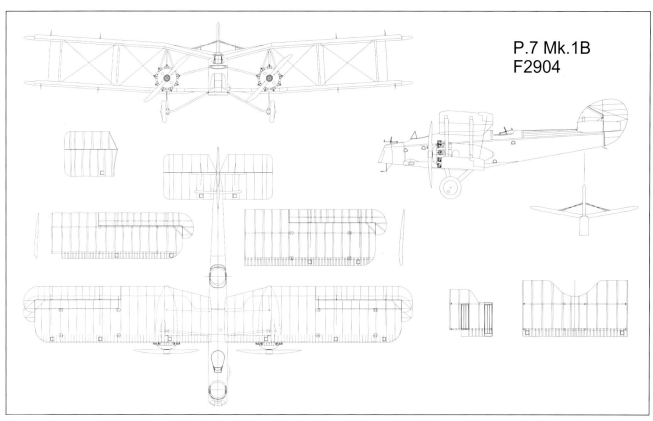

P.7 Mk.1B
F2904

The second prototype, F2904, designated P.7 Mk 1B with Dragonfly units above the bottom wing. B&P patented centre section droop and vee tailplane gave enhanced arcs of fire for the gunners. Flapped ailerons had become the norm.

F2905 was later contracted to utilise Lion engines on an improved structure. By keeping the outer lower wing layout identical to the Mk 1A it was eventually necessary to add 56in to the centre section to accommodate the Lion powerplants at the original thrust centres of 15ft and include revised strutting outboard. To recover fore-aft balance, a 30in parallel-sided bay was inserted at the tailplane position. In this form it became the P.7B Bourges IIIA. Note the revised non-standard twin gun ring design.

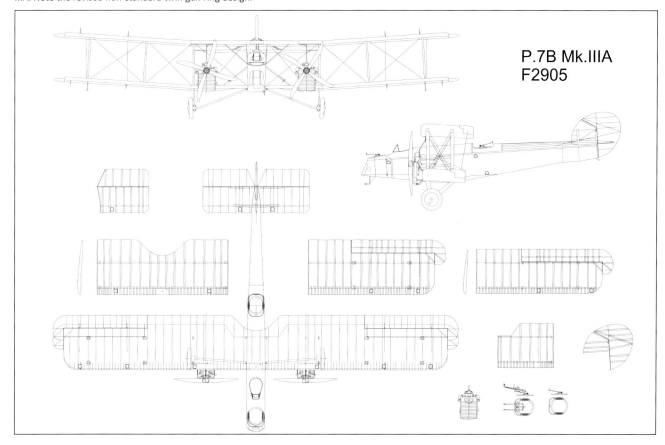

P.7B Mk.IIIA
F2905

also manoeuvrable on the increased-power engines and achieving 124mph. The employment of full 'soup-plate' spinners enclosing the Dragonfly engine body was not as successful as expected, giving poor airflow through the engine body area. This was changed so that the frontal cowling of the nacelle formed a similar shape but with four circular piercings to allow better amounts of cooling air to pass through. Courtney flew the modified Dragonfly engine Bourges IA to Hendon, demonstrating its aerobatics in front of the crowd at the flying reception for Commander Read and the USN crew of the Atlantic crossing team on Saturday, 31 May 1919, the first time it had formally been seen in public. In July 1919 the machine went to A&AEE Martlesham Heath for testing of its engines and sample propellers, undergoing various tests until September 1920.

The second aircraft, having finally got the Air Board approval to complete it as a 'Vee' wing with improved defensive layout, was modified as the P.7 Bourges Mk.IB using serial F2904. The undercarriage had to be raised by 4in to take the lower engine position, altering the angle on the ground. It unfortunately crashed in October 1919, nosing over on to its back at Mousehold Heath. The wreckage was purchased by B&P to salvage parts and to study which parts failed in the crash.

The third aircraft, F2905, was also part-completed as a Mk.IA and then changed and completed as 1B prior to the eventual decision to convert the whole airframe as the new P.7B Bourges IIIA. The loss of the second prototype at Mousehold prompted the move to abandon Dragonfly aircraft and to concentrate on the Lion engine. Development may have been delayed but it had flown sufficiently by July 1920 to issue for trials, when North urgently telegrammed the Director of Research on 24 July to send a pilot to collect the machine by Monday the 26th. Eventually fitted, the Lion engines, though powerful, were heavier and, placed upon the lower wing, the centre of gravity and centre of pressure changed. During redesign, with the engine weight being moved forward (propeller centreline

13.75in forward of the P.7 Dragonfly machine, 31in forward of the lower plane leading edge and thrust line lowered to 10in below gap centre) the tail moment arm was deemed unsatisfactory in design calculations. Since the airframe existed, the C of G balance of the machine was restored in the simplest way: by the addition of a 30in extension to the rear fuselage length. The fuselage to the last bay was retained as before but the last bay was moved back 30in and a new parallel-sided bay inserted so that none of the existing cross sections of the truss-work had to be altered. As redesigned, the large-chord upper wing now still had the same stagger and the interplane struts were approximately vertical when the wing was at 2° incidence and the engine thrust line at zero. By holding the engine centres at 15ft and retaining four-blade propellers, the inner wings had to be extended to take interplane struts outboard of the nacelle. Retaining the same outboard lower wing size as the original two prototypes, this brought the P.7B Bourges IIIA or B up to a stressed span of 61ft 4in and a projected span of 61ft 2.6in uncovered. The struts outboard of the engines were at 18ft 10in centres and the wing joint at 19ft 8in. The redesign allowed the company to experiment with their steel spars within the wings. The P.7B also had the long undercarriage of the P.7A and adjustments to the wheel track with the undercarriage moved slightly outboard for good taxying ability on rough fields, so the undercarriage struts coincided with the new interplane strut location for strength. Performance was exceptional for the time but still considered limiting at 130mph in either Wing A or Wing B form, with similar manoeuvrability to the earlier models. It also met the long endurance requirement, achieving almost nine and a half hours. The main performance restriction was noted to be the drag from the rectangular radiator, which was slung under the thrust line just ahead of the lower wing leading edge at right angles to the airflow. The violent aerobatics to which this machine was subjected at Martlesham caused some movement of the new design upper wing structure, resulting in extra drag struts being fitted before air pageant displays

Third prototype F2905 revised as the P.7B Bourges IIIA. The bottom outer wing panels were identical to those on the 1A and 1B but moved outboard by the centre section revisions.

F2905 appeared in many variants starting with IB and IIB, to IIIA (here), IIIB and IIIA again as the engineers sought to find the ideal layout. However, it was the IIIA version that was recorded on camera.

were allowed. This prompted the later reported conversion of F2905 to a IIIB in 1921. A chance to modify the aircraft to represent a Puma-engined type was finally abandoned as the aircraft was then revised back to IIIA and remained at the Royal Aircraft Establishment (RAE) for testing until June 1924. The Puma engines, which had held such promise at the time of the Armistice, remained in the Experimental Department prototype workshop unused and covered in dust sheets.

A final P.7, the P.7E, was schemed as the preliminary arrangement of the 'New Bourges Mk.VIA' in July 1922. The aim was to propose a Bourges aircraft type with more and improved metal structure to meet the latest specification, probably B.30/22, as a night bomber. Although similar to the basic Bourges, the introduction of all-steel structure resulted in so many basic detail differences that the machine became ever closer to the P.15 layout, a prototype for which had been ordered as early as July 1920, and finally was developed instead into the stubbier P.25 Boulton Bugle to cope with new rules on fuel storage and night operations. Both the P.15 and the P.25 were, however, constructed as completely new structural designs and given unique project numbers.

Summary of B&P Design Options over the 1918 to 1922 period (B&P Designations):

P.7 Bourges IA and B Twin 320hp Dragonfly Thrust line 0.25in below the centreline between upper and lower front spar centres for IA and IB but later reverted to above lower wing for IB at 21in above lower spar centre. Prototype IA had 1° of down thrust on the entire nacelle and engine so that at the prop centre 27.5in forward of the front spars the thrust line was 0.83in below the front spar centres. Lowering the engines on the 1B meant that the lower inner wing leading edge had to be cut away to take the engine body. Note that a wind tunnel model of IB had 1° of up thrust as tested. Another later tunnel model conversion had a vee tail on a IA wing. Wheel centres for IB dropped 4in below IA. Standard twin Lewis Scarff ring.

P.7A Bourges IIA Twin 230hp BR.2 Thrust line 0.25in below the centreline between upper and lower front spar centres as a IIA and had 1° of down thrust on the entire nacelle and engine passing through the front spar centres as above. Initially without balanced ailerons. Direct ejection of heated air from the rear of the cylinders over the smaller nacelle diameter and oil loss drained out of the bottom by holes in the lower cowling. Standard twin Lewis Scarff ring.

P.7B Bourges IIIA&B Twin 450hp Lion Engines above lower wing. Thrust line 28.5in above the front lower spar centreline, propeller centre axis 30.5in front of lower front spar centre, increased stressed span by 56in and length by 30in. Wheel centres dropped for the 1B were retained in this design. Special new twin Lewis Scarff ring.

P.7C Bourges IVA&B Twin 290hp Puma Engines above lower wing, increased span and lower wheel centres.

P.7D Bourges VB Twin 400hp Liberty Engines initially centre interplane but design abandoned before the airframe layout was formally given a drawing number. This designation was later applied retrospectively for completeness and redrawn further for discussion as an alternative to the Puma.

P.7E Bourges VIA Twin engines, Possibly Lion or Jupiter. Only the VIA was drawn up as 'New Bourges' in a single scheme drawing now lost.

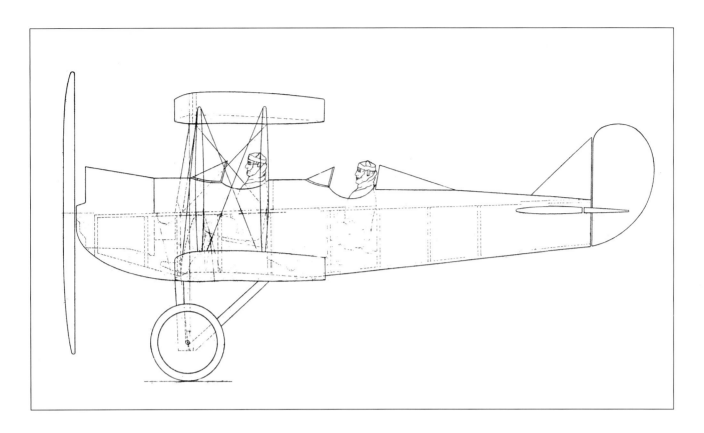

CHAPTER THREE

Early Civil Designs P.6 to P.11

P.6 Project

NORTH WANTED TO TEST wing sections and aircraft models, but also to fit an airframe with their tested wings in full size. The machine needed to be able to revise outer wing sections for differing profiles to prove that the company 4ft NPL wind channel results approximated the full-size wing. With six prototypes expected for the P.3 Hawk design it was thought at first that there would be ample airframes to borrow one and use it for test wings. However, only the first machine would appear in a set format for trials. The part-completed units were held in abeyance and then abandoned. With the P.3 Boblink reduced to a single machine, the alternative was to build, at their own cost and risk, a simple machine to accommodate the changes in section. Such a private venture (PV) project was forbidden unless it was approved by the Air Board. The request was successful and the machine design was given the serial X25. Work on the aircraft was allocated the shop floor Job No 315.

The first GA of the P.6 was D150 in March 1918 and was roughly dimensioned in a sketch as a projected span (P-Span) of 25ft, 4ft 9in upper centre section and 3ft projected overhangs on the upper wing, so the interplane struts were 19ft apart. The undercarriage copied that from the P.3 with identical track. It was extremely simple in layout and designed to use many surplus components already in production for the Sopwith Camel manufacture or left over from the uncompleted P.3 prototypes, the wing design being almost identical in structure to variations of the P.3 series. A two-seat biplane with an RAF 1A engine so familiar to North when at Austin, the aircraft was completed right at the end of the war and was never tried with alternative wings. On 20 May 1919 the P.6 was allocated K-120 and then G-EACJ under the new civilian marking scheme but its civil aircraft registration was not taken up because although advertised for civilian sales at £600 it failed to attract a buyer.

The machine had a 5ft chord and gap to the unstaggered wings. Overall length was set at 19ft and height 8ft. As built, the main wing struts were moved inboard from the tips along the main spar until they were now 42in from the tips in the final design measured along the spar surface. Tail span was 11ft and the 100hp RAF 1A gave it a top speed of 103mph at 1,000ft on a specially modified propeller. A 20.1 gallon tank gave an endurance of 2.37 hours (ie a decimal result, following Air Ministry precedent in recording data). Landing speed was 45mph. The all-up weight (AUW) was 1,725lb and the empty weight 1,100lb. The airframe was eventually broken up into parts.

The P.6 initial scheme by Boudot was unfinished but shows the pilot in the rear cockpit sitting slightly higher than the passenger and having a large headrest. It ignored War Department stressing convention and had projected rather than stress span dimensions on a sketch under the side profile.

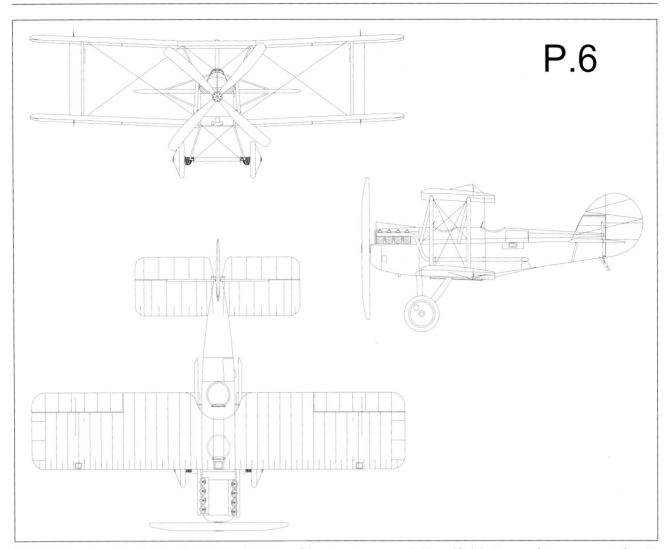

P.6

The P.6 full-size wing section test aircraft serial X.25 as built. Some of the outer wings were probably modified abortive manufacture components from P.3 prototypes Nos 2 and 3. Seating positions have changed and there is no headrest. There is a faired blister over the cine camera on the port rear fuselage.

The imposing gloved and muffed up figure standing in the middle is Department Manager John North.

P.6 at Mousehold Heath when marked with adverts and used for sales trips by company officers.

P.8 Atlantic and Passenger Variants

In early 1918, confident that at some point the war would end, North committed his team to come up with a civil airliner based upon the ideas for the P.7 Bourges. B&P were sending stressing data for approval of the Ministry of Munitions of War, Air Board Technical Department, as early as May 1918, since there was no civil controlling authority operating in a similar manner. The initial concept was a 'P.7 Civil' with a revised passenger fuselage but drawings for this and for additional fins on the tailplane surfaces had the type reference later

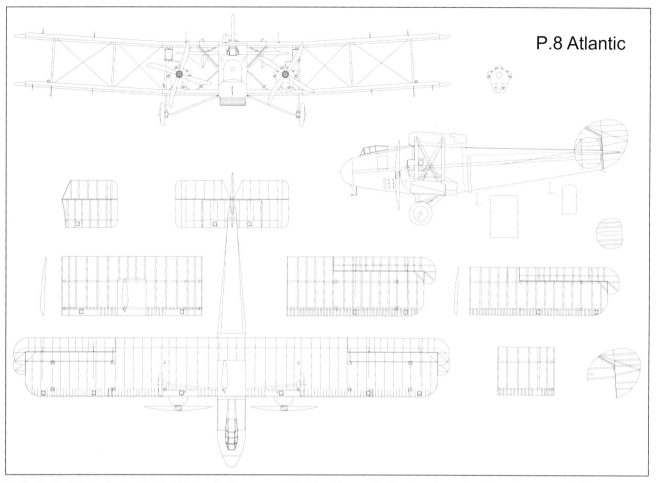

P.8 Atlantic

The final as-built design for the P.8 'Atlantic' aircraft, a longer-span P.7B style with a new fuselage based upon the widened P.7 truss and additions above. Reported span varied from 59ft to 61ft. However, study of the manufactured aircraft proves an identical span for both prototypes as rolled out.

altered from P.7 to P.8 in the records. The company tried to purchase one of the P.7 prototypes for conversion but were turned down. The pilot sat in the normal open cockpit in the nose and passengers could be carried just forward of the wing leading edge and just aft of the trailing edge in glazed areas on the schemes. In order to accommodate them in comfort the fuselage in those areas would reach up to the top wing. To maintain the original fuselage frame, passenger access steps would be needed at airports so that they stepped over the upper longeron of the original frame to enter the seating area and the whole above it formed carriage-style sides and roof. In addition to the pilot three passengers were planned in the front cabin and four in the rear. The initial schemes and artist's impressions by Geoffrey Watson showed incomplete ideas of the best way to present the cowled engine and nacelle. It was based on the streamlined rear nacelle of the P.7 Mk.IA/IB being moved nearer the bottom wing and then faired in by extending the lower portion to touch the bottom wing upper surface. The four-blade propellers then had the 'soup-plate' Dragonfly P.7-style spinners completing the frontal streamlining for the Lion engines. Engine cooling was via a retractable under-fuselage radiator. A mock-up of the fuselage of the machine was built in the works and development on the shop floor was allocated under Job Nos 348 and 371, with a prototype and a production series of six airframes planned at the same time. The machine design continued in parallel with and similar to the P.7B Bourges IIIA, having initially suggested a 796sq ft design of 58ft span in November 1918. This wing area was arrived at by simply adding 4ft to the original P.7 stressed span of 54ft.

A serious revision in the prototype machine design came when the B&P board decided that it was an ideal opportunity to showcase

their work and the reliability of the design by competing for the *Daily Mail* prize for the first aircraft crossing of the Atlantic. Since 1913 the £10,000 prize for the first crossing in either direction had been held in abeyance by the war. The Atlantic machine work was allocated Job No 354. In order to obtain the range it meant a requirement to carry 800 gallons of fuel in six tanks within the fuselage spaced around the position of the main wings. In an emergency the total fuel load could be dumped in 1.25 minutes through ejection piping. It was calculated that at full power a single Lion engine would be capable of holding the aeroplane aloft after two hours of fuel had been consumed, so that the engines could be throttled as far as half power after that period if required. One engine out performance and directional trimming was helped by the ability to clamp the control stick and operate via control wheels to maintain a predetermined course. The control wheel method by which this could be achieved was patented by North under patent 129781. It should be noted, however, that this was a purely mechanical pilot set device and not an autopilot. Extra finlets above and below each tailplane half could be set to reduce the pilot's load as well. A communications radio and a navigation (D/F) radio were to be fitted and a crew of three were to be accommodated in the nose. Mindful of the weather that might be encountered en route, the open pilot's position was soon revised to an enclosed canopy, but the side windows at the radio position were left unglazed for navigation sightings and to read engine instruments on the external wing struts.

Maintaining the basic structure of the Lion P.7 truss in side profile, only lengthening the horizontal fuselage bracing from side to side, meant that the new upper fuselage consisted of merely unstressed

The wood and canvas mock-up of the intended P.8 airliner showing the windows fore and aft of the centre-section fuel tanks for passenger areas. Lower right are two unused SD-Puma engines for the Bourges IVA variant, which was not ordered, and the incomplete forward structure of one of the other P.3 prototypes (Machine No 2 or 3) with open tubular metal upper centre bracing giving better vision above. Bulged P.3 cowl for BR.2 bottom left.

fairings. Being a new-build fuselage, the odd straight section applied to the P.7B penultimate bay was not needed. Where the prototype machine differed from the original illustrations was the lack of passenger areas (taken up by extra fuel tanks), the new pilot's canopy and the more developed engine mount and better fairings. Because of the heavier fuel load, the wing surface increased in span a number of times from the initial 58ft to 59ft and finally to at least 61ft according to publications of the time. Taking the P.7 weight estimate at 57ft span and replacing the centre section of the Mk.I with the new Lion centre section requirement (identical to the P.7B) suggests how the press arrived at a span of 61ft in their illustrations late in 1919. Ultimately the two prototypes placed in build had the span being developed for the P.7B of 61ft 4in since the 'Atlantic' prototype had to carry the enlarged fuel load and the second prototype was under build to the same standard before the Atlantic attempt was cancelled. Small supplementary water radiator matrix units were added to the circuit in front of the inter-plane struts outboard of the engine, sitting below small upper leading edge water tanks. The main water header tank feeding these and the fuselage radiator sat offset above the upper centre section.

Since this was a civil venture, it was possible to release some of the details of the original scheme to the press. Typical of the company, however, which was used to avoiding giving out military data, the dimensions were never given with absolute accuracy. Random figures were rounded or approximated, leading to differences in various publications as the design progressed. Maj. G. ffiske travelled to Newfoundland to survey possible sites to operate from and, as with the Alcock & Brown Vimy, the decision was made to ship the machine across the Atlantic and reassemble it there for a west to east crossing. Two machines were placed in staggered manufacture, the Atlantic attempt to be completed first ready for the best weather to attempt the crossing. Flight approval was delayed when some structural rigging was deemed under-strength, but Report A1101 dated 15 May from Mr Hayward to Maj. Bramwell confirmed that the aircraft was perfectly satisfactory for both first experimental flight and production. Hayward reported from his visit that the machine seen was erected in skeleton form for the fuselage and tailplane and similarly for the wings up to the engine bay, (ie the outer plane joint).

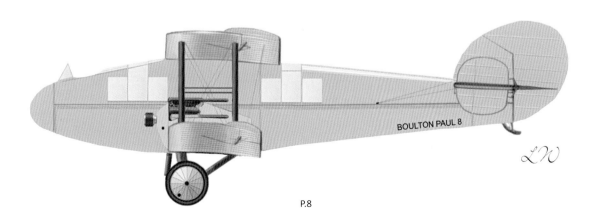

P.8

The 'Atlantic' machine after fuel blockage and engine failure on its maiden take-off.

As-built of second prototype G-EAPE. However, when the production design was advertised at the Paris Salon the proposed wingspan had been reduced to 60ft 4in.

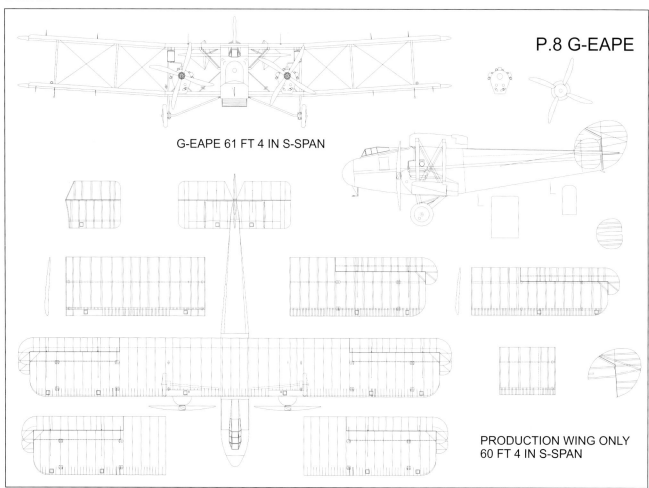

P.8 G-EAPE

G-EAPE 61 FT 4 IN S-SPAN

PRODUCTION WING ONLY
60 FT 4 IN S-SPAN

The same month other events took a hand. From 8 May to 30 May 1919 a US Navy NC flying boat team flew a circuitous route with numerous stops from Massachusetts to Plymouth, England, making the first successful crossing. With the BP aircraft finally ready during late May–early June, Frank Courtney was to take it on its first test flight, witnessed by officials. Courtney was carefully running up the engines and checking everything for taxying out on to the strip at Mousehold. The most senior government official, however, had a set time by which he had to leave to obtain his train back to London. Mindful of this, and with increasing frustration, the managing director finally insisted that the group must see the machine fly immediately. Setting off to the end of the runway, the engines seemed operational,

An illustration by Watson of the planned six production P.8 aircraft before the decision to take on the Atlantic. Only the first two were completed and neither in this configuration.

Second prototype G-EAPE after completion outside the last bay of the factories of the Mousehold Heath 'Old Aerodrome' across the Salhouse Road from the actual flying field of the time. None of the four remaining aircraft planned were completed.

but as the machine gathered speed on take-off a fuel blockage occurred and one engine cut so suddenly that the asymmetric power caused the aircraft to ground loop and shed its undercarriage. The shock broke off the nose immediately behind the crew. Fortunately, having only fuel for a short test flight there was no fire. Courtney and his engineer were able to be brought out of the wreckage relatively uninjured, but the machine was wrecked.

Work was accelerated on the second machine, but way before it could be ready others were in frantic attempts to achieve the prize. It was the Vickers team with Alcock and Brown who managed to cross non-stop the 1,890 miles between Newfoundland and Ireland in just under sixteen hours on 14/15 June 1919. Without the prize to win there was no point risking further expenditure and the second P.8 reverted to its role of proving the design ready for civil production. P.8-2 was completed in October 1919 without any passenger accommodation,

but otherwise correct in form to the same span. Under the Paris Convention it was registered and finally marked G-EAPE after this was approved on 6 November 1919. However, the production line of four more machines was destined never to happen. The machine survived into 1920 and was then broken up. The true span of the P.8 'Commercial' in the company's own sales literature raised in anticipation of the Paris Salon in December 1919 states 60ft 4in. Most likely the four remaining production models were to have a reduced span to improve speed. The only published speed of the P.8 is an originally estimated speed (149mph) since no machine had flown at that time. Because the P.7B itself only achieved 130mph it is likely that the expected performance and/or handling was not achieved during Mousehold flights of the P.8-2. With other designs in the offing the project was quietly abandoned because of cost overrun and lack of interest by potential purchasers.

P.9 Stock Machines

The production decision for a number of P.9 machines was taken at the same time as the P.8 series. The single P.6 design had attracted no purchasers, but there was a potential enquiry from a Lt Arthur Leonard

Long for an improved machine with better load capability, which he wished to purchase with his deferred wartime pay. It was decided that the design of the P.6 would be revised and upgraded so that a stock quantity of nine aircraft would be progressed through the manufacture

Lt Long's P.9 photographed with the propeller and forward cowl of the P.6 temporarily mounted for testing while awaiting new manufactured items.

The P.9 private aircraft (enlarged from the P.6 design) also showing various insets of the integral portmanteau suitcase or cargo system fitted on the rear decking.

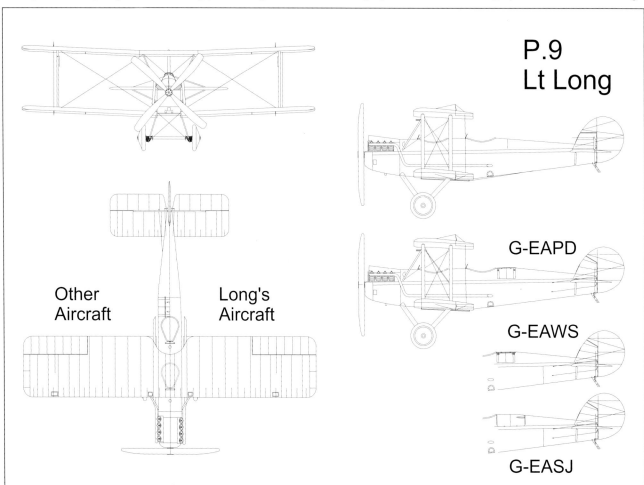

The initial company demonstrator of the P.9, serial G-EAPD, later sold to Australia with its portmanteau system on the rear decking.

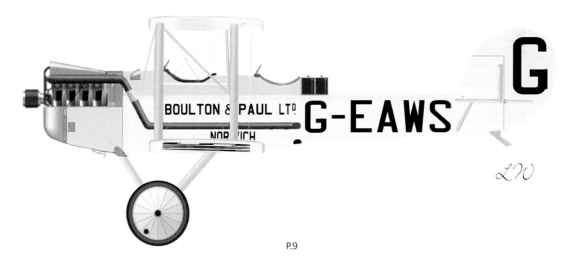

P.9

shops as Job No 367. The wing area was increased by an increase of span, chord and gap and the length of the fuselage was increased. Long's aircraft was the first assembled, representing the prototype. In order to test fly this first airframe early it was fitted and photographed with the nose cowling and the propeller from the P.6 itself while the production items were being made. The four-blade production propeller was cut down from a larger unit to 9ft 3in diameter. Long had the machine shipped to Australia and eventually travelled across to Hobart, where it was reassembled. He made the first aerial crossing of the Bass Straight to Australia on 16 December 1919.

The revised design, still in traditional wood and fabric, had a P-Span of 27ft 6in and 5ft 6in chord and gap. The overall length was 24ft 8in with a tail span of 11ft 2in. A speed of 104mph at 1,000ft was achieved and the larger span allowed it to land at 42mph. a twenty-four gallon tank gave approximately three hours' endurance at full power, although this could be stretched by cruising at a lower speed. The AUW was 1,770lb and empty weight 1,214lb. A design for a metal rib for the P.9 did not proceed since the idea was transferred to the P.10 machine. Similarly, a suggested design for a fully corrugated metal test wing to be fitted to one of the P.9 machines was also not built.

The full total of nine aircraft were eventually made, including the Lt Long P.9 prototype, all others with change of fin/rudder, controls and an integral 'suitcase' system on the rear decking.

P.9-1 G-EAPD: Had a single strap open suitcase bay and was eventually sold to Australia. Possibly the aircraft purchased by Clement John ('Jack') De Garis in June 1920, marked on fuselage as 'Sun-raysed'.

P.9-2 G-EASJ: Various owners and end in South Africa. Had metal cover option over suitcase deck.

P9-3 G-AUBT: To Australia open suitcase option with double straps.

P.9-4 G-AUDB: to Australia. Rear decking design unknown.

P.9-5 G-AUCT: To Australia. Rear decking design unknown.

P.9-6 G-EAWS: B&P. Used to teach B&P employees to fly. Open suitcase option with two straps.

P.9-7 G-AUCP: To Australia.

P.9-8 G-EBEQ: Retained in the UK from a cancelled Australian order. Had metal cover option over suitcases as completed.

P.10 – All-Metal Frame Light Aircraft

While North's team were looking at penetrating the post-war market of civilian sales with the wooden-structure P.8 and P.9, they had also been mindful of the lack of Grade A spruce and the possibility of eliminating wood almost entirely from the structure of aeroplanes. Development of nickel steel in minimum thicknesses as a structural element had been studied as early as the P.3 Boblink and would see great component improvements by the time of last of the P.7 models.

The P.10 all-metal and plastic structure light aircraft exhibited at the Paris Salon 1919 to high acclaim.

North wanted permission to display his P.7 Bourges at exhibitions abroad. The machine was considered much too advanced to be shown to potential enemy countries, so exhibitions in Paris and Amsterdam were refused. Choosing an alternative to display, which would be easy to ship abroad, the P.10 design was just such an 'outside the box' concept and it was a striking contrast to a more regular civil light aircraft reflected in the P.9.

The P.10 revision of the P.9 general proportions and performance for a light aircraft employing all-metal structure and resin plastic fuselage panels to produce a unique design using a simple three-cylinder Lucifer engine.

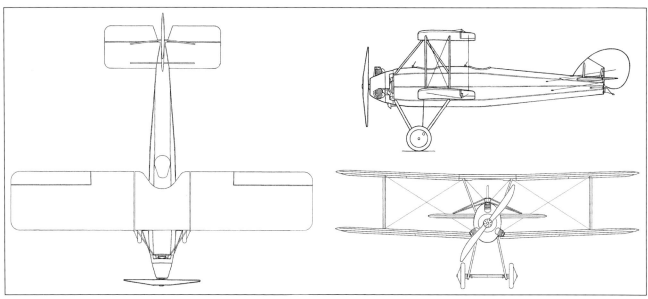

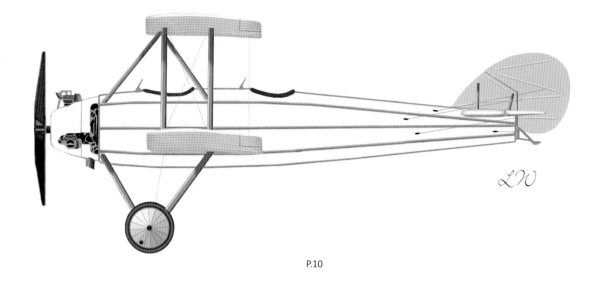

P.10

The P.10 was therefore manufactured as a light tandem two-seater to demonstrate steel structure and plastic covering. In contrast to the P.9 and all current designs, it had a fully oval fuselage section. The forward bulkheads were oval pressings in steel spaced upon four tubular longerons. The aft structure was of hoops of steel and rolled steel sections. Instead of either wood or fabric covering, the spaces between the stringers were filled with plastic sheets. The material was based upon Bakelite-Dilecto-like panels, a moulded sheet product produced by the Continental Fibre Company of Newark, Delaware. A phenolic process was used to develop a resin varnish from purchased Bakelite powder. This varnish could then be used to impregnate either paper or other fillers such as asbestos or sheet fabric to produce Bakelite-Dilecto or Continental-Bakelite, which latter used paper as a filler. This thin moulded material was interposed and riveted between the longitudinal members to form the external fuselage skin. A rounded fin was built into the tail. The wings, ailerons, tailplane and elevators all followed standard wooden practice except that they were all constructed in high-tensile steel with B&P rectangular format and rounded corners to the outline. The ribs retained the current standard of RAF 15 section with the wing chord and the interplane gap being the same as the P.9. There was no stagger in the wing positioning and external rigging was by Rafwire with internal by stranded cable. Power was to be provided by a 100hp three-cylinder Cosmos Lucifer engine held in tubular steel engine mounts and cowled except for the cylinders. Taper bolts and pins allowed the entire engine and cowling to be swung to port so as to access the rear of the engine without having to disconnect services and electrics. The whole was a direct comparison to the conventional P.9. A similar 104mph at 1,000ft was predicted for 1,700lb AUW and 1,104lb empty. The Lucifer engine was to drive a four-blade propeller having a diameter of 7ft 6.25in (but a two-blade item proved easier to ship to Paris for the show). Fuel gave an endurance of 3.75 hours at 100mph and five hours at 90mph at 3,000ft. The P-Span was 30ft, length 26ft and height 12ft, the unstaggered wings were of 5ft 6in chord and 5ft 6in gap. The display at the Paris Salon achieved its aim, becoming the talk of the show from construction aspects. There is no record of the wings ever having been covered or that it flew and there are no fabric or dope remnants on the surviving wing or tail section relics in Norfolk. Even the Lucifer engine was probably a shell model (Job No 374) for the uncovered airframe display, to back up the dual-language English/French sales leaflets given out. Despite the glowing accolades in the press, no one was interested in purchasing such a revolutionary machine design.

P.11 Twin Lucifer Private Venture

The P.10 and P.11, had consecutive job numbers 377 and 378 respectively. Job No 374 was allocated to the construction of a model of the Lucifer engine to aid the project designs. A shop floor job list states that the P.11 was an all-steel, two-seat biplane driven by two Lucifer engines. The fact that the P.11 was multi-engined is doubly confirmed by the issue of drawing C113 on 30 September 1919 for the model shape of the P.11 *engine nacelle* for wind tunnel testing.

The P.11 stuck to the proven box-like fuselage with radial engines mounted similarly to the early P.7 series, simply replacing wooden framework with formed steel. The mid-gap engine nacelles with large interplane gap ensured better ground clearance for the propellers and the square box fuselage meant that the machine could be balanced by seating the two crew side-by-side in the nose, providing the pilots with an outstanding field of view of the forward hemisphere. The innovative machine was intended to have engines with an accessory drive gearbox system at the rear. The two geared Lucifer engines were to be linked together by a cross shaft running from the rear of each nacelle so that both propellers could be run from a single engine if one engine were to fail. In addition a gearbox above the fuselage carried a spur shaft down into the fuselage to drive an electrical generator. The twin-engined concept meant that the P.11 was not only to balance the engine output automatically, it planned to have power to generate additional services. North was eventually to patent his linked engine/gearbox concept using the P.11 as the example in the patent model drawings, which is how we have some idea what the aircraft looked like. The patent discussed the ideas of multi-engine safety by linking a number of engines to the propellers, the linking of additional engines buried in the fuselage or the back-driving of accessories such as large electrical generators buried in the fuselage.

Falling back to the dimensions of the Cosmos Lucifer engine in scaling the sketch fragments, the machine was larger than the P.10. The fuselage now had enough width for a side-by-side arrangement with reasonable wheel diameters on the undercarriage. The fin and rudder remains a conjecture. However, since the front fuselage keel and rear fuselage keel and stringer angles were identical to those employed for the P.12, a smaller P.12-style tail has been assumed in the reconstruction. P.12-style balanced surfaces have been shown, although they could equally have been normal style as the pilot would not have been called upon to fight against engine torque in the event of one engine being shut down.

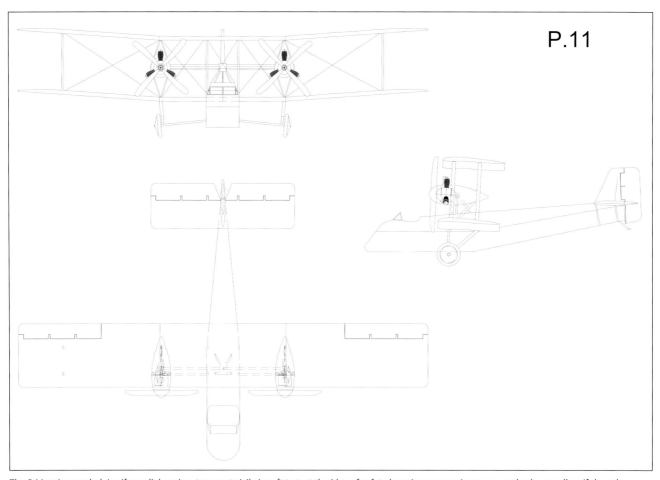

P.11

The P.11 twin-coupled, Lucifer radial engine, two-seat civil aircraft to test the idea of safety by using one engine to power both propellers if the other failed. The tail is a suggested reconstruction as only illustrations of the side (less tail) and the front elevations are known. The front propeller front elevation has been corrected.

The P.11 was destined not to be built. It may well have been a taster for discussions that led to the P.12. However, B&P could not finance both P.10 and P.11 privately. The end of the war was generating a potential major financial slump, which was to come to a head two years later (1921), affecting all departments of B&P. A further factor mitigating against the P.11 was probably the interest that the Air Ministry had shown in the very concept, which led directly to a chance for two larger and much more advanced P.12/P.12As. Not only did this contract make the construction of a P.11 unnecessary, it also placed the company in a difficult position where the very secret developments they were proposing could be compromised if the P.11 were to be shown *sans sécurité* in Britain or at Paris.

However, there were other stumbling blocks that were also a problem. B&P experience with rotary and radial engines to date was that they were right-hand tractor propelled. Only the inlines for the P.6/P.7/P.8 were LH. The drafted patent sketches for use of four-bladed propellers for the P.11 drew RH tractor blades on the port wing. However, the Lucifer was left-hand tractor in operation. What was left out of the patent was a further innovation to run the port engine RH and the starboard engine LH – removing all torque effects in flight and making it even easier and safer to fly. During 1918 and 1919 the Lucifer's design was due to the now famous engineer A. H. (Roy) Fedden, but the design rights passed variously from his initial employers. With development efforts concentrating on the much more saleable Cosmos Jupiter, such changes probably meant that little cash or time was available from any source to advance either of the P.11 engines or the P.11 gearboxes. This was particularly so for an engine structure that might have to be produced in LH and RH versions and be de-selectable through its mainshaft drive

systems and gearing, while still allowing propeller rotation! The P.11 project had everything stacked against it.

Approximate Dimensions of the P.11

Span (Projected):	46ft 9.6in
Span (Stressed):	46ft 10in
Dihedral:	4° (outer panels only)
Wing Incidence to Keel:	3°
Engine Incidence to Keel:	3°
Main Chord:	7ft
Span inner planes:	14ft 5.75in
Engine c/c:	14ft 2.5in
Gap:	6ft 9in
Stagger/Sweep:	None
Wheel Dia:	31.2in
Section:	RAF 15
Props:	RH tractor port, LH tractor starboard: 8ft 5in actual
Length:	31ft 3.8in (this length is based on an aesthetic guess since the tail layout is conjectural)

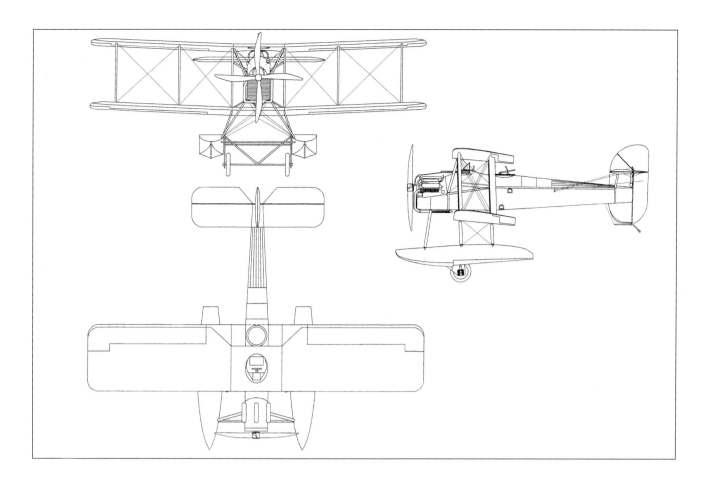

CHAPTER FOUR

The SSP, the All-Metal, Twin-Engine Machines and Metal Bourges

Competition Ships Sea Plane

A NEW BIPLANE requirement to RAF specification XXI was for a shipboard fleet reconnaissance aircraft. Boulton & Paul drew up a front and side elevation for a multi-bay biplane powered by a Napier Lion engine with large nose radiator. The two views of the proposal submitted were oddly numbered 'DWG No 1 RAF Type XXI – General Arrangement Side Elevation' and 'DWG No 2' RAF Type XXI – General Arrangement Front Elevation'. All calculations were done under documentation titled 'Ship Sea Plane' (SSP). The SSP mock-up was contemporary with the P.7 V-wing F2904, so it fell into the design period around the P.7 and P.8. A hint at the explanation lies in a listing of shop floor job numbers where the design is listed as Job No 373 and titled 'Competition Sea Plane Mock-Up'. There was a competition for this specification where the submitted designs were to be unidentified as to the designer/company in the first round.

A complete full-size mock-up was constructed in wood and fabric, together with a four-blade, glued-up propeller blank from B&P/Howes manufacturing stock. This mock-up was an official order using contract sales order number A.2779. Just inside the floats was a conventional undercarriage, but this appears to have been arranged so that it could be raised and lowered to operate as an amphibian or it was dropped after launch from the carrier or turret platform. The fuselage sat between the wings spaced on struts and the Lion engine meant the crew were placed high on the fuselage upper decking with a single forward firing machine gun. The second crew member acted as an observer/rear gunner with a single Lewis gun. There was a large upper and smaller lower fin profile with a full-length rudder. Although the drawings were drawn originally to large scale they were photographed and thereby reduced to glass plate size for printing and circulating. The surviving drawing plates did not have size information listed but the bending moment diagram calculation for the wing spars gave a total structural span (S-Span) along the spars of 40ft 4in. The inner centre

A reconnaissance floatplane with wheeled launch. The pilot sat under an oval opening through the upper wing and the gunner utilised the cut-out in the trailing edge to improve his field of fire. Alighted the aircraft was to three-point by using the fat lower fin as a tail float and the reinforced lower rudder for waterborne steerage.

This view illustrates how the pilot would 'hook on' to the ship's crane through the circular opening in the wing centre.

Side profile with the take-off undercarriage fitted.

section was 5ft 1in span and the outer wings had a dihedral of 3.5°. This gives a true projected span of 40ft 3.2in, which equates well with the competitors' designs at approximately 40ft. A large inter-plane gap of 7ft was applied.

It had a number of unusual features such as very large ailerons on all wings, a thick floating lower fin and rudder plus an oval cut-out above the pilot so that he could hook hoisting strops from the centre section spar positions to the ship's crane. For stowage on board ship the wings folded to the rear with all the struts on the outer panels and the horizontal tailplane was situated above the fuselage on the fin so that the wings passed above and below when folded to lie fully parallel

to the fuselage. Although there is no performance data surviving one would expect a speed of about 110mph from the design.

The company felt that they had a good chance and were receiving positive feedback and encouragement. Work started on drawing up the steel spars intended for the wings in anticipation of further work under the contract. However, a final prototype or production order was not forthcoming. The two aircraft types produced to this specification were the Fairey Pintail and the Parnall Puffin. It seems likely that the design would have been also encouraged as a private venture, but the SSP did not proceed beyond the mock-up and the metal spar design drawing allocation.

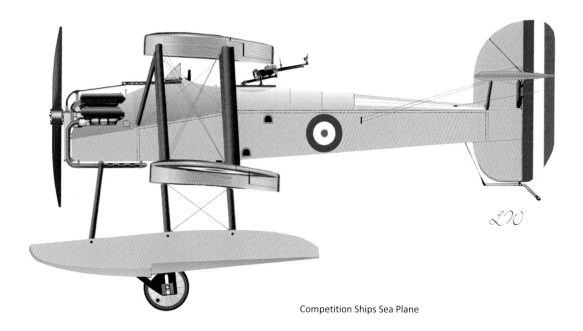

Competition Ships Sea Plane

P.12 Bodmin

Faced with the details of the Boulton & Paul P.11 schemed in mid-1919, the Air Ministry saw an aircraft where multiple engines were connected together to drive the propellers and to drive other accessories within the fuselage. A logical variation was the fitting of the engines (or additional engines) within the fuselage either working alone or also driving propellers on the wings. North's patent was No 154776 relating to multi-engine flying machines of this type. Other constructors, notably Bristol, had looked at fuselage-mounted engines for various projects. However, the transmission systems were not well thought out and problems with them meant nothing had flown. In the meantime, Boulton & Paul had schemed a machine to D of R Specification 3 as a long-distance photo reconnaissance aircraft having fuselage-mounted engines as an alternative to wing-mounted Lion variations of its P.7 Bourges reconnaissance fighter. The source of the suggested town name 'Bodeicre' remains obscure to this day and it may just be a corruption by the local Norfolk dialect. The fuselage layout followed closely the angled fuselage shapes intended for the P.15 development of the P.7 Bourges, but the two 450hp Lion engines were mounted in tandem within a special engine group in the upper fuselage. The engine radiator and power train system was ingeniously designed so that it provided additional stiffness to the drive trains, which then drove four propellers. The forward propellers had two blades driven from the front engine and the rear had four blades driven from the rear engine, to produce a matched output on a smaller diameter that fitted within the wing gap. Propeller rotations were handed and changed hand between fore and aft groups so that there was no offset in torque overall. To achieve this Napier had to change the front end of the engine housing and a gear train.

Specification 9/20 was raised for this type of design and issued to Boulton & Paul as a designated civilian 'Postal' aircraft, although the design retained crew positions that belied its original intention since a second specification was almost immediately issued for conversion of the design to military use. The first schemes to these specifications were being drawn as the P.12 and the P.12A in June 1920. The designator P.12A was drawn first, suggesting that this was the military photo-reconnaissance version, followed consecutively by the P.12 for the civilian version. After some deliberation with the Air Ministry also suggesting that covering with corrugated sheet in the manner of Junkers in Germany might be pursued, the two machines

were ultimately ordered and formally acknowledged under 305919/20 dated 16 August 1921. The delay meant that the P.15 Bolton was then being constructed in parallel and had actually been ordered first. The Air Ministry accepted the English town name Bodmin. The first, serial J6910, was the civil P.12 'Postal' and the second, J6911, was fully kitted out for military load with gun positions appearing fore and aft, internal camera and parachute crew systems as the P.12A. The fuselage section was designed around the need for a forward gun position in the nose and a mid-upper position giving maximum view and field of fire over each side and down to the rear using North's patented shape.

The main structure was of formed nickel chrome steel strip and plate as with the P.15 Bolton, which was then covered in fabric in the normal manner. The locked joint system had not yet been invented for forming the longerons as tubes and the fuselage longerons instead were formed from two strips of pressed plate. The basic plate formed a three-quarter circle section with flanges and the flanged closing one-quarter circle was bolted or riveted to it, forming a circle section with two flanges along its length. Where struts were to be fitted the closing one-quarter circle was omitted over a set length and an angled plate fitted instead to take the strutting and the rigging cable end fittings. For the spars the strips were shaped to provide stiffness in the manner of the experimental spars used on the P.7 Bourges late models. The jointing used a folded seam to strengthen the edges, which was then riveted along its length. For additional stiffness the centreline of the spar had spaced hollow tubular rivets joining the side webs together at set intervals. Some tubular struts were formed into a circular section with butting folded edges and then reinforced with bands at set intervals. Pierced, punched, edge folded, or stamped sheet steel formed other less-loaded items in the structure. Parts of the fuselage upper were formed with limited sheet panelling with stamped or pressed in longitudinal corrugations, but avoided potential confrontation with any Junkers patents by not attempting full corrugation, which was unnecessary and would increase the weight. In various presentations to the Air Ministry and his peers North predicted a weight saving of around 10% minimum, rising ultimately to 20% compared with traditional wooden structures. Only a small number of details were formed in light alloy. The result was a large multi-bay-winged biplane with six fuel tanks and six radiator sections that could be independently

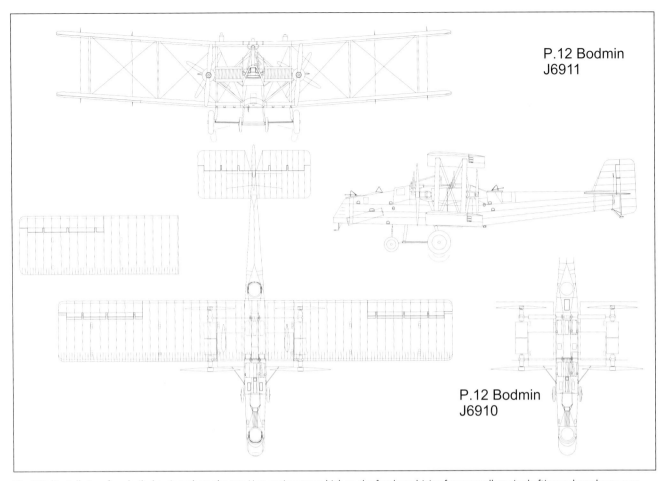

P.12 Bodmin
J6911

P.12 Bodmin
J6910

The P.12 'Postal' aircraft as-built drawing where the two Lion engines were high on the fuselage driving four propellers via shafting and gearboxes was allocated the official name Bodmin. The secondary illustration for J6910 shows the open gun ring locations and details the engines and transmission with the upper wing removed, as well as the BP leading edge balance ailerons. As completed.

The first prototype P.12 'Postal' machine was outfitted as a civil aircraft. This photograph has been digitally repaired from an original broken glass negative.

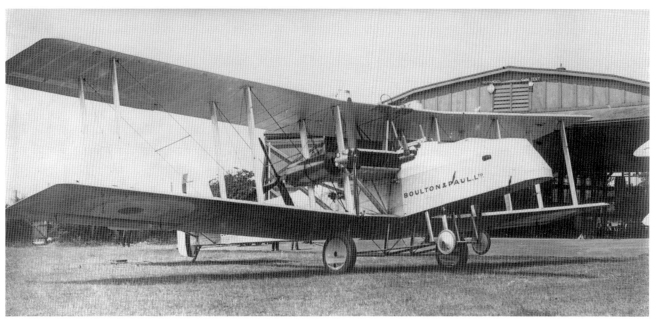

Another view of the first prototype outside the hangar. Just visible to the right are the wing tips of the P.25 second prototype. Reports of large military aircraft nosing over on landing, and the loss of the P.8, resulted in some ideas to prevent this with both the P.12 and the P.15.

controlled to shut off damaged areas. Individual engines could be shut off in flight for maintenance and four main fuel tanks were built around the drive shafts for the propellers. These fed a gravity tank above the upper wing centre section with a second tank available should one gravity tank be damaged. Control surfaces used the B&P-developed, leading edge-balanced, ailerons. For landing the main undercarriage used oleo spring struts with small outrigged wheels forward to prevent nose over. Engine exhausts were fitted with special slotted fir tree uprights and were bolted together.

July 1922 saw the P.12 first prototype to the civil specification rolled out for test flights. During the maker's retention period it was rebuilt with modifications to overcome inevitable transmission problems. A&AEE had it for testing but it survived only until 11 February 1924, when its undercarriage collapsed

during taxying owing to hillocks and unevenness on the Heath. The machine was struck off charge in June 1924. The second prototype, built to the military specification 11/20, first flew on 8 July 1925 and moved to A&AEE on 13 August 1925. It also had a short life, it was hardly flown and was judged to have a heavy rudder control. Despite the general success of the prototypes, it was decided to concentrate on the much simpler conventional layouts in development.

The maximum performance of these large 70ft structural span machines was 116mph at 10,000ft, falling to 112mph at 15,000ft and a service ceiling of 102mph at 16,000ft. Climb to 6,500ft took 8.9 minutes. To 10,000ft 16 minutes and 35.5 minutes to reach ceiling. Length was 53ft 4.5in and AUW 11,000lb.

Sometime believed never to have never been photographed, the second prototype P.12 was a fully equipped military aircraft as the P.12A and was drawn up immediately before the P.12. The primary aim was to test a unique military reconnaissance bomber in the guise of a civil postal machine.

P.15 Bolton

Boulton & Paul were asked to study a metal-framed equivalent of the P.7 Bourges. Designed to the same specification, D of R Type 3. It was then contracted to specification 4/20 for a long-range photographic reconnaissance aircraft. It carried a camera in the nose underside slightly offset to port between the pilot and the front bombing station. The aircraft was to be powered by two 450hp Lion engines standing above the lower wing inboard panels and faired up to engine sump level with radiators angled downwards and backwards in front of the engine plinth and sumps. The largely uncowled engines allowed the smallest radiators to be utilised to cut drag from that portion, with header tanks in the leading edge of the upper centre section. The four-blade tractor propellers were also of B&P design. Although commonly repeated as being a development of the P.7 Bourges, this was ultimately a completely new design with only the nose bomb-aimer's position and the rounded corner rectangular flying surfaces bearing the slightest resemblance to the former aircraft.

A crew of three were to be accommodated in the pilot's cockpit and front and rear defensive positions. The front gunner could also act as the bomb aimer/photographer. The entire centre section was taken up

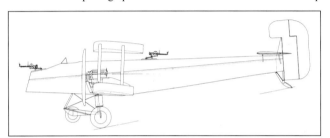

by large reinforced metal fuel tanks and a main header tank immediately behind the pilot's back gravity feeding the engines. No fuel was carried in the engine nacelles or in the upper wings. Although listed as a long-range photo reconnaissance machine, bomb release gear was designed so that there would be a facility for bombs that could be carried externally under the aircraft should that be required.

D1072 was the initial scheme side view and at the point of issue the P.15 was still known as the 'All Steel Bourges'. This first elevation was prepared in September 1920, which is interesting because a contract for its build was prepared as 232562/20 and placed on 7 July 1920, so it was ordered before the P.12 Bodmin. The scheme was never detailed as work concentrated instead on the components used to make the aircraft. The general views had to wait almost 400 drawings later. These GAs were also unfinished. The aircraft had a 62ft 3.2in projected span (62ft 4.8in structural span) with larger-chord upper wings of 8ft 6in compared with the 7ft lower and 7ft gap (spar to spar centres). The fuselage length was originally 49ft moving to 49ft 8in when design was complete, while the upper wing centre spanned 18ft 8.8in with 14ft 7.2in engines c/c. As first proposed, the aircraft had the wings and main struts set square to the aerofoil centreline. This whole frame was then given 3° incidence compared with the Lion engine thrust line, so that the struts and upper wing had negative stagger of 1.875in. This stagger became even higher on the prototype (2.88in) and the rudder was smaller.

Left: The P.15 was first known by the War Department term 'All Steel Bourges' and had variations in the shape of the moving rudder leading edge.

Below: The P.15 photo reconnaissance aircraft to Specification 4/20 as completed. Upper body and nose skinning was also in metal sheet.

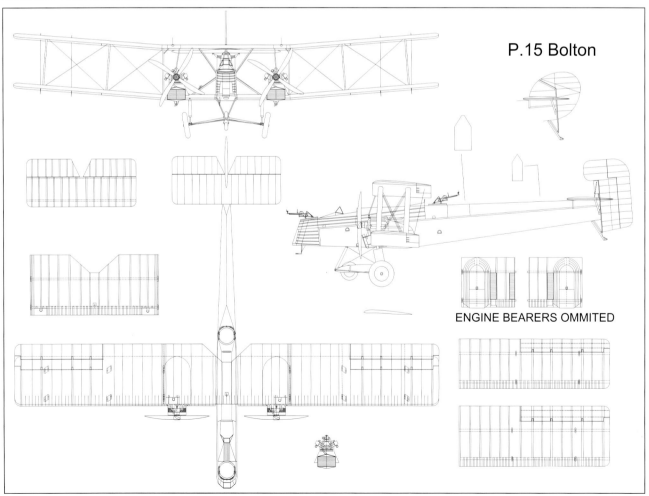

P.15 Bolton

ENGINE BEARERS OMMITED

Above: Uncovered photograph of the P.15 structure on J6584.

Right: The P.15 internals 'as built' reconstructed by the author from a number of rescaled part drawings. The outer port wings are omitted in this drawing as they were on the key original used.

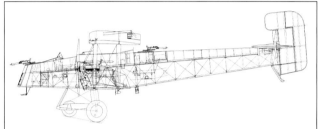

J6584 as covered and flown.

The aircraft had a number of unique B&P features that were also mirrored in the P.12. It was built entirely in metal with fabric covering. The materials being developed were essentially nickel chrome steel rolled into thin strips and drawn into connectable shapes. The sheet metal covering was more extensive than that fitted to the P.12 but essentially similar. Extensive use was made of double ribs at key points rather than thicker ribs. The upper rear fuselage again used John North's patented waisted and triangular-shaped upper cross section to improve the downward field of fire available to the mid-upper gunner. The main undercarriage was a tricycle arrangement where a sprung nose wheel prevented the airframe from nosing over should the pilot fail to three-point the machine on to its tailskid and subsequently lose control. The complicated fin and rudder system was particularly unusual, having a number of trimming and balance adjustments. As well as a trim tab along the trailing edge of the rudder, it also had a trimming leading edge on the fin, which could be used to balance out engine asymmetric power if one engine was damaged or stopped. Thoughts of training pilots and/or the rear gunner taking over if the pilot was out of action resulted in a removable joystick being fitted in the rear fuselage linked to the control runs and instruments in a raised cowl ahead of the gunner.

The first flight was in September 1922 as J6584 and prior to that B&P had been so pleased with the steel frame that it was copiously photographed and subsequent used for publicity. On 29 September 1922 it was flown for the benefit of *Flight* magazine. During October 1922 it moved to A&AEE for testing but it was returned to the manufacturer in June 1923 with the rudder system criticised. While there it was fitted with a conventional fin and rudder, similar to the P.7 design, to compare with the original before returning to A&AEE in May 1924 for more performance tests. Other modifications included work on reinforcing the vertical bulkhead behind the engine, which was deemed to be weak.

Even though the project appeared to be dragging on B&P still had some hope of obtaining some sort of order for a version of the P.15 design. Hearing that there were a number of specifications in preparation for a long-distance bombers, which the P.15 was certainly capable of fulfilling, North had Hughes prepare a complete uncovered side profile of the improved aircraft as a 'Long Distance Bomber' dated 30 May 1924. This drawing differed slightly in the shape of minor areas of the upper fuselage and it had a completely revised fin and rudder, unlike that sent on the P.15 for flight testing but matching a B&P patent. While an interesting project in metal construction, there was no production outcome.

P.25 Boulton Bugle

While the P.12 and P.15 photo-reconnaissance aircraft were in build the Air Ministry released a requirement for a similar three/four-seat twin engine aircraft to the P.15 for night bombing. The requirement was later set out in specification 30/22. B&P responded with schemes mindful that metal construction was still relatively unproven for a whole airframe. Initially a scheme called the 'New Bourges' or 'Bourges VIA' was presented but this served only to fuel the desire for a more detailed new design. The company therefore drew up layouts in November 1922 recorded as the P.25 all-metal structure and the P.25A where the wings remained in wood. The idea was to back up the possibility of success should the steel wing version or earlier prototypes in construction not be accepted. Unlike earlier machines, the design efforts moved away from the Napier Lion and proposed Jupiter II radial engines mounted mid-gap again on the wings. A wide-track split axle undercarriage was fitted together with oleo struts with twin springs fore and aft. The upper fuselage layout was similar to the P.15, with shaped top for the rear gunner and similar nose shaping in plan, but the pilot sat very high in side profile to give maximum view on take-off and landing during night operations. The overall length was foreshortened, however, making the fuselage look even deeper.

The span of the aircraft was one of the largest yet B&P had built bar the P.12, at 62ft 6in along spar tops (S-Span). The 30/22 specification was also to be considered for medium-range day bombing, in which form the prototypes were finally to be tested.

With names still being sought for a two-letter start of 'BO', the company wanted to call the aircraft the 'Bugle'. Since the Air Ministry had also wanted post-war to shorten the B&P designation to Boulton, they submitted the full name of the aircraft for approval as the P.25 or P.25A 'Boulton Bugle'. After acceptance, the prefix 'Boulton' was then quietly dropped when sending data to the press, leaving only the name Bugle to history.

The P.25 structure was essentially the same as that used by the P.12 and P.15 with formed steel strip, folded strip edges and riveting. However, the design differed in detail improvements. The tradition had been to carry fuel tanks in the fuselage, but in this case the Air Ministry had a change of policy and wanted the fuel to be carried over or under the wings. Because of the large amount of fuel specified, the fuel tanks were initially designed as large underwing blister fairings strapped under the top wing inboard of the engines at 8ft 4in centres containing 129 gallons in each tank. The radial Jupiter engines were on swinging mounts and the fairing to the rear was wedge slotted vertically both sides to eject crankcase cooling air either side of the nacelle and add to propeller thrust.

Built to Spec 30/22, Two Machines J6984 and 6985 to 369336/22 Dated 9 December 1922, Jupiter II/III

A contract for two machines was placed as 369336/22 dated 19/12/1922 and a mock-up layout was available for inspection by February 1923. The first machine J6984 was delivered to A&AEE Martlesham Heath in September 1923, a very short time scale compared with other output from the factory. This was partly because J6984 was built initially with P.25A wooden wings. Jupiter engines had problems with the propeller shafts in early prototypes and those on J6984 were no exception. Control loads were also considered heavy on the joystick, which were only part corrected by changes to the control and balance system before reissuing to testing in April 1924. It was shown at Croydon on the 10 November 1923 and returned to Norwich in January 1924 for re-engining with the Jupiter IV between then and March 1924 ready for service trials. It was last recorded at A&AEE July 1925, by which time it had steel wings as on the second prototype. Because of the externally balanced or 'flapped' ailerons, the overall 'along spars' (S-span) of the P.25A wing was initially 65ft 4in.

The second machine, J6985, was completed with P.25 steel wings by March 1924. From A&AEE in April 1924 it was passed to the RAF College in July 1924 after flying at the June 1924 Hendon Pageant. The steel wings had B&P inset balance tabs, less rounded corners and revised ailerons. A B&P rigging diagram drafted March 1924 represented this machine as built. It had a span of 62ft 6in

The P.25 initial as-built for prototype J6984 with B&P flapped aileron on wooden 25A wings and later B&P nose-balanced ailerons on a metal wing. Fuel was carried in tanks slung under the upper wing. There were wedge opening side-vented nacelles immediately behind the engine to extract the heat and provide added thrust.

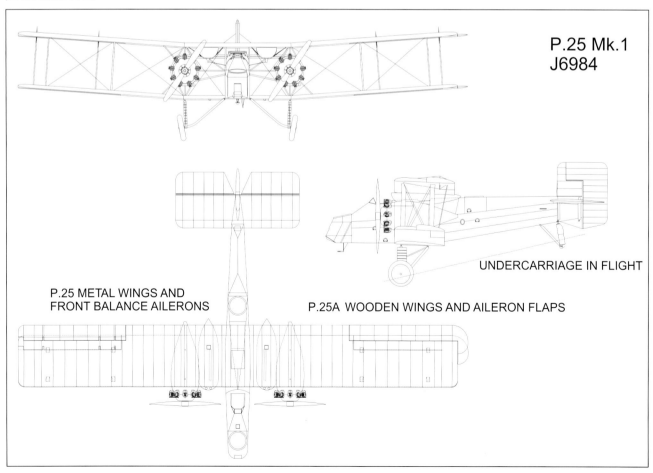

P.25 Mk.1
J6984

UNDERCARRIAGE IN FLIGHT

P.25 METAL WINGS AND
FRONT BALANCE AILERONS

P.25A WOODEN WINGS AND AILERON FLAPS

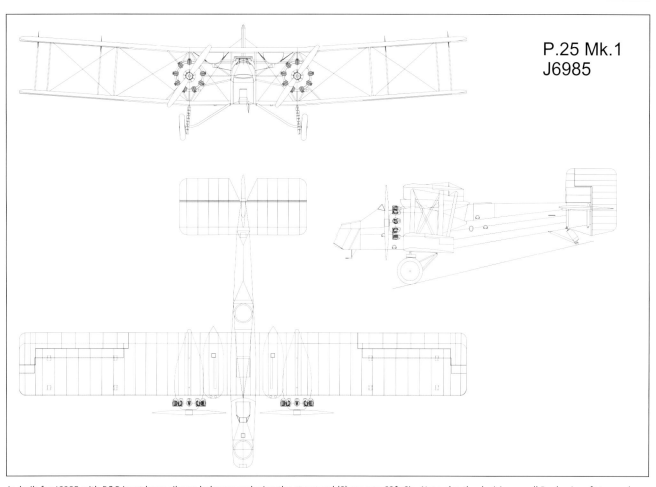

P.25 Mk.1
J6985

As-built for J6985 with B&P inset horn aileron balances reducing the structural (S) span to 62ft 6in. Note also the decision on all Bugle aircraft to employ actuation horns on the upper wing only to reduce drag. The lower ailerons trailed by strutted links. J7259 and J7260 were of the same layout.

Both prototypes at Mousehold Heath. J6984 in the background has had its initial wooden wings replaced by steel with B&P nose-balance ailerons. J6985 has steel wings and B&P inset horn-balanced ailerons. Note the wedge opening behind the engines and the open nacelle rear to drop internal pressure in the nacelle.

J6985 front view with P.12A (military prototype) in the hangar behind.

'measured along the spars', and a 62ft 4.6in projected span. The upper and lower centre sections span was 15ft 3.4in, the engines 15ft centres and length 39ft 9in 'approx.'. Height was 14ft 'approx.' – standing tail down over propellers and 15ft 4in tail up props horizontal. The forward stagger of the wings was hardly noticeable at 0.93in. On this steel wing the horn balances were inset on the standard span to North's patent 221986 released September 1924. The rudder on all machines used the same system. All subsequent machines had the same aileron system but J6984 was retrofitted with B&P nose-balanced ailerons when the wings were changed from wood. The wing area of 924.7sq ft was stated on rigging diagram D2429 along with a dihedral of 4°.

Single J7235 to 439250/23

A single serial J7235 was ordered with a wingspan back to that of J6985 because of the new patented aileron balance system and a fourth crew member in the centre position) under contract 439250/23. It should be noted, however, that all P.25 aircraft had provision for a fourth member and a cut-out in the upper wing where members could stand up and look above for star sights. The revised load of fuel and four persons actually had the effect of reducing the performance by 7mph overall even though the connecting struts for the ailerons were made more streamlined. It went to Martlesham Heath May 1924 for service trials with 58 Sqn and flew at the 1925 Hendon display. All the fuel was carried in the fuselage.

J7235 to initial 15/25 proposals had fuel within the fuselage as the requirements for an additional 'ceiling climb' tank and more fuel made it unrealistic to keep the underslung wing tanks. It also employed a fourth crew member occupying the crew navigation station under the wing.

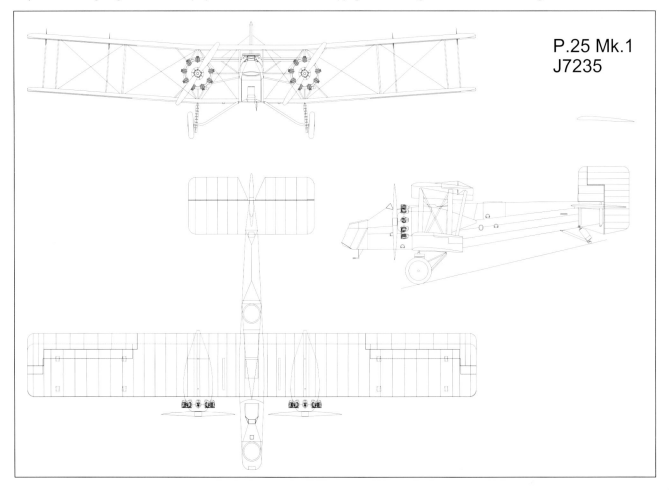

P.25 Mk.1
J7235

Two Aircraft J7259–7260 to 454263/23 Dated 21/1/1924

A further two aircraft, J7259–7260, to 454263/23 dated 21 January 1924 were ordered with Jupiter IV engines. J7259 and J7260 were both flying during 1924. J7260 was demonstrated at Mousehold on 25 February 1927 at the opening of the aero club. As built they still had the underwing fuel tank blisters.

Two New P.25A Bugle II J7266–7267 Ordered Under 469837/23 Dated February 1924

B&P were asked to consider a Bugle-type aircraft with two Lion engines. The project was allocated the design number P.27 and two schemes were drawn up; firstly a basic layout on 28 November 1923 and then a confirmed scheme on 4 December 1923 respectively. As common at the time only a side elevation and a front elevation were drawn for each. Contract number 469837/23 was allocated in February 1924 for two new Bugle aircraft, while the Lion was studied based upon the draft design specification to be agreed. This order was only a month after already ordering J7259 and 7260, making a total of seven prototypes. However, the discussions on design were protracted and the new machines J7266 and J7267 do not seem to have been given a formal order confirming Lion engines under specification 15/25 until January 1925, by which time J7266 was almost complete with Jupiter engines. Since the extra drag of the underslung tanks was a problem, the company had suggested removing these blister tanks and substituting two integral wing section tanks of enlarged aerofoil section on the upper wing. Nevertheless, none of these drawings were approved by the resident

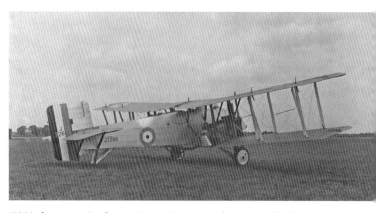

J7266 after converting from Jupiter to Lion power plants set on the lower wing. A metal ribbed fairing covered the engine mount and the rear nacelle. Note the cutaway in the trailing edge at the nacelle position and the crawl way on the rear fuselage top so the rear gunner could crawl forward to speak to the pilot or a second pilot could drop through the upper hatch into his seat.

technical officer as the adaption was rejected in favour of reverting to all main fuel being in the fuselage.

The design was so like the Jupiter engine versions in size and shape that the designation P.25A and Bugle II were to be applied for the Lion version (despite the fact that the P.25A had been schemed originally and its wooden wings used for J6984, the original first prototype, B&P objections were overridden). One can only presume that modification of the two further prototypes of the P.25 were less concerting when applying for funding than to change to a completely new P.27 build designation. J7266 appears to have been tested with Jupiters at A&AEE before being converted to the Lion power plant.

To improve further on P.25 prototypes up to J7267 it was recommended that the fuel could be carried in aerofoil-section fuel tanks built into the upper wing structure, thereby dropping the large problem of mutual interference drag under the top wing. This innovative suggestion was refused for the Lion variants in favour of moving all fuel back to the fuselage as in J7235.

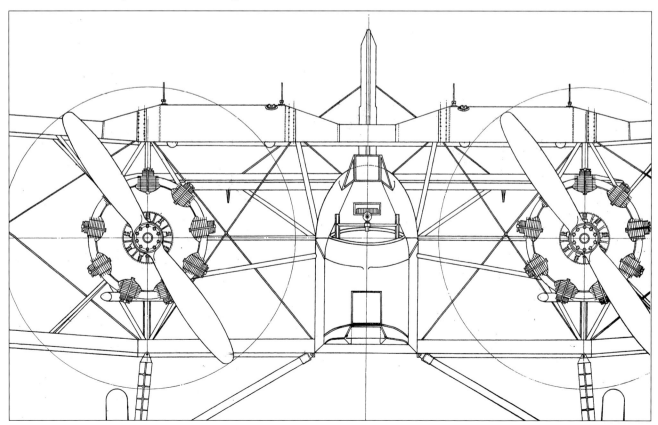

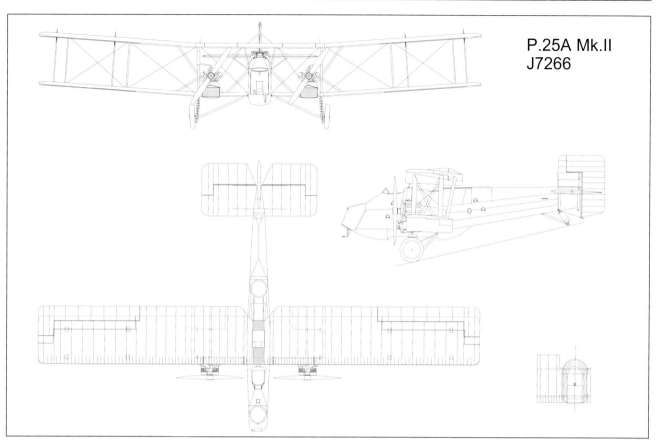

P.25A Mk.II
J7266

Changing the machine from a Jupiter, J7266 extended the span by 4ft 8in to accommodate the Lion engines. The engine nacelles were improved compared with the P.15 style and the lower inboard wing under the nacelles ceased at the rear spar with an under fairing covering the rear spar thickness, looking much like the tail of a racing car of that period.

J7967 as built showing trial modifications using a fishtail nacelle fairing based on the B&P design fitted to Malcolm Campbell's record car.

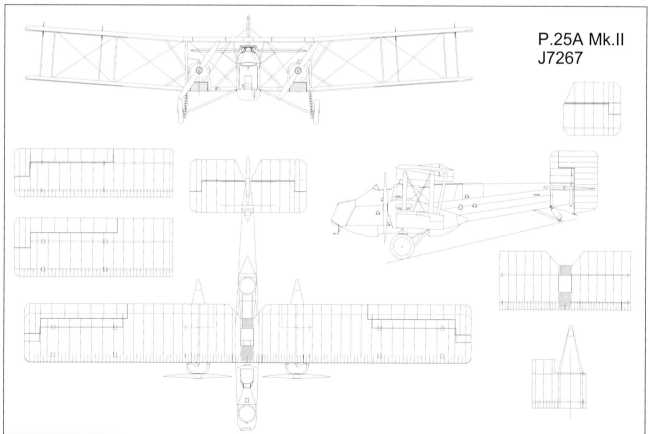

P.25A Mk.II
J7267

Front view of J7966 with faired in bomb locations to form an open-bottom bomb bay. The rudder tip had a small skid to prevent over-compression of the tail oleo.

The main differences were that the Lion II engines were mounted above the lower wing in P.15-style nacelles rather than at mid-span, and the bombs were carried under the fuselage truss in a 'guppy'-type belly fairing, which could be described as 'enclosed' in a bomb bay. All fuel was now in the fuselage. The all-up weight of the machines had increased to 8,914lb with the Lion power plants but also a number of structural detail redesigns took place involving the wings, undercarriage, tailplane and elevator balancing. The aircraft still retained the standard RAF 15 wing section, but B&P were slowly introducing improvements in the structural steel arrangements. The tests unfortunately only offered a 2mph speed increase over the Jupiter IV engines and the type was initially claimed again to have a heavy rudder. The second machine, J7267, was completed with Lions and also went to A&AEE Jan 1927, but it had a revised rear nacelle that was more streamlined than that of J7266, extending past the wing trailing edge to improve form drag aft of the engine and radiators. The J7267 Lion engines were also installed with closely fitting cowls leaving just the camshaft covers exposed, while streamlined feed and return pipes provided feed for oil coolers ahead of the leading edge of the first front outer struts. Essentially these two prototypes were extended in span at the centre section to accommodate the Lions at the same engine centres. They had an S-Span of 67ft 1.5in and a P-Span of 67ft 0.5in. Despite all this work and obvious government interest, no production orders resulted as a new specification was emerging instead.

J7967, the second Lion prototype, had a completely sealed engine location except for the cylinder head oil cover and exhausts. Radiator flow exited out of the nacelle sides over the upper wing. It also had a triangular-section rear nacelle extension beyond the wing trailing edge. In trying to show the centre section the photographer has left the wing tips out of focus, an error he repeated on other views.

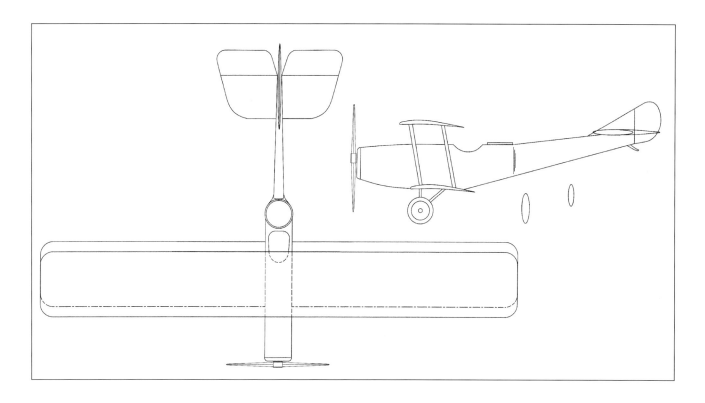

CHAPTER FIVE

The Lost Projects up to P.30

A complete title list of Boulton & Paul P-series projects was not created until a drawing office master series was recorded starting at P.27. Between P.14 to P.26 unless a project actually got built the record only survived in drawing office register books, quite often with a single comment. Most of these projects were stillborn with a single drawing only before they were rejected and/or abandoned.

P.7 (Believed a Type Allocation Error)

An initial layout for a two-seat aircraft with a thin boom rear fuselage to give the gunner better firing arcs was drawn 23 September 1918 and possibly wrongly allocated to the P.7 series in the drawing log. The number had been subsequently added over a straight line (signifying no allocation) in the type number column. The drawing has not been traced.

P.7 Two-Seat Flying Boat

The first known stab at a seaplane design was an aircraft listed as a two-seat flying boat and drawn on 12 November 1918, probably to specification N2. The design was logged in 'ditto' of a P.7 series machine list and then overwritten as P.7, so may have been based on the P.7 wing layout with a new hull. Although nothing proceeded forward from this lost drawing, the work may have been an alternative option to the official requirement for a floatplane titled the SSP/CSSP (See Chapter 3).

P.8 Bomber (Initial Type Issue)

A C-series preliminary layout for a two-seat bomber was logged in October 1918 with the type designation P.8, to be followed a day later by a more detailed scheme for the same aircraft as a larger drawing. However, the type designator P.8 was later struck through

in both drawing logs and a month onwards the same designator was then being used for the civil adaptation of the P.7. The first scheme of applying extra fins on the P.7 tailplane unit was a drawing in late November 1918 and this had continued use of the type designator P.7, in parallel with development of the Puma engine variant, but all drawings related to the tailplane revision then had the 7 struck out and changed to 8. One presumes that the bomber design attracted no official interest and was abandoned, while efforts were redirected to the existing civil development of the P.7 under the new number.

P.14 Biplane

The P.14 dating from 1920 is simply recorded as a 'biplane' with no known numbered outline drawings ever produced. Whatever was sketched probably never reached a formal drawing issue before being abandoned. It is possible, however, that the P.14 was sketched simply to illustrate a possible airframe that would ensue if an idea of North's was taken up related to the P.7 error above. On 15 October 1919 North applied for a patent to increase the field of fire available to the rear

Subject to conjecture, if this was the P.14 biplane then the crude drawing was made even cruder by the patent officer's reproduction to demonstrate the elliptical tail boom concept for improving the gunner's field of fire under the tail. The tail boom differs slightly in cross section – specifically in width – from test pieces made for the initial boom idea of September 1918.

gunner of a two-seat aeroplane. The aim was to make the rear fuselage of extremely small oval cross section and entirely in metal. The rear 'boom' was to have similar engineering properties to and perform as a normal fuselage. Patent 154041's 'biplane' layout was crudely drawn as side and plan only with the cross section of the boom.

P.16 Troop Carrier

In comparison, the P.16 underwent some detailed thought during October 1920, having both GA drawings and an installation detail for a reconnaissance camera. It was intended to be a troop carrier to specification 5/20 and was probably a variation of the P.15 Bolton long-range reconnaissance machine with the fuselage redesigned and reconfigured to have seats. The most significant point for the P.16 was that in its reconnaissance mode it was to carry the heavy (82lb) BM electrically powered and/or the L-Type cameras in a turreted mount that was intended to make them much easier to handle and operate. B&P had received drawings for the mount in October 1918 and these were retrospectively allocated to the P.16 project, but were probably also to be used by the P.15. The Vickers Type 56 Victoria I (a stretched Vimy) and the Armstrong Whitworth Awana were ordered to this specification, while the P.16 was rejected.

P.17/P.17A Fleet Spotter

The P.17 and P.17A was an attempt to scheme a fleet spotter in May 1921, the former with engine ahead of the pilot and the latter with engine behind. The interesting comment in the little information available was that it had a 'floating aileron control system', meaning that the aileron control surfaces sat on struts separate from the wing.

P.18 Reconnaissance and P.19 Bomber

The P.18 was a preliminary scheme for a reconnaissance aircraft drawn as a single sheet in June 1921, while the P.19 was intended to be a twin-engine bomber to specification 15/21, but was quickly abandoned when the specification was withdrawn. It consisted of three views on separate sheets dated 3 September 1921.

P.20 Army Co-operation

The P.20, was an all-steel structured army machine based upon an initial early specification D of R 3A. It was logged officially on 30 September 1921 and then seemingly offered to meet any army co-op specifications as they appeared, vis 10/20, 19/20, 5/21 and 10/21. It was a three-seat corps reconnaissance aircraft very similar in layout to the DH.9A (the metal wings for which Boulton & Paul produced as a design and made parts). The three views of the machine do not survive, but an artist was commissioned to draw the submission in perspective and the art exists. It appears that an AS Puma engine was used and the fin was installed under the tailplane to give the rear gunner a maximum field of fire, plus a wide-track undercarriage to allow operations from undeveloped airfields. In deference to fears that fuselage tanks would place the three crew in danger if they caught fire, the main fuel was carried in over-wing streamlined tanks similar to modern slim drop tanks and held on struts just above the upper surface of the top wing. The Advisory Committee for Aeronautics, Fire Prevention Committee had studied both underslung and over-wing tanks as a means of removing fuel tank fires away from the crew, resulting in government test reports during January and February 1921. There must have been verbal interest somewhere perceived by the company as significant,

Corps Reconnaissance Aeroplane. The original drawings have not been found. This GA is therefore based upon the tone illustrations of artist Geoffrey Watson in 1921.

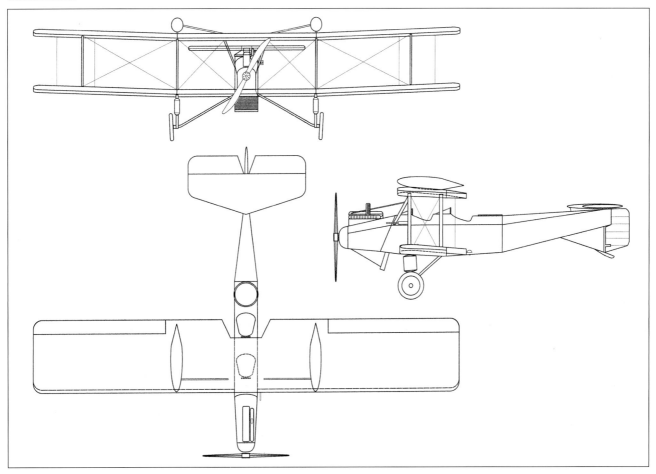

Watson's illustration of the P.20 aircraft. Over-wing tanks conform to one of the positions being studied by the Fire Prevention sub-committee of the Aeronautical Research Committee during 1921–22 (R&M 796 (Appendix V)), but already adopted by North as a safety measure.

because details such as the proposed observer's navigation table for the type were still being drawn afresh as late as May 1923, even though the type never got past the drawing stage.

P.21 Reconnaissance, P.22 Torpedo Carrier, P.23 Amphibian and P.24 Twin-Engine Torpedo Carrier

The P.21 returned to the theme of high-altitude photo reconnaissance and was most likely to be a long-span P.15, while the P.22 issued in the same month was a torpedo carrier for coastal defence. The P.23 logged on 16 June 1922 is listed as a single-engine amphibian. The P.24 was a twin-engine version of a torpedo carrier. The P.26 details for June 1923 simply stated 'cabin aircraft', drawings covering the three views and a detail of the cabin.

P.28 Day Bomber

The P.28 was a single-engine day bombing landplane using a Beardmore 'Typhoon' engine, drawn as a three-view, a side elevation and a series of sections in early January 1924. Because of the late work on the P.20 in 1923, it may have been based on a derivation of that aircraft. The specification that it is recorded as being based around by the company was 10/23, which ultimately seems to have been also used for a single-engine production development of the Avro Aldershot III. The move to a potential inverted engine prompted a number of companies to look at its advantages, but there was no hope of competing with an already anticipated development of the Aldershot. None of the drawings are known to survive and there is no known record of the P.28 being formally submitted.

P.30 Lioness Fighter

A potential new engine design again was the Napier Lioness, Design E.71, a revision of the successful three-bank x four-cylinder 'broad arrow' Lion engine, but able to run in an inverted installation. This immediately attracted designers of potential fighter aircraft because of the improvement of the pilot's view forward and the potentially efficient upper decking of the cowl area. Only a brief side and front elevation was drawn in June 1924. Once interest was shown a plan view was added in July 1924. There the project stalled because the Lioness was only being developed as a potential racing engine with a few prototypes. Although tested in the air, it was not moved to production status and revising the P.30 or any other proposals to an upright Lion engine would defeat the whole point. Once again, no drawings are known to survive.

With each of these projects only the drawing numbers of the general arrangement of the machine or a minor detail remain.

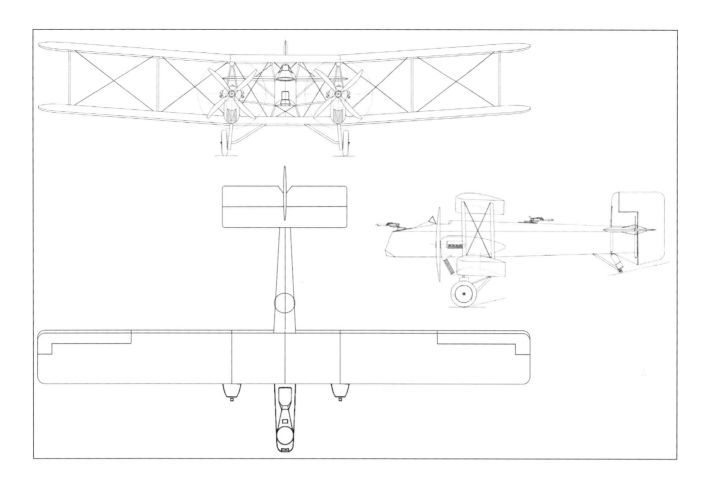

CHAPTER SIX

The P.29 Sidestrand

THE RAF actually had no use for medium twins post-First World War because it had continually seen no speed or bomb load advantages compared with its current application, the Lion-powered Hawker Horsley. However, such aircraft were still studied and 1924 saw the release of a new specification for a twin-engine, medium-range bomber under the designation 9/24, to which B&P allocated project reference P.29.

The P.29 project saw quite detailed changes from its initial issue. It is likely that the initial P.29 layout drawn in April 1924 represented a complete revision of the P.27/P.25 schemes to reduce fuselage cross section and improve radiator drag. Body models of the initial idea and a side and front view were drawn that show a box-like fuselage and engine nacelles suspended between the wings with a highly streamlined engine radiator system between the engine shaft cowling and the lower wing – an improvement of the Campbell land speed record car tail rear nacelle shapes fitted to P.25 Serial J7267, which now also totally enclosed the radiator in ducting with a low-drag cowling. Positioning of offensive load was not detailed. The installation mirrored the cowled radiator designs of later years. A four-blade 9ft 6in prop was schemed with both engines having the same rotation. The design had straight wings and 680sq ft of wing area on a 70ft span, 7ft chord and minimal stagger of about 2.2in.

Above: The P.29 initial design with Lion engines and faired radiators seemed to completely ignore its prime reason for existing, the carriage of bombs, and to concentrate instead on improving the radiator drag that it was believed had dogged the P.7B, P.15 and P.25 Bugle-II. This design may well indicate one layout drawn and abandoned for the P.27 but resurrected for the initial P.29 study to the first issue of 9/24. The similar Bluebird-style tadpole nacelle tail to J7967 is noteworthy.

Right: At the same time B&P submitted this long-range bomber design based upon the P.15. It never received a project number but it had the new rudder system designed for the P.15 in January 1924.

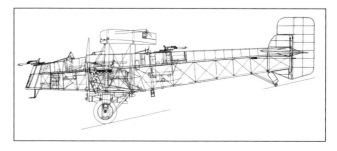

The machine was 39ft 10in long and stood 15ft 3in high. The wing incidence was 3° and the dihedral of the outer wings 4°. The nose and pilot's positions were technically similar to the P.25 but this time both on the same level.

As drawn, the wing adopted a thick flat bottom section, whereas all previous aircraft utilised the old RAF 15. In September 1921 the experimental department had obtained a copy of *Ergebnisse der Aerodynamischen Ersuchsanstalt zu Göttingen* (Results of the Aerodynamic Testing Facility at Gottingen) written by Dr Engineers Wieselberger and Betz and approved by Prandtl himself, dated December 1920. It is likely that Hermann Glauert, brother of Otto, suggested this document or any previous work by Prandtl, Betz and Munk as being useful. From then onwards they did not have to rely on technical memoranda from the Air Ministry or R&M reports to study previous progress, for they now had data on Gottingen sections and German wartime research on body models.

By 1924/25 the sections on propeller/nacelle interference and body interference had been translated from the German for the team to study. It was clear that the way forward would be to adopt thicker wing sections to replace the outdated RAF 15 section. The team studied a whole series of new special sections all based upon Joukowski transformations. Designated sections BP.1 to BP.11 were also tried in the wind tunnel and the first P.29 design drawing displayed a 15% thick flat bottom section. The aerodynamic breakthrough came with a slight under camber section with reflex trailing edge designated BP.10. Although there were a series of variations produced including BP.10A to D, the company adopted the basic BP.10 section of about 12.88% thickness at 35% chord for its future aircraft and a symmetrical section designated BP.11 for its fin/rudder and tailplane. The BP.10 was a variation of the Joukowski formulae as the shape was more akin to the Karman-Treffte transform of the basic Joukowski. During tests on the engine nacelle/radiator fairing combination North's team realised that there was only slightly less than 2mph difference between a good cowled in line with new controlled radiator fairings and a radial engine tightly faired so that only the cylinders were exposed. They concluded that it was possible to negate that difference so neither engine layout had the advantage and even to improve the radial engine with better cowling and flow control. This became the continuation of North's 'anti-turbulence cowling' development well prior to the work by Townend at NPL.

The initial airframe scheme was somewhat compromised by a later requirement asking for an under defence gun position. In addition, discussions on the undesirability of always carrying bombs externally continued the design moves with the P.25 'guppy belly', which would heavily change the initial layout. In order to do this and carry fuel in the fuselage, the P.29 would have to have a deeper fuselage extending to and beyond the lower wing, removing the advantage of North's attempt to streamline the individual radiator installations. The additional requirement to provide a defensive arc of fire beneath the tail also resulted in changes. The use of Lions was proven to reduce the top speed significantly on the P.25 Bugle II when first tested so, all-in-all, the P.29 design team were faced with a serious rethink on the overall layout. The last version of the P.25 had already seen some attempt at streamlining the lower front but the Lion radiators were a massive drag penalty on that aircraft. In that situation North convinced the Ministry that the performance of the aircraft would be better reverting to air-cooled Jupiter radials on the lower wing and a much more streamlined fuselage. The Jupiter chosen was the new VI of 430hp. All of the differences, including the movement of the engine locations forward to accommodate Jupiter VI radials, produced an entirely different airframe and another departure from the B&P design team's norm. The usual straight wing planform was modified by sweeping back the outer wing panels to maintain optimum C of G. Tunnel work with fish-like aircraft models and Sir Malcom Campbell's land speed record car was starting to pay dividends. The new basic fuselage shape was based upon further Joukowski transforms in elevation and plan.

The front nose had an extremely slim entry. The nose area on J7938 and J7939 was skinned in duralumin on steel and duralumin formers with external metal skinning of the cockpit areas and lower fairing forward. Some problems were encountered with hand forming the sheets and in maintaining their stability in use, since both aircraft appear to have had mods to the nose skinning and been reskinned before being released to the service for evaluation. Thin alloys had not always been successful in heat treatment during the First World War and beyond as thin sheet tended to crack in service.

The rear fuselage truss also saw a radical departure from the P.12/P.15/P.25 methods. North's structural team had been improving the process by which they formed longerons and were now making sheet steel tube as a full draw bench job where the materials were formed and the joint closed and folded upon itself internally in what was to become known as a 'locked joint'. This removed the external riveted flanges, which had been common before. The joints between each section of tube, or at mid-positions on the tube, which took all the spacing struts and rigging connections, were now cast and forged from alloy as billets of hexagonal section (for ease of holding and machining offsets). The 'locked joint' tubes were inserted into these joints and bolted or riveted. Boulton & Paul announced the availability of the sections in a booklet A.262 published in December 1925 titled *The Metal Construction of Aircraft*. While the wing ribs remained similar to those made previously, the main spars had been improved tremendously with more corrugations in their cross section and at least two extra horizontal sheet planes across the upright formed and riveted spar, meaning that the rivets were now well

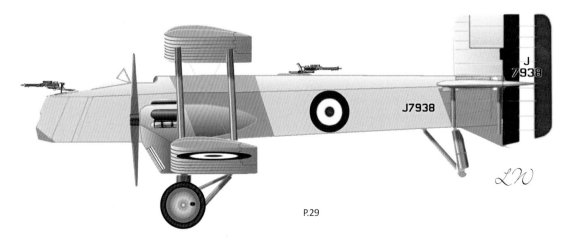

P.29

contained in shear as they passed through multiple thicknesses of sheet. A whole new range of spars suitable for any possible design bending moment and stiffness was created, with the P.29 as the first application. Other changes to the construction publicised were the introduction of stainless steels (although strictly 13/1 was technically known as stainless iron in aeronautical specifications at the time, but the term steel carried more interest for publicity purposes) and improvements of surface treatments and coatings of zinc, anodising and shellac to resist inter-material and external corrosion.

The prototype lower wings were mated to the outer engine under-nacelle on a diagonal rib, while the upper rib joint was perpendicular to the spars. This could be that the intention was to accommodate wing folding with minimum of change if the Air Ministry objected to a span of 71ft 11.3in uncovered and required better hangar storage with folded wings. Wings and tailplane were in steel while the rudder was in duralumin. The angle of incidence of the wings was 4° with outer plane dihedral of 3° 10' and 3° of sweepback. To get the largest-size spar possible into the wing section, both front and rear spars canted forward. Another key to strength in such a large span was the removal of the intermediate nose ribs and the replacement of the majority of these with a full-chord boom sewn into the fabric covering of the upper surface only at each location. This gave the impression when observed from above that there were twice as many ribs at half normal spacing compared with the underside, although in truth the hidden metal rib structure was normal other than double ribs capped with pierced sheet where strength was needed.

Two machines were ordered on contract 555797/25 as P.29 Sidestrand Mk.Is and were completed with inset horn balance ailerons and Jupiter VI engines of 425hp. The fin and rudder reflected the B&P standard used on the P.25. The initial mnemonic on drawings, with the company still worried that the Air Ministry would insist on the first two letters being BO, was the 'Boulton Sidestrand'. This was later changed to 'Boulton-Paul Sidestrand' and, as with the Bugle, only the last name was eventually deliberately used. Serial J7938 first flew in 1926 piloted by Sqn Ldr Rea. Rea joined the company as their full-time test pilot in mid-1926. Sorting a tailplane adjustment error after the first flight, J7938 was delivered to Martlesham Heath in December 1926 for quite extensive trials over at least six months, while J7939 remained at Norwich until the next year. The plan was to have 10ft or 10ft 7in two-blade propellers but by the time the prototype was completed the propeller diameter was set at 9ft for the Jupiter VI. The propeller initially drawn was a 10ft diameter left-hand

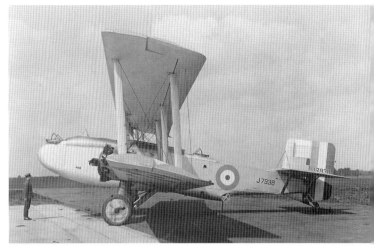

Prototype J7938 on trials. This photograph was later used in A&AEE Report M471 of June 1927. *Crown Copyright*

tractor but was cut down to 9ft 9in and then redesigned at 9ft, the final standard, because of engine vibration and the need to increase RPM out of the vibration frequency during testing.

In a report on J7938 with the maker's two-blade 9ft diameter propellers (but actually both 8ft 9in from minor adjustments), manoeuvrability was the main criticism, with a very heavy rudder and unsatisfactory ailerons, but it was considered very stable for bombing in level flight. The maximum speed reached was 130mph at 6,500ft. It was thought that the machine promised to be excellent for fighting. A larger bombing window and better rudder gearing were recommended. The engine cowlings in aluminium were found to repeatedly fail by cracking and required a thicker material or a material change. There was also trouble with the early engines caused by carburation problems at height. Servicing and access was considered easy because of the swinging mounts. Dual control was fitted with the second pilot accommodated behind the first in his own cut-out when required. It was summarised by the testing pilots that 'the requirements for a medium range day bombing landplane appear to have been well met, subject to minor modifications'. The wingspan of the aircraft stated was the same throughout its life but the fuselage length was changed from both prototypes to improve criticism of the heavy rudder.

Second prototype J7939 showing problems with the hammered hand-formed, alloy-covered nose plating.

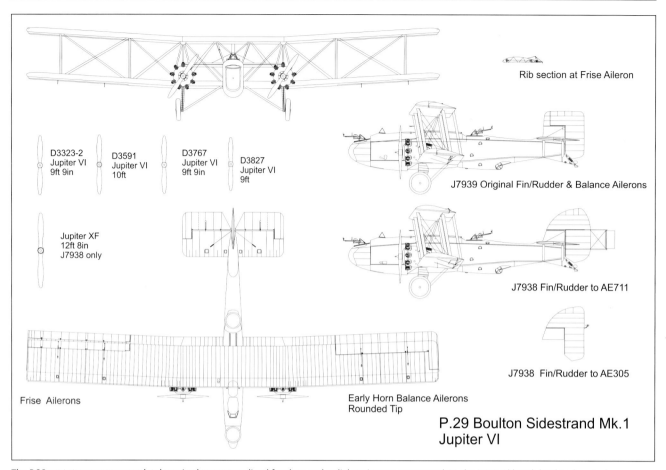

D3323-2
Jupiter VI
9ft 9in

D3591
Jupiter VI
10ft

D3767
Jupiter VI
9ft 9in

D3827
Jupiter VI
9ft

Jupiter XF
12ft 8in
J7938 only

Rib section at Frise Aileron

J7939 Original Fin/Rudder & Balance Ailerons

J7938 Fin/Rudder to AE711

J7938 Fin/Rudder to AE305

Frise Ailerons

Early Horn Balance Ailerons
Rounded Tip

P.29 Boulton Sidestrand Mk.1
Jupiter VI

The P.29 prototypes were completely revised to a streamlined fuselage and radial engines to accommodate the internal bomb load and ventral gun location with a minimum effect on performance. J7938 was refitted with the rudder entirely redesigned and eventually tried a trials Flettner servo system. Note that this was further changed before production machines were delivered and HP-Lachmann slats later added to the upper wings as shown. These slats were retrofitted to the first six production aircraft and installed on all others at the production stage.

Propellers for P.29 Bristol Jupiter Engines

Model	Engine	Drg No	Diameter	No Blades	Comment
P.29	VI	D3323-1	10ft	2	
P.29	VI	D3323-2	9ft 9in	2	Cut from -1
P.29	VI	D3591	10ft	2	As D3323-1
P.29	VI	D3767	9ft 9in	2	
P.29	VI	D3793	9ft	2	On J7938
P.29A – Mk.II	VI	D3827	9ft	2	taper hub
P.29A – Mk.II	VI	8820/1/2/3	9ft	2	taper hub
P.29B – Mk.III	VIII	D3895	11ft 9in	2	
P.29B – Mk.III	VIII	G1257		2	
P.29B – Mk.III	VIII	G1269/70	11ft 6in	2+2	AE test only
P.29B – Mk.III	VIIIF	G1293/94	11ft 6in	4	Bristol P3333
P.29	XF	G1416	12ft 8in	2	J7938 J9186

Note: G1416 required 5.96in longer main leg centres wheel to wing underside in order to increase undercarriage height. Probably also applied to J9186 with circular rings.

After return to the makers, modifications included the replacement of balanced ailerons with the Frise type so that J7938 appeared briefly with flat end-plate wings. J7938, with this new aileron format, was tested in March/April 1928 for control effects. The ailerons gave light and effective lateral control at all speeds and 'should give confidence to the average pilot'. The complete replacement of the square-set fin and rudder with a shaped unit was also carried out under order Ae503 and eventually an improved fin and Flettner servo tab-operated rudder unit was provided under Ae711 for J7938. Tests on the rudder in November 1928 brought positive comments that it gave fair control and could now allow control at full throttle with either engine out. The machine could be controlled straight down to 60mph. However, the fin and curved rudder shape tested was further improved for manufacturing ease on the P.29A. Outer upper wing HP auto-slots were fitted to J7939, along with the new redesigned Flettner system under Ae951. This became the agreed system to be fitted to the P.29A onwards and the scheme drawings for the P.29A production aircraft with the planned original square fin and rudder with approximate 40ft 7.87in overall length were replaced with the new vertical tail unit and a slightly extended last bay in the fuselage, moving the sternpost centre to the rear by 3.05in. The relationship between the wings and tailplane remained the same, although there were internal changes in the tailplane system itself. The length of the machine was now 41ft 11.87in but the extended Flettner rudder servo tab opened this to 46ft 2in overall (although most formal documents consistently repeat an approximate value of 1in less).

A production batch was ordered consisting of only six aircraft under contract 789943/27 as the P.29A Sidestrand II, retaining Jupiter VI engines, a slight change in cowling to take a forward exhaust ring and a taper hub propeller giving the impression of a partial spinner. All six had the final design fin, Flettner rudder and Frise ailerons, the serials allocated being J9176 to 9181. A major difference was the abandoning of the light alloy skinning for the upper and lower fuselage forward of the wing. This was replaced with a wood and moulded plywood monocoque, which was easier to produce and maintain. The wooden nose was also made to open for access to the instrument housings in the pilot's panel and bomb gear maintenance. The other change was to remove the diagonal rib joint on the lower outboard wing and to maintain a straight rib on the wings. The lower outer wing sweepback was similar to before but was now stated in

distance measured at the wing tip for easier rigging to 12.7in at the tip lower wing and the outer upper wing sweepback to 13.6in at the tip, with the wing joint on the upper wing exactly over the engine centreline. J9176 was then the first production aircraft to be retrofitted with the prototype-tested HP auto-slots on the upper outer wings, which were subsequently fitted to each machine. They were initially delivered in 1929 over a four-month period. The company proposed anti-turbulence rings but these were continually refused as an unnecessary complication. Experiments with propellers also occurred throughout the life of the aircraft to try and remove engine problems of over-speeding or rough running, but the biggest change was to eventually redesign the engines, with the Jupiter VI replaced by the Jupiter VIII and 11ft 9in propellers as the P.29B. The two prototypes were also recorded as brought up to P.29B standard after temporary issue to 101 Squadron in April 1928. The changes, however, did not alter the style of nose retained on the prototypes and the nose remained fixed; it also did not alter the last bay adjacent the sternpost. Testing of the first production example, J9176, with its Jupiter VI engines brought some criticism of the engine over-speed again. The design used the same 9ft propellers and various propeller sizes were tried including 9ft 9in. A 12ft 8in propeller was schemed based upon J7938 with a Jupiter XF engine in 1929, which would temporarily result in a taller main undercarriage but still leaving only 9in ground clearance when extended. Tests with Bambridge Automatic Brake Control in mid-1932 were abortive. The system was rejected as unnecessary, complicated and counter-intuitive, since the pedals operated in reverse while taxying and were judged to be more liable to cause maintenance and reliability problems compared with the proper training of pilots in how to land and taxi under power with existing braking designs.

Layout of the P.29A Sidestrand II production model, which had spinner-like taper hub propellers and a Bristol exhaust system similar to the Bristol Bulldog. Originally the prototype fin and rudder were proposed. This also shows the location of a proposed aerial array for a multi-function radio system, which does not appear to have been accepted for prototype or production.

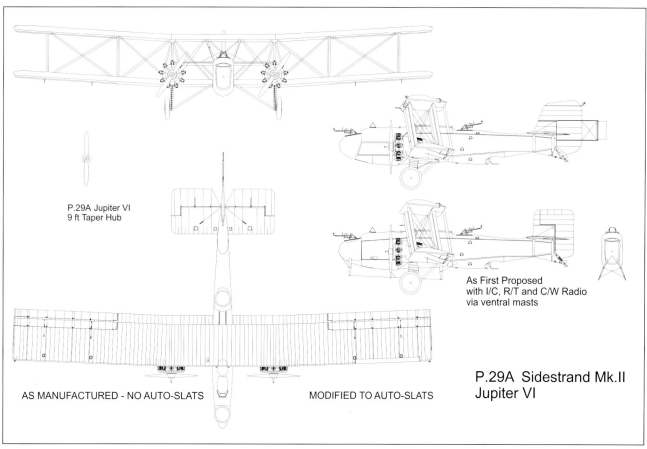

P.29A Jupiter VI
9 ft Taper Hub

As First Proposed
with I/C, R/T and C/W Radio
via ventral masts

AS MANUFACTURED - NO AUTO-SLATS   MODIFIED TO AUTO-SLATS

P.29A Sidestrand Mk.II
Jupiter VI

First production Sidestrand II J9176 on Mousehold Heath compass base before being retrofitted with upper wing slats.

By April 1928 funding had been found for a further five machines and an amendment to 789943/27 was issued. The five aircraft were to have the HP auto-slots as manufactured and improved Jupiter VIII engines, but still had two-blade propellers, which were of larger diameter and still no anti-turbulence rings were approved. These propellers, drawing reference D3895, were 11ft 9in in diameter, leaving a ground clearance again of only 9in 'tail up' on these machines. Stagger varied depending on the how the aircraft was rigged, varying from 17.8 to 18in at the centre section and 17 to 17.2in on the outer panels. The short stagger was known as 'low' rigging tolerance and the latter as 'high' rigging tolerance. Aircraft were acceptable anywhere within that range subject to adequate air test. Aircraft serials J9185 to 89 were allocated but now known as the P.29B Sidestrand III. With the improved Jupiter it was possible to modify the aircraft in the field but all went out as Jupiter VIIIs. By the time the AP for the Sidestrand III was in second issue only the Jupiter VIIIF was mentioned as all aircraft were being upgraded to this 'Penthouse Head' (with angled valve sets) rather than the 'Poultice Head' Jupiter VIII (with vertical valve sets).

Two further key improvements on the later-service P.29B were the introduction of the so-called 'bombing nose', where the under-fuselage bombing slot was replaced by a nose-mounted opening clear window for the bomb aimer, and the replacement of the VIII two-blade propellers with four-blades for the VIIIF (or four-blade 'two+two' units by special order). A further four machines were ordered under 92429/29 in November 1929, with serials J9767 to 9770, and three replacements for unrepairable crashes under 92429/31, K1192 to 1194. By this time any airframe with 101 Squadron had been bought up to final P.29B Sidestrand III standard (specification 10/29) under a series of field modifications or staggered refurbishments at Norwich to Specification 17/30, order 78257/30. The two+two-blade system has not been identified on photographs of the P.29B Sidestrand III, which appear to use two-blade D3895 (Jupiter VIII) or one-piece four-blade drawing reference G1293 (Jupiter VIIIF) assemblies in service, providing a good recognition point. In service the aircraft were continually updated with the newest internal equipment to maintain unit efficiency.

A rare photograph of 101 Squadron recovered from a damaged negative. In the background is J9177, still a Jupiter VI-engine 9ft propeller P.29A, while J9188 is an early P.29B with Jupiter VIII engines and larger two-blade propellers of 11ft 9in diameter. During updating later versions served alongside original ones awaiting conversion.

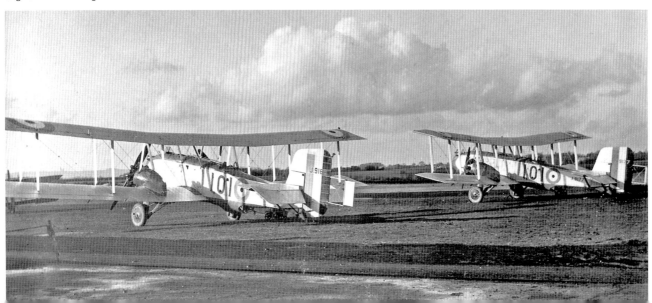

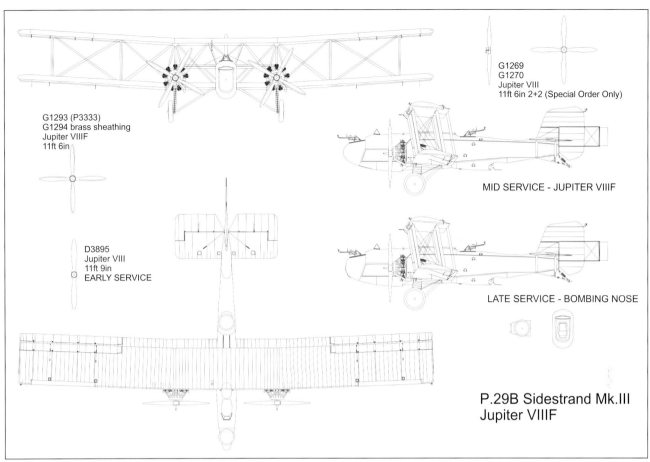

G1293 (P3333)
G1294 brass sheathing
Jupiter VIIIF
11ft 6in

D3895
Jupiter VIII
11ft 9in
EARLY SERVICE

G1269
G1270
Jupiter VIII
11ft 6in 2+2 (Special Order Only)

MID SERVICE - JUPITER VIIIF

LATE SERVICE - BOMBING NOSE

P.29B Sidestrand Mk.III
Jupiter VIIIF

Layout of the P.29B Sidestrand III in second form with retrofitted Jupiter VIIIF and four-blade propellers. Late service has an improved bombing nose.

Although considered a successful machine, there was still no real use for such an aircraft in the RAF inventory other than with 101 Squadron. As the Air Ministry started to consider more improvements or its replacement, the company also began to receive other enquiries for variations. A sales brochure was generated for enquirers with photographs of the serving aircraft and three-view drawings of the P.29B potential variations, pushing particularly the use of anti-turbulence rings. Originally North had always suggested anti-turbulence cowlings for the P.29 but this had never been accepted in each batch and neither had his proposal in 1928 to fit such rings to J7938 for trials. His 1931 sales brochure repeated the suggestion again by including the cowlings on the brochure's P.29B layout for export machines. In December 1927 a proposal had also been made to replace the Jupiter VI engines with either Mercury or Jupiter VII engines in full anti-turbulence cowlings. The Ministry did ask for a proposal for a Sidestrand mounting a tail turret (by which they simply meant a tail gun position). The design result was logged on 15 March 1928 and used a tail with twin fins and rudders similar to the early style for the P.32. In the same month a proposal was made for a Sidestrand with RR FIIY steam-cooled inline engines, perhaps the most interesting potential development which failed to happen. Looking for alternative orders, the production Sidestrand III was drawn up as a rigging diagram late in 1928, a GA in August 1929, and later supported by variants of a floatplane

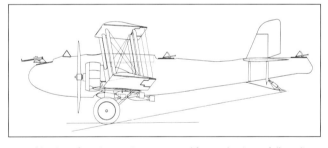

A combination of two innovations suggested for production: a full cowling for either a Mercury engine or a Jupiter VII (or either uncowled) in December 1927, and a design for a rear gun mount with twin fins in March 1928 similar to the early prototype design for the P.32 fins.

Author's negative of 101 Sqn P.29B Sidestrand IIIs in final form all with the Jupiter VIIIF and the new 'bombing nose'.

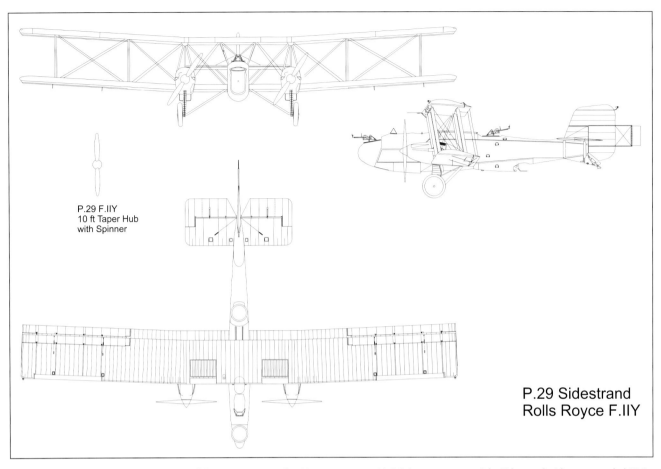

P.29 F.IIY
10 ft Taper Hub
with Spinner

P.29 Sidestrand
Rolls Royce F.IIY

Perhaps the most interesting development of the P.29 was an April 1928 response to an Air Ministry request to trial a Sidestrand with steam-cooled RR F IIY engines. This designation appears to have been used by B&P for the proposed pressure-cooled version of the RR Kestrel F IIS also fitted to the Gloster TC33. The wing-mounted coolers here match the surface area used for the later P.35 fighter but it is not known if the aircraft was also to have the leading edge coolers shown. Had the conversion taken place it would have made an interesting comparison with the Hart/Fury family.

with tailskid removed and lower gunner's bath changed to a smooth underside to create a torpedo coastal defence aircraft with wheeled or float undercarriage, using a Jupiter VIII for 135mph and AUW of 11,500lb, all studied in early October 1929.

In the same week the company also drew an aerial survey machine with an Eyrie panning camera in the lower nose and another camera in the rear fuselage giving 140mph performance at 11,200lb AUW. This was based upon the requirements of the Aircraft Operating Company and pre-empted the later issue of Air Ministry Specification 1/31. The aircraft was essentially a simple direct conversion of the P.29B/Jupiter VIII with all open upper positions converted to low windshields and the gunner's bath removed. The Eyrie camera was intended to pan in a 120° cone under the camera operator's seat in the nose. Wheeled or float interchangeable undercarriage was provided but with floats the sideways pan recording was reduced to 90°. Because of its similarity to the basic P.29, it was not issued as a new project number and no contract was obtained to build the version. November 1931 brought another enquiry from the Air Ministry for a Sidestrand as a night bomber, which involved fitting enlarged fuselage tanks resulting in a slightly revised upper fuselage fairing forward of the rear gunner. Yet another floatplane was drawn in March 1932, but no orders emerged from any of these studies.

Development Sidestrands included J9186, which was fitted with Jupiter VIIIF and then XF engines in anti-turbulence Boulton Paul Townend Ring cowlings of circular form. The Air Ministry seemed to have a change of heart on using ring cowlings when National Physics Laboratory expert Dr Townend issued his reports and patents reflecting what North's team had always argued from several years earlier.

Separately, the aircraft tried a lever suspension undercarriage, tailwheel and brakes under government development contracts. With Pegasus engines and round cowlings it became a full-size proposal for an I.M.2-engined version of the Sidestrand III with the new B&P anti-turbulence units. The second prototype Sidestrand 1, previously upgraded to Mk.II and then various Mk.III standards, was modified with Jupiter XFB and finally to Pegasus I.M.3 for tests without B&P cowlings and became known as the Sidestrand IIIS when fitted with the Pegasus, and the bombing nose, representing part of the P.29C and D design sequence into the Overstrand – although as stated previously J7939 still retained a fixed nose portion and although described as a Mk.III this only referred to the upgraded standard of equipment fitted and not the true structural standard of the original fuselage.

Replacements or upgrades to the 101 Squadron fleet were hoped for and in April 1933 the P.29C Sidestrand IV was drawn up for detailed proposal brochures. This was intended to use Pegasus I.M.3 radials in Boulton Paul Townend Rings and to have a stronger centre-section structure and fittings to take the improved power. The undercarriage was also improved, including better suspension and brakes, and a permanent tailwheel was to be fitted instead of the tailskid.

However, the early 1930s also brought increasing difficulty of handling weapons and ammunition in the slipstream of high-speed aircraft such as the Hawker Demon and B&P Sidestrand. In August 1932 the Air Ministry issued ITPs to the two firms to investigate the problem. In B&P's case it was to address an air shield for the

Sidestrand III Developments

Subject	Main Drawing Reference	Engine Type	Anti-Turbulence Rings	Number of Propeller Blades	Other
Mk.III	D8064	Jupiter VIII	None	2	Original Mk.III
Mk.III	AP1381 2nd ed. diagrams	Jupiter VIIIF	None	4	Re-engine
Mk.III Torpedo	D8065	Jupiter VIII	None	2	1 torpedo
Mk.III Seaplane	D8066	Jupiter IX	None	2	Floats
Mk.III Surveying	D8067	Jupiter VIII	None	2	Eyrie camera, Floats or wheels
Mk.III Export	G2231 and 32	Pegasus IM or Jupiter VIIIF	Polygonal	4 (2+2) or 4	Bomb nose
Mk.III Night Bomber	G2271	Jupiter VIIF	Polygonal	4 (2+2)	Larger fuel tanks, bomb nose
Mk.III Seaplane Export	G2300	Pegasus IM or Jupiter VIIIF	Polygonal	4 (2+2) or 4	1 torpedo and Floats, bomb nose
J9186 AE1025	G1399	Jupiter VIIIF Jupiter XF	Circular	2	AT ring trials, Longer undercarriage leg
J9186 AE1360 AE1769	G1435 G1465 G1255	Jupiter VIIIF Pegasus IM3	Polygonal	4	New undercarriage
Mk.IV	G2340 and 41	Pegasus IM3	Polygonal	4	Stronger fuselage, new undercarriage
J9186 AE3206 AE3808	G2075 G3451 G3766	Pegasus IM3	Polygonal	4	Nose turret, new undercarriage
Mk.V	X1034 Serial J9186	Pegasus IM3	Polygonal	4	Nose turret, new undercarriage
Overstrand Mk.I	G7599 G7606	Pegasus IIM3	Polygonal	4 (2+2)	Nose turret, canopy

Notes:

Export model three-view GA drawings were dimensioned in English and metric.

Export models were shown with three defensive weapons. The Air Ministry only required two.

Eighteen-inch torpedo lengths drawn on D8065 were 19ft, 16ft 7.5in and 13ft 3in.

The IIIS J7939 is not listed as neither J7938 nor J7939 were modified to true Mk.III structures, only to new component fits particularly within the fuselage.

Sidestrand as part of a potential Sidestrand 'update' contract to the Sidestrand IV. The B&P ITP was referenced as 199464/32/C.4 (a) Item k and required an air shield for both upper gunners in the new aircraft. The design team quickly realised that to simply study an air shield was not a long-term solution and requested more information as to the requirements. Following further discussions and clarification, by the close of 1932 it was confirmed that a complete nose redesign might be required and it was decided that some form of 'cabin' having universal movement was needed. A method of interlinked control of the gunner's seat and weapon had been completed. Since there are no indigenous hydraulic systems on the Sidestrand, North and Hughes utilised a lightweight pneumatic system for turret rotation and a sealed oil pressure balancing system for the gun and gunner's seat using static hydraulic fluid. The designs were patented in January/February 1933. Production of a nose mock-up of the 'turret' remained part of the contract and was inspected in June 1933. By September 1933 the turret prototype was fitted in J9186 and the prototype aircraft flown in November.

The Sidestrand update option choices were now a basic update to Mk.IV, already presented with conventional design of nose and gun ring, or the option to update to a production version of the turreted prototype, designated Sidestrand V. Three more aircraft were converted to contract 301584/34 dated January 1934 as Sidestrand Vs and the production type was later redesignated from Sidestrand

V to Overstrand I in recognition of the major change in design and Pegasus engines. The P.29D Sidestrand V differed from the Mk.IV in that it had all the changes of the former plus the new pneumatic operation nose gun turret and a large windscreen shield for the rear gunner. Before the prototype was finished, North also added to the design his new patented totally enclosed pilot's cockpit hood. The Sidestrand Mk.V also had a crew heating system taking hot air from the cuffed engine exhaust and feeding it to all four crew stations. The interim conversions were serials J9185, J9179 and J9770. There is some confusion that J9187 was also converted since it was known to be part of 101 Squadron when fully converted to Overstrands. However, the log book of PO G. Thomas shows that in June 1936 J9187 remained a P.29B Sidestrand III with dual-control capability for pilot checks, since this type of training test was not possible in an Overstrand.

The appearance of the Sidestrand V did not stop all work on the Sidestrand IV. The placing of the early gun turret patents on the secret list meant that as publicity was generated for the freshly named Overstrand the company would only be able to send more detailed information likely to generate an order on the Sidestrand III. Details of the Sidestrand IV with its range of possible engines were therefore redrawn again so as to offer the new structural components, undercarriage, brakes, and engine types to interested parties abroad. The late export models (such as the March 1932 floatplane torpedo

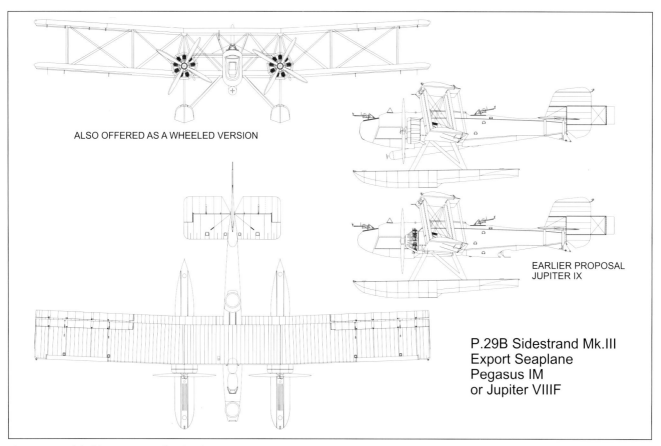

ALSO OFFERED AS A WHEELED VERSION

EARLIER PROPOSAL
JUPITER IX

P.29B Sidestrand Mk.III
Export Seaplane
Pegasus IM
or Jupiter VIIIF

The export model of the P.29B was offered with Jupiter VIII or Pegasus IM series engines in Boulton Paul Townend Ring cowlings, even though the Pegasus series were to actually use the military P.29C structure.

The IIIS, a development towards the P.29C, still had the basic prototype fuselage and therefore was not a true P.29B. Here all gun rings have been removed but Jupiter VIII-style Bristol exhaust rings have been fitted.

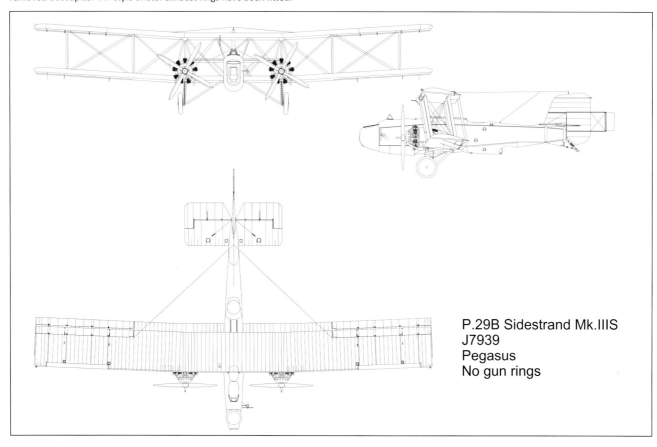

P.29B Sidestrand Mk.IIIS
J7939
Pegasus
No gun rings

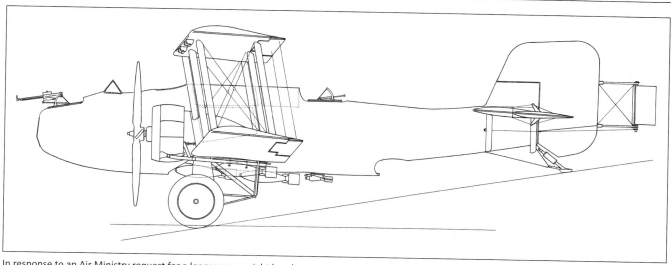

In response to an Air Ministry request for a longer-range night bomber version this view was offered with AT rings, 2+2 propellers and enlarged tanks in the fuselage.

bomber) were proposing the Pegasus IM series of engines in anti-turbulence rings and were actually P.29C airframes of Sidestrand IV structure and engines. For security purposes, since the Mk.IV was only a government proposal, they were all described abroad as the 'Sidestrand Mark III' and sales brochures sent out to enquirers actually had a GA drawing G2341 (Sidestrand IV) hand-modified to state Sidestrand III. Other drawings proposed the Sidestrand III with Jupiter VIIIF engines. These pseudo Mk.III designs were offered

around as far as South America and to friendly Europe, such as the Scandinavian countries. In July 1933 with the P.65 abandoned while everyone watched developments on the sole P.64 prototype, the company also received an enquiry from Sweden for two Sidestrand aircraft fitted with floats to the design the company had drawn in 1932 with Pegasus engines, but no order subsequently ensued. Despite all the efforts, no Sidestrand was sold abroad.

Proposal for a coastal defence model configured as a torpedo bomber. The additional side view shows the proposed survey machine version of the P.29B with float or wheeled undercarriage and a panning Eyrie camera under the nose. By the time this was traced the civil-contracted Gloster AS31 was already close to first flight.

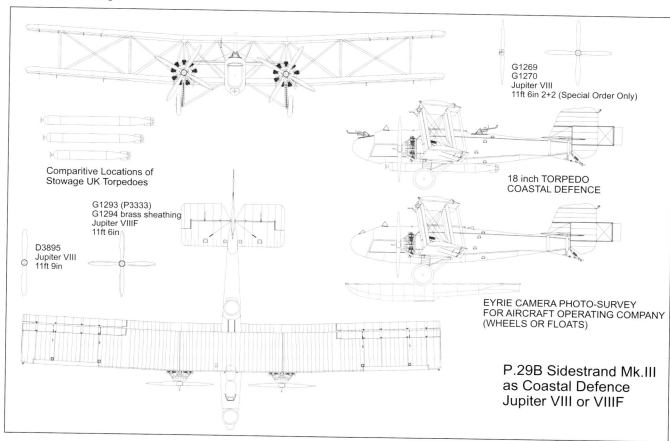

G1269
G1270
Jupiter VIII
11ft 6in 2+2 (Special Order Only)

Comparitive Locations of
Stowage UK Torpedoes

G1293 (P3333)
G1294 brass sheathing
Jupiter VIIIF
11ft 6in

D3895
Jupiter VIII
11ft 9in

18 inch TORPEDO
COASTAL DEFENCE

EYRIE CAMERA PHOTO-SURVEY
FOR AIRCRAFT OPERATING COMPANY
(WHEELS OR FLOATS)

P.29B Sidestrand Mk.III
as Coastal Defence
Jupiter VIII or VIIIF

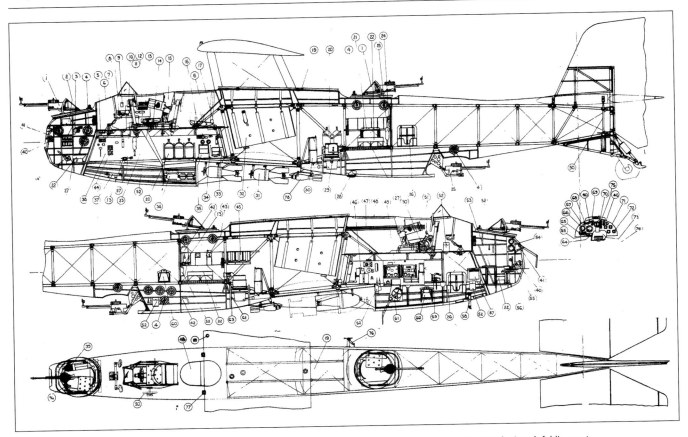

Interior Details – P.29C

1. Gun ring mounting No 7 and 0.303 machine gun
2. Bomb aimer's writing tablet
3. Very pistol and cartridge holders
4. SAA ammunition drums
5. Bomb fusing levers
6. Rudder control
7. Cockpit lamp
8. Oxygen regulator and flowmeter
9. Locking strap stowage box
10. Pilot's writing tablet
11. Aileron and elevator controls
12. Electrical panel and identification switchbox
13. Oxygen connection
14. Pilot's bomb release gear
15. Pilot's adjustable seat with back-type parachute
16. Dual control training set
17. C3 compass stowage
18. Upward identification lamp
19. Catwalk
20. Oxygen bottle stowage
21. Rear gunner's folding seat
22. Firestep
23. Fire extinguisher
24. Electrical panel for rear gunner
25. Special downward-firing gun mounting and 0.303 Lewis gun

26. Parachute stowage
27. Harness anchorage
28. Downward identification lamp
29. F.8 camera and adjustable mounting
30. Gas starter air bottle mounting
31. Special bomb carrier for 4 × 112; 2 × 230 or 250; 1 × 520 or 550, 4 × light series bombs
32. Petro tanks 260 gallons total capacity
33. Navigator's chart cabinet
34. Electrical supply panel
35. 12v accumulator stowage
36. Intercommunication telephone battery crate
37. Tail drift sight stowage
38. Electrical panel
39. Bomb aimer's centralised release
40. Cockpit lamp and dimmer switch
41. Bomb aimer's window operating gear
42. Footstep
43. Mechanical camera control
44. Electrical camera control
45. Camera magazine stowage
46. Intercommunications telephone panel
47. Petrol cock controls
48. Removable folding hatch over second cockpit
49. Wireless panel
50. Tail adjuster gear
51. Engine controls
52. Mic: Bag and telephone connections

53. Bomb aimer's folding seats
54. Bomb aimer's instruments
55. Watch and holder
56. Bomb sight and adjustable mounting
57. Map stowage box
58. Tail drift sight mounting
59. Aldis signalling lamp and stowage
60. First aid outfit stowage
61. Aerial reel mounting
62. Gas starter connection panel
63. Electrical camera motor
64. Compass correction card holder
65. 'Twinob' engine switches
66. Altimeter
67. Air speed indicator
68. Wing tip flare push buttons
69. Cross level
70. Turn indicator
71. Oil temperature gauge
72. Oil pressure gauge
73. Engine running instruction plate
74. P.4 compass and mounting
75. Fore and aft level
76. Windmill drive for camera
77. C3 compass mounting
78. Light series bomb rack

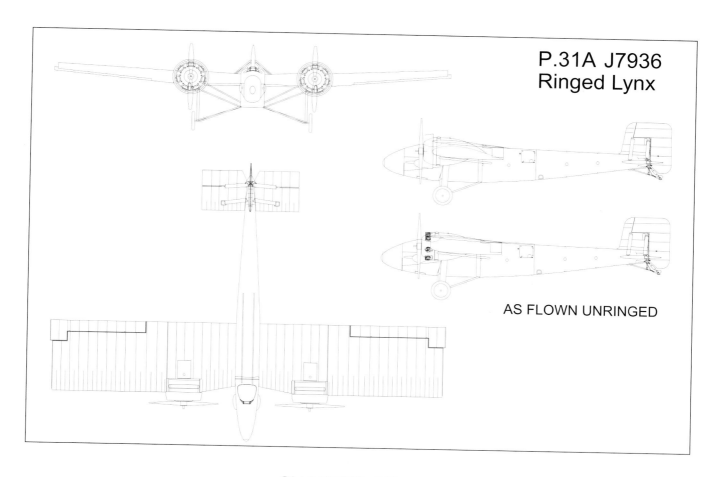

P.31A J7936
Ringed Lynx

AS FLOWN UNRINGED

CHAPTER SEVEN

Single-Engine, Single-Seat Fighters P.31A, P.33/P.34 and P.35

P.31 & P.31A Bittern

DURING THE SECOND HALF of 1924, J. D. North started calculations and concepts for an ideal or 'model' monoplane under project P.31. Considering safety and performance, North felt that his monoplane should be about the same power as a single-engined aircraft but should be twin-engined and he built the idea around the Armstrong Siddeley Lynx, a seven-cylinder radial giving similar power in the machine overall as the then standard single Napier Lion inline.

The P.31 was not built and not even drawn in detail. The scheme drawing seems to be lost. The idea of a twin-engined monoplane appealed as an avenue for the Air Ministry to study, since they were issuing specs for much larger aircraft to be used as bomber destroyers but employing the Coventry Ordnance Works cannon or COW gun. Three months later the revised military design known as the P.31A appeared, in a general arrangement dated 16 February 1925. A contact was placed and the initial wind tunnel body model of the

P.31A was schemed and mock-ups of the nose and controls laid down for construction and approval. The design actually produced was designed to meet specification 27/24 for a bomber destroyer/night fighter. Various model wings or 'planes' were tested for the P.31A into early 1926 with scale body models and control mock-ups, arrangements for aerials for wireless telegraphy, Aldis telescopic sight arrangements, structural frame diagrams, etc. occupying February–March 1926. Decisions on what the Air Ministry would agree upon as regards wing section and detailing were not rapidly forthcoming. Schemes for the elevating sight and weapons were being developed into April 1926, with mock-up drawings a month later and lighting/radio generator schemes in September 1926 to gain approval for manufacture.

The P.31A first prototype, as finally completed after many revisions requested by the Air Ministry. The design accommodated planned fitting of anti-turbulence rings after initial trials without them, so the wing details around the under-cowling area looked decidedly unfinished with these absent.

The eventual design layout was a twin-engined, fabric-covered, metal-structured monoplane with the wing braced to the fuselage by metal aerofoil strutting that ended at the engine nacelles. The fuselage truss was the B&P-patented locked joint tubing, formed from stainless strip and forged and machined alloy end fittings. The outer wing was in cantilever with no struts. To fair into the nacelles, the wing thickened towards the nacelle from the fuselage and thinned again from the nacelle to the wing tip. This meant that, as the wing tip was approached, the section was essentially semi-symmetric and a very thin 'racing' section. The basic BP section chosen looked like an RAF38, the base of the section remaining essentially the same throughout and the upper shape of the aerofoil increased in thickness until the nacelle was approached, when the radius of the lower leading edge changed to fair into the nacelle. It is possible that the section similar to RAF 38 was a section known as 'NEC Thick', which was tested during late 1924 but which remains undefined to this day. The engines themselves were set back so deep in this wing that the leading edges stepped forward of the nacelle cowling and exhaust ring. The rearward position of the buried engines with a strong bare step was because North had an idea of employing an additional ring fairing to this as a means of improving the drag. The B&P team were therefore working on a 'North Cowling' for the P.31A prototypes way in advance of Dr Townend's ring concept. Within the company these types of radial engine fairings invented by North were then known as anti-turbulence rings (AT). When prototypes were allocated under the contract 617051/25 there was always the intention to fit North AT ring cowlings after initial flights.

The first P.31A, serial J7936, was completed and flown in February 1927. It had no North AT ring cowlings and no elevating weapons. Instead it tried the new Vickers 0.303 machine guns in a fixed installation and the airframe therefore had very small bulges over the cartridge ejection area and the weapon blast tube positions were faired over for initial flying. The location of the weapons offered the pilot the opportunity to access and clear breech problems in flight. Test Pilot Sqn Ldr C. A. Rea had problems with the aircraft as it was reluctant to follow his control inputs in turning. Yaw and elevator seemed responsive so it was assumed that the ailerons were not offering roll input and he landed with difficulty. On the second

flight he found that essentially putting an aileron up twisted the wing down and vice-versa until the ailerons were only acting as a control tab and the wing itself was trying to act as the aileron. Looking at the rigging diagram, as the wing got thinner towards the tip the torsional stiffness was insufficient to control the wing. The very thin section at the tip meant that the tip would stall after only about 4° of twist, the resulting tip vortex aggravating the aileron into flutter. ('Racing sections' could only tolerate 8° of incidence before stalling and the tip was already at 4° as built). In the condition experienced there was little point in submitting the machine for trials and no B&P records have been found to confirm that the machine went to Martlesham Heath in first flight form. However, it is believed that the outer wing panels were strengthened and the aircraft delivered in March 1927. Subsequently it is confirmed by verbal reports and drawing records that the North AT cowling was fitted and tested to at least one of the two prototypes in initial form, subsequently being modified by a strengthening ring to the cowling during its tests.

Dr Hubert Charles Henry Townend of the National Physical Laboratory at Teddington was investigating the control of flow over airship nose models and over radial engine cylinders to improve drag and cooling. Townend made application to patent his experimental ideas in two linked submissions during 1928. North made application to patent his ideas in May 1929. North's initial rings were a simple single plate curve as used on the P.7 BR2 aircraft and the P.31A, later with an aerofoil stiffener at the leading edge that could be used as a collector ring if the engine cylinder exhausted forward. In the Lynx it exhausted backward and on the first prototype 'Bittern' the outer half of the aerofoil exhaust ring formed a 'wedding band' part buried in the cowling – although a thin insulating air gap existed between its aerofoil section and a ring depression in the cowling panels. Amendments to the HCHT/NPL patent submissions of rings forward of the engine were further made in March 1929 by Townend and his agent to include an asymmetrical aerofoil cowling, the shape of which hand-copied North's AT cowling already submitted to the Air Ministry for the P.31A and P.29 prototypes and which had already been made, resulting in a 1929 publication of Townend's patent 320131. North's first patent 328481 for his cowling was only published in 1930.

First prototype J7936 as completed had black serials above and white serials below the wings. Note the crawl-way for pilot access and the engine instruments in the nacelles.

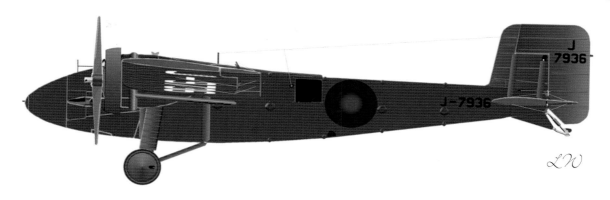

P.31A

At least one of the prototypes was fitted with the North AT cowling in its original form and a full range of drag tests with and without the ring had previously been carried out in model form. In the meantime, the plans to revise the identical but by then cowled second machine (delivered to 15 Squadron A&AEE in April 1928) were on hold with many of the components to be broken down and reassembled. The design of the wing and engine nacelle had been reinvestigated with the aim of strengthening the existing or redesigning in the hope of reinvigorating the programme. A number of potential routes were investigated before it was decided to completely redesign the aircraft main flight surfaces and engine nacelles to match other ring cowling experiments then being undertaken by North and in line with B&P recent acquisition of the Townend patents. The P.31A second machine, J7937, therefore had the entire wing, engine nacelle and strutting system redesigned under B&P's internal cost reference Ae 1558. The engine thrust line was lowered so that the engines were under-slung. The cowlings, of

North's original indigenous design, but alas, now to be known throughout the world as, 'Boulton Paul Townend Rings' were also fitted. The wing chord was revised to be of straight planform of 8ft chord and the actual span of the machine was revised to some 50.54ft compared with 45ft 6in of the original, to increase lift and improve climb. The wing section was replaced by the modified Joukowski section BP.10, developed by B&P and used for the P.29 and P.32 designs. The wing root joints were slightly revised so that the new wings fitted in approximately the same positions on the original fuselage truss and the original landing gear axle was used. The increase in wing chord resulted in the root ending at the rear spar joint and a triangular cut-out appearing beyond that to the trailing edge. The armament originally proposed for the type was finally installed as two Lewis guns at the cockpit sides elevating together with a slaved elevating ring sight. Fairing shapes and the weapons were installed so that the weapon centreline and ammo drums were angled outwards each side to ease case and link ejection. The changes

The P.31A second prototype, as rebuilt using North's BP10 wing section and underslung engines with new anti-turbulence rings divorced from the wing leading edges.

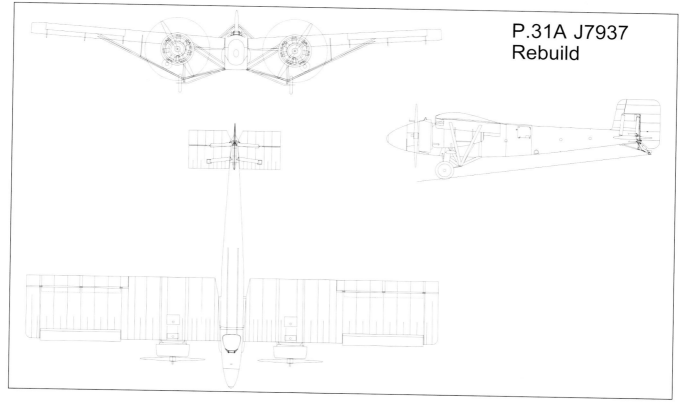

P.31A J7937
Rebuild

J7937 with completely rebuilt wings and engine nacelles with BP10 section and North-designed Boulton Paul Townend Rings.

reduced the fuselage bulges and barrel slot width to a minimum to limit drag. The armament in this case consisted of pivoting 0.303in weapons stripped of their stock and handle grip accoutrements.

The P.31A J7937 in revised form was described by Rea as 'a very pleasant aircraft to fly'. Unfortunately, the increase in speed brought about by the ring cowling was negated somewhat by the increased drag from the extra struts supporting the new wing and only about 9mph was added to the speed of the aircraft in the early cowling form fitted. There is no doubt that the aircraft could have performed its duties as a bomber and Zeppelin destroyer but was simply let down by circumstance. Since the design was now seven years down the road from the specification issue, testing was simply a contractual matter with no views by the Air Ministry of ever entering production. The work to introduce the new wing, underslung nacelles and Townend rings could not save the poor performance from the government free-issue engines that were probably never able to produce the planned 210hp. The adversaries had moved on several years since the specification was issued. The aircraft's speed was some 15mph less than the Bristol Bulldog fighter and only 15mph more than the Sidestrand prototype.

In the meantime, the first aircraft J7936 had already been compromised by undercarriage collapse in August 1931. The new wing and nacelle designs were not approved until about March 1931 but work must have been swiftly incorporated. Photographed at Martlesham in November 1931 prior to trials, the rebuilt second aircraft, J7937, was damaged in an accident there in December 1931 when the undercarriage also collapsed, possibly at the tailskid, on the poor surface of the Heath. This damage, plus the low power of the aircraft, sealed its fate and the P.31A project was abandoned before detailed contractual A&AEE formal flight testing had begun. The machine wreckage was finally struck off charge in February 1933 and some of the parts subject to structural testing. Unfortunately, too much time had passed since the issue of 27/24 and North's 'Model' Monoplane was abandoned by officialdom in its damaged state.

P.33 Partridge

In late 1925 the Air Ministry was considering how to replace the Gamecock in service. The first production order was September 1925, but commensurate with the release of that order was the thought of when and how it would be replaced. The Gamecock was a wood and fabric aircraft and the Ministry technical departments were already embracing the idea of all-metal structures with fabric or metal covering for the future. B&P and Gloster themselves were asked to look at the possibility of a metal structure version. Liking what they saw as initial proposals, contracts were placed for a 'Metal Gamecock'. Serials for the prototypes were allocated, J7959 for the B&P example and J7940 for the Gloster machine. Being a direct revamp of a machine they were already building, the Gloster offering

was named Goldfinch and was sorted and flying within six months, albeit with only metal wings and tailplane but wooden fuselage, to specification 16/25. Boulton & Paul, on the other hand, had drawn up a Gamecock type when the contract seems to have been cancelled, and the layout drawing ideas were reallocated to the new specification 9/26, which it was hoped would now replace both the Gamecock and the Siskin fighters. The designs by North for their 'Metal Gamecock' became of interest as a 9/26 contender.

The two early tracings, by now marked 9/26 and referenced P.33, show an scheme with the guns at hip level of the pilot and a later drawing number traced before the first with the guns in the First World war style inset in the upper decking forward of the pilot. Air Ministry letter 679/471/26/RDI/F of 28 April 1926 informed the design team that 'the gun position should be lower than pilot's hip joint when seated on parachute. Axis of gun should not be more than 12 inches from pilot's seat'. This comment was written in pencil across one drawing. Other requirements were also pencilled in – '1200 rounds of ammunition per gun required'. The machines as drawn prior to that instruction had a 30ft span upper wing and 26ft 3in span lower wing, with a length of 18ft 1.5in. The type had a track of 5ft, upper wing chord of 4ft 9in and lower of 3ft 9in. During the discussions the upper wing chord was altered and increased on the pilot's 'hip' weapons drawing to 5ft 6in in pencil. Presumably from viewing the early P.33 designs compared with the prototype by later authors, much has been made of the change in shape and the change in location of weapons as the reason for the P.33's intimated reduced performance. This view is not strictly true, however, since shape was only part of the story.

The initial scheme tied to the P.33 was a 'metal Gamecock' design, which was quite a stubby aircraft. Although a serial was allocated, the aircraft was not built and was probably cancelled. The issue of 9/26 afterwards resulted in traced drawings of this design carrying both P.33 and 9/26 designations. This is the version with the guns moved down to the pilot's hip.

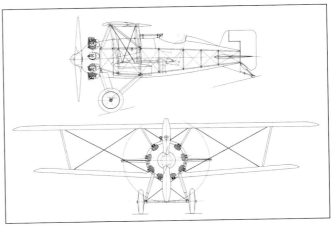

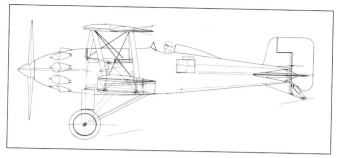

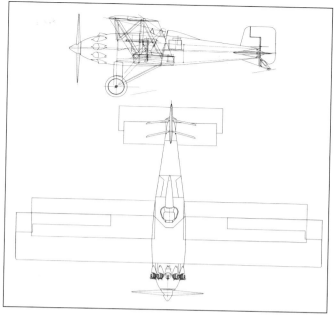

Above: After discussions the P.33 was the subject of much revision. The 'metal Gamecock' schemes had to be heavily redesigned, not just because of the gun locations that are often quoted as a reason for compromised performance. The revised requirements of 9/26 needed the installation of heavy radio equipment and pressurised oxygen bottles, requiring a much longer fuselage. This is the first scheme drawn and it was dimensioned.

Right: The first scheme was followed by an alternative and was unfinished before North and the resident technical officer objected to the heavy stagger and the potential loss of pilot's view downwards, plus the likelihood of poor ground handling, requiring the main wheels to be moved back by 6in.

F.9/26 was a requirement for a day and night fighter, which internally Air Defence Great Britain (ADGB) defined as a 'zone fighter' rather than a high-performance interceptor. ADGB operated at that time with three defensive zones inland from the coast. The first and third employed AA weapons, the middle zone was a free ranging area in which day and night-capable aircraft solely had enemy bombers as their targets. To achieve this F.9/26 would require intercommunication radio so as to be fed towards the bomber formation and sufficient pilot oxygen to enable the type to climb above the bombers. It was this additional weight of equipment and the consequent increase in fuselage size that lowered its performance. In addition, generators were required to power all the new equipment and these external generators with slipstream-driven propellers hung below the fuselage. As a 'zone fighter', however, the overall performance in terms of absolute speed could be degraded to increase climb rate and achieve a lower landing speed to make the airframe safe to land at night. Although the offered designs did not have generators in prototype form as tested, the equivalent weight of radio was carried. It was only realised much later when considering why the Bulldog production failed to meet the prototype performance that external generators, no matter where fitted, had severe effects on the drag of small airframes.

The issued 9/26 specification with Mercury IIA engine (that nearest type test of those suggested, including Jaguar, Orion and Falcon X) was selected by the company, but the requirement was considered so important and of such potential for a large order that at least fourteen competing designs were known to have been schemed or offered as PV designs to cover the specification. In order to respond to the criticisms of the original dumpy (ex-Gamecock shape) fuselage schemes, lack of radio accommodation and unsatisfactory weapon locations, B&P first issued a third drawing in May 1926 showing the Mercury II engine installation front and side elevation in detail and then proceeded to modify the fuselage into a longer, more streamlined, shape.

It was planned to use a modified Bristol spinner FB10212 with the centre point cut off to allow cooling air into the underside of the nose-mounted Bristol exhaust ring. The prototype was ordered under 693540/26 as J8459. The firm allocated a production sequence drawing list to cover the 'P.33 (modified)' revision. The fuselage was considerably lengthened to 23ft 1in and the wingspan increased to

35ft span upper and 31ft span lower wing to carry the loadings. The first attempt at developing drawings for the revision proved somewhat abortive. In trying to produce an airframe to carry all the additional equipment weight now required in 9/26 and to accommodate the best possible view required by officials, the wing and undercarriage position solutions became untenable. The stagger between the increased chord top and bottom wings extended to a massive 3ft 0.25in, while the bottom wing now prevented the pilot largely looking over the fuselage side. Internally a rethink was demanded and the movement of the mainwheel 6in further back to provide a better response on take-off. The pilot's station was also moved in position, meaning the drawings needed to be revised yet again.

On the new production drawing for the prototype the stagger was now 14.5in at the centre section and 15in at the tip, the lower wing being slightly swept back. Overall dimensions stayed the same as the first design attempt at 23ft 0.875in long. A Jupiter Series VII supercharged engine (larger diameter than the Mercury) was ultimately to be fitted because the Mercury was delayed and that engine would have been close cowled so only the cylinders protruded

Shown with upper ailerons only and a Jupiter VII, this was equally representative of the P.34 wheeled version – both were originally intended to have the Mercury engine. The pilot has been brought back forward and raised, resulting in a higher decking in the cockpit area. The front view of the engine (here showing a Bristol exhaust ring) was never applied.

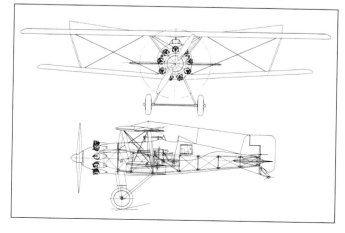

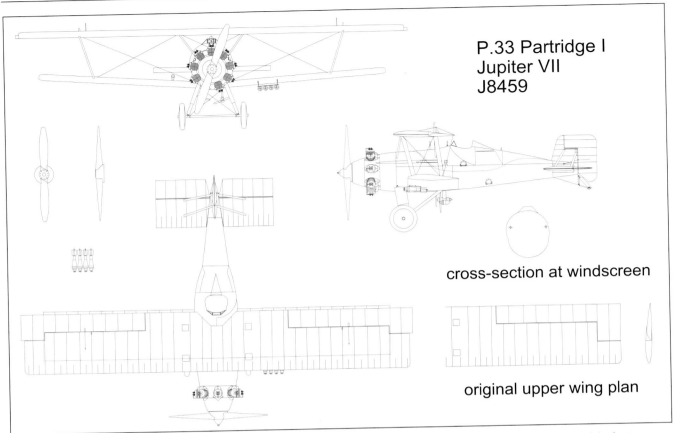

P.33 Partridge I
Jupiter VII
J8459

cross-section at windscreen

original upper wing plan

P.33 Partridge as built. The position of the bomb rack under the port wing is unusual, with the load being taken by the leading edge and the front spar, but a rack never appears to have been fitted to the lugs. Although equipped with aerial fittings, no aerials were strung and no gun camera was issued for the machine. Neither were the generators fitted under the fuselage because the radio was represented only by ballast. The method of applying down aileron via a cable from the bottom wing is also unusual.

Interior equipment of the final prototype shows how the wetted area of the fuselage skin was almost doubled to balance the weights of the radio equipment and the oxygen, plus the additional requirement to carry more ammunition and handle weapon jams. Under the aircraft were also to be two wind-driven generators to power the electrics, creating more drag energy loss.

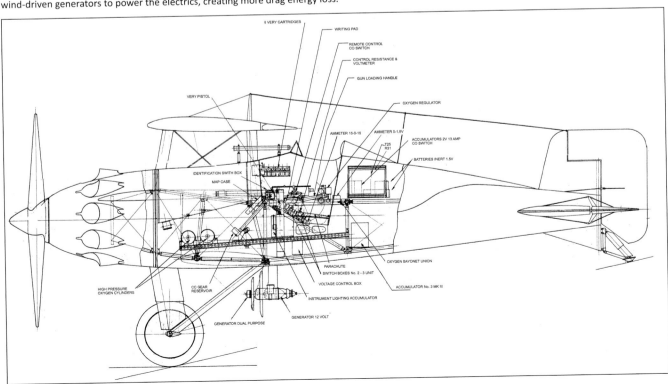

Single-Engine, Single-Seat Fighters P.31A, P.33/P.34 and P.35

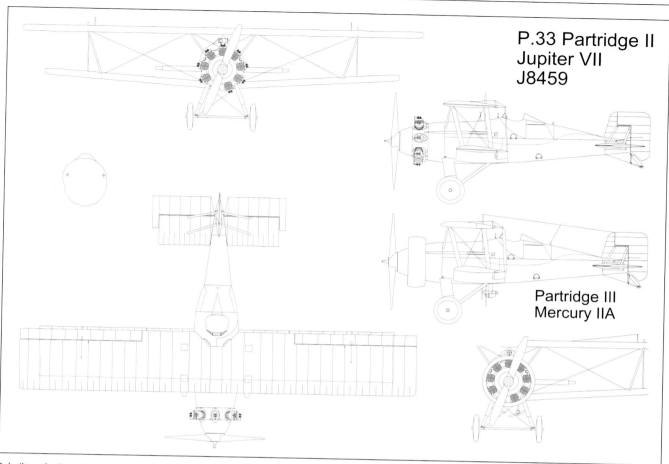

P.33 Partridge II
Jupiter VII
J8459

Partridge III
Mercury IIA

Rebuilt as the Partridge II, the modified wings had Frise ailerons in all positions, the elevators were aerodynamically balanced, increasing the tail span. The strut joining the ailerons was later made streamlined in section. Although helmet cowlings were supposed to fit behind the cylinders they were not mated to the cowlings for the Jupiter. The planned P.33-III model finally with the Mercury IIA engine and Boulton Paul Townend Ring was also never completed.

with small rear helmet fairings, pending development of an anti-turbulence cowling. Exhaust was from short pipes with no forward collector ring, but the manufacturer was quick to point out in its later literature that the design allowed provision for such an exhaust ring should it be required. The oil cooling was carried out by a conformal tank and cooler inset with the starboard side skinning aft of the front cabane strut. The tail span at this stage was set at 10ft 5in. The main reasons for the fuselage lengthening were the introduction of a complete weighty radio set T25/R21 and accumulators behind the pilot, plus the need for more room for the newly specified 1,200 rounds per gun, which could no longer be accommodated under the pilot's seat in a Gamecock-like fuselage. The location of the weapons were therefore moved higher and further forward than the original, with only small weapon budges over the breeches of the guns. As the structure was designed and a mock-up inspected there were further comments on the pilot's position and in January 1927 the design of the fuselage mock-up had to be altered yet again to provide a bulge each side on the current streamlined shape to satisfy the Air Ministry on the ability of the pilot to clear weapon jams and to have room inside to operate all the new services. The positioning and splay of the undercarriage struts also moved the main wheels an agreed 6in further back than originally drawn. The Bristol spinner was abandoned and the nose shape was instead modified to accommodate the Jupiter VII with a solid conically shaped hub propeller, which then mounted a conical spinner and a Huck's starter dog. Not clear on photographs or most drawings, the final fuselage bulge over the weapons was asymmetric, being slightly larger to starboard.

According to B&P marketing records, the overall structure was based upon using Sidestrand-like components selected from the range of standard sizes that were being developed. The fuselage truss work was steel closed joint tube and alloy fittings, then covered in formers and stringers to bulk out the shape into an oval. The main spars and ribs were all based upon P.29 technology and this new range of steel and alloy strip extrusions that were being offered to industry.

The prototype J8459 as completed was left with quite a hunchback as a result of the raised pilot's position and revised upper decking. This version is the Partridge I.

Oxygen for the pilot at altitude was held in two across-axis bottles on a stiffened pressed steel structure that held the rudder bar, stick and pilot's seat. This oxygen supply sat in the fuselage just above and slightly aft of the mainwheels. Below the pilot's position just forward of the windscreen, struts under the aircraft were to hold dual-purpose, wind-powered electrical generators to power the radio and charge the accumulator. To aim the two fuselage-mounted CC synchronised machine guns a ring and bead sight was offset to port and provision for an Aldis telescopic sight to starboard. The wing section seems to have ignored the now popular BP.10 section used for the P.29 and 32, using instead a slightly semi-symmetrical shape of 11% thickness, promising more speed. As with the Sidestrand, the spars were canted forward to fit the section. At least two sets of structure were partly completed and the first prototype, J8459, had ailerons only on the upper wing, with these being non-Frise type, horn balanced at the outer ends – losing a small portion of outer wing forward – while the elevators finished flush on the tailplane. This was later changed by modifying both upper and lower second set of wings to have ailerons of Frise type. These two ailerons were then connected at each trailing edge by a large aerofoil shape strut. This change was carried out after the first set of trials to submit the machine for the second set. The second machine structure manufactured may not have been fully assembled and had no official serial number allocated, although as a private venture duplicate it could have been flown without serial if required. Instead, its components appear to have been used to modify the first machine to the unofficial Partridge II standard and it may have been produced for required static strength tests.

The machine first flew in January 1928 and the competitive trials with the prototype revealed a top speed of 167mph and a warm and comfortable cockpit, but compared with the experienced fighter constructors it received a number of adverse comments on handling, eventually being placed third in the competition of February 1928 behind the Bulldog and the Hawfinch. The oleo undercarriage was considered spongy and narrow, requiring the rudder hard over to taxi and take off in crosswinds. Elevator control was poor and required considerable force to pull out of a steep dive as the machine quickly acquired a pitch-down moment as speed increased and there was worry that full elevator and trim adjustment might not cope with this in service. While the Bulldog was liked by all testing pilots for its handling, the winner was unclear as the speed difference between first and third was a mere 1mph in the initial trials, while the Hawfinch was faster at 171mph. The Partridge outdid the Hawfinch on climb and had a better ceiling than both the others. A later second set of trials after modifications by the makers finally chose the Bulldog as the winner based upon alleged ease of maintenance.

The P.33 J8459 appeared at the Hendon display in late June 1928 as New Types Park No 2 with a number of modifications. Trial mods to enlarge the pilot's coaming to correct the perceived but unproven difficulty of baling out and other mods had resulted in this version of the P.33 prototype being unofficially dubbed the Partridge II. It was demonstrated without the spinner cap, having a Huck's dog extending out on the nose spike. To improve the elevator it now had a horn that was external to the original span. An additional 7.4in was added on each elevator, leaving the common 0.4in gap for fabric. This made the tailplane span now 11ft 7.8in. J8459 returned to the manufacturer in July 1928 and a retrofit Boulton Paul Anti-Turbulence Townend Ring was produced to test on it. The prototype returned to RAE from December 1929 to March 1930 in its Partridge II form for additional tests, but still with a Jupiter VII. The production Mercury engine version, had it been sanctioned, was unofficially the Partridge III. None of this work enabled the Partridge to recover and despite a move to look at a revised 9/26 for a night fighter version only, the Bulldog went into production. Even after the decision, the

Bulldog continued to be thought by some in the Ministry as the wrong choice and they doubted its ability to ever be successfully deployed at night. The potential Partridge III with Mercury engine and sales via agents into South America were abandoned.

P.34 Naval Fighter

The P.34 was intended as the naval version of the P.33. A carrier-based shipboard fighter to N21/26 with a floatplane conversion for catapult launch or crane deployment from capital ships. The basic machine design drawn was identical to the prototype P.33 scheme as initially drawn. The engine type was deliberately left off the drawings from experience with the P.33, although the drawings were based upon the currently unavailable Mercury IIA of 450hp. It was drawn in March 1927 in wheel and floatplane versions, which were the same as the P.33 design having inset ailerons on the upper wing only. The floats took the overall length to 25ft 11.875in, which the company would have quoted as 26ft overall. No aircraft submitted to N21/26 matched the required specification documents exactly as most submissions were a navalised version of the ones submitted to 9/26. The real problem, as with 9/26, was the insistence upon engine choices that were under-developed and unavailable at the time, leading to a proliferation of alternate offers using available engines or a need to delay the project. In the end no N.21/26 offer was chosen as any decision stalled temporarily on the outcome of the 9/26 competition. Had there been a formal fly-off, conversion and assembly of either P.33 airframe as the P.34 might have been justified. There is no doubt, however, that it would have looked like the final configuration of the P.33 Partridge II or III by that time.

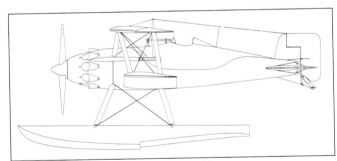

The P.34 in floatplane version and the wheeled carrier fighter were intended to be identical to the prototype P.33 build at the time they were drawn. The engine at this stage was still expected to be the Mercury II. The floats were spaced at 7ft centres by horizontal struts shown on the drawing as circles.

P.35 COW Gun Fighter

Believing that much heavier firepower was required in order to bring down enemy bombers at height according to Air Commodore T. C. R. Higgins, in late 1927 B&P were quizzed as to how they would meet the design for a COW gun carrier that could be faster than the now poor predictions for the twin-engine types. In early February 1928 North came up with a single-engine, two-seat biplane fighter where the COW gun was served from the rear seat behind the wing firing obliquely forwards and upwards at an adjustable 34° to 75° elevation. The pilot sat ahead of the wings behind the Jupiter VII radial engine. As schemed the wing section was semi-symmetrical and the fin and rudder copied the preceding design for the P.33/34 series. A single side elevation was drawn to portray the layout and answer the question, no time being wasted on front and plan views. A short time later B&P drew up details of how they would fit a wind deflector for the COW gun installation in response to official questions. In neither case were the proposals burdened by a specification.

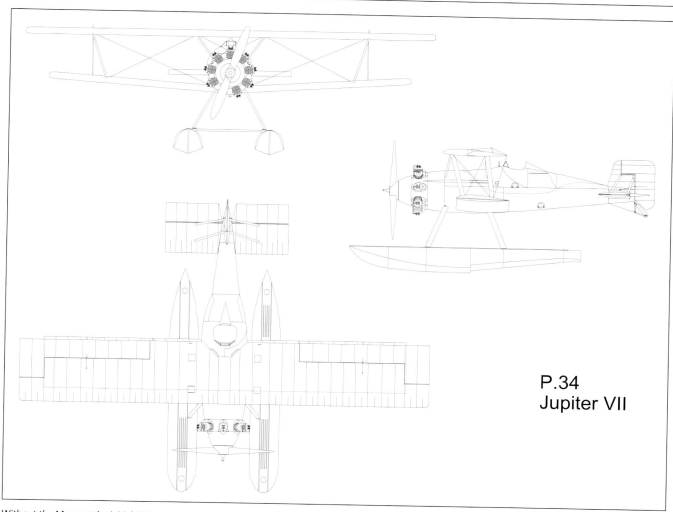

P.34
Jupiter VII

Without the Mercury the initial P.34 prototype would have matched the P.33 first production GA but with a Jupiter VII engine had an order been forthcoming. Since the airframe was to be convertible between wheels and floats it retained the tailskid.

However, the response from officialdom was sufficient to ensure that the company would be asked to study details of the single-seat, single-engine COW gun fighter requirement to be released as F.29/27. The requirement was for a fast fighter capable of both climbing to height rapidly and overtaking enemy bombers flying at 20,000ft and 150mph, just like the F.20/27 standard fighter requirement. The machine was to fly below the enemy bombers and so pour shellfire into the formation from the 37mm pilot-loaded 'shell' gun.

B&P were already scheming a high-speed, single-seat monoplane in February/March 1928, almost certainly for F.20/27. The suggested performance required by the specification was 200mph (reduced later to 190mph) top speed and twelve minutes to 20,000ft. The detailed three views of this did not receive a project reference but these were studied and the design ideas were suggested for F.29/27 at an identical performance requirement. What was frequently ignored in specifications by the time they left the experts' hands and were modified by committee discussion was that high speed and high rate of climb were mutually exclusive aims. In either biplane or monoplane, high climb rate was determined by large wing area and thick sections, while high speed was determined by low wing area and thinner sections. There was also a mismatch between F.20/27 and F.29/27 in that the former required only two machine guns (reduced from four by a preparation error) and the latter had to lift the heavy

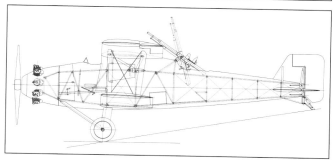

Prior to the P.35 B&P were asked for their opinion of how a COW gun interceptor fighter should be laid out and responded with a side view of a two-seat biplane where the anti-bomber, anti-Zeppelin weapon was served by the crewman. This scheme had no design number allocated as it was simply a discussion piece but a fairing for the cannon was also developed.

COW cannon firing individual 1.5lb shells. The government response was again positive, however, because the design employed an F.II, the early designation for the RR Goshawk steam-cooled engine, which was considered an important and promising development. So in May 1928 the company drew and prepared mock-ups of the fuselage framework, the fuselage fairings, the pilot seating and controls plus a mock-up of the gun mounting for F.29/27. A body model of the fuselage for wind tunnel testing was also completed and the final layout with three complete views was issued on 17 July 1928. Of the five potential tenderers, only the tenders from Westland and Vickers were accepted, neither working with the RR engine, and there is no proof that B&P were actually asked to price their design after it had been studied. Westland went on to produce a fighter with RAF serial J9565 that was very similar in layout to the P.35 but with a Bristol Mercury IIIA radial engine, The Vickers offering was their Type 161, J9566, a Jupiter engine pusher biplane more reminiscent of a more streamlined First World War type with multiple strutting.

The P.35 was a low-wing monoplane powered by an upright Rolls-Royce F.II supercharged and evaporative-cooled inline with fuel tanks fitted in front of and behind the pilot. The engine coolant was passed to wing-mounted radiators flush with the top and bottom surfaces of the inner wings when operating at high speed and at height, with a fuselage vertically retractable radiator for ground running and slow speed. The oil cooler sat flush on the lower cowling side, while the COW gun was offset to starboard immediately in front of and served by the pilot at elevations of 45° to 61°. The weight of the wings when static and the lifting forces were taken by large streamlined section 'Vee' struts from the wing radiator area to the fuselage, supplemented by cables to the outer span. Cables on the underside went from the outer span to the wide-track undercarriage braces, which ensured good ground handling at night. Oleo suspension was used forward of the struts, and the wheels had drum brakes. Frise ailerons were fitted with Handley Page auto slats on the outer leading edge to maintain slow-speed handling on a semi-symmetrical section set at only 1.5° incidence. The slats were used to improve performance at slow speed without needing to have greater wing incidence or flaps. Despite the interpretation of positive noises from the Air Ministry, the selection of this undeveloped engine and its untried cooling system is likely to be the main reason for it not choosing to proceed with the design when the contracted machines used the more common Jupiter VII and Mercury III radials. In hindsight, evaporative cooling was not to be tried in flight until the development of the RR Goshawk series from the F series (Kestrel), by which time the P.35 would have found itself well and truly obsolete. With the Westland machine being very similar in layout to the P.35 one would have expected a credible speed of 185–190mph minimum with the fuselage radiator retracted had a working F.II engine and cooling system been viable. The span was 40ft with square tips and the chord 7ft. The height was 11ft 5.5in over the cannon, the length 32ft 2.5in and track 16ft 11.81in. The dihedral was 3.5° and the wing incidence 1.5°.

After these studies the change in policy away from heavy shell guns meant that the specification was scrapped but the idea of oblique firing weapons remained.

The result of their two-seat submission was an invitation to tender to F.29/27, which resulted in the P.35 monoplane with Rolls-Royce F II engine and evaporative cooling. A streamlined fairing around the cannon would also have been applied if a prototype had been ordered. Despite financing mock-ups and tunnel testing no manufacturing contract appeared.

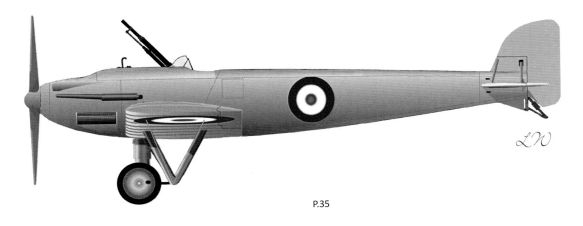

P.35

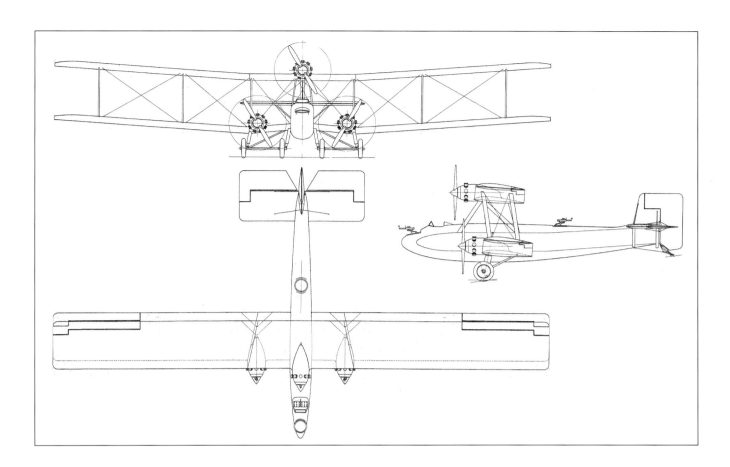

CHAPTER EIGHT

P.32 Night Bomber and Optimum-Span Wings, P.36 and P.40

B.22/27 AND B.19/27 were both issued around the same time but while B.19/27 was issued to tender on the 17 August 1927 for a Vickers Virginia replacement, B.22/27 was only issued to de Havilland and Boulton & Paul. Both were expected to submit bombers of metal structure capable of operating at 15,000ft. The Air Ministry had already been talking to Boulton & Paul about a night bomber version of the P.29 Sidestrand aircraft then in development so there was little point is expecting the company to respond to B.19/27 with anything other than a long-range Sidestrand. Instead they needed to evaluate the advantages of a much larger aircraft with the safety of three engines compared with a two-engine machine. The company had been looking at the possibility much earlier at government request and hence the allocation reference, P.32, preceded the allocations of the P.33 and P.34 fighters even though the machine was only drawn up in detail later.

The company was an advocate of the Prandtl/Lanchester theories on optimum span. An increase in wing area operated as a square of the dimension and weight as a cube so all parties realised that there must be some operating formulae that would yield the optimum span wing, being a compromise between lifting area and structural weight. But how would such a wing be manufactured? The Ministry placed a contract with B&P under specification 29/26 (File 722599/26) to design a steel wing based upon these theories that would represent a constructible wing of optimum span. The Optimum Span Project had

An initial proposal for the P.32 was essentially a scaled up early Sidestrand design and called the P.32-II, suggesting that there was an unknown P.32-1.

three basic sizes of ribs and spars designed to fit along the span listed as rib or spar No 60, No 70 or No 80, with all appropriate fittings and bracing cables. The wing design was intended to be for a biplane with full inter-plane strut and spar joint details, external bracing wires, etc. A total of seventy-nine drawings covered the entire wing detailing and a further thirteen drawings covered the appropriate mating ailerons for the wing. It is not known what wing section was employed. Whether or not the actual design proceeded to build and test is also not known, but the order was essentially for a basic design and that design study was completed and delivered complete with all drawings and GAs for parts. A further government contract to test metal spars was issued as 803572/27.

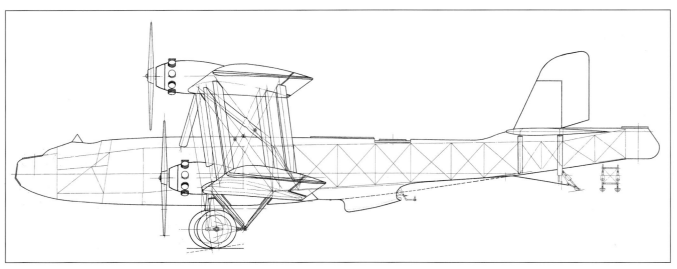

Side profile of the P.32 during manufacture and development of the design now shows twin fins with tail gunner's pulpit, ventral bath, twin tail skids, swept outer wings and Sidestrand III-style 'bombing nose'. This concept was set back by the requirement to have free access down the fuselage to the rear pulpit. The normally cable-rigged rear fuselage truss shown had to be completely rethought.

In the meantime, in April 1927, as a result of discussions with government officers the company had drawn up a GA of just such a large (100ft span) three-engine night bomber based upon an enlarged P.29 Sidestrand prototype and named the P.32. For the P.32-1 design no such drawing was formally recorded, since it was probably a Jupiter VI engine version discussed and sketched around the drawing board earlier and not saved in standard record. The general project record simply stated 'Jupiter' for the engine. The P.32-II of 28 April 1927 alternately assumed the available use of Bristol Jupiter VIII geared engines. The wing chord was 10ft, the overall length 56ft 8in and the wing section was semi-symmetrical. The Air Ministry were pleased to issue B.22/27 to B&P and de Havilland as two businesses who had not been involved directly with the Virginia and other B.19/27 tender programmes. The requirement issued in August, however, was for Mercury engines, not Jupiter. Larger front and side elevations had been drawn in July 1927 and mock-ups were drawn for the P.32 body and the pilot's and front gunner's cockpits in October 1927. The design was ordered under contract 796097/27. Discussions with the Air Ministry representatives immediately and inevitably brought changes, particularly to the bombing nose and pilot's cockpit.

At the mock-up conference held late at Mousehold Heath on 8 August 1928, delivery, planned for 31 March 1929, slipped back and back as the team were hit with more changes required in the design. Trials intended to compare the B&P and DH designs in early 1930 were shelved as the planned Mercury power plants were not going to

appear either. By the second and final P.32 conference on 26 November 1930 the new delivery date had slipped to March 1931 and the free-issue engines were likely to be Jupiter XF or XFBM. There were still numerous changes needed such as the addition of a tail gunner's position and then the improvement of this location into a large gunner's 'pulpit' overhanging the original tail. The P.32 fuselage was quite wide in plan so that with the removal of an added prone position it would be difficult for the dorsal gun position to fire downwards either side of the tail. B&P solved this by having a standard gun ring mount on a cut-out portion of decking that could be slid from side to side on rails to fire down over the necessary side. Since the tail gunner had to access his location, but also had to move forward to take over other positions as necessary, a walkway was demanded right along the keel of the aircraft. The final walkway was a mirror image of the first idea. It started in the nose centreline and then went diagonally to the starboard side to pass the pilot's raised platform to port and the radio operator's seating behind him. Then it moved to port, passing the three large fuel tanks to starboard. Finally it continued diagonally back to the centreline and aft to the dorsal gunner's platform and beyond.

The rough one-tenth side elevation showed an airframe with five crew positions. The bomb-aimer/gunner in the nose, a pilot offset to port, dorsal and prone positions and a tail position. It had large upright twin fin and rudder systems and the tail was supported on the ground by two large tailskid assemblies. The prone gunner bath was removed once the sliding dorsal ring was agreed. It is notable that not one surviving P.32

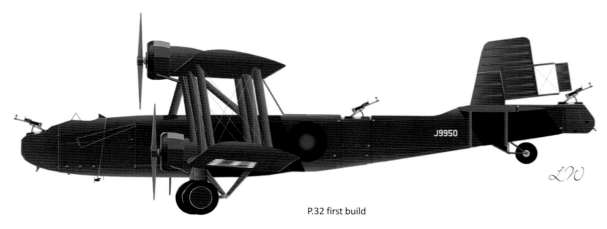

P.32 first build

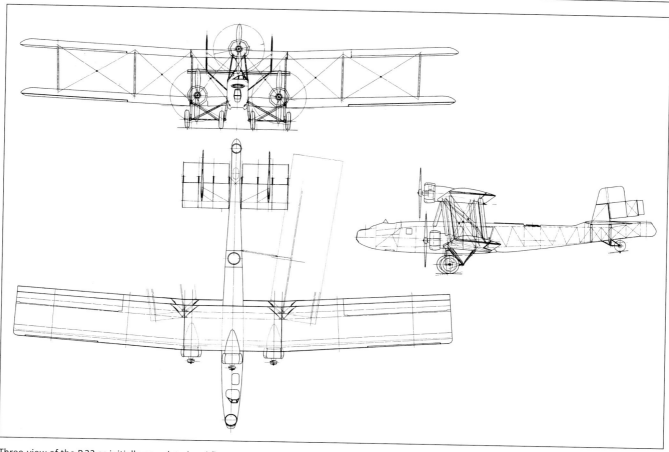

Three-view of the P.32 as initially completed and flown.

drawing known states the engine type, such were the problems the design was under in obtaining a suitably developed and approved power plant for first fit. When the press got wind of the P.32, the engines were identified as early Pegasus, which in unclear form on photographs would be difficult to differentiate from the Jupiter or Mercury, upon which the Pegasus was based. The structure remained of steel and light alloy developed for the P.29 albeit in larger sizes, but then, compared with the 100ft-span, 56ft 8in-long P.32-II the fuselage had grown enormously in section and length. D9040 displayed a machine 65ft 6.76in long overall, requiring a non-contractual special drawing sheet to accommodate scale, while the wing chord had grown to 10ft 9in to lift the increasing weight as requirements for load and equipment changed. The fuselage sides aft of the wing had warren girder 'W' pattern struts rather than traditional vertical ones when photographed as a skeleton in April 1930 because

the keel walkway all the way to the tail precluded the use of cross-bracing cables in the fuselage aft of the wing. The wing section was now BP.10.

The final design emerged in late 1930 as a revised 100ft-span, 69ft 1in-long machine with outer wing panels that could be folded to accommodate the airframe in smaller-width RAF hangars. It had three Jupiter XF engines in fully enclosed polygonal anti-turbulence cowlings with internal nose-mounted collector rings. Four mainwheels carried the landing loads. The large truss under the rear fuselage for the twin tail skids had been retained but left in favour of a single castoring tailwheel. The twin fins had been shortened in height and the rudders each fitted with Flettner servo tabs as on the Sidestrand production. In doing this the hinge line was no longer maintained at vertical to the tailplane but was tilted forwards at 82° to the tailplane centreline, allowing the rear gunner to have a better defensive line of sight below the servo tabs.

P.32 Hendon

J9950, the only machine completed, as first flown. *Crown Copyright*

The first flight of serial J9950 was now to have taken place in January 1931 to meet the delivery date of March, and on 3 February 1931 the Air Ministry sent a team to inspect and photograph the completed aeroplane. It was assigned to Martlesham Heath for tests from March but then could not be delivered because further problems were experienced with overheating engines during ground runs prior to flight. The large boss two-blade wooden propellers did not push

enough air flow through the enclosed cowls for prolonged ground testing and problems with the Jupiter XF early development engines then inevitably led to overheating. At this point the machine had not even flown and the predicted delivery date was slipping once more. By September 1931 all the tinkering with the engines and the overheating on the ground led to failure of the experimental port engine, which had to be changed.

Close-up of the unsuccessful engine cowling, which failed because of the development model engines. The system would have been fine with developed engines but could not cope with the prolonged ground running required to get the supplied engines working properly. *Crown Copyright*

The engine gantry for the middle unit only available after the initial aircraft had been tested.

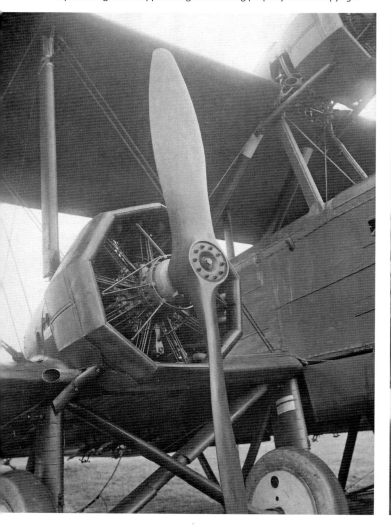

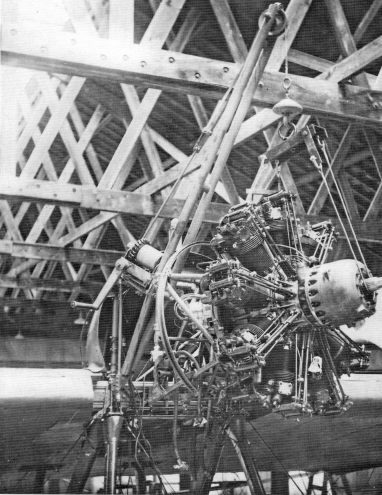

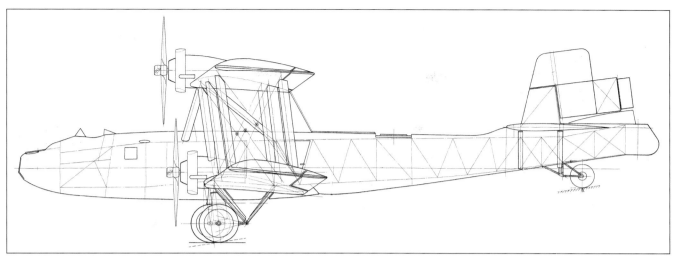

The final physical condition of the P.32 prototype with revised anti-turbulence rings and forward exhaust collector system. The tail gunner now had a fairing to reduce wind blast forward of his station.

Finally, the machine managed flights from 23 October 1931. However, the government replacement port power plant was again proven to be a development non-standard and had a bad gear reduction unit that had to be changed during November. The test pilot himself, Sqn Ldr Rea, was not happy with the handling, but with the de Havilland DH.72 allegedly being delivered to A&AEE for comparison the company had no option but to submit the machine for trials. The machine was flown in this condition at Martlesham and was found to be fairly stable in flight but, as Rea had already commented to North, all of the surfaces were heavy to operate. Throttling back on the centre engine made the elevator both slow to react and heavy to move. Tail trim was difficult to get right, needing unusual amounts of travel as speed and engine power were slightly altered. The placement of pilot controls was criticised to a degree that was uncalled for seeing that the layout had been decided upon in the mock-ups required by the Air Ministry themselves. The narrowness of the cockpit, because the Air Ministry wanted to operate so that a nose gunner had access all the way down to the tail, was also commented upon. The DH.72 competitor had similar problems with engines and forced landings during delivery for the trials, so was unlikely to steal a lead on the P.32.

This view shows the tail wheel fitted aft of the stubs for the twin skids, now forming part of the tailwheel fork support. *Crown Copyright*

With B&P unhappy with the problems of engine overheating, the machine was completely revised at the engine gates, replacing the large anti-turbulence rings with short-chord circular rings – by now known as BP Townend Rings – and the engines were changed to Jupiter XFBMs with four-blade (two + two) units. This allowed a smaller-diameter propeller system and there was no exhaust collector ring integral with the cowling as there had been with the polygonal items, reverting instead to the earlier common Bristol design. The changes were made fairly quickly in 1932 and the aircraft was displayed in new form in the New Types Park at Hendon in June 1932 as Aeroplane No 11. The castor on the added tailwheel was always restricted to 50° and this put a strain on the structure when trying to turn tightly. As a result of this and the poor field conditions on the Heath at Martlesham, the tailwheel had been heavily stressed and collapsed suddenly in February 1933, dropping the fuselage on to the old tail skid upper structure as the machine was being taken into one of the hangars. A redesign to at least allow 180° of arc was recommended. The redesign and repair was at no charge, internal sales order Ae 3646 being issued for the work. The machine was passed to RAE Farnborough on 22 September 1933 for servo rudder tests. There, in less than a month, there was yet another round of comments on issues that B&P thought had been already sorted out by and at A&AEE.

In response to criticism by RAE Farnborough that the airframe was becoming susceptible to oscillation in flight, B&P test pilot Rea, calm and collected as ever, arranged to fly in the machine at Farnborough on 24 November 1933 to determine if the oscillation found by their pilots was similar to some seen and corrected at Norwich. Dr Roxbee-Cox arranged that Flt Lt Stainforth would fly the aircraft initially, with Rea in the radio operator's seat. If he could not reproduce what had been observed at Norwich then they would change places and Rea would attempt to reproduce the oscillation observed by tests at Norwich.

Rea's report to North commented: 'We flew at an all-up weight of about 20,000lb with 400lb of ballast on the front gunner's floor and the rear main (fuel) tank empty. On reaching 8,000ft I stood behind the pilot and he gradually increased speed while flying level, until at about 107mph the oscillation commenced and increased until at 115mph it reached its peak. I understand that if the speed is increased to 125mph the oscillation damps out completely. The movement is exactly the same as we observed at Norwich, except that it is not so violent. The difference may be due to tightening of the control cables after inspection or some similar cause.'

Side view of the final prototype condition with new engines, cowlings and four-blade props.

At Norwich the company had fitted balance weights in the nose of the rudder balances to overcome the problem, so Rea knew that it was just a mass balance readjustment situation, but proceeded calmly down the testing route to teach grannie Farnborough how to suck eggs. Rea continued his report: 'At Farnborough these balance weights were gradually reduced until the oscillation was just discernible with half the weight removed, thereafter the weights were further reduced and finally the aircraft was flown with no weights at

all … it is felt that the oscillation is not due to any obscure cause and, therefore, additional research is not called for.'

Eventually, it was quite obvious that the three-engine bomber was not going to happen as a production order. It was last flown at RAE Farnborough on 22 March 1934 and from there disappears from the records. The Air Ministry gave up on the idea of a three-engine heavy night bomber in preference to the twin-engined Handley Page Heyford biplane and the Fairey Hendon monoplane bombers of B.19/27.

P.36

In September 1928 the team drew up a civil airliner based upon the P.32 layout of that time. This may have been based around specification 26/26 for a three-engine European civil transport but this was cancelled fairly quickly before requests to tender, making the timescale rather late.

The design used P.32 wings except that the wing tips in the swept back outer panels were skewed outboard to remain parallel to the line of flight and ended in blunt end plate tips. The new fuselage followed the shape of the P.32 but was more aesthetically streamlined, particularly around the nose. While retaining the original design's span, the fuselage length ceased just before the elevator trailing edge, giving a length of 63ft 11in. The wing chord was listed as 10ft rather than the 10ft 9in of the P.32, while the tailplane of 48ft 9in span had the same chord. Engines were the proposed new Jupiter VIII, installed in three nacelles as before. There were seven passenger windows each side and the plan was to give each passenger a large and individual view outside, although ten of the fourteen would simply be looking at the wing or engine nacelles and two of them would be looking directly at the propellers. On the port side there was an entrance for the passengers via steps and immediately behind on the starboard was a large door for baggage stowage. Baggage or mail could also be stowed under

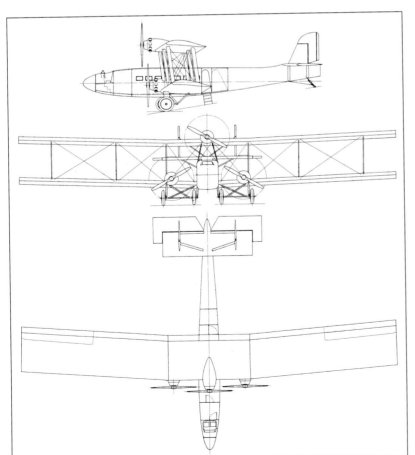

The P.36 civil airliner was based on the P.32 interim prototype design with early twin fins and rudders.

the pilot's position in the nose. A kitchenette and baggage stowage was drawn behind the pilot with a toilet to starboard aft of the passengers directly as they entered the aircraft. While the design looked a modern and purposeful machine it was not taken up by Imperial Airways or any other airline. On the basic drawing (as with the early P.32) there were no anti-turbulence rings shown and the twin fins followed the first planned build schemes of the P.32 prototype.

P.40

Issued to tender in December 1928, specification C.16/28 called for a three-engine, all-purpose aircraft able to carry up to thirty troops or payload of equivalent in stores, spare engines or bombs. For ambulance duties, twelve stretchers were required. The Handley Page Clive and Vickers Victoria used abroad in the Middle and Far East had to be replaced and it was thought the third engine would be useful in such primitive conditions. High speed at 10,000ft, landing restricted to below 55mph, a ceiling of 22,000ft plus a range of 1,200 miles were required. The projected bomb load was 2,580lb and protection was from two Lewis guns in gun rings.

The B&P response was the P.40 drawn up in January 1929. Essentially a P.32 with five windows each side, a large rear entrance door and a roof hatch to help load spare engines, it retained the bombing nose and dorsal gun positions. For the bombing mode a weapon carrier was slung under the fuselage when required. The three-view and the interior equipment layout were some of the first drawings in the G2000 to G2199 series reserved for speculative drawings intended for tenders or small details for ground equipment or modifications. There seems to have been no proposal brochure generated, it being assumed perhaps that its similarity to the P.32 would speak for itself and that a more detailed description would not be required. The engines proposed were Mercury II, III or V geared and the design was unique in that it showed the only engine anti-turbulence ring ever drawn up by B&P that appeared to faithfully follow the Townend patents and hence had the ring forward of the engine cylinder centreline only. The basic aircraft had no tail gunner station, presumably because only two stations were specified in the original tender request, but an alternative had the station dotted in almost as an afterthought.

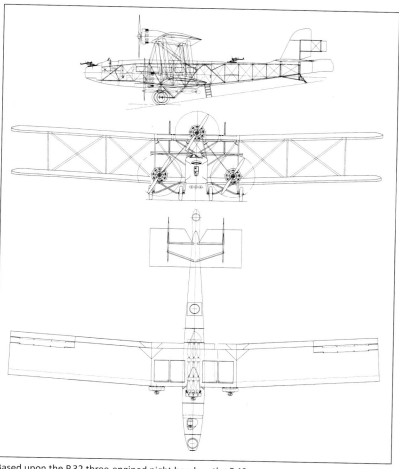

Based upon the P.32 three-engined night bomber, the P.40 was proposed to satisfy C16/28 for a three-engine, all-purpose troop carrier, spares transport and temporary bomber.

The span was 101ft 4in and length 66ft 3in without a tail gunner's pulpit, but 69ft 10.5in with gunner's pulpit. 22ft 6in tail up, 11ft 8in gap and 1ft 6.75in forward stagger on 10ft 8.75in chord wings.

The specification was amended to allow four-engine aircraft and an order was given to Gloster for their four-engine, Kestrel-powered TC.33 and Handley Page for their three-engine, Pegasus-powered HP.43. The main reason for the dropping of C.16/28 was to be confirmed later in 1930 when John Salmond, concerned with yet another 'multi-engined day bomber requirement', pointed out the C.16/28 responses had all been aircraft that would not fit into any existing hangars at home or abroad.

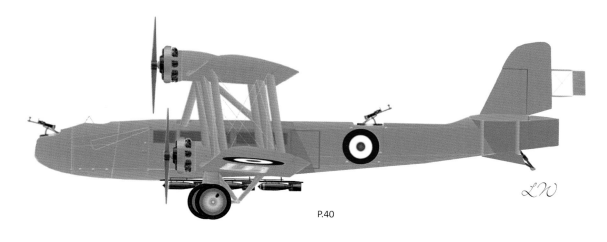

P.40

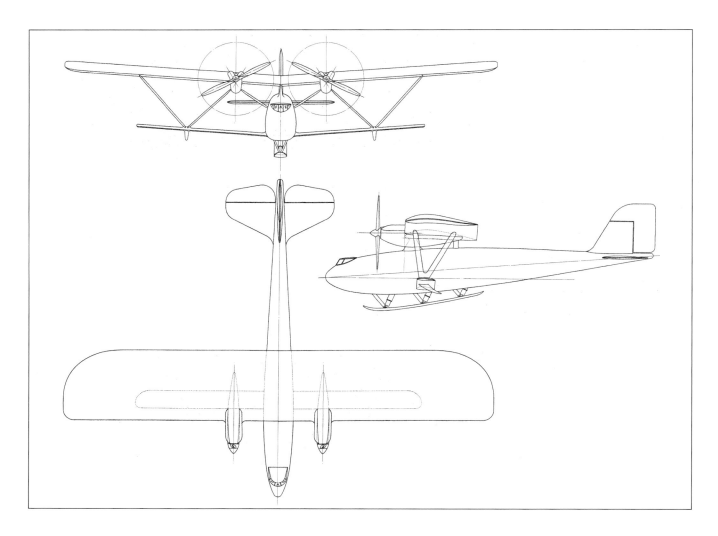

CHAPTER NINE

The 'Streamlines' – P.37 to P.63

P.37

DURING LATE 1928 North considered what best form could be achieved for a high-speed day bomber to attack enemy forces. It is thought that he studied the requirements of specification B.12/26 having seen the new bombers in development: the Avro Antelope, Hawker Hart and Fairey Fox. This specification was for a high-speed, single-engine day bomber capable of at least 160mph, and was considered by many firms to be an impossible task. North felt that it was achievable using inline engines in development, but not necessarily in a single-engine machine. Instead he started on the basis of his ideal twin-engine design, keeping tare (empty) weight to a minimum. Adopting the shape of a fish body and streamlining the rest for minimum interference would reduce drag. North knew that by wind tunnel testing the shapes a low-drag profile could be produced and a good way of achieving both low tare and high speed was to shed all surplus external weight such as the undercarriage. A basic suggested three-view finally drawn in September 1929 was allocated the design sequence P.37.

The machine was noteworthy in having a main supporting wing mounted upon a well-streamlined pylon above the body. To maintain the structural strength and appease a biplane mentality the aircraft had a very small-chord lower wing set at steep incidence and 'Vee' interplane struts, forming a sesquiplane layout. It also had very rounded wing tips from the rear of the centreline to the trailing edge in an attempt to limit the amount of tip vortices generated, assisting drag and fuel consumption.

Take-off was to be via a small-wheeled dolly, which was dropped from a retractable centreline skid, or alternately by catapult launch.

The first attempt to produce a streamlined, fast, unarmed high-speed bomber was the P.37. To maximise bomb load and reduce weight the machine was to use dolly take-off and land on a shock-absorbing skid. North patented the retracting skid concept with shock-absorbing liquid springs in reference 326705 applied for on 9 May 1929 and published on 20 March 1930.

Landing was to be achieved by lowering the skid. Two small outrigger skids provided wing tip protection as the airframe slowed on landing. The pilots sat in a totally enclosed cabin and power was provided by two Rolls-Royce Type H engines (RR Buzzard IMS or H.XIMS). No engine cooling was shown but it was obvious from the layout that the RR H would have to be steam cooled by flush-mounted radiators forming areas of the wing skin, as on the P.35. Similarly, there were no details of bomb stowage and no defensive positions. North expected that the machine would have sufficient high speed to be able to proceed unarmed and to outrun any fighter opposition. Bombs would have to be held in cells either side of the landing skid and dropped vertically or ejected diagonally on release. On one drawing there were no details of aileron layout as so little effort was expended on presenting the idea in detail. North applied for a patent for his pressure extendible and retractable skid mechanism as 326705. The patent included the idea of small wheels within the skid structure to take normal loads while the skid operated when on soft ground.

The idea was circulated as a possible replacement for the Sidestrand and to compete with the Hart and Fox. This was probably the start of the 'High speed H or F engine 1,000lb bomber' discussed later. It had a 71ft 10.5in span upper wing and 47ft 11in span steep dihedral lower wing. Length was 54ft 8.25in, upper chord 11ft 11.75in and lower chord 3ft. The tail span was 17ft 8.75in with engines at 15ft c/c. Two-blade fixed pitch propellers of 12ft 6in diameter were schemed.

P.47

Exactly ten projects after the P.37 high-speed day bomber and only two months after the first aircraft had been detailed, North's team drew up another streamline view of the P.37. This was probably as a taster for someone interested in high-speed civilian mail transport. The same month it was followed by a similar layout intended to be a high-speed mail carrier. It relied upon a retractable skid landing gear, but in deference to civilian pilots and civilian operations it had the tip skids replaced with small trouser-faired wheels and more thought was given to where the dolly would be installed on the skid. Skid operation was altogether more advanced in design and had two-ram retraction rather than the original three. The engines this time were Rolls-Royce Type Fs with long exhausts. The upper wing had ailerons shown and was mounted on two streamlined struts rather than a full pylon. Overall the aircraft was much smaller than the P.37 since it did not have to have either the same range or load. The tailplane was moved up from the fuselage to part way up the fin. It had a reduced size with a 55ft 8.75in span upper wing and 37ft 11.75in span lower. Upper chord was 9ft 3in and lower chord 3ft. The fuselage was 42ft 8.5in long and the height was 12ft 2.875in tail down on the skid. The tail span was 13ft 9.625in and the engines at 11ft 8.675in c/c. Propellers were of 9ft 1.34in (2,777mm) diameter.

In order to suggest a potential layout for a high-speed mail carrier, the P.37 streamline bomber was reduced in size to produce a layout for the P.47. In this case both skid and dolly were drawn in and the tip skids were replaced by faired outrigger wheels, perhaps in deference to the assumed lesser skills of civilian pilots and to reduce civilian airfield damage.

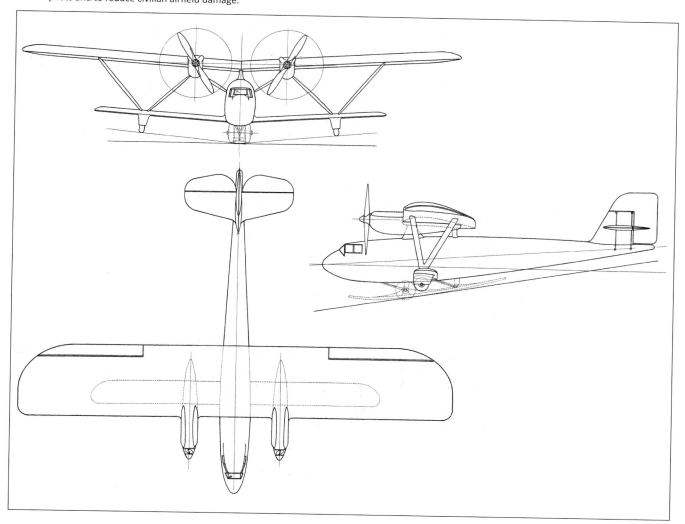

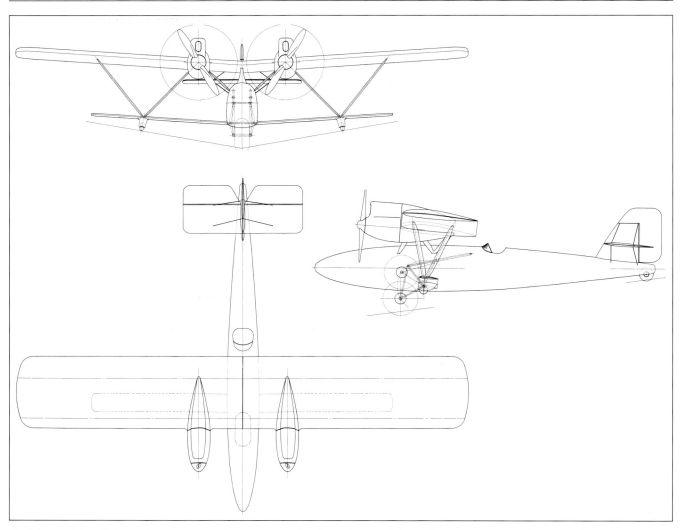

The P.49 sesquiplane high-speed concept was used to present a racing aircraft for potential record attempts. Operations from the airfield employed a single monowheel retractable gear and faired monowheels on the steeply angled lower wing. Twin upright Gypsy engines and the pylon wing mean the pilot had to look out by craning his head to either side to see ahead.

P.49

The P.49 was an attempt to use the sesquiplane streamline concept in order to produce a twin-engine, single-seat, high-speed racing aircraft. The engines were two closely spaced, upright, air-cooled Gypsy units set on the top wing, which was pylon-mounted to a Joukowski aerofoil-form fuselage. The pilot sat behind the pylon with limited view directly forward and the single mono-wheel undercarriage was retractable into the body of the fuselage. The originator of the enquiry that prompted this design is unknown.

P.56

In June 1930 a further attempt was made with the streamlined mail carrier. The airframe was exactly the same size as the P.47 but Panther radial engines replaced the RR F inline, moving the engine centres outboard and partly underslung. Other than that the machine was to have been the same size as the P.47. The P.56 scheme was roughly drawn and unfinished, with the border text pencilled in scribble but not stencilled over by a tracer. It is likely therefore that the P.56 was abandoned before it was formally submitted to a customer.

The ideas of the series accelerated some thinking within the enclave of the Air Ministry but the concept of having no undercarriage and no armament was not an immediately acceptable one. It was in around October 1930 that the department of the Air Member for Supply and Research (AMSR) put forward the idea of a high-speed bomber delivering 1,000lb of bombs and operating with impunity by virtue of its speed or its heavy armament, for home defence.

The response from other departments was that if this was a replacement for the single-engine bomber such as the Hart then it was not required or requested. If it was instead a replacement for the Sidestrand with the lack of the strategic capabilities the Air Staff considered should be procured in its fleet, it was too large and of too much engine capability to carry a mere 1,000lb. The point was missed entirely on bombing at high speed and medium range for defence against already attacking forces, because discussions deteriorated into yet another comparison of the single- and twin-engine bomber lobbies within the Ministry. The consideration of heavy or medium bombing in the lightest possible machine became instead the age-old argument of single- or twin-engine bombers to strike the Continent. Boulton & Paul argued that improvements in the older Sidestrand concept and its more recent developments would ultimately outclass the Hart in speed and, if required, armament. Nevertheless, at this stage of thinking, none of the P.37/47/56 project schemes was taken up by either the Air Ministry or civilian operators such as Imperial Airways.

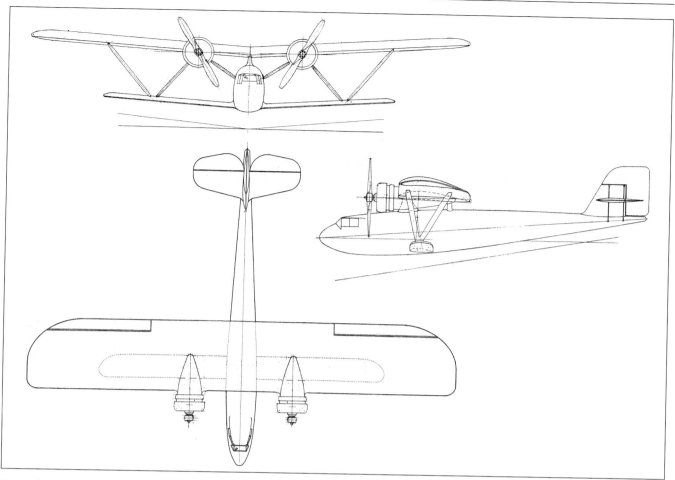

A second attempt to draw up a high-speed mail carrier the same size as the P.47 but with Panther radials moved slightly outboard on the wings. The drawing was unfinished and abandoned when again all potential customers were uninterested in financing the idea.

P.63

The final sesquiplane high-speed project was much smaller again in that it was intended as an interceptor fighter. Back to the P.37-style aircraft, this diminutive fighter was just over 32ft span and was powered by two Napier Rapier air-cooled engines on the rectangular upper wing. Even the skid was dispensed with and replaced by a fixed monowheel and tip skids. The pilot sat in an open cockpit ahead of the wing and therefore had an excellent view forward but was severely restricted to the rear by the upper wing, struts and engines. The design never got past the 1/50th scale pencil-on-paper scheme that H. A. Hughes used to employ for initial discussions prior to drafting larger one-tenth or one-twentieth drawings. It is most likely that this was a pre-study for what was subsequently to be released as specification F.7/30. The airframe drawn had 32ft 3.5in upper wingspan and 20ft 7.5in lower wingspan. The fuselage was 32ft 3.5in in long. The chord was 6ft 6in on the upper wing and the tail chord 4ft 5.125in, with a tailplane span of 10ft 5in. The underwing skids were 15ft 10.625in c/c and the engines 10ft 11.25in c/c.

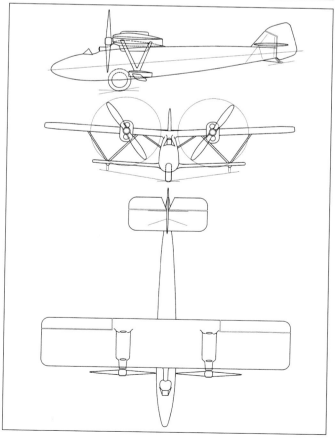

Representing the final high-speed, rapid-climb sesquiplane layout, the P.63 was sketched as a lightweight twin-engine fighter operating with a fixed monowheel in the fuselage and tip skids. Air-cooled engines were intended to keep all services and hence the cooling system drag to a minimum.

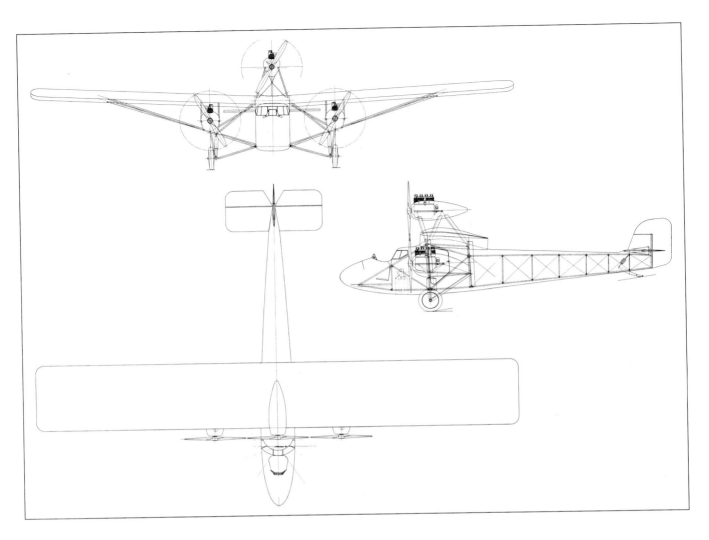

CHAPTER TEN

Civil Aircraft Attempts P.38 to P.54

P.38

THE P.38 was a response to an enquiry for an aerial survey aircraft. The machine proposed was a streamlined-fuselage monoplane with three engines, the third engine being mounted on a pylon above the centre section. The pilot sat in the nose and cameras were installed behind the pilot's position 23in ahead of the wing leading edge and set behind a panoramic glazed window. The engines were upright de Havilland Gypsy units with the cylinders exposed. The wing sat at the top of the fuselage and the side engines were below the wing on diagonal struts. Below each engine nacelle there was an undercarriage unit and main wheel, while the tail unit was a simple curved skid. The tail moment arm was large to provide a smoother control in high and hot air for photography. There were vast tracts of Africa that needed areas and air routes surveying and it is likely that this enquiry originated in Kenya or Tanganyika with Tom Campbell Black and the company of Kenya Airways owned by John Carberry. An order was not received, probably because the enquirers moved on to pastures new before any competitors were assessed.

The aircraft was to have had a span of 50ft and a chord of 6ft 11in. The fuselage was 33ft 9in long, the height was 12ft 10in tail up and 12ft 7.875in tail down. The engines were set with the upper on the centreline and the lower pair at 12ft 10in c/c. All used a propeller diameter of 6ft 4in. The wing dihedral was set at 3.5°, the tail span was 10ft and the chord 4ft 3.4in.

P.42 and P.42A

A scheme allocated the number P.42 was first issued as a tracing on 30 May 1929. The requirement was for two crew and about ten

P.38 triple gypsy-engined survey machine. Cameras and observers were situated behind the pilot in an enclosed and environmentally regulated cabin.

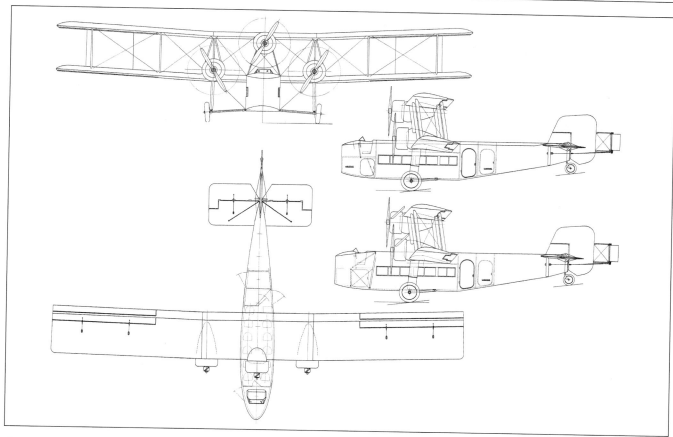

The initial study for the P.42 to 6/29 before the specification had been fully clarified. Only a biplane was drawn and this was subsequently altered to a simplified squared fuselage top with increased baggage capacity in the nose.

passengers, but B&P allowed for eleven passengers and a tip-up seat for a steward/stewardess. They estimated that with the engines based upon three supercharged Lynx they needed 1,000sq ft of wing area using the BP.10 section and Frise ailerons. The span was just 72ft and there were 7ft equal-chord wings on a biplane structure where the lower wing sat just below the upper fuselage longerons. This made the wing structure look like that of the Sidestrand but raised towards the top of a box-like fuselage. The tailplane also emulated the Sidestrand with a Flettner servo tab rudder. It was estimated that the machine would have an all-up weight of 9,815lb. Although based heavily on the proven Sidestrand general layout, one would suspect that the new shapes proposed were by Higley-Sayers because they had a particularly odd nose design. The streamlining was mono-directional in that the leading edge of the nose was purely vertical in side view and was streamlined only in plan as a Joukowski aerofoil. The drawings were signed by Hughes, but whomever calculated and chose the P.42 layout also had no idea of the configuration of the Armstrong Whitworth engine because an anti-turbulence ring enclosed each Lynx but was shown with no exhaust circuit. Only on the final design to Spec 6/29 was there a leading edge exhaust collector and diagonal exit pipes, when in fact such a ring on the Lynx would require North's patent trailing edge exhaust collection. The positioning of the lower wing on the fuselage would have made transfer of the loads to the fuselage truss complicated and within a couple of days the entire aircraft had been redrawn with the wing root almost 6in higher, making the tail-down height 17ft 6in rather than 17ft.

The type was to conform to the requirements of Air Ministry specification 6/29 for a general-purpose landplane for civil duties and, if suitable would be evaluated by Imperial Airways. Although this first scheme was a biplane, the purpose of 6/29 was not initially understood

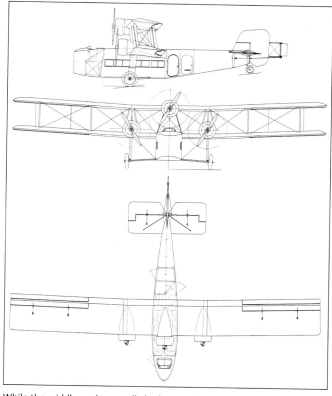

While the middle engine nacelle had originally been underslung, one discussion suggested that the upper wings could lowered to reduce the interplane gap. This was not a normal B&P design feature as they traditionally made the gap the same as the wing chord. Nevertheless, the scheme considered and pencilled on P.42 master drawings would have altered the initial detailing to the layout above.

– it was to evaluate the advantages and disadvantages of a three-engine civil (passenger) aircraft in either biplane or monoplane form. The first drawing G2026 was therefore added to after scrutiny with drawings G2030 to 2035 a month later. The first three of these showed the P.42A, now a monoplane with the upper engine nacelle central on a pylon structure but requiring a larger chord wing, and the other two were the P.42 front and plan to compliment the original side profile and fuselage plan as a biplane. The upper decking of the P.42 was also flattened and simplified. Discussions brought the suggestion to drop the centreline of the top wing so that it met the centreline of the upper engine, but selection of the P.42 was abandoned before this could be drawn. From the side the P.42/42A were so ugly that it is easy to see why the choice for prototype manufacture fell on the Blackburn CA15B and CA15C, which had modern light alloy skin on metal framing. Other competitors were the Westland Type V Limousine and a Fairey project. Even the winners never saw their prototypes evaluated by Imperial Airways. Blackburn biplane G-ABKW was scrapped in 1934 and monoplane G-ABKV was purchased by the Air Ministry as K4241 for wireless transmission testing, finally sold as scrap in 1937.

The airframe for the initial P.42 was 48ft 4in long over the Flettner servo tab rudder and sat 17ft high with a 7.5° static ground stance. The wing incidence was 4° upper and 5.5° lower, and the aircraft was designed for 9,815lb AUW carrying 120cu ft of luggage plus passengers and crew. The chord and centre-plane gap were the same as the Sidestrand.

The monoplane P.42A increased the span by a mere 3.5in to 72ft 3.5in. The length was 49ft 3.25in including the Flettner servo rudder and 45ft 1.25in less the servo rudder tab. The stagger was 16.25in and the gap 7ft 7.25in. The tail chord was 7ft 6in and the tailplane span 17ft 11in. The engine thrust lines were 17ft 6in c/c. The track was 19ft 2in.

The final revised biplane P.42 had a new span of 71ft 1in and was 55ft 3.4375in long including the Flettner servo rudder, 51ft 4.25in less the servo rudder tab. The height tail down was 17ft 6in and tail up 14ft 2in (to top cowl ring). The dihedral was 1° on the outer planes only. The wing chord was 7ft and the gap 7ft 6in, with tail chord 7ft 6in. The tailplane span was 17ft 11in, the engine thrust lines were at 17ft 6in c/c and the track 21ft 10.5in.

P.43

The P.43 was yet another three-engine machine. This time it was a streamlined-front fuselage biplane in conventional format, the lower wing at the bottom of the fuselage and the upper wing above it on cabane struts. The engines this time were three upright Hermes with the third engine central on the upper wing. The three-view was drawn as three sheets in April 1929. The enquiry would most likely have been from Wilson Airways in Kenya, which was preparing to form. Tom Campbell Black became the chief pilot and managing director at its formation on 13 July 1929. Had it been constructed the P.43 would have been a four-passenger biplane with padded bench seats. A single

In order to conform to the clarified 6/29 and provide a comparison monoplane to their biplane version as instructed, the team drew up the P.42A.

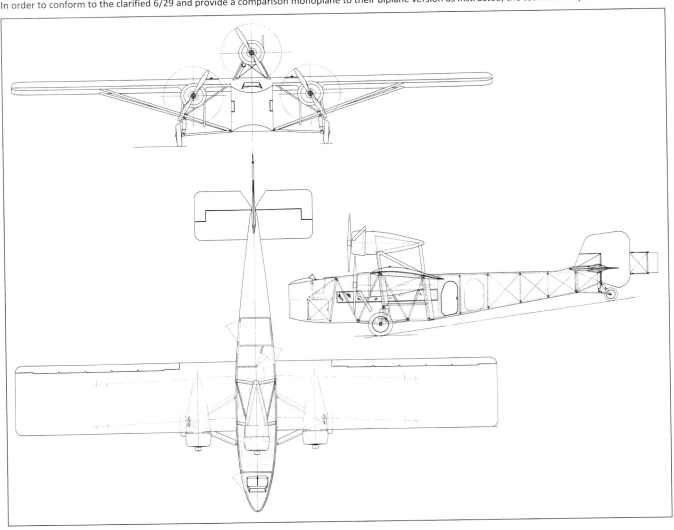

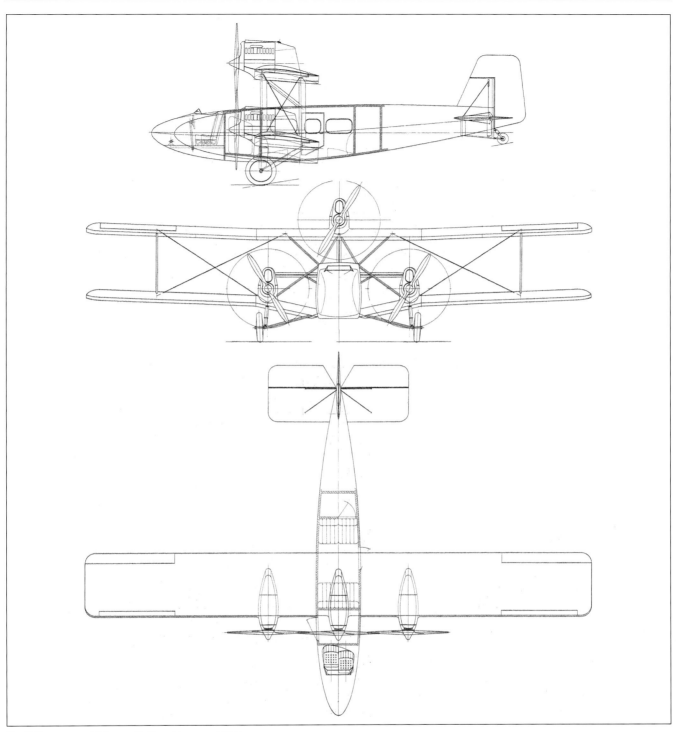

The P.43 passenger biplane with three Hermes engines.

fin and rudder of conventional form ended the rear fuselage and there was ample space forward and aft of the passengers for luggage and freight. The reason for the Hermes engine was probably the fact that it was both air-cooled and also that a number of light aircraft designs had been exported to countries including Kenya, Tanganyika and South Africa with this engine or the DH Gipsy. Mechanics and fitters in the area were therefore familiar with its idiosyncrasies and general build when periodic maintenance was required.

At the same time that B&P were scheming the P.43 in Norwich, Westland in Yeovil were also converting a Westland IV 'Limousine' design as G-AAJI with the same ADC Hermes engines in anticipation of a sale to Wilson Airways. The anticipated sale did not happen for either company. The Westland IV with Hermes was a much more workmanlike aircraft than the P.43 and more like the Fokker Universal that operated there.

The airframe had 42ft 11in span wings and was 32ft long. The height was 12ft 10in tail down. The wing chord was 5ft 6in and the gap 5ft 10in. There was a small backward stagger caused by the whole wing and strut assembly being built square but then set at wing incidence. The tail chord was 5ft 10in and the tail span 11ft 10.5in. The thrust lines of the engines were 11ft 11.75in c/c, with the propellers of 6ft 11.75in diameter.

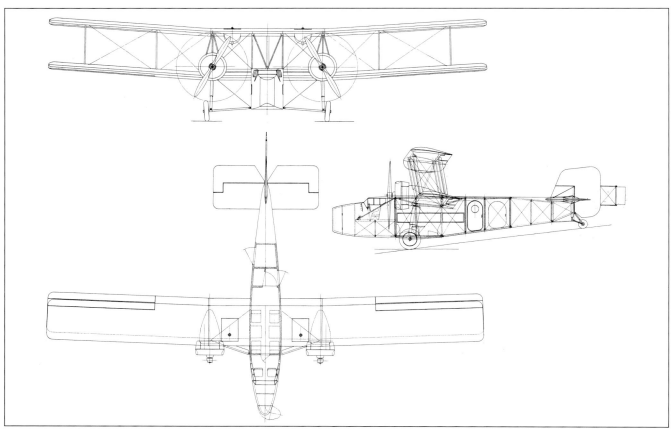

The P.45 with external fuel tanks.

The alternative P.45 with fuel tanks in the upper wing.

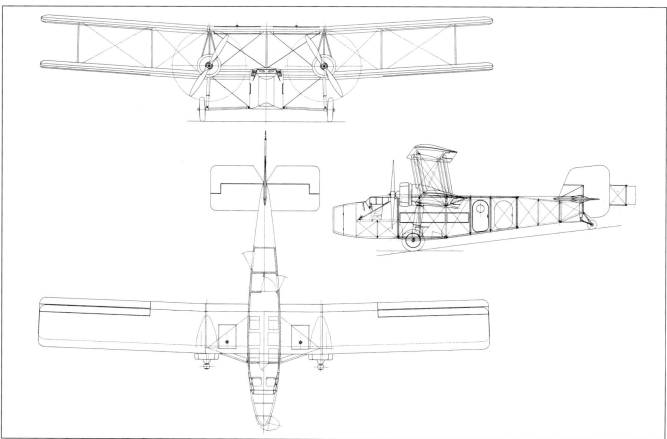

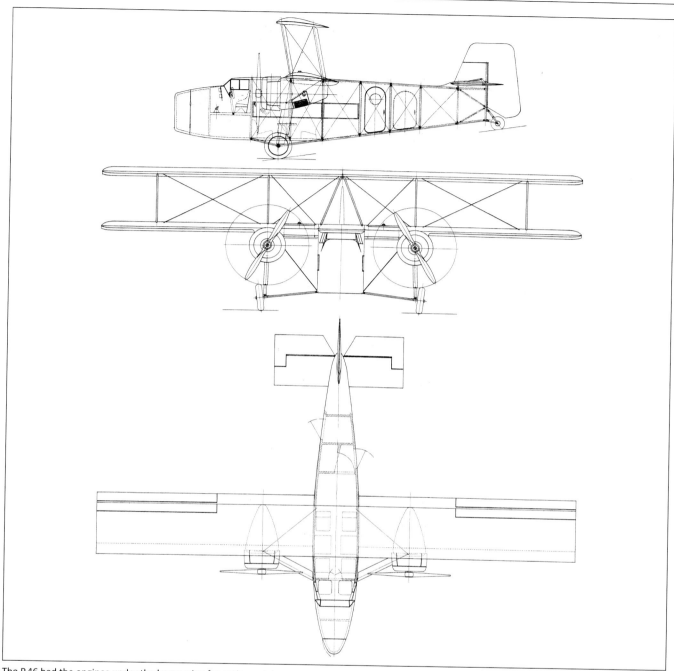

The P.46 had the engines under the lower wing for easier maintenance access.

P.45

The P.45 was another design with an ugly-looking nose, with streamlining in plan view only. Intended as a four- or five-seat commercial aircraft for Imperial Airways, it was offered with a series of engine choices in November 1929. The layout was again a set of Sidestrand wings and fin/rudder assembly, but the radial engines were fitted with full anti-turbulence cowlings later to be marketed as BP Townend Rings, as proposed for various versions of the Sidestrand. Although the Lion V was offered as an alternative, this version was not drawn. The P.45 had an opening nose ahead of the pilot's cabin, which accommodated two crew. There were four passenger seats shown but space for a fifth and the passengers entered to port aft of the wing with more baggage through a door aft of this on the starboard side. Sidestrand-type nacelles were drawn in on the lower wing. The fuel tanks assumed for the Jupiter XIF version had them slung under

the upper wing as blisters. For the Jaguar VI Major engines the fuel was held in the wings themselves. The machine would have been 49ft 2in long over the Flettner tab and 73ft 4in span. The track was 20ft 5in.

P.46

A revision of the P.45 drawn with only geared Lynx engines, the wing was oddly redesigned having no stagger, sweepback or dihedral and the engines were now slung under the lower wing so that they were more accessible for servicing. Anti-turbulence were again applied to the engines. There were fuel tanks in the upper fuselage above the passengers. The span was 50ft 2.5in and the fuselage 37ft 6in long. The height was 15ft 6.25in high tail down. The wing chord was 7ft. The engines c/c was 15ft 11.25in and the track 17ft 1in. The tail span was 17ft 1.625in and the tail chord 5ft 10in.

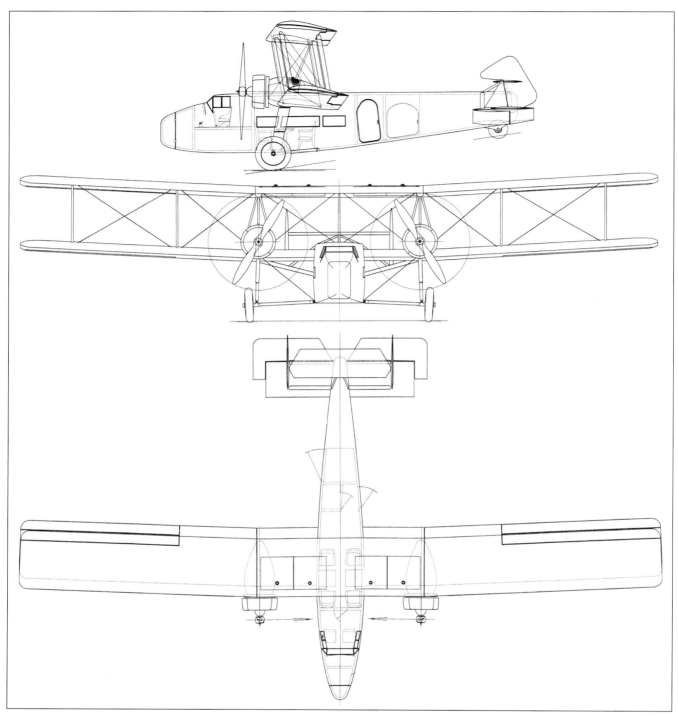

The P.54 was the final design in the twin-engine civil series which started with the P.45.

P.54

The P.54 was yet another imperial Airways scheme for a five-seat commercial aircraft. It had Sidestrand wings with AS Panther engines but with two key changes: the tail area now incorporated a twin fin and biplane tail system, which had previously been designed for a version of the Sidestrand with a tail gun position, the P.52. And at last the ugly nose of the P.42/P.45/P.46 was gone – or at least improved – replaced by a moulded nose cap opening to port as a door to accommodate mail, freight or luggage. The access door was aft of the wings on the port side, while a luggage door was aft to starboard. A table with forward- and aft-facing seats was provided.

Drawn in April 1930 and traced May 1930, it is assumed that the P.45, 46 and 54 actually represent a single design sequence and evolution in discussions with Imperial Airways and others as specified engines and layouts changed. Similar changes were to be seen in the development of the Air Ministry-specified P.64 (spec 21/28) and the eventual Imperial Airways-specified P.71 series. The span was 73ft 4in and the length 42ft 10in. The height was 17ft 0.6in tail down and tail up. Wing chord was 6ft 11in and the gap 7ft 6in.

No orders were forthcoming for any of these proposals.

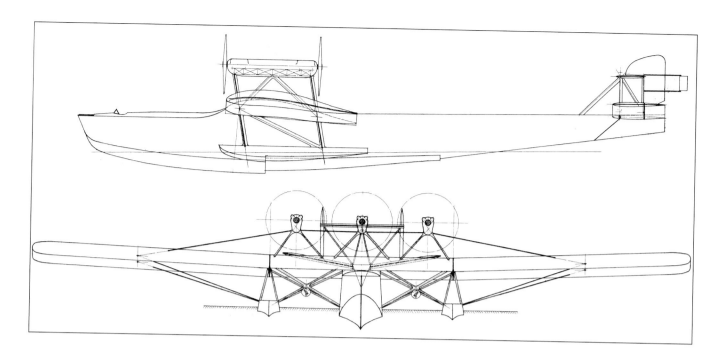

CHAPTER ELEVEN

Large Airframes and the Double-Decker Project

P.39

R.6/28 WAS BASED upon a Short PV design but for fairness it was issued to general tender in late 1928. The responders were Shorts themselves with their S.14 Sarafand, but also Supermarine with the Type 179 and Boulton & Paul. The company had already studied flying boat hulls to obtain maximum hydrodynamic efficiency under Job No 349 in 1919–1920. As a result of this testing they had loaned a scale model double-step hull design in late 1921 for testing in the test tanks for sea state stability. It had been judged the most stable hull tested other than the 84ft and 120ft versions of the Vickers Vigilant (D&M 785 January 1922). This was put down to its long length between double steps of 38.5ft. B&P's only previous flying boat experience was the seventy hulls built for the Felixstowe F.3 and F.5 flying boats at Norwich in 1918–19, and only one two-seat flying boat schemed in November 1918.

The company drew up the P.39 in 1/50th scale and issued it in January 1929 to satisfy R.6/28. The large size of the P.39 at a span of 125ft and 25ft wing chord meant drawings were limited to a side and front profile and described as a 'large multi-engine boat seaplane'. A monoplane wing sat at the top of the hull, which itself was almost 116ft long over the twin Flettner tab rudders. The tailplanes were twin units in biplane format, the upper plane ceasing at the fin centres and the lower having a span of almost 30ft and set with dihedral to keep the unit out of the water spray. The size of the machine could be judged by the outboard floats themselves, which were normal single-engine seaplane floats. They were set part way along the wing at 34ft 10.75in centres. The engines were set above the wing on struts in three tandem push-pull pairs at 17ft 6in centres

P.39 flying boat to R6/28 was a massive six-engine monoplane able to carry out long-range patrols and launch two anti-shipping torpedoes from its underwing cross bracing. The experienced designers of these type of boats were already offering more advanced-looking aircraft with better pilot and crew protection from the elements.

and were proposed to be Rolls-Royce F.II units, which had some oil cooling in the sides of the nacelles between. The engines drove 17ft 11.625in propellers. No other radiators were shown in detail. The P.39 large wing/ailerons of almost 3,125sq ft total was to be supported by cross-braced strutting underneath and long aerofoil section struts from the outboard engine nacelles. Central between the hull and outboard floats it was possible to carry torpedoes from the cross joint of the strutting at 20ft 10in centre to centre. Only a single nose defensive position and mooring location was shown, but dorsal or extreme tail positions could have been accommodated had more detailing been carried out. The wing dihedral was 2.5° and the final design had a length of 115ft 7.5in over the Flettner servo rudders. Conventional single aircraft-style floats 28ft 4.625in long were fitted for stability. The tail span was 15ft 1.25in upper (centres of fins). The lower tail chord was 9ft 2.2in and the upper chord 5ft 5.6in.

The P.39 scheme was much cruder than the other offerings, reflecting B&P's inexperience with flying boat development. If the Air Ministry had been interested in the P.39 and the design proceeded

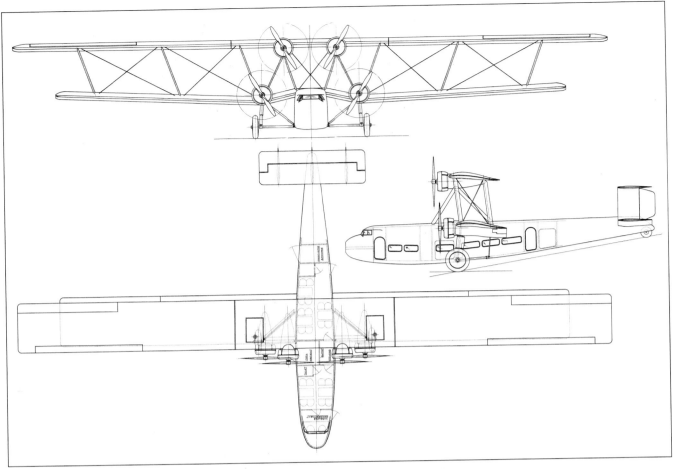

The P.48 four-engine airliner was a competitor to the HP.42 and looked very similar.

to a prototype it would have had to be manufactured in component parts and delivered to a warehouse or seaplane base at the coast or on the Broads for assembly. As it turned out there was no interest shown and neither the Supermarine nor the B&P proposals were ordered, but Supermarine did obtain an order for a civil version to 20/28, subsequently cancelled on cost grounds during the economic downturn. This is a fate that would probably have befell the P.39 had construction been contracted.

P.48

A direct Imperial Airways requirement for a large four-engine commercial passenger machine for imperial air routes across the Continent and of longer range (Far East and Africa) was put to tender in 1928/29. In issuing this there was no Air Ministry specification attached. The civilian specification was tendered in particular by North's friend Handley Page with his HP.42 airliner to cover route variations and engine type changes. B&P tendered the P.48, which was very similar to the HP.42.

The P.48 was offered with either Jupiter XIF or Jaguar VI engines. It had a biplane wing set at the top of the fuselage and above, with two engines on the lower wing and two on the upper. The tail unit was also biplane in layout. Twelve seats with tables were proposed aft of the centre fuselage and eight seats with tables forward. Between the two was a buffet area and steward accommodation to the port side with access through between cabins. Mail and freight could be accommodated to starboard of the corridor. There was a toilet to starboard in both passenger areas and another luggage area aft with a starboard access door. There were two seats

in the pilot's position and a radio room aft of this. Pilots entered the radio room via a door to port and then forward to the cockpit. A full three-view of the aeroplane was drawn in ink on linen. The bottom wing was cranked up to the fuselage inboard of the engines, with 3.5° of dihedral on the outer wings. The manufacture contract was awarded to Handley Page.

The span was 140ft 1.25in and the length 72ft 11in. The height was 24ft 9.6in high tail down and 24ft 8.1in high tail up. The wing chord 11ft 11.75in with 14in forward stagger. The engines were c/c 12ft 6in on the upper wing and c/c 23ft 0.56in the lower wing. The track was 26ft 6.75in. The tail span was 25ft and the chord 8ft 0.875in. The upper wing centre joints were at 37ft 6in span.

B&P Double-Decker

North's 'double-decker' was a civil multi-engine biplane using six Wright Cyclone engines with anti-turbulence rings in an 'M' formation, two on the upper wing and four on the lower. The title was '40 Passenger Airliner'. The fuselage filled the entire gap between the wings and was of aerofoil profile in elevation with a lifting body section, the top being flat and the bottom rounded. The two decks divided the fuselage and the cockpit occupied the forward portion of the upper deck. Angled struts to and from the engines and the outer wing formed the connecting biplane structure and a biplane tail with twin fins and rudders was utilised. The lower tailplane had North's standard dihedral sequence. The drawing survived on a torn remnant of drafting tissue to the B&P normal draft scale of 1/50th, so presumably did not proceed past this very basic sketch and was not given a project number.

The top plane spanned 104ft with 13ft 9in chord and the lower 70ft with 11ft chord. Total area was 2,200sq ft for an empty weight of 19,000lb and AUW of 33,000lb. Payload and crew was 9,000lb, fuel and oil 5,000lb. The length was 48ft 2in and the height 15ft 7in. It was supported on the ground by four large Overstrand-style undercarriage assemblies in linked axle pairs.

P.59

The P.59 in mid-1929 was a specific Imperial Airways enquiry for a three-engine airliner smaller than their four-engine empire specification that resulted in the HP.42/45 and the P.48. The resulting machine was based upon a P.32-style wing of reduced span and a P.48 fuselage shape with the tail unit amended to a twin-fin design developed for the P.54 and P.57. Three-geared Jaguar or Panther MS engines resulted in an 86ft 6in span and a 59ft length biplane using 9ft 4.5in chord wings. Nine passenger seats were to be accommodated with a folding jump seat addition. There were two seats in the cockpit. A corridor led to the pilot's cabin with baggage and mails to starboard. It is likely that this was the airline's own attempt to come up with a better scheme than the Air Ministry 6/29. A three-view was issued on 15 September 1930 with accommodation for either type of engine. The machine did not appear to proceed past its 1/32nd scale initial scheme.

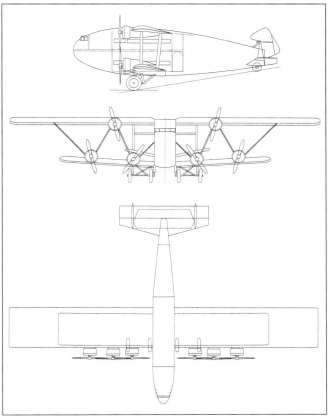

Right: Existing only as a torn-off scrap of drawing sheet, this double-decker airliner was only the second B&P design to choose American engines. It did not proceed past the initial sketch.

Below: Requirements for a smaller airliner than the P.48 for Imperial Airways was covered by the P.59 using three engines and by then the latest design B&P standard twin tail.

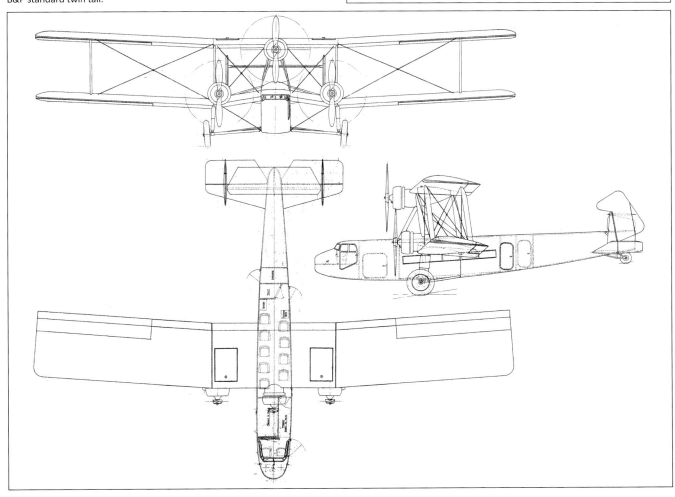

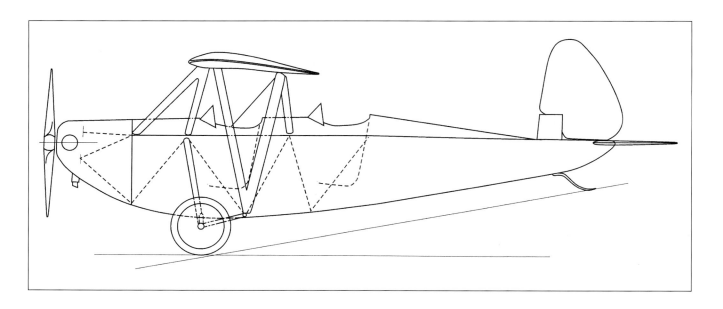

CHAPTER TWELVE

Light Aircraft Market – P.41 Phoenix and P.44

P.41 Phoenix

THE P.41 PHOENIX was intended to test out the civilian light aircraft market. By 1929 the B&P chairman, Capt J. Dawson-Paul, had recently learned to fly under the tuition of Sqn Ldr Rea, the company test pilot, and the local aero club. He felt that the time might be right to enter the civil market again with a cheap product. Rather than competing with the Moth family and other biplane two-seaters, it was decided to undercut these by offering a simple, light-weight, cheap to run prototype, comparable to the simple structures of home-built ultra-lights. The initial layout design and scheme for the P.41 was issued on 26 March 1929 and was, as usual, a collaboration of J. D. North and H. A. Hughes. Hughes drew a little two-seat, high-wing monoplane of 30ft span and 20ft 8in length, which was 6ft 8in high at rest. A neat lever suspension, oleo-pneumatic strut undercarriage was taken between the top and bottom longeron, with two main wing support struts that ran from the rear of the undercarriage wishbone joints on the lower longeron. The track was a wide 6ft 4.5in with the wheels 6in behind the leading edge of the wing. The pilot sat well back in the fuselage, slightly higher than the passenger and behind the trailing edge of the 4ft 3in-chord wing, which had a cut-out so that the view above was exceptional. The passenger sat under the wing in a 2ft 2in-wide fuselage shaped so that the plan view was straight and the fuselage tapered to the tailplane in side elevation. The tailplane was all-moving and to pivot on a single tube at the rear of the fuselage. The tail surfaces and the rudder were identical and interchangeable. The basic fuselage was square in section but had a large rounded upper fairing back to the fin. The tail sat on a simple leaf spring skid.

The neat scheme by Hughes was given to Capt William Higley-Sayers to continue the detail drafting and design. Sayers had designed many small aircraft at the time; the Kitten series, when he served on the Isle of Grain during the war, and a glider, for the 1922 *Daily Mail* competition held at Itford Hill, Sussex. Previously technical editor of the *Aeroplane*, he left in 1928 to join B&P as an assistant design engineer to North. The prototype eventually built was typical of his odd solutions to problems and the use of simple shapes. It seems most likely that Higley-Sayers' and Dawson Paul's enthusiasm for small light aircraft had convinced the board. Changes to the initial scheme started almost immediately. The wing and tail were to be moved rearward by at least 4in, but centre of gravity issues meant the wing then had to be moved forward again. The pilot also had to be moved forward by 10in and the wing chord increased by 3in to 4ft 6in.

Revisions were also made to the wing strut arrangement, which became a strange set of struts compared with Hughes' plan.

What emerged at the end of the hacking and changing was a non-streamlined monoplane of parasol wing design using only a single main bracing strut and a number of smaller supplementary struts to prevent wing twisting, flouting convention. The fuselage was tapered in elevation but with little taper in plan, as was originally envisaged, so that the flat rear end formed the horizontal pivot tube for the all-moving tailplane. The tailplane design was duplicated in the rudder,

The neat little P.41 two-seat monoplane layout drawn by Hughes was not developed as the design deteriorated into a crude amateurish-looking structure under the new design assistant to whom detailing was allocated. Almost immediately changes were implied on the drawing to move the wing and tailplane to the rear by 4in and the pilot (rear) cockpit forward by 10in. Warren girder fuselage was intended eventually to be made in welded steel.

which used the same component fitted on to a small stub fin. The main undercarriage was wishboned and strutted to the longerons on the fuselage but used temporary bungee cord shock absorbers for cost and simplicity in the prototype. The engine used was a designated 40hp two-cylinder ABC Scorpion with short stub exhausts. Although in Scorpion II form the engine produced only 34hp at cruise (2,300rpm) and 39hp at maximum rpm of 2,750, with an emergency burst of 41hp for a few seconds only if it was overrun to 2,800rpm, it has been suggested that the airframe had only a Scorpion I with a rated power of a mere 30hp. In order to cope with the light engine the nose had been extended to be 4ft 8.8in ahead of the forward undercarriage points. The total length of the machine on the drawing office weights' presentation had grown to 26ft 6.3in and was excessively heavy in the aft end.

The mainplane was a simple rectangular section with multiple spaced ribs to cater for the fact that it had no biplane rigging cables. There was now a 30ft-span, 4ft 6in-chord upper wing. The strut to the upper wing was heavily faired, forming a small-chord, high-dihedral surface itself and terminated to the rear of the front spar. The structure of the prototype was mainly of wood, essentially aircraft-grade spruce to Specification DTD36A, and utilised the same BP.10 wing section as the P.29 Sidestrand. There was no option to fold the wings on the prototype but the now single diagonal wing strut proved that it was planned for the future. The spruce fuselage was metal plated at the front and heavily gusseted at the rear with ply plates,

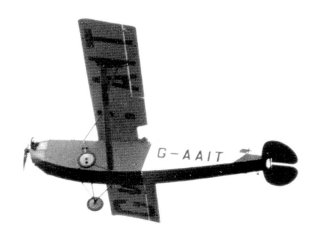

P.41-1 in flight was an entirely wooden structure of crude form. Hughes' planned oleo strut forward legs had become a crude bungee cord system. Note the crustacean-like twin elevators and no fairings on the various legs of the undercarriage at this stage.

and the sides were an N girder at the front, changing to a zig-zag Warren girder aft of the fuel tank. The idea was that the main fuselage truss could be made in tube in any major production run in the future. The bracing aft of the pilot was at 10° to match his seat back angle.

The arrival of Higley Sayers and ideas for simple structures convinced Dawson Paul and North to develop the P.41-1 as a working prototype. The outcome was a rather crude vehicle not considered satisfactory for long-term production but provided useful feedback from potential customers. Variations show improvements during testing.

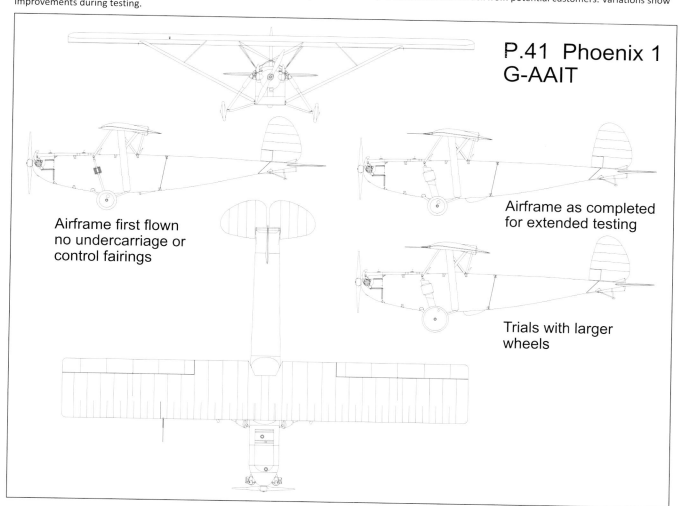

P.41 Phoenix 1
G-AAIT

Airframe first flown
no undercarriage or
control fairings

Airframe as completed
for extended testing

Trials with larger
wheels

The machine was single control, flown only from the rear seat. The excessive length of the fuselage was revised again, bringing the tail forward. The eventual length fixed for the first machine was 22ft 1.5in, with the tail set 2.35in above the fuselage datum. The aircraft in this first configuration made an initial flight on 7 July 1929 but could only complete one circuit and land as the engine revs fell away after take-off, a problem that dogged many light aircraft initial designs of the time. With little power available to start with, it was found to be essential in these ultra-light designs that the engine was set up correctly to make use of every available fraction of power and to avoid overheating.

After some tuning by the ABC mechanic, three flights were satisfactorily carried out, with the engine remaining steady and slow running much improved. Climb was at 50–52mph with a level max of 70mph and a glide of 60mph, engine idling. It was reported by the pilot that Frise-type ailerons would considerably improve the lateral control in the glide and probably 55mph would be achievable with these fitted. Landing speed was 40–42mph. All controls were found to be good except that lateral control was slow and soft in bumpy weather, especially when climbing. An increase from 50 to 60mph on the climb improved control. The blind spot forward and upward caused by the wing/pilot locations was noted, although this was expected to differ when piloted in general use without the pilot

having to sit on his parachute. Rea commented particularly about the easy, stable flying, easy landing and the ground handling on its robust undercarriage. The machine was exhibited at Olympia in July and was offered as an ideal first pilot design at £375. After allowing a large number of mostly amateur pilots to take it up, the general opinion was that it was easy to fly and to land bearing in mind its limited power. There appeared, however, a wide opinion of distrust of the reliance on only two cylinders in cross-country flying. As a result, a search was made for a multi-cylinder engine.

The revised P.41 Phoenix II was rolled out in December 1929. In the meantime B&P had drafted a letter for enquirers explaining the delays and confirming August 1930 as the likely release date. It was proposed that the new model would ultimately be manufactured in all-metal with folding wings and a wide-track undercarriage on oleo-pneumatic suspension. In later press reports, particularly those post-Second World War, it has been taken that the Phoenix II rolled out in December 1929 was essentially a completely rebuilt aircraft with a spot-welded steel fuselage structure. Unfortunately, this is a myth, and one that is difficult to dispel given the abandonment of the design. The Phoenix II, the original Phoenix modified, carried the same registration. The Phoenix II was fitted with a 50hp Salmson 9-cylinder radial engine (54hp continuous climb-rated power) that involved reconstructing the fuselage and improving the fuel tank and oil systems.

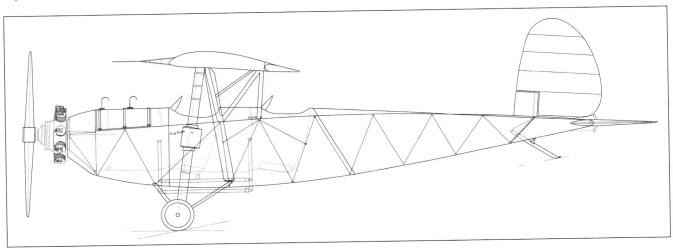

The P.41-II as initially flown.

As first built the P.41-II was modified from the P.41-1 G-AIIT and shows some crude compromises in the forward cowling shape and fuselage to complete the aircraft for flying. The machine was still an entirely wooden structure when it received the new C of A. The rudder was no longer interchangeable with the elevator half.

There were also modifications to many components on the aircraft: rudder details, front seating, rudder bars, elevator trim, the base of the rear cabane strut to fuselage longeron joint and the orientation of all the cabane struts, wing details, reinforcement of the main lift strut, and the fitting of a new undercarriage where the main bungee sprung leg was now taken up to the wing. The aircraft sat higher on the ground with a new tail skid as well so hand grips and step were required to starboard to enter the cockpit. The aileron was extended in chord and made of the Frise type, but appears to have been reduced in area to compensate for the additional control offered by this design.

The machine was now dual control but still predominantly of wooden construction, all of the modification drawings being listed under the title Phoenix II (Wood). The resulting machine had been shortened in length from 22ft 1.5in to 21ft 7in, caused by the weight of the Salmson AD9 engine. This new engine was fitted with 1.5° of up thrust and the fuselage was some 5in slimmer than the original. During flight trials the skid was again modified and a trim system was incorporated for the tailplane. The propeller was reduced to a 5ft 8in from 6ft diameter as the engine could not reach design revolutions otherwise. The best flight reported was obtained on 14 January 1930. Level speed was 90mph and steep side slips could be achieved down

Right: Test flying of the P.41-II resulted in advice from the test pilot Rea that the rudder control could be improved by increasing the surface area. In addition, the crude bungee undercarriage gear was finally replaced by a metal tube leg and an internal oleo strut. The rudder now had no stub fin but was an 'all-moving' unit, again different to the elevator halves.

Below: The same aircraft with crudely modified rudder after the advice of Rea and other improvements.

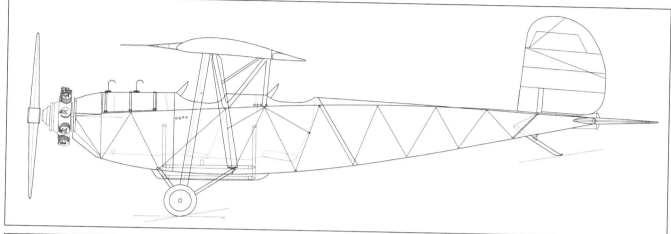

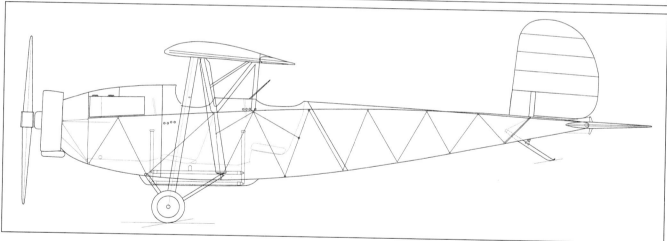

The P.41-III was intended to be the production version and constructed from spot-welded metal and steel tube. The wingspan was increased and one layout considered was a completely faired nose to protect the passenger and a large flat windscreen for the pilot, who sat higher to see over the passenger section. However the P.41-III was to be finally detailed for production, it was to have an anti-turbulence Boulton Paul Townend Ring and some form of folding wings for ease of storage in flying club hangars, which the B&P Steelwork Division were happily supplying to customers.

to 50mph, although it was difficult at this speed to keep the aircraft straight. Rea recommended a slight increase in tailplane and rudder areas. A top speed of 92mph at 2,120rpm was recommended.

By this time (January/February 1930) details were already being planned for a Phoenix III (Metal) as the production model. Following on from this, Rea tended to use the aircraft as his personal runabout. The second state was still listed as a wooden aircraft, while the 'general particulars' of the Phoenix II, G-AAIT, specifically states of the wingspan 'does not fold'. During the life of the Phoenix II a number of experimental changes were incorporated, including the enlarged fin and tailplane as recommended by Rea (still in wood). The external joystick connecting rod was faired in and the original

oleo suspension proposed by Hughes was designed and installed inside a new main strut fairing in anticipation of Phoenix III production.

The Phoenix II generated few enquires and took no orders against the DH Moth family. Any possibility of moving into series production was stopped when the UK engine manufacturer, British Salmson, decided that the aero engine industry was not viable for its products and moved into the design and production of motor cars and car engines. The aircraft continued to be used by Sqn Ldr Rea until its C of A renewal, 2747, was cancelled in November 1935, just as the reformed Boulton Paul Aircraft were planning the move to Wolverhampton.

The production aircraft was to be known as the Phoenix III and several drawings were started for this metal aircraft, mainly the centre wing and the outer wing planform (since the wing was to be foldable), spar and rib details and two or three joint designs, including the wing fold, in the new drawing series reserved for production. Schemes were carried out to try a Townend Ring on the Salmson engine on the Phoenix II to be used on the Phoenix III. There is also evidence that the span would have increased to around 33ft, reduced to 10ft 8in for storage by wing folding, and the length folded became 23ft 6in – these approximate sizes being quoted in a 'stowage requirements by type' list for B&P hangar designs. The planned concept of the Hughes/North reconstruction of the Phoenix into a Phoenix III design with a 'welded steel structure' was intertwined with the press marketing magic of the time to suggest the Phoenix II prototype actually had that structure.

P.44

During the prolific tendering period around 1928–30 the team looked at a specification 18/28 for a four-seater touring aircraft. Just why the Air Ministry should prepare such a specification for what could only be a private aircraft is not clear and the document was cancelled almost as soon as it was issued. Perhaps it was disappointed in the proposals for twin-engine, small-capacity aeroplanes when a single-engine four-seater might do a similar job on air charter. Nevertheless, a number of companies looked at this and started to prepare designs: Avro, B&P, Bristol and de Havilland are known. The DH.80 Puss Moth, although intended as a touring three-seater, went on to achieve many of the firsts for which the 18/28 specification was intended. It was September 1929 before B&P got around to looking at the design in detail and three-views were drawn in October 1929. The proposal was to expand the size and layout of the P.41 light aircraft by filling in the upper fuselage to form a cabin but to retain the idea of identical rudder and all-moving tailplanes. There were to be two bench seats with two port-side entry doors and a large tray aft for cargo. Fuel tanks were moved into the wings, and forward of the cabin front firewall an ADC Airsix inverted engine was proposed to be fully cowled. Unlike the odd strutting arrangement on the P.41, the aeroplane had conventional twin struts supporting the wing and an oleo undercarriage braced forward to the firewall rather than back to the rear. Doubling the persons to be carried by the Airsix compared to the P.41 gave a span of 53ft and a length of 33ft 10.25in. Unfortunately, the Airsix was an upright engine and it is not known if it could ever be utilised inverted without redesign; even the upright version never achieved production. This seems to be another case of Higley-Sayers input; choosing an out-of-date or uninspired set of engine data on which to base the design. With the specification cancelled no interest was shown in the design when the majority were suggesting biplanes for the same role.

An expanded four-seat cabin version of the P.41 generally to 18/28 but with an undeveloped ADC Airsix engine variant. The design was designated P.44.

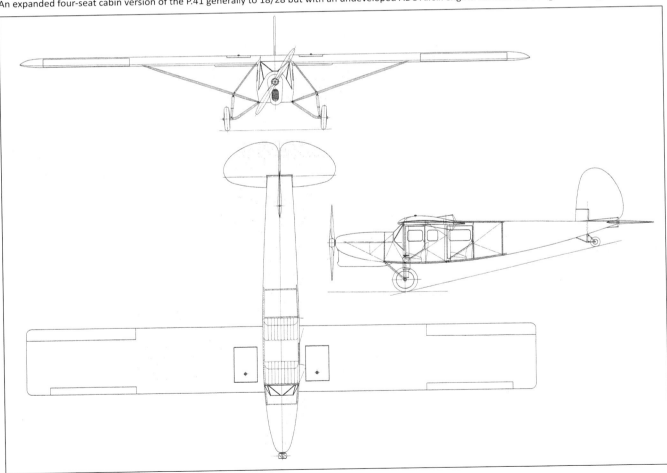

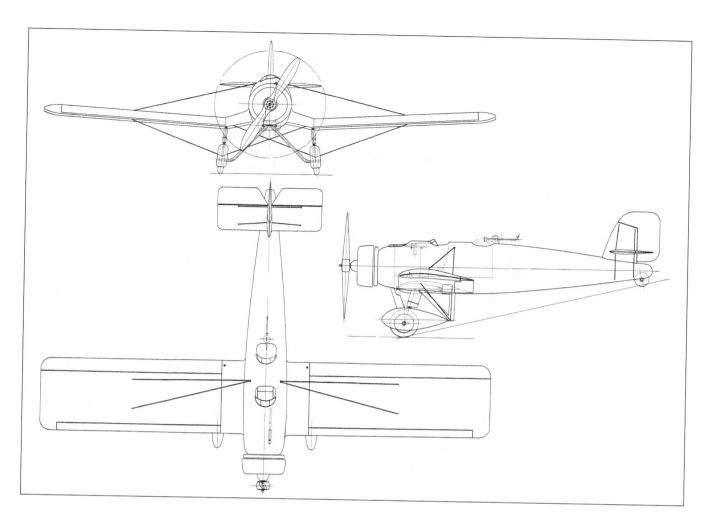

CHAPTER THIRTEEN

General-Purpose Single-Engine Aircraft and Variations on the Sidestrand

P.50 and P.53

THE P.50 was a monoplane with a spatted undercarriage and a semi-buried tailwheel, the layout of which was finalised in April 1930 so it might have been related to the specification 15/29. The semi-buried monowheel of the P.49 generated the idea that the tailwheel of some aircraft could be fixed within the fuselage and partially buried to reduce drag, so that the machine would have to 'hop' turn as with many early fighters if ground crew were not available. The aircraft had two seats with either a windscreen for both crew, or a spigot-mounted defensive machine gun at the rear seat position facing aft. A fixed machine gun was offset to port in the upper cowling for the pilot. The engine was the AS Panther in a BP Anti-Turbulence Townend Ring, which required a collector ring band aft of the cowling for exhaust. Side-by-side bombs were partially buried in the lower fuselage at the wing position, leading to a cranked wing to make the undercarriage legs shorter, and the 9ft track undercarriage was splayed outwards for better stability.

The specification 15/29, along with Army co-op specification 14/29, was cancelled fairly quickly, leaving no customer other than export. A floatplane version was generated as the P.53 only ten days later, retaining all the look of the P.50 and designated 'Reconnaissance

P.50, possibly to 15/29 for a general reconnaissance type but equally likely for export to Scandinavia and South America.

Seaplane'. It is possible therefore that the real potential source of the project for both was Sweden. The fuselage was generally of circular cross section 30ft long and the span was 42ft 1.5in. Other key dimensions were heights of 12ft 6in tail up and 14ft 2in tail down. The wing chord was 6ft 11.75in and the dihedral 3.5°. The tail span was 9ft 9.6in and the propeller diameter 10ft 7.5in.

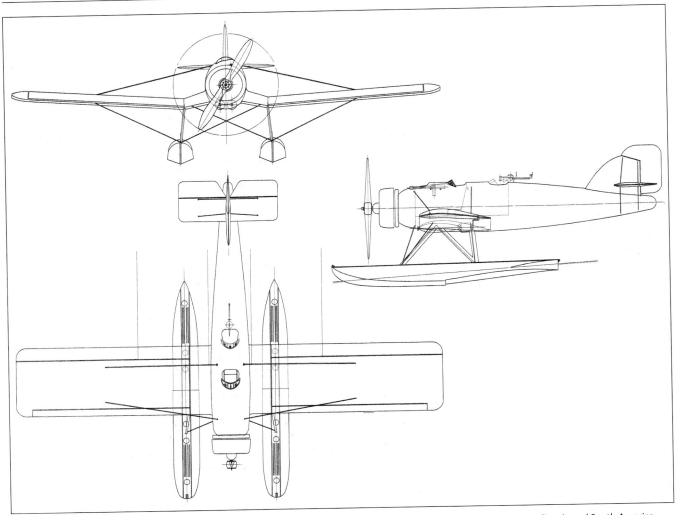

The seaplane version of the P.50 was numbered as the P.53, again probably to 15/29 but it was hoped also to sell it to Scandinavia and South America.

P.51

Based again on the P.50 layout, cranked wing and spat undercarriage, the P.51 was a generally enlarged size to carry six passengers internally on the same Panther engine. The new span was 50ft and the chord increased from approximately 7ft to 8ft. The pilot entered though a port-side car door while the passengers had a door aft of the wing on the same port side. On the starboard side opposite this door was a toilet and further aft a door for cargo/luggage. The length of the machine increased to 35ft 7.5in to accommodate the passengers. Instead of ink on linen this scheme was in pencil on tissue paper and the drawing was never numbered, but must have been drawn in April/May 1930. The height was 11ft 4.25in tail down and the chord 8ft. The tail span was 12ft 6in and the tail chord 5ft 2.5in. The propeller was 10ft 6in in diameter. There was an 11ft 8in wheel track on the splayed undercarriage.

P.55

While numerous other projects both civil and military were being studied, the Air Ministry issued a specification, 26/28, for a five-seater aircraft able to operate from restricted spaces. B&P and Fairey are known to have responded. The P.55 GA was logged on 16 June 1930 and was dated 1 July 1930. A single Panther engine and an open-cockpit, closed-cabin biplane characterised the design, which had a large 50ft span and was 38ft 4in long. With no flaps, the upper wing had HP autoslots and integral fuel tanks. Five seats could be accommodated

with a port entrance door, starboard toilet and starboard luggage door aft. The tailplane was particularly large for landing control at slow speed and, while the machine had no conventional flaps as such, hidden away on the drawing were variable airbrake foils that were attached to the trailing edge of the lower wing to fuselage diagonal strut. When fully closed across the propeller arc these blocked some of the thrust during landing and held the machine back during run up for a short take-off. In intermediate positions they added to the slow-speed control and lift. The upper wing was also at a degree incidence larger than the lower so that both wings would not stall together.

All of this was going on while Imperial Airways were pursuing twin-engine machines of similar passenger capacity. The thought was that there were many places within the Empire where only short strips could be built or the location was 'hot and high' in rarefied mountain air, calling for a smaller, efficient machine to get travellers in and out. The specification called for the absolute minimum 'no-stall' landing speed in descent and the ability to climb at steep angles after take-off. Other dimensions were 14ft 4.5in high tail down, chord 6ft 11.75in and stagger 1ft 6.75in. The tail span was 16ft 10.5in and the tailplane chord 6ft. The propeller had an 11ft 11.7in diameter, and the track was 15ft 5in. The dihedral on the wing was 4°. The specification did not proceed, but North was to revise the design idea to a larger span and length to accompany the P.78 project and his patent for a compound aeroplane.

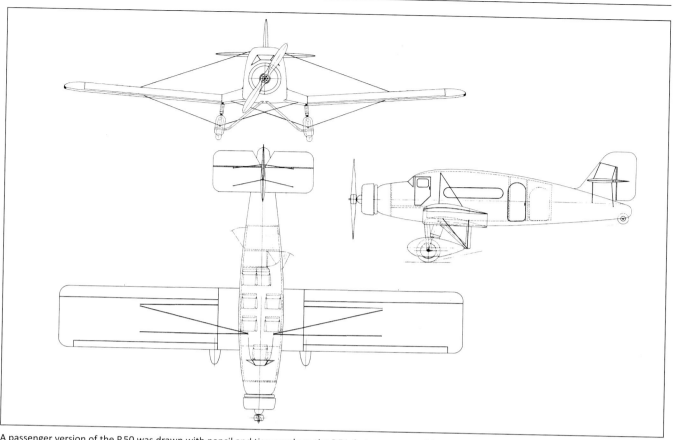

A passenger version of the P.50 was drawn with pencil and tissue only as the P.51, but was never added into the drawing record.

Specification 26/28 wanted a five-seater for operation from restricted spaces. B&P were slow in getting around to the requirement but drew the P.55 with unique air flaps for variable braking during landing fitted on the inner rear diagonal struts.

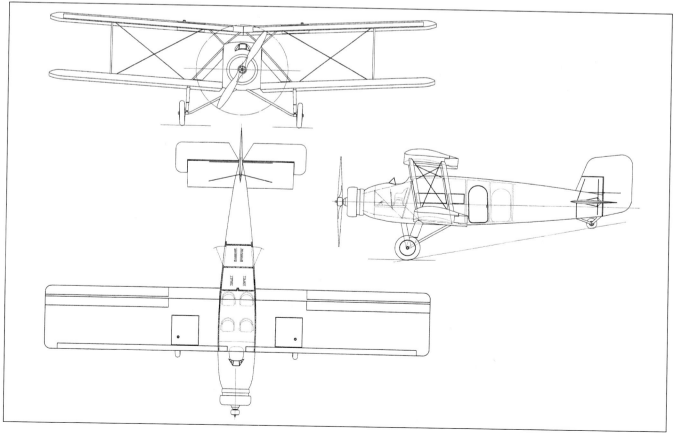

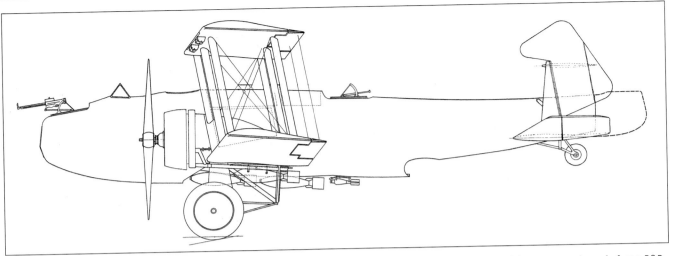

Impression of the Panther-engined Sidestrand layout with new tail unit planned for the P.52. Only the proposed detail changes were drawn before a B&P request to use a development Sidestrand for trials was refused.

P.52

This was a twin-engine bomber in the style of the Sidestrand but with the engines replaced by AS Geared Panthers equipped with BP Townend Rings. There was a requirement therefore to construct an experimental nacelle to cover the potential retrofit. In addition there were also new drawings required for an experimental tailplane and an experimental rudder system – all produced in May 1930. There were no formal three-view drawings generated for this machine. It can only be suggested that this was an attempt to re-engine the Sidestrand layout and potentially to introduce a tail gun position with biplane tail and twin-fin/rudder assemblies also being looked at for the P.57.

Despite the fact that the government had already earlier asked for a tail gun position on a Sidestrand, the request for permission to use a Sidestrand test vehicle for this work was not accepted by the Air Ministry. Therefore the P.52 did not appear to proceed further than the scheme drawings of the suggested new parts and mountings, although the company worked on the project intermittently for about six months, the tail unit mounting being schemed in August 1930. The tail unit layout was also reused on the P.54 for Imperial Airways. It is not known if the Sidestrand sweepback would have been retained or if the wings would eventually have been straight like the P.60 design.

P.57

The P.57 was illustrated by very large 1/10th scale drawings, in side and front views only, on 7 July 1930 as pencil and ink on oiled tissue. The dirty and disintegrating tissue was later transferred on to Ozalid film, making a very poor copy. The requirement was an enquiry from the Irish Free State for a general-purpose biplane. The machine was to be capable of fulfilling all normal general-purpose functions, passengers, freight, photo reconnaissance, survey and bombing. The aircraft was based upon the P.29 Sidestrand with a completely new streamlined fuselage. The Sidestrand swept back outer wing design was retained in total, but the engines were AS Geared Jaguars with BP Townend Rings, which again meant a circular tube exhaust collector around the nacelle aft of the ring. A tail gun position was required so the biplane tailplane with twin-fin/rudder assemblies was set low on the fuselage with a gunner's pulpit aft. Front and mid upper positions were inset into the fuselage, which had a distinctive 'whaleback' shape with a bombing nose and a camera under the dorsal gun position. The undercarriage was upgraded to that tested on J9186 and later fitted to the P.29D or P.75 Overstrand, but with a tailwheel part buried in the lower fuselage. A large windowed centre section finished with a triangular access door to port aft of the wing. Bombs were carried in an open-bottom faired bomb bay below the lower wing. None of the weapon positions were shown with mounting for guns.

Another variation on the P.29 layout was the P.57, a general-purpose aircraft for the Irish Free State. A very large side view drawing seems to have been abandoned before it was completed.

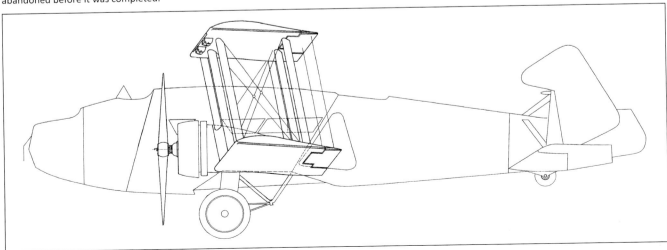

The span was identical to the Sidestrand and balanced by a length of 43ft 4in. The lower tail chord was 7ft 3.5in and the upper tail chord 3ft 11.5in. The overall height was 15ft 1.25in tail down. Neither view as drawn was completed because all of the text normally stencilled on the drawing sheets for civil or foreign offers was still roughly scribbled in pencil. It is certain that the government refused to allow such an advanced machine to be offered to the Irish Free State and the work was therefore abandoned or the requirement was withdrawn.

P.60

The P.60 was drawn and logged on 11 November 1930 in response to a requirement for a general-purpose aircraft for the Royal Canadian Air Force that could be mainly employed as a photo-survey machine. A number of drawings were involved. It featured a slightly enlarged P.29 Sidestrand layout but with unswept outer wings employed. In order to make the aircraft general purpose, the fuselage had to be enlarged and the fuel tanks moved into the upper wing. A total of three wing-enclosed tanks were employed in the centre section of the upper wing. Because the centre fuselage had a cabin, the structure of the centre area had some additional diagonal bracing rather than a more expensive Warren girder redesign. The dual tandem cockpit openings and the Sidestrand Mk.II (no bomb aimer's front window) nose shape was retained but the lower belly was a redesign because a bomb bay was not needed. The undercarriage was upgraded to a style tested on J9186 under AE1769 and fitted to the P.75 Overstrand, including a Goodyear Musselman tailwheel of 10in diameter. The engines used were AS Geared Jaguars with BP Townend Rings, which meant a circular tube exhaust collector around the nacelle aft of the ring. These engines were set at 17ft 6in centres.

A large camera mount was shown within the front gunner's location at the front of the mounting ring. The now clear fuselage interior had side windows at mid-wing chord and a large passenger and cargo door situated aft on the port side. The wingspan was roughly the same as the Sidestrand, stated as 72ft. The whole machine was 46ft 4.8in long over the Flettner tab aft of the rudder, with a tailplane of 18ft span and 7ft 6in chord. The wing chord was increased to 7ft 2in and the gap to 7ft 8.25in. Both a wheeled undercarriage and a float undercarriage for operation from sea and lake were shown, including steel ice runners on the floats. The floats were smaller than those designed for the Sidestrand. No performance data exists but one would expect a similar performance to the Sidestrand for the wheeled version. Despite all the work put in, the RCAF was suddenly hit with parsimonious cuts and a 'new build' machine could not compete with existing civil types (such as the Ford Trimotor) either available or already in service. No machines were ordered.

Yet another variation of the P.29 layout, the P.60 was intended as a general-purpose survey and transport aircraft for the RCAF. The outer wings on this design were not swept back and all fuel was moved to the upper wing. Lighter in weight smaller floats than those on the Sidestrand were shown ghosted on the wheeled version.

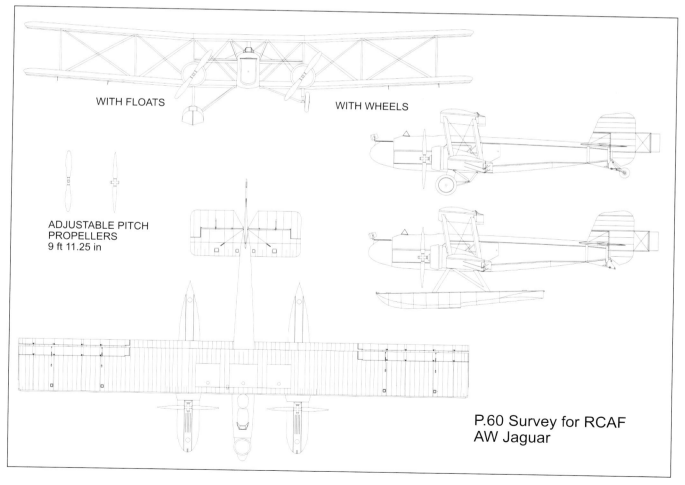

WITH FLOATS

WITH WHEELS

ADJUSTABLE PITCH
PROPELLERS
9 ft 11.25 in

P.60 Survey for RCAF
AW Jaguar

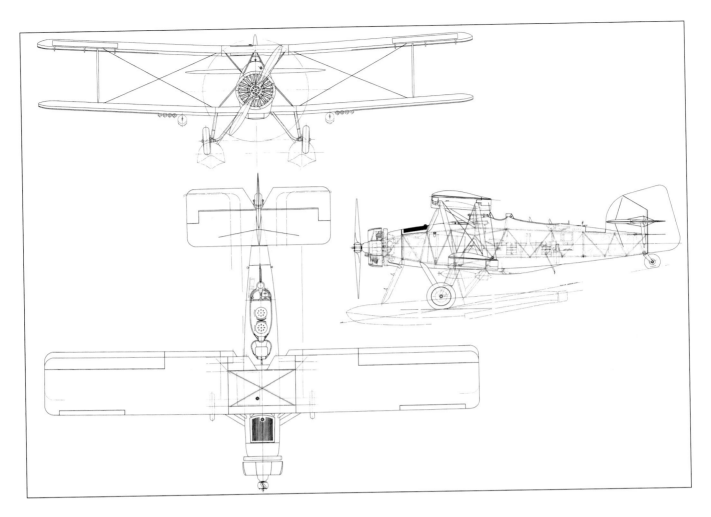

CHAPTER FOURTEEN

General-Purpose Spotter/Torpedo P.58 and P.66

P.58, P.58A, P.58B

A REQUIREMENT for a fleet spotter aircraft was issued as S.9/30 and resulted in a series of schemes under the designation P.58 employing either RRFI2MS inline or Panther MS radial engines. All of the designs covered either wheel or float undercarriage, and all were based upon an upper wingspan of 45ft 2.5in, but fuselage lengths (landplane) varied from 34ft 4in to 35ft 7in approximately, the P.58A being the longest. All the drawings were completed in September 1930 and traced using master ink onto linen over three days from 29 September to 1 October 1930.

The P.58 basic model was a biplane with an anti-turbulence ring cowled Panther MS engine and three crew, a pilot, observer and rear gunner. An aft circular collector ring was needed at the rear of the cowling exhausting along the underside, and the oil cooler was built into the upper decking forward of the cabane struts. A wheeled undercarriage was shown with the floats dotted in for the catapult version. Under the crew positions there was a ventral bath to allow the observer to lie prone and view the sea ahead while deploying the bombsight. The gunner's position had the Vickers K or Lewis stowed in a slot and below that a

vertical camera was installed. All positions were equipped with headrests for crew comfort in normal flight and catapult launch protection. Armament also consisted of a single forward-firing machine gun in the port upper decking and bombs were accommodated underwing.

S9/30 required a three-seat fleet spotter capable of operations on wheels or floats. The first version numbered P.58 employed a Panther engine. Notable is the prone bomb aimer's position below the seats in the belly of the aircraft and the use of headrests to protect the crew during catapult launch. Floats were shown in lighter lines on the same drawing

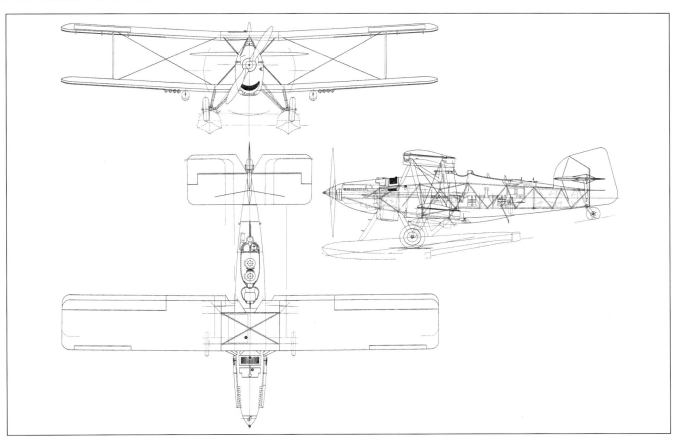

The P.58A employed a Rolls-Royce F12MS in place of the Panther engine.

Revision of the wings into sesquiplane with long oleo strut legs to absorb the landing shock resulted in the P.58B with RR F12MS.

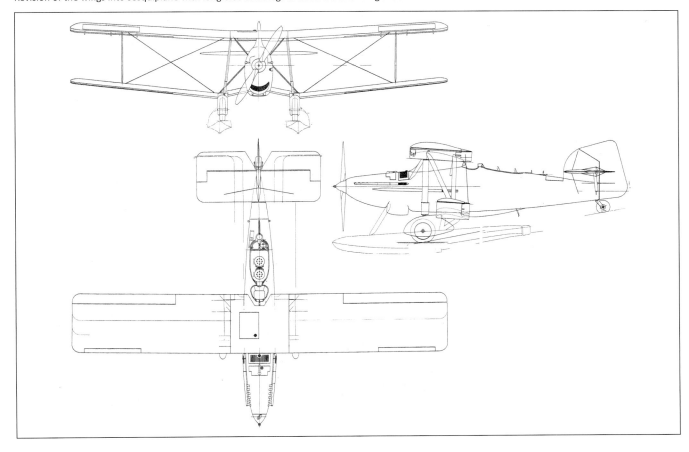

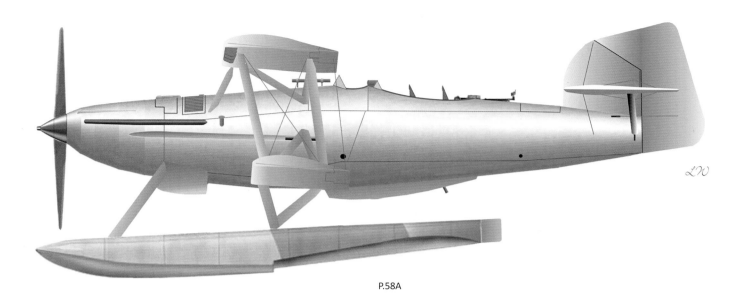

P.58A

The structure was to be standard B&P steel tube and alloy fittings with a circular/oval fuselage of built-up wood formers and stringers, and the wing section used was BP.10. All the designs had extensive flotation bags in the front and rear fuselage to cope with ditching.

The P.58A was very similar except that it had the inline RRFI2MS in a close-cowled nose and spinner. The oil cooler was smaller on the upper decking and a radiator was slung below the fuselage ahead of the wing. The P.58B, drawn last was unusual in being of sesquiplane layout and heavily staggered so that the thin-chord lower wing was almost matching its trailing edge with the upper. This left the undercarriage out on a very long strut from the upper wing, which it was thought would enable heavy carrier landings to be undertaken with long oleo dampers within the strut. The wheels were contained in spats and the outer interplane struts were of vee form. The headrests were removed for all but the pilot. The P.58B was offered with either engine but the drawings were limited to only two sheets with the RR engine.

Six firms responded with designs, however, only two were with full tenders. Although B&P drew up the designs they may have simply sent the drawings as suggestions as there seems to have been no attempt to add extra structural diagrams indicating components in detail or produce a formal brochure. However, the internals on the

large-scale drawings were extensively detailed in finer lines than the main outline. The Fairey tender was ordered as serial S1706 and the Gloster tender as serial S1705. Neither type progressed to production orders and by the time these were physical specimens the Air Ministry were already preparing a new specification, 15/33, which combined M.1/30 with S.9/30 into an updated requirement.

Torpedo Aircraft Studies

Consideration of the optimum layout for torpedo aircraft resulted in two designs being created with alternative single or twin engines. Neither of these proceeded past front and side views and the tail design suggests they were being drawn around the time of the initial P.61/P.64 Mail Carrier proposals. The single-engine machine was a two-seat, two-bay biplane with a Panther engine. The twin machine was also two-seater with a slim 'military' fuselage looking similar to the P.61 in layout and with Double Mongoose engines. Both aircraft employed full wheel spats and the studies may have been related to and encouraged the development of the P.62 PV bomber.

Single Panther dimensions: Span 42ft, Length 34ft 7in, 6ft chord and 500sq ft area, 11ft 3in high static, 10ft diameter propeller. Twin Double Mongoose dimensions: Span 50ft upper, 31ft 6in lower, Length 38ft 6in, 7ft chord upper wing and 570sq ft area, 13ft 9in high static.

At least two comparison schemes were drawn to look at torpedo aircraft around the end of 1930. The twin-engine aircraft, undated and powered by Twin Mongoose engines, was clearly a derivative of the P.61 wing and tail calculations.

The comparison single-engine machine utilised an identical tail unit plus a Panther engine. They had nothing to do with the P.58 but were probably precursor ideas for the private venture torpedo bomber variant of what became the P.62.

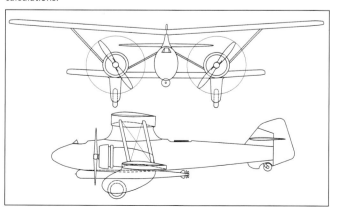

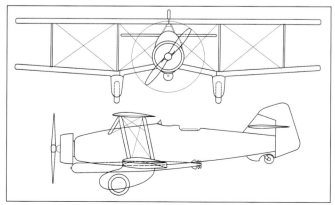

In addition at the same time that B&P were looking at the P.58 spotter there was another specification M.1/30 for a torpedo aircraft. In this case the company decided to align itself with Blackburn in their submission to the Air Ministry and designed the wing structure of the Blackburn prototype aircraft. When this prototype was unsuccessful they again supported Blackburn with the structural design of the wings for the private venture M.1/30A.

P.66

Specification G.4/31 of 2 June 1931 to OR.2, with amendments from Issue 2 of October 1931, was a requirement for a general-purpose bomb and torpedo carrier to replace the Fairey Gordon and the Westland Wapiti in service abroad, providing aerial co-operation, aerial reconnaissance, photography work and casualty evacuation. It was to provide day and night bombing operations abroad from any type of surface and to include dive bombing, coastal reconnaissance and land-based torpedo bomber actions in tropical climates. The coastal and torpedo dropping was actually added to the second issue. The maximum landing speed was to be 53mph and the maximum flying speed 140mph at 5,000ft. The machine was to be able to operate with a torpedo up to 14,000ft and a 500lb bomb up to 20,000ft. An air-cooled engine was preferable for tropical roles and desert equipment for such a role, or dinghy for coastal roles, were required as part of the kit supplied. Various types of bomb and torpedo loads were suggested. Torpedoes, for example, listed the Type K, Mark VIII and Mark X.

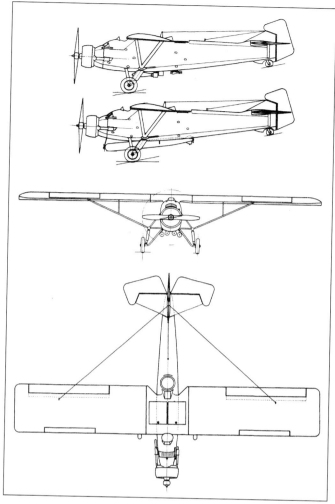

Right: A GP bomb and torpedo aircraft, the P.66 was designed to meet G.4/31.

Below: The requirement included a floatplane version and to meet the requirements of emergency landing and flotation. B&P also came up with the idea that the pilot could power fold the undercarriage outward on a wheeled aircraft so that it could land by aquaplaning on the struts. The alternative action was to blow off the lower legs completely with explosive bolts.

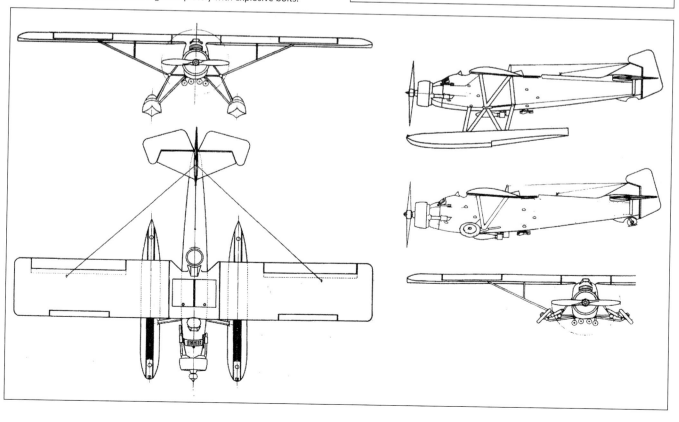

The importance of the potential order meant that nine firms offered proposals with almost twenty designs and of these six were produced by the companies concerned as private venture prototypes. One third of the designs were monoplanes and all were single engine. All the other non-PV prototype companies were issued with contracts with the exception of Boulton & Paul. The Air Ministry may have been put off by the lack of a tender price as the company stated within their submission brochure their primary cost target was a production cost ceiling of £2,000 when ordered in quantity, hence a cheap airframe and cheap spares. By using many interchangeable parts already qualified by long-term testing in the past, it was thought a relatively small and efficient aeroplane could result. As an example, the company pointed to the rudder being identical to and interchangeable with the elevator. The very layout of the monoplane was quoted as having been in extensive service in America and proven that it was the ideal type of machine for service in harsh conditions with little facility for maintenance. The design had been chosen structurally to cope with the humidity and sudden temperature changes of semi-tropical climates. The resulting design was stated to be the best and most efficient of many possible layouts studied.

It is possible that B&P did not submit a detailed prototype cost but they certainly submitted a massive proposal folder on 1 November 1931 including stress calculations, structural frame diagrams and the results of extensive wind tunnel testing with a fully dimensioned drawing of the wind tunnel model. With the torpedo requirement being added only in October many of the detail brochure three-views were only allocated for tracing on 3 October and a torpedo added to the wind tunnel model for checks on the aerodynamic qualities with such a weapon. This load had not previously been drawn into the original model layout.

The B&P design, the P.66, was titled by the company as a general-purpose, bombing and torpedo-carrying aircraft. It was a high-wing braced monoplane with the main undercarriage on outriggers so that the wings could be removed and replaced without disturbing the landing gear of the fuselage on the ground. It also enabled short diagonal wing struts to be used at a large angle to the wing and hence limit wing/strut interference and drag. The monoplane design was also thought to result in fewer parts, better all-around view for the crew and less likelihood of the wing being damaged during landing operations, as might occur with the lower wing of a biplane. There were no external tie-rod bracings and cabling required, everything external being structured on aerofoil section strutting. A choice of engines was offered; the basic drawings showed a supercharged AS Panther but the Bristol Pegasus was suggested as an alternative. All controls used tubes and ducts inset within the fuselage fairings but external to the basic steel and alloy structural frame. Interchangeability included a horn-balanced rudder/elevator half and aileron plus autoslot; fuel tank; oleo leg, axle and radius rod; and all wing, tail and outrigger struts.

The resulting aircraft was very similar in layout to the Westland PV P.7 with the exception that it had a rounded, streamlined fuselage and both cockpits were open as proposed. As submitted the aircraft had a span of 55ft 6in and a length of 39ft 7in on a wing chord of 9ft. The wing area of 500sq ft gave loadings of 11.4lb/sq ft as a bomber (5,702lb AUW), 14.4lb/sq ft as torpedo carrier (7,225lb AUW) and 12.4lb/sq ft as bomber seaplane (6,232lb AUW). Predicted performance was a maximum speed of 144mph at 5,000ft as a loaded bomber and 142mph as a torpedo plane with landing speeds between 50 and 60mph depending on the remaining load on board.

The Air Ministry found enough funding to pay for three G.4/31 prototypes and encouraged all the others, including B&P, to submit their machines as PV build projects. Unfortunately, B&P were getting into serious financial straits across the four divisions of the company and, despite North arguing the case for its development, the board decided that they were not in a position to fund a prototype themselves where there was no guarantee of follow-on production and so many bidders confusing the issue. The company decision to walk away was justified as acceptance and testing of competitor designs was spread over some four years, and the general-purpose requirement of G.4/31 was dropped from the RAF inventory.

Left: Sketch of the P.66.

Below: Wind tunnel model of the P.66 fuselage.

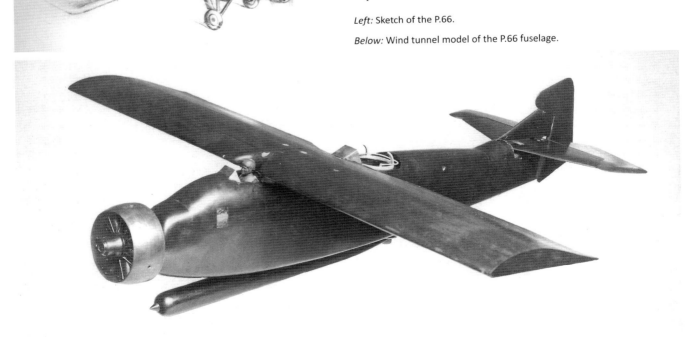

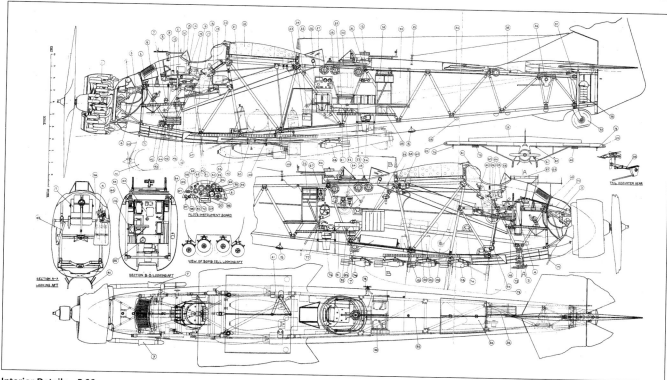

Interior Details – P.66

1. Mod. supercharged Panther engine with Townend ring and exhaust manifold
2. Small oil tank for engine supercharger
3. Engine-driven generator and mounting
4. Engine controls
5. Oil tank with surface cooler
6. Rudder bar with Palmer brake gear
7. Cockpit hot air heating
8. Bar-type torpedo sight
9. Very pistol and cartridge case
10. Control locking strap box
11. Writing tablet with notebook and pencil
12. Cross level on cockpit coaming
13. Oxygen gear panel
14. Pilot's cockpit mirror
15. Identification switchbox and downward lamp
16. Lighting switches
17. Pilot's adjustable seat with safety strap and back-type parachute
18. Fire extinguisher
19. Oxygen supply bottles
20. Navigation lamps
21. Torpedo depth gear
22. Petrol tanks
23. 12vo accumulator
24. Dual control gear
25. Fixed aerial
26. Gunner's parachute stowage
27. Electrical gear panel
28. SAA drums
29. Gunner's adjustable and collapsible seat
30. No 10 Scarff ring and Lewis gun
31. Cockpit lamps
32. Wireless crate
33. Door for removing wireless crate
34. Rubber dinghy and blower

35. Distress signals
36. Tail adjuster gear
37. Elevator control
38. CG balance weights
39. Tail wheel
40. Torpedo pistol stop gear
41. 18in torpedo (alternates type X, Mk. VII and Mk. X)
42. Bomber's instrument board – ASI, altimeter and watch
43. CG gear reservoir and control valve
44. Torpedo release toggle
45. Electrical bomb release switches
46. Control column and flying controls
47. Pilot's map case
48. Bomb alternatives
49. Gas starter bottle and connections
50. Extra oil tank for long-range flying
51. Gunner's firing steps
52. Gunner's harness anchorage
53. Camera magazine stowage
54. F.24-type camera
55. Electrical rotary converter
56. Handholds for lifting
57. Fixed wireless equipment panel
58. Navigational instrument cabinet
59. Hand-bearing navigational compass
60. Petrol collector box
61. Communication door (pilot and crew)
62. Emergency petrol cock controls
63. Jettison valve pull-off
64. Gosport speaking tubes
65. Petrol cock controls
66. 0.303 gun with ammunition and link case collector
67. Aldis gun sight
68. Bead and ring gunsight
69. Oil cock controls

70. Hand-starting magneto control
71. Bomber's windscreen
72. Extra fuel tank for long range flying
73. Course setting bomb sight and mounting
74. Footsteps
75. Windmill camera drive
76. Aldis signalling lamp
77. Wireless aerial and winding gear
78. Holt flare
79. Smoke floats
80. C3 camera gun and mounting
81. Torpedo heating air-driven generator
82. Release pin gear for dinghy cover
83. Air brake bag and gauge connections
84. Control wire and electrical cable duct
85. Watch and holder
86. Holt flare push buttons
87. Altimeter
88. Engine ignition switch
89. Dimmer switch and swivelling lamp
90. ASI
91. Turn indicator
92. Instruction plates
93. Compass correction card
94. Engine rpm indicator
95. Oil pressure and temperature gauge
96. Engine boost gauge
97. Engine starting ignition switch
98. Priming pump and dope cock
99. P.4-type compass
100. Desert equipment including:
    Spare tail wheel
    Bedding
    Fresh water tank
    Personal case
    Ration boxes
    Engine tool bag
    Fitter's tool box

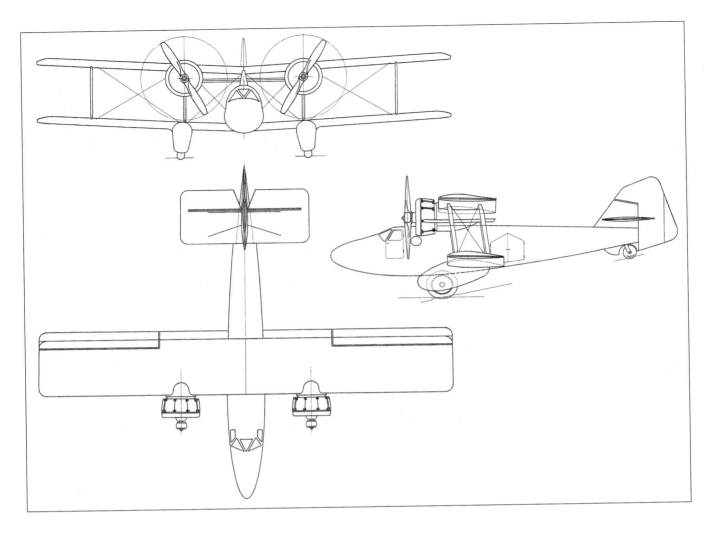

CHAPTER FIFTEEN

Mail Carriers and High-Speed Bombers

P.61

THE P.61 was the first attempt to water down the 'streamline Mail Carrier' concept into a more conventional layout that would be acceptable to the government and Imperial Airways. Prior to this all suggestions had been based upon high-speed dolly take-off and skid-landing sesquiplane machines where the bulk of the lift was provided by the upper wing held above the body on a pylon or struts. Undated, but drawn in the third quarter of 1930, this layout was a conventional biplane with twin Jupiter XFB engines partly slung under the upper wing and a streamlined fuselage that sat on the bottom wing.

The undercarriage consisted of spat-enclosed mainwheels set below the engines and a tailwheel where the wheel was in the open but faired fore and aft ahead of the rudder. The inner wings were cranked downwards to keep the spats for the mainwheels as small and sleek as possible. The machine would have broadly met specification 21/28 with a span of 50ft and a length of 41ft 6.75in. The aim of 21/28 was to propose a pure mail carrier that could transit mail at high speed between key points where the mail arrived consistently at regular times. At this time mail was carried by conventional passenger planes

to random schedules with many stop-overs. The key targets for 21/28 were 1,000lb of mail for 1,000 miles at 150mph and the ability to maintain a height of 5,000ft with full load on one engine. After discussions on this design the company resubmitted a new design referenced P.64. There would ultimately be five bidders for this project

Having failed to achieve anything with their high-speed sesquiplanes, the company produced a layout for the P.61 Mail Carrier using a streamlined fish shape-fuselage but with engines on the upper wing and spats on the mainwheels.

and one wonders why two of them were proposing only single-engine machines when the height capability clause obviously meant a multi-engine machine. This suggests that either the 5,000ft full load on one engine clause was not in the original documentation or was unclear. The wing chord was 7ft, engines c/c 15ft, and track 16ft 0.5in. The tail span was 15ft and the tail chord 7ft 6in.

P.62

During work completing the large-scale drawings for the P.61 streamline Mail Carrier, H. A. Hughes' team was tasked with scheming ideas for torpedo aircraft that could also be high-speed bombers. Two of the comparison schemes did not proceed forward and were undated and unnumbered as they were rejected. These were a 42ft-span, single-engine torpedo aircraft and a twin-engine machine of 50ft span listed in Chapter 14.

North was still determined to back up his suggestions that developments of the Sidestrand or his high-speed bomber concepts would ultimately overshadow the Hart series and that twin engine was the way to go in terms of both speed and defence. His streamline twin-

engine bomber/torpedo aircraft selected took the next project number, P.62, and was very similar to the P.61 Mail Carrier layout. The circular navigation/radio officer's window in the fuselage was retained and the opening nose now held a nose gunner's position and a hinged bomb-aiming window similar to the Sidestrand III. The fuselage was increased in height to allow access fore and aft, so that the dorsal and nose gunner's positions had a full hemisphere or more of clear view above. A ventral gunner was accommodated by a cut out into the bottom monocoque behind the lower wing if required. The fairing ahead of the upper wing formed the pilot's headrest and the fuselage body represented an aerofoil section in side profile. The upper leading edge had HP slats and the ailerons were Frise type; only the elevators were horn balanced. The engines at this time were Jupiter XFAs enclosed within circular anti-turbulence rings and supplied by four large fuel tanks set into the upper wings outboard of the engines.

To limit drag, when not required the nose gunner's ring had a folding weapon mount. Immediately following internal discussion with North, three full views plus a body cross section and a balance diagram were drawn and logged on 2 January 1931. This was followed by a series of sections of the body shape, diagrams of the wing and body structural arrangement, plus the landing gear fairing all within days.

The concept of the P.61 was followed to propose a high-speed day bomber, the P.62. A very detailed proposal was submitted allowing for four different possible engines, although only two were drawn for the brochure. The prime offer was a Jupiter XFAM-engined P.62.

As one alternative, Kestrel inlines were also drawn for the P.62 project. All versions could be adapted to carry bombs or torpedoes, suggesting why the unnumbered torpedo schemes had been produced earlier.

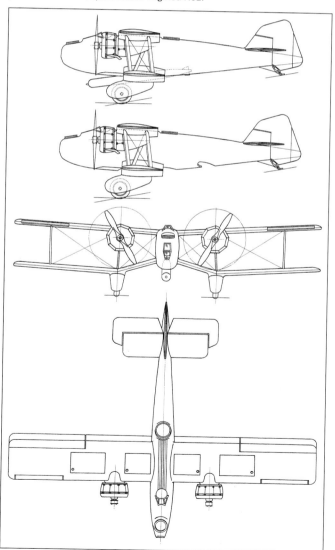

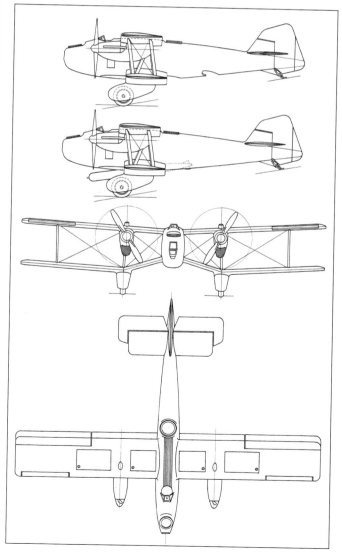

Based upon this idea, a P.62A was also sketched as a high-speed transport on 12 January 1931. Drawings for wind tunnel models of the aileron, engine nacelle and tail followed. Drawings continued sporadically during May and July punctuated by the need to develop the P.64 concept and propose the P.63 interceptor. The P.64 was such a similar machine that much of the concept layout could apply to either and a design to abandon the undercarriage spats for both the P.64 and the P.62 in lieu of a backward-retracting undercarriage was schemed as a wind tunnel model for testing and released on 1 June 1931. Testing of this was disappointing and showed less than a 2mph difference between a rear-retracting concept or a spat undercarriage because of the need to still partly expose the wheels when retracted. As a result, both types continued with fixed spats, avoiding the complication of a lead screw, power-retracted undercarriage. The P.62A was in fact externally similar to the P.64 proposal layout and the P.61 design was abandoned to concentrate on the P.64 proposal to 21/28.

During July and August 1931 all efforts were expended in the office in putting together drawings to be reduced in size and used for the P.62 brochure, which was submitted as an unsolicited proposal for a replacement of the Sidestrand III on 24 August 1931. The P.62 proposal submission was full of varied role models. It offered four basic engine variants: the Jupiter XFAM in polygonal cowlings, the Jupiter XFA with the same, the Panther III in circular cowlings and the close-cowled Kestrel inline with an underslung radiator. In each case two-blade, fixed-pitch propellers completed each power egg. The company reiterated the points that gave a twin-engine machine an advantage: capacity for self-defence; better view for the crew, particularly the pilot and bomb aimer; steadiness for bombing and gunnery because of the lack of fuselage vibration from a single engine; increased confidence for the crew of ability to fly a single engine; and increased gunning accuracy as the gunners were not within the propeller slipstream.

The structure followed the Sidestrand experience but with simplification as a result of developments since the initial P.29. Wing spars, framework longerons and heavily loaded members were of alloy steel, the rest of dural and aluminium alloys. External shape was with wood and fabric fairings. The system had already been proven in the P.29, where experience on aircraft sent for refurbishment had required unusually few replacements. Where the aircraft differed from the original P.62 scheme was in the wing fuel tanks – two pairs had been moved inboard of the engines to reduce fuel supply distances and the load passed from the upper outer wing to the lower wing and fuselage. With the fuel carried in the wings there was room for full access down the fuselage from front to the rear gunner. Surprisingly, however, the walkway/crawl-way from rear gunner to pilot across the fuselage top still retained the shaped wooden handrails at each side that had characterised the P.29, P.31 and P.32 designs. The prone gunner's position followed the planned aerofoil fuselage in being designed as a cut-out into the fuselage shape rather than as an obstruction blistered on the underside. Bomber, torpedo carrier and floatplane versions were all schemed.

The 52ft span, 41ft long machine had 325 gallons of fuel, which gave it a range of 1,000 miles at any stable cruising speed between 75 to 110mph when loaded to 10,150lb, landing at 60mph. the 7ft chord wings had a forward stagger of 15in and the height, tail down was 12ft 6in. Maximum speed was estimated at 186mph between 4,000 and 10,000ft, dropping to 182mph at 15,000ft. Loaded to 10,750lb, the speeds were 185mph and 177mph respectively. Some 1,080lb of bombs were catered for at the maximum range calculations but for special duties two external 500lb carriers increased the load of large bombs to 2,000lb. Three Lewis guns with eighteen double drums, radio, F.24 camera set, etc, were all covered. Air brakes were not offered within the design submission but, knowing the interest within aviation circles, it was assumed that they might be fitted in the future after model and full-scale trials found a good design solution. Trial fuel tank manufacture in Elektron metal was undergoing strength testing as the brochure was submitted. More than double the range, up to four times the bomb load, three times the defence capability, the P.62 as proposed far exceeded all the capabilities of the Hart day bomber with the exception of the top speed, which it was expected to match.

The presentation of the PV proposal in August 1931 was made at the time of internal discussions over the future need for multi-engine day bombers (if any) and the internal arguments at the Air Ministry over these plus the unfortunate perception that any

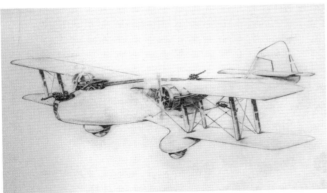

Left: Sketch of the P.62.

Below: Sometimes wrongly stated to be Sidestrand interior, the P.62 had full-length access amidships.

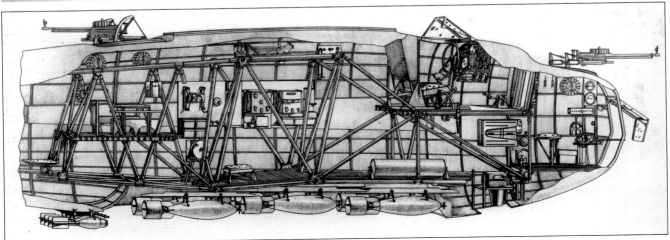

requirements formed a multi-engine Hart replacement rather than necessarily a proposed Sidestrand replacement. It was stated by Burnett that 'the new PV B&P proposal' met or exceeded all their requirements, with the exception of the landing speed. This was the 55mph or less speed required for landing during night operations. Pushed, he stated a landing speed of 65mph being the maximum he personally could accept, which was already over that actually predicted for the P.62. The result of these internal discussions at the Air Ministry was not a decision on the P.62 in detail but rather an attempt to rationalise specification requirements of the next multi-engine bomber. A new specification was ratified as B.9/32 (OR 5) to account for all of the discussion points, including limit of wingspan, and the offered PV P.62 was simply lost in the change.

P64 and P.65

The P.61 had been abandoned when more effort was put into the basic layout to produce the unsolicited P.62 High Speed Bomber and this generated a similar layout as a civil mail plane in the P.62A. In order to respond to 21/28 more fully the developing concept was once more reduced to a series of scale outlines by H. A. Hughes. The first of these was produced in early February 1931, with a cleaner series in early March. The P.64 scheme was nothing but a renumbered P.62A

Right: Sketch of the original P.64/P.65 proposals. The shallow windscreen of the P.62/P.64 was found inferior to a steeper structure throwing the airflow over the wing placement.

Below: The initial P.64 proposal was intended to formalise the P.62A design to tender for 21/28, a high-speed mail carrier. The P.65 design submitted to Sweden was absolutely identical.

offered with Jupiter XFAM 'or suitable other' engine. Detailing and general services layout drawings followed throughout March 1931, broken only by the need to produce a similar scheme for the P.65, a 'Civil Mail Carrier' enquiry generated by Aerotransport of Sweden. The P.64 and P.65 were to be identical, sired by the P.62A and differing only by their drawing number issues. The infilling of the side profile up to the powered upper wing was retained but, having no need for gun mountings, the depth of the forward and rear fuselage had been reduced in the series compared to the military P.62. The main difference was in the seaplane version, where the tailwheel was removed but the additional fin effect provided by what had been the tailwheel fairing formed a lower strake to counteract the mass and drag of the floats. On both types the floatplane version included an ice runner on the bottom of each float ahead of the step so the aircraft could land on frozen lakes and winter tundra.

The initial sketches maintained the cranked lower wing inboard panels of the P.62/P.62A but as the proposal reached submission this had been abandoned for a straight centre section and a slight change in lower lines to produce an imperceptibly deeper body.

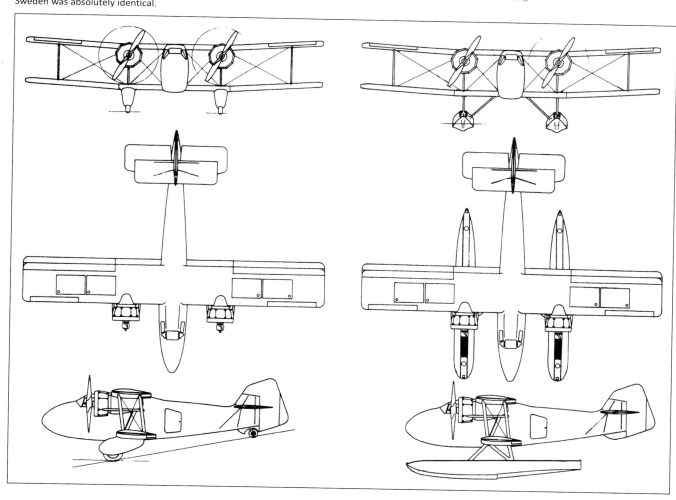

The full proposal was submitted in March 1931 with a Pegasus I.M.2 engine and a Jupiter XFMA alternative. Unlike the P.62, the four main fuel tanks remained in the outer wings, where it was thought they were well removed from the mail should a forced landing have to be undertaken.

Almost two dozen design projects were produced over the proposal period from at least eight contractors. The BPA proposal aimed to have C of G at 27% chord to give the M6 wing and fuselage ample stability. Jupiter XFA engines were proposed in circular BP Townend Rings with forward exhaust collectors, although both Pegasus and Panther were options. Wood airscrews for the prototype would be changed to metal when appropriate. Within the cabin, facility for green anti-glare screens was made and entrance for the crew on the starboard side. Mail weight of 7lb per cubic foot was allowed for. Corrugated Elektron metal on duralumin formers was suggested for the cargo cabin walls, otherwise a fabric on metal lattice was proposed. An ability to pick up and drop mail was not to be proposed until the nature of the method was available from the

Ministry. The proposed aircraft size itself was 52ft span, 7ft chord, 7ft 3in gap wings at 2° incidence and 3.5° dihedral. Four panels of the upper wing were attached to the fuselage. A trouser-type undercarriage or an alternative retraction type was suggested using a lead screw system. Horn balance rudder and elevators with Frise ailerons and slats were utilised. Maximum speed was predicted at 207mph at 13,500ft and 1,090 miles range. Speed at ground level was 162mph at an initial climb rate of 1,200ft/min and the service ceiling 27,500ft. Flight at full load and one engine out was computed to be possible up to 14,000ft. Drawings of the same machine were submitted to Sweden as the P.65.

A contract was slow in coming for anyone as the Air Ministry had allowed the specification to be open for so long, new money now had to be found to fund any prototype decisions. In the end the original file for the projects, 868473/28, was closed and a new file, 170576/32, was opened. The contract was awarded to B&P once new funding was available during February 1932 with a completion date 'ready for flight' of 22 March 1933 and Pegasus engines were chosen

Once an order for 21/28 was obtained further wind tunnel testing introduced a more streamlined fuselage and revised tail areas. Side views show: Top: basic prototype with fairings on the rudder, which were compromised by the need to have large cut-outs for the controls. Middle: The truncated fairing removing the areas over the rudder in an attempt to improve control. Bottom: Finlets added to add further control at the rear to counteract the large forward fuselage surface.

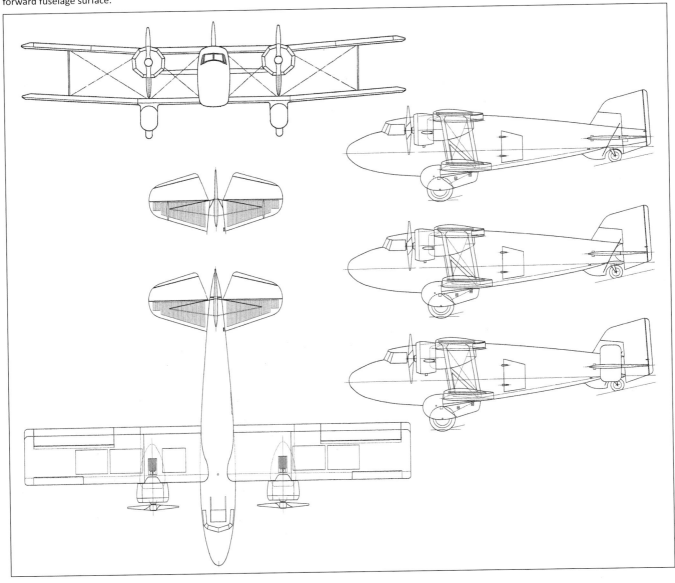

Wind tunnel model of the P.64 as built.

for the prototype. From the start of the go-ahead for build the fuselage shape started to change back towards the fish-like aerofoil body shape of the P.62 bomber as body model testing proved this to be more efficient, and the entire tail unit was revised in outline. The angle of the windscreen was found to be critical to the airflow over the fuselage top and was made steeper than that suggested for either the P.62 or the early P.64. The rudder became truncated with a much smaller control tab area at the trailing edge, and the tailplane was completely revised into a double taper with rounded tips and a trailing-edge tab. The body shape continued on to the rudder surface itself, whereas before it had continued even on to the aft servo part of the rudder in the early schemes. The central surface of the tailplane was corrugated for stiffness. Assembly of the design commenced mid-year, with 'first flight' date still held as contracted and the aircraft registered for C of A 3853 as G-ABYK on 14 July 1932.

As was normal, a series of Air Ministry photographs were taken of components prior to final assembly. The company also started to photograph large components and main sub-assemblies and date them in order to prove progress using one of the employee's box cameras. On 3 January 1933 a progress meeting stated that load testing of tailplane was to be undertaken that day to prove flight status. If tests required an increase in stiffness it was deemed more economical to build a new one rather than revise the existing. By the opening of February 1933 double shifts, overtime and weekends were being sanctioned to meet the target, with bonus payments if it was met. The aircraft was rolled out on the 22nd as complete. It took to the air on the 23rd with Rea at the controls. He found the machine pleasant to handle during the initial flight at minimum loading. Subsequently he started to notice some handling idiosyncrasies when faced with adverse winds. However, on 30 March, Rea was at the controls with Dawson Paul in the crew seat in order to demonstrate some of the problems. The aircraft landed at fairly high speed and, touching down, Rea found himself unable to counteract a swing during a crosswind. To avoid damage to the machine wings, as it moved towards a fenced area he aimed the aircraft towards some of the wooden palisade sheep fencing so that the mainwheels would flatten the fence as they ran over it. Unfortunately the tightly rigged

fence sprang back up rather quickly under the rear fuselage and the aircraft was flipped on to its back and damaged.

At a meeting on 7 April 1933 regarding damage to the Mail Carrier, discussions took place on a rebuild of the cabin such that previous visual criticisms by the Air Ministry's officers could be addressed and corrected. These included the lack of concealment of wiring, cables, etc, the sliding roof mechanism and the interior finish. For taxying (tendency to swing), a three-quarter power stop was to be incorporated so swinging could not occur by virtue of holding RPM until rudder control became effective. The following corrections were agreed by the company:

a Enlarge rudder and modify stop design to eliminate existing spring box.

b Provide partial static balance of elevators.

c Replace fuel tanks by riveted type, simplified design and eliminate extra ports included for interchangeability.

d Re-design sliding roof.

e New petrol cock controls.

f Revise control run throughout by demonstrating new run in the mock-up.

g Nose shell as before but underneath portion to be detachable.

The corrected 'ready for flight' offer to the Air Ministry was 14 June 1933. By 24 April the changes had increased with direct and servo elevator operation to be investigated, and the rudder to be intercoupled. The tailwheel was to be spring loaded to centralise it. Dunlop were asked to alter the method by which both brakes had to be applied before any steering became effective, which was considered totally unsatisfactory. The tail trimming gear had failed to trim properly and needed tests to ascertain why and develop a solution. It was agreed to interconnect the elevators via a torsion shaft, which would eliminate the need to have a large aperture in the rudder and improve rudder effectiveness. By 8 May it was decided to refit the old fuel tanks as otherwise the flight date would be compromised because new ones could not be designed and constructed within the remaining timescale.

An enquiry from Brazil for the Mail Carrier was discussed on 22 May 1933, but the decision of the meeting was that it should be ignored. At this stage it was felt to be premature to suggest that the company could offer the machine design for sale until its performance could be proven. At the 12 July 1933 meeting an enquiry from Australia for the aircraft was also put on hold as the company thought they would almost certainly get the same approach via official channels. The machine was complete prior to the agreed date but first flight was delayed awaiting improved weather. Finally, on 13 June 1933, with improved weather conditions, Rea managed four flights totalling one hour twenty minutes. Rea reported 'the rudder does not seem satisfactory and after a discussion with Mr. North he decided to have a flight in the machine and investigate himself'. Rea continued his report: 'After a flight of 15min, when we reached 5,000ft approx.. and attained an indicated air speed of 170mph, Mr. North was able to decide that the rudder was unsatisfactory as it stands and he considers it unadvisable to send the machine to Hendon unless we can improve the rudder very considerably.'

In that state, if flown at 120–130mph with the feet removed from the rudder the machine would swing left, and to counteract this one engine had to be run at 1,750rpm, the other 2,000rpm. If, however, the rudder was pushed slightly to the right and then feet removed, a violent turn to the right took place and had to be again corrected by engine speeds. On the glide with the engine throttled back and feet off the aircraft would go into a gradually sharpening left turn. It appeared that the rudder was ineffective compared with the surface pressure on the large forward fuselage if the machine was not dead straight, because the machine had a mind of its own once a turn in either direction was initialised. Lateral control was also very light and less spade grip movement was recommended to avoid over-control.

Press displays were mounted at Mousehold Aerodrome on the next Thursday, 15 June, pending display at Hendon on 24 June. North, however, had already determined that display at Hendon would not take place until the aircraft was safe. Rea carried out contractor's trials on 16 June 1933 but the speed trial was limited to a cruise speed of 160mph at 5,000ft, concentrating instead on climbing capability at 90mph ASI to 10,000ft with Z.1010 two-blade airscrews. Slats deployed successfully at 69/70mph as speed was reduced. The aircraft had never been taken up to full speed so the press could only be told that, pending official trials, a speed in excess of 190mph was expected with a cruise of 172mph at two-thirds power and a maximum range of 1,000 miles at 150mph cruise. Pegasus IM2

engines of 565hp were fitted that enabled cruising at 4,500ft and maximum speed at 6,500ft.

Further tests on a model found that the airflow was blanketed by the fin and fuselage unless coarser rudder deflection was applied, leading to over-control. The tests of rudder effectiveness had been subcontracted to RAE but had only been checked at 1–2° and maximum deflection. Without more extensive testing of the whole model, the problem would only ever be noticed during detailed full-size trials. The first action was to remove the rear fuselage fairing, which was built on to the rudder structure. This truncated the fuselage and allowed the airflow to sweep inwards on to the rudder surface. It had been hoped that this would improve the control problems but it was not successful.

Following on from North's brief testing and the press day, the Air Ministry insisted on receiving the machine at Hendon, so despite North's protests it had to be delivered. 16/17 June *Flt Lt* Boothman and *Sqn Ldr* Maitland flew it at Martlesham Heath. Both were displeased with the rudder and all staff were disappointed to decide that the machine could not be risked at Hendon. Two rectangular finlets were eventually added above and below each tailplane, increasing control authority and rudder forces. Manufacturers' contractual testing continued prior to delivery for government testing.

The problems appeared to have been cured to a large extent and the machine was delivered to the A&AEE on 16 October 1933. It was found that at full load 11,300lb (some 800lb heavier than had been planned) the rudder system was still exceedingly heavy at small angles, only becoming effective when outside of the body shadow. Other axes were fine, straight and level was fine, but firm control of the rudder was needed in turns, particularly if the air was 'bumpy'. Two flights had been made without incident by A&AEE pilot Flt Lt Boothman when it was decided to get a second opinion with a different pilot. Unfortunately the new pilot seemed to lose control and the aircraft crashed. Sqn Ldr Rea reported to Mr Carter, copied to several company managers including North and Hughes, on 23 October:

'As Boothman told me flying would be likely to take place Saturday morning I went to Martlesham along with Major Stewart on that day, 21 October. As we were travelling along the Woodbridge Road I noticed the mail carrier taking off and drew Maj Stewart's attention to it. It took off into wind and climbed straight ahead very slowly. When 3–4 miles away the pilot did a gradual turn to the left, increased into a normal bank turn and flew straight back across the aerodrome towards Ipswich at a height of 700ft. All this time except for the initial turn the machine was on an even keel.'

Appearance of the P.64 as revised for its final testing by Martlesham Heath. In this configuration the aircraft received positive comments from Flt Lt Boothman but crashed when it stalled during too tight a turn over the airfield at low speed and height flown by a less experienced pilot.

Stewart and Rea had by this time stopped and got out of the car to observe.

'When the machine reached the end of the aerodrome it appeared to me to bank to the left as though the pilot was turning in to land. It struck me that the bank seemed rather steep in the circumstances, but was otherwise normal. Just after this the machine dived vertically and lost about half its height and resumed level keel for a moment, then it turned right evidently out of control and disappeared behind a small knoll.'

Having seen the crash, Rea and Stewart picked up Collins, another B&P man, at the airfield and proceeded to the crash site to give assistance. When reached the pilot was already on his way to Ipswich hospital. Rea was sent off by Sqn Ldr Maitland to try and find Flt Lt Boothman and bring him to the wreck. Boothman, however, was en route by other means.

The machine was entirely smashed except for the tail unit, the port wheel and legs and the throttle column. Both throttles were noted by Rea to be shut and the altitude levers in their stowed position. When a message was conveyed to Rea from Grp Capt Maund not to touch the machine it was thought to be better to stay away and Rea gave Boothman and another a lift back to the main airfield office. On the way Boothman volunteered that he thought the flying qualities of the machine were very much improved and that he had his own theories about the cause of the accident. Stewart and Rea then went to the hospital to enquire about the pilot, Flt Lt Richmond.

Rea knew that Boothman had flown and landed the machine twice before Richmond's flight and had no real problems. Rea stated that in his opinion the machine was flown too slowly and consequently stalled on the turn when steeply banked. This was agreed by Maj. Stewart, except that these two eyewitnesses could not

agree on the direction of the final turn, left or right, even though they had witnessed it standing side by side.

The loss of the only prototype brought the programme to a standstill. Firstly it was necessary to decide on the crash cause, secondly to determine if there was any culpability on behalf of the company. There was assurance that there would be funding for a second prototype, but in the end this was not forthcoming as the Air Ministry had already struggled to get this agreed for the first machine. The P.64 project was the only contract that could not be transferred to the new Boulton Paul Aircraft Ltd in 1934, because liability had not been determined at that time. Although no blame was ultimately assigned to B&P when investigations closed in early 1935, the P.64 project was finished.

P.69

The P.69 to specification C.26/31 provided yet another possibility of obtaining a military contract. OR.4 required a fast transport capable of performing general goods and personnel transport duties but also standing in as a bomber when required. C.26/31 was issued as a specification on 9 March 1932 but B&P did not get to a stage to start putting together detailed and numbered tracings of proposal drawings until 3 September 1932 because of all its other commitments. Many of the trial drawings were not numbered or were taken as a block in pencil and filled in later when ink outlines were drawn up for the proposal. This was submitted on 28 September 1932 under heavy pressure to achieve the end of September submission date and some of the drawings had to be rushed through in pencil. For example, the starboard-side 'equipment' layout was ink drawn, while the port side was a pencil drawing dyeline printed on to very poor light-sensitive silvered paper when North and Hughes discovered that this would not otherwise be ready in time.

P.69 military bomber/troop transport and cargo carrier to C.26/31 based on an enlarged P.64 Mail Carrier.

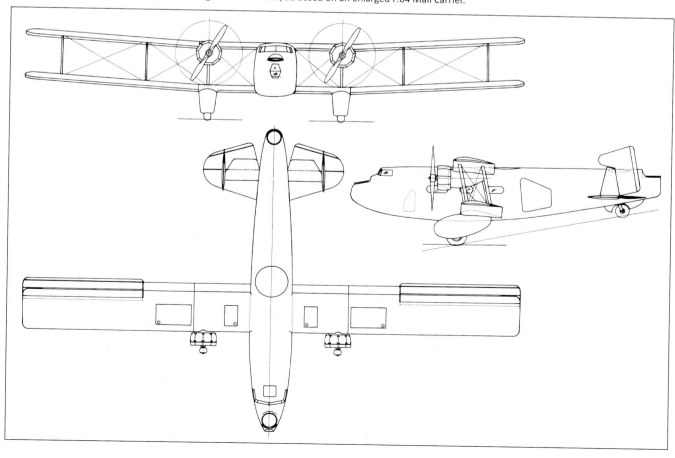

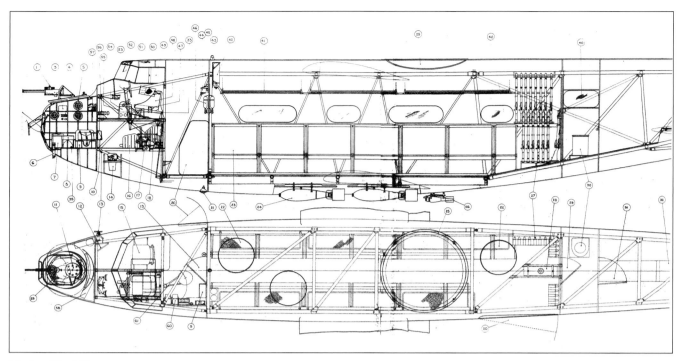

Interior of the P.69.

The area of operations specified in the OR was tropical and/or desert with easy to repair structures under desert and field conditions. A minimum military load in excess of 3,000lb or ten fully equipped troops for ranges over 900 miles on a maximum 18,000lb AUW was required. Paragraph nine of the specification asked that all performance estimates were made on an assumed 15,100lb AUW. Cruise at rated power had to be more than 95mph at 10,000ft. It should be able to carry twenty-four troops, three engines at 1,000lb each or ten stretcher cases, and their equivalents in tanked fuel or water or general cargo. Only two crew were specified on the assumption that they would be trained to cover flying, navigation, radio and bomb-release duties. Since bow and stern gunner stations were required it is assumed that in the bombing role or for defence either extra RAF personnel or selected passengers would man any free weapon stations. Eight 250lb and eight 20lb bombs were to be carried on suitable carriers, released by the crewman filling the aiming and navigation role. A number of parachute exits were required in the floor to cover the case that the machine had to be abandoned in flight.

The design drawn by B&P was an enlarged and bloated-fuselage Mail Carrier employing all the structural layout of the P.64 in planned build but returned to the BP.10 wing section. The biplane format drawn had a span of 89ft 6in and a chord of 7ft 6in. Unsure of the best layout and worried that almost 90ft might be unacceptable in some Far Eastern hangar sizes, an alternative of 80ft span with the chord increased to 8ft 5in was also offered at a slightly reduced performance. The second size was a last-minute addition to the brochure made after the basic drafting and was not provided with supporting drawings.

The construction was again listed as an improved method of that used in the Sidestrand but benefiting from the wide wheel track and heavy landing capability of the Mail Carrier. The fuselage length remained the same in both variants at 56ft. The two Pegasus I.M.3 engines were located in the Mail Carrier positions on the upper wing in polygonal BP Townend Rings with swinging engine gates for servicing. Below the engines and the lower-wing Mail Carrier-like spats formed the trouser wheel location. The enlarged span required double bays on the outer wing panels, while the fuel tanks equipped the upper inner wing either side of the engines. Warren girder fuselage truss design surrounded the passenger area, while the tubular structure aft of this followed that of the Mail Carrier again. The front gun station sat in the nose ahead of the windscreen, and there was an opening bomb-aimer's window in the extreme nose like the Sidestrand III updates, which would also open for access to the rear of the instrument panel.

In order to accommodate the rear weapon station, a rounded tail portion in wood completed the rear fuselage, with the biplane tail attached to the top and bottom areas of the fuselage and twin fins and rudders sitting outboard on the lower tailplane. The rudders were dynamically balanced at the top with actuation tabs on the trailing edge. There were no leading-edge slats on the large wing but as a concession to ensuring the aileron loads were not excessive for the pilot, trailing-edge actuation tabs were fitted on the lower ailerons only and extended back from the wing trailing edge as an additional area.

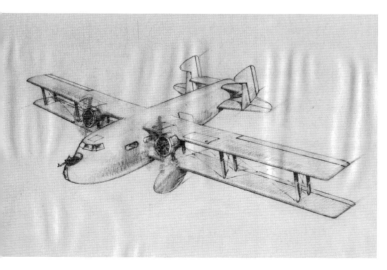

Sketch of the P.69 in flight.

In order to load engines or any pre-filled fuel containers, items were loaded into the fuselage via a demountable crane, which could be connected on to the fuselage truss and upper longerons, loading through a large circular roof hatch just after the trailing edge of the upper wing. Each load consisting of three engines or three fuel storage tanks could then be slid along inbuilt tracking on the lower structure and locked in their respective stowage positions. For the light bomb carrier duty two sets of four rack assemblies were provided on opening hatches in the floor of the bomb bay. This enabled the crew to carry more than the eight 20lb bombs specified, up to a stored maximum of 100 plus eight on the racks. The crew could therefore replenish the racks in flight, giving twenty-seven full rack loads in total.

Troops were accommodated in folding canvas seats, thirteen to starboard and eleven to port, one of which became the attendant's seat when used for ambulance duties. There were rifle racks opposite the port entrance door so that troops could be seated comfortably as possible without having to hold on to kit, but which would be immediately available if the troops were to be discharged during an active battle. In addition to the light bomb rack doors, the parachute exit scenario also was covered by a rear door in the floor aft of the cabin. Other emergency exits were three 'rip-panels' in the roof and knock out windows, which were rectangular with rounded ends fore and aft. The cargo hatch in the roof could also be discarded for emergency exit.

Performance estimates presented included calculations based on the specification paragraph nine requirement of 15,100lb loaded. These gave an estimated speed of 138mph at ground level, 147.5mph at 4,500ft and 144mph at 15,000ft. Landing speed was expected to be 55mph. The optimum cruise was thought to be 135mph on maximum boost and 2,000rpm. Service ceiling was estimated at 23,650ft and an absolute maximum possible of 26,000ft. The maximum AUW condition was the case for carriage of fuel in the storage containers to be supplied with the prototype, which was 18,965lb. This was followed closely by the troop transport case at 18,758lb. Absolutely empty the aircraft tare was expected to be 9,513lb. No data was added to suggest the likely reduction in performance if the 80ft span wing was chosen for the design but it was estimated and stated to be a loss of 1.5mph.

Competition came from four other companies at least: the A.W.23, the Bristol Type 130 Bombay, the HP.51 and a scheme from Supermarine, the Type 231. All of these were either high-wing or low-wing monoplanes compared with the biplane format of the B&P offering and the first three received prototype orders, with Supermarine likely to be doing a general scheme at Vickers' request but probably not proceeding further. The P.69 was likely to have been ignored in the first instance for an order as the P.64 would be completed and flown to prove its concept before any great movement was seen on the more interesting other three designs, which were all ordered as prototypes.

P.70

OR.5 required a high-speed bomber aircraft and specification B.9/32 was drawn up to fulfil the requirement, dated 17 December 1932. Although a day bomber, it was made clear that the aircraft might start out before dawn and return after dark. The maximum tare weight was to be restricted to 6,300lb (amended to 6,500lb by hand as AL.1). Although not stated, this weight was the result of inter-country negotiations to limit certain bombers' weights by treaty to 3 metric tonnes. All component parts were to be rail transportable to stores or units and the span must be less than 70ft unless a folding wing system was installed. All strength-contributing items were to be in metal except for the main wings and coverings. Tensioning rubber was to

be excluded from the undercarriage, which in fact suggested oleo-type shock absorbers would be required. Range was to be 720 miles at 15,000ft, or overload condition with auxiliary tanks of 1,250 miles at the same height.

Four crew were required: pilot, radio operator, navigator and gunner, unless, by invoking clause 2(b), the use of a single weapon station aft of the wings allowed full rear coverage, when it could be reduced to three crew. (This clause it seems may have been written in to cover a potential tailless machine or machine with a single rear gunner in the fuselage extremes.) Regardless if this occurred, nose stations were required for bomb aiming, navigation and front weapon operation. Carriage of variations of virtually every RAF bomb in its inventory, young and old, was specified in a long list and a second list of potential bomb carriers. An enclosed cockpit was specified. To the rear in the non-clause 2(b) configuration two weapons stations were required aft of the wings so that anything outside 50ft from the machine could be fired at and any two guns together of the three stations must be able to fire at the largest killing zone possible.

The response from B&P was the P.70. Essentially this was its upgraded PV design P.62, or to look at it another way, a P.64 Mail Carrier as in build at that time, but retrospectively redesigned to the bomber format from which it was sired. By this time, however, North's enclosed cockpit and sliding hood design was in vogue so the aerofoil section side profile of the fuselage was broken by a fully glazed raised centreline cockpit canopy with sliding hood. Behind the wing the rear fuselage was stepped down and shallower to the tail, incorporating a retractable open-topped dorsal gun turret above and a ventral bath free gunner's position below. The nose was formed by a rotating gun turret pivoted top and bottom and based upon the

P.70 high-speed bomber to B.9/32 was based upon upgrading of the P.62 with P.29D nose turret and pilot's canopy.

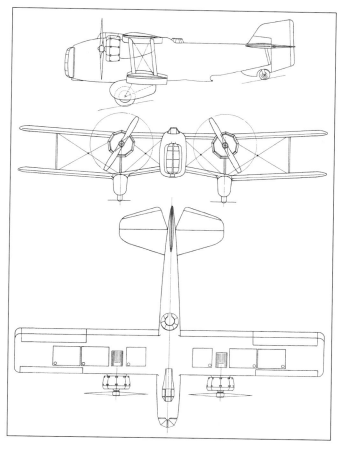

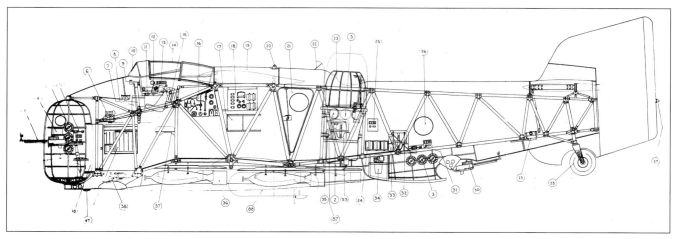

Interior of the P.70 starboard wall.

Interior of the P.70 port wall.

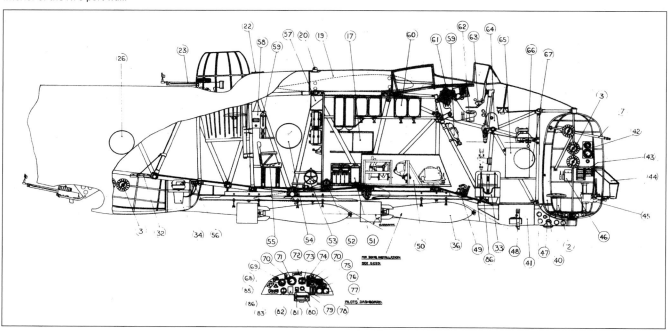

ideas being developed for the P.29D Sidestrand V. The company rejected the clause 2(b) option as in their experience a tail gunner, as opposed to two weapon locations nearer the centre of gravity, added more weight to an airframe that was already target limited on weight. It also required twin fins and more complicated control runs and adjustment gear. To give the best field of fire and gunner's view it would also be necessary to place the tail position a considerable distance aft of the rudders, most likely at an impractical distance, with poor inter-communication forward and, if the gunner was also required to operate the wireless, he would be a long way from his station if attacked. Instead, the layout offered seated gunning for both turret positions and shielding from airflow for all three positions and the pilot. All three gunners' positions together covered all areas to within 50ft of the aircraft with overlaps. In addition, the full performance required with a degree of reserve was suggested. All control runs were in tube and rod where inaccessible. Finally, normal gun positions were offered if gun turrets were unacceptable.

The proposal offered drawn bomb load configurations for each of the considerable number of bomb types listed in the specification, to which were added external racks on a standard bomb carrier under the lower inner wings and light racks for small bombs partly buried in the inner wing underside, the carrier being covered by a cover plate when these racks were not required. The outer wings had slats on the upper and Frise ailerons on both but no flaps, following the format of the P.62/64 series. For poor field conditions the spats had a wheel-cleaning brush at the rear end of the opening that brushed the tyres as they entered the spat.

Two types of engine mount were offered, the swinging type where the engine could be swung away to access the back or a fixed type. A derrick could be mounted on the wing spars to remove the entire engine and bearers as a power egg for changing or maintenance at ground or bench level. Several engine types were offered. The primary choice was the Pegasus II.S.2 in polygonal Townend Ring cowling, both of which had passed type test. Possible alternatives were any other Pegasus series, the AS Panther, AS Tiger or the RR F.XI series with appropriate changes to the weight, horse power and fuel consumption calculations. The Boulton & Paul Townend Ring anti-turbulence unit with its exhaust collector was stated to have been proven by tests to be inaudible on the ground when the aircraft was above 10,000ft. Seventy three gallons were carried in a tank outboard

Interior Details – P.70

1. 0.303 Lewis gun on special mounting
2. Balancing gear and seat with Sutton harness
3. Ammunition drums
4. Gunner's writing tablet
5. Gunner's oxygen and electrical connections
6. Pilot's rudder bar
7. Pilot's map case
8. Elevator and aileron control column
9. Control column locking strap stowage
10. Windscreen wiper
11. Pilot's oxygen connections
12. Identification switchbox
13. Pilot's electrical connections
14. Sliding roof of pilot's cockpit
15. Pilot's adjustable seat with parachute stowage
16. Engine starting panel
17. Sliding window for navigational duties
18. Electrical supply – control panel
19. Removable hatch for fitting dual control set
20. Upward identification lamp
21. Entrance door for crew and baggage
22. Windscreen for rear gunner
23. 0.303 Lewis gun on special mounting
24. Camera magazine stowage
25. Rear gunner's electrical connections
26. Prone gunner's window light
27. Navigation rear lamp
28. Castor type tail wheel
29. Tail adjusting mechanism
30. Prone gunning 0.303 Lewis gun on special mounting
31. Prone gunner's electrical and oxygen connections
32. Prone gunner's folding seat
33. Parachute stowage
34. F.24-type camera
35. Oleo-pneumatic elevating gear
36. Bombs
37. Folding footstep for access to pilot's seat
38. Course setting bomb sight stowage
39. Navigators instrument cabinet
40. Entrance doors to front gun turret
41. Front gunner's parachute exit
42. Bomb aimer's navigational instruments
43. Bomb release switches (electrical)
44. Adjustable bombing window
45. Bomb sight mounting
46. Front gunner's inter-telephone connections and mic stowage
47. Downward identification lamp
48. Tail drift sight mounting
49. Aldis signalling lamp stowage
50. Automatic pilot control plates
51. Electric batteries and accumulator stowage crate
52. 80w motor generator
53. Bead type aerial and winch
54. Window light for wireless cabin
55. Wireless operator's folding seat
56. Electrical motor for camera
57. Wireless and inter-telephone panel
58. Rear gunner's electrical and oxygen connections
59. Fire extinguisher stowage
60. Oxygen and air bottle stowage
61. Signal pistol and cartridge holders
62. Pilot's inter-telephone connections and mic stowage
63. Pilot's fuel cock controls
64. Pilot's engine controls
65. Navigator's folding table
66. Bomb fuzing levers
67. Window light for navigational duties
68. Altimeter
69. Holt flare push buttons
70. Instrument lamp and dimmer switch
71. ASI
72. Cross level (if required)
73. Reid Sigrist turn indicator
74. Fore and aft level
75. Oil temperature gauges
76. Oil pressure gauges
77. Engine boost gauge
78. 'Record' engine revs indicator
79. Watch and holder
80. P.4 compass
81. Compass correction card holder
82. Standard engine instruction plate
83. Fuel contents gauge
84. Twinob engine switches
85. Bomb jettison switch
86. Stowage for tail drift sight
87. Rear gunner's oxygen bottle
88. Long-range fuel tank

of each engine and 33 gallons in a smaller tank inboard. For the extended range case a single streamline circular section tank was also to be carried on the bomb gear.

The fuselage concept section in elevation and plan was a modified Joukowski aerofoil providing for the best drag factor possible short of an airship profile. With minimum interference by following the results of Mail Carrier testing, the calculated performance with the Pegasus engine chosen and 10ft 6in two-blade airscrews was 197mph at 13,500ft on full boost, maintained at 196mph at 15,000ft and dropping to 191mph at 20,000ft. At ground level the machine would achieve 160mph. Best climb rate to 13,500ft was 1,000 to 1,040ft per minute, with the maximum of 1,100ft per minute at 1,500ft. Service ceiling was approximately 26,500ft and landing speed 65mph. Tare weight was stated at 6,500lb and AUW with full military load and fuel as 11,096lb. In order to achieve this tare weight a very detailed estimate was provided even down to covering individual components for the engine and brake system such as sparking plugs and pipe unions. Some 390lb of fixed military equipment brought the total to exactly 6,500lb. B&P seemed to be the only manufacturer who did not suggest that the 6,500lb limit might be unreachable. The first wind tunnel and outline schemes seem to have been thought about in August/September 1932, with the main proposal drawings completed in December 1932 and two or three additional illustrations for the proposal allocated in early February 1933. The typed proposal copy was not dated but on the basis of the drawing dates it is likely that the master document was hand dated and submitted before the end of February 1933.

Again, because of its perceived importance there were a number of firms either looking at or submitting against the specification. The ones destined to become important were the HP.52 Hampden by Handley Page and the Vickers Type 271 Wellington prototypes. The twin rear weapon positions on the Hampden resulted in a very small tail boom and twin fin and rudder assemblies to keep blind spots to

a minimum. The Wellington prototype assumed a bulbous tail blister, which might contain an as yet undefined gunner's location. Both machines chosen to prototype were monoplanes, the Hampden being metal monocoque and the Wellington a Barnes Wallis geodetic metal framework covered with fabric. In both these cases the international agreement limit of 6,500lb tare were objected to by these manufacturers and an agreement was finally reached most probably regarding what could be considered as standard inclusions in the tare and which could be moved into the added military load. Other studies were carried out at least by Bristol, Gloster and Westland. The speed offered by the P.70 was considered much too low, even though it matched Air Ministry thinking of the time, compared with the estimates of the front-runners in the competition. No one was going to order a P.70 when the Hampden and Wellington were forecast at around 50mph more. No wonder the ultimate customer thought it might be possible to use the B.9/32 aircraft as bomber interceptors against the enemy.

Although there was no order forthcoming, the internal feeling within the Air Ministry that heavy bomber interceptors were a desirable asset did filter back to some of the companies. In particular the possibility of using B.9/32 bombers converted as 'Novel' heavy fighter aircraft. The Ministry thinking was that they might not need to be as fast as the bomber version and the top speed requirements talked about were lower, essentially close to the P.70. In response to this North and Hughes raised project P.72 as a Pegasus engine 'Novel' fighter devoid of heavy bomb load, fuel and some of the defensive weapons stations.

P.71

The P.71 was a project study for a twin-engined 'Feeder Line' aircraft to Imperial Airways specification. It was based essentially on the P.64 Mail Carrier. The original P.64 had undergone some fuselage and lower wing design rationalisation during post-proposal design, however, and the P.71 reflected those changes as applied to the eventual physical P.64 airframe rather than the original P.64/65 proposals. By the time the project study for the P.71 came out, therefore, the two machines, P.64 and new P.71, had become similar in layout. However, the airline's requirements were for a machine with less range than the P.64. The P.71 aircraft was therefore slightly smaller and was to have been powered only by Armstrong Siddeley Double Mongoose radials in circular cowlings on a polygonal nacelle, abandoning the polygonal-cowled Pegasus IM2 of the P.64. The P.71 also differed from the P.64 in that it was to be both a passenger machine and a cargo carrier, requiring the installation of windows in the cabin. The prototype Mail Carrier was already in production with a completion date of 22 March 1933 when the proposals for the civil P.71 were issued on 5 January 1933 in response to the airline's requirements.

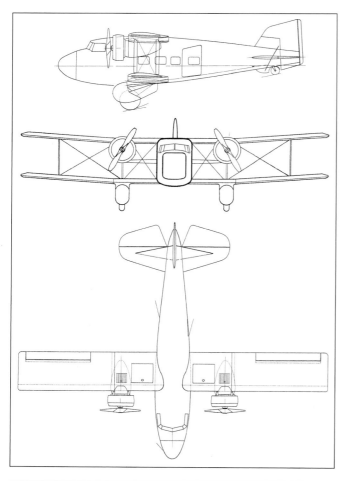

The aircraft was to have given a top speed of 175mph at 4,500ft with a cruise of 155mph at the same height for a range of 450 miles. The gross design weight was initially 7,000lb. Accommodation for two crew and seven passengers (normal passenger quantity six since the last seat at the rear could be occupied by a flight attendant, an additional passenger or the second crew member if he moved back from the cockpit – or the equivalent in freight). Only one pilot's station was envisaged in the side-by-side cockpit, although dual control could be provided if required (obviously at extra cost). Baggage could be carried in the nose and/or rear fuselage, and there was an access corridor and a toilet between the passenger cabin and the pilot's cockpit. Large fuselage windows were provided; the aim being to give every passenger the best view possible and attract speculative travellers. The total payload capability was estimated to be 1,690lb, with which the aircraft was capable of maintaining flight on one engine. The rate of climb was 1,000ft per minute and there was a theoretical service ceiling of 21,000ft. The landing speed was 57mph on an essentially flap-free and slat-free wing.

The P.71A was a revised and slightly more detailed proposal submitted on 22 July 1933 in response to a more detailed specification from the expected user, Imperial Airways, which was issued around March 1933. The engines were now to be Armstrong Siddeley Jaguar VIC with a reduced cruise speed of 150mph at 4,500ft but an improved climb rate of 1,150ft per minute and a range of 420 miles. Service ceiling was revised to 20,000ft and a stalling speed (rather than the previously quoted landing speed) was stated to be 62mph. The payload capacity was 1,870lb and normal load was expected to be two crew plus six passengers and 180lb of mail for an all-up weight of 9,000lb. Flight on one engine could be maintained at 1,500ft at full load or 3,600ft with half fuel consumed. Extra tanks were provided within the airframe to increase the range to 600 miles if they were filled. Essentially the proposed P.71A was still identical in concept layout to the P.71 airframe but had become larger, approaching the dimensions of the P.64. The performance was now guaranteed within the following margins: 1.5% for weight empty; 3% for speeds; 6% for climb provided the engines develop their stated power and the fuel consumption conforms to the values given in the specification.

What made the loss of the P.64 more complicated for the P.71 order was that the question of liability for the crash had not been settled by the time B&P became BPA. The P.64 project assets could not therefore be transferred to the new BPA company. With the P.71A moving towards a possible order and no prospect of a second P.64 prototype

Designed to Imperial Airways' specification, the P.71 was based on the P.64 Mail Carrier then under construction revised as a passenger aircraft with a squarer, larger-section fuselage. Minor changes to wing area and performance covered the initial and revised specifications from Imperial.

The smaller machine is notable if its basic dimensions are compared with the P.64 prototype and the eventual P.71A

	P.64 Mail Carrier (as built)	P.71 Feeder Liner (as proposed)	P.71A Feeder Liner (as proposed)
Span	54ft 0in	47ft 6in	52ft 6in
Length	42ft 6in*	36ft 10in	40ft 6in
Height	13ft 0in	11ft 1in	12ft 6in
Wing Chord	7ft 0in	6ft 2in	6ft 10in
Wheel Track	18ft 3in	16ft 0in	18ft 0in
Wing Area	756sq ft	586sq ft	717sq ft

* 42ft 9in according to *Flight* drawings, 42ft 6in according to B&P press releases.

being built, technical discussions and drastic redesign were considered necessary in the P.71A proposal. The solution applied was to considerably extend the rear fuselage and employ a central fin and two additional all-moving rudders outboard operating above and below the tailplane. Improvements were also made to introduce more modern rounded wing tips with sweepback on the outboard wings to balance the longer tail moment arm. The concept of sweeping back the outer wing panels had already proven satisfactory during the design of the P.29 Sidestrand and its development into the P.75 Overstrand.

The need to keep costs down on the P.71A meant that many of the production drawings were only created as pencil on tissue originals. The customer could only afford two aircraft and minimal documentation costs. The centre fuselage structure of the P.71A allowed North to use more built-up and pierced plating in light alloy and to cover the passenger section in corrugated sheeting, a technique also successfully used in the wing structure of the P.82 Defiant.

While all this work provided Imperial Airways with a technical solution, as with many concepts, by the time it was available both the government and the airline seemed to be hesitant and unsure what the need had been in the first place. The potential P.64 requirement for large numbers of high-speed mail carriers to link the main long-distance mail route stopovers with smaller airfields had faded away, and with it the interest by all in carrying mail only. Similarly, Imperial Airways seemed to view the original idea of a feeder liner, attracting affluent travellers eager to hop abroad and connect with other longer-distance aircraft, as something of a non-starter. Now in the autumn of 1934 they were saddled with two finished P.71A aircraft complete with Certificates of Airworthiness and no priority to accept them into service. Boulton Paul were continually put on hold regarding acceptance as Imperial's engineers were 'far too busy to schedule in acceptance at present'.

A number of months after completion, engineers from Imperial Airways monitored and cross-checked BPA trials, and BPA/IA trials continued into February 1935. The acceptance of the machines dragged on through into April, when on the 17th Imperial suggested that an opportunity to use the machines might arise during Easter but that this did not mean that they were fully accepted by them. On 21 May a letter from Imperial finally agreed that they would not raise any claim for delayed delivery or for fuel consumption levels, in view of the exceptional (weather) difficulties that had been encountered during the trials.

The airline put them to work on Croydon to Paris and Brussels runs carrying some passengers but mainly shipping freight. Sadly, both aircraft were lost within thirty-two months. P.71A c/n 2, G-ACOY, *Britomart* belly landed at Brussels on 25 October 1935 with no casualties. The other, P.71A c/n 1, G-ACOX, *Boadicea*, disappeared over the Channel on 25 September 1937 with the loss of both crew, although, fortunately, only carrying outbound mail and freight rather than passengers.

Faced with the loss of the P.64 prototype, B&P decided that revisions were required to the P.71 design once a two-machine purchase was placed. The revision was designated P.71A and two machines were delivered. Experimental slat detail was abandoned.

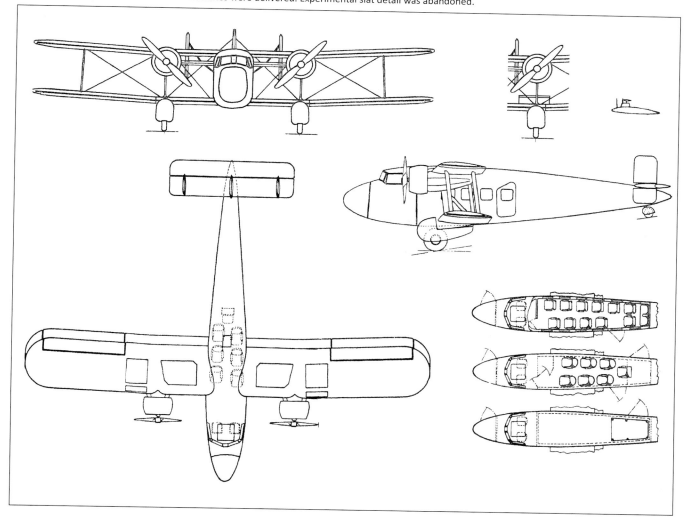

P.71A being run up at Mousehold Heath across Salhouse Road from the airfield outside the B&P assembly hangars.

The airframe completed and supplied had a span of 54ft 1.5in (the bottom wing) and 54ft (the top wing) plus a length of 44ft 2in. The chord of the wings was 6ft 10in and the height 15ft 2in. The tail span was 16ft 8in and the chord 4ft 11in. The wheel track of 18ft 4in was also the centreline distance between engines. The aircraft theoretically cruised on its Jaguars at around the specification value of 150mph at 4,500ft using two-thirds power. The maximum AUW was 9,500lb and the stalling speed 57mph.

During acceptance trials with Imperial Airways observers the aircraft was worked up to a cruise speed of 154.5mph true (ie corrected). Martlesham Heath had achieved 172mph in a dive in October 1934, but no one at Imperial seemed interested in what absolute maximum was possible from the airframe – perhaps, one might think, not wanting to risk damage to their own engines. Joint BPA/IA trials in November 1934 also included trying the machine with Z.1770 propellers with and without special slats in use, and Z.1490 propellers without slats. It was decided that Z.1770 units gave the best performance as the other design was heavier and that was with the design operating in the slatless configuration. In response to aeronautical press pressure later, Imperial Airways finally stated a maximum of 175mph without any physical proof, which was at least 10mph less than that of which it should have been capable.

However, notes by W. H. Sayers on the final January/February 1935 trials reveal that the weather was particularly adverse for flying and results could only be snatched here and there with the dogged assistance of BPA and IA staff to have the machine ready and loaded for the slightest break in the weather. Both BPA and IA instrumentation matched to a reasonable amount but pressure conditions were so variable that it was impossible to get a match of performance from each engine operating only 18ft apart. Imperial engineers settled for proving that the important 150mph minimum cruise requirement was achieved. Sayers himself acknowledged the tremendous skill and dedication of the pilot, Cecil Feather, in achieving even that with G-ACOX.

Home and overseas sales of the design were attempted by BPA with Pegasus III engines, which were judged to allow a maximum speed of 195mph and a cruising speed of 166mph at 5,000ft, but these efforts were unsuccessful. The tare weight increased to 7,300lb and AUW to 11,500lb. The best range was at a cruise of 130mph, when 900 miles +/- 3% should be achieved. The stalling speed of this configuration was 62mph.

Structure of the P.71A fuselage.

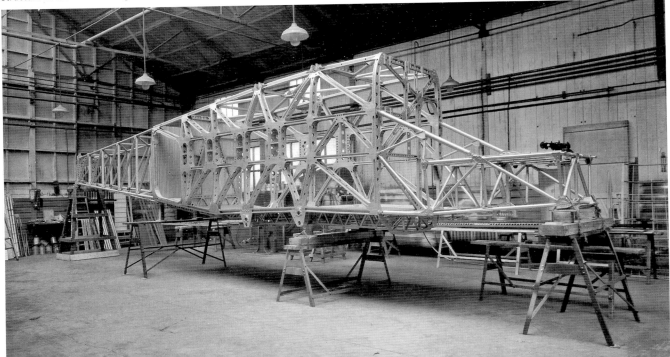

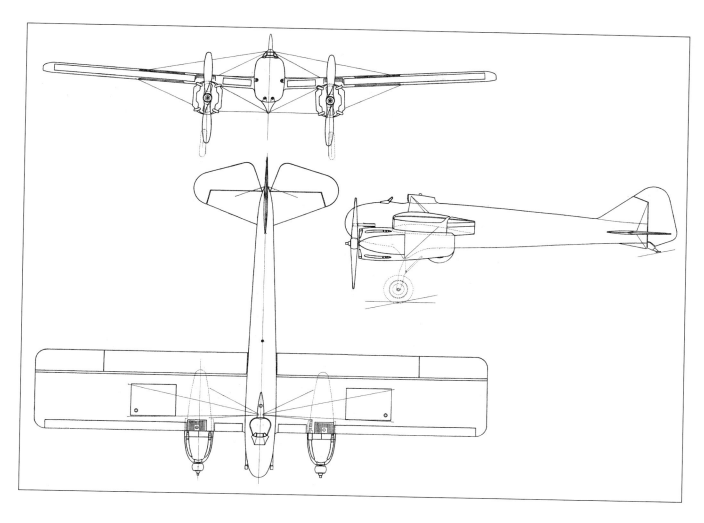

CHAPTER SIXTEEN

A Mixed Bag – P.67 to P.73

P.67

F.7/30 WAS THE SPECIFICATION for the first of the Air Ministry Operational Requirements issued as OR.1. In April 1930 the internal draft by DTD called for a single-seat day and night fighter to replace the Bulldog, a zone fighter for bomber attack. Although the government file was opened in 1930 the specification was not formally issued until October 1931 and B&P were not in a position to allocate formal drawing numbers against their calculations and drafts until pre-Christmas week 1931. There appears to have been some confusion in drafting of the specification as the term interceptor is said to have appeared in some documents, which was normally a completely different type to the day and night zone fighter in Air Ministry circles. Nevertheless, there was a move to delay issue of the specification while other fighters were being evaluated. As with the P.66, the Air Ministry followed the same carrot-dangling format: substantial orders were promised to the winning design following competition in 1934 but only a limited number of prototypes would be ordered and all others would be invited to submit PV prototypes. F.7/30 called for a high maximum speed above 195mph. The climb rate, service ceiling, range and manoeuvring were all to be better than current fighters. Also important was the ability to undertake a sudden steep rate of climb for night interception, and an optimum pilot's view. Radio equipment was essential and a Kestrel IV steam-cooled engine was suggested but not insisted upon. Again, as with the P.66, a large number (at least eight) companies looked at the potential layout because of the production quantities that were likely. With contract placements limited, a large portion of industry was again potentially financing its own airframe submissions.

For F.7/30, unlike many other competitors, North returned to his twin-engine, high-speed monoplane concept for the P.67, using air-cooled inline engines.

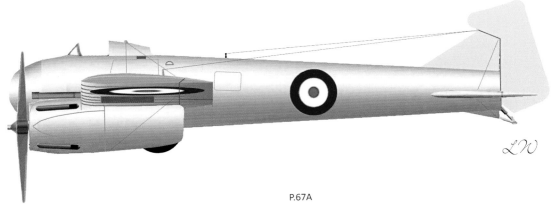

P.67A

The P.67 design took the form of a twin-engine monoplane with the pilot in the extreme nose for good view and controlling four Vickers machine guns. Two were fitted alongside the pilot, where he could clear stoppages, and two under and behind his seat in the lower belly. Hence the pilot would always be able to service at least two of the weapons in combat. The company suggested that this was the cleanest possible aerodynamic efficiency to give high performance and low drag, while the twin-engine format not only gave the best view for the pilot, it also was the best and safest for night flying, with the ability to fly on one engine in the event of a failure. In this case the absence of external struts was given as a positive feature despite the supporting cables used on the wing instead.

The undercarriage was retracting and folded backwards to seat in the lower engine nacelle under the wing with Dowty internally sprung wheels. Stressing calculations and wind tunnel results were included in the proposal based upon a 1/10th scale model of the aircraft, 1/5th scale models of the engine nacelle and a portion of the wing. A wingspan of only 40ft was chosen and a length of 29ft 4in, with a 7ft 3in wing chord. A wing area of 290sq ft gave a light loading of 16lb/sq ft using a NACA Munk M6 section at 2° incidence and a planned AUW of 5,650lb. It was hoped the climb rate and the ceiling of 30,000ft would mean that the machine was unlikely to have to

zoom climb and fire into the underside of the enemy as inferred.

North and Hughes were not drawn to the steam-cooled Goshawk suggested as all their previous designs using this development engine family had failed to be accepted, but offered instead the air-cooled Napier Rapier engine in a close cowling having upper and lower cooling intakes. Wooden airscrews for the prototype to be changed to metal for production were proposed. There would be welded Elektron metal fuel tanks, and either aluminium or tinned steel-riveted tanks as an alternative. Tanks were to be interchangeable and tank levels transmitted to the cockpit from their locations in the wings. Oil tanks above the nacelle in the wing leading edge were cooled via the airflow, there being no other cooler for the oil in the system. Gas starting was to be via RAE starters and the high-pressure bottles also supported the landing gear, wing flaps and wheel brakes. Exhaust collectors exited through slots in the tail end of the nacelle and the top inner on the left-hand engine had a heater muff to draw cockpit air for the pilot and thereby also heat the gun mechanisms for the four 0.303in weapons in the fuselage. The right-hand engine powered the electrical generator within the rear nacelle for instruments and radio. Square thread lead screws driven by air motors performed the undercarriage retraction and extension via co-axial nut and struts, with electrical switches to indicate if the gear was up, down or locked, etc.

Interior Details – P.67

1. Lower gun loading mechanism
2. Ring and bead gunsight
3. Swivelling cockpit lamp
4. Voltmeter and ammeter mounting
5. Very pistol and stowage
6. Identification switchbox
7. Reflector sight and operating gear
8. Oxygen gear
9. Electrical switch
10. Stowage bag for knee-type writing pad
11. Lighting and gun heating switches
12. Stowage for very signal pistol cartridges
13. Gas starter press cock and change over switch
14. Two-pin socket for inspection lamp
15. Pilot's escape door and locking pin
16. Button type pilot's fighting harness
17. Ammunition boxes for lower guns
18. Upward identification lamp
19. Petrol priming pump
20. Oil cock control
21. Magneto change-over switch
22. Hand starting magneto and mounting
23. Voltage control box
24. 12v accumulator
25. Pilot's rudder control with Palmer brake gear fitted
26. Upper Vickers 0.303 guns with empty link chute
27. Ammunition boxes for upper guns
28. Pilot's control column and flying controls
29. Pilot's adjustable seat with back-type parachute
30. Lower Vickers 0.303 guns with empty link chute
31. Pilot's map case
32. Engine controls
33. Compressed air bottles for gas starter and air motors
34. Oxygen supply bottles
35. Gas starter connection and gauge panel
36. Trigger for firing upper guns
37. Trigger for firing lower guns
38. Self-contained wireless gear
39. Air motor and operating gear for flaps
40. Canvas bag for diagrams
41. Tail adjuster operating gear
42. Compressed air bottle controls
43. Wireless remote control
44. Petrol cocks control
45. C3 camera gun and mounting
46. Locking strap box for control column
47. Wing tip flares
48. Wing tip navigation lamps
49. Downward identification lamp
50. Light series bomb rack and 20lb bombs
51. Petrol gauge pressure pump
52. Petrol pressure gauge
53. Dimmer switch
54. Wing tip flare push buttons
55. ASI
56. Engine instruction plate
57. Twinob engine ignition switch
58. Retractable undercarriage indicator lamp for left side
59. Altimeter
60. P.6 navigation compass
61. Retractable undercarriage indicator lamp for right side
62. Compass correction card holder
63. Engine boost indicator
64. Oil pressure gauges
65. Engine revs indicator
66. Oil temperature gauge
67. Turn indicator
68. Locking strap box for rudder control
69. Cross level
70. Watch and holder
71. Air motor and operating gear for retractable undercarriage
72. Cockpit hot air control
73. Light series bomb release gear
74. Wireless aerial lead-in

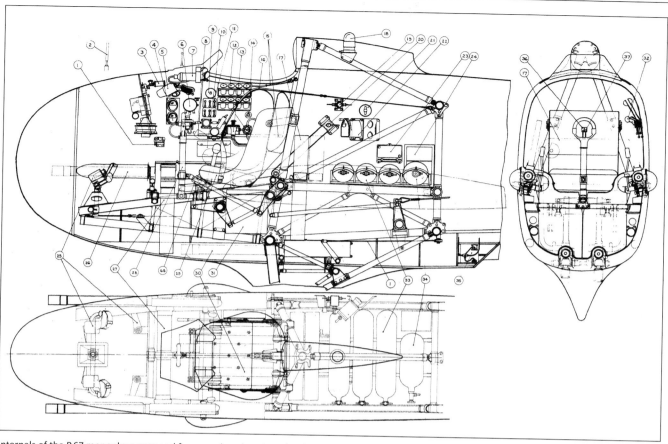

Internals of the P.67 monoplane proposal framework and starboard wall.

Internals of the P.67 monoplane proposal port wall.

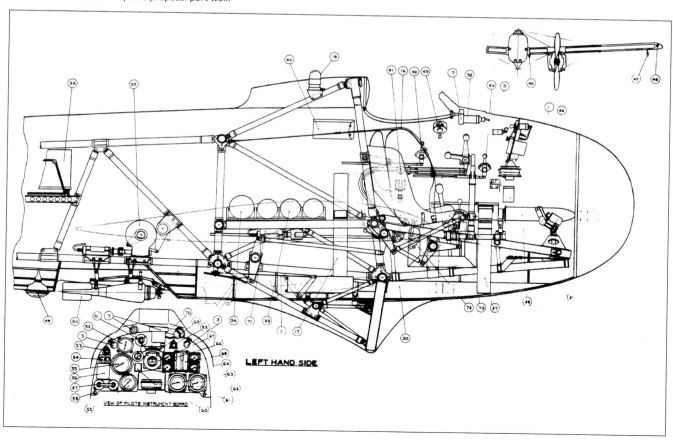

Sketch of the P.67 in flight.

Wind tunnel model of the P.67.

Standard sections were used with hard-drawn tube for all sections over twenty gauge and closed joint for all sections under that gauge. The wing was twin sparred with 4ft between spars and a 17in leading edge. The spars used 2in upper and lower tubes with corrugated web between them, the rear spar being of smaller depth in the web and set high to allow the Frise aileron vent. The fuselage truss was of Warren girder form faired with timber and fabric covering. The pilot's section forward of the wings was a monocoque structure of three-ply on spruce formers while other fairings were spruce formers and stringers on fabric covering. Everything reflected the work being done on the P.62–64 series. The P.67 full proposal was submitted during February 1932 in a brochure as detailed as that for the P.66.

All the F.7/30 tenderers thought that 200mph could be exceeded but that 250mph was not achievable. This was a common theme at the time circulating within the Air Ministry, that industry (and some of the Air Ministry themselves) thought that the performances being asked for were not realistic, requiring a step change in either engine design or airframe design to achieve it. Just such a change had been seen with the Kestrel engine but manufacturers were still toying with the choice between wood, fabric and metal covering. F.7/30 was potentially but one more possible step towards the latter. The P.67 was estimated to achieve 227mph at 12,500ft and to climb to that

height in 6.55 minutes. This was on a par with most other aircraft actually built with the exception of the PV Gloster Type 133, which achieved 260mph on a Bristol Mercury VIS engine.

The ultimate winner was the PV Gloster SS37, which eventually became the Gladiator. Although North's team design had projected comparative speeds with all but these, the choice of engines for the P.67 could not have been appealing to anyone involved in Ministry decisions and while all the arguments appeared sound to North's team, their offering was the only twin-engine machine in at the tender stage. While the team knew that Air Ministry global thinking tended towards twin-engine fighters, only time and war would prove the choice of twin engines for a night fighter to be correct. Instead this layout put too much design emphasis on the night missions as opposed to the replacement of the single-engine fighter force as a whole and turned the assessment team off funding the proposal themselves. In contrast, some of the more esoteric offerings were allowed as PV but were not funded, the exception being the cranked-wing Supermarine 224. Unfortunately, as with the P.66, B&P were unable to fund a PV prototype in the company's financial climate immediately after the proposal issue, and with the Air Ministry failing to provide a contract order for this machine the project had to be dropped.

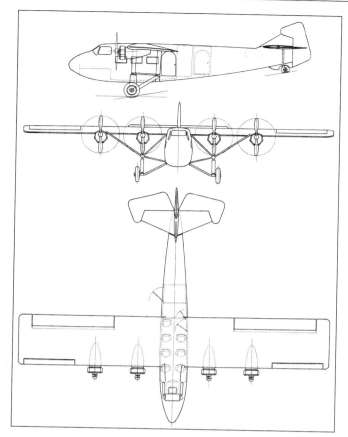

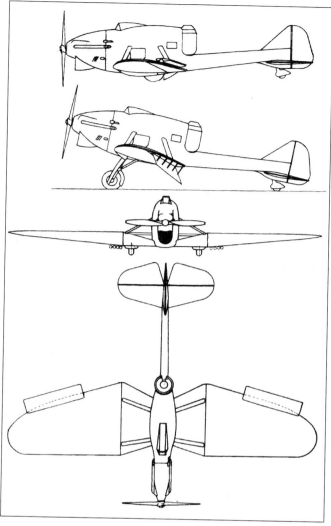

Above: The P.68 four Pobjoy-engine, high-wing monoplane passenger aircraft did not proceed past a 1/50th three-view set.

Right: One of the more weird-looking proposals was the P.73 single-engine bomber with a Type II turret for rear defence. Being a monoplane with full span flaps and retractable undercarriage, the ailerons had to be carried off the wings in a 'park bench' manner.

P.68

On 16 December 1931, Hughes drew a three-view for an eight-seater, high-wing monoplane passenger aircraft with four Airmotors Pobjoy engines. The exact model of Pobjoy is unknown but these were relatively low-power units. It is unlikely that this was a rather late study of the Imperial Airways specification that led to the Armstrong Whitworth A.W.15 Atalanta but it is possible that it originated in Kenya with Wilson Airlines, who were going to meet competition from Imperial Airways. The IA spec was released a year earlier and orders placed with AW for delivery before 1933. The first Atlanta flew in June 1932. It is also possible that this was an attempt to produce a smaller aircraft than the Atalanta for other IA routes but having four engines for safety.

The machine had a 53ft span, was 41ft 6in long and had the standard port entry door, starboard luggage and an aft toilet and washroom. The height was 10ft tail down and the wing chord 8ft 9in. The wheel track was 7ft and the inner engines were 6ft 1.5in from the aircraft centreline with 7ft 8in between the inner and outer engines. The small drawing was not physically numbered and the designation P.68 is only known from the description in a formal list and by cross-referencing the drawing record. It did not proceed beyond the 1/50th scale discussion sheet.

P.73

The period around 1930 saw some particularly odd-looking aircraft being drawn as designers tried to think 'outside the box' in order to find solutions to the ideas thrown at them. The Boulton & Paul P.73 was perhaps not as odd as some types but it was considered odd even by its designers, as the second sentence in the proposal described it as 'a single-engined low-wing monoplane *of unusual design*, incorporating a Rolls-Royce "Griffon" engine'. Proposed to meet specification P.27/32, which called for a two-seat, single-engined monoplane to operate as a bomber, the specification covered OR.7. There were eight known companies looking closely at the potential tender. As with the early B.9/32 tender, the tare weight was limited to 6,300lb in the specification released on 12 April 1933.

The P.73 design at first viewing might be perceived as an attempt to produce a Type Y 'Novel' fighter aircraft, and indeed the thoughts of the design team were controlled closely by information being received on desirable features in that sort of aircraft and the Type W. In particular the need for proximity between pilot and gunner so that, if necessary, they could exchange tasks. CAS Ellington had already voiced the concept of crews being interchangeable as dual pilots/gunners – although in that case he was referring to bomber interceptors and not bombers. The company also wanted to make use of its recent invention, the pneumatic gun turret, to provide maximum field of fire for the rear gunner and with the enclosed sliding canopy together providing maximum comfort for both crew.

The result was a stubby insect-like front fuselage with the pilot ahead of the wing and the gunner sitting in a standard preliminary Type I turret at the trailing edge. In order to give maximum field of fire to the rear and down each side, the rear fuselage was simply a boom formed of a monocoque structural beam, harking back to 1920, which the designers stated was a well- known and well-tried solution. Even the wing was based upon a moth-like shape. It was smaller in chord and thinner at the root but expanded past the undercarriage position, which accommodated a ratchet retraction system. This folded back into the wing when retracted, leaving part of the wheel exposed. To manage the landing and air loads, two large aerofoil-section struts each side braced at just past the undercarriage bay area back against the fuselage. The outer wing then tapered again into a rounded tip. Full-length 'Zap' flaps along the entire trailing edge of the wing meant that there was no room to accommodate ailerons, which had to be fitted on extensions above the outer wing trailing edge. The wing section was stated to be M.6 (modified) and the chord varied from 9ft in at the root up to 13ft outboard of the wheels and down again to 7ft 5in just before the tip rounding. The sections were M6 at root and tip and M6 thickened in between. Structurally a standard Warren girder front fuselage with wood and fabric covering was proposed. Standard metal structure wings with fabric covering. Ailerons were to be ribs threaded on to a tubular spar and the Zap flaps were corrugated duralumin. Only the rear fuselage and tail frame was actually a metal monocoque.

The result was a 60ft span, 43ft long machine where the pilot then sat some 15ft off the ground when static. The Griffon Mk.I engine power was not stated directly, just that it would provide the performance. At the stage of the tender the Griffon I had not even been run and was just in development from the 825hp Buzzard, so, it was hoped that it should improve on the Buzzard family. It was essentially an unknown entity other than on RR datasheets. However, the propeller – for the prototype only – was a wooden 13ft 3in diameter two-blade absorbing 1,080hp at 200mph at 13,000ft, with the engine running at 2,750rpm, which gives a good idea of what Rolls-Royce were predicting for the experimental Griffon. Expected performance was 203mph at 13,000ft, with 170mph cruise at 2,400rpm at the same height. Service ceiling was 24,000ft and landing speed with Zap flaps deployed was expected to be less than 65mph. It was stated, however, that with careful fuselage design the company thought they could attain a maximum speed some 5mph better than the brochure predictions.

Competitors were all looking at much more conventional and advanced machines, which were offering a step change in speeds, while B&P were following and interpreting information fed back from their contacts in order to promote their own specific details. Competing designs predicted higher speeds than possible from the P.73. The proposal was not well received compared with the two that received prototype orders. The P.73, being the only one needing the Griffon engine, was rather a problem when the Griffon Mk.I was never to run. Instead, development pressure switched to the PV.12 and the more promising Merlin. RR would not return to the Griffon until 1938/39. B&P, on the other hand, could not afford to offer a PV development and it was not worth trying to redesign back to any other engine.

Interior Details – P.73

1. RR Griffon engine
2. Oil tank and surface cooler
3. Ring and bead gunsight
4. Water header tank
5. Fire extinguisher
6. Camera indicating lamp
7. Control locking strap box
8. TR9 wireless set controller
9. Controls for three-axis controls
10. Electrical bomb release and oxygen panel
11. Lighting and gun heating switches
12. Stowage for signal pistol cartridges
13. Sliding roof to pilot's cockpit
14. Pilot's sliding seat, seat parachute and safety harness
15. Oxygen supply for pilot
16. Three-axis autocontrols
17. TR9 wireless set
18. TX38 wireless transmitter on swinging mounting
19. Upward identification lamp
20. Wireless panel, TR38 receiver, Morse key, writing tablet, etc.
21. Reserve petrol tank
22. Sliding window
23. Identification switchbox
24. Lewis gun on wind balance gear
25. Oxygen gear panel
26. Lap type safety belt
27. SAA drums
28. Hydraulic balancing gear and seat
29. Air motor and driving gear
30. Oxygen supply for gunner
31. Downward identification lamp
32. Entrance and exit doors for turret
33. Motor generator and switch panel for wireless
34. F.24-type camera, mounting and folding seat for navigator
35. Aerial winch and lead in for trailing aerial
36. Accumulator and battery stowage for wireless
37. Light series bomb racks
38. Bomb aimers instrument panel, electrical bomb release, ASI, altimeter and oxygen connection
39. Drift sight
40. Flying controls
41. CG gear reservoir and air valve
42. Steam evaporative cooling condenser
43. Exhaust manifold
44. Cockpit heating collector muff
45. Wind shield for bombsight opening
46. Air bottles for gas starter and air motors
47. Control for long range petrol tank cocks
48. Gosport speaking tubes
49. Signal pistol stowage
50. Tail adjuster hand wheel
51. Engine controls
52. Control for main petrol tank cocks
53. 0.3030 Vickers gun on adjustable mounting
54. Ammunition box 400 rounds
55. Course setting bomb sight and adjustable mounting
56. Footstep for access to pilot's seat
57. Entrance door
58. Engine starting and doping panel
59. Electrical gear panel
60. 12v accumulator and stowage
61. P.6 compass and stowage
62. Map case and chart cabinet
63. Mechanical camera control
64. Electrical camera motor
65. Fuel contents gauge and changeover switch
66. Holt flare push buttons
67. Bomb firing switch and stowage
68. Air speed indicator
69. Bomb jettison selector switch and master control
70. Standard engine instruction plate
71. Cross level
72. Turn indicator
73. Fore and aft level
74. Engine revs indicator
75. Engine switch
76. Boost gauge
77. Oil temperature gauge
78. Oil pressure gauge
79. Compass correction card holder
80. Watch and holder
81. P.4-type compass
82. Steam cooling warning light
83. Undercarriage warning light
84. Altimeter
85. Radiator temperature gauge
86. Removable hatch when training set fitted (dual control)
87. Louvres for crankcase cooling
88. Electrical generator
89. Air compressor

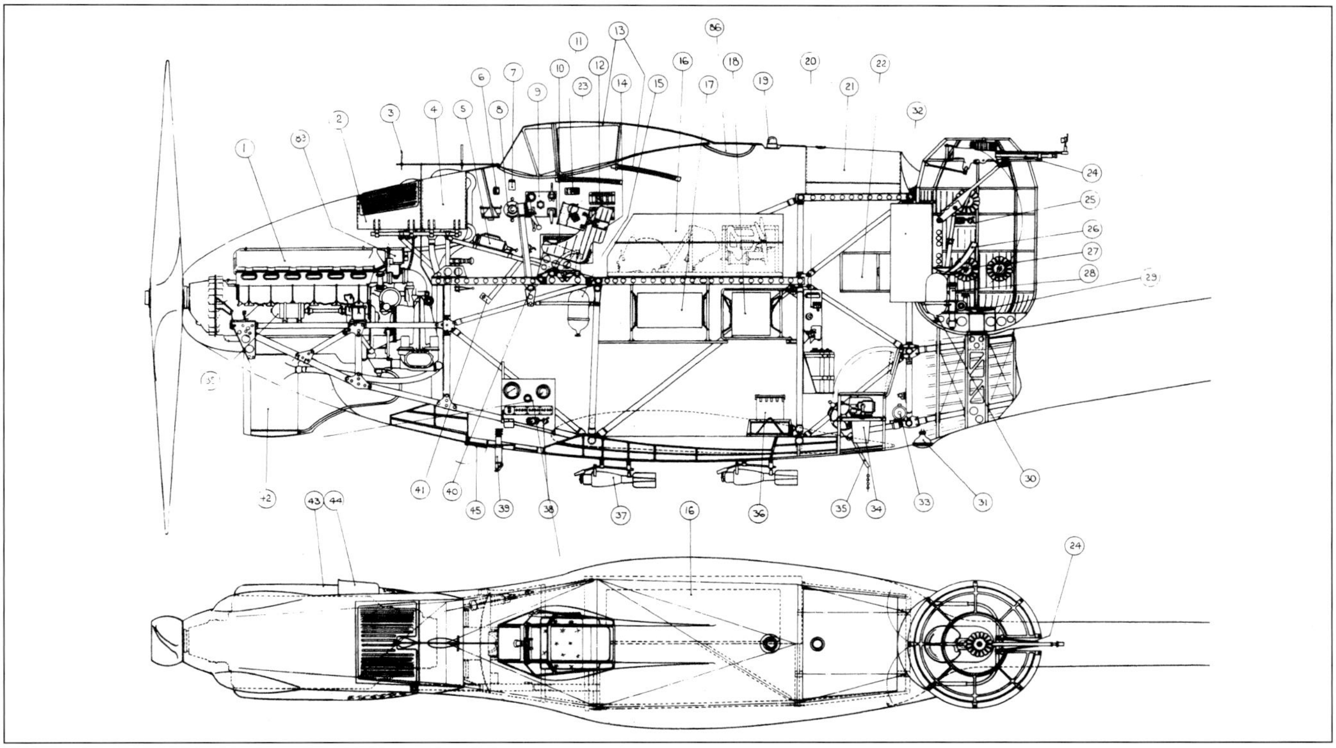

The insect-like P.73 fuselage in plan was designed to allow pilot and gunner to converse and even change places. Such a logic was based upon rumours from within the Air Ministry actually related to the 'novel' fighter concepts. Note that the Griffon engine was unusual in that it was to be steam cooled despite a conventional-looking radiator.

P.73 interior opposite side.

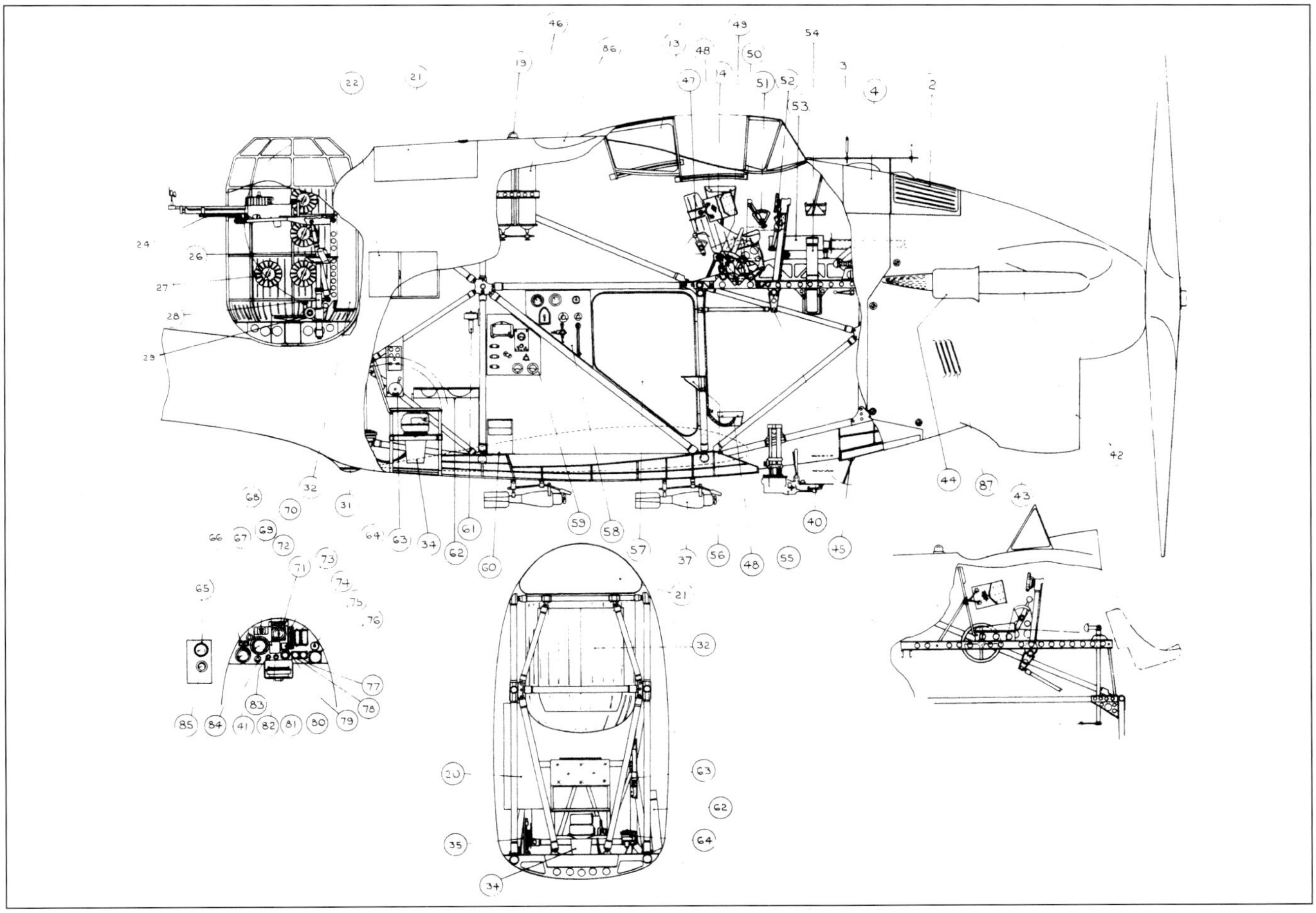

CHAPTER SEVENTEEN

Sidestrand Developments – Overstrand and Beyond

P.75

THE DEVELOPMENT into the Overstrand occurred during the 1932 to 1934 period. This was just at the time that Boulton & Paul had decided to cut their losses and remove the least profitable of the four works divisions from their portfolio. By 1934 the Aeronautical and Research Department was to be sold into the hands of investors. Even though the idea of a power-operated turret was being worked upon and the Air Ministry, always indecisive with budget, were still looking for a viable application for the twin-engined bomber in terms of an update for the Sidestrand, the decisions were made. Boulton & Paul would finally remove itself from the manufacture of aircraft. North had to gather new investors and raise the capital to continue with the business divorced from Boulton & Paul. In 1934, the newly formed Boulton Paul Aircraft Ltd moved almost exclusively to the airfield site, Mousehold Heath at Norwich, with a lease that would allow them two years of tenure before needing to move on.

The sole prototype of the P.29D Sidestrand Mk.V was the J9186 conversion to specification 29/33 and contract 199464/32, which first flew on 11 November 1933 under the control of Sqn Ldr Rea. It was decided that there was such a difference between J9186 now and the original Sidestrand that this prototype would be considered the prototype of a new production batch designated P.75 and renamed Overstrand. Sometime after March 1934 therefore photographs of J9186 were then stated in the press kits to be the P.75 Overstrand prototype.

The P.29C and D proposals had specified an increased area tailplane in order to cope with the Pegasus I.M.3 power and, in the case of the P.29D, to balance the mass of the nose turret. Although schemes had simply shown an increased area, rounded-corner tail unit with a servo-tab equipped trailing edge, the initial drafting of the conversion used quite sharp corners and a mass balance had been added forward of the hinge line for the elevators. The undercarriage geometry was that already tested on J9186 itself, as was the tailwheel, replacing the skid. The Pegasus I.M.3 installations finally

The P.29 Sidestrand V prototype. Photograph from A&AEE Report M471c4 of March 1934 covering Sidestrand J9186 with Pegasus IM3. Later renaming the design P.75 Overstrand I for production resulted in the company pictures of J9186 being retitled. *Crown Copyright*

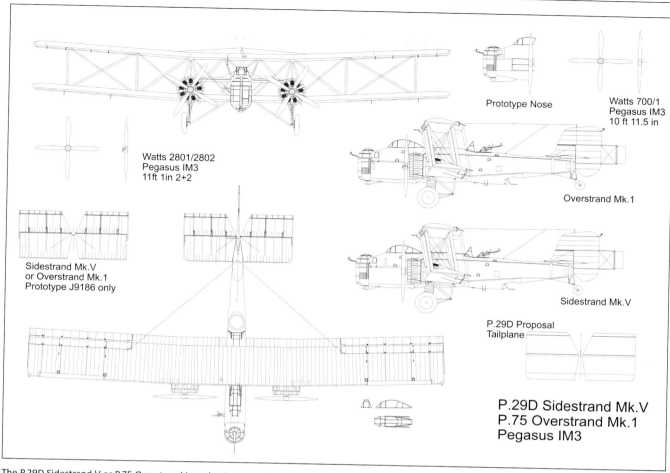

Watts 2801/2802
Pegasus IM3
11ft 1in 2+2

Sidestrand Mk.V
or Overstrand Mk.1
Prototype J9186 only

Prototype Nose

Watts 700/1
Pegasus IM3
10 ft 11.5 in

Overstrand Mk.1

Sidestrand Mk.V

P.29D Proposal
Tailplane

P.29D Sidestrand Mk.V
P.75 Overstrand Mk.1
Pegasus IM3

The P.29D Sidestrand V or P.75 Overstrand I production aircraft 'as built'.

had a BP Townend Ring and the propellers were four-blade Z.800 by Watts of 3,940 to 3,956mm diameter (12ft 11in). During the trials at A&AEE two propellers were damaged striking objects and it was suggested that the trailing edges on the outboard sections were too thin, making them brittle to stone impact. Thickening of the trailing edges was recommended.

Internally, however, there had been a large number of changes. The system of electrical heating required by the crew suiting was gone, now replaced by a duct system fed from cuffs on the outer exhaust pipe of each engine. This channelled hot air taken in from ahead of the exhaust pipe over the hot element of the pipe and out to feed each of the crew positions. In the A&AEE Form 897A reporting on testing Sidestrand J9186 and released in March 1934 the only criticism of this system was that the turret heating was poor and severely reduced the heat available to the pilot when used. Nevertheless, the pilots testing the aircraft, used to sitting muffed up in extreme cold conditions, reported that at no point did the cockpit temperature become uncomfortable.

Initially the P.29C Sidestrand IV catered for a radio suite below the pilot's cockpit and the front gunner was also the radio operator. With the increased weight of the turret in the nose the sets were moved to just forward of the rear gunner for the P.29D Sidestrand V and he became the radio operator. In production P.75 Overstrand aircraft the location was further aft to behind the rear gunner's ring. Pneumatic power was provided by a pump on the starboard engine that fed storage bottles. This air then fed the turret drive and was available on the ground for the gas starter system. The aircraft managed 145mph true at 6,500ft. With a glide approach at 80mph, tail up landings were easy.

The best climb rate speeds were 84 to 87mph indicated. The test weight was at 11,245lb with four 250lb bombs, two internally and two on the wings, and four HE practice smoke bombs.

Three conversions had been ordered from P.29B Sidestrand III to Specification 29/33 (see P.29). The actual production had a new specification 23/34 as a medium day bombing aircraft to contract 349906/34. The Air Ministry were by this time confident enough in the design history to order nineteen Overstrands, serials K4546 to K4564. These now had two+two-blade propellers, type Watts 2801 and 2802. The turret fitted had also been revised from the prototype Mk.I to a Mk.II production unit that was slightly larger in diameter.

The aircraft entered service with 101 Squadron, forming the training C flight. Replacement machines were subsequently ordered under contract 414975/35 with serials K8173 to 8177. Although the company was now Boulton Paul Aircraft Ltd, all Overstrands were completed at Norwich and assembled and flown at Mousehold Heath. Some machines were converted for specialist roles. The P.29D Sidestrand V, J9770, was used for air-to-air refuelling experiments during the 1935 to 1938 period. It was also re-engined with Pegasus IV engines prior to this in connection with the design of the P.80 Superstrand.

K8175 and K8176 were utilised for experiments at Wolverhampton and A&AEE/RAE for two types of aircraft turret. Type A Mk.I turret was the turret being developed onward for the Defiant and Roc fighters, while the single-cannon turret Type F Mk.I was an experimental design using a single Hispano 404 20mm cannon. Both types were air tested for live firing in the nose of an Overstrand. The Type A Overstrand K8175 was then used to test the A Mk.II production turret in mid-1937. The nose design used to house

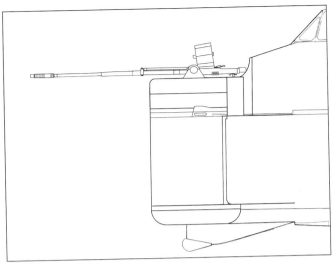
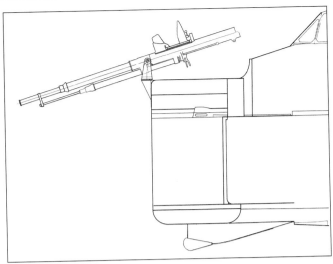

The nose of the P.75 fitted with a Type F 20mm cannon for trials and considered by the Air Ministry during June 1940 as a possible 'tank hunter' for the defence of Britain after invasion. Fortunately only one Type F existed and was not available at the time since it was in the prototype Defiant.

The same nose variation fitted with a COW gun considered briefly as the likely retrofit for 'tank hunting' if sufficient Overstrand machines could be located for conversion in 1940. Fortunately for Overstrand and other bomber crews the situation envisaged never continued to hardware.

either turret was that which had been developed for the lower nose of the P.80 Superstrand. K8176 subsequently became the company spares hack, delivering parts to active Defiant units during 1940/41. It undershot landing at Blackpool in a thunderstorm 30 May 1941 and was wrecked while trying to deliver spares to 256 Squadron. Fortunately both occupants, Robin Lindsay Neale and engineer Slim Bunkle, were unhurt. As 101 Squadron gave up its Overstrands for the Blenheim, four aircraft were allocated to 144 Squadron complete with crews pending the Anson in January 1937. Others moved to AOS units as trainers of potential RAF crew members.

After Dunkirk, the British government were now as afraid of the tank on the ground as it was of being bombed. Having failed to prevent the loss of northern France and Belgium, by failing to develop ground attack aircraft for the Army, the Air Ministry were forced in early June 1940 to consider how the country should guard against the tank with a limited choice of airborne anti-tank weapons available. It was known from French sources that the smaller tanks (Panzer I and II) were very vulnerable to 20mm fire, while the larger (Panzer III) could be knocked out by lucky hits. One possibility fell to the Overstrand. It was already known that the nose structure of the Overstrand could be modified to take a 20mm cannon. Just such a

conversion had been used to demonstrate the Boulton Paul Type F Mk.I powered 20mm cannon mount. However, Churchill himself was demanding that the limited supply of this cannon should be installed in fighter aircraft in fours or pairs, as had been contemplated in the P.88 and Whirlwind. There was only a single BPA Type F turret structure in Britain and this was being tested more importantly in the dorsal position of the prototype Defiant Type W fighter. The 37mm COW gun, some sixty or so of which were in storage along with some thousands of rounds of ammunition, was available. A suggestion was made that older airframes such as Sidestrand, Overstrand and Virginia bombers could be quickly converted to take the COW gun in a new mounting. The thought that the massive Virginia could go around the front at low level combatting the Panzer was, in hindsight, horrifying, but that scenario was seriously contemplated. Fortunately, no Sidestrands and only six Overstrands could be found in serviceable condition and only two ever had the strong P.80-style nose meant for the Type A or F mounting. Doubts were also set, however, that the 37mm ammunition propellant and explosive heads might not be safe after so long in RAF storage. The Overstrand's swansong as an anti-tank aircraft was fortunately abandoned.

Model of the Overstrand 1 made from a combination of the author's original production drawings and the drawings of the late Alan W. Hall. *Model and Photo by champion Greek modeller Aristidis Polyzos*

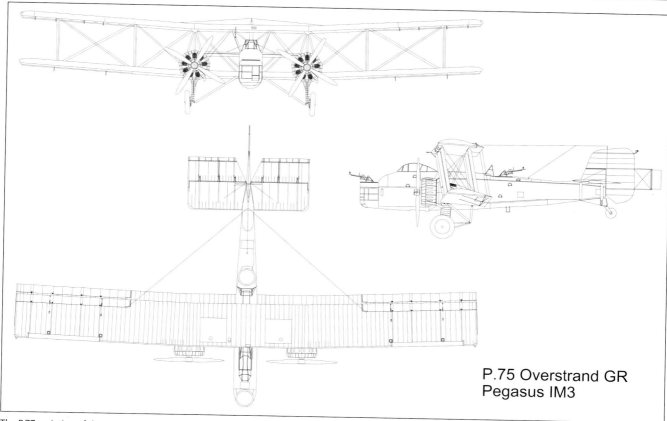

P.75 Overstrand GR
Pegasus IM3

The P.77 variation of the P.75 Overstrand for coastal patrol with front observer/navigator's station and internal walkway between all stations. Fuel tanks have been moved to the upper wing. The nose layout is conjectural, being based upon descriptive documents since submitted drawing X1104 has not been traced.

P.77

The P.77 was the result of an Air Ministry letter 327629/34/C/4(a) of 7 May 1934, which was responded to by a layout drawing on 26 May. The letter requested a study of the feasibility of the Overstrand for conversion to general reconnaissance duties with the ventral gunner's bathtub removed. BP recommended that it was not logical, because of space, to retain the nose turret. Instead they designed a replacement nose with extra glazing and a Scarff ring above. Other than this there were no external changes for the basic outline, simply the internal accommodation of necessary equipment. The major internal change was the moving of the fuselage fuel tanks into the upper wing and the opening up of the fuselage space left by this to incorporate a full internal walkway between the nose and pilot's positions and the dorsal rear gunner. This would allow full communication and physical movement between crew locations for all-around observation. Nothing further happened on this conversion to Overstrand GR, but in 1935 specifications M15/35 for a shore-based torpedo bomber and G24/35 for a general reconnaissance machine were released and BPA were instead requested to tender against these specifications, submitting the completely new P.83 and P.84 designs.

P.80 Superstrand

Based on what looked at first instance like an improved and extended Overstrand, the P.80 was significantly different. It had an Overstrand wing layout in plan, but the BP.10 wing section was entirely replaced by Munk M6. Because of the section characteristics, the company noted that autoslots were not required but could be added to special order. The structure had better streamlining and a retracting mainwheel undercarriage that folded backwards so only part of the mainwheels protruded from the bottom of the wing. The tailwheel was enclosed within a spat and the Overstrand-style ring cowlings hid Pegasus IV engines in its initial design. Following the success of the Overstrand horizontal tailplane with its trailing edge servo actuator tabs on the elevators, the rudder was also to have a servo tab trailing edge, deleting the ugly Flettner tab stuck out in mid-air.

Contrary to some published assumptions based purely on the visual presentation of the aircraft, the machine was proposed only for export and had no powered turrets as such. The Turret Types I and II were initially placed upon the secret list by the government and unavailable for export until released. The gunner stations were simply Scarff rings with canopy enclosures. The nose was a standard Scarff ring with a cupola. The dorsal position had a lobster-tail clear segmented folding hood. There has been a suggestion that about five Superstrands were ordered to replace the Overstrand and then quickly cancelled, but there is no record of that at BPA since the design was purely for export and a sales brochure in dual English/Metric was produced based upon that premise of promoting the aircraft abroad. It is possible that the Superstrand was briefly considered (with turrets) as a heavy fighter in the place of the B.9/32 fighter with the abandonment of the F.22/33 and F.5/33 series. In total there were four versions of the P.80 listed as P.80 to P.80C but only the basic sales brochure layout drawing X1179 has survived. It is most likely that the variations, based upon normal practice, were for various potential engines that overseas customers might specify.

In Pegasus IV form this day and night bomber aircraft was estimated to achieve 187mph at 15,000ft if it was fitted with standard four-blade wooden airscrews. Three-blade, two-position metal airscrews at extra cost (to special order) would give an estimated 191mph. Span was as for the Overstrand at 71ft 11.3in (21.92m) and length 45ft 6in (13.85m). The wing area was 980sq ft (91.04sq m), giving a loading of 15.3lb/sq ft (74.6kg/sq m) at 6,198lb (2,810kg) AUW.

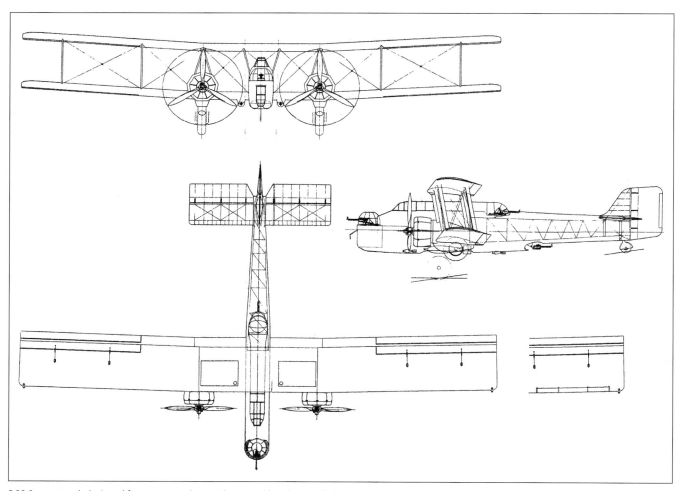

P.80 Superstrand, designed for export markets with covered hand-controlled gun positions but no turrets. HP autoslots and three-blade metal propellers were optional.

An enquiry from Turkey for fifty-five aircraft was received for a day and night bomber to a specification similar to the Superstrand but this never evolved into an order. Unfortunately the enquiry from the Turkish government appeared as an exclusive request via a London agent, Giffard & Goschen, so the company was not dealing directly with Turkish sources and had no idea if the agents were officially engaged or merely attempting to become potential middlemen. The BPA financial outlay on such a potential order was tremendous and great difficulty was encountered in getting the agent to define suitable terms and conditions from Turkey upon which it would be placed. In exasperation the company finally insisted that the terms must be essentially those it had already laid down if no clarity was forthcoming to mitigate the risk, otherwise the agents were free to look elsewhere. On 13 August 1935 a letter from the agents indicated that they would indeed be seeking machines elsewhere. Turkey's requirements seem to have eventually been filled by early versions of the Heinkel He 111 bomber.

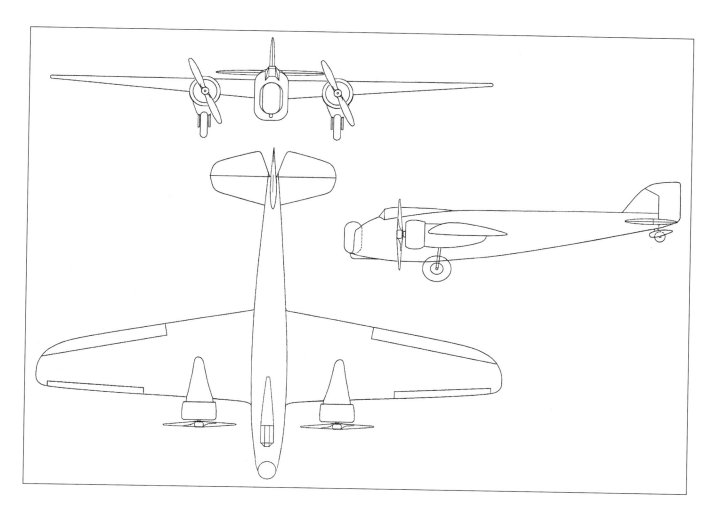

The likely basic layout of the P.78, based on a larger P.76 for heavy bombing.

CHAPTER EIGHTEEN

P.78 and Composite or Compound Aircraft, P.79 Bomber

AMID THE BOULTON & PAUL Aeronautical and Research Department's struggles to maintain production viability and new developments, the company filed patents for an idea to enable heavily laden aircraft to get airborne. The concept was not new in the aeronautical world, but the approach with well thought-out calculations was so clearly a new variation of important merit. North's three patents were all filed upon the same day, 11 December 1933, before B&P decided to sell the Aeronautical and Research Department. North called his concept a 'Compound Aeroplane' and it related to one aircraft being carried or assisted by another. Perhaps unknown to North, Major Robert Hobart Mayo had cross-filed a composite concept slightly earlier than North in April 1932. Mayo continued to file related patents in both Ireland and Germany during 1934–36. As with North, Mayo was at pains to point out that the concept was not new because both Junkers and Dornier in Germany had proposed such machine combinations.

Claims were subsequently served against Mayo and a rejection was received 8 November 1935 from Bristow, Cooke and Carpmael acting for the Mayo Composite A/C Company. North and BPA formed the APD company to exploit the patents but also limit the liability if it came to a fight. The patents 429948, 430068 and 430071 (for North) and 40029, 402895 and 402997 (for Mayo) were involved but the

significant patents would be those pursued in other countries, particularly in Germany, France, Russia, USA and Canada. As a consultant for Imperial Airways, Mayo was already deeply involved with Shorts, Imperial and the Air Ministry. On 12 March 1936 North reported to BPA Board that he had interviewed Mayo, Borroughes and Stewart (in February) suggesting they might take a 5 year option on his patents at a price to be assessed by an independent arbitrator. At a second meeting in April he tried again with a few figures of an

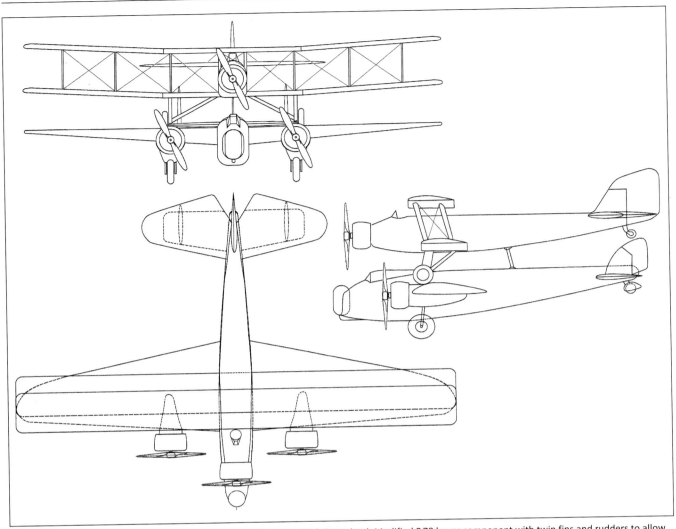

Composite aircraft for getting a heavy bomber P.78 type airborne with full overload. Modified P.78 lower component with twin fins and rudders to allow an 'assistive' unnumbered biplane on the top based upon an enlarged P.55 design.

aircraft which would meet the as yet unreleased specifications for 1936 bombers. Mayo thought that the concept had great worldwide potential and obviously so did North. The Air Ministry support for Mayo eventually faded away when the Geneva weight restriction limits on bombers was not ratified. At the 17 December 1937 BPA board meeting it was announced that APD was abandoning any claim against the Mayo patents, having failed to come to any sort of settlement either way. This meant the shelving of the three North APD patents and one filed in France but retaining that in the USA.

North's concept was developed around the need to get heavily loaded aircraft (such as advanced high-speed bombers or passenger machines) off the ground and into the air without the need for catapulting or rocket assisted take-off, or even with the addition of catapulting as well. Even if North was aware of Mayo's patent applications it is clear that his detail concept was different from all of the others and warranted an application. Again, the fact that a machine could fly with a much heavier load than that it was able to lift from the ground was well known, as was the need to design the high-speed machine's propellers for operations when airborne rather than when at take-off. North's patents revolved around his specific latest project, the P.78 day and night bomber, itself developed from his P.76 two-seat, twin-engine fighter. North's idea provided a solution by temporarily increasing the lifting wing area and avoiding the need for longer take-off runs. North's first patent specifically describes an unnumbered

variation of the P.76/P.78 concept as the lower component. The layout is P.76-style but slightly larger at 63ft span to accommodate the bomb load. The original P.78 may well have had a P.76-style single fin and rudder but here the tailplane has twin fins incorporated so that the upper component can neatly fit above the fuselage. North proposed that, in order to get the heavily loaded machine off the ground, a lightly loaded, slow-speed biplane of similar size should be fixed above. In this way a triplane, triple-engined layout was formed for take-off and climb at low speed. At height the biplane would be detached rapidly and climb away due to its light loading. The P.78-style aircraft was then free to operate at maximum load and range. The upper machine, also 63ft span, appears to be based loosely upon the P.55 concept for a single-engined biplane for operating using short take-off and landing in confined spaces. The machine is more refined and is otherwise unrelated to any other project. North's second patent shows a slightly different machine from the basic P.78 series. In this case the centre fuselage terminates as a pod with turrets at both ends, while the separated tail booms extend from each engine nacelle with full-height fins on each. North also proposed the possibility of trolley or catapult take-off to save undercarriage weight, and so we can suggest he was probably also thinking again of skid or buried wheel landing. The nacelles/tail booms were swept downwards aft of the engines, which would allow both the accommodation of skid landing and potentially extra (bomb) cells within the booms. North's third patent was for a

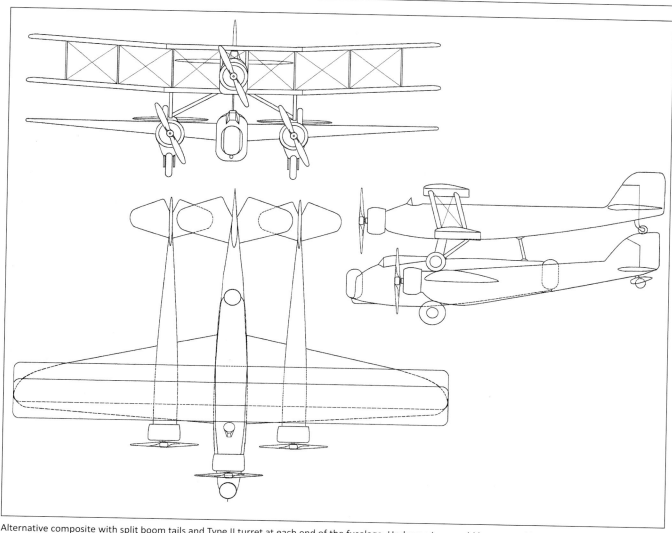

Alternative composite with split boom tails and Type II turret at each end of the fuselage. Undercarriage could be retractable or jettisonable (the bomber landing on the forward tail boom fairings).

release mechanism – including overload and altitude (pressure) release – using the first patent machine design as a basis.

Some interest was shown in North's proposal in military/civil circles. The P.78 bomber itself failed to attract any interest and its very draft scheme drawings seem to have been eventually destroyed, having been reused to generate layouts on the composite aircraft for the patent agents. North's idea was not discarded out of hand, however, and provision for a large aircraft based around various options of catapult launch, air refuelling, or launching by other aircraft appeared in the cost estimates for 1935 prompted by DTD. So the Air Ministry was not unaware of either North's or Mayo's patents. Specification B.4/36 was issued to Shorts for a catapult-launched aircraft but it was eventually abandoned and merged with the other 1936 bomber specifications B.12/36 and P.13/36. Nevertheless, if the airframe design could stand the estimated g-load of launching, the catapult scheme provided the cheapest form of take-off assistance with the minimum of equipment needed.

P.79

In the meantime other, more favoured, companies than the now renamed BPA were obtaining work by private venture demonstration and detail expertise linked to the latest high-performance specifications. Specification B.3/34, which followed, was a complicated document for

a bombing/troop-carrying Heyford replacement that eventually spawned three detailed documented requirements. The third was drafted following the DTD delegation's visit to USA, where they saw a number of new designs, but particularly the Martin 139 (to become the B-10 bomber) and the Douglas DC-1, progenitor of the DC-2 and DC-3 series. But it was the turning of a Nelson-like blind eye to the international tare weight limit and its eventual removal that allowed sensible airframes to be offered again.

The allocation of the project number P.79 on the B&P major project list was initially for a project conforming to B.3/34 and an engine type 'Perseus' was tentatively allocated – an engine with similar power to North's familiar Pegasus in theory but based upon the new sleeve-valve principle in development. The engine was destined never to appear in the final submission, being overshadowed by its developing sister power plants with the Pegasus as a final back-up. The initial work was probably based around obtaining a design to conform to an early draft of B.3/34 No 3 since the newly received specification was announced in November 1934 and initial drawings had already been prepared. During redrafting B.3/34 to version No 3 and before actual formal issue to constructors around March 1935 it was renumbered B.1/35, calling for a 230mph bomber carrying 2,000lb of bombs for 2,000 miles and 4,000lb for 1,000 miles with three gun positions for defence. The specification drew on much that DTD had seen and reported on in the USA.

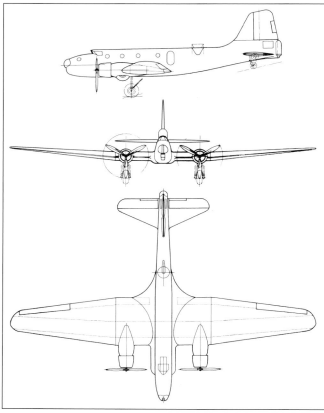

North had already obtained details of the DC-1 and its intended production series, the DC-2 and, impressed with its advanced metal structure and skinning, he studied it in great detail. He saw the possibility to licence produce the DC-2 in the UK and it is likely that he was on or closely associated with the DTD team visit to the USA. Hearing that Fokker were exploring licence production of the DC-2 in the Netherlands (for KLM), North wrote to Fokker proposing that

North's P.79 bomber based on Northrop and Douglas-type civil designs of the time. It featured North's patented rotary bomb bay ejector racks in parallel bomb bays and was the first design to be submitted by Boulton Paul Aircraft Ltd.

there was some scope for a USA/Fokker workshare collaboration or alternatively a UK sub-licence from Fokker for the UK market. Unfortunately, he reported on 13 December 1934 that Fokker had not even bothered to acknowledge his request, let alone reply. What he did not know was that the Fokker licence only allowed them to import US-produced DC aircraft, not build them in Europe. Had such a move been possible it is likely that the P.79 could have been a DC-2 wing with a military fuselage – as developed in the USA.

North also announced, in addition to the new specification stated above, that separately studies were continuing into the composite aircraft concept, even though the P.78 had obviously temporarily been pushed to the rear. North thought that in the box spar, steel-skinned monoplane, with semi-buried retracting undercarriage, gun turret technology and some thought to a method of loading and safely dropping the increasing number of bombs required he would have enough pre-developed ideas to make the Ministry sit up and take note. Despite the financial situation, he planned to spare no expense in preparing a proposal to win draft B.1/35.

North commenced with an obvious Douglas-style layout; a twin-engined, single-fin, low-wing monoplane. The low wing of the Douglas had been in order to have a capacious passenger seating area throughout the fuselage; in North's case it allowed him to build sufficient strength and streamlining into the lower fuselage to employ large, hollow, bulbous bays fore and aft for his new bomb delivery system while avoiding mating these to a mid-wing joint. The ability to employ such a low wing on a streamlined fuselage stemmed from new work on trailing edge filleting also carried out in the USA. Home-based wind channel testing confirmed the efficiency of adequate filleting and resulted in North's team employing a massive trailing edge fillet fairing up to half of the centre section span. The wing was to be a full-depth box spar with metal leading edges.

The prototype working rotary ejector rack for the P.79 bomber. The idea probably started during internal discussions on the twin-boom P.78 composite variant.

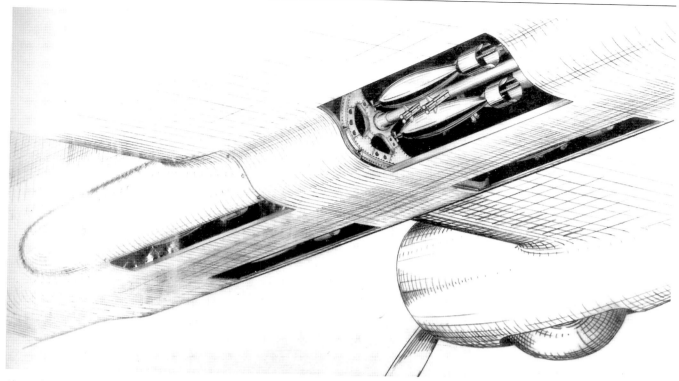

Above: Sketch from the brochure showing the small doors through which the bombs would eject and larger doors used for rearming.

Right: Wooden mock-up of the twin Lewis tail mount for the P.79 formed with two clamshell doors aft when the mount was not in use.

Douglas had a completely metal wing, which was immensely strong. If North followed conventional UK thinking in one respect of the design, however, it was to avoid metal skinning of the rear wing structure (to save weight). Instead he proposed exactly the same type of structure that was used for the Whitley to B.3/34 No 2 – he used fabric over metal ribs for the wing aft of the box spar. It is likely, however, that had the B.1 /35 been built under contract this would have developed into all metal. This decision was also coloured by his idea to prove the system cheaply – he intended to first build the rear wing structure in wood and to then replace it with metal after the machine had been proven.

Traditionally bombs had been slung externally or accommodated within slab-sided fuselages. North had already broken the mould on that one with his Sidestrand where copious streamlining included open-bottomed fairings enclosing all but the bottom of the bomb bay. Work on the P.76/78 and studies of others convinced him that internal carriage was essential, but this led to large drag penalties in huge powered doors when all the bombs now being specified might have to be salvoed in sequence. Similarly, the advantages of a low-wing design might have to be offset in an unusually long undercarriage to allow access to the underside bays. North wanted a short undercarriage with a DC-style half-buried mainwheel, which could be used for landing in the event of extension failure. He had already developed a patented multiple rack idea and with the B.1/35 he could demonstrate it for use. His solution was to utilise an electro-mechanically indexed method of carriage similar to the revolving pistol, which could be loaded on the ground as a complete module through side-accessible hatches that were not needed to launch the bombs. With four separate large weapon bays, all four could be loaded at the same time without the crews stumbling over each other or having to crawl under the fuselage. Towards the rear two smaller bays could carry lighter bombs, flares or incendiaries in a similar manner. The B.1/35 centre section would therefore be a triple bubble or clover leaf shape.

North's rotating bomb carrier Patent was 579310. It covered multiple bombs being carried on a rotary launcher and indexed with phased release so that the balance of the rotating launcher was maintained. Release of all bombs on a launcher would take two complete revolutions of the carrier. In the P.79 North reverted to a smaller x-rack configuration. A maximum standard bomb load 6,000lb (eight × 500lb and eight × 250lb) plus light rack bombs were offered using the system, 75% greater than required in the initial specification. In addition, 5,000lb of the new, secret, Type B anti-battleship bombs could be accommodated by installing one per bomb bay in place on the X-shaped crutch and carrying a further six on partly faired wing racks. The carriage of these meant that the lower X crutch had to be used and the B bomb casing protruded half an inch or so into the airflow without bomb doors, a slight compromise on the whole concept. In addition, North had to put two bays side by side to accommodate the number of bombs. North had offered to revise the design of his system and the lower fuselage bay to accommodate all four of the fatter Type B bombs on his rack but was advised by the Ministry officials that this was not necessary, the proposal would be perfectly alright as it was. In fact, the political pressure and enthusiasm from the Ministry for the system to be fitted to British bombers was such that during the February 1935 BPA board meeting North revealed to the board that he had been forced to assign the rights of his Patent 36270 for the rotating bomb carrier to the Secretary of the Air Council – this meant that the whole system had, once again, been placed on the secret list. Probably as a result of this agreement, he was able also to reveal that some of the gun turret patents had now been released from the secret list and could be published.

Certainly no expense was spared in mock-up and experimentation for North's Rotating Carrier or anything else on the coming B.1/35 proposal. The company was at pains to point out the amount of effort that could not be presented within the proposal for lack of space. The list of work available for scrutiny at Norwich was appended. Fuel for the bomber was carried in a series of standard identical replaceable tanks installed through underside hatches into the box spar, with a larger tank in the same spar within the centre section. Prior to this it had been normal to propose fairly small fuel tanks to form the leading edge of the wings. An overload tank could be installed within the fuselage above the spar. Engine cooling was to be by labyrinth coolers as used on the Overstrand and alternatives of three engines could be accommodated: Bristol Taurus TE1 S (Double Aquila), Bristol He 1S Hercules or Pegasus VSM, all using 13ft Hamilton Standard VP propellers.

The specification called for three turrets and all were new developments. The nose turret was an angled powered ring with a clear cupola carrying a single Lewis gun. The tail turret was similar to an Overstrand Mk.II but, since it was facing rearward, could have opening clamshell-type, full-length doors to accommodate twin Lewis mountings with maximum field of fire. A thickened rear fuselage accommodated the turret under a large single fin, considered superior and simpler to construct and control than the twin-fin types. The upper turret was retractable on a central hydraulic jack, completely enclosed and shaped at the top so that when retracted it conformed to the upper surface of the fuselage, the weapon being accommodated in a slot in the fuselage to the rear. No mention of overload take-off solution by composite take-off was necessary since an alternative possibility had been placed in the specifications, that of refuelling the bomber in flight after take-off. However, in view of the secret nature of the refuelling system, BPA were not given the details and simply had to accommodate the possibility of refuelling from a single point in flight. BPA proposed a system to connect at the nose, handled by the bomb aimer/gunner/navigator. The fuselage was to be manufactured entirely in metal in two halves, split vertically about the centreline with a separate bolt-on nose and tail and a capping strip covering the longitudinal joints above and below. The windscreen for the pilot was offered both in the American style with inward-sloped panels to reduce glare or the conventional pattern. North pushed the Bristol Taurus TE1S (Double Aquila) as his lead engine, probably because he had more data on that than the others. The best performance prediction was with the Hercules, which matched exactly that predicted by one of the competitors, the Vickers design. The top speed was projected to be 261mph at 15,000ft, with a ten-minute climb to that height, and a full-load range of 1,500 miles. This was achieved on a smaller span and wing area than the others because of North's choice of large trailing edge flaps. Every proposer struggled to cruise at 230mph, the P.79 managing a predicted 228mph. The new design had a span of 87ft, length of 61ft 3in and stood 15ft 10in tail down.

Despite the Ministry's detailed interest in the work and the working mock-ups, they awarded prototype contracts to three of the other six competitors. As North had thought, many of the design features would have been world-beaters if proposed by a favoured firm. So just why was North not favoured? One suggestion is that in pushing the low-wing concept with rotating racks the P.79 had shot itself in the foot. It was believed (wrongly) not to be capable of adaption to either the larger B-type anti-battleship bombs nor to torpedo carrying (even though neither had been specified at the time) because of its restricted-length dispenser bays. This seems initially unlikely, however, because no one thought to tell the firm, who continued to promote the rotating rack concept on both their P.13/36 and B.12/36 designs. The main problem may have been that BPA had tendered £50,000 for the single prototype in July 1935, which may have appeared to be too pricey. BPA were instead on the favoured list of tenderers for the 1936 specifications.

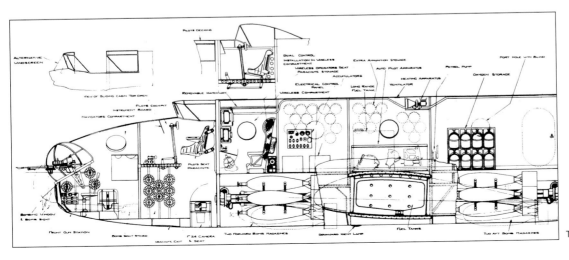

The P.79 fuselage interior.

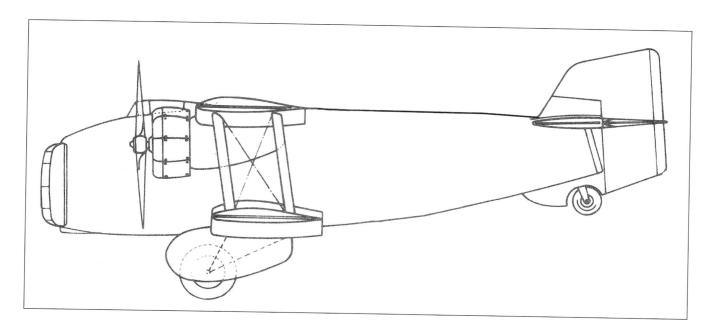

CHAPTER NINETEEN

The 'Novel' Fighter Programme (Stage 1)

THE SEARCH FOR A 'NOVEL' idea for fighter design stems from the studies for fighter development involving higher speeds and greater firepower but also the perceived need for a uniquely different method of attack for the forces of ADGB. After the First World War various members of the Air Staff put their minds to how they could combat, not just a bomber, but a whole formation of bombers with cohesive defence. In the heat of combat against a defending aircraft 'hits' inevitably went down when compared with training results, but it was assumed the ratio between a turret gunner and a pilot gunner firing would stay the same. This fuelled the impression that a formation of bombers with gunners positioned in specific positions within the aircraft in the formation would always be able to provide multi-gun defence and much higher firepower. The resulting formation would be hard to break.

One idea was that in order to destroy a formation, you must attack with a formation, just like a traditional naval battle. The enemy formation might be stopped by a formation attack of normal fighters, cutting the enemy formation in two, or alternately by flying alongside the enemy 'line-astern' pouring broadsides into the bombers. The problem was that it was impossible to maintain a formation and fire at the enemy in a normal single-seat fighter. The pilot was just not able to multi-task as all his effort would be required to avoid collision. Hence a two-crew fighter would be required, preferably one with the advantages of a dedicated pilot for flight control and a dedicated free gunner to attack the enemy by concentrating his aim on them. Air Vice-Marshal Edward Ellington strongly favoured a multi-turret fighter formation where the position of the gunner could be selected depending upon the formation. During 1933 the Deputy Chief of the Air Staff (DCAS) Air Vice Marshal Edgar R. Ludlow-Hewitt listed the fighters that should be looked at as a priority. These were:

A Type W two-seat fighter with stern armament.

A Type X single-seater with heavy firepower (eg: cannon) to stand off from the formation.

A Type Y two-seat fighter with trainable guns forward.

A Type Z single-seater with the highest performance for shock attacks, also known as an interceptor fighter.

P.72

During issue and work on B.9/32, the Air Ministry considered the possibility of employing a high-speed version of B.9/32 as a fighter. Since it was expected that B.9/32 would lead to an airframe as fast as many fighters of the day it seemed logical that this could easily be configured as either a heavily armed gunship or perhaps as a 'Novel' fighter for attacking formations of the enemy. Boulton & Paul's submission to B.9/32 was the P.70 high-speed bomber covered earlier. At the submission stage of the P.70 the Mail Carrier was still an unknown entity but Boulton & Paul had applied the results of this

The P.72 started out as a twin-engine fighter designation when the Air Ministry deemed to consider if turreted bombers to B.9/32 such as the P.70 and Wellington might also be utilised as heavy fighters. The P.70 drawings were thought to cover the layout so no other drawings seem to have been done. This sketch suggests the layout of a Type Y 'Novel' fighter based on the P.70 airframe.

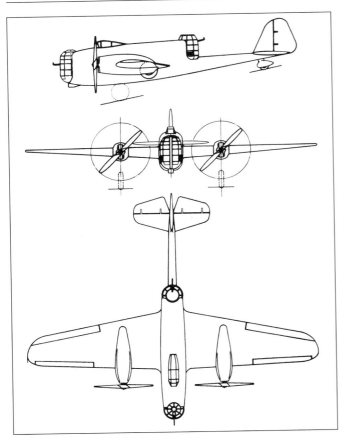

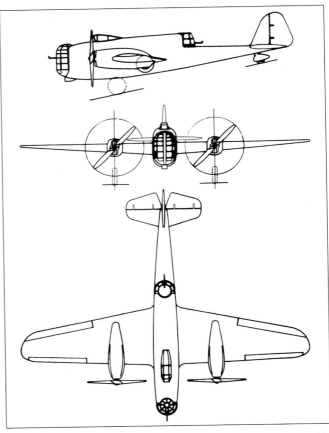

Version A of the P.74 'Novel' fighter with Napier air-cooled inlines, full Type II turrets front and rear and a thin tail boom.

Version B of the P.74 has a Type II nose turret and a Type III non-retractable rear turret.

testing and their Joukowski aerofoil fuselage elevation to the P.70. It was only a small step lightening the all-up weight of the aircraft by removing the large bomb bay and stores carriers and replacing these with more Lewis gun ammunition to produce a heavy fighter. By further removing the dorsal and ventral weapons stations and crew to enhance performance, but retaining the nose turret and gunner, a high-speed, two-seat, twin-engine P.72 'Novel' fighter resulted. The P.72 would be capable of being configured as either the Type W with mid-upper armament aimed astern or the Type Y with its nose turret.

No drawings or calculations of the P.72 survive, merely the listed facts that it was a two-seat, twin Pegasus-engined fighter aircraft. Given the highly detailed submission of the P.70 in December 1932 very little would need to be revised to offer the unofficially sanctioned P.72 as a possible solution, and that is perhaps why no further data remains. The Air Ministry did not pursue the point, but the feedback from B.9/32 tenderers to that idea helped formulate the specifications for 'Novel' fighters issued into the 1933 round of tendering.

On 22 December 1933 Air Ministry specifications F.5/33 and F.22/33 were issued. F.5/33 called for a two-seat fighter aircraft with a front gun station, while F.22/33 called for a two-seat fighter aircraft with both front and rear gun stations meeting both W and Y ideas. Feedback made it clear that the officials studying the requirement had favoured monoplanes, and the Mail Carrier layout was to be abandoned with the loss of the prototype in October 1933. F.22/33 was the more complicated design and the company allocated the designation P.74 for a design to conform to the specification and P.76 for the fighter to F.5/33. Boulton & Paul prepared to offer both fighters with the advantage of its newly developed pneumatic Type I turret.

P.74 with two gun stations

Four versions of the P.74 were prepared. The P.74A and B were based around the Napier Rapier V (E.100) engine, which the company considered was the only inline engine that was sufficiently tested and showing promise of suitable power to meet the performance requirements in the airframe proposed. The P.74C and D were much larger machines but used the more powerful Pegasus IV radial with BP Townend Rings. Other than size, the general proportions and shape were similar in each airframe. Designs A and C utilised two complete B&P Type I turrets fore and aft of the pilot together with a slim beam tail boom carrying the fin and tailplane surfaces. The rear turret had the upper hatch of the turret omitted, so it acted essentially as a windshield for the gunner. The B and D designs had instead a lighter powered cupola on a gun ring in the rear station for arcs above horizontal, allowing a more substantial conventional rear fuselage to be utilised. This rear gun ring (described as a 'powered fighting cockpit') again had no roof capping, being a non-retractable version of the dorsal turret proposed in the P.70 programme. In both B and D rear cases the gun slot was sufficiently wide to allow the Lewis gun to be depressed outside its normal arcs to fire downwards either side of the rear fuselage. Provision was mentioned to allow additional fairings behind the rear gun station if that was considered necessary. In all cases the power for the turrets/gun rings was pneumatic, using the same services that would retract and lower the undercarriage and techniques already proven with the Turret Type I prototype. All aircraft had retracting undercarriage, spatted tailwheel and North's patented sliding cockpit canopy for the pilot. In deference to AVM Ellington's concept of a gunner who could move station, the B and D (Pegasus) versions had removable panels in the fuselage ahead of the turret, allowing extra Lewis guns to be free-mounted to fire abeam if required.

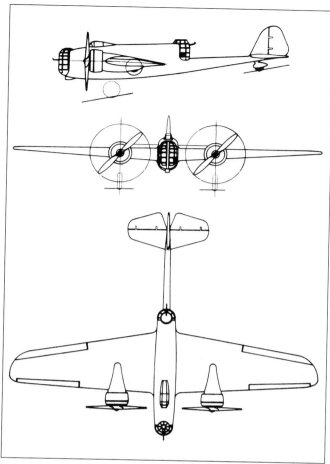

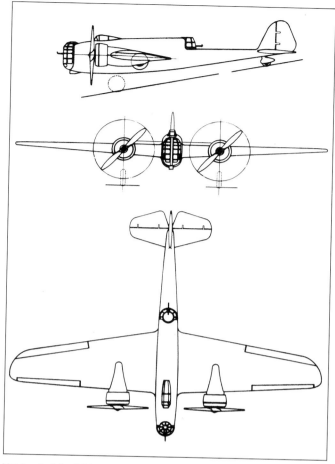

Version C was a larger aircraft using Pegasus engines but otherwise similar to the P.74A.

Version D of the P.74, a Pegasus-equipped P.74B.

Performance with the E.100 engine was 195mph at 15,000ft, reached in 12.5 minutes for the P.74A, and 203mph and twelve minutes for the P.74B. A full model engine for the Napier Rapier had already been wind tunnel tested for the P.67 programme to F.7/30 (Air Staff Requirement OR.1). The Pegasus IV predicted 226mph at 15,000ft reached in eight minutes for the P.74C and 232mph on the same parameters for the P.74D. The E.100 machine had a 48ft span and was 39ft 3in long, while the larger Pegasus machine had a 60ft span, was 44ft 9in long and 33% heavier.

Five other companies are known to have tendered in competition to the P.74. The two-seat Armstrong Whitworth A.W.33 with Double Genet Major engines appears to have been a front runner with a predicted 225mph at 13,000ft. This was followed by a Fairey proposal and both were initially allocated contract numbers. Bristol proposed the Type 141 with a pilot and two gunners and Westland schemed a Pterodactyl type with twin tractor engines and turrets fore and aft.

P.76 With Front Gun Station

The P.76 to F.5/33 was offered in two versions: the P.76A with Napier Rapier V (E.100) engines and the P.76B with Pegasus IV. Again both machines were identical in shape and layout but in this case had conventional rear fuselages. The nose-based gun turret had been given some additional thought and had two Lewis guns incorporated by lying one weapon on its side under the first so that both weapons fired through the central gun slot. There was also homage to anti-Zeppelin concepts in that options were offered for two forward-firing Vickers guns in the wings and/or two oblique no-allowance weapons in the rear fuselage firing upwards at 45°.

Performance with the E.100 engine was 217mph at 15,000ft, reached in 11.2 minutes for the P.76A, and 247mph and 7.5 minutes for the P.76B. The E.100 machine had a 48ft 6in span and was 39ft 6in long, and the larger Pegasus machine had a 58ft 6in span, was 44ft 6in long and 51% heavier. The company suggested that it was worth them offering the larger alternative machine because of the performance increase with the RR Pegasus, whilst they could not predict better performance with the E.100 engine over that given because of the current results of testing by the manufacturer. Both P.74 and P.76 designs were said to meet their respective specifications and to represent the best performance obtainable in the immediate future.

Six other companies are known to have tendered in competition with the P.76. There was the two-seat Armstrong Whitworth A.W.34 with AS Terrier engines and a Fairey study. Bristol proposed the Type 140 pusher with a nose turret, while Gloster favoured a turreted scheme. Parnall proposed a tractor with turret and Westland schemed a Pterodactyl type with pusher engine and turret in the nose.

AVM Ellington was talked out of support for the twin-turret machine by DCAS with the view that some of the proposals (including B&P) schemed it as a requirement for a three-seat crew rather than two seats with a gunner who had a choice of positions. The enthusiasm to develop either specification type was lost by scepticism that the performances would neither be adequate for the task nor offer anything new to Air Defence Great Britain plans. F.5/33 and F.22/33 were quietly allowed to fade away in anticipation of a series of new specifications, including one that fitted the DCAS Type W idea, F.9/35.

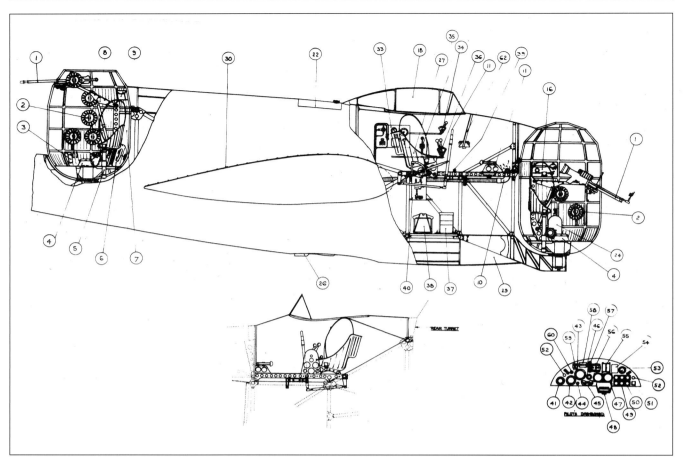

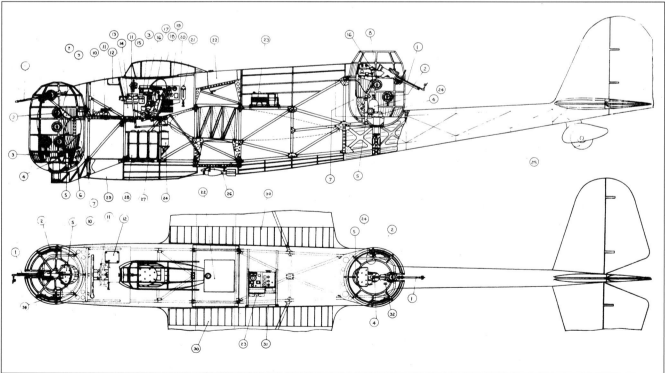

Interior of the P.74A and C series.

Interior Details – P.74 A and C Series

1. 0.303 Lewis gun and wind balance gear
2. SAA drums
3. Microphone stowage bag and sockets
4. Air motor and driving gear
5. Hydraulic balancing gear and seat with Sutton harness
6. Parachute stowage
7. Entrance and exit doors to turret
8. Gun arm with underslung gun mounting
9. Spare parts holdall for gun
10. Heating louvre for pilot
11. Flying controls
12. Removable panel for access to instrument board
13. Map case
14. Stowage bag for knee type writing pad
15. TR9 wireless set remote controller
16. Oxygen panel
17. Signal pistol stowage
18. Sliding roof of pilot's windscreen
19. Electrical panel
20. Signal pistol cartridges and stowage
21. Fire extinguisher
22. Gravity fuel tank
23. TR9 wireless crate
24. Oxygen supply
25. Castoring tail wheel
26. Light series bomb rack and 4 × 20lb
27. Pilot's adjustable seat with parachute stowage and Sutton harness
28. Compressed air supply for turret motors and gas starter
29. Parachute exit for front gunner
30. Running boards for access to tank, wireless, etc
31. Hatchway for removal of wireless crate
32. Foot release valve for hydraulic balancing gear
33. Gas starter panel
34. Fuel cock controls
35. Tail adjuster gear
36. Engine controls
37. No 3 Mk.III accumulator
38. First aid outfit
39. Gas starter press cock
40. Gas starter hose connection and atomiser
41. Tail setting indicator
42. Altimeter
43. ASI
44. Undercarriage warning lamp
45. Twinob engine ignition switches
46. Watch and holder
47. Boost gauge
48. P.6 compass
49. Oil temperature gauge
50. Oil pressure gauge
51. Compass correction card holder
52. Lamp and dimmer switch
53. Fuel contents gauge and change-over switch
54. Standard engine instruction
55. Edgewise engine electrical rpm indicator
56. Turn indicator
57. Fore and aft level
58. Bomb firing switches
59. Bomb jettison switch
60. Bomb firing switch
61. Sliding panel for access to cockpit
62. Pilot's dashboard

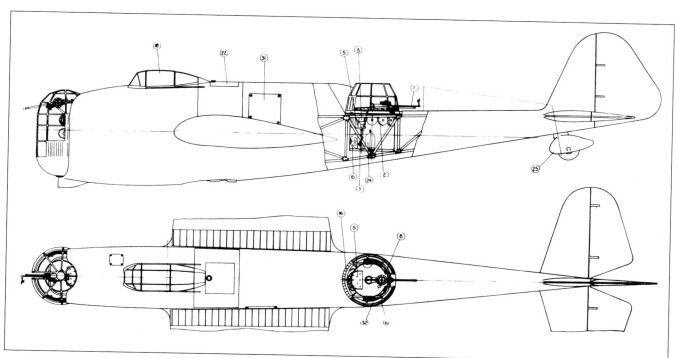

Details of the P.74B and D series.

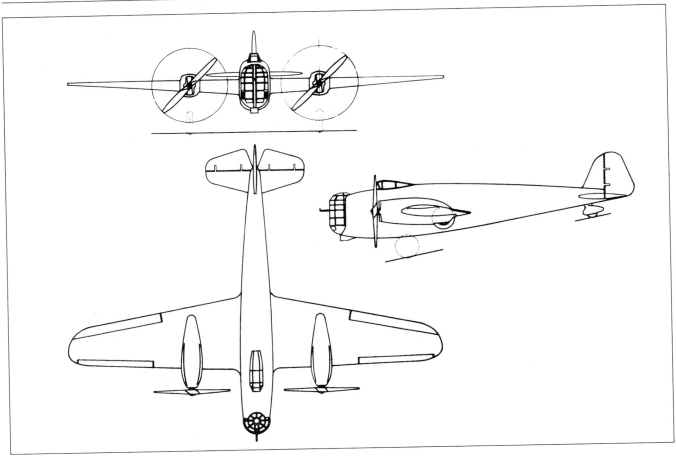

Version A of the P.76 'Novel' fighter with Napier air-cooled inlines.

Version B of the P.76 'Novel' fighter with Pegasus alternatives.

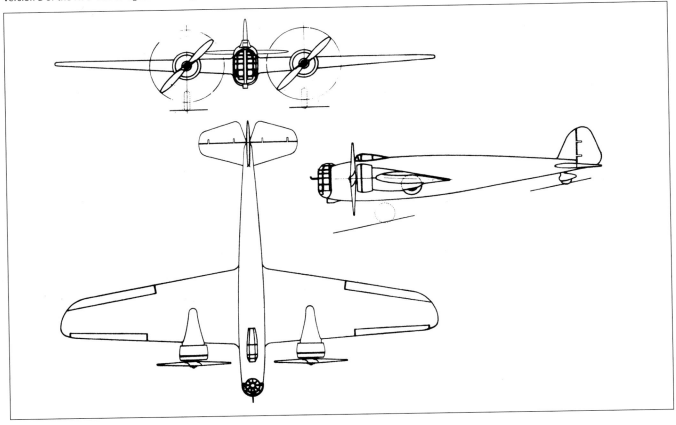

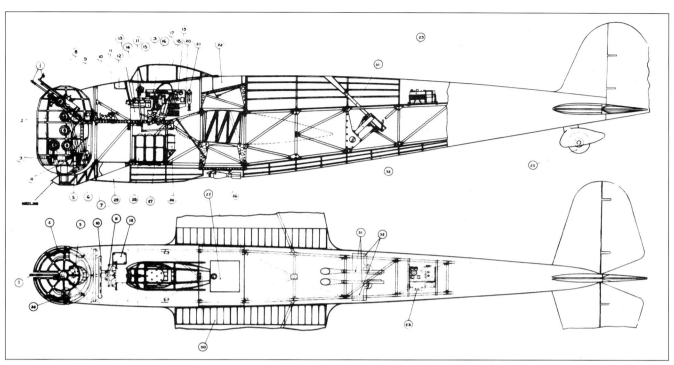

P.76 Interior. Note twin Lewis turret and twin browning no-allowance anti-bomber weapons in the rear fuselage.

Details of the P.76 interior.

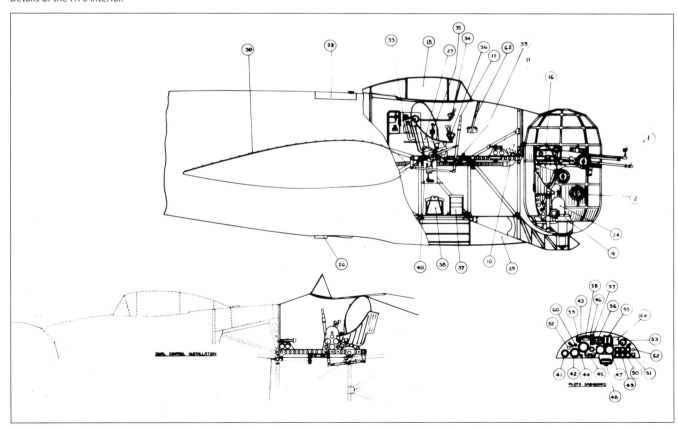

CHAPTER TWENTY

The 'Novel' Fighter Programme – Single Engines (Stage 2)

P.82 Defiant

WITH ELLINGTON and DCAS agreeing that specifications F.5/33 and F.22/33 were unlikely to offer anything new, opinions moved to a Type W fighter, with two seats and with the armament in the rear or mid-upper. The initially favoured 'Novel' designs for a Type W or a Type Y were generally ignored for the alternative of a single tractor or twin-engine tractor or pusher aircraft of conventional design. It was decided there was no need to insist upon a nose turret as a gunner-controlled mid-upper could do the same job.

While the Type W fighter F.9/35 specification was in preparation for a Demon replacement, the deployment of P.29D and P.75 Overstrand machines were under way. Despite the turret having many of its patents held on the secret list for twelve months, sufficient information appeared in the press to gain attention from abroad. The result was that a French engineering firm SAMM (Societe d'Applications des Machines Motrices) contacted John North with the news that they had a number of hydraulic weapon mount designs developed in anticipation of sales to the French government. At that stage North had only toyed with hydraulics as an idea as most of the work had been done on pneumatic drive more appropriate to the Sidestrand development.

The SAMM two-gun unit seen by North at Boulogne-Billancourt was the AB2J twin-Darne test model, which coloured his decisions on the P.82 and the nose and ventral turret proposals for the P.90 and P.91.

During a visit to Paris, North took the opportunity to visit SAMM at Boulogne-Billancourt and view the designs of de Boysson. What was drawn was easily recognisable as a potential powered gun mount and far in advance of anything done in Britain. He saw specifically a vertically placed two-Darne gun experimental hydraulic mounting with gun ring and immediately realised that this could be duplicated by mirror image of the powered weapons about its centreline into a four-gun mounting. The chance of obtaining French-designed turret schemes operating four machine guns rather than one or two, thereby doubling the rounds fired per burst, offered another step forward. What would result was a turret with the theoretical hit ratio of an eight-gun interceptor fighter.

A meeting with Boulton Paul Aircraft took place in 1935 in the office of E. D. Davies (later to be Air Vice-Marshal Davies) at A&AEE Martlesham Heath, at which a turreted fighter was considered with a four-gun package. The aim was to discuss the likelihood of a BPA submission with a turret based on combined BPA and SAMM concepts being accepted for F.9/35. While favourable, North's team was told by Davies that if they included forward-firing weapons for the pilot the proposal could be rejected without consideration. Davies believed that the Bristol Fighter was a failure in the First World War because the pilot used it as a fighter and left the gunner to defence.

The initial proposal had a straight taper wing that was split outboard of the wide-track undercarriage with an external flange joint and the fuel in the outboard section. To the rear of these tanks a light bomb rack was buried in the outboard trailing edge behind the tanks and, when not used, was covered with a metal under-surface. A single landing light was in the port outer near the tip and the wheels retracted into the wings with a single-piece door intended to totally enclose the gear after retraction. The gunner was to sit comfortably in the fuselage behind the pilot during take-off and landing, only moving into the turret when targets were presented. Two turret variations were offered initially: one had the French design layout with the trunnions 'mirror imaged' in plan port to starboard, but with all four guns grouped as a block at the aft edge inside the turret ring. As an added scheme, there was one where the weapons were split into two pairs either side of the gunner. This British-developed scheme gave better balance and better gunner view within a limited cupola height. Neither was ideal in such as small fighter and the proposal pointed out that the best layout needed to be formulated in a mock-up. When full details of the turret were received from SAMM the turret hydraulics were clearly self-contained, requiring only electrical power generated from the engine. This meant that the turret was much better equipped, but turned out heavier than first thought. In deference to the advice of Davies, no forward-firing weapons were proposed.

The design had a 39ft span, was 35ft long and 9ft high static. An initial track for the undercarriage was set at 9ft 8in on a straight dual-taper wing. A straight trailing edge, swept leading edge, tailplane already designed was employed of 13ft 8in span. Maximum speed predicted was 323mph at 15,000ft reached in 6.2 minutes (2,450ft/min), and 306mph at 25,000ft reached in twelve minutes. At sea level the top speed dropped to 265mph. At the specified height of 15,000ft a two-position airscrew would cruise at 274mph and improve to 293mph with a VP airscrew. The airframe was expected to stall at 80mph flaps up and 67mph flaps down. A 1,000hp RR Merlin was expected to power the machine with a three-blade, 11ft 6in diameter Hamilton Standard propeller. The predicted weight was 5,774lb, 204lb of which was the armament. The turret was not calculated as a removable item, rather its weight was hidden within the fuselage structure 'and its value was considerably less than eventually needed.

During discussions with the Air Ministry and the inspection of mock-ups, etc, more fuel capacity was now to be required for F.9/35 to increase endurance, compromising the wing tanks and the semi-buried bomb rack design. Much of the equipment was moved inwards to maintain the fuel masses nearer the centre of gravity. The wing panels became greater in chord at the panel joint and the joint was moved outboard, giving rise to the double wing taper seen on the final design with joints now held within the wing section covered by a flat metal and rubber strip. The cockpit was moved 4in back; the bi-fold 'car door' canopy entry in the fairing roof was removed because an opening turret cupola was agreed; the fuel tanks were moved to the inner wings; and the radiator was re-sited under the centre section. The latter change was because during tests with the body and wing alone in the wind tunnel early onset of pitch down was caused by the nose radiator. The under-fuselage radiator, similar to that of the Hurricane, cured the problem without revisions to the wing and tail positions and without needing to add negative incidence to the tailplane. The fuselage structural design was revised so only the lower area took all the loads. The original split halves became split halves aft of the wing and below the turret ring with horizontal decking at the turret level. There was some worry about the ability of the turret to power four weapons when turning across the slipstream. North suggested that there would be no problem with power and offered to fit aerofoil fairings on the barrels if this turned out to be the case. Fortunately fears about the drag effect were unfounded.

B&P formal proposal for a Type W 'Novel' fighter to F.9/35 was initially second choice against the Hawker Hotspur and of very similar layout.

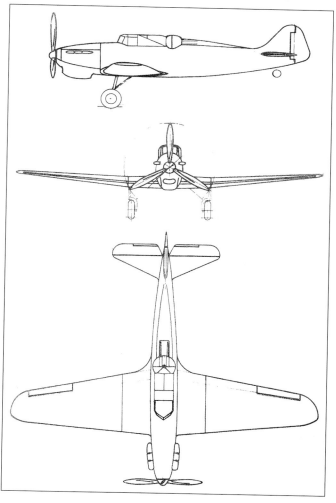

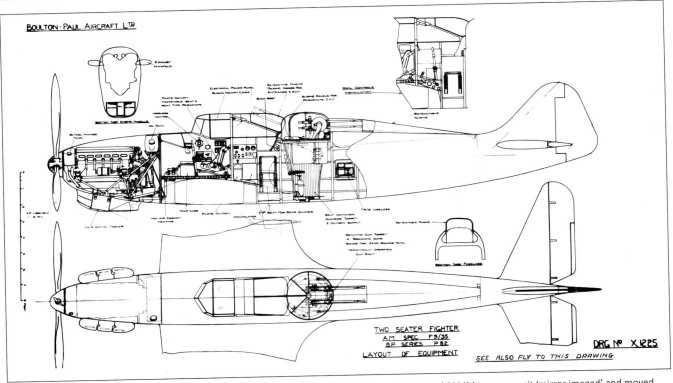

Fuselage interior equipment for the P.82 and configuration of a basic turret based upon a BPA revised SAMM two-gun unit 'mirror imaged' and moved inside the gun ring.

Not having forward weapons, the company arranged an option that the turret could be operated by the pilot. If the gunner turned the turret around forward and elevated it to 17.2° or above he could set the turret fixed and change to pilot control of guns. The pilot could fire the turret guns forward and upward over the propeller arc as fixed weapons in a perfectly valid anti-bomber installation already known as the no-allowance position. The excuse was that this allowed the gunner to pass control to the pilot if he was himself wounded. It also meant that, provided the correct ballast for CG purposes was carried in the turret or weight boxes, it was possible to operate the aircraft as a single-seater with no-allowance shooting – although this latter single-seat operation was not as efficient.

The structure relied heavily on a Z stringer rectangular internally corrugated wing upper surface with two spars, a leading edge and a lightly stressed underside requiring the minimum of wing ribs. The patented structure was totally unlike any other fighter of the time and the main skinning was capable of being pre-drilled on boilerplate jigs using unskilled labour. By splitting the fuselage into three aft of the centre section it was possible to use the corrugated structures as a reinforced decking plate beam at turret ring level carrying the two lower fuselage halves. Above this decking there was no further structural need so upper fairings aft of the turret could be manufactured in light non-strategic materials of wood and fabric with the minimum of metal skinning to save weight. One employee came up with the idea of a weight box on this decking in the rear upper fuselage so that fine tuning of the centre of gravity could be made and the machine could be trimmed out fore and aft even if the turret was unoccupied or the machine used for target towing or training with the turret removed. This was both a formal possibility and a fall-back position drawn in 1938 in case the design be cancelled in favour of a new specification or the P.92.

While it was down on speed because of the two crew and the turret weight, the Hurricane-style wing, modified and productionised by North and Hughes into only two straight tapers, which approximated the Spitfire's ideal ellipse, and the thick NACA Munk M6 aerofoil section,

meant that the Defiant could out-turn the Spitfire, Hurricane and the Bf 109. What it could not do was outrun or out-climb any of them. The Defiant prototype, K8310, was flown at a speed of 320mph during official tests (Initial Assessment December 1937) and achieved 7.5 minutes to 10,500ft, but at that time it had no turret and was therefore much lighter than the planned machine. The turret was fitted by February 1938 and it undertook speed trials in early October, where speed was reduced to 303mph and it took 15.1 minutes to reach 20,000ft.

Initial manufacture was recorded at a maximum speed of 303mph in level flight at 16,600ft with 6.25lb boost. With 12lb boost and 100 octane fuel this rose to 312mph at 10,000ft. The two machines tested would have had three-blade, two-position airscrews. A constant-speed airscrew improved climb: five minutes to 5,000ft, eight minutes to 10,000ft and twelve minutes to 20,000ft (8,350lb AUW in service and fully armed).

The new turret system and the redesign had resulted in an aircraft that was 45% heavier than the original estimate but improvements in the engine (now a Merlin III) and the better shape had resulted in a machine only 2mph slower than the average general production Hurricane with 87 octane fuel.

Six variants were eventually to be manufactured:

The TT Mk.III was a conversion of service F. and NF Mk.I to target tug with either normal or Mk. II enlarged radiator and a new nose intake that performed a cheaper form of tropicalisation to cater for dusty conditions. The original proposal for the F Mk.II was a Merlin 24 and so the TT version was designated TT Mk.II. However, the Air Ministry selected the Merlin XX for the F Mk.II, so the TT Mk.II was never built. N1550 Defiant Mk.II with a Merlin XX had a much better rate of climb even at 7,690lb AUW. This was two minutes to 5,000ft, 3.9 minutes to 10,000ft and 8.3 minutes to 20,000ft, although the top speed was only 313mph. The conversion of N1550 and N1551 to Mk.II was covered under contract B.28069/39/C.23(a).

The production aircraft had a 39ft 4in span, and were 35ft 3.9in long with the Merlin III and 35ft 10.3in long with the Merlin XX.

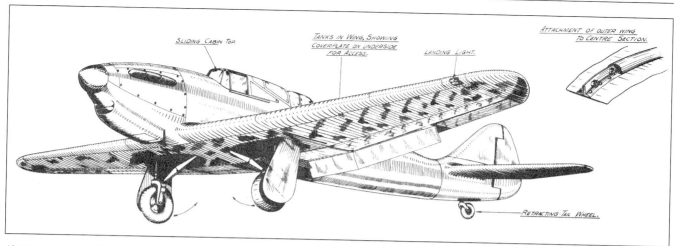

Above: Impression of the P.82 Defiant as proposed.

Right: Not entirely happy with the four gun mirror-imaging placing all four weapons in front of the gunner's forward view, an addendum by BPA to the equipment drawing was inserted in the proposals splitting the two gun pairs apart and rearranging their position. Note the ammunition moved down under the turret ring. The final turret after mock-up discussions followed neither proposal as all ammunition and case collection was moved forward of the gunner for ease of rearming.

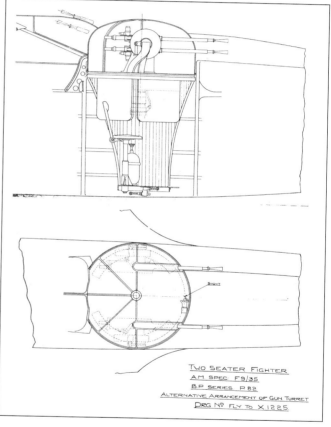

The track was 11ft 2.5in. The Merlin XX versions had the increase all forward of the firewall. At the rear end, the rake of the rudder was increased to add area but the rudder base width and trailing edge distance at the tail light remained the same.

A key test model was the replacement of the Type A four-gun turret with a Type F Mk.I single cannon turret for trials on the installation. Under 961941/38 the prototype aircraft K8310 was fitted with the turret and a cupola for trials at A&AEE. The Type F was tested in a number of Defiant airframes in 1939–43 despite the initial 1940s ban on cannon turrets, and a Defiant so equipped was last seen at CFE West Raynham in 1943. A fishtail section barrel fairing (invented by North in 1935) had to be applied to try and get the torque down as the early SAMM-designed pump/motor system incorporated in the Type F could not cope with the air loads of full rotation. The single Type F prototype therefore never went into production for any airframe design.

At the height of the Battle of Britain work was on-going to cover advanced versions of the Defiant. It was thought that a large number of fighters would have to be despatched to tropical climates. Therefore 'first fit' equipment would have to be installed and tested in prototype or development aircraft to match the expected production build. The Defiant Mk.I (tropical) would have to be tested as a one-off machine converted from the basic Mk.I. For the more advanced Mk.II there were expected to be the Mk.IIA, which would be the tropical type delivered abroad, and the Mk.IIB, which would be the home front day fighter. The Mk.IIB variant was that initially represented by both serials N1550 and N1551 with Rotol airscrews of 11ft 3in and 11ft 6in diameter available for fit by 24 August 1940. Both were later tested with the tropical equipment and large filter intake required by the Mk.IIA. As it happened, the Mk.I (trop) and Mk.IIA or B were not put into production.

Following on from initial tunnel testing and complete revision of the fuselage cockpit and radiator positioning plus a wing shape change, the P.82 now looked very similar to that seen in service. Still looking odd, however, was the shape of the upper cowling and the 'soup plate' spinner. This model has been painted up in accordance with initial camouflage instructions. The heat of the photography lights has caused part of the rear upper fuselage (where a turret or a TT operator's position could be interchanged) to peel away.

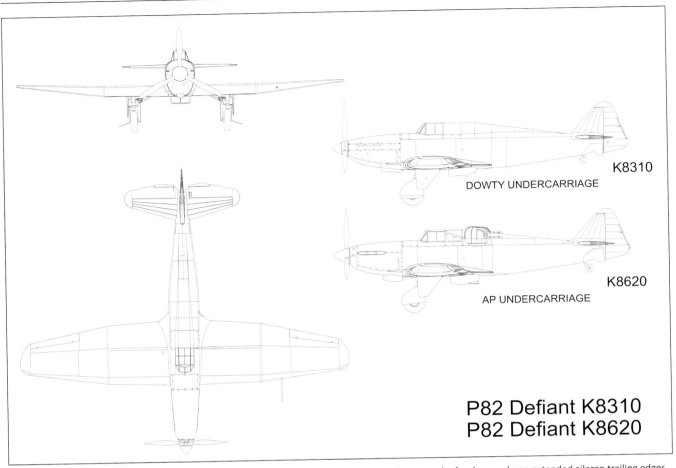

P82 Defiant K8310
P82 Defiant K8620

K8310
DOWTY UNDERCARRIAGE

K8620
AP UNDERCARRIAGE

Prototype K8620 below the prototype K8310, which had a tailplane and fin/rudder 1.45in lower on the fuselage and non-extended aileron trailing edges. The Type A turret was now based on the BPA-designed alternative to the SAMM unit but these prototypes had less framing to the rear doors.

K8310 P.82 first prototype finally fitted with its Type A turret.

Above: Serial L7012 was a production F. Mk.1 delivered in early 1940 with split colour undersides.

Right: The original quarter plate negative had damaged film on the left side prior to being exposed. Nevertheless, this slightly cropped version proves to be one of the best air-to-air close-ups of N1650 being flown by Flt Lt J. C. Colin Evans. Evans was killed on 27 November 1945 while testing Firefly PP463. These pre-MOD 140 aircraft had a single clear panel in the top of the hood.

P.82 variants

Model	Use	Engine	Comment
F Mk.I	Day and night fighter	Merlin III	Basic airframe with no specialist night equipment. Could carry dinghy containers when on air sea rescue duties
NF Mk.I	Night fighter	Merlin III	Dedicated NF. AI radar retrofit on some
F Mk.II	Day and night fighter	Merlin XX	Prototypes and conversions back from NF Mk.II*
NF Mk.II	Night fighter	Merlin XX	Dedicated NF. All equipped to take AI radar
TT Mk.I	Target tug	Merlin XX	Conversion and production inc. tropicalisation
TT Mk.III	Target tug	Merlin III	150 conversions of F Mk.I

Note: *These conversions back to day fighter were those used for special duties such as 515 Squadron employed on radar jamming and were not carried out at the factory.

With camouflage changed to night finish, this tactical development machine AA357 has AI Mk VI radar and the final form of exhaust stacks of the NF.Mk.1. Suggestions that this made the machine a Mk.1A are not confirmed by any company Mods, Air Publications, or the design's formal Type Record.

Main visual changes to the NF.Mk.1 were the introduction of six stack exhausts for a period in early 1941 and the replacement of these with the later standard three-stack fishtail type (right). The TT.III version is below. It had the deeper radiator 'when stocks are available' and a cheap form of tropical protection to the oil cooler/carb intake.

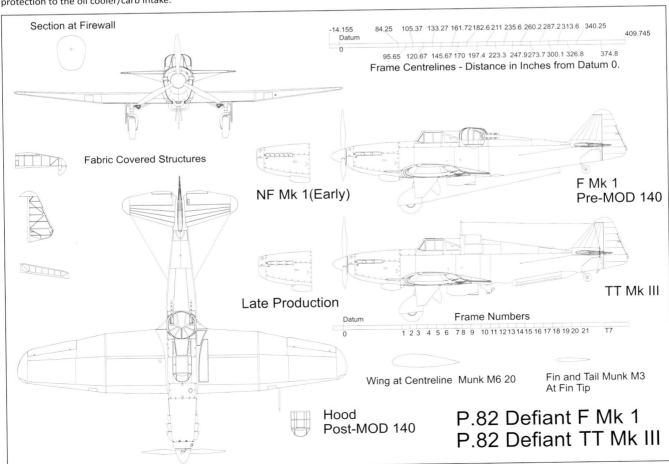

Section at Firewall

Fabric Covered Structures

NF Mk 1(Early)

Late Production

Hood
Post-MOD 140

-14.155 84.25 105.37 133.27 161.72 182.6 211 235.6 260.2 287.2 313.6 340.25 409.745
Datum
0
95.65 120.67 145.67 170 197.4 223.3 247.9 273.7 300.1 326.8 374.8

Frame Centrelines - Distance in Inches from Datum 0.

F Mk 1
Pre-MOD 140

TT Mk III

Datum   Frame Numbers
0   1 2 3   4 5 6   7 8 9 10 11 12 13 14 15 16 17 18 19 20 21   T7

Wing at Centreline Munk M6 20   Fin and Tail Munk M3
                                         At Fin Tip

P.82 Defiant F Mk 1
P.82 Defiant TT Mk III

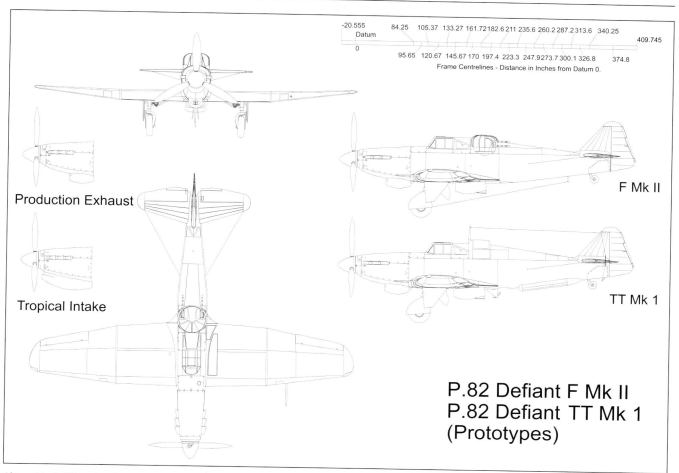

-20.555 Datum
0

84.25 105.37 133.27 161.72 182.6 211 235.6 260.2 287.2 313.6 340.25
409.745

95.65 120.67 145.67 170 197.4 223.3 247.9 273.7 300.1 326.8 374.8

Frame Centrelines - Distance in Inches from Datum 0.

Production Exhaust

Tropical Intake

F Mk II

TT Mk 1

P.82 Defiant F Mk II
P.82 Defiant TT Mk 1
(Prototypes)

Above: Merlin XX engine, longer cowl, steeper rudder trailing edge and enlarged radiator and oil cooler/carb intake identified the F.Mk.II and NF.Mk.II. TT variant as the TT.Mk.1, the TT.Mk.II was abandoned as its Merlin 24, preferred by BPA design staff, was not approved.

Right: Defiant Mk 1 fitted with the F. Mk 1 20mm cannon turret for trials. Several Defiant airframes were fitted with the prototype turret at various times and the last one was seen at 9 AOS in 1943. The cupola on the mounting was a temporary one made from plywood and Perspex with only limited vision aft and portholes on the side.

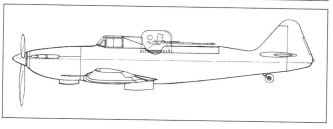

EAST GODAVARI III

P.82

Opposite top: N1551, second prototype of the F.Mk.II, completed at the height of the Battle of Britain. N1550 was completed both as a standard fighter and then with tropical nose intake. (Crown Copyright)

Middle: Production TT.Mk.1, serial DR972, on the compass base at the factory. The prototype DR967 differed in having a long tropical intake under the nose, first tested on an F.Mk.1.

Bottom: Production TT.Mk.III conversion by Reid and Sigrist as MOD 356. The two silver coin-shaped items in the intake are part of the dust screen protection system and would be opened once the machine was airborne. *Crown Copyright*

Models of the Defiant planned during 1940 but not ordered

Model	Use	Engine	Comment
F Mk.I (tropical)	Day and night fighter	Merlin III	Modified Mk.I test aircraft only
F Mk.IIA	Day and night fighter	Merlin XX	Tropical kit and air filters as standard
F Mk.IIB	Day and night fighter	Merlin XX	Intended standard Mk.II day aircraft
TT Mk.II	Target tug	Merlin 24	Rejected by Air Ministry for Merlin XX as the TT Mk.I

By the time the first production Mk.II was available in mid-1941 it was simply designated NF Mk.II at the factory, just Mk.II in the Air Publication and the RAF, and all aircraft were equipped with brackets to take AI radar fit for the night fighter case even if this was not initially fitted. The production tropical kit including a tropical rudder (simply more drainage to get rid of condensation inside) was eventually fitted to some versions of the TT Mk.I sent abroad depending where they were destined.

This table above summarises the types not built beyond prototype trials of components.

P.85 and P.93 Roc

P.85

While the Air Ministry were working on the F.9/35 'Novel fighter' which attracted the P.82 tender they reasoned that if this was the potential anti-bomber destroyer for the RAF then a similar type was required for the Navy. Specification O.30/35 was generated for this requirement and issued at the end of 1935. The specification called for a single-engine, two-seat fleet fighter that was capable of operating from an aircraft carrier or from shore bases and could be equipped with floats for catapult from capital ships. The second crew member was to be an air-gunner/telegraphist and the armament of four machine guns and ammunition fitted into an amidships turret.

The P.85 design was generated by BPA to meet this specification and it was decided to offer two alternatives. The P.85A was a conventional layout low-wing monoplane with a Hercules HE1SM engine and the P.85B a similar aircraft with a Merlin E engine. The proposal and diagrams favoured the A version with the Hercules; the B Version was a potential alternative. Because of the requirement for a good view for deck landing, the pilot sat higher than in the P.82 proposal compared with the thrust line. Construction and turret were to be similar to that proposed for the P.82 prototypes. In view of the need to stow the floatplane with wings folded and minimum hangar height, the tail unit was blended into the upper decking as much as possible to give the cleanest and lowest lines. Compared with the P.82 proposal, the M6 section wing could not be continuous taper because the two fuel tanks were moved to the non-folding centre section, between the wing spars, which was made with parallel leading and trailing edges to accommodate them. The twin-leg main undercarriage followed the P.83/84 style where the legs carried their own fairing down and around the wheel. As the legs folded backwards just inboard of the wing joint they formed their own wing under-surface with a portion of the wheel protruding into the airflow. The main gear could be removed and cover plates fitted in converting the aircraft to a floatplane and back again easily. Slats improved deck landing.

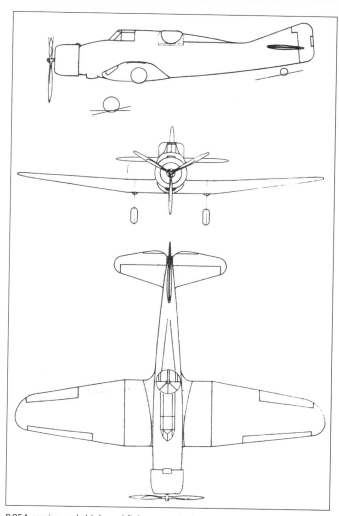

P.85A carrier and shipboard fighter as a deck aircraft.

The P.85A had a span of 42ft 6in with 318sq ft of wing area. The length was 37ft 8in as a landplane and 39ft 9in as a seaplane. The landplane height tail down was 12ft and 13ft 9in as a seaplane. The height on a catapult was 16ft 6in and the width 15ft 9in folded. The weight of the landplane was 5,000lb tare and 6,862 AUW, the seaplane was 5,375lb tare and 7,227lb AUW. Maximum speed was 318mph (276 knots) at 12,500ft and cruise 256mph (223 knots) at 15,000ft for the landplane. Maximum speed was 267mph (232 knots) at 12,500ft for the seaplane.

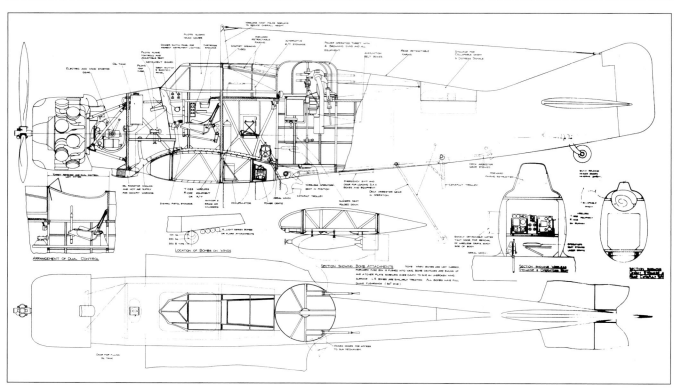

Details of the proposed P.85A interior.

Impression of the P.85A.

The P.85B differences were a slight area reduction to 313sq ft. The length was 38ft as a landplane and 39ft 9in as a seaplane. The landplane height tail down was 12ft 3in, the weight 5,038lb tare and 6,750 AUW. The seaplane was 5,413lb tare and 7,125lb AUW. All other data was the same as the A version. The maximum speed was 308mph (268 knots) at 12,500ft and the cruise 258mph (224 knots) at 15,000ft for the landplane. The maximum speed was 258mph (224 knots) at 15,000ft for the seaplane.

A full proposal was made in March 1936, while Blackburn Aircraft submitted their own O.30/35 proposal as the B-25. The B-25 was a revision of the existing O.27/34, B-24 Skua dive bomber, layout but having the Boulton Paul Type A turret already being developed.

From there the waiting dragged on without a decision but with both companies being told they were well received. Boulton Paul expected to get the order and at least one Blackburn programme showed production with the 'Boulton Paul Fighter' amalgamated into overall output. After a year of procrastination the Air Ministry were finally galvanised out of their thoughts by strong admonishment by the Admiralty about a lack of movement forward. Although the P.85 was attractive and the BPA turret was essential, it was not as attractive as the thought of having two almost identical designs on the carrier, the B-24 and the B-25, with similar engines and spares requirements. The Air Ministry decided upon the B-25, to be named the Roc.

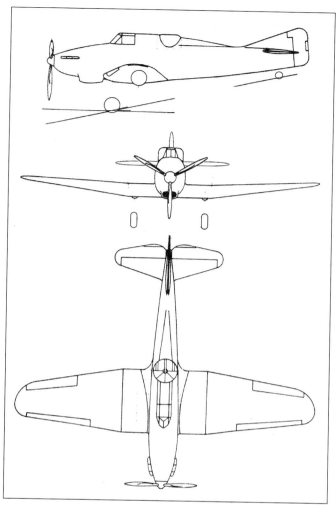

P.85B carrier and shipboard fighter as a deck aircraft.

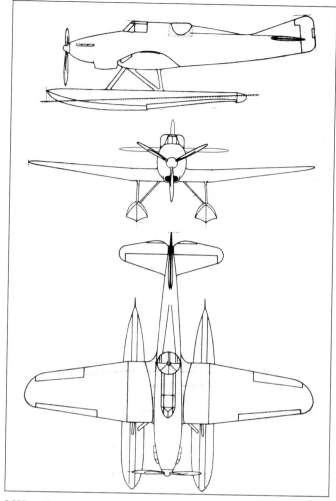

P.85B carrier and shipboard fighter as a floatplane. The same floats fitted the P.85A.

P.93 Roc

The order was placed with Blackburn with the proviso that it could not hope to produce the B-24 and B-25 in parallel. Blackburn were informed that the entire Roc production batch was to be placed with Boulton Paul and they were to be made responsible for the redesign of the fuselage structure from the engine firewall to the connection with the tail unit, complete with BP Type A turret.

Blackburn were responsible for the design of everything else. While the choices appear logical the difference between the potential airspeed of the P.85 and the production B-25 Roc was enormous: over 300mph for the P.85 compared with 223mph for the B-25 Roc and

225mph for the B-24 Skua. It was probably the ability to operate Roc and Skua as mixed formations that flavoured the decision. Eventual attempts to increase the B-25 airspeed by propeller selection were pursued for some time on the development aircraft. BPA had allocated the project designation P.93 for the Roc partial design and total build to Specification O.15/37.

What proved a disaster for BPA was that while Blackburn were overwhelmed with the Shark and Skua, the Air Ministry thought that placing orders for both the P.82 Defiant and the Blackburn Roc with BPA in the same month would not be a problem. Because of the

Air Ministry Model of the B-25 turret fighter proposed by Blackburn, selected for production, but built by BPA as the P.93 after further detail design by both companies.

The B-25 Roc proposal was considerably changed by the time detail design and manufacture was contemplated because by then the B-24 Skua, on which it was to be based, was already being built.

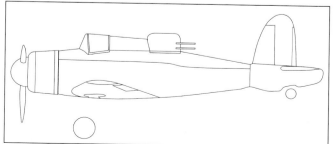

P.93 Blackburn Roc fuselages being built at Wolverhampton. In the foreground of the second line is the first of the production P.82 Defiants.

annoyance with the Air Ministry by the Admiralty over the delay, BPA were instructed to manufacture both in parallel but that their subcontract Roc was 'to always have absolute priority over the P.82 Defiant'. Manufacture was delayed by numerous officially led changes to the wing design in particular, such that by the time approved wing drawings were received the wings were always fifty aircraft sets in arrears compared with the fuselage. The manufacture was also not helped by the Roc not being given formal priority for materials supply until the war started. The sixth Roc tested at Worthy Down found that the overall airframe was nose heavy and resulted

in a change of tailplane incidence on all eight delivered Roc aircraft and all subsequent deliveries of the 136 aircraft manufactured. Additional delays appeared once the aluminium paint schemes were replaced by camouflage as aircraft had to be finished in naval colours if allocated to a naval base for carrier squadrons and RAF colours if allocated to land bases. Only a couple of carrier fighter squadrons started receiving Rocs alongside the two-seat Skua in the fighter role before the type was withdrawn and reduced to coastal defence, training and some target tug work.

Roc aircraft being prepared for delivery in schemes depending where they were theoretically to be deployed.

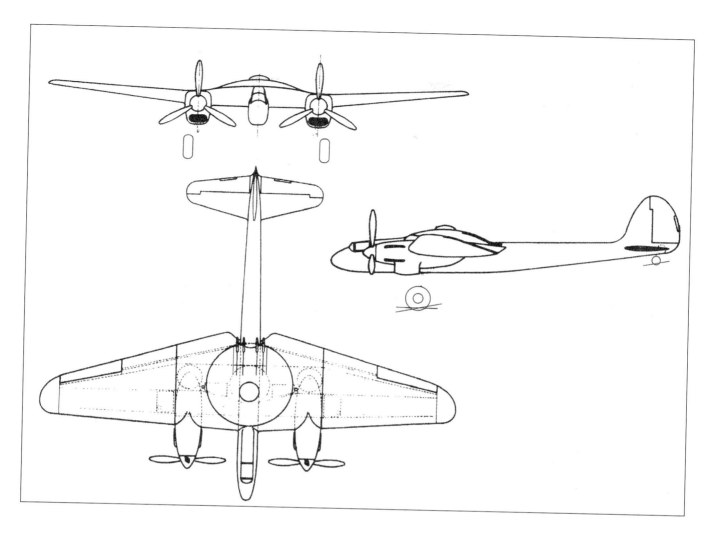

CHAPTER TWENTY-ONE

The 'Novel' Fighter Programme – Twin Engines (Stage 3)

P.89 Turret Fighter

THE P.89 IS LISTED by BPA as a two-seat, four-cannon fighter for which twin modified Kestrel XVI engines were chosen. When raised in early 1936 the allocation had no specification listed. It is most likely that this design was a study to early discussions about draft F.18/36, which BPA were worried might leapfrog and replace the F.9/35 P.82 Defiant, the design allocation being too early for F.9/37 of almost two years later. The project number was taken out well before both specifications were written. Since BPA were into the cannon dorsal turret requirement even before F.11/37 was issued this was almost certainly a result of the first of North's and Hughes' studies of how to fit turreted cannon armament into a twin-engine fighter aircraft. Looking at the P.92, the turret and wing design patent (based upon mathematics of the shape only) was applied for a mere twenty-three days after the date of F.11/37 release. The P.89 was therefore probably the first time a conformal turret was considered and a patent was raised using extracts from the design to patent the concept.

North considered the possibilities of a two-gun turret where the

P.92 'Novel' fighter to F.11/37. It was a Type W fighter with four 20mm cannon but presented by BPA with four additional 0.303 machine guns in a conformal turret. This layout represents the final bound proposal design.

blister was a smaller portion of the centre wing shape, a four-gun turret and he also envisaged two × two gun turrets across the span on larger aircraft. One can only assume that these would fit above the engine nacelles of a twin-engine aircraft or above the inner two nacelles on anything larger. The centre section wing shape was a very

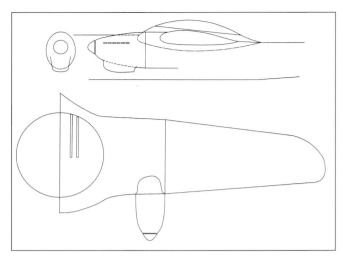

The wing centre and turret sections of the P.89 appear to be the only details that have survived simply because they were reused to patent the idea of the turret/wing combination.

early mathematical calculation for a conformal turret blister requiring a large rounded plan for the leading edge. At that stage the idea had not been subject to tunnel tests. North and Hughes had come up with the concept of making a large area of the wing centre conform to an enlarged aerofoil section from which the 'solid of revolution' formed by cutting a plane through this area became the turret outer skin and its rotation axis. In this manner the surface presented the same aerofoil low-drag blister shape whichever way the turret was pointed. By May 1936, with the official decision to revise and renumber F.18/36 to a dorsal cannon turret of North's shape, F.18/36 became F.11/37 issued to BPA.

P.92

OR.50 generated the requirement for a large cannon-armed fighter to operate with home defence units or with the field force. The worry that opposing machines and eventually bombers would be equipped with cannon armament and/or armour that rifle calibre bullets could not penetrate meant that a Type W or similar anti-bomber fighter would also be needed. The idea was that the new specification F.11/37 would require four cannon in a gunner-controlled turret where the operator could fire from a comfortable seated position. At 15,000ft a speed of not less than 370mph was required at maximum power. It had to be able to reach 15,000ft on one engine alone but climb rate in any mode was secondary to speed and offensive capability. Any engine approved by 100-hour type test was allowed and fuel capacity was to be defined by a number of minutes at power settings in various modes. Four 20mm 'automatic gun' (ie cannon) were required with 240 rounds of ammunition, an internally carried 250lb bomb and a crew of two. A number of companies had started looking at the potential for F.18/36 and transferred their work to F.11/37, including Armstrong Whitworth, Avro, Bristol, Fairey, Gloster and Hawker. With the dropping of F.18/36, the initially released specification to F.11/37 was dated 26 May 1937. An errata, prompted by BPA feedback, pointed out that only drum containers were available for the 20mm gun. At the prototype stage therefore only drum-fed Hispano cannon could be employed.

The BPA design was allocated the designator P.92 as a twin-engine, two-seat day and night fighter. It seemed quite clear from the outset that this was intended to be an anti-bomber formation fighter and a potential replacement for the Defiant, but had to accommodate four high-drag cannon barrels in a rotating gun turret. North and Hughes had already decided that the best solution was an aerodynamic design that integrated with and formed part of the upper wing surface of the aircraft, The four cannon, when lowered into slots in the turret

Fuselage details of the P.92 proposal. Note the six gun slots. The outer slot of each side held two vertically stacked 0.303 machine guns like the Type A turret design in case the gunner ran out of cannon ammunition.

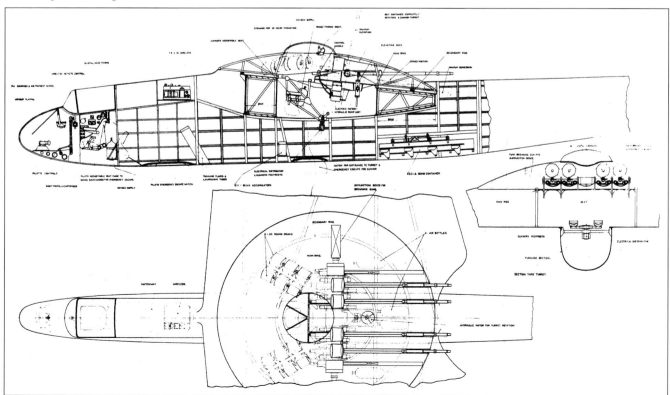

surface, were almost totally enclosed, with the slots covered by movable strips. The gunner was given a small clear cupola for sighting, complete with a BPA-developed azimuth correcting sight mount integral with the cupola. A rangefinder sight being developed was also offered. It was noted that the gunner therefore had more than a 360° hemisphere of view at all times compared with any sort of retracting turret scheme. The pilot was to sit in the nose of the aircraft ahead of the airscrews and, in order to provide safe escape, his seat could be released to fold rearwards and he could then slide backwards down a chute to be automatically dropped from underneath the machine clear of the propellers. The gunner could escape by releasing his small bubble canopy or he could also drop out from a hatch directly underneath his station in the underside of the body.

The undercarriage was an Automotive Products design with a single main leg and outboard wheel that retracted backwards and rotated to lie flat, wheel uppermost within the wing, the main leg then being enclosed below the wing in the rear of the engine nacelle. The tailwheel and leg retracted backwards into the rear of the body. The wing surfaces and the turret blister were entirely designed as one integral aerodynamic unit. The company patent 554855 based on the P.89 was held on the secret list and only released for formal publication in July 1943. A second patent application showing the P.92 turret and wing structure was not published until January 1946, reference 574413. Work on the design on the shop floor were carried out under BPA Aes 2859.

Right: Another view at Pendeford, in this case the covered centre section and turret. In the background is the cockpit mock-up of the proposed P.82 prototype.

Below: Mock-up of the cannon turret with 4 × 20 mm photographed for inclusion in the P.92 proposal brochure.

Because of the large size it was expected that the turret's soup bowl-like blister would cause some constructional difficulties. It was intended to use a rigid inner turret powered azimuth ring, within which the four cannon were situated, and a more flexible outer ring of greater diameter, but well inside the overall blister diameter. The overall diameter of the blister was 157in, the rigid inner ring approximately to 73.25in diameter and the outer ring to 124.3in diameter. By this method it was expected that the flexibility imparted to the outer portions would allow for movements of the aircraft's structure during the stresses of flight and combat. The basic details were laid out in mock-up structures of the aircraft centre section but the gun turret as illustrated in drawing X1577/T had the three diameters above and did not match the mock-up. The concept was further altered prior to assembling the tender. The thought was that weapons may jam during combat, leaving the fighter defenceless, or the gunner might be caught between drum changes when he needed to attack or defend. Pencilled in outboard of the cannon on each side during the discussions and added to the drawing therefore

Front view of the Air Ministry model shows this to be the Napier Sabre engine second prototype, which was later to be fitted instead as the new third prototype. Noteworthy are the blast tubes emerging from each spinner centre for either single cannon or single machine gun mounted in the French manner as a 'moteur cannon' through the engine block of the twin crankshafts in the Sabre.

were two vertically opposed 0.303 machine guns in the style of the Defiant Type A turret, which were added together on the main elevation shaft axis, each with belt-fed ammunition boxes. The design then offered a purely optional armament of four cannon and four machine guns. The four-cannon turret for the P.92 was designated Type L Mk.I for development work. For each cannon a total of four thirty-round drums were detailed, three of which were replenishments and carried on a slide rail mechanism so they could be moved to the weapon breech. The design therefore provided 120 rounds for each weapon in thirty-round containers, but sixty-round containers could be accommodated giving 240 rounds per gun. The azimuth drive provided for 360° rotation, an elevation of 85°, and depression either side of the rear quarter of -10°. This did not meet the specification requirement of -15°, but it was thought that this might be achieved once detail design was under way. The standard pump and motor units in the normal BPA turrets were insufficient in size and essentially they would be uprated pro rata with new larger units of the same basic design. The complete tender finally was submitted in August 1937.

Predicted performance, based upon a 1/20th scale wind tunnel model loaned with the tender, at 17,700lb AUW was a maximum speed of 371mph at 15,000ft where the rate of climb was 3,220ft/min. Level flight attainable on one engine was 20,000ft and the service ceiling was 38,000ft. All of this was based upon a Rolls-Royce Vulture engine with an underslung honeycomb radiator, rams-horn exhausts and a three-blade VP metal airscrew of 13ft diameter operating at a gear ratio of 0.4. Rolls-Royce provided the recommended layout of the proposed engine, radiator and cowlings. The overall dimensions as submitted were 62ft 6in span, 52ft 3in length and engine centres at 18ft.

There was discussion internally at the Air Ministry after tender receipt, including comparison of the Hotspur, Defiant and P.92. The reviewer of performance, R.N. Liptrot, disagreed slightly with the top speed of the P.92. However, the differences were not considered significant. The most interest, though, was generated by the basic turret concept, which was seen to be potentially adaptable to other aircraft, in particular the soon-to-arise 'ideal bomber', because of its use of

The 1/20th scale model supplied with the tender submission photographed by the Air Ministry. *Crown Copyright*

heavy cannon armament placed at or around the centre of gravity of the machine. The decision to build prototypes of the P.92 almost became essential in Air Ministry eyes because of the unique turret idea. Initially two prototype aircraft were contracted under Order 708600/37 in March 1938. These were to be completed with Vulture engines for L9629 and Napier Sabre engines for L9632. Once an order was received, development of the large powered turret ring proceeded.

The improved mock-ups were examined on 31 May 1938 by Air Ministry representatives. As with most design schemes, the development of the aircraft saw discussions on wing planform where an alternative sweepback outboard of the engines and wing slits (slots) was suggested by RAE. There were changes in the fuselage shape, which was simplified to a more rectangular side and profile and the rear fuselage increased in angle upwards, to enable the turret to achieve more firing area under the tailplane in lieu of the 15° depression. The fin/rudder, tailplane and the tail cone had striking changes compared with the original proposal. The Air Ministry may have been less interested in the Vulture machine, which purely allowed the prototype to get airborne as early as possible, than in the use of the Sabre. The Sabre variant ordered was intended to become unique. Because the Napier-Halton Sabre engine had two crankshafts, a version was to be developed where a blast tube passed concentrically through the compressor impeller, between the crankshafts in the

Viewing the SAMM 404 cannon pedestal mount purchased as a mere example of the type. In the background are two P.92 Vulture engine 'power eggs' mounted in wooden jigging, probably to speed up the completion of fuel flow tests on the twin system.

The true shape of Vulture prototypes under construction. The fuselage shape was completely changed for the prototype manufacture. The wing was more swept back, achieved by pivoting the complete outer panels backwards and redesigning the centre section. The fin and rudder and the elevators were changed, the latter based upon the style of the Defiant. The lower fuselage from nose to wing rear was a 40in diameter half circle and the rear fuselage was tilted upwards to give a better view under the tail. Sections shown represent the distances from the nose in inches. The radiators of the prototype were to follow the RR design. The production might have been moved forward to try and make both Vulture and Sabre radiator systems and lower cowl roughly the same had the project got that far. There were no inset aileron trim tabs on the aircraft.

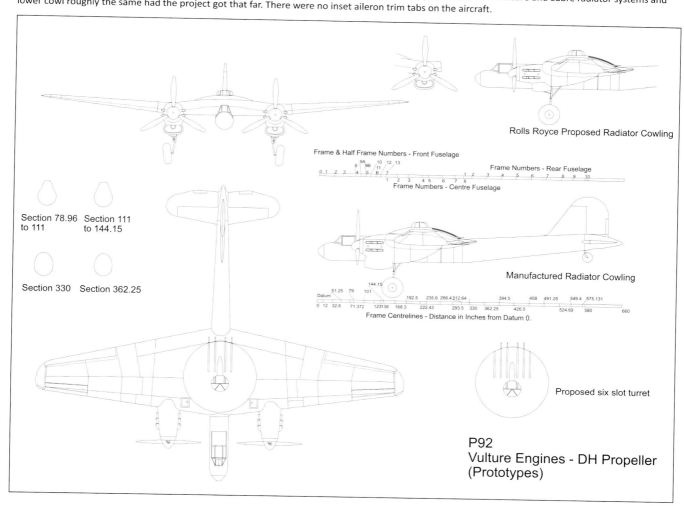

P92
Vulture Engines - DH Propeller
(Prototypes)

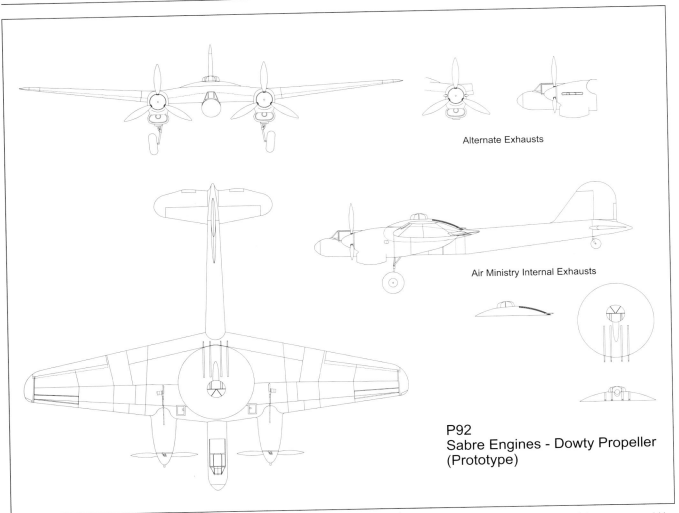

Alternate Exhausts

Air Ministry Internal Exhausts

P92
Sabre Engines - Dowty Propeller
(Prototype)

Sabre prototype as being constructed. The suggested position of the two forward-firing weapons is approximate as it is not known if the cannon would be upright or placed upon its side like the P.88. Certainly for the prototype, the Sabre was incapable of taking a blast tube through the air compressor, engine block and prop shaft. The radiators are further forward for the Sabre than on the original Vulture proposal as this was recommended by Napier. Note the 'fixed slits' positioning on the outer wing requested by RAE for both engine types. The nacelle was longer than the Vulture model to accommodate the mainwheel below the cannon installation rather than in the wing.

engine crankcase and through the propeller hub/spinner. This could then take a 20mm cannon (or a 0.303in machine gun) buried in the wing to the rear in the form of a 'Moteur Cannon'. So, while the production Vulture variant could have its specified four cannon and an optional four machine guns in the turret, the Sabre variant could add two forward-firing cannon or machine guns. The latter could be initially fired no-allowance by the pilot while turret cannon were being rearmed or by the gunner if the turret was aimed forward. Project summary revisions dated 9 March 1939 now gave a span of 65ft 10in, a length (tail down) of 54ft 4in and a tail down height of 13ft 10in. The 1,720hp, 3,000rpm, 13ft 6in, three-blade system based upon the Vulture was now 21,000lb AUW (or 24,700lb overload condition), giving 355mph at 15,000ft and a cruise of 300mph. The Sabre engine alternative 1,920hp, 4,000rpm with the same three-blade propeller of 13ft 6in at 20,500lb AUW (or 24,700lb overload) gave 370mph at 15,000ft and a cruise of 315mph. The large performance decrease shown in the Vulture version was due to a number of factors including increases in expected weight of the engine and reduction in the available gear ratio compared with the original predictions.

The final layout in-build had the fuselage nose tip defined as 'Station 0' and the extreme tail cone as 'Station 660' in the construction drawings, giving a length of 55ft. The wingspan was to

become 66ft 3.3in by the time of skinning panel layout for the prototypes. Work eventually included a 2/7th scale model for the RAE 24ft tunnel with standard wing layout based upon the tender, and a later 1/7th scale model for the NPL tunnel where the panels were pivoted back slightly to give more leading sweepback. The design drawings eventually utilised the sweep of the 1/7th model, as did the later P.92/2 flying model. Tunnel tests with the turret turned (45° elevation and 45° abeam) showed that drag increased as much as 35%, indicating how much the electro-hydraulic system had to be increased in size if a full 360° azimuth was to be achieved at all elevations out of the stowed position. The barrel turbulence also acted as a lift-dump owing to airflow spoiling and altered the lift co-efficient by about 25%. Operating the turret might therefore require some anticipation of rotation and elevation trim changes on the part of the pilot. This happened to a degree in the Defiant, the jinking being perceived by the pilot as wind gust effects. Because of this it was decided as late as 1939 that a half-scale flying model was desirable to investigate the flight characteristics and the effect of turret movement. This was planned to eventually have an electric turret drive to position the mock-up weapons. However, it seemed highly unlikely that such an airframe could be flying before the first full-size prototype. It was expected therefore that the first machine would fly with only the

The work by Leonard Lord's assistants to locate and destroy any P.92 drawings on the shop floor was aimed at preventing any further work on the P.92 and the Type L cannon turret continuing after 26 May 1940. Lord wanted BPA to merely become a shadow factory for non-BPA airframes. The lack of restricted information fuelled 'misinformation' rumours during the war and after. Workers would talk of it as an 'escort' fighter intended to take the combat into Europe and still being developed in secret. In 1943 *Flight* published a short article that the aircraft was a three-seat machine, requiring a navigator. Neither was true of the original design. Here, based upon the P.92-2 and the *Flight* article, an unsigned fictitious tone painting in the BPA collection – possibly by Colin Evans as a sample Christmas card or calendar cover – attempts to squeeze in three crew with a 1944/45-style cockpit canopy system but 1941 markings.

aerodynamic fairing and be fitted with the turret later. Nevertheless, development of the turret would proceed in parallel to ensure the structures would mate correctly after initial flights.

Development was slow because of commitment to the P.93 Blackburn Roc and the P.82 Boulton Paul Defiant airframes and the numerous other turret projects fostered by the company. Manufacture started in mid-1939 with the RAE tunnel tests only half done. There were problems with getting sufficient stiffness and accuracy into the centre wing/turret structure on such a large-diameter turret ring, which had never been built before. Rivets and flanges tended to fail as the turret ring was hand rotated and even from the stresses induced by the simple task of riveting in any strengthening pieces. The initial two prototypes, which were to be fitted with the alternate engines – Vulture and Sabre – were revised to speed up approval since in November 1938 it was recommended that both examples would have Vultures and a third machine was to be contracted for the delayed Sabre engines with serial allocation V9258. At that stage completion was forecast as January 1940 for the first machine and the second in about May, the major problem being the inability of the company to recruit more staff because of the general expansion of defence work. Virtually all existing staff were dedicated to the Defiant and Roc production designs.

In January 1939, with detail design still fluid, the programme moved back again with a first flight date now not earlier than March 1940. On 5 March 1940 it was reported back to the Air Ministry that the firm was 'energetically pursuing the building of all three prototypes'. When the HM the King and Queen visited to open the turret extension to the factory in April 1940 it has been suggested that only about 5% of the first aircraft had actually been assembled and they had to look more at the jigging and mock-up frames than an actual machine, although something like 90% of the rest were available as component parts. A month later, on 26 May 1940, the entire project was cancelled along with any work on cannon turrets and indeed many British aircraft designs that relied upon cannon turrets. The dire straits that the country found itself in after Dunkirk and the appointment of Lord Beaverbrook as head of the Ministry of Aircraft Production (MAP) by Churchill resulted in his decision that cannon turrets at this stage of the war were a development leap that the country could not afford to waste energy upon. Beaverbrook's allocated production manager a few days later was Leonard Lord, a main advocate of the shadow factory system. Regardless of Beaverbrook's opinion on the subject, Lord's assistants were instructed to ensure that no shop floor documentation remained on the project so that it could never be resurrected.

P.92/2

With the cancellation of the P.92 it was decided that the P.92/2 half-scale model should continue. With no capacity to build at BPA, and since it was to be in wood anyway, the Air Ministry awarded the build contract to Heston Aircraft under their design designation J.A.8. BPA had to provide Heston with all P.92 drawings and assistance necessary to produce the machine. Twin Gypsy Major II engines were chosen to represent as closely as humanly possible the Vulture or Sabre installation of the P.92, but the prime concern was accuracy in the aerodynamic form of the wing and turret blister in relationship with tail surfaces. The result was that the pilot could not be placed forward of the airscrews. His position was set hard against the wing leading edge and his vision to each side was blocked by the Gypsy

cowlings. However, vision forward was good within an arc of about 85°. Additional windows were cut into the nose at the pilot's position to enable him to look down and to the side, but during taxying he would have to weave from side to side to avoid obstructions. The canopy was so small that it could only be fixed in place from outside.

Worries that the narrow chord and taper of the outer wings in this small scale would lead to tip stalls and spins resulted in the fitting of fixed aerodynamic slots in the outer wing, as had been designed for the P.92 prototypes at the insistence of the government aerodynamicists. Despite having to do this the company still claimed that there would be no problems of that sort on their plain wing design, but they had outer wing slit designs on the prototypes just in case. The pitot head for airspeed was placed on a mast below the nose where it could do least

The P.92-2 half scale model on the Wolverhampton compass base tried to accurately reproduce the wing and turret blister and the tailplane location, but with large compromises for the engine nacelles and pilot's position.

This view of the P.92-2 shows the tight pilot position and the lower intakes for the outboard 'wing slits'. Argued by North as unnecessary, tests with them open and taped up showed virtually no difference on trials. RAE still recommended their use if the project proceeded. However, at that stage it had been a dead project for two years. Note the Defiant-style struts on the flaps. *Crown Copyright*

harm to the airflow on the wing and a spike was added above the nose to assist the pilot's judgement of ahead. AP1480X for ROC observers listed it under the special recognition identification number X127. The official serial was V3142 and the contract was carried out under B.19037/39. Following test flights at Heston by BPA test pilot Cecil Feather, it was delivered to BPA in the first half of 1941, being subject to a complete round of photographs on 17 May 1941. Feather was a fairly robust man and found it a tight squeeze to get into the cockpit without assistance. How he might escape was covered by a knock-out panel in the port side aft of the seat, but the catch could only be reached by tying a piece of string to the handle and leading it to the pilot's side. The arrival of the aircraft at Wolverhampton was followed by instructions to build a dummy turret with electric or hydraulic power to revolve it in July 1941. BPA and DTD estimated that it would take twelve months to build and iron out any problems. It was therefore decided not to expend the costs since the likelihood of the turret or the aircraft design type reappearing was very slim.

Feather habitually flew the aircraft until it was eventually decided that it should really be delivered to RAE for handling trials, which were started in July 1943. The test report A&AEE/812 Part I indicates how easy it was for pilots to criticise a specific machine. They admitted to having no data on what typical service operations were required and although it was known to be only a half-scale model, they proceeded to attack the cockpit size and positioning as if this was the expected layout. Only a back parachute could be worn because of the shallow cockpit. Beyond 85° the pilot's view to the side was obscured. There was no rearward view below a 30° angle but above it was good. The wing tips could only be seen if the pilot craned his neck, which would impact upon formation flying. No clear

view panel was fitted and the window to port, which slid back, was too small to take the pilot's head. The temporary Heath Robinson method of abandoning was criticised. Once they got to test it the flight characteristics were considered fairly good, although ailerons were used a lot in bumpy weather. Test with slots in use or with slots covered, required for the full size, found no difference in general, confirming that they might not be required.

The full report was sent to BPA and received 25 August 1943. On 1 September 1943 Flt Lt Feather sent a memo to North and Production Manager Beasley responding to the report. He agreed with the remarks regarding control, cockpit, instruments layout and emergency exit but noted that they could not be considered adverse when this was only a half-scale model. All of the qualities of ground handling and cockpit were specific mainly to the P.92/2 and matched Feather's reports issued internally at BPA. In closing Feather commented: 'In general I think we can say that the report is a good one and we are not in serious disagreement over any particular point.'

All the sundry points would have been found and corrected fairly easily on the full-size aircraft, while the pilot location problems commented upon would never have arisen in the first place. Following the return from RAE the P.92/2 was used by Feather as a general runabout for spares delivery and off-site meetings, even given its difficulty of ground access. When Feather's health started to deteriorate in 1945 and he was moved to lighter duties, this usage finally ceased. The engineless aircraft frame was consigned to a shed part way down the perimeter track access from the factory to the airfield. It was given the ignominious fate of being dragged out and burned one bonfire night in the early 1950s.

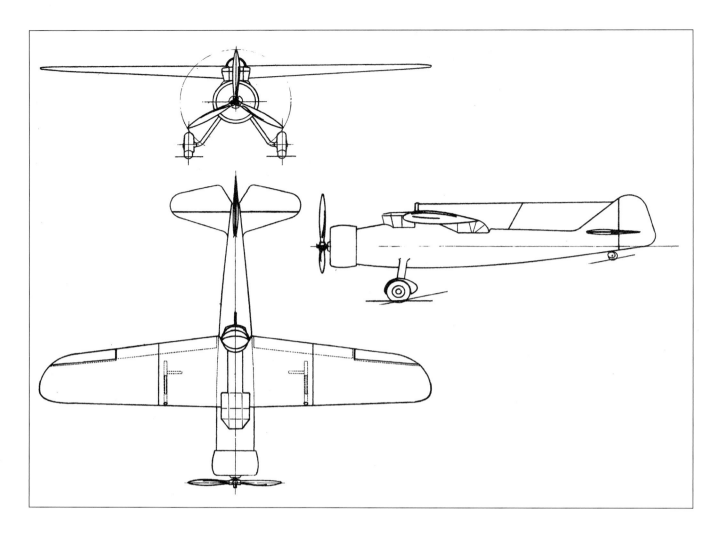

CHAPTER TWENTY-TWO

Army Co-operation and Coastal

P.81

OR.18 CALLED for an Army requirement for a co-operation aircraft for artillery spotting and reconnaissance duties. A monoplane was required to replace the biplane Hector and Audax. Although required by the Army, as was usual the Air Ministry drew up the specification A.39/34 and would evaluate the tenders. Avro, Bristol, B&P, Fairey and Hawker all looked at the requirement. The B&P offering was the P.81, which was submitted in brochure form in April 1935. The P.81 was a high-wing monoplane of conventional layout powered by a Pegasus V or X radial engine. The wing was a three-piece cantilever unit requiring no struts or bracing to support it and no rigging. It consisted as a centre section up to and including wing machine gun installation and two outer wings bolted on. Frise ailerons occupied the outer wing towards the tips and full-length flaps occupied 15% of the chord all along the trailing edge from the canopy to the aileron inboard edge. There were no leading-edge slats because the specification dictated that the aircraft should be capable of performing spinning, while auto-slats would act to prevent that. However, it was commented by the company that tip stall causing one wing to drop was known to be associated only with aircraft having a much sharper taper than was proposed. With a fixed tailplane it was also noted that the aircraft would have to be held firmly in a steep dive and would be rather stiff in that dive, so dive bombing was one of the roles considered.

A large box spar was utilised and the outer wings were bolted to the inner with raised flanges, which were then covered by an external capping strip. All of the wing, including ailerons was metal construction and metal clad. The monocoque fuselage was to be built in two sections: the forward portion from the firewall to the tail ahead of the tail unit and the tail unit itself as a detachable rear section carrying the tail fin and tailwheel. The joint between the two was made by a series of sunken

P.81 for the Army.

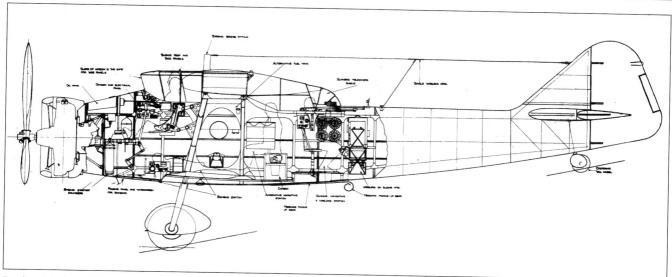

Fuselage interior equipment for the P.81.

dips in the skin where bolts passed through the mating flanges between the two parts. The engine was mounted to a ring and the forward cowling was a BPA Townend Ring collector, with the aft being an attached cowling/fairing. The tail unit was all metal and the undercarriage was a Dowty cantilever type with a sprung wheel. The wheels were detachable without having to remove the spats and the rear edge of the spats incorporated brush scrapers to clean anything picked up by the tyre on rough fields. Surprisingly there was no discussion on short take-off and landing despite the ultimate appearance of the Westland P.8, but camera and message pick-up hook were in the design. This begs the question as to what degree the equivalent of the currently termed 'STOL' was actually in the documents or only appeared during discussion. The Bristol 148, for example, was a low-wing monoplane development of the 146 and not the type of machine one might chose for small field duties, yet it was considered during later trials to have met the A.39/34 requirements well.

Performance of the P.81 was based upon a two-blade wooden propeller and a Hamilton-Standard three-blade was offered if required, but in the later performance section it was noted that the three-blade system added 400lb to the weight for no increase in performance other than during take-off. It was thought that the reduction of initial take-off performance with a wooden propeller was of little consequence compared with the addition of the three-blade unit. Three options for fuel tank positions feeding the engine were discussed with no strong preference for any particular configuration. All tanks were to be duralumin De Bergus riveted. The oil tank in the upper forward fuselage was to have a labyrinth external surface to assist cooling. Bombs were to be carried on racks under the wing. Light bombs were on internal racks under the wing upper skin so they were only out in minimal airflow at the rear of the wing. The rack was covered by an under-surface cover plate when not in use. A gun was carried off the rear face of the main spar through blast tubes just inboard of the wing joint on each wing with 500 rounds of SAA ammunition. The rear gunner sat behind the wing in a lobster shell canopy and had the BPA balanced seat and mounting. He also could lie prone for level bombing forward of his station. Exits in an emergency were multiple roof hatches, the canopy opening plus a side door entry between the pilot and gunner. The roof and aerial was strengthened to hold the canopies clear of the ground and assist exit should the aircraft overturn. The pilot, ahead of the wing, had a forward canted windscreen like the P.79 design with flat panels for best observation and visibility.

At 8,000lb AUW, predicted speed was 222mph at ground level, increased to 242mph with full boost, giving an initial climb rate of 3,000ft/min. Maximum speed was 256mph at 6,000ft and a climb rate at that height of 2,380ft/min. Service ceiling was an impressive 31,000ft and the aircraft would stall flaps up at 69mph and flaps down at 60mph. A tapered wing section of NACA Munk M6 to technical note 487 and 42ft span gave a wing area of 275sq ft. The overall length was 36ft 3in. All of this was with the simple two-blade wooden airscrew. Beyond the data described it was obvious that the proposal was submitted in haste since a large number of paragraphs in the specification were simply listed by their titles with the footnote 'The specified requirements under the above headings are noted and will be fully complied with.' Two types were built to the specification, the Westland P.8 Lysander and the Bristol 148, but only the Lysander later received the production order. In hindsight the all-metal P.81 could well have made an efficient machine for battlefield duties and precision bombing at the front had the Army had a chance to try it.

Twin-Engine Coastal Aircraft P.83, P.84 and P.86

P.83

Air Ministry transmittal letter S.35706 launched Specification M.15/35 to request tenders against OR.22. This called for a shore-based torpedo bombing landplane using two engines and utilising a crew of three: the pilot, a navigator – who also assumed the roles of W/T operator and bomb aimer – and a rear defensive gunner. The specification was unusual in that it called for 'illuminated sighting'. This idea consisted of a series of electric light bulbs fitted to a framework some 5ft ahead of the pilot, the distance between bulbs being fixed so that they subtended an angle of 4° each and allowed pilot judgement of 'angle-off' from the target.

BPA produced the P.83 scheme, a conventional layout monoplane utilising the wing and tail planform of the original Defiant proposal but with an added rectangular centre section to the engine nacelles. Two differing engine schemes were suggested, either the RR Goshawk with underslung radiators or the Pegasus X radial in a BP Townend Ring cowling. The Goshawk installation following the cowling and radiator lines shown in the Defiant proposal, the Pegasus version utilising a labyrinth oil cooler on the top of the nacelle aft of the

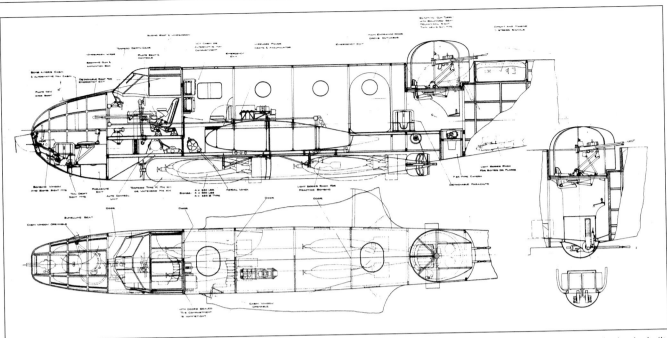

Interior equipment of the P.83 variants. Inset right is the slaved gun version. If the aircraft was also a torpedo carrier then the slaved turret had to be built in further back. Only the bomber version could cope with a slaved turret in its original position.

Impression of the P.83 as a torpedo carrier with ventral slaved browning guns controlled by the dorsal turret gunner's positioning of his upper turret.

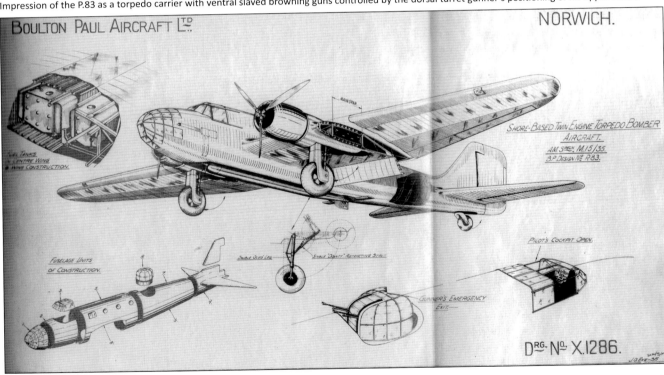

circular cowl. Construction was entirely in light alloy except that a section aft of the wing spar might be in fabric or thinner metal and the control surfaces would be fabric covered. The joint between the wing portions was again a raised flange and capped bolted joint. A twin-leg Dowty retractable undercarriage carried the fixed nacelle shape to enclose all except a portion of the mainwheel when retracted backwards, while the tailwheel also retracted backwards into the rear fuselage. The multi-task navigator was accommodated in the nose for bomb aiming and moved to the rear aft of the pilot for W/T operations. Each area was divided and screened by doors on the starboard side.

Through the aft door was the gunner, who was equipped with twin Lewis guns in a turret cupola. The design had three options:

a Twin fixed Lewis guns on a supporting arm with the turret power operated with a double hand-grip control.
b The same system but with the guns being able to be released from their power mount to allow the gunner free fire either side downwards under the tail.
c As A., but with additional slaved Browning weapons that mirrored the movement of the upper turret in reverse. When the upper turret guns were horizontal the slaves

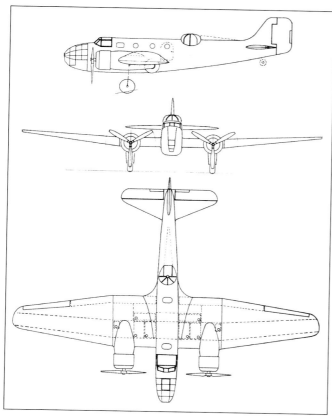

The P.83 and P.84 designs were virtually identical. This P.84A to 24/35 with Aquila engines also illustrates the P.83 second version with Pegasus engines.

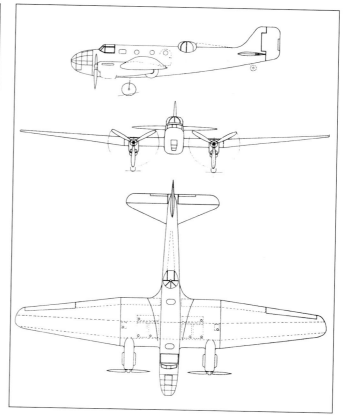

The P.84B or P.83 first version with Goshawk engines.

would be depressed and when the turret guns were raised the slaves would be horizontal. Two Browning guns and 500 rounds were suggested. In this case the turret would have to be moved further aft on the fuselage spine to allow the torpedo to be carried.

In additional to the torpedo on the centreline, the 'semi-buried' following variations were available: four 250lb or 500lb bombs plus four light bombs; and four 250lb 'B' Type plus four light bombs (doors removed). In the event of turret scheme C, twin light bomb racks would be moved to the outer wings and F.24 camera moved to the nose. Both engine variants produced a span of 67ft using an M6 section 18% thick at the root. The overall length was 47ft 9in and the height (tail down) 12ft. The Goshawk machine was heavier by tare at 8,624lb against the Pegasus weight of 8,453lb, maximum AUW being 14,060lb and 14,286lb respectively. Maximum speed was forecast as 257mph with either engine at 5,000ft.

P.84

As the transmittal letter for M.15/35 was dispatched it also circulated a second specification, G.24/35, for a general-purpose reconnaissance landplane to fulfil OR.25. The specification desired a maximum AUW of 9,500lb and a crew of four: a pilot, a second pilot who was also navigator and bomb aimer, a W/T operator and a rear gunner/observer. BPA produced the P.84 schemes, but pointed out immediately that it was technically impossible to produce a machine of such low weight and yet able to perform the functions listed and carry four crew. The general layout followed that for the P.83 and two schemes were offered. The P.84A used Bristol Aquila AE3M radial engines and the P.84B a derated version of the RR Goshawk B. It was also pointed out that with a large number of Kestrel IX

engines going into service there might be some advantage in the fact that the Goshawk and the Kestrel were virtually interchangeable. All of the turret and bombing equipment applied to the P.83 were included in the P.84 except that the 500lb bombs were limited to two. The P.84A Aquila machine had a span of 60ft compared with the Goshawk at 67ft. Lengths were 45ft 6in and 47ft 9in respectively and heights 11ft 8in and 12ft. The Goshawk machine was again heavier in tare at 8,539lb against 7,150lb. The maximum AUW came to 12,915lb and 11,430lb respectively. Maximum speed of the Goshawk was 245mph from sea level to 5,000ft. The Aquila machine was lower at 239mph at 5,000ft, dropping to 220mph at sea level.

P.86

Neither the P.83 nor the P.84 have a stated submission date but the key drawings were all dated November 1935, suggesting submission of both before the end of 1935, fitting the tender conference dates of 10 December 1935 and 8 January 1936 respectively. Following feedback immediately after these conferences, a merging of the two specifications was recommended and endorsed on 26 January 1936 by the Chief of Air Staff (CAS). The main contenders were Avro, Blackburn, BPA and Bristol, who would be asked to resubmit as each had provided good responses. In February 1936 BPA submitted a third brief brochure. The object of this proposal was to confirm that the specifications M.15/35 and G.24/35 were so similar that the work could be carried out by one single design and to provide that amalgamated design. The design offered was the P.86, which was similar to the P.84A with Aquila AE3M engines and some exceptions. The nose was lengthened to accommodate a 36in × 24in chart table with improved navigation facilities. Four (blistered) windows were provided for observation points, two in the nose cabin and two forward of the rear gunner's turret (one in the crew access door).

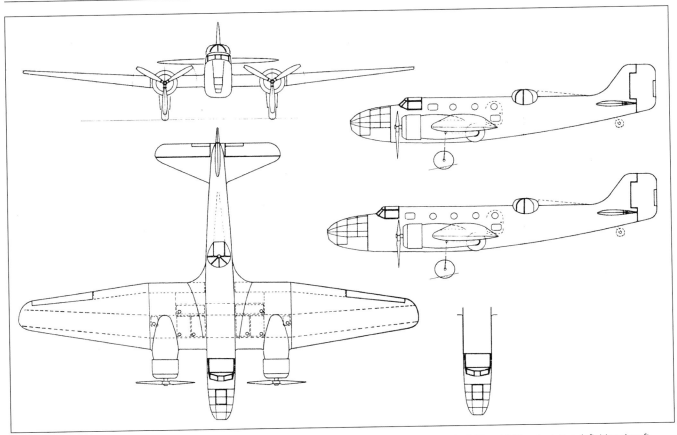

Above: Combining the P.83 and P.84 series into a definitive aircraft resulted in the P.86, which was offered as a version with pilot behind the engines and one with pilot ahead of the engines. No X series drawings (X1332 to 1335) of the P.86 appear to survive. This impression is based upon the P.84A drawing (stated to be identical to the P.86 and front fuselage mock-up so should be considered conjectural as regards the exact positions of the pilots cockpit and overall length).

Left: Forward cockpit mock-up of the P.86 with extra chart table room.

There was alternative torpedo accommodation and tankage increase for the torpedo bomber case. A further alternative was also offered to bring the pilot's cabin forward of the airscrews, moving the wing back and hence increase his all-around view. The trade-off in this case was a reduction in speed of 2mph and an increase in weight of 120lb. As requested during January discussions, a wooden mock-up of the new nose was constructed and photographed. Unfortunately, in the only proposal record found, the drawings X1333 to X1335 were all omitted from the binding except for climb rate curves. The detail outline can therefore only be predicted by combining the P.84A drawings with the pictures of the wooden nose mock-up. The overall length was unfortunately only shown on the missing drawings. A new specification was finally issued only to Blackburn for their B.26 Botha and to Bristol for their Type 156 Beaufort. All of the earlier specification offerings were put to one side.

P.87

The P.87 was listed as 'a twin-engine heavy bomber with modified Merlin engines' and was raised early in 1936. When raised there was no specification attached to the design. Either it was a revision of the P.83/84/86 series as a Bomber Command aircraft or an initial stab at revising the P.79, B.1/35, to a new layout incorporating North's fresh idea for a rear defence system, the four-gun barbette turret (later designated Type B) or a remotely operated rear barbette (later the Type G). It could simply be a sketch based upon initial discussions to the upcoming B.13/36. Nothing survives for this scheme other than that stated above, so it is currently impossible to confirm if the scheme was ever finished or what modification was intended for the basic Merlin engines.

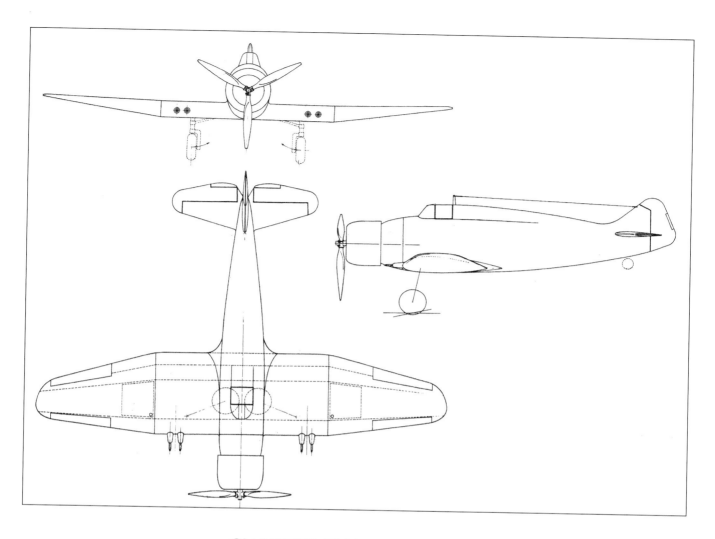

CHAPTER TWENTY-THREE

Cannon Fighters and Close Support

P.88

O R.31 AND F.37/35 raised in February 1938 called for a single-seat day and night fighter armed with four 20mm cannon to operate with greater firepower than the current eight-gun fighter designs. The requirement was looked at by at least Bristol, BPA, Fairey, Hawker, Supermarine and Westland. Hawker offered their Hurricane and Supermarine the Spitfire Type 312 or a twin-engine Type 313. Westland looked at a number of ideas before settling on the KV26 (Peregrine)-engine P.9.

For the P.88, Hughes drew a rather tubby oval-section American fighter-style fuselage with a Hercules radial engine enclosed in a long-chord BP Townend Ring cowling. This version was designated the P.88A. The wing section was M6 and the centre portion was rectangular in plan with the fuselage placed over the wing as with the P.82. The four 23mm or 20mm cannon sat in the outer section of the inner wing outboard of the propeller. The installation was made with the cannon on their sides so the outer weapon had its drum container outboard and the inner weapon inboard. As with the P.92, there were

no means at that time of belt-feed for the cannon, so the drums limited the ammunition load possible. Heavy diagonal struts ran between the two vertical planes of the box spar to enclose the gun bay and take the shock of firing, while blast tubes pierced the leading edge from the front spar out ahead of the wing. The gun bay was heated and hydraulic means of cocking, loading and firing was to be fitted. Inboard of the weapons the wide undercarriage folded inwards and backwards. The tailwheel retracted by pivoting about the top of its fork forging, while the oleo system for it sat above the pivot. The fuel tanks were in the outer wing panels, while the ailerons on the trailing edge were complemented by leading-edge slats. A P.82 plan tailplane

Radial-engine version of the four-cannon fighter to F.37/35.

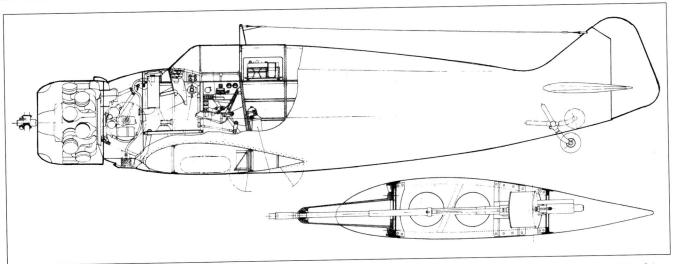

The main proposal side detail was of the radial version but included the substantial bracing of the wing cannon to prevent distortion and jamming during firing.

Impression of the P.88A.

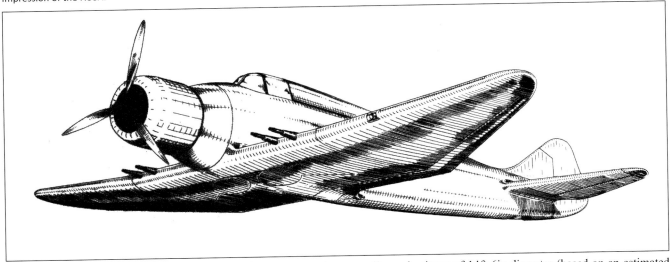

and a more rounded P.82 fin and rudder completed the empennage. A raised thinner shape on the fuselage top formed the headrest and faired in the rearward-sliding canopy behind the pilot. A three-blade, two-pitch propeller without spinner of 12ft 6in diameter completed the design. De-icing was via Dunlop Glycol and a rubber leading edge on the tailplane. The wingspan was 29ft 6in and the fuselage 32ft 8in. At 25.3lb/sq ft the performance predicted was 337mph at 15,000ft.

As an option the P.88B was a much larger machine but was powered by the heavier Vulture II engine with a similar three-blade

propeller and spinner of 14ft 6in diameter (based on an estimated Vulture gear ratio of 0.4 because true values were not available to the design team). The radiator was fitted under the centre section of the wing. The wingspan was 44ft and the fuselage 36ft 3in. At the same 25.3lb/sq ft the performance was 358mph at 15,000ft. Both machines provided a performance well above that listed within the specification but the data on the Vulture was so limited that fuel tank size had to be calculated by assuming a 1.7 uplift of the consumption of the Merlin E. All of the interior and build sketches concentrated on the Hercules version. The combined proposal was submitted in May 1936 and was quoted at £20,500 for prototype 1 and £17,500 for prototype 2.

Although take-off performance was lower, it was the Vulture model, the P.88B, which interested the Air Ministry. A long time in gestation, the P.88 was ordered towards the turn of the year under 556966/36 with allocated serials L6951 and L6952. L6953 was allocated for the Supermarine Type 313 but subsequently cancelled. The Westland P.9 was also ordered as L6844 and L6845. On 11 February 1937, before many drawings could be produced and released, the P.88 contract was cancelled by mutual agreement between the Air Ministry and BPA, the amount spent by the company

Model of the P.88B version ordered, photographed by the Air Ministry at the time. The nose taper seems out of proportion with the original drawings and too slim to take the Vulture. *Tony Buttler*

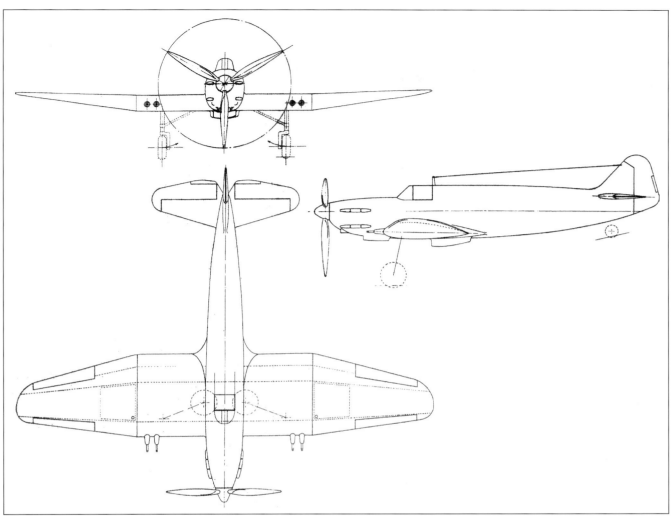

Vulture-engined version of the four-cannon fighter to F.37/35. Two prototypes were ordered to this version but subsequently cancelled.

on the project at that date being some £600. The reason cited was that there was no hope of any suitable (powerful) engine being available by the time the airframe was ready to receive it. The Air Staff decided to rely solely on the Westland P.9, of similar predicted performance to the P.88B and to be named Whirlwind.

Had construction continued to prototype and the Vulture eventually become available, the airframe may well have looked very different. When the P.88B was proposed the Vulture weight used was 1,700lb. For the P.91 submission in January 1937 it was 1,800lb. By the time the P.92 brochure was made in the next year, it had risen to 1,908.5lb, and even this was struck out in the P.92 brochure prior to submission and replaced by a new RR figure of 2,120lb, a 25% increase on the calculation used almost a year earlier.

P.94 Single-Seat Fighter

The driving force for this proposal was feedback from the Air Staff that future fighters would require 20mm cannon to attack fully armoured bombers and cannon fighters, or up to twelve machine guns to deliver sufficient weight of fire to bring down lightly armoured bombers and fighters. The aim was to provide a fighter that could be rapidly converted from the basic Defiant airframe structural design into an interceptor fighter or a long-range fighter with this amount of armament. In addition, the Air Staff had long considered how they could rapidly get aircraft overseas into Middle East or tropical climates without having to dismantle and ship crated machines by

sea. The proposed technique worked on enabling the machine to carry sufficient fuel to allow direct flight to its destination and was known as 'reinforcing'. For a number of years tenders had quite often included a reinforcing role. With transit stops through France lost to the RAF, reinforcing conversion could be an important method of quickly getting aircraft directly to places such as Malta, Greece and Egypt, with or without having to necessarily stage at Gibraltar.

With the prototype Defiant returned from RAE and the Type F Mk.I experimental turret removed, BPA faired in the turret position and upper rear fuselage with a fixed wood and fabric fairing and refurbished the paint scheme to the June/July 1940 service standard. The idea was to provide a demonstrator of the single-seat version of the Defiant, to confirm potential handling and speed benchmarks for such a conversion. The new build using the planned Defiant II engine, the Merlin XX, was intended to produce a fighter with superior performance and armament to the cancelled P.88, or alternately a twelve-gun fighter that had been discussed for F.18/37 Type R and Type N fighters, the future Tornado/Typhoon. In the context of the situation at the time, the twelve-gun P.94 version was uniquely offered with short barrel-weapons firing through blast tubes in the leading edge of the wing. Six guns were carried in each inner wing half, outboard of the undercarriage, and all fuel in the fuselage. When used for ground attack, the pilot could select all twelve guns on a pivoting surface plate under the wing to point downwards at 17°. The pilot would then be able to carry out ground

The P.94 single-seat fighter. Essentially a single-seat Defiant with either four 20mm cannon or twelve machine guns. The latter could be selected to 17° depression for ground attack.

The proposed P.94 single-seat fighter produced with Defiant Mk.II components compared with K8310.

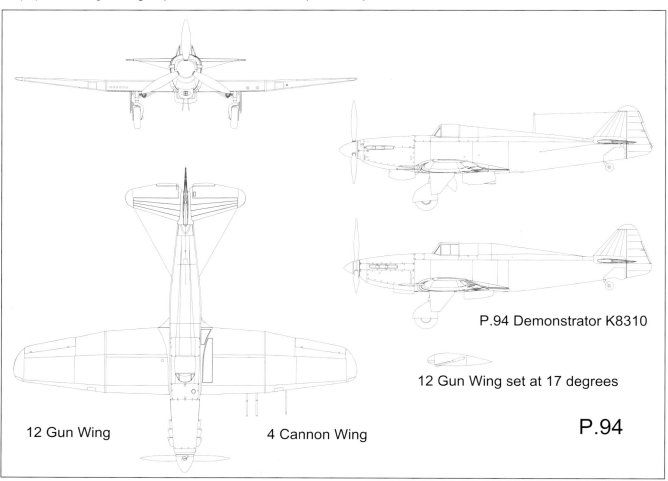

12 Gun Wing

4 Cannon Wing

P.94 Demonstrator K8310

12 Gun Wing set at 17 degrees

P.94

The fitting of four 20mm cannon was refused but North was seconded by Beaverbrook to the team that was investigating unsustainable cannon fit in RAF fighters, which was hampering their deployment in combat.

attack strafing runs simply from level flight without necessarily pointing the machine at the target. On the ground the plate pivoted the other way and the guns could be rearmed underneath the wing with 750 rounds per gun in an immediately replaceable cassette, meaning rapid rearmament for the machine to fly the next sortie. The imminent potential invasion of Britain in June 1940 and the need for ground attack aircraft to destroy the invasion force on the beaches led many to assume in hindsight that this had been the intention behind the idea of two-position machine guns. This was in fact never discussed in the P.94 proposal, although the selectable weapons angle would have been obvious to anyone seeing the concept at the time.

The basic version proposed was the cannon fighter carrying four 20mm Hispano cannon and four machine guns with 150 rounds and 750 rounds per gun respectively, normal fuel (approx. 98 gallons) stowed behind the pilot and a weight of 7,855lb. The alternative was a twelve-gun fighter with extra ammunition to 750 rounds per gun. As a long-range machine gun fighter, twelve Browning guns and 300 rounds per gun plus 160 gallons of fuel gave a weight of 7,675lb and a range of 580 miles. Finally, the reinforcing conversion had two options. By fitting additional tanks in the place of the weapons, in the form of two standard Defiant tanks, an additional 104 gallons of fuel was available, or alternately two fuselage tanks to a total of 202 gallons gave 1,254 miles, but allowed the aircraft to retain an offensive load of six of the twelve machine guns. If the two extra long-range fighter tanks were fitted with the Defiant wing tanks, the aircraft was unarmed but the range became 1,620 miles on 254 gallons of fuel. At that maximum range figure the weight of the aircraft reached 8,000lb at take-off. Based directly upon a known airframe design with improved performance, once relieved of the gun turret and second pilot the Merlin XX engine airframe would have a predicted top speed of 380mph at 23,500ft if the Merlin XX gave full rated power, comparing favourably with the 326mph at 30,000ft that had been deemed good enough for the Vulture engine P.88 five years earlier. For reinforcing at maximum weight the top speed dropped to 350mph at 8,000lb take-off weight but a cruise of 228mph at 13,500ft was possible and reached in 4.65 minutes. In addition, the light wing loadings without a turret (28.6lb/sq ft for the gun wing and 31.42lb/sq ft for the shell gun wing) would enable the airframe to out-turn all current fighters.

The unsolicited proposal was undated but submitted in late August/early September together with a request to fit cannon. The Air Ministry were not particularly interested in converting existing Defiant components to a single-seat fighter, they were still considered too important as Type W anti-bomber fighters. When the company sought permission to convert it to four cannon to prove the wing installation, this was refused in September 1940. There was a 'behind the scenes' reason for this, however, which North found out at the same time. Fitting Hispano cannon into a fighter aircraft was not that simple and the RAF was having serious problems with two cannon squeezed into Spitfires. They caused vibration and distortion in the airframe, and they were prone to jammed rounds, partial breech cyclic action and incorrect ejection of cases. North found himself in direct discussion with Beaverbrook about the problems and immediate secondment by the head of MAP to a team tasked with solving the service problems of the weapon.

P.95

Specification B.20/40 was released for a close support, bombing and tactical reconnaissance aircraft. A specific requirement was that the crew members should be placed close together so that the gunner had access to the pilot. The arrangement was thought by BPA to be a compromise as better rear defence could be achieved by placing the gunner in the tail. In order to offset this compromise, the rear fuselage design was made as a boom of thin cross section forming a tadpole shape in plan. A tricycle undercarriage was then chosen to help such a tail shape. The gunner was hence able to fire at a considerable angle downwards either side of the fuselage. Twin fin/rudder units were also adopted to provide the best situation to defend against a rear diving attack. A speed of 280mph had been requested, with a Merlin as the likely power. The engine offered by BPA was either a Hercules VI radial engine or a Griffon, both being in the form of power egg designs to enable rapid engine changing. It was pointed out, however, that even with a radial engine the engine change limit of one hour required by the specification could not be met.

The two crew of the P.95 sat under a clear cupola with the pilot having a mechanically operated sliding hood. The gunner sat under the rear of the cupola protected from the air stream with an open area aft uncluttered with framing and two Browning guns with 1,000 rounds of ammunition.

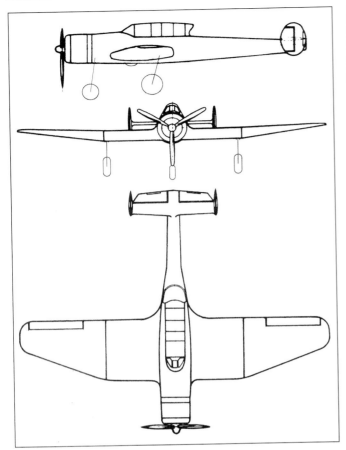

P.95 close support bomber and ground attack aircraft to B.20/40. Aircraft to this specification were outclassed by planned specialised fighters and outdated before it was issued.

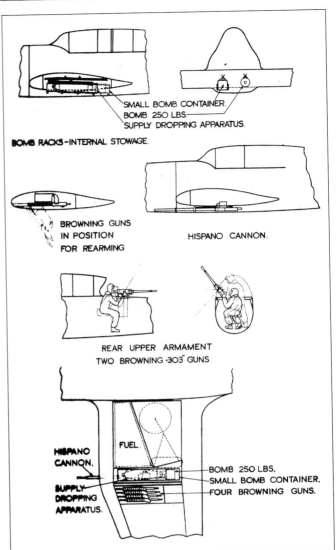

Armament details of the P.95, which included underslung cannon with the drum magazine buried in the wing.

The weapons were manual in elevation but the pivot point was power operated to either side so the gunner could fire down over the fuselage sides. The centre wing was rectangular in section, while the trailing edge was straight but the leading edge swept back on the outer panels to allow maximum view for the pilot. Four Browning guns, all identical, were carried in the inner portion of each outer wing with 600-round containers, or 1,000-round alternatives if required. Bombs could be carried internally within the fuselage and 250lb bombs in the wings immediately outboard of the undercarriage. These outer bombs could be replaced on their racks with a 20mm Hispano cannon instead, the cannon hanging under the wings but the ammunition drums buried within the wing. Two F. 24 cameras and radio equipment occupied the space immediately forward of the gunner. Anti-bomber aerial mine units were also be accommodated and deployed but the details could not be shown in the proposal as the government had not provided sufficient information on the system to decide the location of components. Alloy angled protection was to be employed instead of 9mm steel armour plate to save weight. Although the mainwheels were completely enclosed, the rearward-retracting nosewheel left a chord of its wheel protruding beneath the fuselage skin.

The submission was undated and perhaps the most annoying point in the document was the complete omission of dimensions for the airframe, which had to rely on scales on the crudely traced

and reduced drawing. The dimensions approximated to a span of 44ft 10.4in, a length of 36ft 2.6in (35ft 1.6in with engine, propeller and spinner removed but cowling in place) and a height of 10ft 4in static. The Hercules engine gave a weight of 12,440lb AUW and maximum speed of 323mph at 16,000ft. At sea level this reduced to 273mph. Service ceiling was 27,500ft and as a reinforcing conversion the range after already reaching 10,000ft was 1,510 miles. For the Griffon engine at 12,500lb AUW, maximum speed was 316mph at 18,000ft and 265mph at sea level. Service ceiling was 30,000ft and range after a climb to 12,000ft was 1,525 miles. In both cases dive bombing could be carried out at 60° and the flaps set to 90°, when the dive speed was stated to not exceed 300mph. Only the Hercules machine was drawn and it may be that the cancellation of the specification came before a full brochure could be completed and submitted. All competitors were disappointed by this early cancellation.

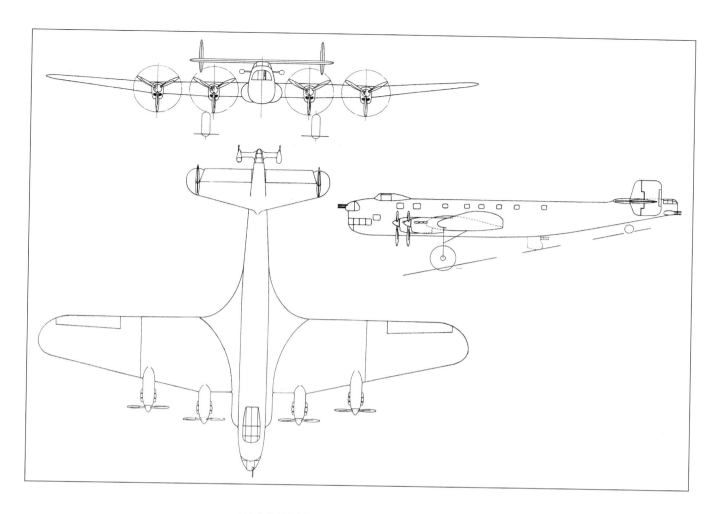

CHAPTER TWENTY-FOUR

P.90 and P.91 Bombers

P.90

THE ISSUE of B.12/36 (OR.40) dated 15 July 1936 turned all attention away from B.1/35 in being the first requirement for a four-engine heavy bomber to appear for some time. To make the specification even more technically difficult, it required that the machine be able to take the stress of a catapult take-off under heavy overload conditions. The Air Ministry had ignored North's P.78-based 'Compound Aeroplane' concept in favour of ground-based catapults. A speed expectation was 230mph at 66% power. The maximum range was 3,000 miles, with at least 2,000 miles carrying 14,000lb. Three gunners were required: one as a bomb aimer/observer, one as an engine fitter/amidships under and one as a tail gunner. Bomb load specified covered all variations in the inventory: twenty-eight 250lb or 500lb bombs; seven 2,000lb AP, or twenty-eight 250 or 500lb containers or practice weapons.

The P.90 became a four-engine, low mid-wing aircraft with an M6 modified wing section and large outboard wings. The trailing edge was straight and the leading edge swept back from the inboard engine location. The fuselage utilised double circular-section bays at the bottom extending forward of the wing and at the rear half of the wing. The centre bay within the wing was triple bay (ie with three bomb racks side by side each in its own bay). Each bay held a BPA rotating and indexing

bomb rack. Only the 2,000lb bomb would require special single adaptors, all others could be launched from the rotating racks. In order to carry the Type B and 500lb bombs, however, the doors would have to be replaced with special doors. In addition each cell could transport RR Merlin, RR Goshawk or RR Kestrel KV26 spare engines. If required, slightly larger cells could accommodate Pegasus or Hercules engines. Alternately, the space of 4ft diameter, 6ft long allowed containers for fuel, oil, water or other supplies to fit. Accommodation for twenty-four fully armed troops was by removable deck-chair type folding seats above the bomb bays. Heating would be piped from the radiators on each engine.

P.90 heavy bomber to B.12/36 with KV26 (Peregrine) engines. Note the Type B turret with rear outrigger guns.

The cockpit, centre and rear fuselage were to be built as two halves each, with a plug-on nose and tail support sections. The tailplane was of the twin fin and rudder variety and sat on the top of the fuselage tail support. For the engines the RR Kestrel KV26 (later Peregrine) inline was selected with Hamilton Standard three-blade, variable-pitch metal airscrews. The front gun turret with two Browning guns was the first draft design Type C and was based essentially on an adjustment, a re-gunning and re-sighting of the SAMM AB2J layout, having the ammunition boxes as curved containers on the right side above the gun ring and two vertically stacked weapons on a single trunnion mount to the left side. The advantage of this layout with the weapon mount pivot point over the gun ring edge was the large arc of elevation and depression that was available – elevation +85 and depression -65 to 70° – with azimuth from wing tip to wing tip of about 200°. Firing was pneumatic with interrupter systems to avoid the airframe and 2,000 rounds per gun. The under turret was a retractable version of the same vertical-stacked 2,000 rounds per gun, two-gun mount, but fitted to the right side of the turret from the gunner's view. The under turret could be retracted and was the first design of the Type K series. With 360° azimuth the turret would have not less than +20° elevation on each beam and not less than -65° depression. The tail turret on the other hand was an entirely North patented design, which was designated Type B and which North described as a Dumb-Bell. This was a four-Browning gun station with two gunner positions. As in the P.79, the 'easy position' was a seat location 2ft ahead of the 'action' station. For firing the gunner moved to action and sighted and fired the guns. Two guns each were mounted on outboard arms and the streamlined pod provided elevation and depression of +90 to -90°. For azimuth the arms were pivoted at about mid-span and also operated for aft +/-90°. The gunner could therefore protect a complete hemisphere aft of the aircraft with 2,500 rounds per gun belt-fed from large circular drums hung in the sides of the rear fuselage. The main gear sat under the inboard engine and retracted outboard into the wing. The tailwheel retracted by pivoting aft at the top of the wheel fork to leave only a segment of wheel protruding into the airflow.

The wingspan was exactly the 100ft limit and an area of 1,450sq ft. Overall length was 77ft 3in and height tail down 20ft 3in. The chord was 18ft at the centre section and 9ft at the tips. The empty weight was 21,495lb, normal AUW 33,451lb and maximum specified – with 2,000-mile range and carrying 14,000lb of bombs – was 47,922lb. Maximum speed at 15,000ft was 290mph and at sea level 232mph. Cruising speeds were 267mph and 208mph respectively. The design stalled at 81mph flaps up and 66mph flaps down. The service ceiling was 35,000ft. The best flying endurance based on a specific load of 8,000lb of bombs and 3,000-mile range condition was twelve hours and twenty minutes. Sufficient fuel allowed 3,000 miles plus a 25% safety margin.

The P.90 was submitted on 1 October 1936 and the initial conference was heartening in that the P.90, with its rotary bomb cells and unique rear turret design, was placed second behind the geodetic Vickers 293. Further inputs by DTD favoured the P.90 as a back-up because of its perceived ease of manufacture. Two negatives to this were further positive interviews with Supermarine and the fact that BPA had not produced a modern bomber structure. By January 1937 a further round of discussions decided that the Short S.29 Stirling and the Supermarine 316/317 were to be contracted as prototypes, while the BPA P.90, AW, Fairey, Vickers and Bristol designs were rejected.

Interior of the P.90 showing early Type C nose turret based upon the original French layout and North's Type B rear system, plus his rotary bomb dispensers.

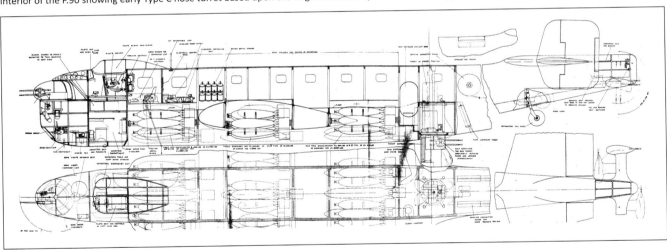

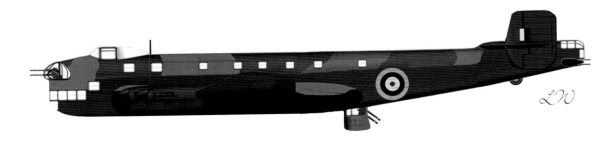

P.90

Although some writers have suggested that the seven rotary bomb bay cells in 2-3-2 formation would have resulted in a design that could not be adapted to larger bombs, this is not strictly correct. As with the Defiant upper decking, the design loadings were taken by only the fuselage structure down to wing level. The bottom half of the rotary bomb bay structure was unloaded and hence could be cut back to hollow. It would have been possible therefore to adapt to the Blockbuster, Grand Slam or even two Tallboy bombs semi-buried by either changes to bulge the lower doors or leaving them off the aircraft. In these cases the range would have been limited to around 1,000 miles. The main problem that the P.90 would face was the same as the Westland Whirlwind, the lack of KV26 (Peregrine) production, with the Merlin taking preference. One can only envision the airframe eventually being adapted with Merlins.

P.91

Specification P.13/36 (OR.41) was dated 8 September 1936 for a medium bomber that could also cover GR and GP classes and carry two torpedoes. All of the basic information about requirements laid down in B.12/36 applied, including the stressing for catapult launch. The speed requirement was 275mph at 66% power. The maximum range was 3,000 miles, with at least 2,000 miles with 4,000lb of bombs. Two gunners, nose and tail, were required. The specified bomb load was sixteen 250lb or 500lb bombs; four 2,000lb AP or torpedoes with 'Bull' gear; or sixteen 250 or 500lb containers.

The company offered two alternate magazine designs, a widened lower fuselage below the wing spaced so that bombs could be accommodated four abreast, or four large rotating bomb magazine cells, two forward of the wing and two aft at the wing trailing edge. Two light carriers were in the rear fuselage belly. In addition each cell could transport an engine or storage containers as with the P.90. BPA drew a scaled down version of the P.90 wing except that the wing outboard of the engines was swept back slightly to maintain the centre of gravity. The Type C with 1,000 rounds each gun and Type B with 2,500 rounds per gun were carried as before, although a conventional turret was possible in the rear if required. The design Type was not specified but could only have been the Type E draft already offered for the AW Whitley. Turret operation remained as the P.90. The engines chosen were the RR Vulture 12ft 6in from the centreline of the aircraft, driving 14ft diameter three-blade continuous VP propellers. Twin mainwheels under each engine nacelle retracted backwards into the rear of the nacelle. Span was now 83ft, area 950sq ft and overall length 71ft 3in, although the drawing was incorrectly dimensioned to show overall length over the gun barrels, which was not the normal way of dimensioning. The wing chord was 14ft 6in at the centre section, 6ft 9in at the tips. The tail down height was 18ft 9in.

The empty weight was 1,680lb, normal AUW 24,060lb and maximum specified 3,000 miles with 3,500lb of bombs gave an AUW of 35,734lb. Maximum speed at 15,000ft was 321mph and at sea level 258mph. The cruising speeds were 297mph and 230mph respectively. The design stalled at 84mph flaps up and 69mph flaps down. The service ceiling was 38,000ft. Sufficient fuel allowed 3,000 miles plus a 25% safety margin.

Reduced detail Interior of the P.91 configured to show a low bomb bay for two fully tailed aerial torpedoes instead of the deep rotary dispenser bay alternative.

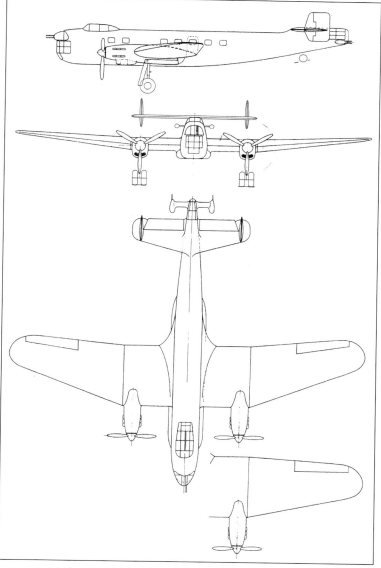

P.91 heavy bomber to P.13/36 with Vulture engines. The swept wing was not liked and the shown alternative was pencilled in during discussions.

Submitted on 6 January 1937, the P.91 failed to generate interest in a prototype. The swept back outboard wing was not received well and there was some discussion on internal equipment changes that would have resulted in a more normal shape but this still failed to get the P.91 chosen. It may well be that despite the rotary bomb rack design, the decisions initiating the rejection of the P.90 at the time the brochure was submitted were read across to the P.91.

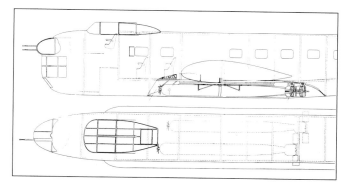

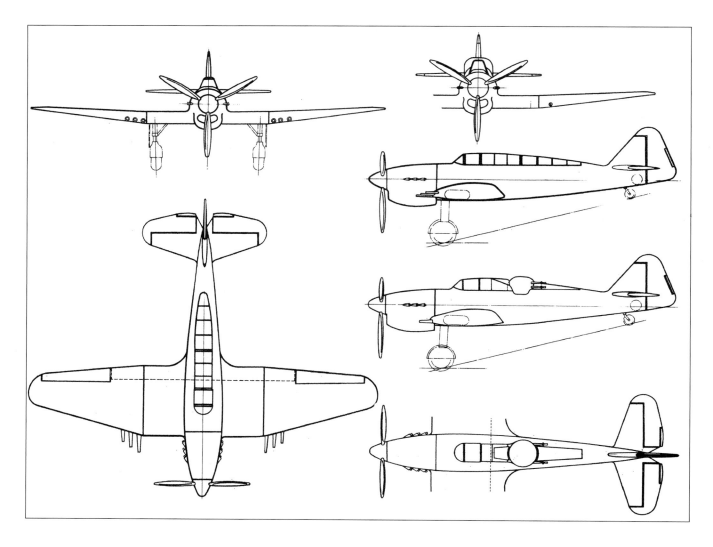

CHAPTER TWENTY-FIVE

The 'Novel' Fighter Programme
Night Fighters (Stage 4)

D URING P.82 DEFIANT production late in 1940 BPA looked at further improvements in performance not then available from any variation of the current range of Merlin engines. It also added forward-firing cannon to the improved design. The issue of government specification F.18/40 dated 31 October 1940 provided a means of submitting formal proposals for a version with forward-firing weapons only, but amendment Corrigendum 1 added 9 December 1940 asked for alternative armament to include a dorsal power-operated turret and increased endurance. The specification required a speed of 380mph minimum at 20,000ft and two speed blowers to give maximum speeds at lower altitudes. BPA prepared two designs, the P.96 single-engine and the P.97 alternate twin-engine aeroplane, for the role.

P.96

Initially the P.96 submission had two variations, the P.96A with six cannon and no turret, meeting the initial requirements of F.18/40, and the P.96B with two cannon and gunner-operated Type A dorsal turret to meet the amendment. Both aircraft were powered by the Napier Sabre NS6SM or alternative NS3SM and moved back to a

chin radiator as proposed for the original P.82 Defiant. The wing cannons were fitted with special BPA hemispherical auto-shutters at the end of the barrel fairings to close off the weapons. Boulton Paul universal recoil dampers, developed in solving the problems

P.96A night fighter to F18/40 with six 20mm cannon and a radar operator or P.96B with two 20mm cannon and turret.

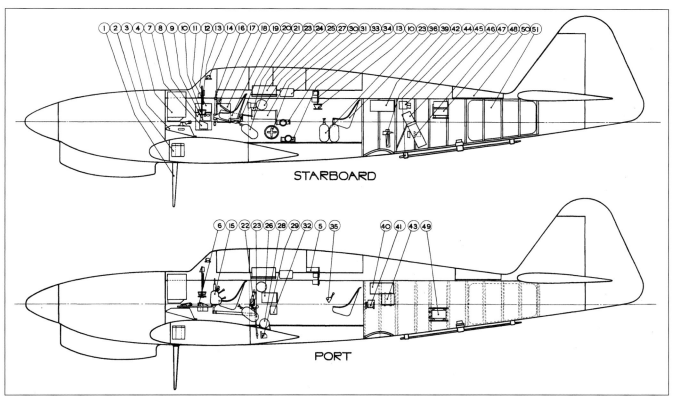

STARBOARD

PORT

Interior Details – P.96A and B and revised P.96C illustrations

1. Aerial mast for W/T
2. Accumulator
3. Rudder pedestal
4. Oil tank
5. Cathode ray tube for AI
6. De-icing tank
7. Map case
8. Electrical panel
9. Electrical panel
10. Compass
11. Electrical panel
12. Instrument panel
13. Flying instrument panel
14. Gun sight
15. Engine controls
16. Control column

17. Switchbox-identification
18. Electrical panel
19. Pilot's seat
20. Hand pump lever
21. Hand pump
22. Selector valves u/c and flaps
23. Oxygen bottles
24. R/T unit TR1143
25. Air bottle
26. Control panel for AI
27. Receiver for AI
28. Aileron unit – auto control
29. Aileron servo – auto control
30. Elevator and rudder unit – auto control
31. Blind approach unit
32. Blind approach unit
33. Elevator servo – auto control
34. Rudder servo – auto control

35. Throttle control – AI operator
36. Seat – AI operator
37. Turret
38. Service hatch
39. Modulator (or desert equipment)
40. Transmitter (or desert equipment)
41. Master contactor
42. Axe
43. First aid outfit
44. Dipole aerial
45. R3003 IFF Mk II unit (R3090 IFF Mk III for P.96C)
46. Flare tube
47. R3003 IFF Mk II unit (R3090 IFF Mk III for P.96c)
48. R3003 IFF Mk II unit (R3090 IFF Mk III for P.96c)
49. Blind approach unit
50. Dinghy stowage (tail anti-spin parachute on prototype a/c)
51. Flotation bag

with Hispano cannon in service, were proposed. The airframe was estimated to achieve 389mph at 20,000ft and 410mph at 34,000ft in the non-turret version, dropping to 379mph at 20,000ft and 400mph at 34,000ft with a turret. The machine looked like an enlarged Defiant with the outer wing panels swept back on the leading edge and parallel at the trailing edge to take the heavier Sabre engine. Indeed, the main selling point was the speed with which the machine could be designed because of its broad similarity to the original Defiant structure, enabling the use of all the standard parts. The P.96 had a number of other interesting features including beam approach equipment to allow easier night landings and an autopilot system in the non-turreted version so that the pilot could be searching with the aircraft in flight, while the radar operator could impose gentle control input over the top to follow the target he had obtained on his scopes. That control was to be via electrically operated trim tabs on the flight surfaces.

A second brochure was submitted for the P.96C, which had four forward-firing cannon in the wings and a Type A dorsal turret. The P.96C abandoned the non-turreted machine except when, as with the A and B versions, it was a single-seater 'reinforcing conversion', adding two hours of additional endurance at 320mph cruise. The wingspan was increased from 44ft to 46ft and a performance identical to the P.96B was predicted. Finally, with reports that the Napier Sabre development was becoming rather protracted, a fourth design, the P.96D, was proposed. This had a completely new straight-tapered outer wing design of 46ft span and a Bristol Centaurus CE4SM radial engine as a standard Bristol power egg. Both a six-cannon, two-seat fighter and a four-cannon plus Type A dorsal turret fighter were proposed in the single brochure. Speed was predicted as 400mph at 22,500ft or 390mph at 22,500ft when equipped with a turret. A full-scale mock-up was made for photographic purposes using a Defiant fuselage and mated wooden structure to provide a resemblance to the as-built shape.

Painted wind tunnel model of the P.96A.

Interior equipment of the P.96B.

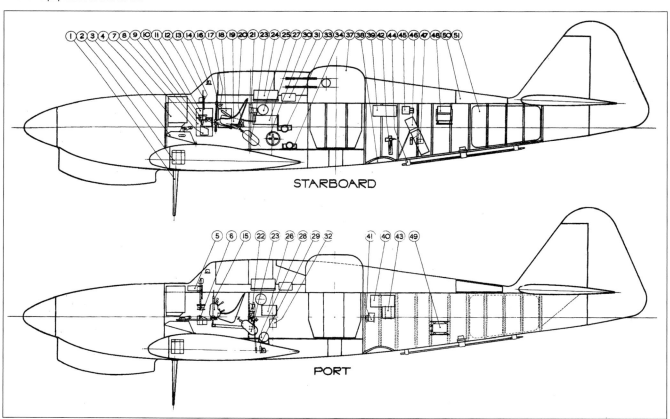

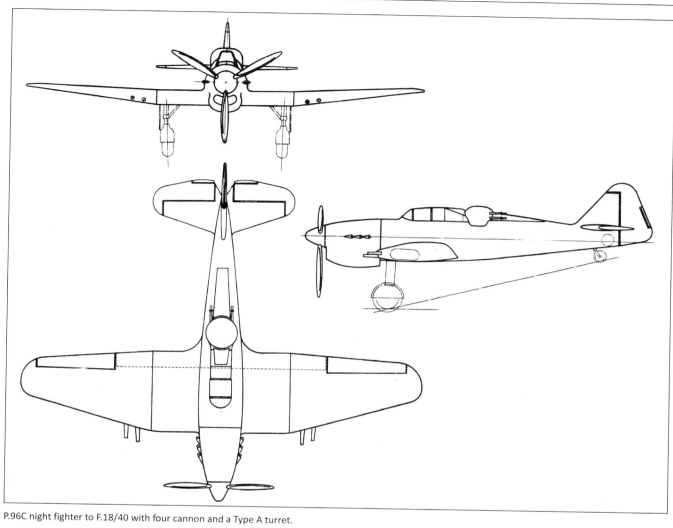

P.96C night fighter to F.18/40 with four cannon and a Type A turret.

Model of the P.96C turreted 'Super Defiant'.

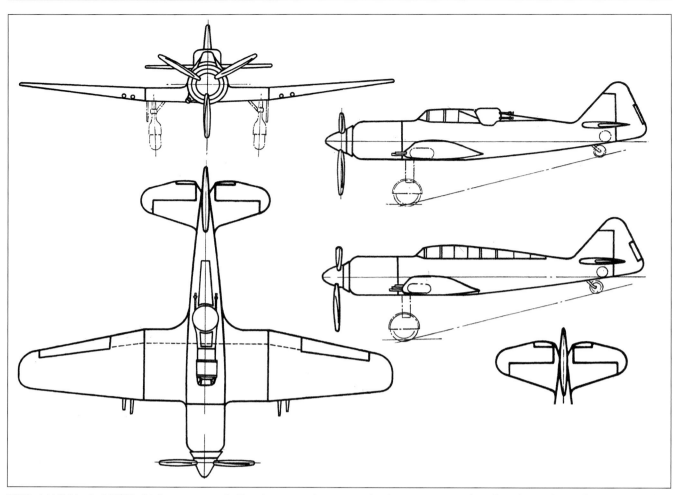

P.96D night fighter to F.18/40 with four cannon and a Type A turret or six cannon and radar operator. Note the enlarged trim tabs on elevator and rudder to improve radar operator's extra input on the six-cannon machine.

Model of the radial-engined P.96D.

Full-size mock-up of the P.96D using a real Defiant fuselage clad forwards with plywood.

P.97

While the P.96 was offered as suitable for night fighter defence over Britain, the P.97 to the same specification was intended to have twin Napier sabre NS6SM engines for improved safety when over Britain and as an intruder over Europe. Again two versions were offered, the P.97A had a conventional radar operator installed in a raised cockpit well behind the pilot or the alternate option of a radar operator immediately behind the pilot in the nose, while the P.97B replaced the radar operator with a gunner and Type A turret. It was intended that either version could be employed in the field by modular conversion of the specific airframe at squadron level. The radar operator's position (forward or aft) was, however, expected to be chosen prior to the design progressing to flight.

P.97A night fighter to F.18/40 with six cannon.

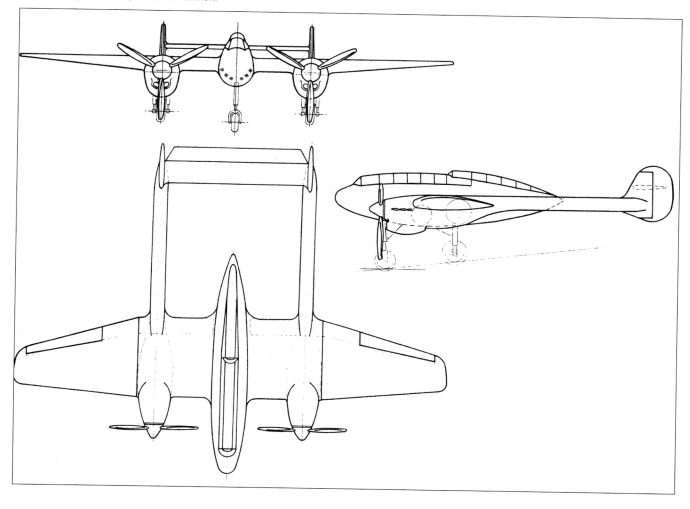

Tunnel model of the P.97A with forward radar operator's position.

A central podded fuselage, twin-boom layout with twin fins and rudders with a high-set horizontal tailplane between the fins was chosen. The undercarriage was tricycle type with a nosewheel retracting between the cannon bay. Although the specification called for only two cannon with a turret, the firm commented that it was well within the capabilities of the aircraft to carry both six cannon and the four-gun turret simultaneously, so that is what was proposed, but with rapid conversion by removing the four central cannon to revert to a twin-cannon machine. Similarly, modular conversion as a light bomber was possible with a bomb aimer's position if the AI operator

was accommodated directly behind the pilot. Internal bombs could be used in the place of the central four cannon. As with the P.96, the radar operator was to be equipped with the ability to add control adjustment to follow his target over the autopilot system while the pilot was searching for visual contact. As with the P.82 and P.96 series, the Type A turret was given a forward position where it could, if required, be fired by the pilot. This 'no-allowance' position was at the standard elevation firing directly forwards, although it would have been perfectly feasible to operate at 0° forward. Maximum speeds were 425mph without a turret and 418mph with a turret at 34,000ft.

P.97A interior for two seat conventional night fighter with aft radar operator's position.

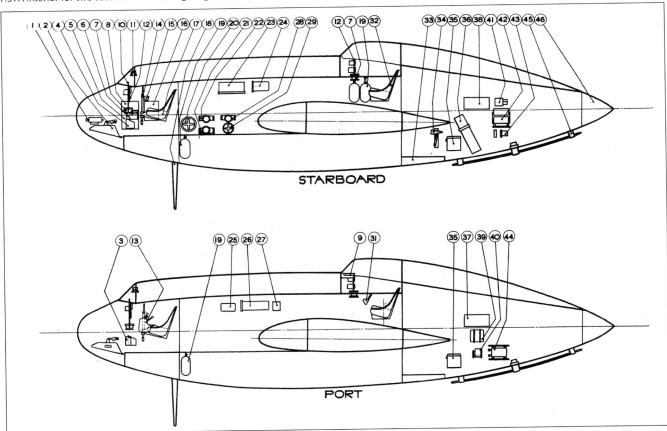

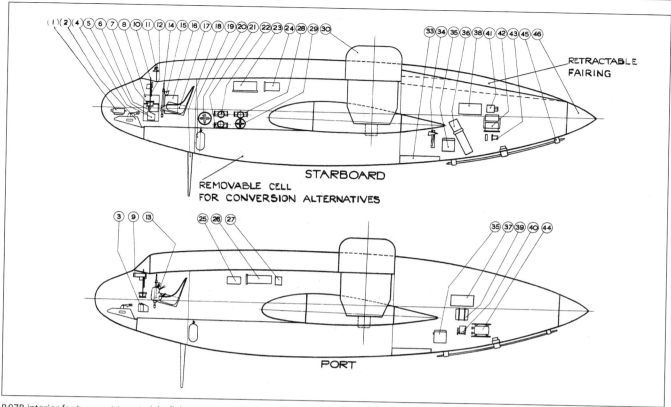

P.97B interior for two-seat turret night fighter.

Interior Details – P.97 series

1. Camera
2. Rudder pedestal
3. De-icing tank port
4. Map case
5. Fixed electrical panel
6. Electrical panel
7. Compass
8. Electrical panel
9. Cathode ray tube AI port
10. Instrument panel
11. Gun sight
12. Flying instrument panel
13. Engine controls port
14. Control column
15. Switchbox identification
16. Electrical panel
17. Pilot's seat
18. Aerial mast W/T
19. Oxygen bottles port and stbd
20. Elevator and rudder unit – auto control
21. Rudder servo – auto control
22. Elevator servo – auto control
23. W/T unit TR1143
24. AI unit control panel
25. Blind approach unit port
26. Receiver AI port
27. Blind approach unit port
28. Aileron servo – auto control
29. Aileron unit – auto control
30. Turret
31. Engine throttle control – AI operator
32. Seat AI operator
33. Service hatch
34. Axe
35. Accumulator port and stbd
36. Flare tube
37. Modulator (or desert equipment) port
38. Transmitter (or desert equipment) port
39. First aid outfit port
40. Master contactor port
41. R3003 unit
42. R3003 unit
43. R3003 unit
44. Blind approach unit port
45. Dipole aerial
46. Dinghy stowage

Perhaps the most unusual feature proposed for the P.97 was the ability to save strategic materials of alloy and steels by manufacture of the identical and interchangeable circular tail booms and fins, plus potentially the tail and outer wing surface, removable panels and the body superstructure in moulded resin plastics and resin-impregnated compressed paper and fabric materials. These had been developed on the Defiant as replacements for metal parts. At this point in time, however, a conventional airframe was schemed. As with the P.96, it was noted that both Sabre and Vulture power egg schemes for interchangeability had been defined for the F.11/37 and previously approved.

The specification F.18/40 and some of the British ideas were studied closely by the USA. Interestingly, the Americans were already looking at a twin-engine night fighter based upon RAF feedback and developed by Northrop, and although independent of the UK, it embodied much of the thinking passed into F.18/40. That machine was the P.61 Black Widow, which, typical of the constraints following a specification, had the same layout as the P.97. Of particular interest looking back at the eventual Northrop Black Widow success was the fact that Liptrot of RDT.1 looked at the BPA design and stated that: 'This type I suggest has no merits for a night fighter and introduces severe structural problems. I have therefore not bothered at this stage to do any performance estimates.'

Gloster modified its F.9/37 aircraft, which was already in prototype form. Other tenderers were the Miles M.22A, Hawker P.1008 and Fairey with a variation of their N.5/40 'Firefly' – only the latter and the BPA proposals being seriously reviewed. The Air Ministry decided not to proceed forward with the specification. All development work on the P.96/P.97 series was finally abandoned by the company in early 1942. Even with the potential for rapid development of the P.96, intrigued 264 Squadron pilots were destined never to receive their anticipated 'Super Defiant'.

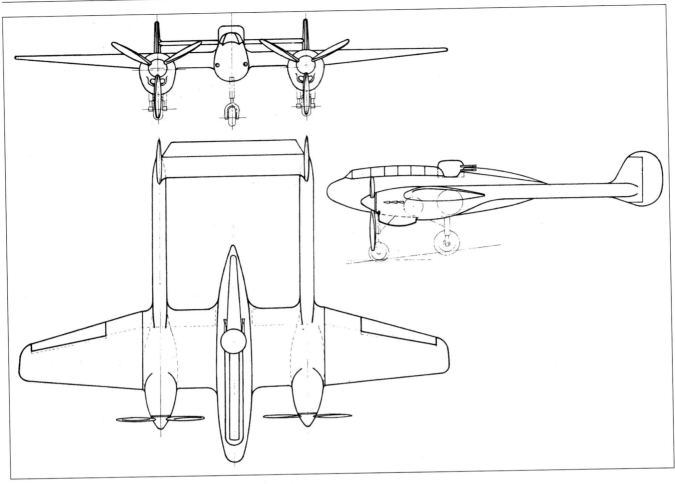

P.97B night fighter to F.18/40 with two cannon and a type A turret.

Tunnel model of the P.97B night fighter intruder.

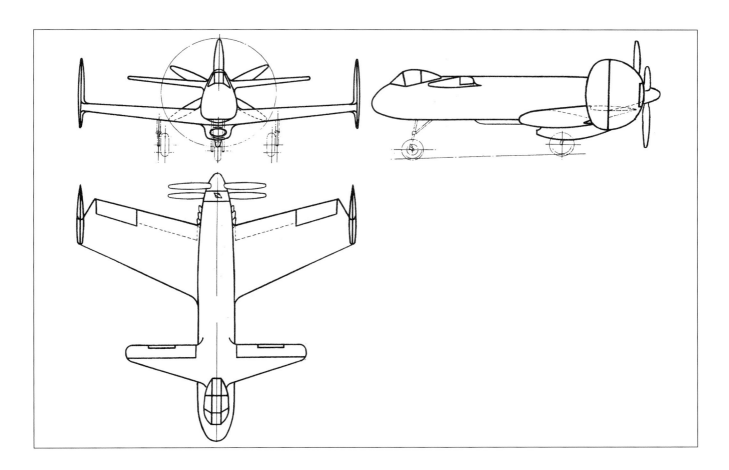

CHAPTER TWENTY-SIX

Light Fighters, Ground Attack and a Short Dalliance with Jets

P.98

SPECIFICATION F.6/42 for a single-engine, single-seat fighter with medium-altitude ability was raised in September 1942. Folland was the suggested contender, but not all were convinced that the team that could be fielded was up to it and other companies were therefore asked for their ideas. Engine choice was limited to Griffon, Centaurus or Sabre, and to save weight less than one hour of internal fuel was required. Companies specifically approached included BPA, Hawker, Vickers and Westland, plus Folland and Airspeed. BPA were looking at draft concepts from early in 1942. With Beaverbrook's insistence that BPA must concentrate design assistance on production of the Defiant variants and support of the Gloster Reaper, few projects had been worked upon since June 1940. With North and his assistants committed on other work by Beaverbrook and Lord the quality of its aircraft proposal submissions fell dramatically. From the P.94 series onwards the beautiful drawings of Hughes and his staff ceased. Any proposal sketches were extremely crude outlines, produced by the female tracers as very basic ideas, with the dimensions only applied by the scale placed on the drawing. The proposal documents also reduced in size. In the case of the P.98 to P.100 series there were no overall dimensions stated in the written proposal copies at all, leaving anyone to sift through government paperwork to glean what the Air Ministry guesses were on sizes. Hence numerous three-views for various engines did not have to be produced and submitted in the first instance. North was too busy to have absolute influence in what detail was finally submitted. The proposals lacked the technical rigour of North, Hughes and Clarke, and interest by the Air Ministry may have suffered because of it. Air Ministry reviewers had to rely on artist's impressions to gain the barest of simplistic views of the few machines offered.

A whole series of designs were considered for the format of F.6/42 leading up to the P.98 variants. No drawings are known to survive of the light fighters. This provisional layout of a single design is based upon the recorded dimensions of one submitted aircraft and the knowledge that it had its wingspan and length enlarged to be resubmitted as the P.100 ground attack machine.

The raising of P.98 was based on a Griffon engine and, as with the P.99/P.100, initially had no allocated specification, having only unnumbered bare details and generalised enquiries. When given the formal F.6/42 request via Rowe, BPA initially wrote to say they thought that all existing engines would be too weak for the specification. They could only see a sensible approach with a Sabre on a tail-first aircraft, although they thought that this would be a good lightweight fighter. Government feedback disagreed with BPA assumptions and felt the machine would be overweight. North insisted on an internal second look at the problem. The company therefore came back on 8 September 1942 with a very brief standard tractor machine (Griffon or Centaurus), probably based on the P.96C at reduced size but with a laminar wing, along with contra-rotating propeller machines carrying a Sabre or Griffon. Any proposal drawings of these types no longer exist but the company allocated the suffix letters A, B and C to the initial three types.

The two key BPA P.98 selections used by Liptrot for comparison with others in mid-September were a 33ft-span, Griffon-engined, tail-first aircraft of 225sq ft area and 8,861lb (39.4lb/sq ft). Fitted with a contra-rotating pusher airscrew of 11ft 6in, it would achieve an estimated 440mph at 20,000ft. The larger 34ft 6in-span Sabre machine had 247sq ft area and 9,892lb (40.05lb/sq ft). The airscrew was larger at 12ft 6in but achieved 446mph at 20,000ft. The overall length was thought to be about 35ft. All of the tractor machines were slower, between 414 and 437mph at the same height. All the P.98 designs aimed at about 40lb/sq ft loading. The company argued that this was so as to be able to turn inside the current Focke-Wulf Fw 190.

Liptrot's interest was such that he did not even bother to check the size calculations or performance of the BPA canard machines using his own RDT.1 staff or his personal formulae, taking the company figures as rote and concentrating instead on the submissions from Westland, Supermarine and Folland. In his opinion all BPA designs selected in the series were 'far too advanced for service use' at the current time. Liptrot commented that he did not intend to waste his time and investigate any of the BPA machines further. The conventional airframes were totally ignored and unlisted, although they were similar to the Folland offering. It was hardly a fair study. As it was, machinations around F.6/42 continued into 1943. The specification was referred to in relation to many variations of existing designs and the Folland F.117 contra-prop tractor machine with Centaurus was ordered in September 1943, but with English Electric to build the six prototypes. However, the F.117 did not progress from drawing board to hardware and F.6/42 was abandoned.

P.99 to P.100 Low Attack

One of the few specifications to which the company did respond, again with no reference number, was described simply as a 'Low Attack Aircraft' and initially issued in early 1942. The need perceived the replacement of the Hurricane IID in the ground attack and anti-tank role. Heavier armament than two 40mm cannon, more manoeuvrability and ease of sighting the target were key requirements and the machine need not be finished to high standard externally. Low weight and simple construction was required, but suitable for worldwide use. Even wooden construction and a fixed undercarriage would be considered. The machine design had to be in production by January 1944. The maximum speed should be around 280mph or more, with 200mph during attack in daylight and 90mph for attack in night conditions. The loaded range must be over 750 miles. Despite the highest performance possible outside the attack regimes being requested, landing runs were still maintained as the Air Ministry standard. It was also thought that all the weapons should be grouped together for concentration of fire, and the need for excellence of view for the pilot would suggest a nacelle location, which it might be

expected would preclude a single-engine aircraft. The cannon should be four 20mm; or two 40mm and two 20mm; or three 40mm Vickers S; or one 47mm and two 20mm. In addition, six rockets or two 500lb bombs, 500lb SCI containers or bomb containers should be carried, or two auxiliary fuel tanks.

P.99

With the designs already likely to be put forward by BPA for the P.98 it was obvious that one solution was to utilise a single-engine pusher or canard, the forward fuselage of which would become the 'nacelle' for the pilot and underfloor weapons tray. The P.99 with Griffon II therefore again used the unusual variations studied but not necessarily all drawn for the P.98. It required an area of 360sq ft and span of 44ft 8in to lift the heavier cannons and bomb load of a ground attack machine because of the choice of Griffon engine. This was a pusher but not a canard, utilising twin booms holding a central cruciform tailplane, at the bottom of which was the tailwheel. The machine was considered by BPA as an orthodox monoplane and could suffer only from breakdown of turbulent flow over the tail, or rotational components in the slipstream. Both of these had been proven not to occur in wind tunnel tests, the latter because of the use of contra-props. Tail flutter at high speed in the Lockheed P-38 Lightning had been identified as stiffness problems and adverse pressure gradients plus disturbed radiator flow aft of maximum camber of the wings. These would not occur in the P.99, BPA argued.

The choice of tailwheel versus tricycle led to a tailwheel to allow operations from advanced landing fields. Plastics would be used for components as far as necessary if judged suitable. Proposed pilot ejection to avoid the rear propeller was by the entire fuselage floor being blown away and rotating backwards at a point behind the wing root. At a point in the jettison the pivoting weapons tray carrying the pilot's floor would reach the end of its hinge movement and the frangible fuselage skin behind the floor would be crushed as the floor ripped away and flew backwards. In the meantime, the pilot would automatically have been released to fall downwards away from the aircraft while the aircraft, relieved of some 2,700lb of structure and pilot weight, would lift upwards away from the escapee.

Loads suggested were four 20mm; or two 40mm and two 20mm; or three 40mm Vickers S; one 47mm and two 20mm. Also to be carried were eight rockets or two 500lb bombs, SCI containers or bomb containers, or two auxiliary fuel tanks.

The proposal text noted that the rocket installation drawn was subject to high drag (being the normal rail launch system used for the Typhoon) and that careful development might yield much simpler suspension and launch methods, depending on how accurately the rockets needed to be discharged. At 13,700lb AUW the wing loading was 38lb/sq ft, giving 282mph at sea level, 291mph at 3,000ft and 315mph at 17,000ft. Up to 3,000ft the climb rate was 1,775ft/min and on emergency boost 2,140ft/min. Liptrot, investigating for RDT.1, felt that the use of the Griffon (brought over from the P.98) was overkill and resulted in a much larger machine than necessary. He also criticised the employment of elaborate means to save the pilot as an unnecessary adornment. Tied mentally to performance and weight, he was unperturbed by the risks of baling out of a pusher aircraft with a rear propeller.

P.100

As an alternative to the P.99, a true canard version of the P.98 was enlarged in span to carry heavier weapons, rockets and bombs. The same RR Griffon II and contra-prop was utilised. The propeller blade diameter was the same as for the P.98 at 11ft 6in. No areas appeared in the brochure but a wing loading of 40lb/sq ft is stated and a

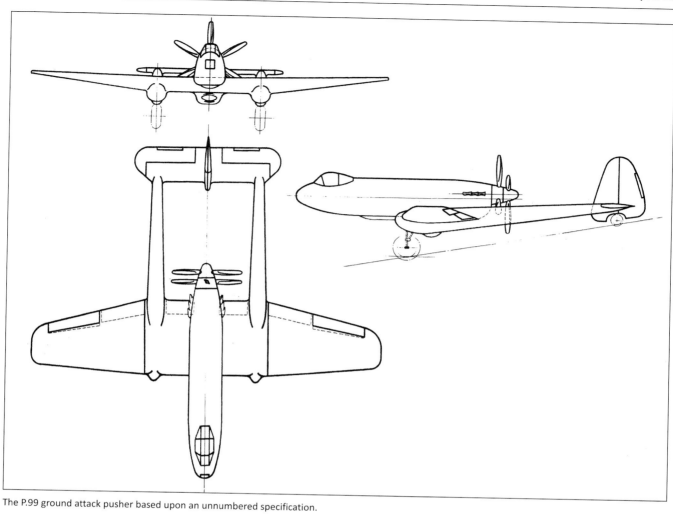

The P.99 ground attack pusher based upon an unnumbered specification.

Artist's impression of the P.99.

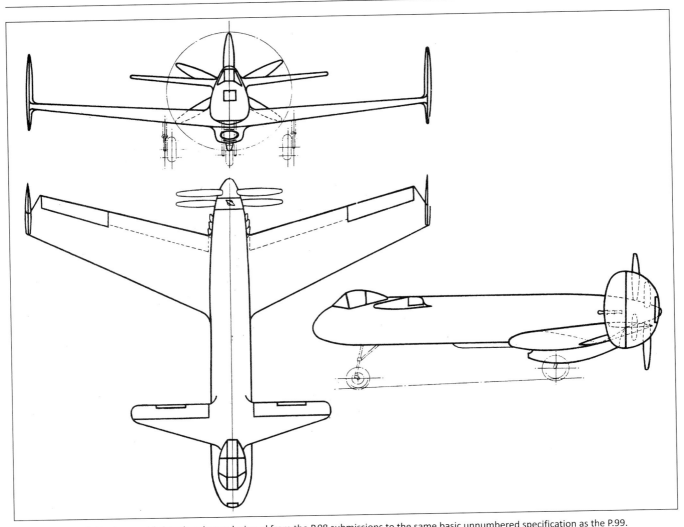

The P.100 ground attack canard fighter bomber redesigned from the P.98 submissions to the same basic unnumbered specification as the P.99.

Artist's impression of the P.100.

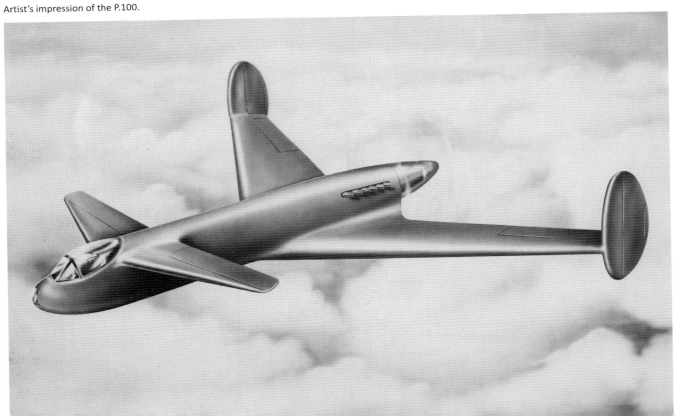

performance calculation weight of 13,450lb, which gives an area of 336.25sq ft, while Avia documents give a weight of 13,150lb (from a different part of the brochure dealing with weight estimates, not the performance summary) but areas of 270sq ft wing and 67sq ft foreplane – giving a comparison of 337sq ft total lifting area. The span of the main wing was stated in the official reviews as 40ft 2in and the foreplane (stabiliser) span as 20ft. All Liptrot's assumptions were based upon the three 40mm gun package.

The main difficulty in studying brochures or glass plates produced for the figure numbers was the inaccuracy of the crude tracings. The drawn span appears to be approximately around 41ft 2in on plan and front-view drawings. The poor tracing of the side and plan make it difficult to check accurately the fuselage length, which comes out on original prints as 36ft 2in. The best sketch in the brochure was Fig. 4, an internal equipment fuselage side view, which had a length of exactly 35ft including the spinner. It is thought that this internal side section was taken as a duplicate from the P.98 proposal and is the fuselage design length of the P.98 lightweight fighter.

While the P.98/P.100 was being rejected as too advanced for the specifications, Miles were building a flying scale model of exactly the same layout in the M.35 Libellula and offering their own canard designs. It was considered that the canard-type aircraft offered the best layout to solve the problems of the specification but that the length of time required to develop such a type would preclude it from being available. The most favoured design was the Armstrong Whitworth A.W.49, which was similar in layout to the P.99 but had the armament spread in fuselage and wings and no contra-prop propeller.

P.101

The P.101 was again a ground attack machine alternative to the P.99 and P.100. The paper request had been for a machine that could be designed or adapted to ground attack rapidly. It had to be conceived, made and in service by early 1944, and to carry heavier armament than the Hurricane IID. Obviously it was an almost impossible task for any bidder unless something could be adapted. The company stated that the main reason for putting forward the P.101 design was that it satisfied the specification requirements as regards service date, simplicity and size to be in production by January 1944. Because a biplane would be more manoeuvrable and taking the fixed undercarriage as a hint, in order to carry the heavy weapons the company suggested a design using two Defiant wings sandwiching a large radial-engined fuselage to produce a strut-less biplane. The design used a Bristol Centaurus 12SM engine modified for low attack duties and the two Defiant wings were backward staggered so as to give the pilot maximum visual arcs. The undercarriage was buried in very large spats so that the heavy weapons could be carried within the spats either side of the oleo legs. All three wheels of the undercarriage were therefore non-retractable.

Method of pilot escape from the P.99 and P.100 submissions.

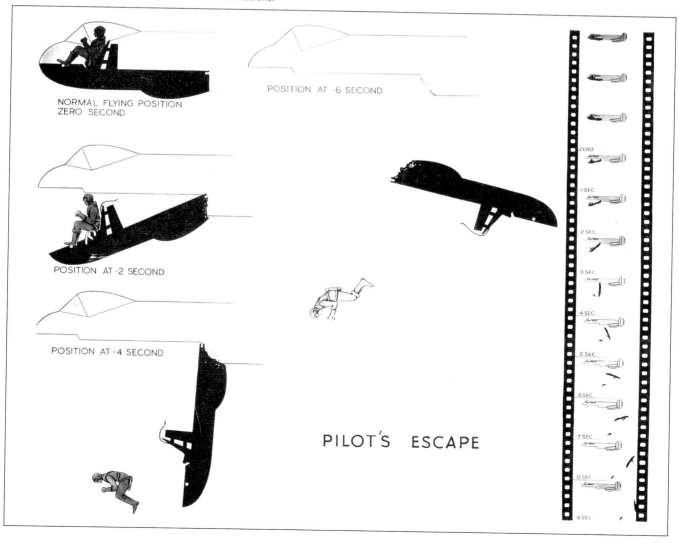

NORMAL FLYING POSITION
ZERO SECOND

POSITION AT ·6 SECOND

POSITION AT ·2 SECOND

POSITION AT ·4 SECOND

PILOT'S ESCAPE

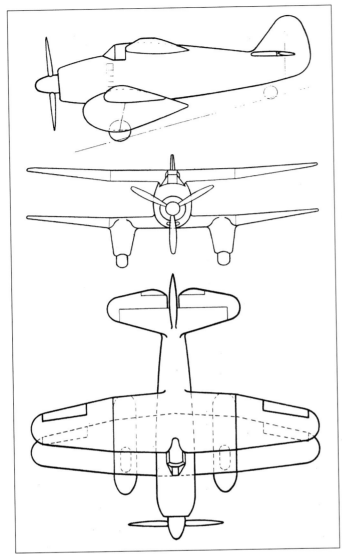

The P.101 heavy assault ground attack aircraft utilised two whole Defiant wings in an attempt to get a robust machine that could be produced in the impossibly short timescale set.

design BPA also included a separate larger drawing of the biplane's outline aimed at clarifying the layout. While seemingly a step backwards, R N Liptrot wrote in December 1942 that the design would certainly be available sooner than the other studies.

Abandonment of the Low Attack Specification

DTD argued, in an about-turn when returning the circulated drawings internally, that there was no rush to develop these designs as the Hurricane IV would suffice for the moment while other designs were being studied for adaption to the requirement and this precluded the need to develop new machines. One such design was the fitting of two 40mm cannon to the Mosquito and ultimate conversion to take the six-pounder gun and underwing rockets (unrotated projectiles or UP). The second was the development of a low attack wing for the Mustang and retrofit to Mustang airframes. Ultimately by 1944 the RAF made use of all of its existing developed fighters but specifically the Typhoon and Tempest for land duties and the twin-engine Beaufighter and Mosquito for anti-shipping.

P.97 Low Attack Variant

One other possible development studied by BPA during that period turned towards Liptrot's opinion that a twin-engine design was warranted for low attack duties despite its increase in size. The BPA choice seems to be more of a powered gun mount approach than a specific airframe, although the illustrations utilised a variation of the twin-engine P.97 as a possible aircraft to describe the weapon mount. It is quite possible that this was one variation of DTD's twin 40mm Mosquito, but where the guns were not a fixed mounting. The initial introduction of the low attack specification stated the machine was to be used in 'operation against military forces on the ground, aircraft, invasion craft and shipping … destruction of tanks and similar targets'. The company went right back to the ideas of the P.31A and the initial thoughts of a possible single-seat 'Novel' fighter attacking bombers with the idea of pilot-controlled guns. These large 20mm or 40mm weapons were to be installed in the nose of suitable aircraft either side of the pilot-gunner nacelle.

The large panoramic canopy was supported by a central window in the nose, giving a similar view ahead and down to the attack windows in the P.99 and P.100. A special spectacle type control column allowed the pilot to fly the aircraft and select and control the guns. The package had a pilot selection system via a small computer that auto-trained the position of the weapons to the relationship between the attacker and the target. The weapons had high elevation and depression angles so that the aircraft could attack while simply flying level, rather than having to undertake the dangerous dives at the target, and could be given limited traverse. Strafing a column of tanks or U-boats was therefore simply a matter of overflying them. In air-to-air combat the elevation would allow the pilot/gunner to fire inside the turning circle of the enemy. Once target firing commenced the computer maintained the variable bearing on the target point until the pilot chose the next target.

Nothing came of these suggestions so neither the machine nor the pilot-controlled weapons were built at the time. However, the concept became the Type G gun turret system mock-up post-war. The computer idea was part of a number of North's tests on hull motion simulation and control of a turret fitted to a tank. Army requests for such a system to be developed for British tanks came to nought when MAP objected to the diversion of BPA turret resources to help the Army. They stated that turret work at BPA 'was a MAP domain and the work was by far too important to waste effort on the Army'.

As the Vickers 47mm gun was unlikely to be available in time, it was left out of the provisioning, but all others could be accommodated outside the airscrew disc. For better view by the pilot the Centaurus 12SM was drawn in with down thrust giving a 15° view down from the horizontal. Rocket racks sat under the wings and bomb racks or a long-range tank were fitted under the fuselage. Construction was to use many parts drawn directly from Defiant stock; the entire Defiant wings would be used and the tail unit would be scaled up from the Defiant design. While Defiant raw materials and extrusions would be used for the fuselage, the new design could still use existing Defiant jigs for basic fuselage manufacture using the unit construction principle developed for the Defiant.

A weight of 15,200lb was used for performance calculations, giving a low wing loading of 37lb/sq ft and maximum speeds of 285mph at sea level, rising to 294mph at cab rank loiter altitude of 3,000ft, and a top speed of 317mph at 18,000ft. Normal climb rate up to 3,000ft was calculated as 1,470ft/min but with emergency boost a rate of 2,200ft/min was achievable. Cruise speed in the case of reinforcing flight was not decided because of lack of data on the Centaurus cruise power from Bristol Aeroplane Co. In submitting the

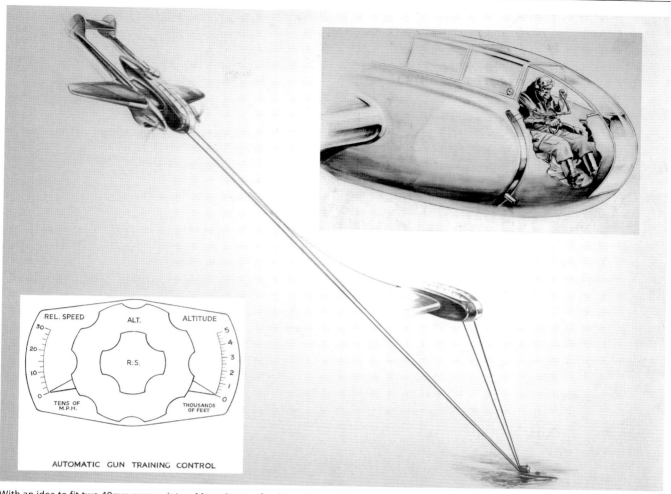

With an idea to fit two 40mm cannon into a Mosquito as a fixed installation doing the rounds of the Air Ministry, North's team had already come up with this concept for a twin 20mm or 40mm pilot-controlled nose armament. Once the pilot had started the aiming sequence an electro-mechanical computer kept the weapon firing on the selected target through changes in elevation until the pilot switched targets. The P.97 airframe was used as an example of such a mounting.

P.102

No drawings or data remain of the P.102. According to the omnibus listing, the P.102 was a single-seat jet fighter design with a W2B engine. It should not be confused with the 'Jet Barracuda', which was a very short-lived conversion project. Most probably the P.102 did not get past a basic layout. Discussions with drawing office staff from the time in the early 1970s suggest perhaps a laminar flow P.103-like planform with a jet fuselage. It should be stressed, however, that at that time nothing remained and North's personal file 'Jet Propulsion Projects 1944' had already been sanitised of most project information, leaving only the correspondence on the Barracuda described below.

Jet Barracuda (Project not numbered)

MAP correspondence dated 26 February 1944 to the company asked if BPA could carry out a study involving the Fairey Firefly naval fighter. It was desired that a jet engine be fitted within the rear fuselage as a method of boosting the overall speed so that cruise and search range could be obtained from the piston engine and fighting attack speed from the jet addition. North wrote back that he was wary of taking on the Firefly airframe as the study subject. North was not happy to deal with a new outside aircraft company in the light of the very poor support from Hawker on N.22/43. His feeling was that a

similar negative relationship with Fairey would ensue in the contraction of contracts as the war ran down. He suggested the Barracuda as a jet project since all details were already available for the Mk.II and III without commitment from Fairey. Unknown to North, Fairey had already partially undertaken such a study themselves as a new design similar to a low-winged Barracuda to S.11/43 as early as June 1943, but had since been told to concentrate on piston-engine projects by DTD. It was the DTD's opinion that other firms with less strategic commitments had the capacity to carry out such studies without hindering basic development.

Brochures were sent to MAP on the Jet Barracuda on 15 May, based upon the Mk.II with Merlin 32 and W2B/37 jet engine – BPA would already have had available a basic outline of this engine for the P.102. A letter on 26 May 1944 from MAP confirmed that the design submitted for the Jet Barracuda was not as required. What was required was a Mk.V Barracuda with a W2/700 engine. A further letter on 29 May confirmed that the aim was purely and simply to 'double-bank' the Blackburn Firebrand as an alternative in case that project failed. North tried to get W2/700 data but was delayed by the secrecy surrounding jet engines. Despite all of North's efforts and authority, since the engine or even Barracuda V information could not be obtained in the short term allowed, the project stalled and was not completed.

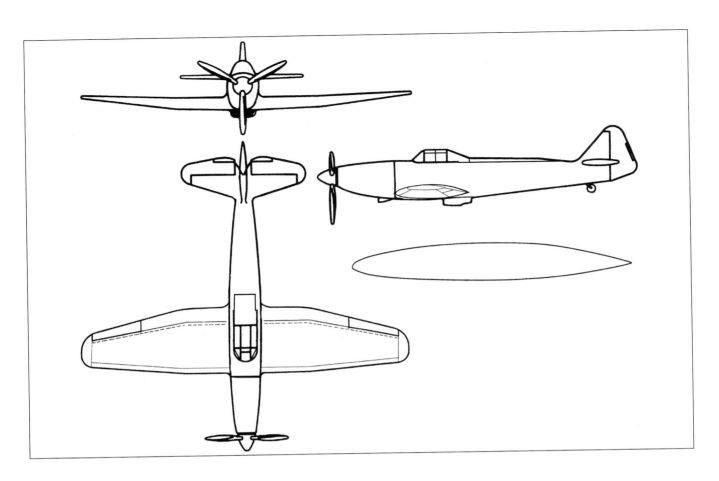

CHAPTER TWENTY-SEVEN

Laminar-Flow Aerofoils

NORTH, CLARKE and Dr Seymour Cunningham Redshaw, Chief Engineer of BPA, were aware of the properties of laminar flow sections since one of the early production attempts at achieving laminar flow was the Mustang, an aircraft that North admired greatly. However, it was clear from his own experiments that achieving true laminar flow compared with simply utilising a laminar section was another matter entirely. The first attempt at a whole laminar wing design was as early as the beginning of 1941, when an enquiry from RAE suggested the construction of a new EC/EQ type wing that could be tested on one of their Defiant aircraft. The internal details allocated were under reference 4978 and Aes 1790, utilising an EC1650/1550 section with 18 to 9% thickness taper. BPA advised MAP and RAE how difficult it was to ensure a completely smooth surface and the desirability of having as few rows of rivets in a span-wise direction on the forward half as possible to ensure the laminar state. The advantage of the Defiant aircraft was the method of how the entire wing was fitted by having the fuselage placed over it, requiring only a spacer piece. The centre section of the Defiant planform was reduced in span and the outer wing increased so that the wing area was slightly lower at 232sq ft compared with a traditional BPA fighter wing of 250–260sq ft. It was forecast that the new wing would drop the drag of that surface by 26% (0.0273 reduced to 0.0202) and increase the level speed of the aircraft. It was hoped to test the wing up to around 550mph by strengthening the pilot's hood and tailplane.

To ensure a smooth surface, the method suggested by the BPA Chief Designer, H. V. Clarke, was to mould over the entire external surface or part surface with plastic resin sheeting, to cover any defects. While BPA continued with the basic design and manufacture of the pure metal wing, RAE were to consider funding a second wing covered in such a sheet of material. It appears that the test wing sample was completed to a usable stage and the sample was tested by RAE for strength. By then a new method of achieving a smooth surface had already been proven without riveting from leading edge to 72% of chord by stringers being attached to the 14 SWG-thick skin by thread cutting screws from inside, subsequently any emerging points being ground off to finish flush. Good joints were then possible at the leading edge and at 72% (the attachment point of ailerons), having been proven by ARC Report 6436/Ae.2147/Struct.649. All ailerons and flaps were conventionally riveted but covered in stretched metal to minimise distortion under load.

The laminar wing Defiant planned by RAE with an enlarged approximate wing section based upon the RAE EQ1650/1550 series section derived by alteration of NACA0015.

A Xylonite model of the laminar wing structure finally decided upon during the design of the Defiant laminar wing project. Upper and lower halves are joined by long bars through hinge joints, with leading edge and flaps/ailerons added front and rear.

Full-size test piece of the experimental EQ 1650/1550 laminar flow section with a completely smooth centre portion for flow tests. The centre has the highly polished cured fabric/resin coating proposed by BPA.

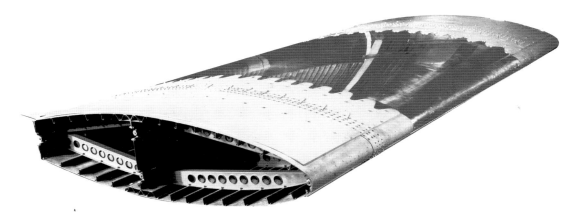

The contract SB.27528/C.38b was completed for a cost of £6,000 against a government agreement of £3,000 fixed price, the difference being absorbed by the company in overheads up to the end of July 1945.

Between 1941 and the war end BPA also continued to study the manufacture of scale models of structures in a clear plastic material called Xylonite. A Xylonite model of the optimal structural wing design post-1943 was manufactured. It consisted of an upper and lower half to which the leading edge was pinned and trailing edge flaps and ailerons were attached. The two halves had a central vertical spar at approximately mid-chord. Connection was by inserting long rods through interlocking tubes to hold the parts as a piano hinge. The exercise resulted in improved internal designs of how such a wing might be constructed but the P.103, P.105 and P.107 series utilised NACA laminar sections rather than the RAE EC/EQ studies. The company was destined to employ these NACA sections but with conventional riveted construction in the P.108/109 series. There was no airframe project number ever allotted for the laminar wing/Defiant combination.

P.103 and P.104

The P.103 and P.104 were designs against the draft specification series N.7/43, subtitled '1943 Supplementary Programme', for a single-seat, single-engine naval fighter to operate worldwide. The key requirement was comparable speed to the RAF fighters in development. AUW was to be kept as low as possible and the height with tail down limited to 17ft. 'Folding wings must result in an aircraft capable of being folded and spread within 20 feet and to do so and be hoisted in wind speeds of 35 knots.' Take-off against a 17-knot headwind required an absolute maximum of a 500ft run. Landing with two-thirds engine power must have an approach speed of about 75 knots. Notwithstanding a small fuel load internally, auxiliary (drop) tankage was to be the maximum possible. Any British engine could be used but a radial was preferred. There was to be four cannon armament with an average 150 rounds per gun. A standard carrier drawing was supplied in which to work out a stowage pattern.

A number of companies seized the opportunity to study the scenario. The quality of new proposal content reflected the return of North to overview of the submissions, although some sketches included continued to be very basic because of wartime constraints. Other designs started by rival companies were the P.1022, Sea Fury X, Westland N.7/43 Griffon or turbojet variants and the Folland 118. BPA were already working on the requirement prior to the formal release of N.7/43. North had approached Hawker Siddeley about submitting a tender based upon modification of their Hawker Tempest/Fury aircraft rather than a BPA new design. On 14 April 1943 he wrote again to appraise them of the fact that the N.7/43 tender had been updated as a design study with weight, performance and an outline drawing to be submitted by 24 April. The update also insisted that the design be based upon a Griffon engine. Hawker Siddeley replied on the 26th of the month suggesting that he should proceed as advised for the new submission date and forget any question of modifying an existing Hawker type based around another engine as this would be almost as difficult to modify as producing his own ab initio design. Unknown to North, Hawker were being crafty, stringing him along and already submitting their own Sea Fury X aircraft in direct competition to North's plan.

The own-design P.103 brochure was proceeded with and finally despatched to MAP on 22 May 1943, complying with N.7/43 (Issue II). Crossing over in correspondence, a letter was received from MAP dated 20 May 1943 stating that N.7/43 had been abandoned as a Type. There would therefore be no new design and MAP would endeavour to meet requirements with the development of existing designs. At the same time the company received a formal typed copy of N.7/43 dated the same 20 May 1943. The P.103 was therefore dead even before the full brochure reached MAP. Although BPA updated their P.103 brochure to the new 20 May 1943 amendment one presumes that it was a record copy as it was the initial issue with an amendment slip in the rear and no updated charts.

Taking as a basis one of the early schemes for F.6/42 and developing it as a laminar wing carrier fighter resulted in the P.103, seen here in the A version.

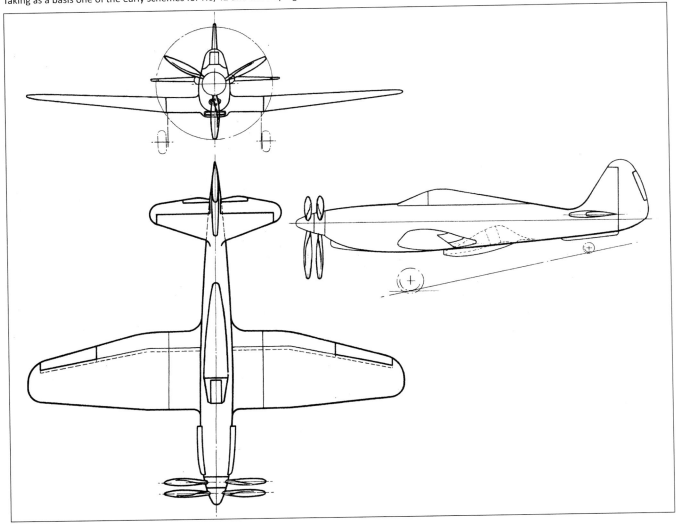

Artist's impression of the P.103A.

The P.103 layout was based upon standard format of a tractor monoplane with two versions. The specification wanted aircraft of the lowest weight but the highest performance, which could not be achieved in the same aeroplane as the two requirements were somewhat mutually exclusive. The criteria of highest performance was taken. It also suggested a radial air-cooled engine, the Admiralty favourite, but an optimum performance above 25,000ft. Again these were mutually exclusive requirements at this stage of engine development. The April 1943 draft specification amendment changed this to Griffon 61. (The 20 May 1943 specification says 'any engine … with alternatives' making the changes even more confusing). It was felt best to submit two versions of the design. The P.103A utilised a Griffon RG5SM engine, while the P.103B utilised the Centaurus CE.12SM and, because the time allowed for submission did not allow for two full sets of documents, the one brochure was to cover both, with the superior performance Griffon variant taken as the lead design in drawings where the details of both were common. Both engine types were to be power eggs and contra-prop installations. For cooling of the Griffon, an under-fuselage radiator scoop was added below and aft of the fuselage fuel tanks and the radiator was buried within the fuselage. In the event of ditching, the scoop was to have frangible mountings so that it would break away rather than force the aircraft under the surface.

The advantages of the Griffon were the use of a smaller undercarriage to obtain an over-nose view on landing and with its highly flapped wings the approach could be shallow where the shorter undercarriage was an advantage. The wing was 'Defiant-like' in planform, roughly conforming to the experimental BPA/RAE laminar wing, but utilised NACA 66-2-216 aerofoil section varying from 20% thick at the centreline down to 12% at the tips. With the supercharging height of the engine at 24,000ft a good performance was available at 25,000ft. The Centaurus allowed less cooling system design and could allow less armour protection, plus it gave more static waiting time if there was prolonged deck running while awaiting the carrier to turn into wind. The Centaurus all-around performance was better from take-off up to 15,000ft, being more of a low-altitude engine. The actual speeds were not stated within the brochure but had to be gleaned from within the performance curves. The best turning circles in combat controlled the design. The Griffon P.103A was predicted at 463mph at 28,000ft, rising from 404mph over the range 7,000ft to 15,500ft. The Centaurus P.103B gave 435mph at 23,000ft, rising from 405mph at 9,000ft and 402mph at 15,000ft.

The wing was to have a large full-span box spar with stressed skins and to be created in thick formed sheet so that it did not require stringers and only the minimum of ribs fitted by rivet countersinking and not by dimpling the skin. In this manner it was hoped that the outer surface would retain a smoothness and cleanliness required for laminar flow to operate efficiently. The leading edge extrusion had upper and lower skins leading to the box spar and the spar would follow the generating lines of the wing surface. The tailplane was again of Defiant planform and identical in size to the Defiant unit but the material sizes were increased and fitted with a matching metal-covered elevator system as per RAE studies. The Defiant structural detail was to be used for manufacture. For carrier operations the undercarriage was retractable via a hydraulic system and similarly the tailwheel, but the latter via mechanical linkages to reduce vulnerability. The wings were to be hydraulic power folding, first rotating forwards until approaching vertical and then folding backwards to lie along the fuselage. This was changed from manual at the last minute.

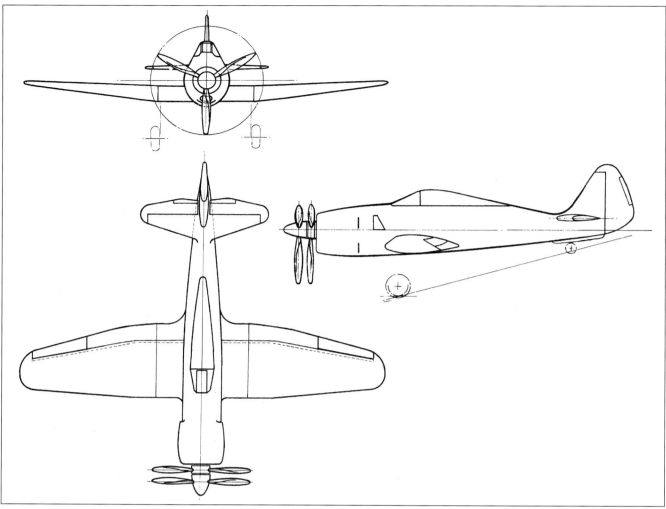

The P.103B was a radial-engine version of the same airframe.

Artist's impression of the P.103B.

Two 20mm cannon per wing were carried just outboard of the propeller arc and the ammunition could be replenished with the outer wings folded since the fold was inboard of the cannon, not on the planform break of the wing. Both versions had the same span of 38ft 8in and folded to a width of 13ft 10in. The length was 36ft 4in for the P.103A at 250sq ft area and 10,221lb AUW. The P.103B was 37ft long, and the wing chord was increased to give 260sq ft at 11,180lb AUW. Forty-four of the P.103 machines could be stowed within the standard carrier deck, four abreast.

P.104

As an alternative to the P.103, the company looked at the P.104. This was a tail-first pusher with a Griffon engine and contra-props. Although no drawings or documents remain It is most likely that the P.98 and P.100 design layouts were utilised to offer a similar tail first (ie canard) design – a hooked P.98 with perhaps an arrester hook forward of the air scoop under the fuselage. Exactly how the wing folding might have been accomplished is unknown and after earlier criticism by Liptrot on the P.98–P.100 series the P.104 was quickly abandoned at the drawing board to concentrate only on submitting the P.103.

N.7/43 Itself Abandoned

Unfortunately N.7/43 as a specification was also abandoned by pooling the requirements of N.7/43 and F.2/43. F.2/43 had been issued to Hawker May 1943 for six Fury prototypes with three differing engines, which had already been ordered two months earlier. By the pooling of the two a production specification 22/43/H was raised for Hawker to build two prototypes of its F.2/43 Fury fighter as naval prototypes. After all of the BPA design studies, the Air Ministry quite liked the idea North had originally of adapting the Hawker Fury and had adopted that approach in their decisions. They rewarded North's foresight by issuing a production run of 300 machines as the Sea Fury X to Boulton Paul in May 1944 as contract SB.27021/C/23a, on the basis that Hawker were too busy with other projects. The first production/prototype was to be VB857.

Hawker were not happy with the subcontract after their subterfuge and delayed collaboration as much as possible by withholding drawings for as long as possible and supplying unsatisfactory parts that had already been rejects from their own manufacture. Although BPA manufactured and part-assembled the components for VB857, with the end of the war with Germany in sight BPA were instructed to hand all materials procured over to Hawker for VB857 and the block-split production range in the sequence TF200 to TF600 series. It was Hawker who finally assembled and flew VB857, while the production materials were absorbed into Hawker product.

P.105

Prompted by the N.7/43 specification and study requirements that spawned the P.103 design, the P.105 was a unique concept at the time. North investigated what might be required to defeat the Japanese over the vast tracts of the Pacific Ocean and how the Royal Navy might view their role of policing the sea from aircraft carriers in the future. It was intended to be the smallest airframe that, by on-board modular conversion, was capable of performing all of the carrier aircraft functions of an air fleet at sea. It was proposed that in this way a greater number of small aircraft and their conversion units could be loaded aboard, thereby increasing the number available for the diverse operations that they were called to accomplish. The high performance of the aircraft was also meant to ensure effective penetration of the enemy defences. The designers chose the Griffon 61 engine with contra-prop propeller, with power wing folding for rapid deployment on deck. Also unique was the use of electric power for elevator tab

trimming and an automatic aiming cycle for bombing and torpedo dropping. The trimming was to be semi-automatic by sensing the load on the elevators and trimming for minimum load when the pilot selected auto-trim by pressing a button on the control column.

The design started with torpedo operations and worked to find the smallest and fastest aircraft capable of carrying a torpedo 500 miles, attacking the target and returning to base. All other potential operations were left as subordinate to that role, leading to a lighter aircraft. The torpedo role was therefore looked at as an unarmed fast machine with minimal radio equipment. This resulted in an aircraft with a fighter performance even when laden with its torpedo. Following North's mathematical approaches, various formulae were derived to control the design. Using formulae and graphs, a weight for the aircraft was chosen followed by a wing loading, and graphs of fuel and wing loading at cruise plotted. Drag and range was estimated for several cruising speeds. Various other graphs were then studied and cross plotted. During these calculations it was decided to abandon the Griffon 61 and to substitute the Centaurus CE12SM radial engine (best power at 9,000ft for low-altitude operations and fuel injected to avoid cutting out in negative G). Fortunately, since all calculations were based upon 12,500lb AUW rather than engine, heavy recalculation was not required and the bulk of the design read across.

The P.105 could be altered on board the carrier to cover any role. The P.105A represents the torpedo attack aircraft.

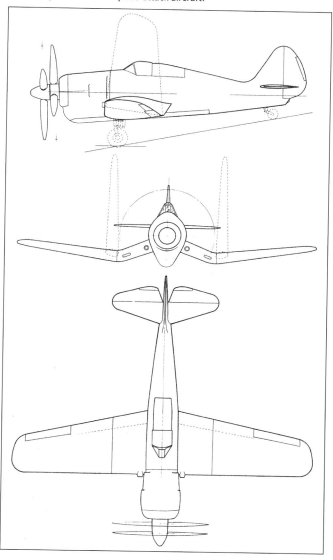

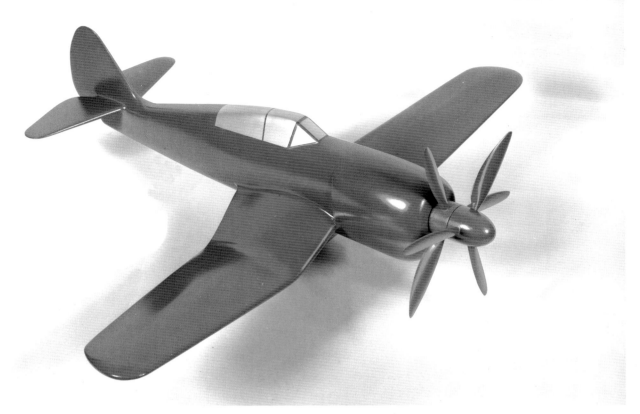

Model of the P.105A torpedo configuration.

A 12ft diameter broad-blade propeller using two × three blades was selected. The final layout was a crank-winged, single-fin monoplane of conventional form with a span of 38ft, a length tail down of 34ft 5in and a height tail down and folded wings of 16ft 11in. Once folded (by upward fold of the outer wings) the width was 15ft 4in. The wing chosen was NACA 65-318-220 section with 8ft 9in chord at the centreline of the aircraft. The tip chord was 4ft 7in and the tip section was NACA 65-318-316. This gave a wing thickness of 20% chord at the centre and 16% at the theoretical tip. The total weight of the torpedo version (AUW) was 12,285lb.

Top speed of the torpedo aircraft gave 463mph (402 knots) at 20,000ft, and 400mph (347 knots) at sea level. When reconfigured as a fighter the top speed was 469mph (407 knots) at 20,000ft and 406mph (352 knots) at sea level. The service ceiling was 30,000ft normally and 32,000ft at combat power. Take-off was 400ft with a deck wind of 27 knots and an overall airflow speed of 85 knots. For dive bombing or decent for the torpedo run the propeller could be used as a dive brake by selecting either windmill or reverse thrust, giving a terminal velocity of 174 knots and 2g deceleration in the dive. This meant the aircraft could drop from 440mph at 6,000ft to 125mph (108 knots) level speed at sea level for the torpedo attack in thirty seconds.

Model of the P.105B recon configuration (with armed rear fuselage).

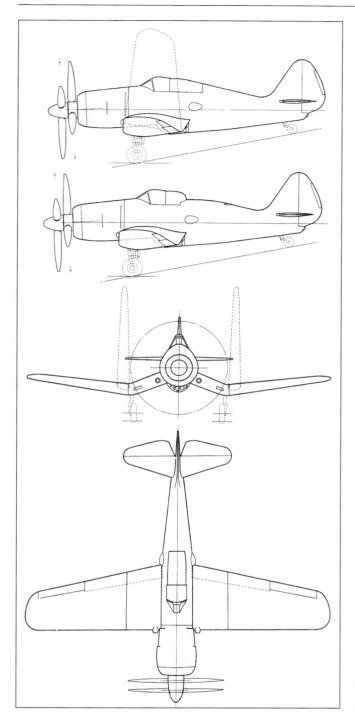

The P.105B reconnaissance aircraft. The lower side view shows the version with a rear defensive armament.

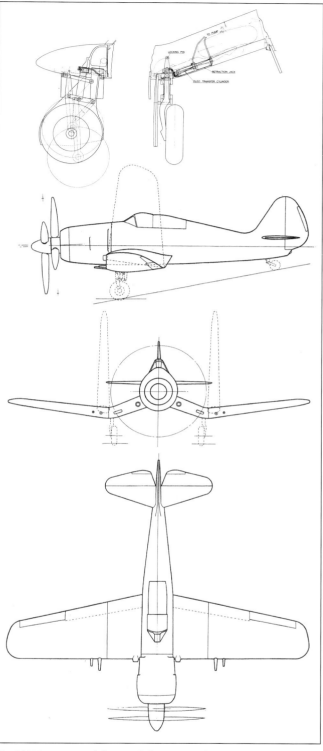

The P.105C represented the pure fighter version for CAP patrol or ground/shipping attack. Larger-scale inset shows the innovative main undercarriage.

The structure of the wing, in order to obtain the laminar-flow capability of the section, required an extremely smooth surface finish; even then only on the outboard wings would the laminar flow be possible. The basic torpedo aircraft was designated P.105A and carried the torpedo internally at the correct launch angle to clear the propellers. All 18in torpedo types including the folding air-tail variant could be carried. The modules A and B fitted for this role were the torpedo housing and launch doors under the belly and the rear extension to the pilot's hood to complete the fuselage streamlining. The bomber variant converted from the P.105A required modules C and B, module C being a lower fuselage fairing containing the bomb

doors and housing for two 1,000lb bombs. The P.105B was the Escort and Reconnaissance (no rear defence) version requiring Module D, a lower fuselage with an observation window, and Module E, an observer's rear canopy and seat behind the pilot. A second P.105B variant was the addition of rear defence in the form of internal 0.5in machine guns aimed by the observer. The two 0.5in guns were pivoted around the muzzle so as to keep their entire swept volume

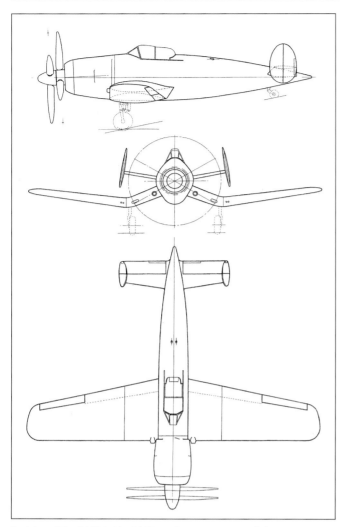

Revision of the P.105 to the P.107 as a long-range escort fighter to escort RAF bombers to Japan and the Japanese-held islands.

within the fuselage and could achieve arcs within +45° elevation, 3°depression and +21.5°either side of aft. This fitting was termed module F. The P.105C was the pure fighter version using Module B as in the P.105A plus a light fairing to seal off the lower fuselage. The P.105C forward weapons (four 0.5in) could, if required, be replaced by two 20mm cannon. It was pointed out, however, that this would considerably compromise the laminar flow of the inboard section of the outer wing and require more complicated structure including the cannon fairing leading edge extensions. The study documents actually looked at the performance losses for all machines and variations in armament.

Plans for the carrier stowage gave Case A, fifty main deck and five extension hangar machines and Case B, forty four main deck and four extension hangar machines. The complete proposals, overlay transparencies and models were submitted in January 1944 but attracted only a study of its features if tried on a Defiant at that stage.

P.107

A spin-off from the P.105 design was the P.107 submitted to DTD in April 1944 as a PV suggestion, which seemed to fall partly on deaf ears. It was based upon one version of the P.105A multi-role carrier aircraft, but reconfigured as a two-seat escort fighter landplane for the escort of long-range bombers, such as Lancaster or Lincoln (FE), from island chains in the Pacific to attack the Japanese mainland and other

enemy-held islands. The airframe used the same fuel-injected Centaurus CE12SM with contra-rotating propellers and differed only from versions of the P.105 by having twin fins and rudders to improve the rear defence fire from the second crew member armed with two 0.5in electro-hydraulically controlled rear weapons with 600 rounds per gun. The guns were pivoted around the muzzle so as to keep their entire swept volume within the fuselage and could achieve arcs within +45°elevation, 3°depression and +27° either side of aft. For forward firing the pilot controlled two 0.5in guns within each outer wing root with 300 rounds of ammunition. For best performance the NACA 65 section was to be particularly smooth over the outer wings. The fully retractable main and tailwheels followed the P.105 design practice. The control surfaces were to use tab operation and the power control method for tab actuation, and trim was again electric push button.

The span was 38ft with an area of 250sq ft. The overall length tail down was 34ft 8in and the overall height tail down was 14ft 5in (over the canopy). The track was 11ft and the same undercarriage as the P.105, which was shorter when retracted than when extended. With a total AUW of 15,900lb and 635 gallons of fuel, 140 gallons of which were carried in external drop tanks, cruising speed was 270mph, rising to 330mph depending upon weight shed. Absolute top speed was 470mph at 22,000ft. A range of 3,000 miles at 25,000ft was predicted after using fuel for take-off, climb to height and thirty minutes at combat power defending the bombers. Without drop tanks the range in the same situation dropped to 2,200 miles. As a single-seat photographic reconnaissance platform without rear gunner and rear defence the range was 3,560 miles with thirty minutes combat and 3,900 miles at fifteen minutes combat. Unarmed the range was 4,250 miles as a photo-reconnaissance aircraft. Configured as a fighter-bomber with bombs on the tank racks the range was 700 miles. Service ceiling was 39,000ft.

Defiant 'Special Features'

The P.105 studies also raised a number of potential details that were relevant to future naval aircraft and a Defiant was again identified as a test aircraft for some of these suggestions. On 14 June 1944, rather than build the P.105 an MoS instruction was placed to build a test aircraft known as the Defiant 'Special Features' under contract t/4227/c.23(a).

1 This machine was to be fitted with a special undercarriage based on note SME7/5195/PAW/61. The essence was that the design was of long travel to absorb the landing shock on carriers and could be pulled up so that it was shorter when retracted to fit in the wing accommodation.
2 The elevator was to be fitted with automatic electric trim tabs selectable by the pilot.
3 The propeller was to be a two × three-blade contraprop with dive brake blade reversal and automatic undercarriage door opening to simulate bomb doors opening in the dive.
4 Auto closure of the simulated doors.
5 Stick force balance on the control column to be introduced as convenient.

By 29 August 1944 it had been agreed that a Mach number meter would be fitted and eventually an automatic observer, which filmed a duplicate instrument panel during flight. The selected trials aircraft was Mark II Defiant serial AA413, which would be fitted with a Merlin 22 engine with a two × three-blade contra-prop system of 8ft 5in diameter. Optimum centre of gravity was regained by the fitment of special weights on pegs in the rear fuselage. A series of fin outlines were also wind tunnel tested, increasing in height and ranging from 21.9 to 32.5sq ft, with the tallest version being chosen for the modifications. The design work dragged on through 1944 into 1945. TT Mk.I DR895 was also used to test motorised electric elevator tabs and an

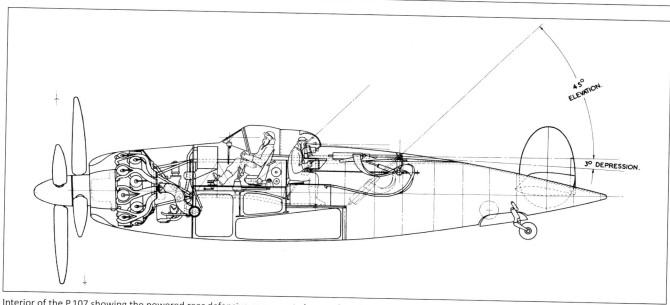

Interior of the P.107 showing the powered rear defensive armament also employed in some P.105 variants.

experimental auto observer for fitting into AA413 in late 1944. AA413 was at BPA from June 1944 and was passed for actual conversion on 30 August 1945 under scrutiny by the CRO. However, the programme suffered a setback when this machine was declared unfit for flight soon after it was viewed by the CRO. It was subsequently struck off charge on 12 November 1946 as uneconomical to repair. The airframe was dumped at Bridgnorth and last seen as a hulk there in 1952.

The second test aircraft, DR895, was then the contender for the fast-disappearing trials programme with cutbacks after the war. The machine was used for windmill winch trials at RAE in June 1946, returning to BPA in August. It was hoped by the company still to continue the experimental aircraft. In order to ensure that the Defiant was suitable for carrier landing tests DR895 was purchased by BPA on 31 July 1948 and on 12 August 1948 it was landed on to a carrier from A&AEE by Captain Eric Melrose Brown. In order to get the correct balance for deck landing, the TT gear had been removed by BPA and the aircraft reconverted, the target tow gear being replaced

The Defiant 'Special Features' intended to test many of the devices believed to be needed for advanced carrier aircraft such as the P.105. Second design has North's drooped tips and additional tailwheel protection. The project started at the same time as the P.105 design.

temporarily with a Type A turret again. One item that J. D. North also intended to explore was the destabilising effect of drooped wing tips as seen on some German late-war designs. The programme to convert DR895 into the Defiant 'Special Features', by now as a private venture, continued into 1949, when it was finally abandoned. The drooped wing tips were eventually tested on the P.108 Balliol prototype.

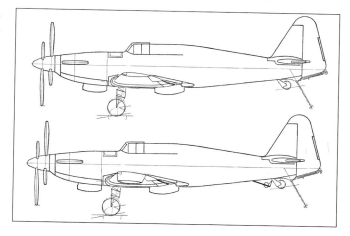

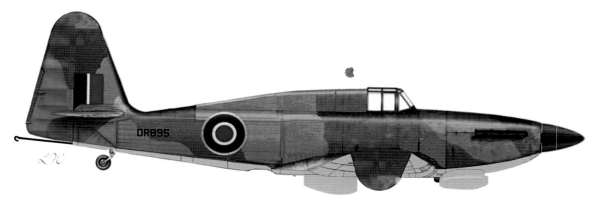

P.82 Special Features

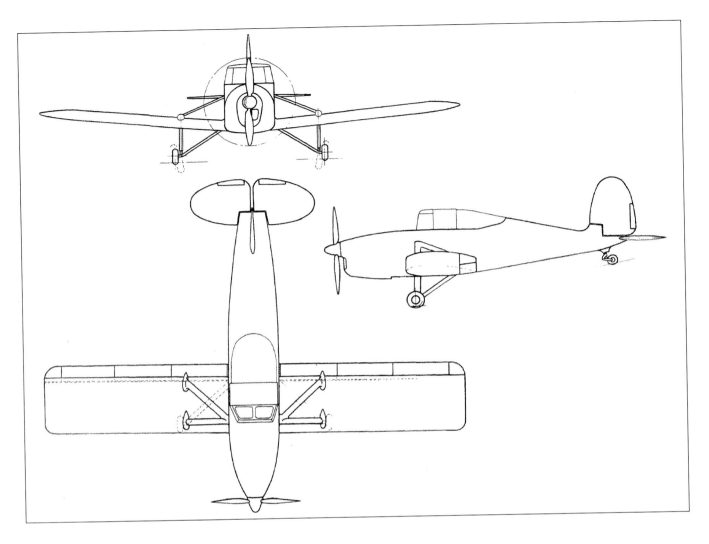

CHAPTER TWENTY-EIGHT

Esoteric Structures – P.106 and P.110

P.106

T.23/43 (OR.131) WAS A SPECIFICATION dated 28 November 1943 and issued to tender on 2 December 1943. A single-engine elementary trainer aircraft was required to be constructed in wood with steel as an alternative if valid arguments could be made for it. It should have side-by-side seating plus a third crew member behind. The speed target was 120mph with endurance of three hours and the design, including undercarriage, was to be able to withstand training mishaps. The engine specification required was a Gypsy Queen Mk.II.

BPA responded with a single basic layout but with three potential variations. They chose to revert to a pre-war tubular steel and alloy structure that was fabric covered so that the machines could be repaired easily by component replacement and fabric patching. Synthetic training requirements were taken as a first priority for design. The aerodynamic shape of the windscreen, for example, had been sacrificed to make the best installation of the two-stage blue scheme for night flying training. The design was based upon the engine requested but an extra 42hp was available from the Gypsy Queen III if required. While the company would agree that the design might not appeal in the aesthetic sense, it believed the design

advantages far outweighed this consideration.

The P.106A covered the specification request of side-by-side tutoring but only with a two-seat aircraft. The P.106B was a side-by-side tutoring, third seat to the rear, version as required by the specification. The P.106C was a two-seat tandem tutoring version with a very much thinner fuselage. The aircraft was a low-winged monoplane with a marked dihedral wing, supported by large faired vee struts from the fuselage framework. The wing itself used 1930s figure of eight closed-joint spars and wing ribs stamped from steel.

P.106A side-by-side dual elementary trainer.

Model of the P.106A.

Multiple part blanking would produce the nose, upper and lower sections and the rear control shroud parts of the wing ribs. The wing section was listed as a 'specially developed Boulton Paul section'. Full-span trailing edge flaps and ailerons were made from identical components repeated in order to gain economies of scale. The rudder and elevators reverted to the P.41/44 style of identical components. The fabric covering of the wing was to be manufactured as a bag and slid on to the wing structure, being laced only at the control surface shroud and the wing root. Tensioning of the fabric was to be by tensioning wires built into the rib and wing design. The fuselage was a tubular truss covered with fabric and laced, the lacing joints then being covered by a weather strip. The blue filter system was designed to slide into position within the existing canopy and screens and the four filters, identical and interchangeable, could be slammed out of the way in an emergency. Variable trimming was designed into the controls so that any control setting from light to heavy might be applied. To cover the all-world application, an oil cooler was provided with an adjustable cooler flap setting.

The span was 34ft 6in, chord 5ft 10in and the length 28ft. The height was 7ft 10in tail down but propeller horizontal and 10ft tail down but propeller up. The propeller diameter was 7ft 6in. An undercarriage track of 12ft 2in ensured stability and the leg root attached at the same location as the wing vee strut span to take landing loads. Weights of the three types spanned from 2,267lb to 2,831lb AUW depending upon the version, crew and equipment. The P.106A at 2,280lb had a predicted maximum speed of 147mph and

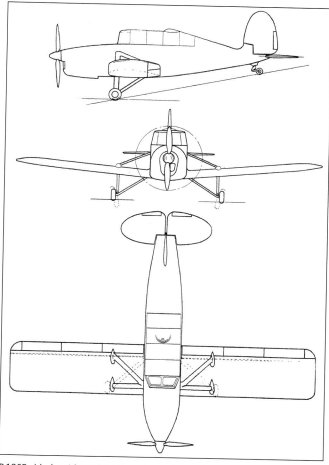

P.106B side-by-side and tandem elementary trainer.

stalled at 48mph. The P.106B at 2,541lb predicted 145mph and stalled at 50mph, while the P.106C of 2,267lb predicted 149mph and stalled at 47mph. With the Gypsy III engine these A to C weights and speeds increased to 2,480lb, 156mph and 49mph; 2,741lb, 154mph and 51mph and 2,467lb, 158mph and 48mph respectively.

Model of the P.106B.

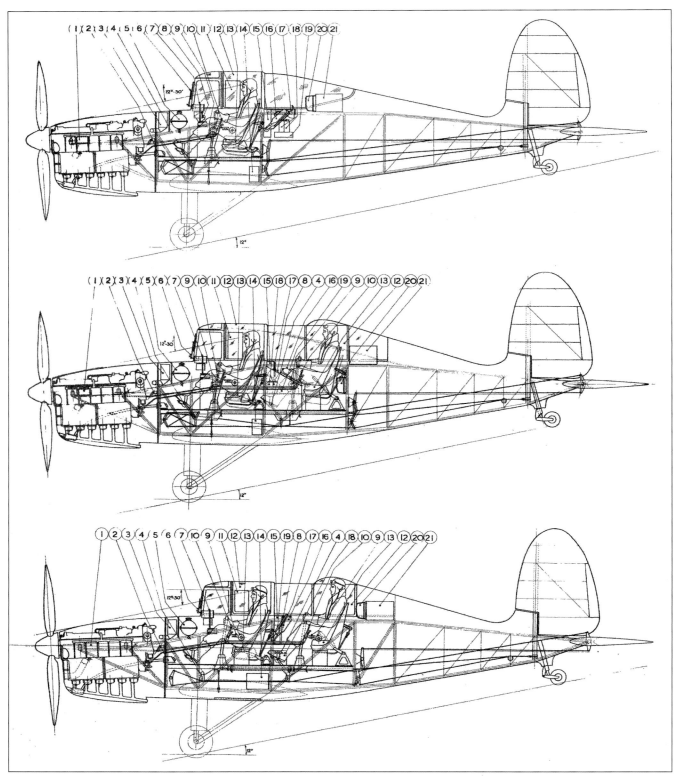

**Interior Details – P.106 series
(top to bottom) P.106 A, B and C**

1. Oil cooler
2. Cockpit heating
3. Oil tank
4. Rudder pedals
5. Water tank
6. Windscreen wiper
7. Instrument board
8. Amplifier A1134
9. Tab controls
10. Engine controls
11. Clear vision panel
12. Sliding hood
13. Parachute and dinghy
14. Accumulator – general purpose
15. Filter storage cabinet – blind flying
16. Fire extinguisher
17. Axe
18. Accumulators, instrument lighting and W/T
19. Battery HT
20. First aid
21. Desert equipment

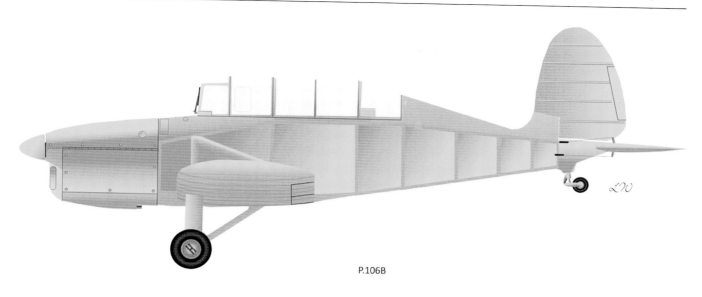

P.106B

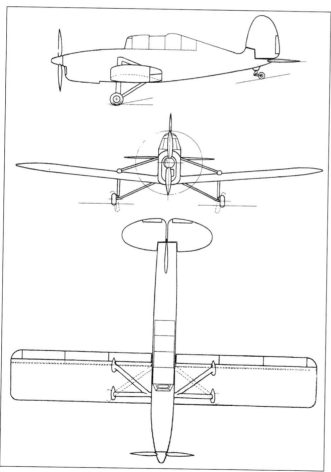

P.106C tandem elementary trainer.

The proposal was submitted in January 1944. In August 1944 Issue 2 of the specification was issued to Percival for their T.23/48 design specifying the Gypsy III engine, with amendments in January 1945 to cover winter operations. The DH.105 design was also ordered in August 1944 but then cancelled. By mid-1945 it was at issue 3 for the Percival design known as the Prentice. The P.106, Heston JC1 and the Miles M.53, on the other hand, failed to attract prototype orders.

P.110

Little is written concerning the P.110 other than available wind tunnel model photographs and the project listing that it was a three-seater light monoplane with a Blackburn Cirrus Minor Mk.II engine. The fact that the company had been studying the machine was revealed to the board as a whole on 26 March 1946 with the statement that it was intended to be a simple three- to four-seat machine with a target sales price of £5,000.

The machine was designed to present a futuristic light aircraft for a pilot and three or four passengers, who experienced panoramic views from a clear bubble nose. This was achieved by placing the engine as a pusher above and behind the cockpit and carrying the tail surfaces out on a thin tubular boom emerging from the cockpit fairing base. The aircraft had a minimum-size fin stub, giving it an all-moving fin/rudder arrangement. The tail surfaces were the same, although the two elevators were joined together at the centre so as to move as one. The fin and tailplane stubs were identical and the rudder and elevator halves were also identical. This interchangeability stemmed back to the P.41 and P.44 machines in the late 1920s. Although the wind tunnel model had no ailerons, it seems highly unlikely that there was any plan to control turns by differential use of elevators, simply that the initial model tests with ailerons operative was not needed. A study of the photographs reveals a heavily fabric reinforced trailing edge on the model, suggesting that it would be removed and reconfigured to represent flaps and ailerons later in the testing. The revised model engine pod also suggests a move to a Lycoming flat four style of engine in a three-seat design.

What was perhaps less obvious was that the design was to be based almost entirely on the use of resin plastics. It will be remembered that as far back as the 1919 P.10 design North had advocated the employment of plastics for structural panels. Prior to the Second World War and before B&P Aeronautical and Research Department had become Boulton Paul Aircraft, North was still thinking of formed plastic materials, where they might be used and how to convince the Air Ministry to employ them in airframes. There were also many experiments with moulding resin-based components with metal particle fillers, and even the production of filled resin as moulds to manufacture large-run Bakelite components. Experiments included forming complete boom sections with integral stiffeners and taper wing sections in the same manner. The resin component parts were assembled and then bonded together by enclosing the parts in shaped bags and pressurising the inner bag to force all the ribs or

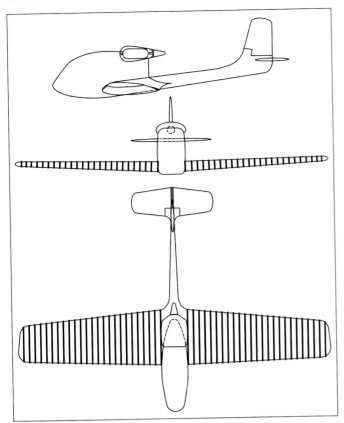

stringers against the inner surface and the outer bag to hold the wing surface itself until the materials were bonded and set. Smaller parts used the metal particle-filled resin moulds. The system could also be used to bond metal items to the resin parts.

In the case of the P.110, there was a reversal of the original plastic skin and former experiments as the strengthening parts were outside of the structure. All of the fibre and resin-impregnated wing ribs were aerofoil profile and external to the surface, not internal. The shaped surface was to be formed by internal pressure and forced against the ribs so as to bond them together as an integral one-piece resin wing. The wing design formed a straight taper with the external surface looking like a metal sheet with fore-aft widely spaced reinforcements, twenty-four in all per wing, but which could be made to form a one-piece assembly with the minimum of manual labour. Xylonite models of the wing structure at quarter scale were manufactured and strength tested in September/October 1946. The potential three-/four-seat light aircraft design was studied only during the period 1945 to 1946, when North's personal file on the type was closed. The P.110 concept was sound had BPA been able to finance the detail development of large plastic mouldings, but any military financing had long been viewed with scepticism during the war.

Left: The initial drawing office engine allocation for the P.110 was a Blackburn Cirrus Minor Mk II in an inverted pusher configuration but this was altered as the design progressed.

Below: Front three-quarter view of the P.110 design. By this time the wind tunnel model had been converted to a flat-four engine.

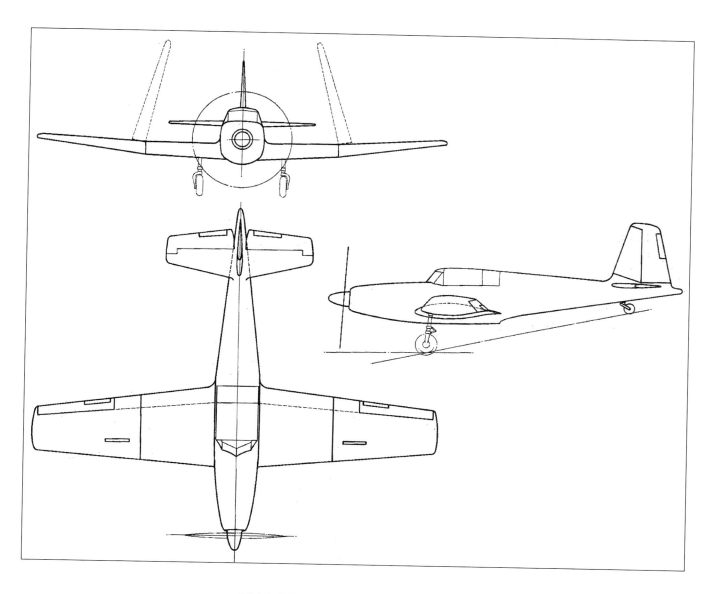

CHAPTER TWENTY-NINE

Trainer Developments

P.108

T.7/45 Issue 1 was dated 16 March 1945 and called for a single-engine advanced training aircraft to meet OR.159. The company response was submitted in May 1945 as two designs. The P.108 was a turbine-engine machine and the P.109 a radial-engine machine. Issue 2, dated 7 August 1945, revised the P.108 and dropped the radial requirement. The design was also to serve as a navy trainer and the engine was to be a gas turbine propeller engine of around 1,000hp.

The P.108 initially had a squared box-like fuselage with the proposed RR RB53 engine, later named Dart. The exhaust ejected under the cockpit as a central duct. The undercarriage was outward folding with capacity for two drop tanks side-by-side at the wing

The layout of the first version of the P.108 to T.7/45 Issue 1 differed considerably from the resubmissions as new issues of the specification appeared.

roots, and there was an up thrust of 3° on the engine. When the P.109 was dropped the round fuselage of this was suggested to be adopted for the revision of the P.108 submissions. By the time version B of the P.108 proposal was submitted the airframe had therefore become a barrel-like fuselage with the cockpit turtleback fairing removed, exhaust ejecting under the starboard side below the wing at about 30° down and starboard to counteract torque, an inward-retracting undercarriage and drop tanks outboard of the undercarriage.

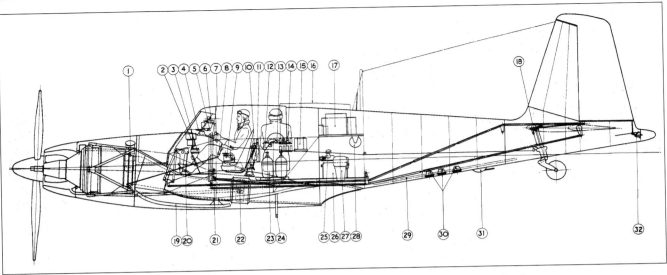

Interior Details – P.108 First Design

Note the 3° up thrust of the Dart engine.

1. Oil tank
2. Instrument panel
3. Compass P.11
4. Instrument board, cowling and sodium lamp
5. Clear vision panel
6. Gun sight
7. Control column (wheel port. Split stick stbd)
8. Engine controls
9. Trimmer controls
10. Fire extinguisher
11. Stowage for chartboard, computers and personal equipment
12. Signal pistol
13. Chartboard
14. Signal cartridges
15. First aid
16. Sliding hood (jettisonable)
17. Radio
18. Tail wheel steering control
19. Crash skid
20. Rudder pedals
21. Slinging hook
22. Bleed air for cockpit heating and jet pipe muff
23. Oxygen bottles
24. IFF aerial
25. Drift recorder
26. Accumulators 24v 40 amp
27. Downward identification lamps
28. Air bottle
29. SBA di-pole aerial
30. Downward identification lamps
31. VHF B/A di-pole aerial
32. Glider tow hook
33. Bomb rack
34. Retractable landing lamp

Illustration of the P.108 initial proposal.

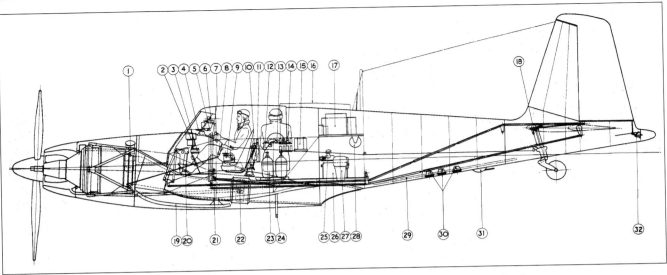

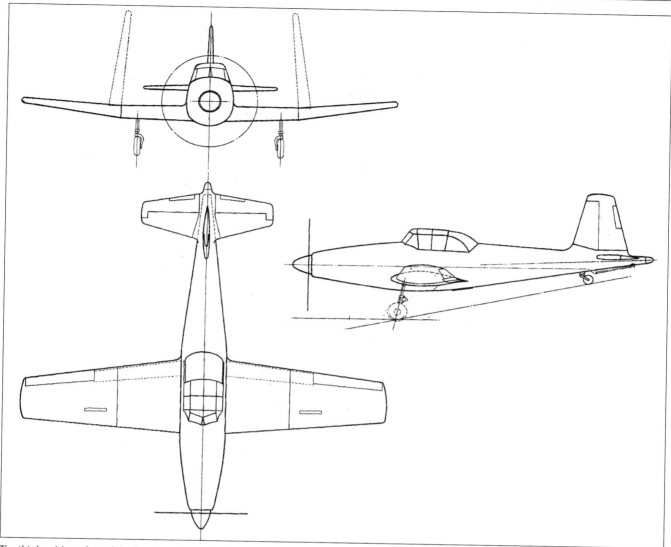

The third revision adopted the fuselage shape of the P.109 and the jet efflux was set to one side to counteract torque of the Dart propeller.

BPA advised at its initial conference meeting on 18 August 1945 that all prototypes would have folding wings and none would therefore be produced as a pure naval aircraft. Rolls-Royce at that meeting specifically asked if the engine thrust line and the fuselage centreline could be standardised. The version C and subsequent outlines used the engine centreline matching the fuselage centreline. A section of NACA 65 20% to 12% was used. The aircraft followed the wing planform of the initial P.108 study with three crew. The navigator/observer sitting athwart-ships behind the other two crew members was changed for a central seat facing forward where he could observe the others. The raised canopy was designed so the hood slid back for the side-by-side pilots and the third member could escape via knock-out windows in the side when the canopy was jettisoned. Since it was a training aircraft the underbelly of the centre section was proposed to have reinforcing skids built internally so a belly landing could be made with minimum damage. This three-view had an arrester hook shown. While the first A version had a length of 33ft 3in the length of the new C machine had increased to 37ft 6in.

Turboprop engine choice all through initial discussions fell to the Dart engine. However, the RR Dart was so protracted in development that the first prototype, VL892, was sanctioned to be completed with a Mercury radial to gain flight experience. Continued delays in the Dart led to the agreement for completion of the other three prototypes

– Balliol prototypes VL917, VL935 and VL954 – with Mamba engines. VL954 was to be a naval prototype with deck gear. This airframe was later cancelled and the parts fed into the Merlin prototype parts pool. VL892 had a tubular structure centre-body with removable panels and underwent a series of full-size trials with its Mercury radial to determine the best shape of the canopy and rear fuselage. The length of the Mercury engine prototype was reduced to 35ft 3in by the loss of the turbine power plant. The height with tail up was 14ft 6in because of a taller rounded top rudder compared with later machines. The height with wings folded was 15ft 8in and the folding was manually obtained by ropes and bracing struts. The expected speed of this version was 280mph at 10,000ft maximum and 230–250mph cruise depending on mixture setting. The AUW was 7,529lb. The aircraft prototypes finally had a generally circular cross section except for a distorted, rounded section at the cockpit and the rear fuselage cone was raised at 2° 32' to the engine and fuselage datum. The tail cone itself was further raised along its axis to 7° 10', this change being approximately at the tailplane leading edge with the tailplane at zero incidence to the fuselage/engine thrust datum. The datum line for the thrust and front fuselage were the same on Mamba aircraft. The rest of the aircraft was to utilise conventional metal-clad framework structure and riveted wings. The turboprop prototypes were designated P.108 Balliol T.1 with the Mamba engine.

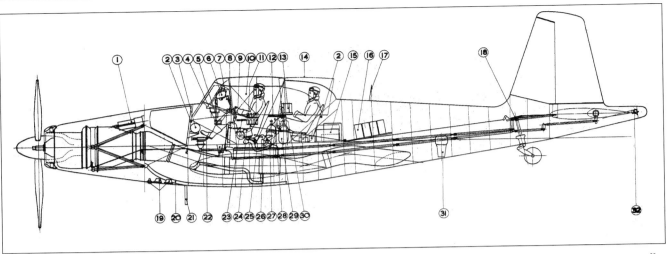

Interior shows the engine now on the dual thrust/centreline of the fuselage as requested by Rolls-Royce, after technical meetings with Air Ministry staff and themselves.

Interior Details – P.108 Third Design

1. Accessory drive
2. Slinging points
3. Air bottle
4. Instrument fuses
5. Clear vision panel
6. Gun sight
7. Instrument board, cowling and sodium lamp
8. Engine controls
9. Trimmer controls
10. Hood closed
11. Signal cartridges
12. Chartboard
13. First aid
14. Sliding hood (jettisonable)
15. Radio equipment
16. Accumulators
17. Radio aerial
18. Tail wheel steering control
19. Downward identification lamps
20. Crash skid
21. IFF aerial
22. Rudder pedals
23. Chartboard
24. Stowage for chartboard, computers and personal equipment
25. Seat mounting
26. Oxygen regulator
27. Cockpit heating feed pipe
28. Crash arch
29. Oxygen bottles
30. Drift recorder
31. F.24 camera
32. Glider tow hook
33. Bomb rack
34. Retractable landing lamp

Elaborate mock-up of the P.108 in the Pendeford factory.

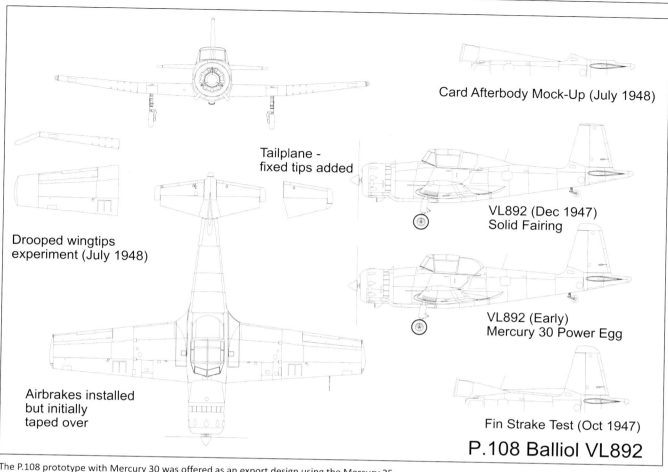

Card Afterbody Mock-Up (July 1948)

Tailplane -
fixed tips added

VL892 (Dec 1947)
Solid Fairing

Drooped wingtips
experiment (July 1948)

VL892 (Early)
Mercury 30 Power Egg

Airbrakes installed
but initially
taped over

Fin Strake Test (Oct 1947)

P.108 Balliol VL892

The P.108 prototype with Mercury 30 was offered as an export design using the Mercury 25.

Structure of the prototype differed from the production, having more removable panels around the cockpit area.

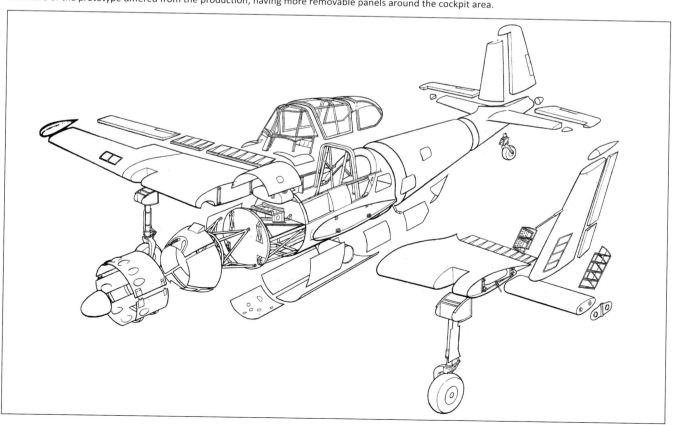

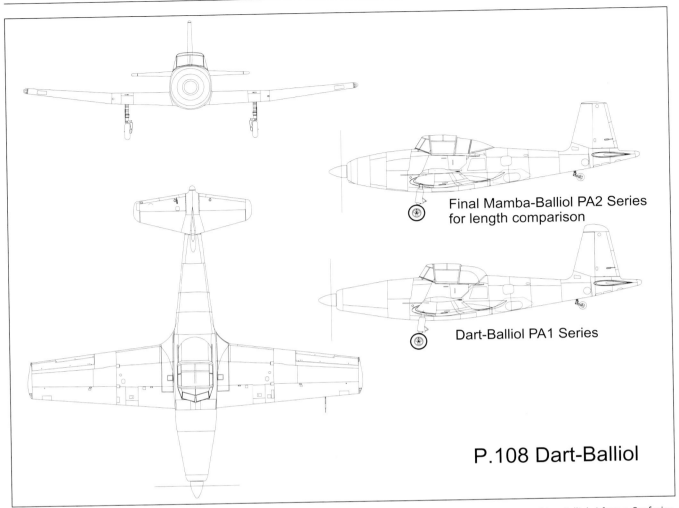

Final Mamba-Balliol PA2 Series
for length comparison

Dart-Balliol PA1 Series

P.108 Dart-Balliol

The Dart-powered Balliol was longer than the Mamba design but delays in the engine development meant it was never mated to a Balliol airframe. Confusion occurs because the T.1 Prototype Notes GA wrongly adapted the Dart drawings with the Mamba dimensions superimposed rather than correcting to the true Mamba shape.

Painted up wind tunnel model of the Dart engine P.108 in trainer yellow.

First prototype VL892 fitted with a Mercury engine because of non-availability of the Dart. One of a set issued to BPA Ltd. *Crown Copyright*

The T.1 aircraft finally had the common span of 39ft 4in and a length of 36ft 6in. The tail span was 13ft 10.25in and the track 15ft. The wing chord at the centreline (theoretical) was 8ft 6in, virtual tip (theoretical) 4ft 3in and the outer wing joint 6ft 6in. The span with wings folded was 21ft 8in. The height with wings folded was 15ft 8in, the height, tail down – at tail, was 9ft 6in, and the height, tail up – at tail, was 13ft 9in. The predicted speed was 307mph maximum at 20,000ft and a cruise of 269 to 272mph depending upon height. The AUW was 7,860lb. The Dart-engine version was to be longer at 38ft 0.5in.

Non-availability of the Dart resulted in Mamba engines for the T1. Conversion of VL892 to the Dart was also revised to Mamba as it needed less reconversion work and therefore cost.

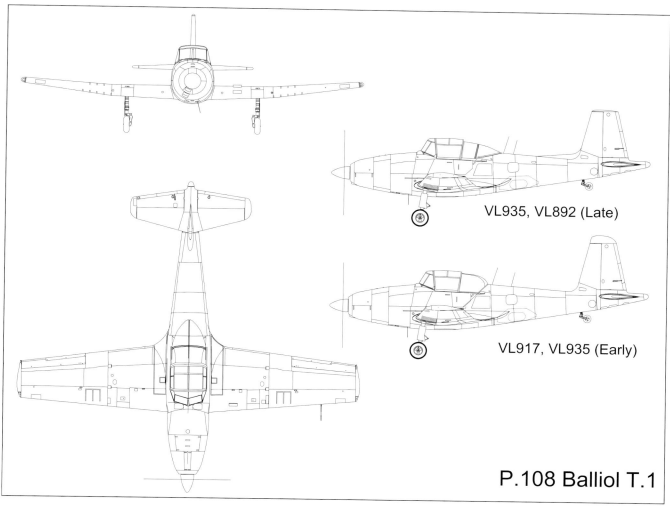

VL935, VL892 (Late)

VL917, VL935 (Early)

P.108 Balliol T.1

VL197 was the first aircraft to be fitted with a Mamba power plant. Usually retouched, this original picture shows a weight attachment under the fuselage for balance tests.

VL892 re-engined with a Mamba.

The problems with producing sufficient turboprop engines and their high prototype costs led to a search for other engines, several being considered including various Merlin models starting with the Merlin 24. The government decision eventually fell to a Merlin 32 variant redesignated 35. The plan to produce twenty pre-production aircraft, ten with Mamba, ten with Dart, was changed to ten with Mamba, ten with Merlin, but then put on hold. Four prototypes were ordered with the Merlin 35 for trials. The first to be tested, VW900, therefore became the fourth Balliol prototype after VL892, 917 and 935. The prototypes ordered to be fitted out with Merlins were VW897 to VW900. There were seventeen pre-production aircraft with the order of VR590 to VR606. The Merlin 35-equipped design was known as the P.108A Balliol T.2 and conformed to specification T14/47 and finally production specification 29/46P. The predicted performance was 305mph maximum at 11,500ft with a cruise of 240 to 250mph depending on mixture setting. The AUW was 8,175lb.

Unable to utilise the Defiant Special Features aircraft to experiment with the effect of drooped tips, an experimental tip was added to VL892 for flight tests prior to it having a Mamba power egg.

The prototypes of the Merlin variant required not only a revision of the engine compartments from Station 120 forward, but also the movement of the cockpit area and windscreen aft by approximately 12.25in. This was achieved by moving the location down the canopy slide rail axis and shortening the sliding canopy itself; the third seat being removed. The rear of the sliding portion also had a better rear fairing added. The fixed clear portions at the rear were completely changed to blown bubble halves. Most of the pre-production had no dive brakes as the original forward-mounted raising slatted blind units called lattice brakes were not liked. They also still had flaps on the outer wing underside. Dive brakes were fitted to production aircraft and some pre-production, so that the outer wing flaps were replaced by a smaller dive brake segment, solid below and with a large slotted segment above.

A problem was found with the Merlin version having a change to trim and an increasing pitch down in a dive. The decision was made to move the pitch down point so it exceeded the maximum diving speed of 450 knots by adding negative tailplane incidence. Flights to determine the cause with a negative tail incidence to about -0.8° applied to reduce the severity resulted in windscreen failure of the already thickened screen design when the dive speed was exceeded. This resulted in the loss of Robin Lindsey-Neale and Peter Tisshaw when the aircraft crashed at Coven, Staffordshire. Unable to put more incidence on the tail unit by adjustment, the planned change was introduced at the fuselage joint to give -1° 40' incidence on all production aircraft. T.2 Balliol data was as for the T.1 except the new length was 35ft 1.5in.

Reduction of an original large-scale master cutaway drawing of the P.108A Merlin 35-powered production model in the author's collection.

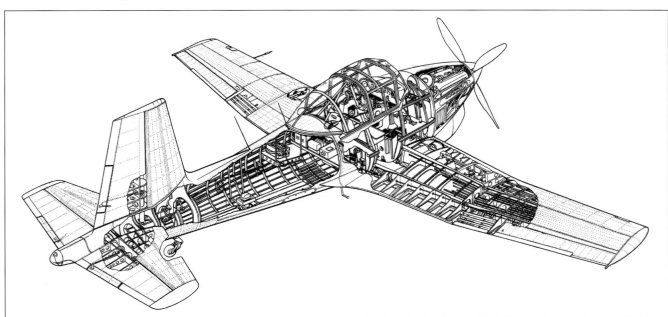

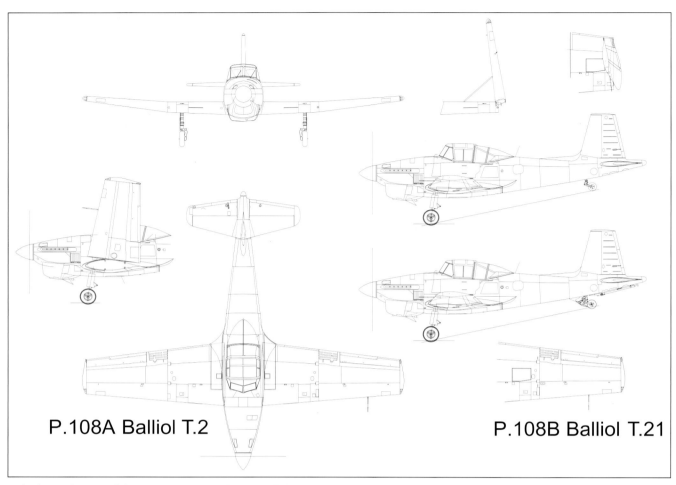

P.108A Balliol T.2   P.108B Balliol T.21

Author's CAD drawings of the P.108A Balliol T.2 and P.108B Balliol T.21.

Production of P.108A Balliol T.2 was undertaken by Boulton Paul Aircraft while a small batch of thirty were assembled at Blackburn Aircraft. Production never reached the 'thousand' predicted by the government in the original 1945 plan and was lucky to reach into the hundreds. As production progressed MoS asked that BPA find overseas sales for some of the production batches as the required quantity for the RAF might need to be reduced. A number of proposals were made using the basic Balliol fuselage design such as a drawing for an aircraft with a Pratt and Whitney engine said to be a T.2A, while the Air Ministry investigated the availability of surplus US Wasps. The company had already produced a catalogue and drawings for the radial-engined P.108 using the Mercury engine utilised initially in the prototype VL892, plus a catalogue showing all three types. The hope was that this would eventually generate foreign radial engine aircraft orders and, if necessary, use up MoS production already on the shop floor.

Only thirty naval aircraft were produced as the P.108B Sea Balliol T.21. There were many changes required to this variant to conform to naval requirements in addition to deck hook systems, strengthened undercarriage and articulated tailwheel. All access doors had to be on chains or cables to prevent loss overboard and electrics with external connections needed to be covered by access doors. An external plate acting as a skin doubler was added on the upper surface of the inner wing to prevent skin distortion with the increased landing forces of the new beefed up undercarriage legs.

In February/March 1949 the Indian Navy enquired about obtaining twenty Sea Balliols (subject to the attitude of the Ministry of Supply, MoS). India also required one aircraft with rockets for test by August 1949. Because of airbrake mods and a lack of enough completed pre-

production airframes, this was impossible. The foreign trials had to be postponed because of the bringing forward of competitive Balliol and Athena trials by the RAF. In March 1950 the Indian requirement was optimistically considered to be as many as 300 aircraft over five years of production and the Balliol was favoured. This quantity had reduced to a more realistic 108 aircraft by April 1950. Eventually the trials aircraft for India was delayed at their request and the inference was that the resumption of Harvard production in the USA and the then dollar/pound rate meant that the American type would be ordered. Nevertheless, the trials aircraft VR597 was planned to visit Lebanon, Syria, Iraq and Egypt from June 1950.

Towards the end of production of the T.2 (February 1952) enquiries were received from Iraq and Ceylon for small numbers. Iraq had already enquired about the Mercury-engined machine as a trainer for its air force as early as June 1948. In October 1952 Egypt enquired about twenty Balliols, but the reply was deferred pending the attitude of HM government towards Egyptian purchase. By June 1953 it was clear from MoS correspondence that the Air Ministry now argued that it required all RAF Balliols manufactured (140) and BPA did not have to find sources of foreign sales to offload RAF surplus units. Any others would be purely new build export orders on BPA. Nevertheless, a Ceylon order for twelve aircraft was finally fulfilled partly by taking existing production line aircraft and partly by stored low-hour RAF aircraft reallocated and refurbished. A tour of the USA was made by two aircraft, and tours of the Middle East during the production period. With no more orders forthcoming for any variations, the company-designated P.108A and B therefore became the last serving types of pure BPA design. North's file on foreign sales was closed in 1955.

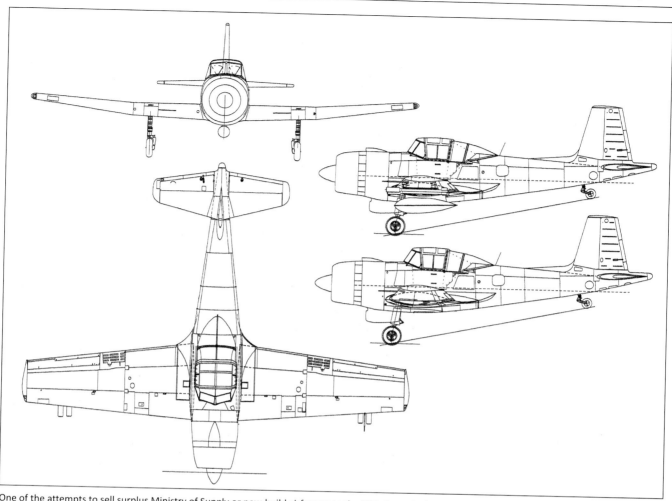

One of the attempts to sell surplus Ministry of Supply or new-build airframes to the USA, Egypt, India and others was to delete the Merlin power egg forward of the firewall and to equip the T.2 fuselage design with a P&W R1820 radial engine, additional dust filtration and cooling for the sump oil. As with the radial engine version of the P.108 prototype, all of the Balliol features of gun, drop tanks and rockets would be available to the operating country. The unbuilt design was initially designated T.2A but failed to generate an order.

Artist's sketch of the T.2A.

P.108B Sea Balliol T.21 serial WL723 of the Junior Officers Air Conversion course landing on.

Balliol T.2 finished to Ceylon Air force Standard as Commercial Production No 1, Serial CA301 was originally Production No 96, Serial WG226, taken from the MoS contract before delivery to the RAF.

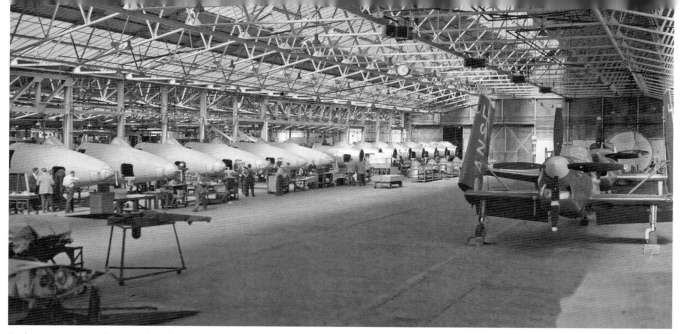

As the company own design projects became based upon technical studies for RAE and the Ministry of Supply with ever reducing chance of manufacture, the expertise continued with subcontract design and manufacture. Here in the workshop the company civil Balliol G-ANSF and probably Sea Balliol WG333 to the rear. On the production line are Canberra front fuselage and nose sections being outfitted for batch conversions under contract from English Electric. It is most likely that these are for Indian PR.57 and B(I).58 airframes.

P.109

The initial release of Specification T.7/45 called for two types of single-engine advanced training aircraft with the second having an airspeed in excess of 210mph. The radial engine was covered by the design series P.109 with the government-specified New Perseus engine. The aircraft followed the wing planform of the initial P.108 study with a raised rear fuselage and three crew, the navigator/observer sitting athwart-ships behind the other two crew members under a one-piece sliding canopy. The design had a circular cowling and a circular rear fuselage; only the cockpit section diverted from this slightly to accommodate the crew. The undercarriage was within the inboard section of the inner wing and retracted outwards, and just at the wing roots two drop tanks could be carried. Electric gear retraction and cartridge-operated emergency extension was provided. Within the outer wing panels there were folding slatted blind air brakes (called lattice brakes), which disappeared into the wing surface above and below. Construction was intended to be all alloy, with the fuselage sides to wing trailing edge using extensive removable panels on a rectangular-section tubular lattice. The rest of the aircraft was to utilise conventional metal-clad framework structure and riveted wings.

The wingspan was 41ft, the length 33ft 9in and height 13ft 3in at rest on the ground at 12.5°. A section of NACA 65 20% to 12% was used. The wings, when folded, gave a width of 22ft 9in. A three-blade, constant-speed, Clark Y airscrew of 11ft 6in diameter was suggested. Maximum speed was 284mph at 4,900ft and maximum cruise 274mph at 8,000ft (stated as 270mph at least at 10,000ft). Stall with flaps up was 93mph, with flaps down 77mph. The ceiling was 30,000ft.

The brochure, submitted in May 1945, described the aircraft as fully aerobatic and having a 'fighter-like' performance, able to perform all the specified roles. The P.109 was abandoned when the next release of the specification dropped the requirement for a radial engine, but as discussed, much was read across into the P.108 development.

The P.109 radial-powered alternative to the P.108 was abandoned after the requirement was deleted from T.7/45 Issue 2, but the idea of a circular fuselage was liked and was adopted by the P.108 revisions.

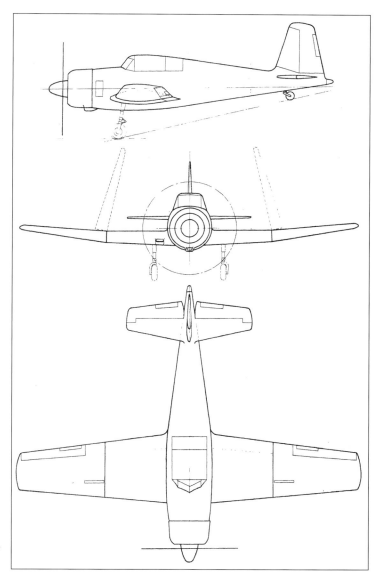

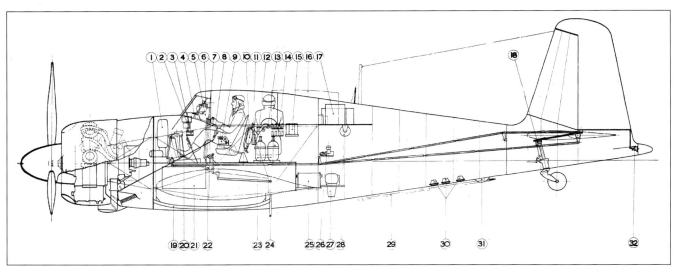

Interior Details – P.109

1. Oil tank
2. Instrument panel
3. Compass P.11
4. Instrument board, cowling and sodium lamp
5. Clear vision panel
6. Gun sight
7. Control column (wheel port. Split stick stbd)
8. Engine controls
9. Trimmer controls
10. Fire extinguisher
11. Stowage for chartboard, computers and personal equipment
12. Signal pistol
13. Chartboard
14. Signal cartridges
15. First aid
16. Sliding hood (jettisonable)
17. Radio
18. Tail wheel steering control
19. Crash skid
20. Rudder pedals
21. Fuel tank
22. Slinging hook
23. Oxygen bottles
24. IFF aerial
25. Accumulators 24v 40 amp
26. Drift recorder
27. F.24 camera
28. Air bottle
29. SBA di-pole aerial
30. Downward identification lamps
31. VHF B/A di-pole aerial
32. Glider towing hook
33. Bomb racks
34. Retractable landing lamp

Illustration of the P.109.

P.112

The possibility of converting the P.108 Balliol design into a primary trainer was mooted in late 1947 and proposals submitted at the end of the year. By the end of January 1948 North poured cold water on the idea as he was aware that MoS were looking at the DH Chipmunk as the future trainer for that role. Nevertheless, on 20 February 1948 it was reported the P.112 had been well received by AM Coryton and by AVM Boothman and copies had been submitted to MoS. There were two P.112 designs for an elementary trainer, but known details are now limited to about five glass plate pages of the illustrations which were placed in the proposal brochure. There is no known surviving detail text on the design other than selection records. The related design specification is not stated either on the illustrations or on the master P-series project list because there was no specification at that time. The P.112A drawing was dated January 1948, a month before drafts of T.8/48 for the Chipmunk and some eight months before the first issue of T.16/48 was released. The design was raised as possible simplifications of the P.108 with the same wing section and fuselage but alternative radial engines as an elementary trainer private venture in anticipation of specification release T.8/48.

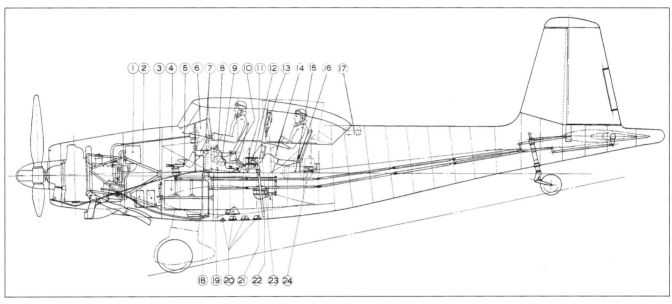

Interior Details – P.112

1. Oil tank
2. Accumulators
3. Instrument fuses
4. Fuel tank
5. Rudder pedals
6. Instrument board, cowling and sodium lamp
7. Control column
8. Engine controls
9. Trimmer controls
10. Seat adjustment
11. Chartboard
12. Signal cartridges
13. Fire extinguisher*
14. First aid
15. Air bottle
16. Oxygen
17. Tropical survival kit*
18. Compass
19. Retractable landing lamp
20. Downward identification lamps
21. Aerial
22. Controls
23. Maps and computers stowage*
24. Radio equipment

* Information missing from original key.

P.112 illustration made by airbrushing over a P.108 photograph.

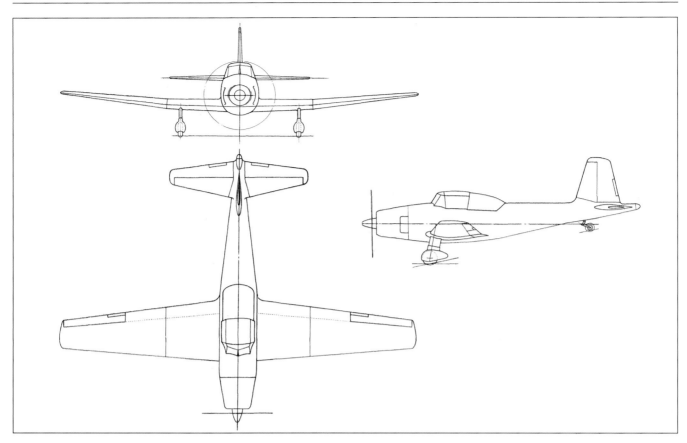

Design simplifications of the P.108 as an elementary trainer resulted in the P.112 radial-engine aircraft with fixed undercarriage and a larger wingspan to make landing slower. The engine was the Alvis Leonides LE IVM.

The P.112A alternative with a Pratt & Whitney Wasp R1340.

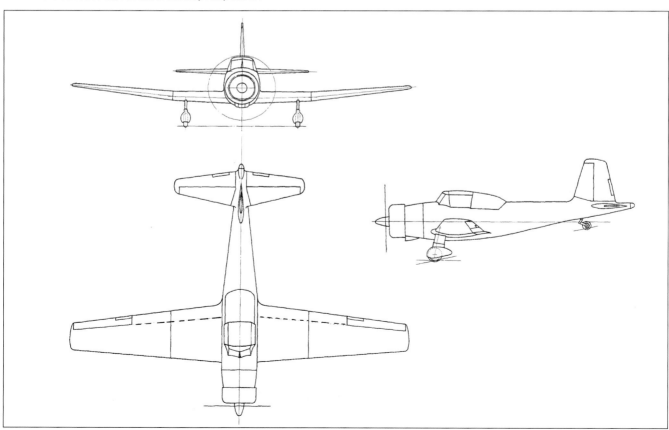

The P.112 was based on the final thoughts for the P.108 Balliol again but with a fixed undercarriage and an Alvis Leonides series IVM radial engine. The P.112A was a similar aircraft but with a Pratt & Whitney Wasp R1340 engine. Both aircraft were tied to the three-seat concept like the early P.108, two tandem seats for pilot and tutor with a third seat behind in the middle for an observer. It retained the P.108 wing section. Performance was 147 knots, exceeding the specification, but with the extended span to reduce landing speed the stall was still over requirement at 55 knots. The P.112's span was 45ft 4in by government records, the length 35ft 2.4in (drawing undated). The engine was the LE-IVM. The P.112A's span was 45ft 8in, the length 35ft 4in (drawing dated January 1948) and the engine was a Wasp R-1340, potentially from US surplus.

P.115

Issues of T.16/48 requested a trainer using a Gypsy engine and two individual designs were submitted in detail. The first used the more powerful DH Gypsy Queen 71. The design layout was based upon the P.108 Balliol fuselage with a new engine forward of the firewall. As in the P.108 development, the crew had now been reduced to two. The undercarriage was fixed but in order to achieve emergency landings could be released to fold backwards by the pilot as the aircraft touched the ground. Pneumatics were used for flaps, wheel brakes and the actuation of windscreen filters for simulated night flying. The wing section was changed to M6 and the aircraft had a span of 38ft 10in, a root chord of 7ft 6in and a tip chord of 3ft 7in. The tail span was 13ft 10in and the length 32ft 6in. The wing incidence to the thrust line was $2°$ and the aircraft sat at $12°$ static. The propeller was a three-blade light alloy DH hydromatic that was 9ft diameter and 0.711:1 reduction geared. The AUW was 4,106lb and 4,229lb with desert equipment. The maximum speed was 162 knots at 6,200ft, the cruise was 149 knots at 7,000ft (all in excess of the specification, which required 110 knots). Stall would occur at 63.5 knots flaps up and at 52.5 knots with flaps at $60°$. The service ceiling was 22,000ft.

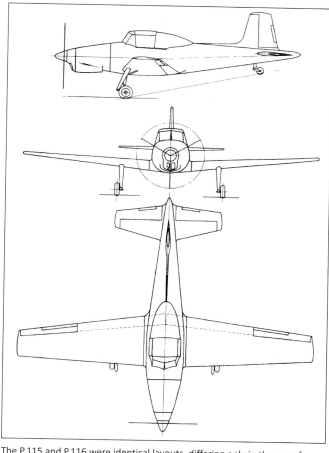

The P.115 and P.116 were identical layouts, differing only in the use of Gypsy Major 71 or 51 engines respectively. The company were worried that the 51 engine would produce an underpowered machine so offered the higher power as their preference.

Interior of the P.115/116 aircraft design.

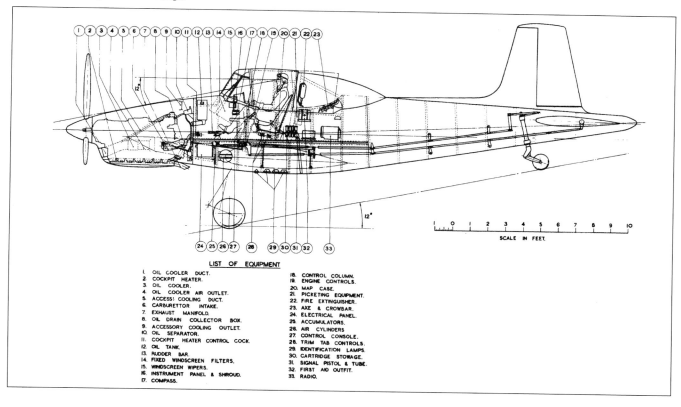

LIST OF EQUIPMENT

1. OIL COOLER DUCT.		18. CONTROL COLUMN.	
2. COCKPIT HEATER.		19. ENGINE CONTROLS.	
3. OIL COOLER.		20. MAP CASE.	
4. OIL COOLER AIR OUTLET.		21. PICKETING EQUIPMENT.	
5. ACCESS: COOLING DUCT.		22. FIRE EXTINGUISHER.	
6. CARBURETTOR INTAKE.		23. AXE & CROWBAR.	
7. EXHAUST MANIFOLD.		24. ELECTRICAL PANEL.	
8. OIL DRAIN COLLECTOR BOX.		25. ACCUMULATORS.	
9. ACCESSORY COOLING OUTLET.		26. AIR CYLINDERS.	
10. OIL SEPARATOR.		27. CONTROL CONSOLE.	
11. COCKPIT HEATER CONTROL COCK.		28. TRIM TAB CONTROLS.	
12. OIL TANK.		29. IDENTIFICATION LAMPS.	
13. RUDDER BAR.		30. CARTRIDGE STOWAGE.	
14. FIXED WINDSCREEN FILTERS.		31. SIGNAL PISTOL & TUBE.	
15. WINDSCREEN WIPERS.		32. FIRST AID OUTFIT.	
16. INSTRUMENT PANEL & SHROUD.		33. RADIO.	
17. COMPASS.			

PLATE I

Model of the P.115/116 aircraft.

P.116

Although the P.116 met the specification, it was suggested the performance was marginal with the DH Gypsy Queen 51 for aerobatics. This aircraft was therefore submitted under a separate number. The wing section was again M6 and the aircraft had a span of 36ft 9in, root chord 7ft 1.25in and tip chord 3ft 4.75in. The tail span was 13ft 6.5in and the length 30ft 8in. The wing incidence to the thrust line was 2° and the aircraft sat at 11° static. The propeller was a three-blade light alloy DH type with a 7ft 6in diameter and direct drive. The AUW was 3,839lb and with desert equipment 3,962lb. The maximum speed was 154 knots at 4,700ft, the cruise 147 knots at 6,200ft. The stall came at 65 knots flaps up, and 54 knots flaps down at 60°. The service ceiling was 20,500ft.

In both the P.115 and P.116 generous control surfaces were to allow aerobatics if required. Both designs were submitted in February 1949. Within a month the company were invited to quote for two and four aircraft plus production quantities. In fact, T.14/48 as a basic release found more than two dozen designs being tendered and only Handley Page and Percival received prototype contracts for aircraft similar to the P.112, all others being eliminated during tender appraisal. In June/July 1949 BPA were informed that they had not been successful in gaining a full manufacture contract, but that the Ministry would provide an engine and other facilities if the company were to agree to provide the prototype as a private venture. On 12 July 1949 it was decided to inform the government that 'BPA did not wish to avail itself of their offer'.

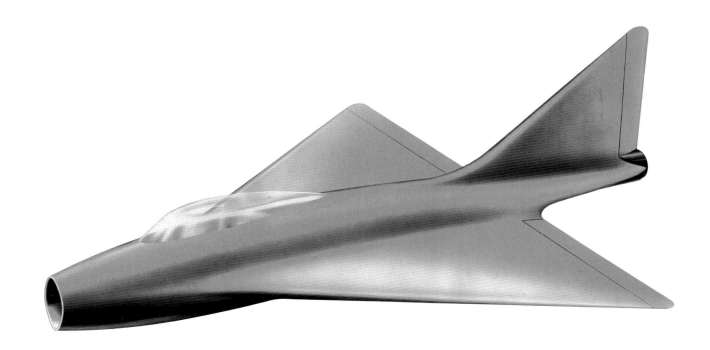

CHAPTER THIRTY

The Jet Deltas

P.111

OR.241 CALLED FOR a jet-propelled tailless research aircraft to investigate the problems of a delta airframe constructed for near sonic speeds and similar problems of a low aspect ratio delta planform powered by one Nene Mk.I jet engine.

The project started during May 1946 when North was asked by the Air Ministry to discuss with the Deputy Director of Research and Development the possibility of constructing an experimental high-speed delta aircraft. Designs were studied and proposals submitted back very quickly, based upon an RAE Nene Delta Concept No 64. The concept version had a ducktail fuselage extension, and the BPA version was aimed at fitting the engine and wing in the smallest body while maintaining the strength at the wing roots and ensuring the correct amount of air was available for the engine plenum.

The eventual MoS/RAE decision was for the BPA design to be mocked up as air intake and cockpit area in July 1946. Instead, the company built a complete wooden fuselage and one wing half to full size. By October it was made clear that the contract would be for the two prototypes and that the price would be tied to the cost of

construction. A fixed tender request for the two aircraft was received but the company suggested that this might be inappropriate in the case of such a programme requiring both new shapes and structural methods to achieve the performance. The Ministry instead set notification and not-to-exceed costs for features of the programme.

The specification E.27/46, dated 10 January 1947, was issued to BPA on 31 January 1947 along with an initial design coverage of £50,000. Contract 6/ACFT/969/CB.7(b) dated 7 February 1947 followed. The programme might be cancelled at any time based on reviews of the expenditure. Serials VT769 and VT784 had been allocated on 29 of November 1946, but these were withdrawn. Serial VT935 was the reallocation for the first prototype and VT951 for the second. By December 1947 the whole programme for two prototypes, a third airframe for test purposes and test pieces was estimated to cost £300,000, made up of £60,000 design, £50,000 for test pieces and the balance on production.

BPA Artist's Illustration of RAE concept No. 64.

Photograph of the full-size wooden mock-up where the photographer has then masked out the background. There is no starboard wing structure.

Completion by March 1949 was agreed in November 1948, but within two months it had slipped again to June 1949. Possibly in order to progress the first flight, Dr Redshaw reported in May 1949 that an official at RAE suggested that there was a possibility of an attempt on the world speed record if the first prototype could be completed quicker. This was not possible and the programme continued to extend. Following taxi trials at Wolverhampton, the aircraft was finally shipped to Boscombe Down and was in the course of reassembly for flight in June 1950.

The P.111 section used was agreed with RAE as Squire's High Speed C at 10% thick. This section had maximum thickness at 35% of chord and the rear surface formed a straight line from 80% to

Wind tunnel model of the P.111.

Above: The P.111 stress and flutter model was manufactured with all structural components to scale in Xylonite and was filled with hundreds of stress gauges wired back to BPA-designed electronic computing modules.

Right: From the complicated to the ridiculously simple. A high-speed taxi stability model for the tricycle undercarriage utilised a model aircraft Jetex solid propellant motor for power.

100%. The section drawn as the theoretical outline of the body was Young's High Speed Body based upon Aero Report 2073. By using a larger outline in plan compared with elevation the new oval-section fuselage looked like a fish on its side, the virtual BPA body in plan running from station zero to station 440 (440in) and the body in elevation from station 60 to station 440 again (380in). In both cases the virtual shapes were truncated and rounded at station 72 by the nose of the aircraft and truncated at station 384.8, the jet pipe tail. The jet pipe shroud and tail end slightly altered this ideal shape.

Construction was to be by an egg box conventionally riveted fuselage structure, with the pilot sitting in the middle of a bifuricated intake, which then divided above and below the wing front portion within the fuselage and continued to the engine plenum chamber. The 45° delta wing was of three-spar design with spars at 35, 59 and 79.5% and elevon hinges at 85% of chord. Only the first spar and the structure in front of it passed entirely through the body, the second and third spars met a hoop structure to allow installation of the Nene engine and the jet pipe. The theoretical aspect ratios of the wing were 4.0, 3.0 and 2.28, but differed very slightly in the actual airframe depending which tip was fitted. The maximum span was 33ft 5.8in with reductions to 29ft 9in or 25ft 8in, and the length 26ft 0.8in static. The height above the fin when static was 12ft 6.5in. The mainwheel track was 14ft 5.3in and the gross mainplane area 290.13sq ft. The maximum speed for the design case was 750 knots (Mach 1.0) at 35,000ft and the maximum level speed 675 knots.

Because of the decision to fly from RAE it was also decided that RAE pilots would undertake testing straight away, with no initial contractor's flights. The first was made by RAE CO Sqn Ldr Bob

Smythe in early October 1950. Flights by service pilots required care as the aircraft was found to be very sensitive to control inputs because of its small size and very early flight control system design with spring feel. The variations in the springs and their point of individual application led to some grey control areas and these could be particularly dangerous at the high speeds to be employed. An improved spring feel with stick-mounted push-button trim was then incorporated, but even that failed to produce a satisfactory control. A force of one 'g' could be created by simply moving the stick ¼in at 500 knots under a force of 2lb. The thought of a pilot giving a shock reaction that was perceived by the system as an input did not bear thinking about, according to RAE pilot *Lt* Jock Elliot. Feedback from the USA (NACA/NASA) that delta types in the States had suffered from catastrophic 'tumbling' near the stall made for some hairy airborne moments. Other problems were encountered with tyre usage and a weak nosewheel fork. On 29 June 1951 Geoff Gwilliam, the BPA service engineer in charge, was asked to incorporate a requested change to the windscreen. This involved replacing the curved egg-like pilot's screen with a flat centre for better clarity. This was incorporated in July 1951 at twenty-eight flying hours.

First prototype undergoing fuel flow tests. The access hatches in the fuselage were later used for airbrakes. Three airframes were initially required. In the background either the second prototype or the strength airframe is being constructed.

The heart of the programme was not just the delta planform, but the electro-hydraulic flight controls using systems based upon those previously developed for its gun turrets.

The first prototype being flown by RAE pilots.

Ultimately the machine was damaged by another pilot, Jim Harrison, having to pull off a credible belly landing when faced with an undercarriage hang-up, most probably due to the difficulty of getting reliable microswitch settings and locking arm adjustments, which altered in the stresses of high-speed flight. Jock Elliot had already come up with the idea of variable rate springs and selectable gearing between the pilot and the flight control actuation system. The idea, after testing, was discussed with North by Elliot and Dennis Higton in October 1951 for incorporation in the rebuilt P.111, to be known as the P.111A, and also in the second aircraft.

Following the damage to VT935, completion of the second aircraft, the P.120 (P.111 Mk.II), was put back from March 1952 to mid-May 1952 so the changes could be introduced. It was also intended to test all-moving wing tip control systems on both aircraft. The total costs had unfortunately risen to £700,000 on the programme as a whole, with an estimated total of £810,000 at close and a recoverable cost by BPA of only £563,000 in progress payments. A meeting at MoS in August/September 1952 discussed two options: continue the rebuild and modify VT935 or completely replace the also-crashed P.120 (P.111 Mk.II). It was decided financially by MoS to simply continue with the basic rebuild of the VT935 as the P.111A.

The P.111 at the Farnborough show after refit with a flat windscreen and coloured striping to hide the revised windscreen position. As well as the anti-glare panel, a thinner spray has been used to form three fuselage stripes. *Only known original colour of this finish courtesy T. Panopolis*

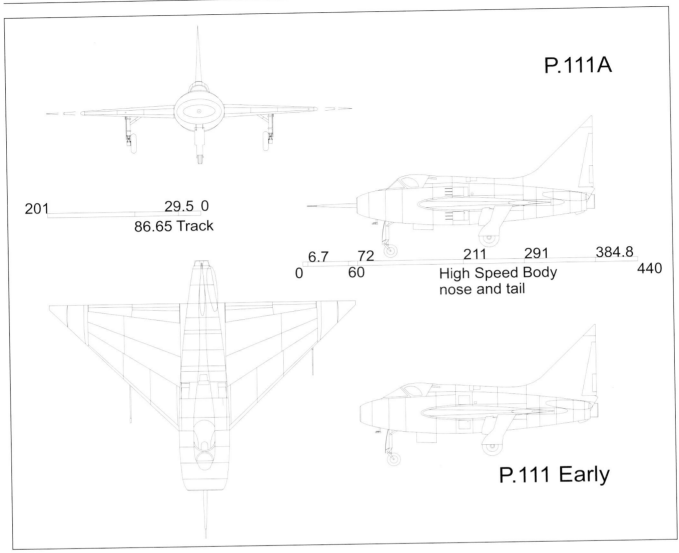

P.111A

201   29.5 0
86.65 Track

6.7   72   211   291   384.8
0   60   High Speed Body   440
nose and tail

P.111 Early

P.111A with side profile of P.111 as first flown.

The rebuilt P.111 was known as the P.111A. The aircraft was now experimentally painted by Titanine in a high gloss overall yellow with black pin-striping. After a number of years at Cranfield it may now be inspected at the Coventry Air Museum, although storage outside has taken its toll.

The differences on the P.111A were airbrakes behind the pilot area; the new variable gearing flight control system runs; a nose-mounted spike increasing the overall length to 31ft 6.1in; larger wheel doors but smaller leg doors; and a new bright yellow with black trim paint scheme. The aircraft was subsequently taken up to its Mach 0.97 flight envelope but no attempt was made to break the sound barrier. The aircraft is still extant at the Midland Air Museum at Coventry airport after previously being part of the Cranfield Institute, Cranfield having offered it to Dowty Boulton Paul in the mid-1970s, whose managing director at the time was uninterested when all likely means of display were proven unsatisfactory for preservation.

OR.252 E.10/47

OR.252 called for another tailless delta aircraft for research purposes. Rather than a near sonic performance, however, in this case the RAE experiment was to launch vertically and utilise additional control during flight by gimbal action of the jet pipe. With BPA in deep discussion on E.27/46 at RAE, they were asked to briefly study the

requirement based upon what expertise they already had. It was not expected that OR.241 and OR.252 would necessarily be placed with the same company but BPA knowledge of both delta wing-form and flight control actuation was thought to provide useful input. The core of the study was again the basic layout of RAE No 64. Specification E.10/47 was eventually generated on 13 September 1947 and issued to Fairey on the 19th. BPA probably felt that a horizontal tailplane might help initial tests and this was one of the requirements added as late as 1950. BPA seem to have done their limited study as part of the P.111 work and did not allocate a project number or, as far as is known, draw up a project design.

P.120

The P.111 Mk.II, the second prototype, which it had been hoped would feature the all-moving tailplane and possibly tip-mounted, all-moving control surfaces, was stalled in part-designed and part-built condition. The rescue came with the redesignation of this second aircraft as the P.120 and extensions to the programme while the P.111 was rebuilt.

Revisions to the P.111 Mk II and the obtaining of fresh funding meant it was finally completed as the P.120 prototype. The track was 5in wider and main legs moved 1.25in to the rear. This illustration shows the framing of the egg box structure for the new fin and tailplane section.

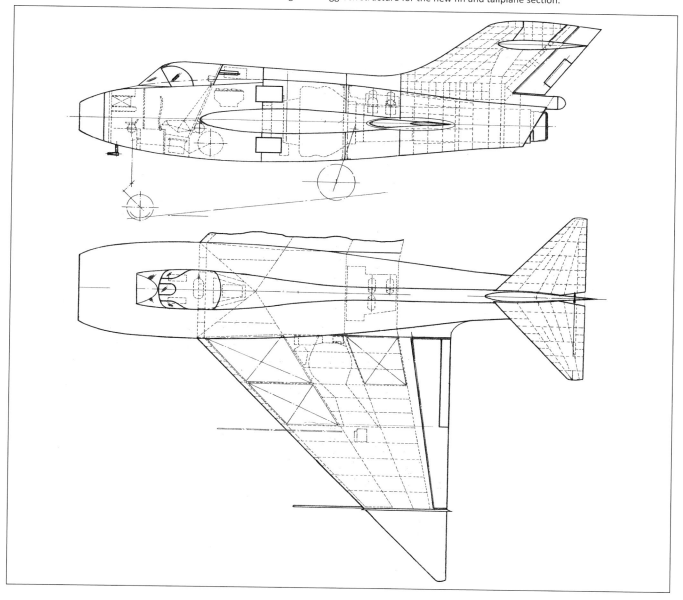

Wind tunnel model of the P.111 Mk II/P.120 showing the wing fences and all moving tips, which were intended to be tested as an alternative to its normal control surfaces.

The P.120 finished in the BPA factory with all markings added on to an area of green primer.

The P.120, painted up for photography and the forthcoming Farnborough Airshow, is seen airborne on Flight 19, the last flight before the fateful Flight 20, the one during which it lost an aileron.

The P.120 (P.111 Mk.II) was identical in basic outline to the P.111 but was equipped with fuselage-mounted air brakes behind the cockpit, a revised fin shape carrying an all-moving tailplane near the top of the fin, and an integral braking chute housing central to the rudder base just above the exhaust of the engine. Wing fences near the delta wing tips divided the shed airflow from the wing and prevented it from distorting as the wing tip controls operated. Minor changes to the position and rake of the main undercarriage were made to improve ground handling, moving it 1.25in back, while the track had been increased by 5in. A larger tail bumper was built under the rear fuselage and pitot systems for both high- and low-speed operation installed. The windscreen was also a flat panel-centre type that had been similarly fitted to the P.111 prior to its belly landing.

Flying started on 6 August 1952 after a fast taxi the day before and nineteen flights had been completed by 19 August. For the last two the aircraft had been painted overall gloss black with a gold fuselage stripe, so that Shell could make an aerial film in preparation for the Farnborough display in September. For all these flights the tailplane was set in a single selected position and the all-moving wing tips had no actuators, instead they were locked solid at zero with struts.

Flight twenty on 20 August 1952, went very well until the pilot, A. E. Ben Gunn, decided to continue with advancing the flight programme from 425 to 450 knots. At 450 knots the aircraft suffered high-speed elevon flutter and detachment of the port elevon from the aircraft, causing a high-speed roll rate to port, a situation that could only just be held by full starboard elevon, and full starboard rudder. Eventually disconnecting the power controls and feel system, using manual controls at extent of travel, it was possible to regain height. Gunn tried every effort to return to base but once over Boscombe at low level he was forced to eject, with the aircraft crashing on Salisbury Plain. With the loss of the P.120, the programme of high-speed flight reverted back to the P.111A only. It was decided on the grounds of cost not to replace the P.120 or to convert the P.111A into a tailplane or moving wing tip configuration.

The span was 33ft 5.64in, the length 28ft 9.7in and the height 9ft 6.3in. The tailplane was of identical planform to the wing but of only 9ft 4in span. The track was 14ft 10in. The speed predicted 650 knots in level flight, although at the time of the crash this was limited to 500 knots by the pilot's notes. Approximate Mach 0.93 or more was estimated. The airframe design was stressed for a speed of Mach 1.

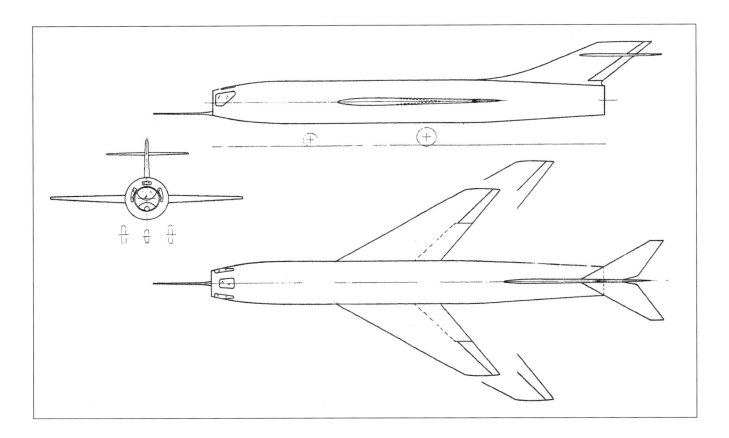

CHAPTER THIRTY-ONE

P.113 and P.114
Supersonic Research and Fighters

T HE MINISTRY OF SUPPLY released a design study in 7/ACFT/3723 calling for an aircraft that could reach 700 knots at an operational height of 45,000ft and which could be employed usefully as a fighter aircraft or a research machine, with the fighter case dominating. RAE Aero 1928 and 1960 had already shown likely useful loads of 3.7% and 9% respectively and BPA felt that for a military load of 2,700lb the fighter case would need an airframe AUW of around 28,000lb. This dictated the need for, by example, two Avon engines with reheat or their equivalent. If, however, a pure research machine was required as soon as practicable, the smallest possible machine would be required. This could be met by a single Avon, perhaps with reheat or rocket boost, and would weigh perhaps 12,850lb AUW in operational condition. The company therefore decided to submit two designs, one for the pure research aircraft and one for the fighter and research type. A contract for the design study was placed in August/September 1948 with no guarantee of production. By January 1949 the company was told that their study had not been accepted for prototyping.

P.113

The P.113 was designed around the smaller research machine requirements. It was pointed out immediately that such a machine would not reach the intended Mach 1.21 without the use of reheat or rocket boost. Six versions were considered:

■ Single Avon engine with reheat (P.113A).

■ Single Avon engine without reheat.

■ Single Avon engine without reheat but with rocket boost.

■ Single Sapphire engine with reheat (P.113S).

■ Single Sapphire engine without reheat.

■ Single Bristol BE.10 High Compression engine without reheat.

The versions 2 and 5 were quickly eliminated from the study as not meeting the requirements. The version 6, with the BE.10 engine, was found to require a much larger machine and reheat, and that too was eliminated on the grounds of insufficient performance. This brought

The P.113A supersonic research aircraft showing the proposed wing size and the possible smaller size sketched in during discussions on the Avon-powered airframe.

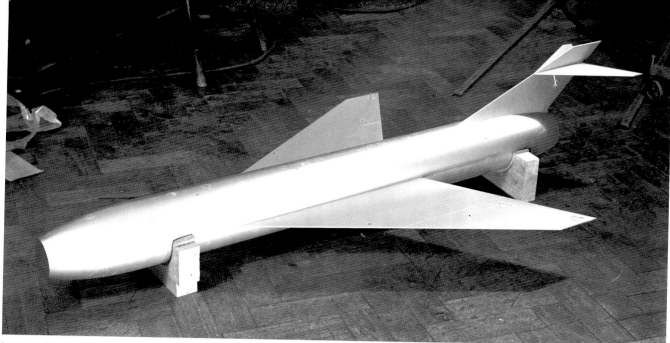

Large wind tunnel model of the P.113.

the potential down to three designs (1, 3 and 4), for which the airframe outlines P.113A and P.113S were generated. In size the two aircraft were identical except that the P.113S required more wing area, which meant an increase in the span by simply extending the wing to a new tip position.

For the fuselage lines it was decided no protrusions should interfere with the fuselage aerodynamic surface. The pilot was therefore to be enclosed within the circular fuselage behind the bifurcation of the intake duct. Seating alternatives were a normal seat with ejection upward and rearward, and prone seating with downward and rearward ejection. The upward seat had a clamshell hood that dropped down to protect the pilot's face and upper body during ejection. The downward seat fired down an extending rail of the couch support, providing similar protection.

Full power control systems with manual reversions were proposed with conventional controls when reclined and either single-hand controls of elevons and rudder or hand elevons and foot rudder bar. The flaps, airbrakes and all-moving tailplane were fitted with electric tabs on the elevons and mechanical tab on the rudder. If version 3 was to be chosen then the rocket boost was by producing an oval section at the tail cone and installing two rocket motors, one either side of the centreline. The rocket motor system and design layout was that recommended by MoS, who provided the system diagrams. The rocket engines were to use 'C' fuel (a British version of the German C-Stoff methanol formula) and hydrogen peroxide. This combination had been studied by Westcott and used in the Armstrong Siddeley Beta engine design development of the German HWK109-509 engine for the Me 163 rocket fighter, although none of this background was provided to the company at that time.

Interior of the P.113.

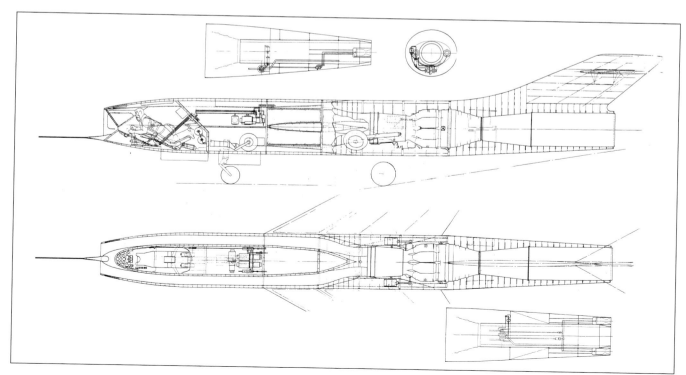

Above: Artist's impression of the P.113A.

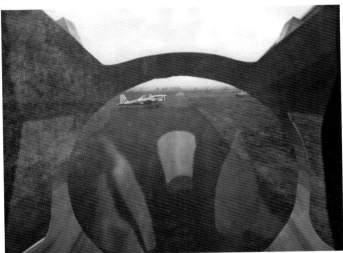

View of both prone and seated pilot positions were taken from a mock-up cockpit.

The P.113S sapphire-powered airframe, which needed more wing area than the Avon and hence had extended wing tips.

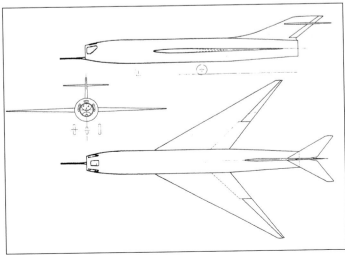

Construction of the P.113 intended to follow the 'egg box' fuselage structure utilised for E.27/46 - P.111 within the fuselage areas. The wing was intended to be made from a thick-skinned box having three spars and no ribs. Each half could be manufactured from three planks of light allow, fully machined inside and out by transverse machining. The trailing edge flaps and elevons were of conventional manufacture. Wings were to be removable so that alternate planforms could be tried if required. Squires High Speed C section was chosen. Considered initially as a double wedge after the design paper 'Aerodynamic Performance of Delta wings at Supersonic Speeds – A. E. Puckett and J. J. Stewart', the section was revised with coefficient of drag (Cd) increased to allow for the rounded nose.

It was thought that the Avon engine was most promising for the first aircraft with a reheat performance in the region of 1.21 to 1.42 Mach. The Sapphire was the logical follow on, installed within the same space. However, if the Sapphire reheat could be increased to that which Rolls-Royce thought possible then there was no reason to doubt that the airframe was capable of in excess of 1.5 Mach without using all of the reheat available. The design was therefore not limited to one engine or one boost source, if rockets could be used instead of reheat. Although the wing had been designed for 1.5 Mach, a redesign could considerably increase this with the same power systems. At 45,000ft and Mach 1.5 the endurance at that speed was quite small at seven minutes. Eleven minutes were available at Mach 1.2. With rocket power endurance was reduced to 30% of the reheat scenario.

The span was 26ft 2in (P.113A), 31ft 8in (P.113S) with net areas 201sq ft and 216sq ft. The length was 48ft 4in (54ft 7in with pressure head fitted to the lower nose). The height was 11ft 3in at static. The sweepback was 57° at 25% chord and constant thickness to chord ratio (t/c) of 0.55. A nosewheel undercarriage with a track of 5ft on the mainwheels completed the landing gear. Flap at 30° were required for take-off and 45° for landing. The maximum AUW (Avon and rocket motors) was 13,500lb, the Minimum AUW (Avon no reheat) 12,250lb.

Artist's impression of the P.114.

P.114

The P.114 was intended to represent the smallest airframe that could fulfil the dual purpose of fighter and pure research aircraft with either two Avon (P.114A) or two Sapphire (P.114S) engines. One could consider the airframe as an enlargement of the P.113 or vice versa. Both were designed together and submitted together in October 1948, although the simplified wind tunnel model for tests was of the P.113. In order to carry sufficient offensive load a two-engine design with an oval cross section for side-by-side engines was drawn with the circular cross section pilot's cockpit sitting between and forward of the side intakes for the engines. Two cannon were installed behind the cockpit between the air intakes, either side of the nosewheel stowage. As Appendix A to the specification had not been issued at the time of submission, a number of standard items of RAF equipment had to be assumed, in particular radios and 30mm cannon. E.27/46, P.111-type construction was anticipated for the forward fuselage and wing area, while from the engine location aft it would be conventional, with the rear fuselage removable.

As with the P.113, it was expected that the aircraft would achieve 1.5 Mach. As before, more reheat temperature on the Sapphires would easily exceed that figure. Take-off speed at 20,000lb assumed for the P.114A was 126 knots with flaps at 30° and landing speed 116 knots at 45° flap and an assumed landing weight of 24,600lb. For the P.114S the performance would be similar but the take-off weight increased to 30,500lb. Rockets rather than reheat were not seriously considered for the fighter as similar performance was available by reheat. It was recommended that 2,000°K reheat be a serious development for the Sapphire engine.

The span was 41ft (P.114A), 46ft 4in (P.114S) with net areas 470 and 500sq ft. The length was 88ft including pressure head. The height was 17ft at static. The sweepback was 57° at 25% chord and constant t/c of 0.55. A nosewheel undercarriage with a track of 8ft on the mainwheels completed the landing gear.

The P.114A twin-Avon supersonic fighter was a much larger aircraft than the P.113 but based upon its structure with a pilot's cockpit at the front and two cannon under the cheek intakes.

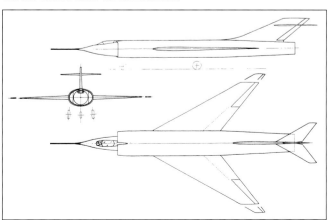

The alternate twin-Sapphire engine supersonic fighter, again with larger wingspan.

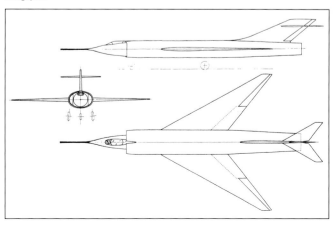

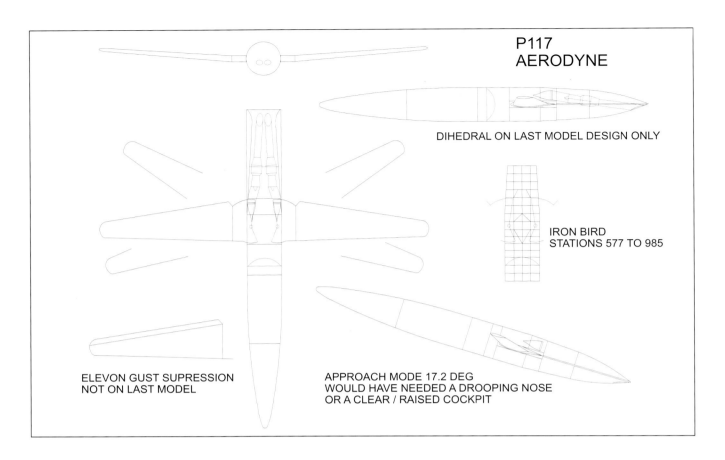

**P117
AERODYNE**

DIHEDRAL ON LAST MODEL DESIGN ONLY

IRON BIRD
STATIONS 577 TO 985

ELEVON GUST SUPRESSION
NOT ON LAST MODEL

APPROACH MODE 17.2 DEG
WOULD HAVE NEEDED A DROOPING NOSE
OR A CLEAR / RAISED COCKPIT

CHAPTER THIRTY-TWO

Aerodyne and Narrow Delta Sweepback Research

P.117

THE P.117 WAS A DESIGN STUDY for a 'Wing Controlled Aerodyne'. The concept of an aircraft having no flight control surfaces and being controlled only by the sweep of its wings either together or asymmetrically had been thought about for some time, most notably by the Vickers engineer Barnes Wallis with this military 'Grey Goose' free-flight models. What was required by government engineers was to understand if such a concept expounded by Barnes Wallis would work and particularly what sort of power control system would be required for the actuation of the flight control surface (wing). The design study covered wind tunnel experiments on a fuselage and wing shape to determine the correct aerodynamic characteristics, then a design for a full-size test bed consisting of a set of wings and a centre section to be equipped with appropriate power controls of suitable size. In the iron bird it was assumed the engine bay would be behind the wing in the tail of the aircraft. Following on from this it was thought that a full-size design or a scale design might progress to physically explore the dynamics in flight.

Studied from the first quarter of 1949 to develop range and payload values, other calculations continued for a year. The first tests in September 1949 utilised a model having forward sweep, through to sharp rearward sweep to determine the pitch characteristics of the body shapes. Despite being a wing-control aircraft, this model assumed full-span flaperons moving the whole of the exposed trailing edge of the wing. The use of the trailing edge surfaces was because it was assumed some form of gust alleviation might be needed to decide between a gust and a true control input.

The overall length of the initial 1/40th scale model was a scale 100ft and the quarter wing mean chord was at 62.5ft. The wing pivoted at 65ft. Forward sweep of 10° and aft sweep of 60° were suggested, and this form would balance at a scale 45ft from the nose.

The P.117 was a study of a 100ft span, 100ft long, 60,000lb airliner controlled only by symmetric and asymmetric sweep of its wings using fully powered and controlled wing sweep mechanisms. The project considerably assisted the understanding of sweep mechanisms and their loadings during actuation.

Spread span was the 100ft. The pure circle-section body shape had 12% fineness ratio and followed RAE report Aero 2073. The body was initially semi-symmetrical as in the Aero report and was apparently not very successful. A number of semi-symmetrical rear fuselage shapes were tried for pitch stability and it was eventually decided to give the aircraft a ducktail strake either side of the rear fuselage similar to the RAE E.27/46 Concept No 64 to assist with stability. This model utilised the improved, fully designed wing shape with correct root pivots and no trailing edge devices.

In parallel with the wind tunnel tests and performance calculations, the Aerodynamics Department and the Technical Office jointly drew up the requirements for the centre section 'iron bird' test unit during February to April 1950. It was hoped that the development would also yield useful data applicable to other variable-sweep aircraft. The design was again based upon an aircraft with a 100ft span when unswept with a 1,000sq ft wing area, with an aspect ratio of ten and of 60,000lb AUW. A bomber or civilian type airliner flight envelope up to 600mph and +2.65 to -1.3g was applied. The revised wing pivots were placed 8ft apart at Station 760 and the overall length retained 100ft. The maximum diameter of the circular fuselage was a scale 12ft 6in. The wings were of 13ft 4in chord at the aircraft centreline and 6ft 8in at the tip. The wing section used HS.2 symmetrical modified and there was zero incidence. Spars within the wings were provided at 25, 51 and 75% of chord and the wings were to be constructed of conventional 'Z' stringers and graduated skinning. The design sweep system was now specified as 15° forward to 35° aft and asymmetric positions within that range. Because of the control parameters and the centre-section design of the aircraft, however, the theoretically usable sweep angles were from 28° 28' forward to 41° 36' aft.

Three key performance cases were calculated. At a flight speed of 220mph, a thrust of 11,400lb, the aircraft would be stable in pitch at 17.2° incidence and the wings forward by 8.7°. At a flight speed of 600mph, a thrust of 10,800lb, the aircraft would be stable in pitch at 4.6° incidence and the wings forward by 0.6°. At a flight speed of 600mph, a thrust of 10,800lb, the aircraft would be stable at 6° incidence and the

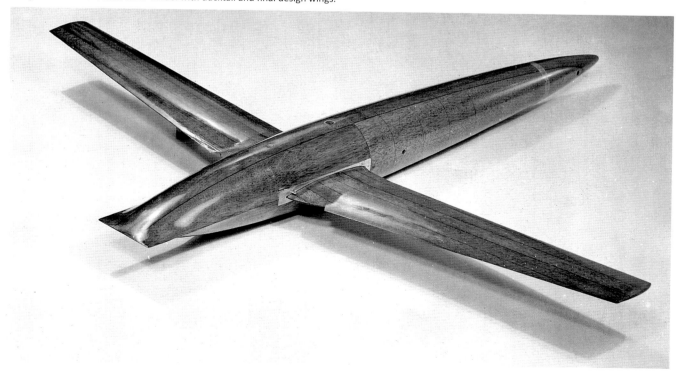

The P.117 aerodyne study started with a basic model shape seen here.

wings swept aft by 30°. Studies of gust loads were made for power and stress calculations but it was assumed for the study that the machine would have no gust alleviation system as such a system requirement had not been defined. One can only assume that the 220mph and 17.2° pitch-up, nose-high mode would be the landing approach, giving the sort of nose-high requirements similar to a highly swept delta. It will be noted from this data that the body of the craft would be in nose-up pitch in all of its key calculation points, even when flying straight. The likely asymmetric flight capabilities for manoeuvring the craft were issued in a different document in March 1950.

Wings neutral on the final P.117 model with ducktail and final design wings.

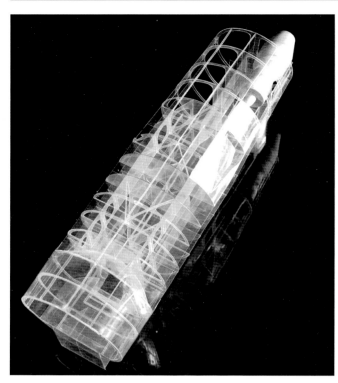

P.117 Xylonite model of the wing box and engine section of the P.117 showing from front (left) to back, the aft pressure bulkhead of the passenger cabin and access steps, the wing root boxes, the port NACA air intake to one engine and the port engine model.

A Xylonite model of the structure required for the centre section, the wing pivot boxes and the engine installation was made. This provided for a twin-engine design with individual NACA flush intakes on the upper surface immediately aft of the pivot boxes taking air into the engines set side-by-side in the upper half, exhausting towards the centreline of the body. This would then have required exhaust ducts just below the centreline of the aircraft at the ducktail extremity.

Forward of the pivot boxes was a full pressure bulkhead for the crew and passenger area. The engines specified were not listed but from the shape the model appears to have twin Avons. Unfortunately the undercarriage design, number of crew/passengers, the cockpit design and the passenger section interior concept remains unknown.

With such a variation in pitch, to be comfortable it would have probably been necessary to develop a wing system that could vary in both sweep and incidence. However, the project did not progress past publication of any reports. An aircraft that had to fly continually in a pitch-up mode, constantly vary pitch with wing sweep and for general directional control, was quite simply an interesting academic exercise, but unlikely to be performance efficient as a military aircraft or passenger friendly as a civil machine. The iron bird calculations yielded useful data on the actuation forces likely and the overall pitch loads trying to twist the wing structure but such a large trial actuation system seems to have been unfinanced before the project was terminated.

P.118

The P.118 was another design study to generate the requirements for a highly swept wing test aircraft powered by a Nene jet engine. BPA were first aware of the requirement in late September 1949, when details were awaited. No detail documents are known but it is believed that a 76° delta planform was selected and the scaled 26ft span, 52ft-long highly swept wing was later revived for the P.134 VTOL aircraft, so one might suggest that the P.118 looked like a single-engine P.134 without lift fans. The very basic club-shaped body wind tunnel model also used later for initial work on the P.134 was that developed for the P.118 calculations. The whole aim of the study was to cover an aircraft with a highly swept wing that would investigate the slow-speed characteristics of such a wing design. By February 1950 Dr Redshaw reported that the Ministry had decided that such an aircraft was not now required, so the design did not appear to proceed further than design calculations and the basic tunnel model wing. BPA continued to apply its design data to later VTOL layouts but formal investigation of the slow-speed requirements of this type of wing did not reappear until the Supersonic Transport Committee was formed in the mid-1950s, resulting in ER197D and the HP.115 test aircraft.

The 'club' model intended to test the initial geometry of the P.118 wing at slow speed was later changed at the rear end (as here) to be used for early tests of the P.133 and P.134 series wing planform. The programme was cancelled, only to be resurrected by other committees when the supersonic airliner project that led to Concorde was started.

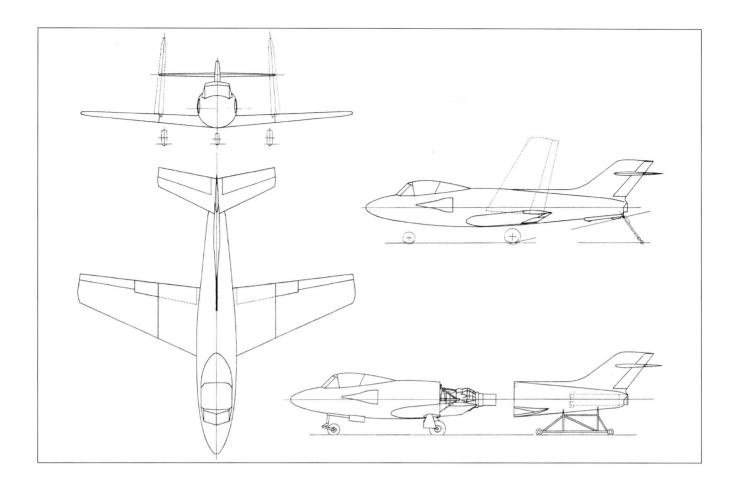

CHAPTER THIRTY-THREE

Post-War Turbojet Training Aircraft

P.119 and P.119N

IT HAD BECOME clear to the board that the development of the P.108 trainer, rather than leading to the 1,000 aircraft originally expected, was to deteriorate into smaller quantities, shared contracts and even disappear to the lowest tender. The turboprop system had been leapfrogged by the jet engine and the need for an advanced fighter-type trainer would move into pure jet designs. The P.119 was therefore a private venture offering for a twin-seat side-by-side jet trainer aircraft using a RR Derwent engine. The initial preliminary study information was released in February 1950 and this was followed by a more detailed proposal brochure in May 1950. By this time folding wings and an arrestor hook had been added to the design variants to provide a P.119N and comparisons were undertaken for Derwent or Nene engines. The design was initially well received. A full-size wooden mock-up was authorised and was manufactured, complete with cockpit layout, gun bay and nose access hatches, internal weapon armament of two 20 mm cannon and systems, being completed in August 1950. Although a PV design the company followed information from MoS and understood at the point of submission in February 1950 that a specification for which the design was suitable was likely to be issued shortly.

The wing section chosen, Squires High Speed C, was an extremely efficient low-drag section used on the P.111 and the P.120 research aircraft. The swept wing was set low on the fuselage, giving a short tricycle undercarriage, and the air intakes were NACA shape set into the fuselage sides behind the crew and feeding into the engine bay aft of the

Private venture proposal to the Air Ministry for a jet trainer. The basic P.119 was land based and the P.119N was a naval version. Folding wings were incorporated in both versions during development of the project.

cockpit. Based on maintenance ease, the entire rear fuselage and jet pipe could be quickly disconnected and wheeled away from the rest, leaving access all around the engine. Under the crew position, two cannon barrels entered from the bay behind. The access to this bay for re-arming, radio maintenance etc, was from underneath through the nosewheel undercarriage bay. Cockpit pressurisation and heating took air from an intake on the fin, fed it to the jet pipe via a cuff and thence forward to the cockpit. All fuel was carried in a main tank between the intake feeds

P.119

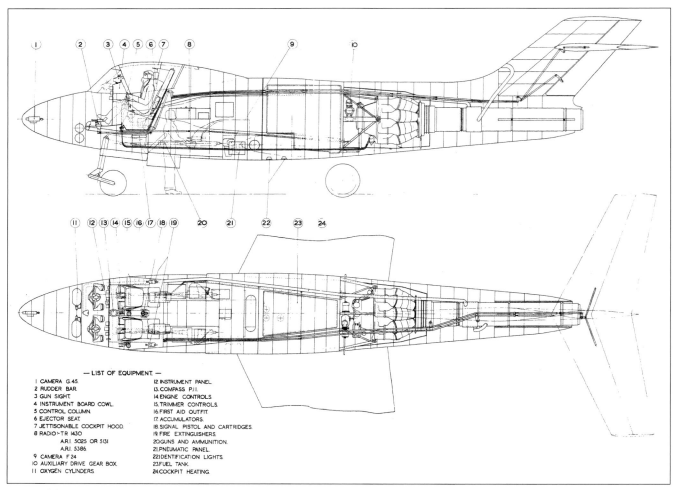

— LIST OF EQUIPMENT —

1 CAMERA G.45.	12 INSTRUMENT PANEL.
2 RUDDER BAR.	13. COMPASS P.I.I.
3 GUN SIGHT.	14 ENGINE CONTROLS.
4 INSTRUMENT BOARD COWL.	15. TRIMMER CONTROLS.
5 CONTROL COLUMN.	16. FIRST AID OUTFIT.
6 EJECTOR SEAT.	17. ACCUMULATORS.
7 JETTISONABLE COCKPIT HOOD.	18. SIGNAL PISTOL AND CARTRIDGES.
8 RADIO - TR 1430.	19. FIRE EXTINGUISHERS.
A.R.I. 5025 OR 5131	20. GUNS AND AMMUNITION.
A.R.I. 5386	21. PNEUMATIC PANEL.
9 CAMERA F 24	22 IDENTIFICATION LIGHTS.
10 AUXILIARY DRIVE GEAR BOX.	23. FUEL TANK.
11 OXYGEN CYLINDERS.	24. COCKPIT HEATING.

Interior of the P.119.

to the engine plenum just forward of the main undercarriage. An F.24 camera and all pneumatic services were accessed via the pneumatic panel in the lower fuselage. There were no flight control actuators as it was expected that neither the Westland/Irving ailerons nor the elevators or rudder needed boosting. In fact, all hydraulics had been left off the design in lieu of simpler pneumatic services. The canopy opened by moving upwards and back on a pantograph system and could be jettisoned in order to fire the crew ejector seats.

Structurally the design was conventional riveted light alloy and the wings on the mock-up folded to 18ft 6in span. The N version drawing also featured wing-mounted airbrakes. The span was 38ft 8.72in for the 3,600lb thrust Derwent 5-powered version with a

fuselage length of 37ft 3.6in to the jet pipe end, 42ft 5in overall. The height was 12ft 3in over the fin at a ground line of zero incidence. The wing was at 1° and the tail at -1° incidence with a wing dihedral of 2°. The AUW for a normal load was 9,496lb, the tropical version 9,619lb and with 200 gal fuel in drop tanks 11,296lb. The performance was 475mph at 22,500ft, with optimum cruise between 250mph and 350mph depending upon height. The landing angle was 14°, and to accommodate deck landing or landing mistakes the undercarriage was capable of an impact of sustaining 14ft/sec. Ultimately no interest was shown in the design as it stood. The fuselage of the P.119 mock-up was still in existence in February 1955.

A fully rolling full-size mock-up was constructed of the private venture P.119.

The canopy was to be powered to swing upwards and rearwards.

Model of the P.119 in the RAF training scheme.

For engine maintenance the whole rear fuselage was detached on a special trolley.

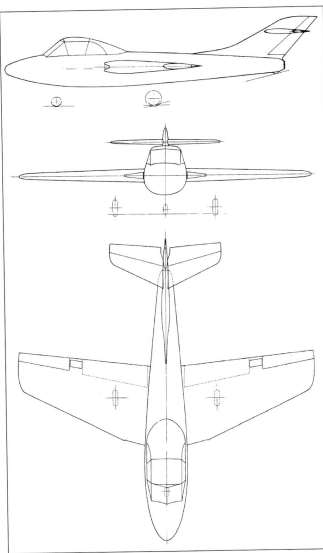

P.124

A similar airframe was submitted July 1954 with an Armstrong Siddeley Viper ASV5 engine designated P.124. The object of the design was to provide a basic jet-powered aircraft to assess the merits or demerits of pupil pilots both during training and prior to incurring the cost of full jet training at an early stage of their career. In this manner the RAF hoped to speed up the progress through training command on piston aircraft into advanced training on jets. Developed to drafted MoS Specification H182074 PDRD ACFT, the proposal was submitted on a non-tender basis to gauge interest.

The view forward was in excess of 15° down and all around exceeded the requirements of AP.970, the basic design reference. Vertical decent capability was designed into the undercarriage of 14ft/sec. Since the designator P.124 was allocated before the P.125, its initial concept may have been a similar requirement. This aircraft had a slimmer fuselage of less pleasant appearance aft of the cockpit than the P.119, and wedge-type intakes at each wing root like the Hunter. The wing was moved up on the fuselage and placed just below the fuselage centreline. The area to the rear of the opening canopy was made clear to give an all-around view. Armament capability suggested comprised a single 0.5in machine gun, two 250lb bombs or eight practice bombs or six rocket projectiles underwing.

In detail the aircraft design was quite obviously developed from the P.119 layout. The span was 32ft, the centreline chord 10.5ft and the tip chord 4.16ft. Sweepback at quarter chord was 22.5° and the gross area 235sq ft. The surface sections had been changed to RAE102 throughout. The tailplane span was 12ft, the hull length 30.5ft and the overall length 34ft. The height was 9.75ft and all incidence, dihedral and ground line angles were zero. Flying controls and control tabs were all incorporated. The aircraft was to be fully aerobatic with a top speed of 330 knots at 30,000ft. Stall was at 77 knots flaps up and 65 knots flaps down. The service ceiling was 35,500ft at maximum continuous power, and 41,000ft at maximum full power rating. A two-seat development of the Hunter eventually made such a design unnecessary, and the P.124 was not developed.

Left: P.124 jet trainer to MoS specification issued as H182074 PDRD ACFT.

Below: Model of the P.124.

P.125

Drawn up long before the P.124 was submitted in brochure form (in the first half of 1952), the P.125 followed the same ideas that many manufacturers were to try worldwide, the installation of a turbojet in the nose of an existing machine. The aircraft was proposed in response to Standard Jet Trainer Working Party (SJTWP) Appendix C requirements and was a conversion of the existing P.108 design mixing T.1 and T.2. The P.125 merely took out the propeller engine and installed a pure jet engine, adjusting the location to suit the centre of gravity. The engine was mounted within the same area and similar firewall design as the Balliol T.1. Because it now had no propeller, a tailwheel undercarriage was unnecessary and a slightly offset nosewheel design was used. The main undercarriage was to be a new design now sat outboard of the wing fuel tanks and retracted inboard but angled forward ahead of the fuel tanks. The engine suggested was a RR Derwent 5 as proposed in the P.119 private venture. There was no need to change as much as 60% of the original, and 20% on top of this were only modifications to existing components with 20% new. Key areas of change were a new windscreen to cope with the increased performance and revision to the jet pipe to exit on the centreline under the aircraft.

A normal dual load for training was 9,316lb AUW rising to a maximum of 10,336lb AUW in dual-occupancy ferrying role with full desert equipment. The naval version added 160lb to any of the weights to allow for catapult spools and arrester hook. At a weight of 9,350lb

A prototype Balliol photograph was skilfully airbrushed to show the P.125 in flight.

the maximum speed achievable was 400 knots at 20,000ft and 396 knots at sea level, with a service ceiling of 41,000ft. The speeds above sea level were limited by Mach number. The maximum Mach numbers usable were 0.65 for a clean aircraft and 0.60 for gunnery training. All the potential training roles used for the Balliol were available: gunnery, camera gunnery, bombs and rockets. The 240 gallons of fuel gave an endurance of one hour and twenty minutes approximately depending on the flight envelope chosen on the sortie.

P.125 pure jet trainer proposal based upon revision of the original P.108 T.1 turboprop airframe and a tricycle undercarriage to requirement SJTWP Appendix C. Had a P.125 Derwent Balliol been built using 60% of P.108A components it would have looked like this.

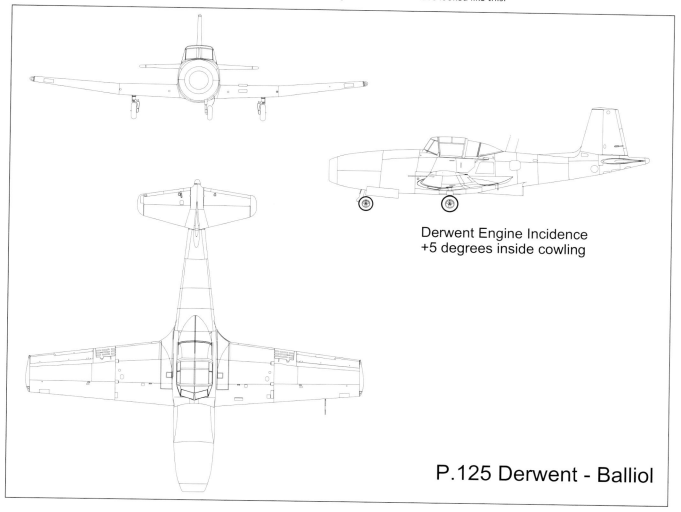

Derwent Engine Incidence
+5 degrees inside cowling

P.125 Derwent - Balliol

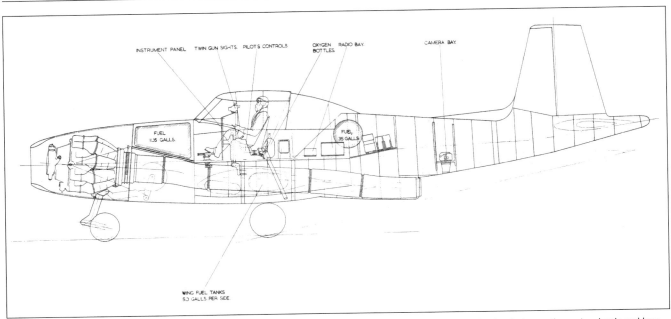

INSTRUMENT PANEL   TWIN GUN SIGHTS   PILOTS CONTROLS   OXYGEN   RADIO BAY.   CAMERA BAY.
BOTTLES.

FUEL
105 GALLS.

FUEL
35 GALLS.

WING FUEL TANKS
50 GALLS PER SIDE

Rushed through in the brochure submission, it was not noticed that the 50 gallon wing tanks would have required redesign as the main wheels and legs would occupy a main part of the tank space when retracted.

P.131 jet trainer for the RAAF.

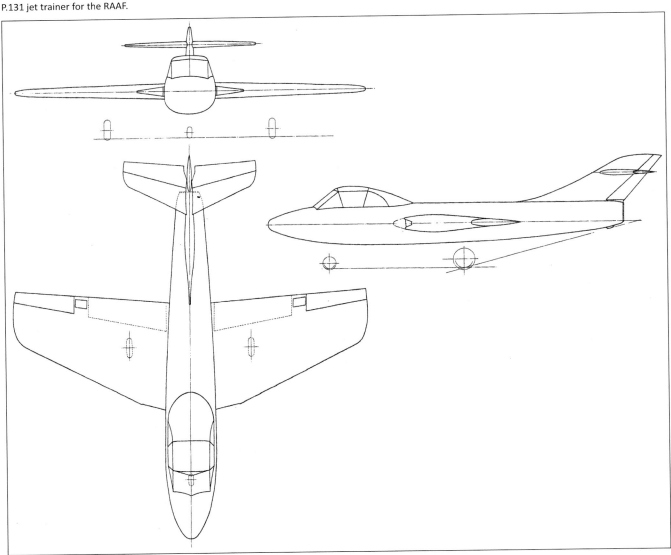

A 'Summary of Characteristics and Performance' document raised by the BPA Technical Department initially followed the formal requirements with only one rocket installed under the outer wings. When the brochure was submitted in June 1952, however, the number of rockets had increased to two under each outer wing following the requirements for the Balliol. To supplement the proposal, an in-flight photograph of Mamba T.1 prototype VL892 was modified by airbrushing using the company's skilled technical publications artist Eric Evans, adequately representing the appearance of the P.125 had it been built. There was no recorded response to the brochure, which disappeared into committee.

P.131

Similarly, in November 1954 the P.131 was submitted to Specification OR/Air/37 of 27 May 1954 with a Bristol Orpheus engine. The requirement was for a Royal Australian Air Force trainer and BPA employed the same wing as the P.124 of 32ft span, but the root and tip chords were adjusted to 11.67ft and 4.67ft, increasing the gross area to 260sq ft. The hull length increased to 32.5ft and the overall length to 36ft. The height was 10.5ft and all incidence, dihedral, ground line angles were zero as before.

Model of the P.131.

Solo, dual, rocket, bomb and gunnery roles were catered for but the two 0.5in guns were in pods and not internal because the specification requested all the alternate role equipment be located in the same position and be interchangeable. A view of their location in hindsight suggests that there might have been ingestion of firing vapours into the intakes during gunnery. Maximum speed was 490 knots (Mach 0.8) at 20,000ft, 440 knots at sea level and 460 knots at 40,000ft. With 50% flap take off at 7,500lb was 80 knots to climb away at 130 knots. Flaps up stall was 86 knots and flaps down and undercarriage down 69 knots. The best approach was flaps down at 95 knots. Again no response is recorded.

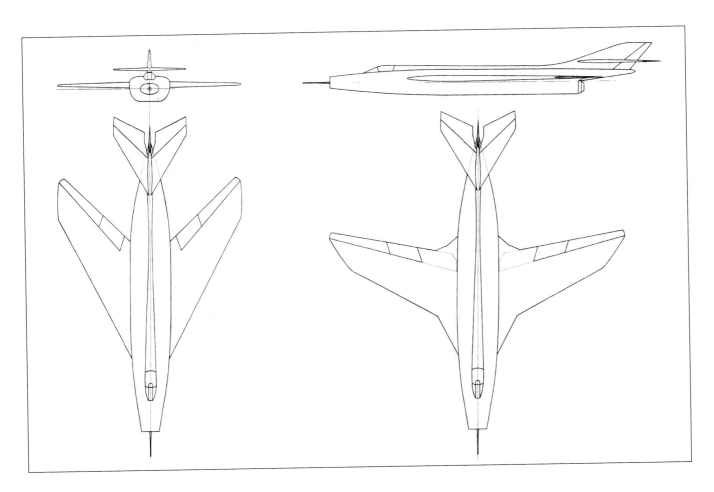

CHAPTER THIRTY-FOUR

Interceptors and Bombers P.121 to P.123

P.121

A NUMBER OF EXPERIMENTS had been conducted to reduce the range of problems of naval jet aircraft by the removal of the undercarriage, saving approximately 7% of the airframe weight, Catapult launch and undercarriage jettison systems were considered, together with landing upon a rubberised mat. By the end of 1952 the whole concept had been abandoned because the cost of the deck systems did not justify the small increase in performance. Nevertheless, prior to that other uses of the concept had appeared.

ER110T of February 1951 called for a supersonic, variable-geometry (swing-wing) aircraft suitable for operation as a fighter and to develop a working swing-wing principle. The aircraft offered could, if desired, have no undercarriage to save weight and therefore boost performance. In which case it was to land via the airfield 'rubber deck' principle. The wings were to be two-position: 25° generally and 60° for high-speed flight of Mach 1.2 at 45,000ft. There would be translation between the two but selection and locking at intermediate positions were not required. Sweep action was to take place above 290mph. Avon or Sapphire engines with 1,500°k reheat were suggested.

The new technical director of BPA, following the move of Dr Redshaw back to academia, was F. F. Crocombe, who had been deeply involved with swing-wing research at Blackburn and had decided to leave Blackburn when all his work on swing-wing designs was moved from Feltham to Brough. His desire to continue this innovative development was why BPA were interested in ER110T. Certainly it had been raised as the result of much previous work by Blackburn and others. BPA proposed to follow the undercarriage-less route and In order to accommodate this requirement, the P.121

was designed with a reinforced flat belly to the fuselage, which took on a trapezium-like cross section. It was also equipped with an arrester hook to retard the landing slide on the mat.

Full details of the wing operational mechanism was provided in the company brochure as they had already studied wing sweep mechanisms under the P.117 project. BPA proposed a fixed pivot point

The P.121 supersonic swing-wing, undercarriage-less fighter proposal to ER.110T.

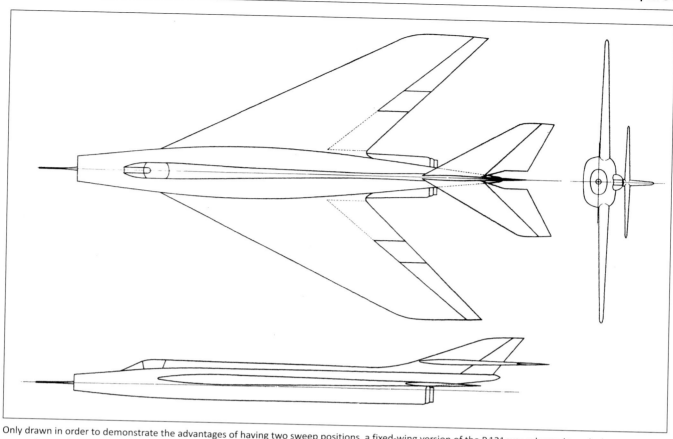

Only drawn in order to demonstrate the advantages of having two sweep positions, a fixed-wing version of the P.121 was schemed to calculate comparisons. There was never any intention that this version would be built.

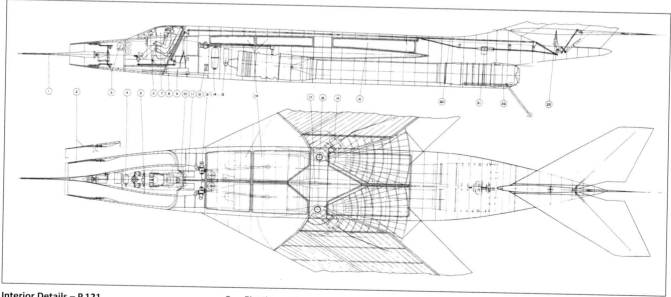

Interior Details – P.121

1. Plastic pitot head
2. Extendable nose intake
3. Radar ranging
4. Oxygen cylinders
5. Instrument panel
6. Gyro gun-sight
7. Jettisonable hood
8. Ejection seat
9. 30mm gun
10. Radio
11. Ammunition boxes
12. Accumulators
13. Auxiliary drive gearbox
14. Fuel accumulators
15. Hydraulic accumulator
16. Fuel tanks
17. Wing operating ram
18. Wing hinge bearing
19. Aileron hydraulic unit
20. Rudder control rod
21. Elevator hydraulic unit
22. Arrester hook
23. Tailplane actuator

for the wings rather than a translating slide, and noted in their proposal that much time and effort had been wasted by others to obtain a rearward movement of the mean chord by the wing group to give the required static margins for high subsonic flight. Instead, BPA ensured that a constant static margin existed for both forward and aft positions of the wing. By creating a solid of revolution of the wing around the pivot point, a near perfect seal of wing to forward wing fairing root cuff was obtainable. The landing speed was estimated to reduce by 27% in the wing-forward location. Catapult launch and arrested landing energy reduction was 37–38% compared with a fixed-wing aircraft. Any difficulties of control were expected to be easily overcome by the use of large tail surfaces and BPA designed power controls with synthetic feel. The pivot point chosen represented 58% of chord when swept and 48% when open. The small wing slot remaining fore and aft of the wing profile was to be made airtight by an inflatable rubber tube. A 1/20th scale model of the sweep mechanism was manufactured to accompany the proposal. Accumulator pressure would bring the wings into slow-speed position when operated in an emergency.

The pilot sat in the centre of the bifuricated duct in a pressurised, ejector seat-equipped cabin. Below his position were two 30mm

cannon and ammunition. It was expected to eventually fit the radar in the nose duct ahead of the pilot and to develop a non-metallic pitot head system on the fore part of the duct. RAE technical notes were complied with in respect of ventral catapulting and flexible deck landing, but for initial trials a fixed tricycle undercarriage would be included with the two main wheels splayed from the fuselage. BPA chose two side-by-side RA8 Avons exhausting under the tailplane and an open nose intake with pitot spike in the immediately bifuricated vertical duct divider. To allow extra intake air at slow speed without a translating radar blister, the entire nose cowl could be actuated forward to open an intake gap around the nose. Full afterburner system was incorporated well back from the engines in the under-tail ducts either side of the arrester hook.

With the Avon RA8 8,500lb static thrust at no reheat and 1,500°k reheat a speed of Mach 1.34 at 45,000ft was expected, to be improved when the 9,000lb static-thrust RA9 became available. Maximum diving speed was 500 knots spread and 625 knots swept, with a sweep operation envelope from 175 to 500 knots. Span with wings spread was 57ft equivalent, 60ft actual, and swept span was 37.83ft. The aircraft overall lengths were 72.74ft over the pitot head and 67.32ft with the pitot head removed. Thrust datum, wing datum and body datum were all at 0° and the wing section was the high-speed RAE101. Sweepback at quarter chord was 55° when set in the swept position. The tailplane span was 15ft and permanently swept, while the fin height reached 10.71ft with the aircraft sitting on the landing mat.

Calculations were also made for a fixed-wing version, since it was appreciated that some comparison of the two would illustrate the advantages of variable sweep. The fuselage cross section was now smaller but the wing area was increased by 25% to give the same performance for comparison. The fixed-wing swept span was now 42.45ft. The variable wing gave an immediate improvement in slow-speed landing performance, which dropped from 127 knots

Left: Impression of the fixed-wing version (for comparison only).

Below: Impression of the swing-wing P.121.

to 100 knots, and the kinetic energy reduction noted earlier for an arrested landing. It was never intended that the fixed-wing alternative was a design option in the proposal since it was simply to point to the swing-wing advantage. Competitive submissions included the A.W.59, Blackburn B.90, Bristol 183 and Saro P.149. The main fighter constructors were deliberately left out of the tender because of their existing workloads, but there was no prototype contract or even mock-up stage eventually awarded under this tender. Abandonment of the rubber deck system would have revised most designs.

P.122

The P.122 was an unsolicited proposal for the interception of high-altitude, high-performance bombers. The need was to attain height quickly enough to combat the potential Cold War bomber menace. Germany had used the Messerschmitt Me 163 with mixed success and the Bachem Natter, which failed to enter service. Nevertheless, the development of British rocket motors took off with the AS Snarler and DH Sprite, then the AS Screamer and the DH Spectre. The development work involved experimenting, like the German projects, with particularly nasty combinations of fuel and oxidant.

In May 1951, detecting a growing need for such a fighter, BPA submitted its brochure for the P.122 design, which it thought was one possible solution to the problem. The machine was to be capable of radar beam riding to the target, attacking with missiles and descending back to earth power off with the aid of an omni-directional homing system. The company submitted its own specification, there being none forthcoming from government at that point:

- A single-seat, rocket-propelled interceptor.
- High-performance with the greatest possible rate of climb.
- Good duration at altitude at high thrust rate sufficient to accomplish a set mission. This was defined as beam riding to target, one attack, glide down to base under a broadcast control. Duration not less than three minutes at 0.9 Mach at 60,000ft. At 0.75 Mach total duration not less than eight minutes.
- Sufficient air-to-air rocket projectiles for one attack.
- Launch by auxiliary-powered trolley on rails, ramp or from ship's deck.
- Low costs, maintenance and repair to be priority, compatible with high performance.
- Simple design with minimum number of components stored as assemblies or units classed as spares that can be easily repaired or replaced quickly, in the field, by service personnel.
- Lightest and smallest aircraft using a rocket motor already in advanced development and available for general use within the next two years.
- Complete cockpit jettisonable by the pilot for emergency escape. To be as compact as possible commensurate with the ability of the pilot to carry out his duties. To protect the pilot until an altitude is reached when he can abandon this capsule and escape by personal parachute.
- Designed for refuel and servicing in the field and equipped so that it can be readily hoisted on to a trolley, or motor vehicle, for transport to the launching site. A quick turnaround is essential.
- To keep structure weight as low as possible, the pilot should be provided with pressure suit and breathing apparatus in lieu of a pressure cabin. Because of the short duration at altitude, heating for the pilot and equipment is considered unnecessary.

- Centre of gravity change for all conditions of flight to be as small as possible.

This draft specification identified some of the problems that would appear in later airframe designs.

The use of an AS Screamer rocket motor was selected and the aircraft was stressed for 6.7g at 6,000lb equivalent to 4.5g take-off weight and a design speed of 455 knots. Basic structure weight was kept low by a small design having no undercarriage and a twin-boom layout. Airbrakes were provided inboard of the ailerons but no flaps. It was decided that slats and flaps offered no advantages for a skid-landing machine and were more likely to be damaged. Instead the air brakes could be utilised until touchdown or braking parachutes streamed from the twin booms, the air brakes being equivalent of two 1.4ft-diameter braking chutes. Flight controls were limited to cable-operated systems. Behind the cockpit the rest of the fuselage was filled with the fuel for the Screamer motor and the motor itself at the aft end.

BPA proposed a rocket motor-powered, fast-climbing interceptor to combat high-flying Russian bombers in the P.122 private venture specification. The Air Ministry took this specification to heart as their own and modified a couple of the parameters to release it as OR.301 and F.124T with higher speed and reduced flight time. However, later amendments to achieve supersonic speed over 30,000ft and use mixed power for endurance could not be met by the small P.122 design.

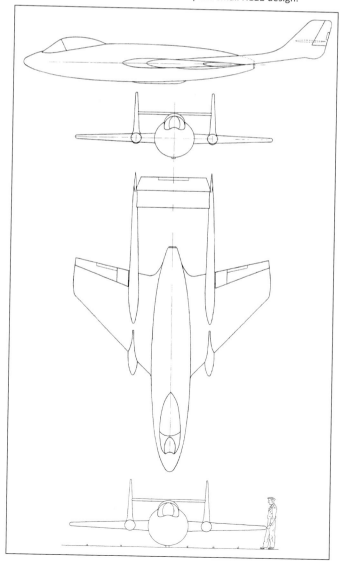

Artist's illustration of the P.122.

Two 'whisker' skids were to be deployed from the aft booms to steady the skid landing. Armament consisted of twenty-two unguided rockets in the jettisonable nose fairing at the front of each tail boom extension forward, an electric release being actioned to drop the nose cap immediately prior to firing and releasing all forty-four rockets at the target. All the structure was to be in light alloy.

With RAE102 section on all surfaces, the design was capable of reaching 60,000ft in three minutes with sufficient fuel to provide 5.7 minutes of cruise at Mach 0.8. With such a small span, area and wing loading the maximum roll rate was 380°/sec at Mach 0.9 and 60,000ft. The technique for landing was a zero-power 'fly-on' at 100 knots with air brakes and/or chutes deployed. The span was 21ft 2in and the net area 129.5sq ft. There was 40° sweepback at 25% chord. The fuselage body length was 25ft and the fuselage diameter 4ft 3.84in. The overall length was 33ft 4in and the height 7ft 6in. This was a really diminutive craft and a drawing in the original P.122 brochure showed an airman holding the port wing tip to emphasise the small size.

Simplified 'club' wind tunnel model of the P.122.

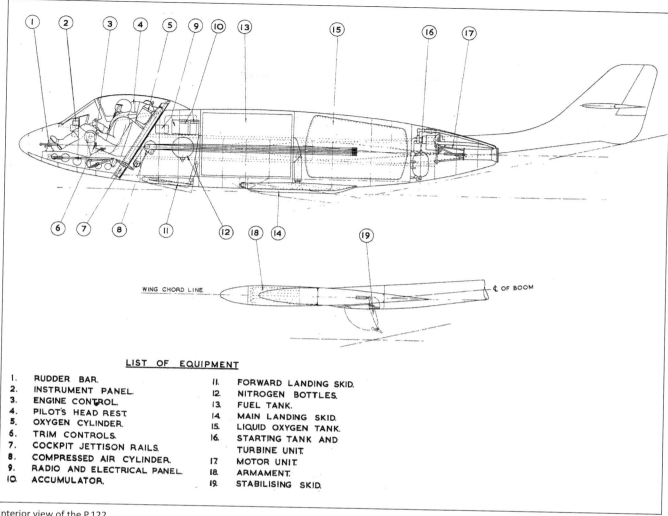

LIST OF EQUIPMENT

1.	RUDDER BAR.	11.	FORWARD LANDING SKID.
2.	INSTRUMENT PANEL.	12.	NITROGEN BOTTLES.
3.	ENGINE CONTROL.	13.	FUEL TANK.
4.	PILOT'S HEAD REST.	14.	MAIN LANDING SKID.
5.	OXYGEN CYLINDER.	15.	LIQUID OXYGEN TANK.
6.	TRIM CONTROLS.	16.	STARTING TANK AND
7.	COCKPIT JETTISON RAILS.		TURBINE UNIT.
8.	COMPRESSED AIR CYLINDER.	17.	MOTOR UNIT.
9.	RADIO AND ELECTRICAL PANEL.	18.	ARMAMENT.
10.	ACCUMULATOR.	19.	STABILISING SKID.

Interior view of the P.122.

To some extent the proposal must have generated or at least heavily coloured the eventual release of OR.301 (January 1952) and F.124T. BPA received a copy of F.124T, probably because of their P.122 design, and did not attempt to change their previous submission. What F.124T actually did was take the draft suggestions of the P.122 and stretch the requirements further. The speed at 60,000ft was increased to 0.95 Mach, the climb to height was therefore reduced to two and a half seconds. This left the P.122 still a viable contender. However, the eventual aim was stated to be an aircraft that would go supersonic over 30,000ft altitude. This change was a step too far for the P.122, which was not designed to pass the sound barrier. The later modification to the specification in May 1952, allowing mixed-power interceptors with jet and rocket equipment, placed the P.122 in even more of an untenable position against any mixed-power proposals, which were bound to be more complicated. BPA let the company's hydro-mechanical actuation section become tied instead with the Avro 720 flight controls.

P.123

P.123 was a response to MoS Specification UB109T of 9 February 1951, calling for a short-range expendable bomber capable of carrying a 5,000lb charge for 400 nautical miles at 500 knots and 40,000ft (ie Mach 0.87). A committee set up to investigate the problem concluded that what was required was a machine of extreme simplicity with the minimum number of components. Expendable working party papers

35, 59 and 68 were consulted along with RAE Technical Notes 107 and 176. It required a high performance but manufactured perhaps in materials and methods little used by the aircraft industry.

Since the design would have to be allied with extensive development of automatic and radio control equipment, not currently available, the main focus was on the airframe. To maintain a constant centre of gravity all consumable fuel was placed about the C of G and not in the wings. The design, with agreement of RAE experts, was split into two 2,500lb units fore and aft of the centre, which would detonate simultaneously. The explosive/bomb containers added either side of the wing and fuel centre could therefore be either this single charge or multiple bombs, incendiaries, etc, in an identical-size module forming the fuselage. The design was finalised as a cylindrical fuselage with streamlined nose and tail caps and a vee tail of two identical surfaces with combined 'ruddervator' trailing edge units. The wings were swept with the engines at mid-wing slung below the underside. A Rolls-Royce expendable engine of 1,750lb thrust was selected with the help of that company, designated RB.93. The bomber divided into seven distinct storable units, two of which were the identical weapons bays or weapon modules.

BPA had studied the RAE Durestos (asbestos phenolic) material for the manufacture of plastic components and their test specimens. While they had no doubt it could be improved by productionising, they felt that glass fibre or paper as a filler had been too lightly rejected and could be handled better in production. Calculations and

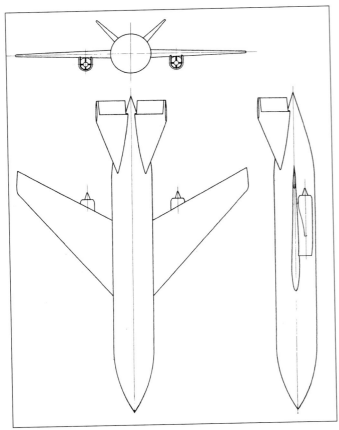

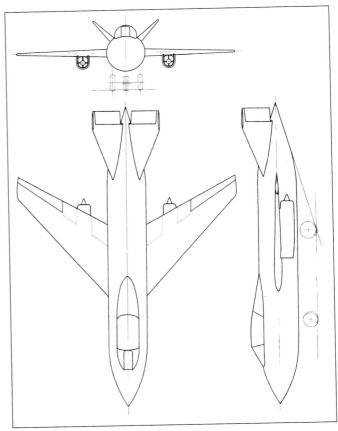

The P.123, an expendable pilotless bomber or a radio-controlled 5,000lb charge blast bomb.The wheeled and piloted version of the P.123 proposed to prove the initial airframe design was sound.

The wheeled and piloted version of the P.123 proposed to prove the initial airframe design was sound.

tests convinced the firm that the torsion capability and weight would be acceptable with a glass-reinforced plastic (GRP) or paper and resin wing. The wings were therefore to be made from thermosetting plastic reinforced with either glass fibre or long-fibre asbestos. Moulding was to be in one unit, one curing operation including all fittings, with tip and root ribs then added. Air ducts were to cool the surface of the wing where the engine attached. The fuselage centre was to be of welded steel and also to form the fuel tank area. Radio equipment would be housed in the rear fuselage, including controls and autopilot, and would be a one-piece plastic moulding. The tail cone, fin and rudder parts were also to be one-piece plastic mouldings. The bomb sections were plastic containers for the blast weapon with internal diaphragms. For the eight 500lb bomb design version the units were to be a steel cruciform structure complete with ejector gear and fitted with moulded plastic doors, which were ejected on bomb crutch release.

Launching by catapult was expected to be the limiting factor on the rate at which the units could be despatched. It was therefore proposed to launch the aircraft from rocket-boosted trolleys on a railway track. By having the track form a circuit, the used trolleys could be replenished and returned to the launch area to sustain a firing rate of four P.123 units per minute. Rather than expend test aircraft in the first instance, it was proposed to produce the prototype as a metal manned aircraft with conventional ailerons and flaps, which could then be flown by the pilot with the ailerons finally locked. Once proven they would introduce the automatic pilot, then the radio control gear and any automatic evasion devices. Finally, remote

control from take-off to landing would be attempted, with the pilot present to take over only in an emergency. In this version a fully retractable nosewheel undercarriage and ejection seat would be fitted into the fuselage design with pilot reversion from the auto-gear in the aft fuselage.

The span of the aircraft was 21ft, with 45° sweepback at 25% chord and the use of RAE101 aerofoil section. The length was 30.33ft, the fuselage diameter was 3.75ft and the height 5.13ft. The AUW was 9,047lb with eight 500lb bombs or 9,297lb with a 4,300lb split explosive blast charge in two 2,350lb modules. The manned version was 5,854lb AUW and would be ballasted to the design weight of the weapon versions. The maximum diving speed was 800 knots after 515 knots cruise.

The proposal was submitted in September 1951 and the competitors were Vickers with their Type 725 and Bristol with their Type 182. Vickers were well ahead, having looked at the projects earlier. They were also expecting to use three tail-mounted RB93 Soar engines and to carry out testing with a manned version first. In the end they had to settle for a scale model for tests and had a programme awarded under the designation Red Papier. Bristol went fully for the RAE Durestos material on production but built a light alloy test vehicle and utilised a Bristol Engines BE17 single engine and a Folland Gnat wing planform as Red Rapier. The BPA P.123 was not proceeded with and none of the projects resulted in production airframes. However, BPA apprentices continued to be trained in GRP/resin mouldings way into the 1970s.

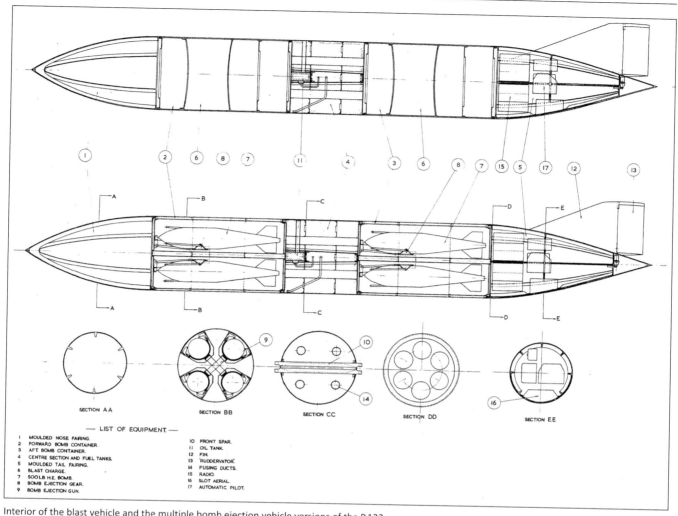

— LIST OF EQUIPMENT —

1   MOULDED NOSE FAIRING.
2   FORWARD BOMB CONTAINER.
3   AFT BOMB CONTAINER.
4   CENTRE SECTION AND FUEL TANKS.
5   MOULDED TAIL FAIRING.
6   BLAST CHARGE.
7   500 LB. H.E. BOMB.
8   BOMB EJECTION GEAR.
9   BOMB EJECTION GUN.
10 FRONT SPAR.
11 OIL TANK.
12 FIN.
13 'RUDDERVATOR'.
14 FUSING DUCTS.
15 RADIO.
16 SLOT AERIAL.
17 AUTOMATIC PILOT.

Interior of the blast vehicle and the multiple bomb ejection vehicle versions of the P.123.

Artist's illustration of the proposed P.123.

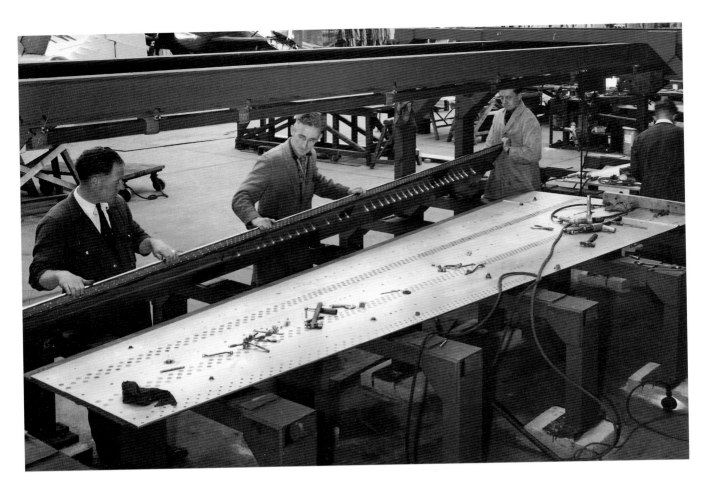

CHAPTER THIRTY-FIVE

Supersonic Research P.126 to P.129

P.126

ONE OF THE DEFINING REQUIREMENTS for high-speed supersonic flight up to Mach 2 in 1951–54 was thought to be the need for thin wings of approximately 3% thickness. This essentially meant either a solid/multi-spar alloy, or a titanium, magnesium or stainless steel structure of extremely smooth finish. Thoughts of how this could be achieved started with Air Staff project discussions as early as 1951 and pressure for a research machine mounted during 1952. If the wing was to be built up in sections, BPA thought that these would possibly be manufactured by machining from forgings/extrusions and then assembled into a wing shape instead of the traditional riveted skin. At this point the outer surface could be formed by an overall machining process on a specially developed machine. Steel materials were rejected because of the difficulty of machining steel extrusions thinly enough. The P.126 'Very Thin Wing Project' awarded to BPA was an MoS contract issued by the Aircraft Production Development Department. The contract 6/ACFT/9615/C.5(c) to investigate, manufacture and test such as wing structure was issued with the design application being a supersonic fighter aircraft capable of Mach 2. The basic layout of such a fighter wing was proposed as a single-seat thin and streamlined fuselage with straight-taper, multi-spar planform wings of small aspect ratio, and with two engines on the wings at the approximate mid-span of each. The layout was one of two studied in RAE Aero 2462 issued in June 1952. Such a design was ultimately to become the part basis of experimental specification ER134T fostering the Bristol 188 and the P.128. For structural simplicity, in the case of the P.126 the engines were assumed to be underslung from each one-piece wing half.

BPA generated a draft specification P.126 V.T.W. on 26 May 1953 for the surfacing machine design, The wings were to be in aluminium light alloy to DTD 364 and of integral construction made in extruded and heat-treated planks for a six-spar wing, which were then machined and assembled by riveting into drilled and cut holes and the two halves

assembled by bolting with special taper pin bolts left proud of the surface. A semi-span of 15ft and a root chord of 8ft, tapering to 4ft at the tip, became the basic layout. The section after machining was to

The wing planks being assembled for one half of the section.

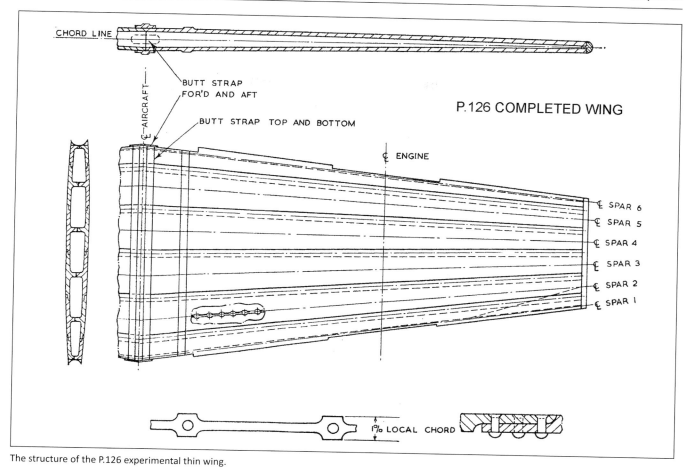

CHORD LINE

BUTT STRAP
FOR'D AND AFT

BUTT STRAP TOP AND BOTTOM

P.126 COMPLETED WING

ℂ AIRCRAFT

ℂ ENGINE

ℂ SPAR 6
ℂ SPAR 5
ℂ SPAR 4
ℂ SPAR 3
ℂ SPAR 2
ℂ SPAR 1

1% LOCAL CHORD

The structure of the P.126 experimental thin wing.

be bi-convex of 1,363in radius at the root tapering to 681.5in radius at the tip, the respective finished wing thicknesses being 4.8in and 2.4in. BPA determined that the whole surface, mathematically modelled, formed a segment from an oblique circular cone.

After assembly the entire outer surface of the upper and lower wing halves were machined to accurately form the bi-convex section and cone segment upper and lower halves, the protruding portions of the bolts and nuts being removed by the process to leave a smooth finish. In order to achieve this it was assumed that the machine bed would need to be accommodating of a span of 21ft and a chord of 9ft 9in to allow for machining runs and variations in specific aircraft sizes. Ultimately however, in the largest types considered, a production machine design might have to accommodate a 25ft semi-span, 10ft root and 5ft tip chord in order to be useful to other airframe designer's proposals for interceptor aircraft. The system finally employed a planning machine equipped with a milling head. The head was designed with its rotation axis span-wise and a taper cutter machining along its rotating taper side pointing towards the wing root. In surfacing terms the inaccuracies would still leave small steps or flash between planks, particularly at the span-wise edges, which would have to be hand finished.

The wing was manufactured from extrusions formed in the shape of a circular 'Ϲ' which, when heat treated and tensioned under pressure, opened out into a 'T' section. The cross of the 'T' formed the unmachined skin and the leg formed the spar for half of the wing thickness. Each plank was then fully machined from the solid 'T' to suit its location within the wing, overlapped and riveted to its neighbour, and finally the upper and lower halves of the wing, with any internal wiring, etc, bolted together for final machining. On this prototype test wing the upper and lower halves were extensively

fitted with strain gauges and recorder wiring prior to assembling the two halves in anticipation of structural testing. The wing was then fitted to a manufactured centre section traditionally riveted and a representative riveted underslung nacelle centre structure was built on to the lower surface of the port and starboard assemblies.

The problem remained how to apply loading to test the whole structure without having to build the traditional rig with tension rods along span and chord. One bright young engineer, R. C. 'Bobby' Briggs, suggested adding fore and aft metal water tanks to the fuselage and engine modules and using varying quantities of water to represent the significant loadings (Bob Briggs was later to finally retire having risen to Quality Assurance Manager of the company and played a significant part in the development of VTOL lift fans for later projects). Construction and testing continued from 1954 through 1956 and the MoS file on the project was finally closed in 1957. The wing construction was patented by 767674 dated 6 February 1957.

P.127

The layout of the P.126 wing and the draft fighter layout on which it was based was detailed as the P.127 supersonic interceptor using two RR Avon engines. The P.127 utilised the P.126 wing centre with leading edge droop and trailing edge flaps and ailerons, including the potential to droop the ailerons as flaps. A bicycle undercarriage was used with added outrigger wheels under the nacelle. A long slim fuselage with potential for AI radar in the nose and armament in the underbelly were specified. In fact, all of the design traits laid out to generate the wing layout for the P.126 project were grouped under the reference P.127 as one possible solution for a Mach 2 fighter.

Thin wing test rig using water loading suggested by engineer 'Bobby' Briggs.

In order to demonstrate and design a 3% section high-speed metal wing suitable for a Mach 2 fighter under the P.126 contract, the P.126/P.127 set out the shape and structural parameters to be used for such a fighter. It is not believed that the P.126 was ever intended to be procured as a machine but the P.127 was considered just such a viable production airframe.

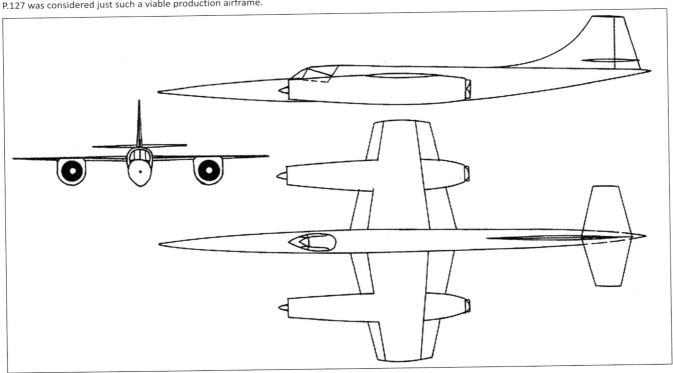

Any possibility of taking this essentially unsolicited design to build was scotched, however, by the existing efforts to meet a new specification that had already been released in December 1952 and was again based upon RAE Aero Report 2462. To produce an operational interceptor with cannon and radar, the nose of the P.127 would have to be increased slightly in diameter over the P.126 machine. Although BPA had sight of the later RAE interceptor design and F.155T specification they do not appear to have attempted to propose a larger aircraft and were not on the F.155T tender list, being more involved with RAE and MoS on experimental machines.

P.128

ER134T, issued December 1952, required an airframe suitable to achieve Mach 2 in level flight for ten minutes using engines then in development, so as to explore the flight regime and control problems that would be evident in a similar fighter aircraft. The overall design was to be of a 'fighter type'. It was expected that surface temperatures in the extreme would reach 150°C, which again would require stainless steel or machine from solid alloy structures as being investigated in the P.126. BPA had already rejected steel and threw their lot in at that point with aluminium light alloy to fatigue strength DTD364 that was being proposed in parallel for the P.126 wing project. A rectangular 4% wing was chosen of zero taper and a single-engine layout was rejected in favour of a twin-engine machine. Rather than complicate the structure by placing the engines in an intermediate position along the wing, they were moved along during internal studies until they occupied the wing ends. The end plate effect of the engine nacelles was argued to negate the need for leading edge devices on this test aircraft, and drooping ailerons on the trailing edge were all that were needed to control the machine in landing mode. Dive brakes, in the form of outward and forward-opening air brakes, were built into the engine nacelles at 45° to horizontal, two in each nacelle.

The layout chosen kept intake and efflux air clean and away from the rest of the airframe and tail. The company felt that ER134T clashed with Aero 2462 as the 30,000lb AUW would conflict unless endurance was severely sacrificed to use reheat. Reheat was eventually rejected as a consequent waste in fuel. Investigation of a translating centre-body in the nose of the intake and a convergent-divergent nozzle in the aft jet pipe in conjunction with the engine manufacturers, convinced BPA that with the structure weight kept lower then reheat was actually unnecessary to attain Mach 2. The proposal was therefore submitted with straight Sapphire SA7 engines and took advantage of a specification amendment to keep the weight to 26,500lb. Flight control actuators were incorporated to add additional damping to the roll characteristic of the layout chosen. In the event of a single engine failure there was sufficient power available to commit the airframe to land using the other working engine. A tricycle gear arrangement with fully retracting and folding outrigger wheels at the tips was chosen with full anti-skid system on both twin wheel main gears. The forward gear retracted backwards and the rear gear retracted vertically into the aft body. For a fighter layout it was proposed to replace the forward test fuselage design to aft of the pilot and test gear with an armament-equipped nose design of the same form.

The wing structure was a constructed and machined multi-spar/multi-plank construction of eleven spars and 155in chord with symmetrical bi-convex section thickness to chord ratio. It differed from the wing being designed for the P.126 project in that the plank extrusions formed a vee shape with two external spar protrusions, and one side of the vee had a rebated end to reduce machining work. The sections were limited to 40in sq cross section by virtue of the material and machines available, so hence had to be constructed of more planks than might otherwise be chosen. The size limitation was the capacity of the largest stretch press in the country to stretch the material after extrusion and minimise machining. Extrusion was used because forging such sizes was also impossible at the time. The wing would finally be machined overall using a milling machine already in existence. An all-moving tailplane employing a large circular pivot within the fin was proposed. The two tailplane halves were to follow the same practice as the wing,

The P.128 twin-engine research aircraft to test out supersonic flight of a P.126/P.127-type project lost out to the Bristol 188.

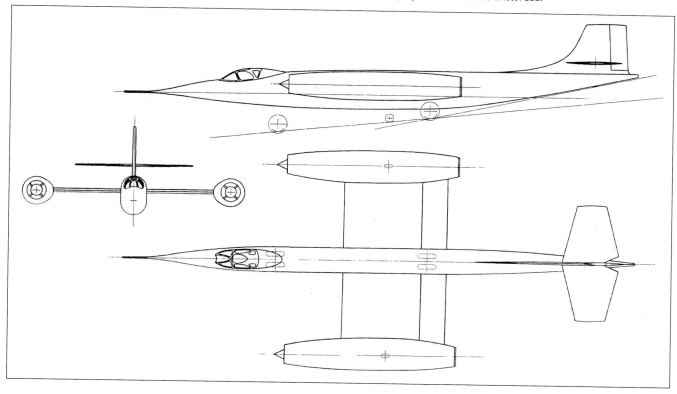

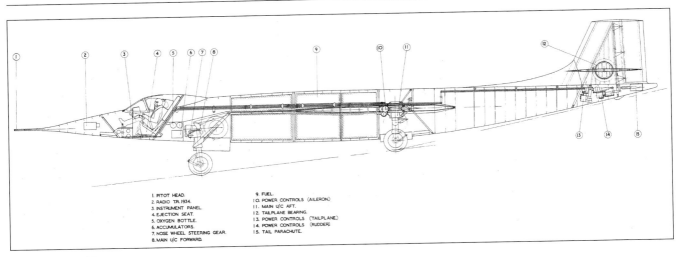

I. PITOT HEAD.	9. FUEL.
2. RADIO TR.1934.	10. POWER CONTROLS (AILERON).
3. INSTRUMENT PANEL.	II. MAIN U/C AFT.
4. EJECTION SEAT.	12. TAILPLANE BEARING.
5. OXYGEN BOTTLE.	13. POWER CONTROLS (TAILPLANE)
6. ACCUMULATORS.	14. POWER CONTROLS (RUDDER)
7. NOSE WHEEL STEERING GEAR.	15. TAIL PARACHUTE.
8. MAIN U/C FORWARD.	

Interior of the P.128

while the fin was of double-wedge cross section and parallel only where the tailplane pivot was located. Mounting of the engines was to be in the form of large trunnions attaching the engine to the wing, with a centre cowling hinged at the top and fully removable front and rear nacelle fairings for engine maintenance.

The pilot was to be housed in a pressurised cockpit with a Martin-Baker ejection seat and was assumed to be equipped with a full pressure suit system in the event that he had to escape the aircraft. For any instrumentation required, accommodation was provided between pilot and the forward undercarriage bay via removable fairings above and below the area. Power controls for the three axes were one system for each axis consisting of two electric motors and two pumps driving a hydraulic motor and a screw jack. The self-contained units therefore allowed one pump to replace another in the event of failure. Fuel supply to the engines was from six 'bag type' fuel tanks in the fuselage.

The AUW on take-off was 26,493lb. The values in Armstrong Siddeley brochure AEDO/S7 was used for 11,000lb at sea level, but uprated by the centre-body and jet pipe changes agreed with them to achieve Mach 2 at 36,000ft on 12,800lb thrust and an AUW remaining at that height of 24,000lb. The span to the engine centrelines was 24ft 6in and the wing chord 12ft 11in. The total span was not stated but based on the best drawings of the engine and nacelle installation to the outside of the nacelles (speedbrakes retracted) was 28ft 3.4in. The overall length was 64ft over the pitot head and with the pitot head removed for storage it was 60ft. The tailplane span was 14ft 8in, with tapered 7ft 4in chord at the root and 3ft 8in at the tip. The fin and rudder was 6ft 3in high, with an 8ft 4in chord at the root and 5ft chord at the tip (although the lower leading edge was faired into the afterbody by a substantial fairing). When static the ground line of the body was +6° and the height at this static sit was 10ft 3in. The maximum diving speed of the design was 750 knots Equivalent Airspeed (EAS). The endurance at Mach 2 specified was to be ten minutes, but BPA stated that they could only guarantee 7.5 minutes unless the 1,500lb specified instrumentation package was reduced to 1,000lb.

The proposal submission was made in May 1953 just as BPA were drawing up machinery specifications for the P.126 project. The end plate effect of having engines on the ends of the wing were a total unknown to the reviewing team, so was not liked and neither was the lack of reheat – despite the accessories agreed with Armstrong Siddeley suggesting that this was not necessarily required

Painted up wind tunnel model for the brochure submittal. The translating bullet in the engine intake was patented by 750420 dated 13 June 1956, having been applied for in 1953.

and the engine location being one covered in RAE Aero 2462 of June 1952. One suggestion was that the BPA team might not be strong enough to pull off such a development. While perfectly logical in the BPA presentation, these points clouded the case and discussions went on to perhaps have additional portions of wing outboard of the nacelle. Such a variation was sketched in pencil on a P.128 wind tunnel model photograph, taking the P.128 potentially back towards the P.126/P.127 design.

Three companies put in similar proposals in terms of outline shapes: the Armstrong Whitworth A.W.166, BPA P.128 and Bristol 188. Of all the other offerors, only English Electric utilised this type of layout in one of their designs, the P.6B variant. Bristol embraced stainless steel as the prime material for their 188 type and expected to manufacture the aircraft by conventional means of frames and riveting with thin sheet skin. The contract, 6/Acft/10144/CB.7(b) was finally awarded to the Bristol 188 on 4 January 1954. BPA staff thought this was partly because the choice of stainless steel was unique among the key tenderers.

P.129

As a smaller-scale model for the development and understanding of the characteristics of high-speed supersonic aircraft at low-speed regimes, the P.129 proposed to follow the layout of the full-size P.128 but in simpler materials and with smaller engines. The title of the proposal was 'A Research Aircraft for investigating the low-speed Characteristics of Supersonic Aircraft'. While it would typically take some three to four years from outset to produce a full-size machine, there was the possibility of building a simpler machine within eighteen months. Such a machine needed to be capable of being converted to and testing several differing planforms. The proposal submitted in November 1953 reflected the idea pencilled on the photograph of the P.128 at that time for wing forms added to the outside of the engine nacelles and suggested phases of testing:

Phase 1 Twin-engine planform similar to RAE Aero 2462 controlled by conventional ailerons and flaps, with or without a nose flap (ie leading edge droop). The outboard wings were tapered and shown with ailerons only. Span of 32.5ft.

Phase 2 As Phase 1 but a delta planform (swept back) outer wing with blunted tip and with ailerons only. Span of 32.5ft as drawn, but during subsequent discussions a suggested smaller span with stub outer wing tips was projected.

Phase 3 As Phase 2 but the delta wing tip is all moving and incorporates a flight control actuator system to operate the tip. A later option once the airframe existed was to introduce an artificial damping unit into the flight control circuit. Span of 32.5ft.

Phase 4 A reduction by removing the outer wings or stub wings to form a tip-mounted engine planform identical to the P.128. Power control system but span now reduced to 18ft.

The airframe was therefore identical other than the interchangeable wing tips and the experimental flight control system in Phases 3 and 4. Estimated AUW was successively 3,790, 3,750, 3,900 and 3,650lb. Using two 880lb take-off Blackburn Turbomeca Marboré turbojets a sea level speed of 395 knots was predicted, dropping to 365 knots at 20,000ft.

There was some interest shown in the proposal and a more detailed design data document was generated in January 1954 in support of discussions and design of the airframe. This new document gave details of a Marboré engine version and an AS Viper ASV5 engine version. The interest generated by the initial brochure was not necessarily in the low-speed characteristics suggested, but if it was possible to exceed Mach 1 and explore the supersonic

A smaller version of the P.128 concept for development work was suggested with a range of interchangeable wing tips. It featured Marboré engines.

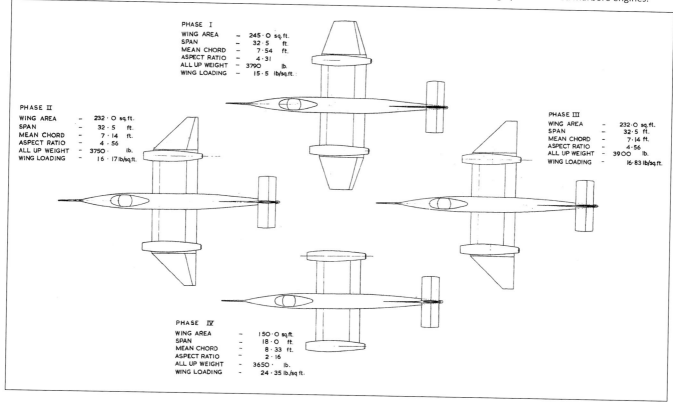

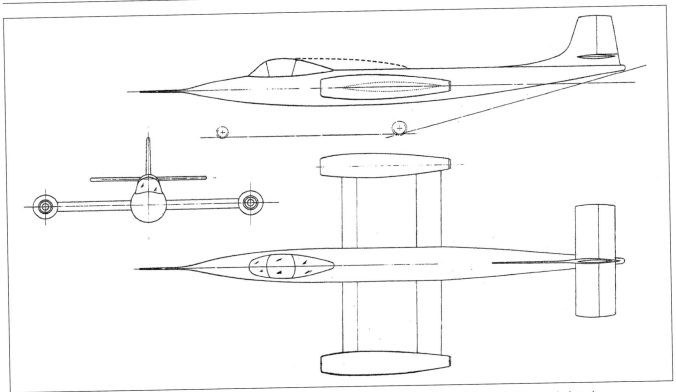

Phase IV design of the P.129 was to have no tips. Discussion of an improved flow aft of the canopy by a fuselage spine increase is dotted.

Marboré-engined revision with a fuselage shape change and tips to allow Mach 1.1.

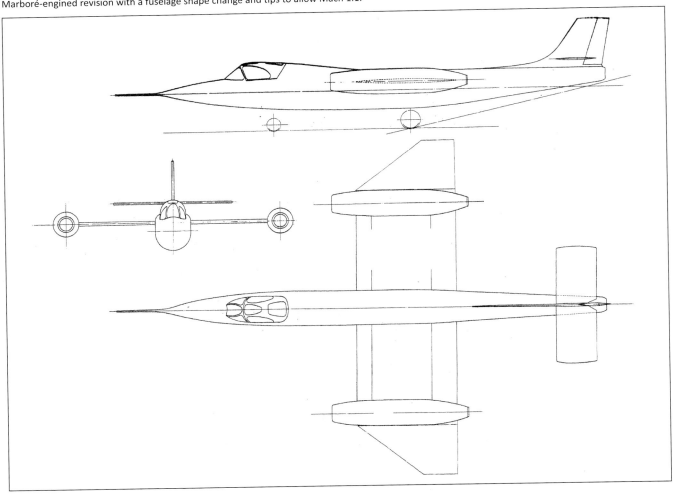

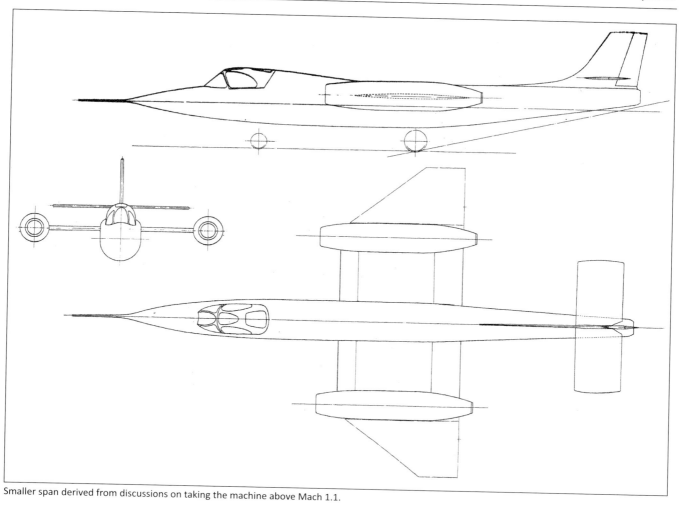

Smaller span derived from discussions on taking the machine above Mach 1.1.

Comparison of the Marboré machine with that of the Viper/Snarler combination. The fuselage was to be identical so either choice could take the Snarler if the design developed.

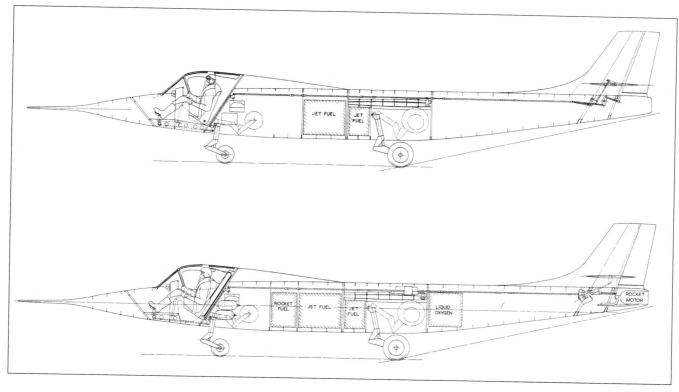

region with a much cheaper aircraft than ER134T. Officials probably eyed a potential back-up programme to ER134T in the event that their favoured design failed since they had already committed to the Bristol design. Both engine schemes had moved to a more streamlined, faired-in rear deck behind the pilot to reduce drag rather than a blister canopy. The Marboré version had a 28ft 9in span with wing tips and a 20ft 1.2in span without tips, 8ft 4in centre section chord. The wing was of P.128 form but with three spars and eight integral stiffeners made as three span-wise sections with integral ribs, forming a 16ft 4in span module to which the engine nacelles, leading edge and trailing edge components were fitted. The AS viper version had the same planform dimensions but varied the wing construction slightly, having a front and rear spar plus six auxiliary spars and no ribs forming a 16ft 5in span module. The Viper version also had a Snarler rocket motor fitted in the fuselage rear, although the drawing for the Marboré version now had the same tail shape without a Snarler shown, suggesting it could be added later. In both cases the data had reduced directly to the Phase 3 and Phase 4

versions only. The aircraft was expected to achieve Mach 0.8 without rocket assistance and Mach 1.1 with the rocket – the latter between 36,000 and 40,000ft. By this time the simple structure originally proposed was becoming more and more complicated and with additional equipment the airframe now weighed 4,400lb totally unequipped, 4,943lb equipped, 7,585lb AUW to achieve Mach 0.8 and 9,032lb AUW to achieve Mach 1.1.

Still MoS officials looked to reduce the weight further. A reduction in span of both the Marboré and the favoured Viper/Snarler design was pencilled in by moving the Viper nacelles and outboard wing more towards the centre of the aircraft, making the tip-equipped aircraft span approximately 25ft 4in and the tip-less version only 17ft. The final Viper version known changed the wings to full swept tips and underslung engines plus a swept leading edge on the tailplane. No calculations remain of what this version could achieve and it might not have been formally submitted, but one would expect perhaps 1.2–1.3 Mach. It was unfortunately not enough to maintain the idea.

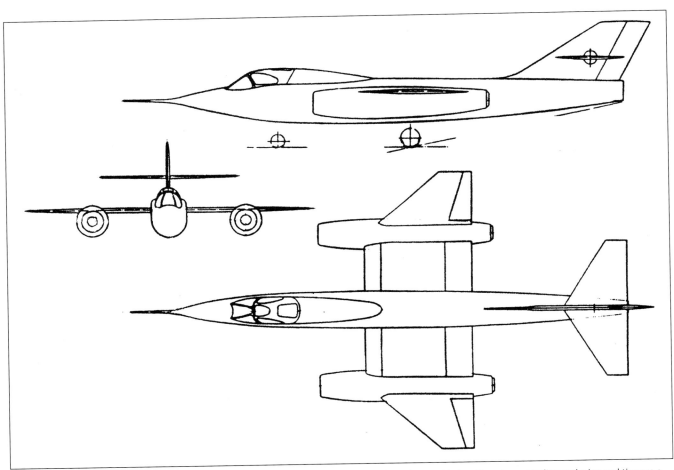

Final known design of the supersonic fixed-wing Viper/Snarler P.129. The engines have been lowered below the wing centreline and wing and tips are a fixed structure.

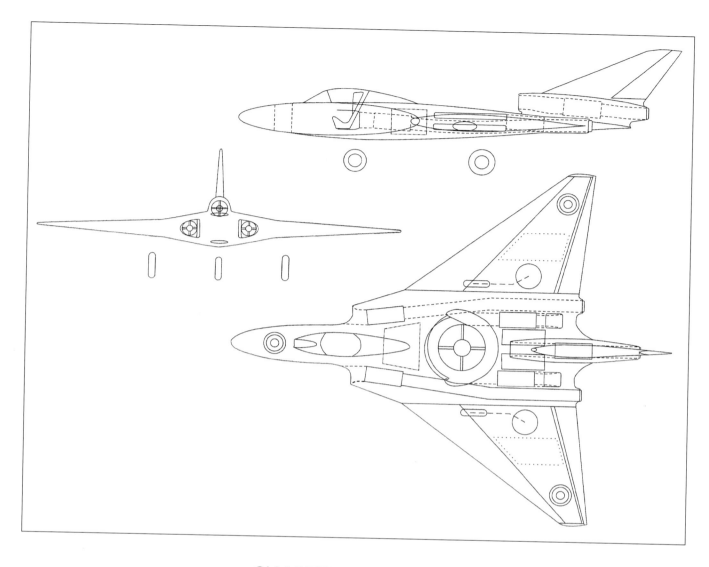

CHAPTER THIRTY-SIX

VTOL Studies P.130 to P.137

P.130

THE P.130 SERIES started as a result of R. A. Shaw's thought-provoking piece on the use of fan lift as an amplification method for VTOL issued in October 1954. BPA were asked to look at a number of layouts in which this fan lift could be utilised, essentially in fighter-type aircraft. From November/December 1954 through into 1955 a total of twelve airframe layouts were studied. Unfortunately a copy of the document or documents describing all twelve has not been traced and only two of the designs have information surviving. The 'Hot Fan' system was being studied by the National Gas Turbine Establishment (NGTE) and consisted of an outer turbine ring of blades that were driven by hot exhaust air from the engine and then drove co-axial, contra-rotating cold air fans to provide the lifting force. The limiting aim was the thought that no more than three engines should be needed for forward flight.

The sixth version of the P.130 studies was a five-engine delta. It had one pure propulsion engine at the base of the fin, two propulsion and lift engines and two dedicated lift engines at the rear. In lifting mode all four engines less that in the tail fin drove the central contra-rotating hot fan. The three fans for stability control at the extremities have no details shown of how they were powered but probably used engine bleed air.

P.130 Scheme 6

Scheme 6, drawn December 1954, considered a five-engine, single-seat, delta-winged fighter of 53° leading edge sweep. The fifth engine sat at the base of the fin within a nacelle-shaped cowling and provided thrust alone. Aft of the root intakes either side were engines two and three also giving forward flight thrust, but by bleed from the exhaust aft of the engine feeding the driving blades for large 54in contra-rotating hot fans central to the fuselage and centre wing, they were also being used during lift and transition. Buried in the rear of the wing were operable intakes feeding two more engines facing backwards. During VTOL these engines took air from above the rear of the craft and fed exhaust forward to add to the power of the central contra-rotating fans. All five engines were Rolls-Royce RB108s. In addition to the large central lift fan there were small air bleed fans out on the wing and in the aircraft nose to provide control function in the hover. No armament was shown within the surviving scheme. Having no scale on the preliminary drawing, the use of an identical planform to that of Scheme 8 yields the approximate calculated dimensions: Span 34ft 2in and body length 38ft 2in. The overall length was 41ft 3.5in. The height over the fin was 12ft 4in.

P.130 Scheme 8

Scheme 8 was drawn for the report in February 1955. It considered a twin-engine machine, again of delta planform 53° sweep, but having no structure above the cockpit height. The outer wing panels had the same shape, planform and size as Scheme 6. Instead of a dorsal fin there were twin fins sitting under the rear of the wings that provided fin/rudder stabilisation and also contained retracting tailwheels in each fin tip. These were supplemented by a long nosewheel leg. In this manner the machine would sit high off the ground or deck and be less affected by the ground effect or the heat of the exhaust. Two engines, Bristol Orpheus in format, provided forward thrust and their exhaust diverted into swirl ducts to drive

blades for 75in contra-rotating hot fans central to the body. There were small fans out on the wing and in the aircraft nose to provide control function in the hover. Both wings folded upwards outboard of the engine intakes, so the aircraft was expected to be a naval fighter for deck operation. Long-range drop tanks could be carried under the outer wings and outboard of that there was accommodation for wing-mounted cannon. Airbrakes sat above and below the central trailing edge between the fins and opened to vertical to slow the machine and ultimately bring it to the hover or to a short take-off and landing (STOL) landing. Based upon the drawing scale, the approximate calculated dimensions were: Span 34ft 2in and body length 43ft 3in. Length overall 46ft 5in. Height over canopy 9ft 6in. Width wings folded 15ft 10in.

P.132

During gestation of the P.130 studies, R. A. Shaw, Assistant Director/Assistant Research Director of the Royal Aircraft Establishment Research Department, suggested that there might be an alternative and better solution compared with the work by Dr A. A. Griffiths into divided propulsion and lift groups. This could be by integrating flight, lift and transition power from one engine group alone. The initial fan design looked at, as in the P.130 series above, had been a contra-rotating system with the main fan unit driven by a peripheral turbine from butterfly valve diverted jet air. Stabilisation by small fans at the extremities was driven by bleed air. The use of fans gave the order of three times thrust increase. For example, the P.132 in a direct jet thrust only situation would have required up to twelve rather than four of its finally chosen standard engines at that

The eighth design studied for a fan lift delta. In this case a twin engine naval fighter.

Basing a small experimental VTOL delta on an aircraft such as the P.130-6 resulted in a three-engine machine because the concept of the RAE P.130 study deliberately limited the number of forward or dual-propulsion engines to a maximum of three. Once an engine designer had been involved at RAE suggestion the three-engine solution was seen as a bad choice if a particular dual-use engine on either side failed. The P.132 design rapidly evolved instead into a fighter layout with four engines and twin fins. Tunnel Model No 1 worked on this new four-engine layout as a fighter design but reduced in size.

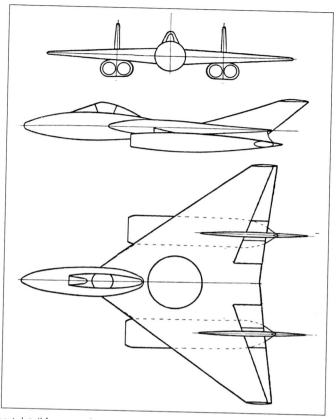

time. Although the study was originally to consider only three dedicated engines needed for forward flight, the nature of the type-tested engine choices was to change opinions.

As BPA was involved with the NGTE on the development of hot gas-driven, contra-rotating fans used in the P.130 projects, the new P.132 was a design for a research vehicle to operate by fan-driven VTOL using the same hot contra-rotating fan system with air bled from the engines. Key technical and experimental resources were allocated to developing this design for a VTOL research aircraft. A series of wind tunnel experiments were commissioned within the BPA 4ft tunnel to determine the best airframe layout and size of lift fans and to determine the inflow and outflow dynamics of these sizes when inserted vertically through a wing planform of the delta type. It was then mutually agreed with PDSR(A) that a jet engine firm be brought into the team and Armstrong Siddeley motors joined the design investigation. Since a fully type tested engine was required, the Viper ASV8 was chosen for the project. The overall propulsion and lift engine project was designated P.175 by AS Motors (having no relation to the BPA numbers).

Final submission for the P.132 and AS P.175 joint project completely changed most detail features of the machine, retaining only the basic layout. Severe friction losses calculated in the hot gas and the cold control bleed duct runs resulted in the gas drive to hot periphery turbine/cold centre fans switching to turbine-driven mechanical fan power shafts with the driving turbine divorced from the fan module and fed by two engines each.

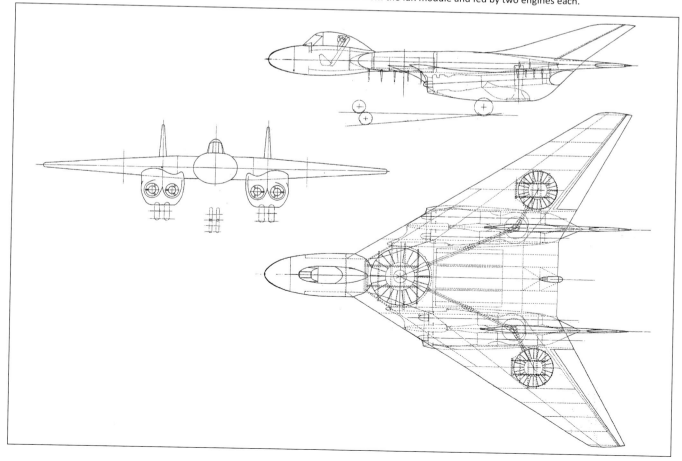

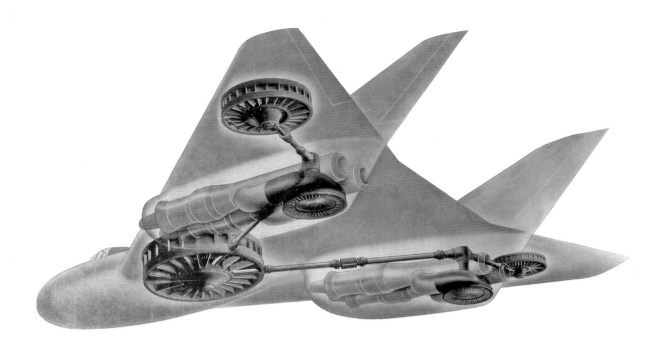

Above: Artist's impression of the AS P.175 engine system installed in the P.132 airframe.

Left: The second P.132 wind tunnel model set up for fan lift experiments.

precious little area for recording packages, the wing being occupied with lift fans and the inner underwing with propulsion engines. The pilot was to sit in a small pulpit-like pod on the extreme leading edge of the delta centreline. Although test models had a centre-swept trailing edge, the design evolved into a straight portion between twin upright fins and more swept-back trailing edges outboard of the fins. The engines now consisted of four Viper turbojets installed in two nacelles, a pair of engines under each wing. The exhaust from the engine pair could be diverted downwards via butterfly valves to drive a turbine and excess hot air shed under the nacelle to add to lift. The turbine then drove the cold lift fans via mechanical linkages and gearboxes. The fans drafted for the wings were 54in, with a 79in fan for the central portion of the forward delta wing.

The joint study was submitted in February 1956. The submission gave a span of 38.6ft and an unstated length. The wing section was RAE104 and the fin rudder section RAE102. Test Phase 1 suggested an initial triple-point undercarriage of fixed units for conventional take-off and landing without any VTOL system operating and a +6° nose-up ground attitude. Then Phase II involved a modified fixed undercarriage with the nosewheel leg reduced in height so the wings were horizontal (under-surface 48in above ground level) and VTOL trials with conventional landings but not wing-borne take-off. Phase III required a fully operable retracting undercarriage for operations in full in either mode, again 48in from the ground to wing under-surface. Wing-borne landings could be made by streaming the centreline anti-spin parachute at the extreme trailing edge of the wing. At a weight of 17,250lb the aircraft take-off was a lift-only state until at a forward speed of at least 90 knots at a fixed incidence. At that point two of the engines were directed into forward flight and lift reduced as speed increased. The thrust available from the lift system was ample at 23,880lb. In the event of three-engine operation (single failure pre-transition) there was just enough thrust from the three to lift an 18,500lb machine.

The joint work by AS/BPA/NGTE showed that there was considerable loss of efficiency using a hot air-driven system of fans because of the air ducting. Pending solutions to the air duct losses a mechanical alternative was studied and finally adopted using the diverted jet thrust on short ducting to drive a turbine below the engine pairs and thence three lift fans. A second study by Armstrong Siddeley also determined that by using both the butterfly valves for diversion of thrust and a variable exhaust nozzle within the main flight tailpipes it was possible to have sufficient control to maintain a complete and accurate transition from lift to forward flight without having to change engine power at all. As a result of these ongoing experiments a specification was drawn up for the research aircraft as ER166D in draft form as at June 1955. The specification was therefore a result of the work rather than the originator of it.

The overall design was an integration of a specific engine/tailpipe group for forward propulsion, with a divertible exhaust driven hot turbine set. This latter then used mechanical linkages to drive the cold fans. At this stage hot fans were not now being considered, although development work on them was to continue. The P.132 retained the overall wing layout of the known P.130 schemes, being a delta aircraft, but it was considerably reduced in size. There was

Appendix 1 gave a slightly revised take-off procedure if a continuously variable butterfly valve was used for diversion since as the aircraft lifted the power required could be reduced with height. In this variation take-off was vertical with lift thrust doors to give 30° aft flow until a speed of 50 knots forward with the aircraft still level. At that point the nose was tilted upwards until half the required lift in forward flight was reached and fan lift further reduced as the aircraft climbed away. The result, compared with a normal lift off, was a reduction in the VTOL transition pitching moments to two-thirds of those previous. In normal take-off the machine would only unstick at 140 knots. Landing conventionally at 140 knots, the airbrake could be popped on landing and the brakes could be applied at 50 knots. At sea level the maximum speed was 445 knots. The maximum height at which the aircraft could enter and remain in hover was 12,500ft. A full quadruplex fly-by-wire system was proposed using tandem hydraulic rams on each surface and single or tandem rams on the fan and air supply systems. The detail of the combined P.132/P.175 brochure went as deep as basic design of the aircraft fans, turbines, centre-body-propelling nozzle in the aft jet pipes, gearboxes and valves. It concluded with a forecast of the performance increase available if a new dedicated engine was used instead of the available ASV8. The P.132/P.175 joint concept was the subject of a BPA and Bristol Siddeley Motors patent 846300A dated 31 August 1960.

P.133

The P.133 project, submitted June 1956, was a supersonic single-seat fighter aircraft of lifting body design formed from a 79° sweep body. The engines were installed near the wing tips with straight-through jet pipes and convergent-divergent nozzles in the extreme aft end to boost thrust at speed. Exhaust bleed during the hover drove two hot turbines, one from each engine. So that failure of one engine would not lead to total collapse of the hover phase, the two centreline turbines were linked by shafting and shafting extensions then drove three fans forward of the turbines and three fans aft. In the extreme tail a bulb fairing covered a Spectre rocket motor with rocket fuel fed from centreline tanks between the turbines and forward fans. At 71ft, this was the longest of this series.

P.133A

The P.133A was submitted as a single-seat supersonic fighter with 'fan-assisted take-off and landing'. The design shape had changed little externally other than a larger set of fins and enlarged intake cones. Internally, however, the fan system had reduced to a single centreline fan and two wing fans driven from a single hot turbine fed by both engine exhausts. The wing fans were smaller than the centreline fan and all were significantly reduced in size compared with the set first forecast for the P.133. The entire aircraft was significantly smaller than the others in the series with an 80° swept leading edge.

P.133B

The P.133B stated more boldly that it was a 'naval search and strike aircraft with fan-assisted take-off and landing'. It was submitted in November 1956. The existing operational requirements for this type of aircraft were already to be met by the Blackburn B.103 (Buccaneer). However, in order to provide a comparison with this conventional aircraft, the P.133B had been schemed to conform to the specification for Naval Air Staff Requirement NA39, Issue 2, Part 2. The aircraft had therefore been designed to be catapult launched at 5g in zero relative wind conditions and, with fan assist, to take off at 100 knots. Typical landing was expected to be 55 knots relative air speed at a weight of 36,000lb. To maintain controllability, a landing speed of 50 knots minimum was recommended. The AUW was 40,120lb but 45,000lb could be managed by the use of 20–25 knots over the deck wind and catapult launch.

Two DH Gyron Junior 10,000lb static thrust engines were inboard of the earlier schemes. There were two seats in the cockpit and a distinct fuselage upper spine equipment bay aft of the canopy area that faired down aft to the single fin and rudder. Bleed from the engines fed two two-stage hot turbines cross connected and exhausting under the aircraft. These in turn drove four cold fans of 32in diameter, two inboard of the engine positions and two at the rear wing tips. Differential thrust and controllable inlet vanes on the fans allowed pitch and roll control in the hover or transition. Some 34,000lb of thrust was available during take-off from the fans and turbines.

Design of the P.133 initial study, with two engines each driving a turbine mechanically linked to six lift fans for VTOL and a rocket motor. Note the section shapes of the flatfish-style lifting body, not generally shown on other drawings.

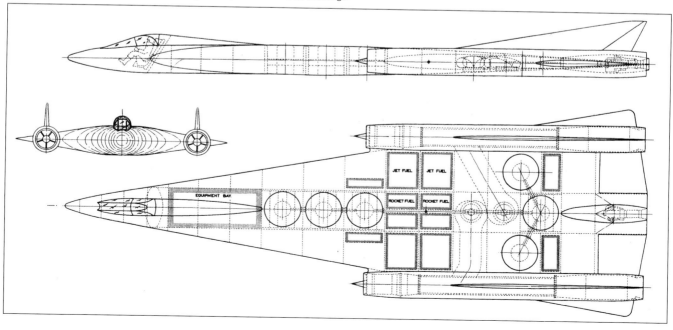

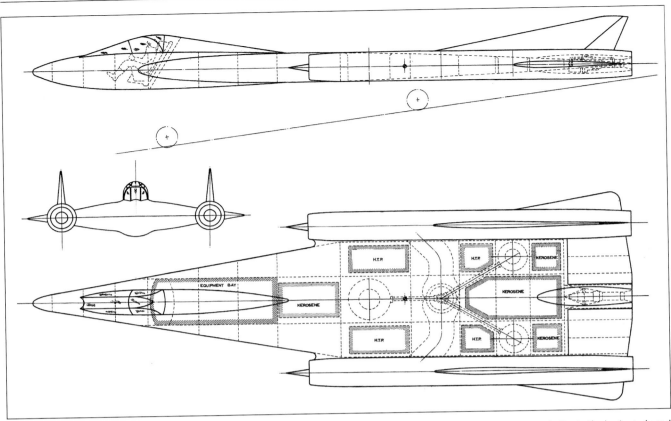

Design of the P.133A revised to two engines driving a single turbine mechanically linked to three lift fans, but otherwise very similar to the basic study and still with a rocket motor.

Tunnel model of the P.133 and P.133A.

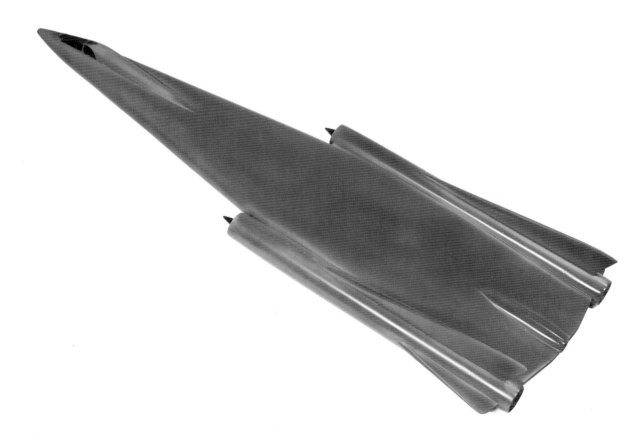

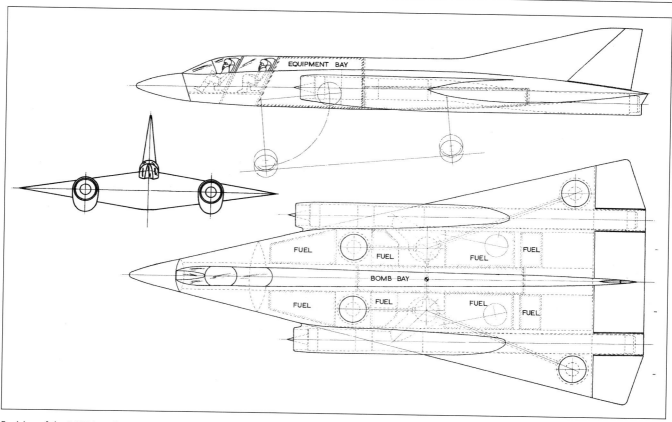

Revision of the P.133A as the P.133B, a two-seat strike fighter. It had an individual turbine for each engine cross-linked and driving four lift fans.

By setting the system with centre of lift aft of the centre of gravity, the nose pitch-up during catapult launch was avoided. At 28ft span it was the largest span of the series and had a 76° sweepback.

A full central internal bomb bay could carry two 2,000lb bombs or one target marker (Case 2), or four 1,000lb bombs (Case 3). Externally five triple RP packs, OR.1126, or eight triple RP packs, OR.1099, could be accommodated (Case 1).

P.133C

Submitted in October 1956, the P.133C version was a 'supersonic single-seat tactical strike aircraft' similar to the B version but with a single-occupant cockpit. It had four equal-size cold fans driven by two hot turbines and shafting. Each engine fed a single turbine that drove two fans on that side of the aircraft. There was no cross shaft

Offensive load of the P.133B.

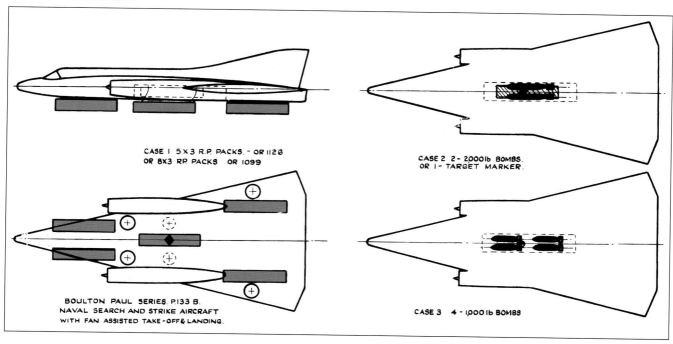

CASE 1 5 X 3 R.P. PACKS. - OR 1126
OR 8X3 RP PACKS OR 1099

CASE 2 2 - 2000lb BOMBS.
OR 1 - TARGET MARKER.

BOULTON PAUL SERIES. P.133 B.
NAVAL SEARCH AND STRIKE AIRCRAFT
WITH FAN ASSISTED TAKE-OFF & LANDING.

CASE 3 4 - 1,000 lb BOMBS

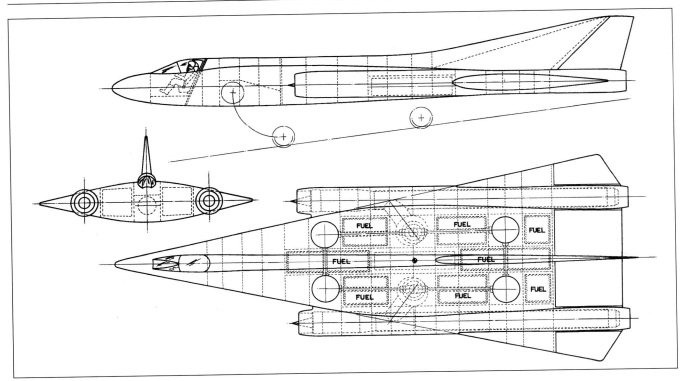

P.133C as a single-seat strike fighter.

connecting the two turbines because the entire area between the turbines was occupied by the internal weapons bay. The decision was made that any loss of capability in V/STOL after an attack would be accommodated under reduced conventional landing power. The sweepback was increased to 78°.

P.134

The P.134 September 1956 submission was another 76° sweepback delta wing aircraft to research the results of the P.133 series design studies. This initial proposal was a lifting body delta aircraft in the same format as the early P.133 with two Orpheus engines. The intakes were set outboard at mid-span and the propulsion ducting then followed a gentle curve inboard to exhaust under each of twin fins. For VTOL capability there were three fans; the largest set behind the cockpit on the centreline of the aircraft and the two smaller at the rear towards the wing tips. All three were 'cold' fans, being mechanically driven from a turbine unit taking hot air from the engines and exhausting it under the middle of the aircraft. The wing fans used a single shaft aft and a gearbox and cross shaft at the rear to each of the fans.

First version of the P.134 VTOL Delta, a variation of the P.133/133A with engine flow paths and fan positions revised.

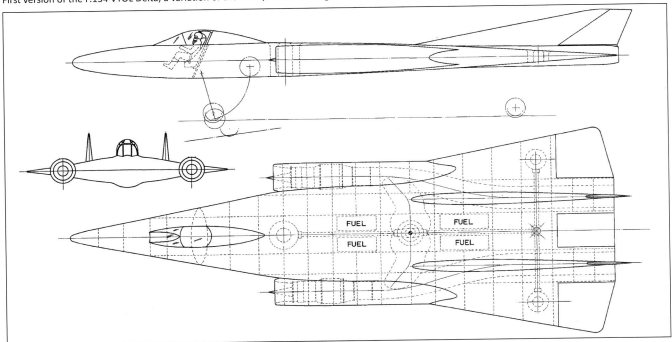

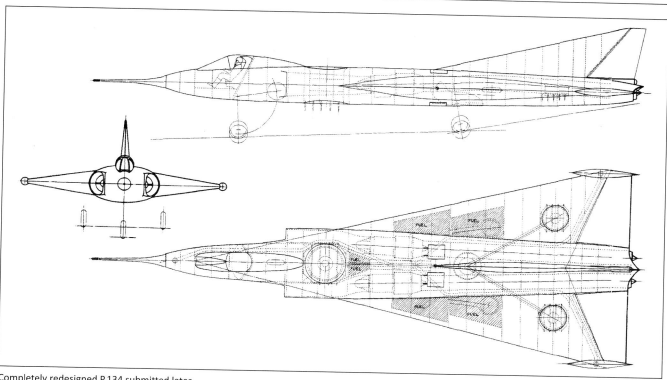

Completely redesigned P.134 submitted later.

A second submission was presented in January 1957. The design of the aircraft had been completely revised. It was still a 76° sweepback delta wing, but this time it had a distinct fuselage with cheek intakes either side aft of the cockpit and exhausting together at the extreme tail under a single fin and rudder. The same three-fan configuration and single-power turbine was used but this time the shaft power to the wing fans drove directly at diagonal angles from the turbine, reducing the shaft length and removing the aft gearbox and cross shafts. Control of stability in the hover was via air bleed ducts to wing-tip pods and the extreme nose. The engines were Orpheus BOR11 and just aft of their installation four airbrakes could be deployed above and below the fuselage. The maximum speed was 1.34 Mach at 37,000ft.

Assembled cross section model of the P.134.

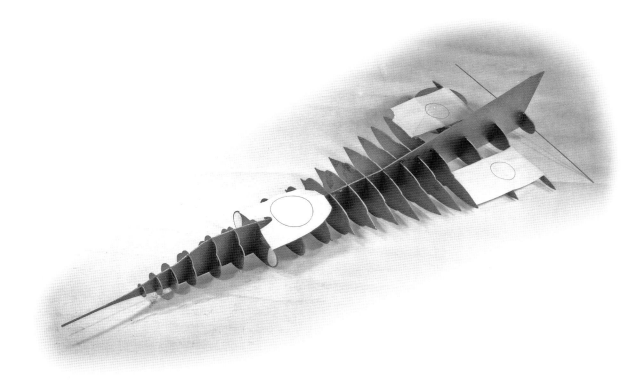

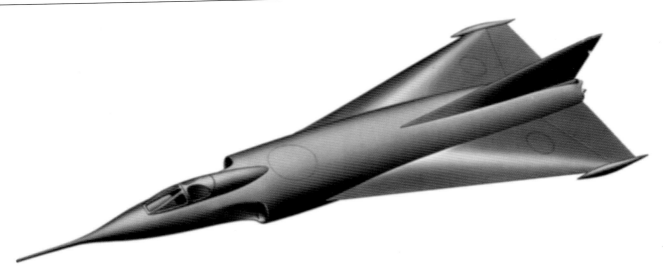

Artist's illustration of the P.134.

P.135

The P.135 was a study in May 1957 incorporating all that had been learned to date and expanding on the P.134 proposals. Since the P.134 very narrow delta proposal further investigations had been carried out on delta wing aircraft with less sweepback and, for efficiency in quantity manufacture plus to keep development costs low, having four equal-size fans. The fan diameter chosen was 45in to keep fan inlet velocity subsonic. The transition was around fifty seconds with these fans, by which time the aircraft would have a forward speed of 150 knots. Two designs were presented, the P.135A having a double sweep leading edge of 71° 34' inner and a 60° 45' outer wing, while the P.135B had a 67.5° constant sweep. Supersonic capability was put to one side for a moment and the aim was to generate a machine with high subsonic speed. Using

Orpheus BOR12 engines the maximum speed was 625 knots at sea level (Mach 0.96), dropping to 590 knots at 20,000ft and 560 knots at 36,090ft. Both designs were 65ft long including the nose-mounted pitot head, but the P.135A had a span of 38.33ft and a height of 12.5ft. The P.135B span was 35ft and the height 12.75ft.

All four fans were powered by taking the jet efflux, part-diverted from the engines, to drive a turbine exhausting under the centre of the aircraft. The power generated mechanically by the turbine was then used to drive the fans via shafting with two fans on the forward centreline behind the cockpit and a fan on each wing. At an operating weight of 21,314lb, the aircraft would be able to hover for 27.5 minutes using a fan thrust of 20,500lb total, a turbine exhaust

P.135A VTOL delta had a double sweep planform.

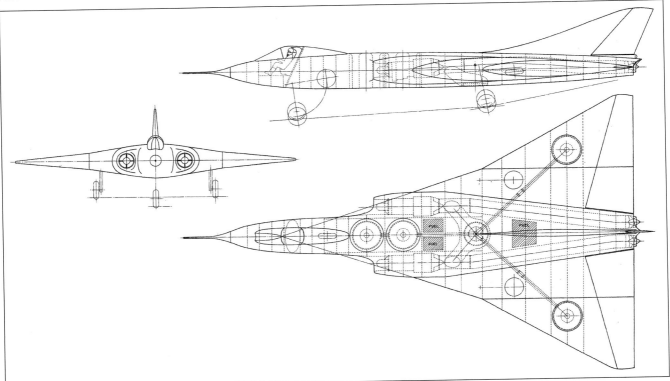

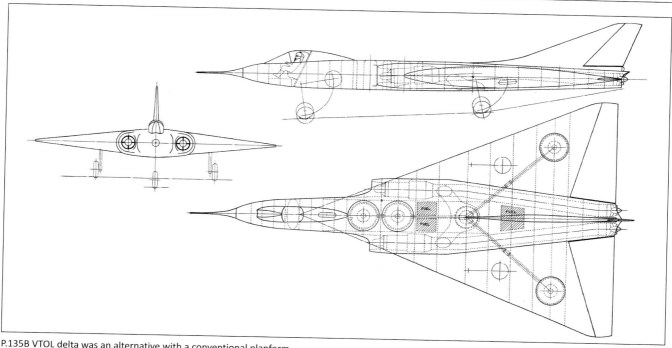

P.135B VTOL delta was an alternative with a conventional planform.

contribution of 4,300lb and control nozzle thrust of 1,200lb using 10% of the compressor bleed. It was not clear from the testing so far if the machine would need control nozzle action at the extremities of the machine or if it was possible to utilise fan differential lift for the same control. Part of the differential lift was to deflect the efflux 30° aft during transition. Some 87.5% of the engine availability would be required for pure hover, leaving 12.5% to start the initial forward motion from the hover. The use of a low wing loading of 24.6lb/sq ft was to allow a 25,000lb AUW take-off and landing or a 30,000lb AUW conventional take-off from a carrier using 4,000lb-thrust rocket assisted take-off (RATO) units. Powered steep approach deck landing was possible at 50–60 knots. Prior to that the aircraft could race to the target area at high speed, carry out a slow-speed search in hover for submarines for a period of fifteen minutes or so and then return to the carrier or airbase.

P.136

The general studies of lift design up to May 1957 had followed two routes, either the general use of lift engines to provide the power for VTOL or the use of a free turbine driving lift fans mechanically. The disadvantage of the pure lift engine was its high fuel consumption and operational problems unless hovering time was limited. As regards the all-up-weight (AUW), however, there was little difference between the two methods for V/STOL.

The P.136 was a comparison design for the P.135 using turbofan lift engines only.

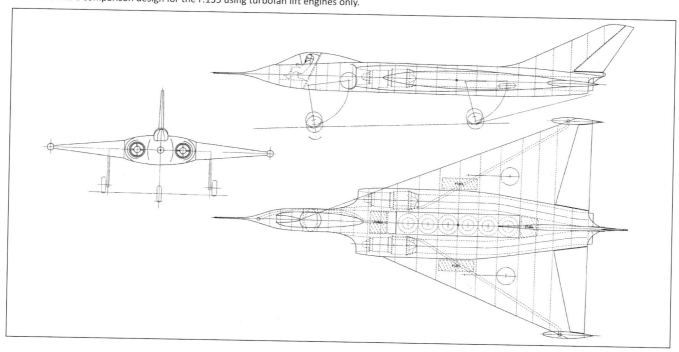

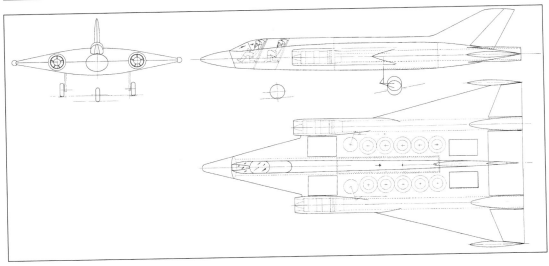

The P.137 was produced upon a request to provide a comparison of the earlier NA39 specification P.133 fan lift strike aircraft but using turbofan engines for lift.

BPA studies had been in the latter area of fans. While all this was going on a third school of thought at NGTE suggested that a possible solution was the use of lift engines but of the 'ducted fan' variety. NGTE advanced a ducted fan engine design known as a 'Rostat'. The high financial cost of developing such an engine quickly scotched the suggestion. However, it had been proposed only recently that it would be possible to modify an RB108 engine design into a ducted fan unit at much lower cost. The Ministry of Supply therefore requested that BPA look at a design of such a VTOL machine using RB108 (modified) ducted fan lift and comparing it with the P.135B. The results of that study were submitted in August 1957. The P.136 design had a similar layout to the P.135B and the same Orpheus BOR12 engines, but instead of BPA mechanical fan lift it was to use six RB108 (modified) engines installed vertically down the central spine of the delta-winged fuselage. Ten per cent compressor bleed was drawn in, feeding streamlined blisters on the wing tips and under the nose cone because differential fan lift and 30° deflection of fan lift aft during transition was no longer available. In trying to make the equal comparison P.135B to P.136, however, it was found that the values of control in hover without the fan differential were too poor in the P.136 and use was made of an R. A. Shaw suggestion of jet nozzles to assist lift experiments in the wind tunnel. BPA modified this to study these in the air bleed tip control circuit. The result was to improve control significantly, although still slightly below the lift fan system. To prevent adverse pitching moments with the ducted fan units it would be necessary to cut the units progressively from forward to aft during transition as the wing lift built up.

NGTE estimates gave these engines a 36in diameter and 48in length, producing 3,800lb direct thrust plus 200lb compressor bleed. They weighed 390lb each. The outer wings of the aircraft could be made thinner as they did not need to accommodate lift fans, and for the same AUW the length of the aircraft was now 62ft including pitot head and the span was 32.8ft. Because of the Orpheus power being available at all times, transition could be undertaken in seventeen seconds rather than the fifty seconds of the lift fan P.135B. Maximum speed was 631 knots at sea level, dropping to 611 knots at 20,000ft and 575 knots at 36,090ft. The company summarised the advantages and disadvantages of each design.

P.137

Representing the last of the fighter layout VTOL work, the P.137 was the result of MoS requesting a study for aircraft having a similar layout to the P.133B Naval Strike and P.135 VTO Research series but using ducted fan lift engines. While the P.136 submitted in August had done this to some extent, the P.137 chose to carry this comparison forward based on the P.133B layout. In order to appreciate the results of the work it was necessary to view all of the studies P.133B, P.135, P.136 and P.137 together. The same Naval Air Staff Requirement NA39 and Gyron Junior development engines were utilised as in the P.133B. Instead of fan lift, however, the centre portion of the aircraft carried ten vertically set lift fan engines, assumed again to be of the RB108 (modified) variety. The engines could not be set exactly on the centreline because of the need to carry internally stored weapons and consequently they were offset into the wing either side of the weapons bay in groups of five. The aircraft t/c ratio had to be increased to accommodate these with a consequent reduction in the aircraft performance, but with a leading edge sweep of 75° the machine could perform all of the take-off and landing conditions suggested for the P.133B at identical speeds.

The normal AUW of 46,465lb gave a 103-minute sortie with a radius of action of 400 miles covering start and catapult launch followed by climb to 20,000ft at M = 0.9. At 250 nautical miles from target, the aircraft would descend to sea level below radar and proceed with its target run at 525 knots for 100 nautical miles to target. Combat for five minutes at sea level was followed by 100 nautical miles at 525 knots, then a climb to 30,000ft and a return to base at M = 0.94. The remaining loiter time was ten minutes at 10,000ft before landing on. The maximum speed at sea level was calculated at 822 knots.

The dimensions of the aircraft were 31ft span and 56ft long. The radar nose portion was to fold for stowage, reducing the length to 51ft and the aircraft stood 13ft 6in high at the fin tip. There was little difference in AUW between the P.133B fan system and the P.137 ducted fan lift engine system. Because of the criticism by Howell at NGTE, the P.133B 40,120lb AUW had been revised to 46,255lb AUW. The P.137 was heavier by only 210lb, some 160lb of which was extra fuel for the engines. Again the company listed the advantages and disadvantages compared with the P.133B.

P.132 to 137 summary

These studies brought forward no requirements for prototypes or developments. Although NGTE continued to look at fan lift and BPA to work on fans. Of interest, when the National Physical Laboratory at Teddington was allowed to open its doors to the press in 1962, *Flight* magazine illustrated a large 3/25th model of a fan lift delta layout, which was described as the BPA P.135 project. The model was, in fact, a large wing and engine pod model of the P.132 project with only the central forward fan piercing the wing. It is more likely that this was being used to provide data for the whole series but perhaps particularly the P.135 development.

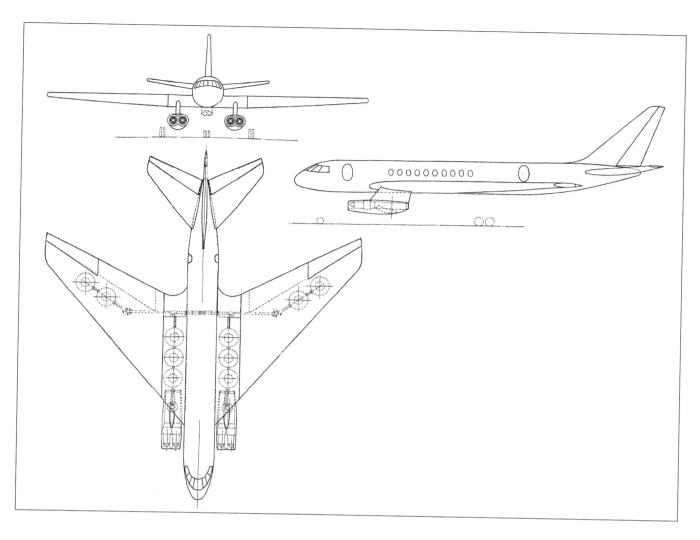

CHAPTER THIRTY-SEVEN

Civil VTOL Ministry of Supply-Funded Studies and BEA/Industry Discussions

P.138 to P.146

BPA HAD DONE LITTLE in the civil airliner market after the Second World War. The electro-hydraulic gun turret and actuation side was deeply involved with flight control systems development and when asked by MoS to tender the Medium-Range Empire Transport Project (MRE – Specification 2/47), this was turned down. Other than the P.117 project and subcontract work the company did not move towards indigenous designs until shortly before the BEA requirement for a Civil VTOL airliner in 1957. The attraction was obviously the civil application of S/VTOL as an extension of its existing military fan studies.

The likely layout of the P.138 study. The design was abandoned very early in the sketch stage when it was pointed out the using only four engines and two turbines for civil VTOL was a very high risk strategy only truly acceptable for a military or a research type. Based upon staff opinions, this reconstruction must be considered purely provisional and the engine pairs may well have been further out on the wing in alternate ideas.

P.138 VTOL Airliner

The P.138 was a first look at the civil airliner VTOL market, having thirty-two seats and powered by four Bristol Orpheus BOR12 engines driving associated mechanically driven lifting fans via hot gas turbines. The design was abandoned because there was a high risk with passenger aircraft in the single engine out situation (which would result in 25% loss of propulsion or lifting effort). This problem

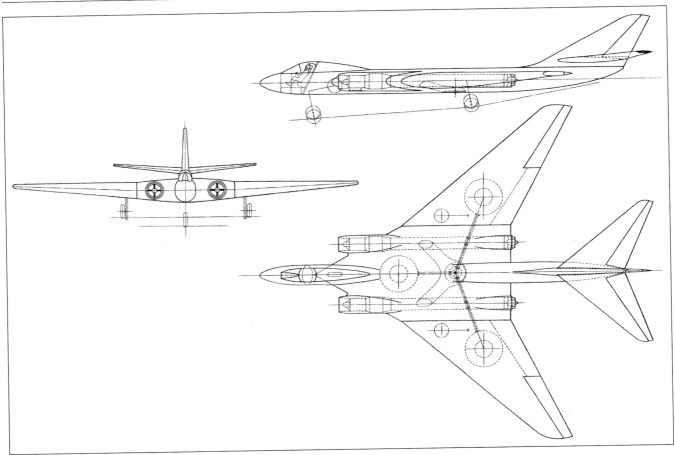

The P.139 was a reduced-scale test-bed proposed as a development stage for the P.138/P.140 VTOL airliner.

was accepted as requiring the need for more than four engines in a civilian VTOL aircraft. No drawings have been located to show what the P.138 looked like since it seems to have been dropped rapidly, but, talking to ex-staff, one might predict a smaller version of the follow-on P.140, looking essentially like a twin-nacelle aircraft having two nacelles of paired engines similar to the P.140. The design was started in mid-1957 before the formal issue of the BEA specification since by then both the P.139 and P.140 designs were in existence. Most probably, the design was to an early draft of the idea before the specification was officially released.

P139 & P.140

P.139 VTOL Airliner Test Bed

Although BPA suggested that the optimum fan lift solution would turn out to be a larger aircraft, a December 1957 paper also discussed an experimental version having a scaled-down planform based upon the P.140. Bearing in mind that no fan lift machine had been built or tested at this stage, the P.139 study proposed such a machine. The lift units were to be identical to those in the P.140, so that development work on the fan units was already carried out for the larger airliner. By using two Orpheus BOR12s driving a power turbine and thence three fans mechanically, the P.139 would have a quarter of the system required for the P.140. The lifting thrust would be 38,350lb, a quarter of the P.140, and 25,569lb AUW. The lift ratio was therefore 1.5, larger than would be needed on an airliner, but more useful to investigate transition on an experimental machine. Pitch and roll during the lift was to be by differential control of the fans, only aided by tip nozzles if it was found necessary.

The scaled-down machine had a span of 58ft, a length of 67ft and stood 14ft 4.8in above the runway. A plan root chord of 24ft and tip chord of 5ft gave an area of 840sq ft in normal flight. The fans were 6ft 4in (76in) in diameter. The aircraft was to be capable of 542 knots at sea level and 474 knots at 50,000ft. A full load of fuel gave a pure hovering endurance of 26.4 minutes. Conventional take-off needed 250 yards to unstick and 690 yards landing run from touchdown. Initial climb capability was 11,000ft/min.

P.140 VTOL Airliner

The P.140 was drawn in October 1957 and was a study for what became a seventy-two to eighty-seat civil airliner. The paper released in December 1957 laid out the background behind the P.140 design. Prior to this much of the work by BPA had been towards high disk-loaded fan lift for military aircraft, which required high thrust to weight ratios to carry out their missions. In the extreme of these cases the fan lift system approached closely the use of conventional jet lift systems. The company therefore decided to look at passenger aircraft systems of lower overall performance that could therefore make best use of fan lift systems.

The airliner layout developed went some way to meeting a recently drafted specification by BEA for a VTOL transport, although it was made clear that the design was produced before this actual specification was released. No claim was made regarding the complete conformance to the requirements, but the design concerned a larger and faster aircraft. It was noted that BPA would be studying the BEA requirement in the near future. A higher standard of furnishing than the BEA specification had been assumed in the P.140. After the decision to look at an eight-engine airliner as a minimum

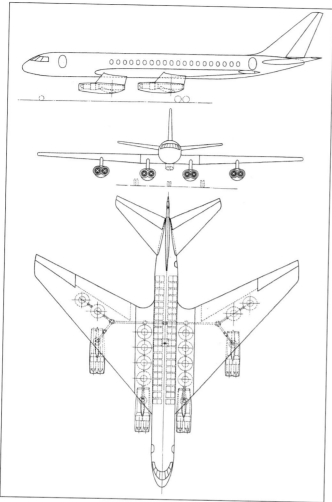

The P.140 VTOL airliner using eight engines for safety, driving four turbines and twelve mechanically driven lift fans.

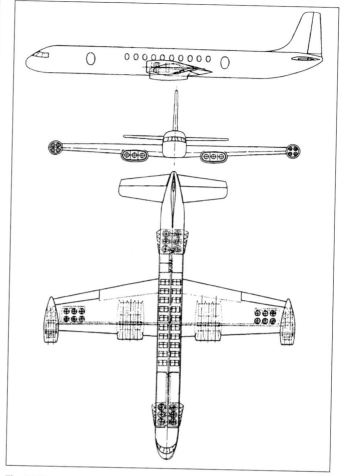

The P.141 was unusual in that eight engines sat in two pods on the wing tips. As pure gas producers, these drove six forward propulsion fans and twenty-four lift fans. The propulsion fans could be diverted downwards to add to lift and provide transition.

safety case, an arbitrary range of 300 miles was assumed and the number of passengers that could be carried calculated by the study. Operators' requirements for cargo, seat layouts and furnishings were kept open by assuming the highest standards of furnishing and comfort in the first instance.

The P.140 had a span of 116ft, a length of 132ft and stood high 42ft 6in overall. The plan root chord was 48ft 6in, the wing area 3,393sq ft and the leading edge sweep was 40° 37' (45° at quarter chord). The take-off weight was 134,225lb with a lift ratio of 1.14 on a lifting thrust of 153,400lb. The cruise at 40,000ft was Mach 0.7. Seventy-two seats represented the highest standards for the passengers with a maximum of eighty passengers in lower seat spacing.

P.141 VTOL Airliner with Clustered Gas Producer Engines

The P.141 was such a radical concept in civil aviation that its VTOL capability was almost a by-product of this. The design was aimed at a forty-seat civil airliner with VTOL capability to fly from city centre to city centre. What was radical was the propulsion design arrived at by discussions with industry. Because of this, the later-issued project numbers P.142 to P.145 bypassed the final scheme of the P.141.

The P.141 starting layout was the same as the P.143 as regards the airframe. It was as a result of the above BEA specification released for forty passengers over a range of 300 miles. Shortly after submission

of the P.140, an alternative form of drive was suggested by D. A. A. Griffiths of Rolls-Royce using compressed air, which A. R. Howell of NGTE, at the request of R. A. Shaw, had used with a Bristol BE53 engine. The difference with the RR suggestion was a lightweight engine would supply compressed air for hovering but would function as a normal bypass engine in conventional flight. In addition to this it was suggested that the hovering could be improved by preheating the air from the compressor. This preheat might be up as high as 725°K by passing it through special burners in ducting before passing it to single-stage lift fans driven by multi-stage turbines.

The P.141 was a brief study of such a system, but without the use of the preheating stage. It had no specific forward-propulsion engines. Eight RB108 modified engines were carried as a pod of four on each wing tip. These engines were pure gas producers and for forward propulsion once airborne these drove six fan systems, three in a nacelle on each wing. For VTOL the same eight RB108 gas producers also fed air to twenty-four fans, twelve with intakes that popped partially out of the forward lower floor and rear lower floor. Six were buried in each outer wing. A lift fan diameter of 2ft, propulsive fan diameter of 2.25ft and 12,500lb static thrust each was selected. To help with lift, the waste air from the tip pods would be deflected at 45°. A total of 54,000lb of thrust was available to lift an aircraft that was 33,522lb empty and had an AUW of 52,427lb. The span was 92ft, root chord 24ft 6in and tip chord 12ft 3in, giving 1,690sq ft of wing area. The length was 117ft with a fuselage 10ft 7.5in deep and 9ft wide.

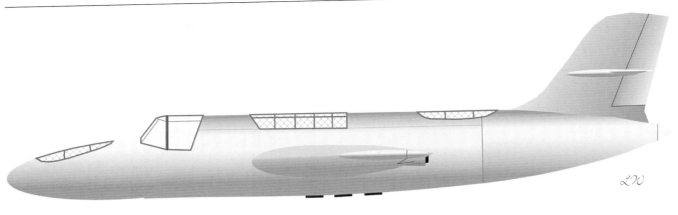

P.142

The P.142 was proposed as a VTOL development machine to work on the hot fan propulsion development suggested for the P.141 airliner. This included not only the hot fan air but additional heating by burning additional fuel in manifolds to raise the temperature en route to the fans. Such as design would replace duct losses by burning additional fuel.

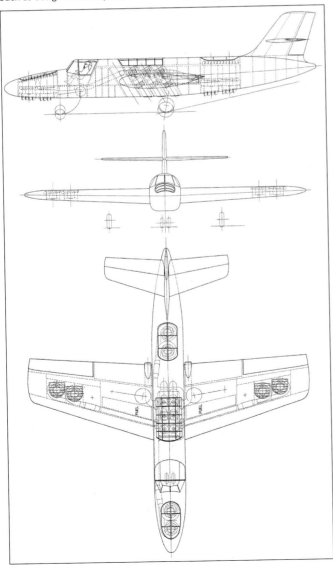

Even as the proposal was being written it was learned that the design of the RB108 was being changed by Rolls-Royce. Only a basic sea level power figure had been available anyway but now RR had suggested that in the new design it would be possible to do away with the ducted fan wing propulsion units entirely. This statement made the proposal document next to useless even as it was being put together. BPA could only comment that a redesign of the aircraft would be required once the nature of the changes to the RB108 and its performance were available. As a result of these potential changes the final drawing of the P.141 layout was delayed until January 1960, still with the original ducted fan wing system.

P.142 VTOL Experimental

The redesign of engines and air drive systems for the P.141 might take several years to achieve, so BPA proposed that attention should be briefly turned to how to proceed with essential research before this engine became available. The P.142 suggested a test vehicle to carry this out using existing power plants. It was proposed to use RB108 engines and to modify these from 1,900lb thrust to 580lb by increasing the bleed air taken off to 33% bleed. This air was then to be passed to a manifold from several engines and preheated by burning fuel. The hot air passed to the lift units, which were each a multi-stage turbine driving a lifting fan. It was suggested that a temperature of 650°K might be used rather than the maximum of 725°K to maintain some adjustment to the final design, and also the air bleed might be acceptable at an alternative rate. The design therefore looked at six engines and eight fans or eight engines and ten fans at the 33% bleed. Alternatively, six engines and ten fans at revised bleed. The successive airframe weights were 13,095, 16,080 and 14,010lb in each case.

The aircraft had a conventional mid-wing layout with six (or eight) RB108 (modified) engines sitting at the quarter chord position within the fuselage and angled forwards so that the waste efflux exited at 30° to the vertical. The air bleed was to be fed into four preheater units and thence to eight (or ten) turbine fan units, two in the nose, two in the rear fuselage and four (or six) in the wings. For horizontal flight an exhaust either side of the fuselage in the wing trailing edge diverted the engine bleed air at initial supply temperature and pressure overboard. Interconnection allowed for individual engine or fan failure. Since control relied on supply temperature and pressure to the fan turbines, in the event of a fan failure a small divert nozzle adjacent to the fan was to be used to maintain control thrust. Because the RB108 engines allegedly had a very fast response to throttle opening it was proposed that the engines be used to control total overall lift.

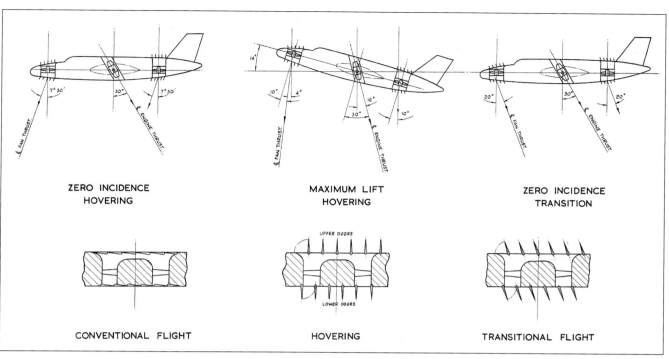

ZERO INCIDENCE HOVERING

MAXIMUM LIFT HOVERING

ZERO INCIDENCE TRANSITION

CONVENTIONAL FLIGHT

HOVERING

TRANSITIONAL FLIGHT

Control phases and key fan control flap positions on the P.142.

Control, in the sense of aileron control, was to be by interconnecting the throttle valves giving pressure and temperature to the aileron jack, having input from the pilot and the auto-stab unit. This type of interconnection was not possible for the elevator jack. Instead, the elevator control rod had an electrical pick-off and this signal, via an amplifier, was fed to hydraulic servos governing the preheat units. Control of pitch and roll in the hover therefore followed the same as in normal flight using the joystick. The fans had span-wise hinged flaps so that, for example, the efflux from the RB108s at 30° aft could be offset by fan thrust directed forward at 7.5° for zero-incidence hovering. Door controls could be operated progressively by a button on the joystick or by a standby lever in the cockpit. In hovering, both upper and lower doors were open. In transition, both upper and lower doors operated in opposition to each other to divert airflow forward or aft, and in normal flight both were closed. The expected transition angle for the doors was 20° aft in horizontal flight, while maximum lift thrust hover was nose up at 14° and fuselage flaps at 10° aft of centreline.

The span of the design was 45ft, the root chord 13ft and the tip chord 7ft, giving 450sq ft of area. The dihedral was 1.5° and the sweepback at 25% of chord was 15°. The overall length was 50.3ft with a fuselage 6.5ft deep and 5ft wide. The overall height (fin tip) was 16ft above the ground.

High speed was not important to the aircraft design but was quoted as 265 knots after a take-off run of 440 yards as a conventional aircraft. The use of fuel employed in the engine and burner units suggested a run-up, take-off and transition taking three minutes, just fifteen minutes in cruise and five minutes landing. The transition method was to hold the aircraft at just zero lift level until a speed of 90 knots, with the fan doors at 20° aft. At that point increase incidence to increase lift and shut down the fans as the aircraft climbed away. The total time for transition was thirty seconds. After transition the aircraft operated conventionally at 150 knots at sea level with a fuel consumption of 5,200lb per hour, matching the specified consumption of 2.2lb/hr/lb of thrust. All of this was based upon six engines, eight fans and 12lb air pressure fan bleed using the Rolls-Royce turbine/fan unit of 25.8in diameter.

P.143 VTOL Airliner

Released in July 1958, the basic airframe layout of the P.143 was a taper-winged civil airliner with zero sweep at 25% chord, similar in layout to the P.141 but having variations in engine positioning and tail group details. It was based upon the same BEA requirements and discussions with industry. The brochure was issued to Dr Cawood, Director in charge of the Aircraft Research Department at RAE, with copies to the chief engineers of RR and BEA, plus Sir Arnold Hall of HSA. The propulsion and VTOL capability came from ten Rolls-Royce RB144 engines and no fewer than forty 25.8in diameter Rolls-Royce lift fans. There were to be six RB144 in pods of three under the wings and four RB144 in the extreme rear lower fuselage. The RB108 could not be used because they were hot gas producers and noisy, far too noisy to be in the fuselage under the passengers. While mechanical-driven fans would be cheaper, this had not been liked by the airline industry, who favoured ducted air for fan operation to reduce mechanical maintenance. Hence, BPA proposed the air-driven fans.

The study had looked at RB108 direct-lift jets, shaft-driven fans, RB144 air-driven fans and RB144 air-driven fans using titanium to lower structure weight. The eventual choice of RB144 for propulsion and air drive for the fans had eighteen fans in the lower forward fuselage ahead of the main spar, ten fans aft of the auxiliary spar in the lower aft fuselage and six fans on each wing in a group inboard of the ailerons. The RB144s providing lift added to the air-driven fans by exhausting from the lower rear fuselage at an angle of 35°. The triplet of RB144s on the wings also drove the wing lift fans when in VTOL as well as being used for forward propulsion. All ducting was cross-connected so all fans could be used if a specific engine or engines failed. The most notable items in the layout were that, other than where the undercarriage, fans and engines were fitted, the entire wings were filled with the necessary fuel tanks and the passenger cabin underside with fans. Most luggage would presumably have to be carried as cabin baggage, which the airline considered likely to be normal in a 'city hopper'. The seat capacity range was forty to fifty-two seats.

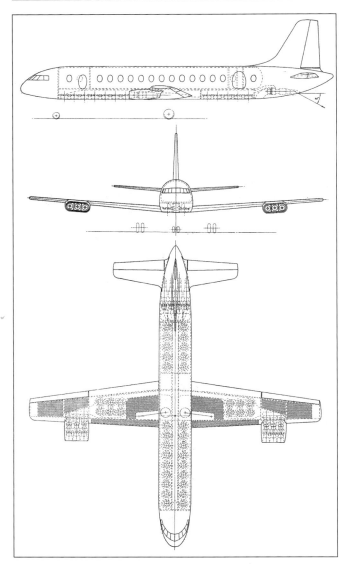

The P.143 conventional engine and hot air fan lift passenger aircraft.

P.145 Twin-Boom VTOL Transport

The P.145 was a design for a VTOL transport aircraft requirement. During its design, reference was made to a BEA report 'Provisional requirements for a VTOL aircraft for Passengers, Mail and Freight – BEA P&D Report No. M/94 Issue 1', to conform to sensible payload and block transition times. The company considered three options. In the transport case it would be necessary to shut down some of the propulsion engines and fair in the intakes and exhausts with doors in order to give optimum cruise fuel economy (where most fuel would be consumed). Instead, independent lift units became most attractive with the development of ducted fan lifting engines giving good weight to thrust ratios and fuel consumption. The BPA philosophy in the P.145 was therefore to calculate the correct propulsive requirement to obtain as much lift from that source and to install high augmentation from a calculated number of ducted fan lifting units.

Four bypass RB154 engines were chosen for forward propulsion, giving both fuel economy and cooler bypass air. When hovering, the hot exhaust would be deflected downwards at 30° and the bypass air directed to rotatable nozzles set apart on the booms of the transport. These nozzles not only added to lift but also provided transition control. The major part of the lift and transition provision came from a total of twelve RB153 lifting engines. The design layout was of a bulbous fuselage with fully opening tail door and ramp access at the rear. The double-taper wing had the lift engines installed in a fore and aft long pod at an increasing range of angles moving aft. Bypass air was added to the aft fans of these engines from the wing engines via ducting. At the rear end of each wing pod a tail boom continued aft to the fin and rudder, while the tailplane sat between the booms high enough to allow loading and unloading of the fuselage. Outboard of these pod/boom structures was the leading edge pod for two forward propulsion engines on each wing. One advantage of this layout was that during normal flight the propulsion noise was shielded from the passengers to a large extent by the boom and pod arrangement of the lift engines.

The final design had a span of 100ft, a root chord of 14.67ft and a tip chord of 8.5ft. Wing dihedral was 2° and area 1250sq ft. Overall fuselage length was 70.5ft, width 11.5ft and depth 10.5ft. The tail boom system made the overall length 86.6ft and the height on the tarmac was 28ft. Capacity for the 7ft high hold provided 52.5ft × 10.3ft.

In terms of performance, the total lift from propulsion engines was 2,600lb and from the twelve lift engines 107,600lb. For a range of 1,000 miles and a take-off weight of 104,300lb (19,166lb of payload) the appropriate remaining weight at landing would be 88,576lb. The flight regime that might be taken in a civil role would be a short take-off of 550 yards fully loaded and a vertical landing at the end of the flight. To achieve this 755 gallons of additional fuel would be carried in tip tanks as well as 2,000 gallons internally. The aircraft could, of course, take off vertically at this weight but only at the reduced safety margins acceptable in the military role. The cruising speed of the aircraft in level flight would have been 385 knots at 36,090ft.

Performance and costs were studied for 200- to 500-mile blocks as VTOL and 500- to 1,000-mile blocks as S/VTOL using data from BEA and SBAC. Compared with a fixed conventional aircraft the difference of an S/VTOL was found to be less than 1 pence per passenger per nautical mile. Seating drawn allowed for sixty seats, two crew, a stewardess and a large aft compartment for freight. Alternatively the whole of the area could become a cargo hold for pallets of freight and vehicles. On completion of the study it was submitted in June 1959. Frederick Francis Crocombe (Technical Director) and Charles Vivian Kenmir patented the layout of the lifting system in 889340A, dated 14 February 1962. Discussions on the aircraft as a civilian or a military transport continued and BPA were also having discussions with other manufacturers on their VTOL military transport studies with a view to collaboration.

The span was 65ft 6in, the root chord 15ft and the tip chord 6ft 4.8in, giving 916sq ft of wing area. The length was 92ft with a fuselage 10ft deep and 9.8ft wide. The height was 30ft. There was a 4° 30' dihedral on the wings. The maximum take-off weight (AUW) was 64,100lb. The documentation also considered the case where the engines could be uprated by the manufacturer to produce more power, when the potential AUW could rise to 75,556lb.

As a result of these studies, Sir Harold Roxbee-Cox reported back to the board in October 1958 that it did not appear that the project(s) were progressing very well from a viewpoint within the Ministry. Their interest appeared to be particularly devoted to the Tilt-Wing concept (of the Bristol 199) plus deflected airstream designs. Their aim was not to cease the work on fans but to limit it to the investigation and production of models. Ultimately it was noted that the official view of lifting fan development was that it was now being regarded as a power plant problem to be dealt with by the engine manufacturers. The official view was that fan lift was not necessarily the best VTOL solution and official progress through government departments was therefore deliberately slow.

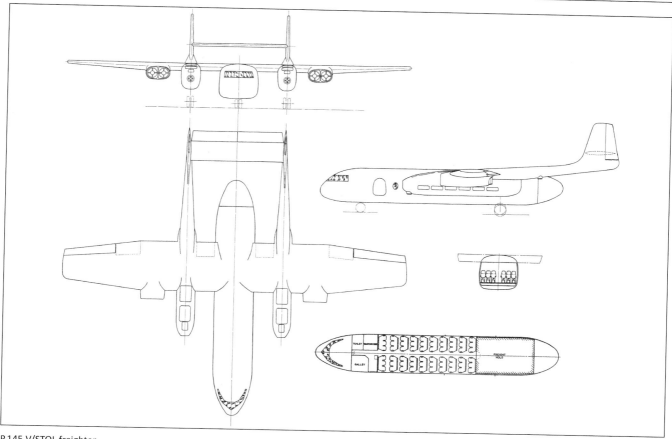

P.145 V/STOL freighter.

Engine, fuel and cargo layout of the P.145. Patent 889340 dated 14 February 1959 covered the angled lift engines in the booms.

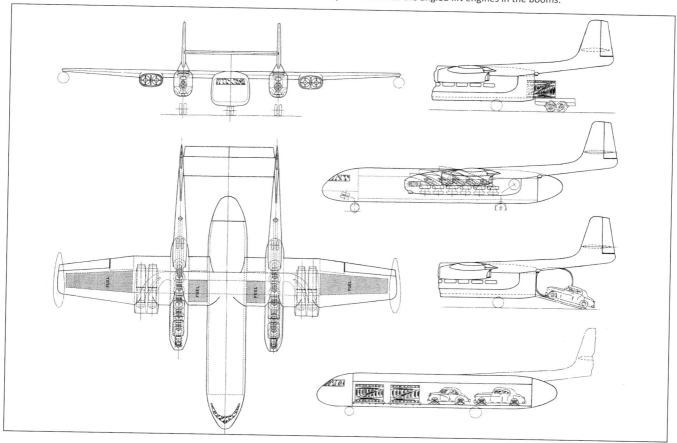

In December 1959, however, it was reported that there had been a change in VTOL long-range transport policy as a result of current Air Ministry thinking. The current ideas were to utilise standard aircraft for long range, the VC11 or the Shorts Britannic (Belfast); STOL only for medium range; and VTOL via the Fairey Rotodyne or similar layout for short hops. The decision was brought about by the recognition that VTOL for long range would be little employed and in studies proved not enough utilised to justify its development costs.

P.146 Canard VTOL Airliner

The final design in the series that represented an aircraft was the P.146. The P.146 came about around December 1959 because of confirmation during discussions with BEA that they had a requirement for a 100-passenger VTOL airliner.

After some years in the study of fan lift the trend to integrate the lift fan and engine together was recognised as the most likely way forward. The use of a fan as part of a ducted fan engine was to reduce the fuel consumption and gas-producing size for a given lifting capacity. If it was then necessary to bleed off air to provide VTOL control functions, this reduced the power available for control compared with a pure jet engine and compressor bleeds might rise from 10% studied into the 15 to 20% range in the future. In the P.145 previously studied, bypass air was utilised instead of reducing compressor efficiency with bleed air, the overall result meaning a more efficient system. However, depending where the engines were sited this could mean the large ducts

of low pressure required to reduce losses would take up an unreasonable proportion of space within the aircraft.

The consideration of these problems brought a decision that, rather than keeping the lift engines close to the centre of gravity, they should be moved to the perimeter of the design as four groups. Also, these groups should be multiples of engines so that in a failure of an engine the others could make good the deficiency. Such a move was difficult unless the design was unconventional and the best solution was in the form of a two-wing, tail-first layout. The lift engines on the forward wing were grouped into a nacelle of five engines per nacelle. In the larger-span aft wing they were grouped into four engines per nacelle. Conventional foreplane elevators and aft-wing elevons were employed during horizontal flight. The three propulsion engines sat in the rear of the fuselage. Two intakes for these were at the base of the tail fin feeding two engines that exhausted directly aft of the intakes and a third engine buried in the rear fuselage and exhausting right at the tip of the rear fuselage.

The lift engines (eighteen required) were RB155 or BE59 ducted fan units of 7,000lb static thrust each and the nacelles had large closing doors above and below when not in use during normal flight. The propulsion engines were scaled up from the RB163 design and were 15,000lb static thrust. The propulsion engines added to the lift during VTOL by diverting up to 24,000lb vertically downwards from the two outer flight engines. It was necessary in this case for the groups to supply only 5,780lb per engine, leaving a margin for engine failure and 7,700lb after an engine failure, comparing favourably

P.146 canard VTOL airliner.

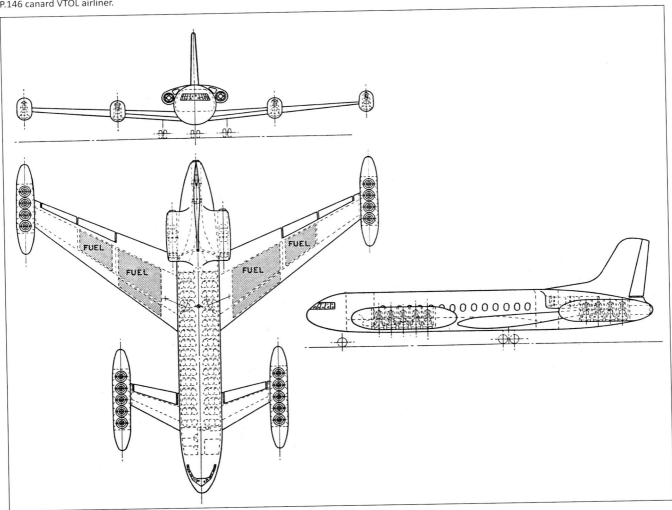

with the lift engine emergency power rating of 8,060lb. All fuel was carried in the aft main wing.

The design proposed was therefore an inter-city centre to centre carrier of ninety-six passengers. The machine was of canard form with a fuselage fin and four tip nacelles, having a span of 100ft, main wing chord of 25ft and tip chord of 8ft. The total wing area was 1,650sq ft, dropping from 15% to 12% thickness and having 4.5° dihedral plus a quarter chord sweepback of 35°. The overall length was also 100ft and the fuselage was a circle of 12ft diameter. The height over fin on a tricycle undercarriage was 31.25ft. The take-off weight was 128,000lb maximum and the basic weight 84,495lb. There were sixteen rows of seats in paired triples and a central isle.

The design and proposals were submitted in November 1960. In addition to drawing on engine data, fan data and tunnel testing, a large-scale model of the P.146 was made for exhibition purposes. The overall design of the type was considered unique and was patented by BPA and engineers Frederick Francis Crocombe (Technical Director) and Charles Vivian Kenmir as 912150A, dated 5 December 1962.

By May 1960 it had been determined that there was no interest from BEA in the project. In addition, the move to split the industry into two main aircraft groups meant increasing confusion as to who BPA could effectively pursue regarding any work on VTOL projects. The decision was made that no more money would be expended on the P.146, which had effectively become a private venture. Six weeks later this decision was reconfirmed and the P.146 project was abandoned other than as a visual marketing tool.

A large display model of the P.146 concept was made for use at exhibitions. As a canard, the foreplane added an additional 430sq ft to the stated main wing area.

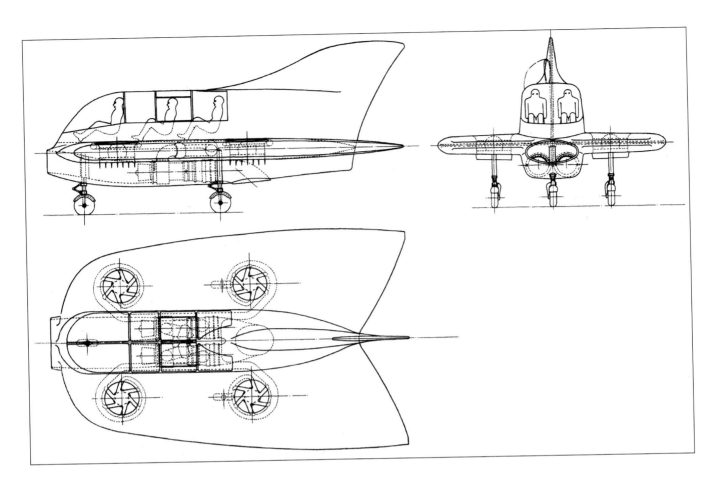

CHAPTER THIRTY-EIGHT

Flying Cars and Jumping Jeeps
– P.144 and P.147

P.144

THE P.144 WAS a design for an airborne vehicle of futuristic shape employing the development lessons learned from aviation design capability for lift fan systems. On 15 May 1959 Sir Harold Roxbee-Cox, chairing the board meeting in the absence of John North, requested an update on the project. The design, then known under the project name 'Flying Jeep', had evolved as a fully glazed cabin body seating one crew member and capable of carrying five passengers or 1,000lb of freight over a range of 120 nautical miles at speeds up to 160 knots, with pure VTOL operation. The design was a viable alternative to helicopters for transport purposes. Technical Director Frederick Crocombe confirmed that the design and a scale model was presented at the Royal Military College of Science, Shrivenham, during a design conference in April/May 1959. Roxbee-Cox observed that the original requirement seemed to be for a craft that could permit a 'quick lift' over obstacles, his inference being that the resulting vehicle was neither roadable nor designed with the Army in mind.

By using two Rolls-Royce RB144 lift engines with an auxiliary compressor stage providing air take-off, the supply ducting from this stage entered a preheat section before being passed to four turbo fans mounted in streamlined stub wings. For forward propulsion and lift the lift fan doors acted as control and transition elements. The engines sat side-by-side on the centreline below the passengers and the air ducting. A fixed tricycle undercarriage with integral mudguards was proposed and the vehicle had a length of 27.75ft, width of 17.5ft and height overall of 13.5ft. Endurance was fifty minutes and with one crew the empty weight was 6,050lb, leading to an AUW of 10,050lb when loaded.

The final design had first been proposed in February 1959 and had the shape of a fat fuselage with thick, short-span, full-length wings at the base and a streamlined fin. There were no flight control surfaces in the conventional sense, all being accommodated by the fan lift system. In competition, Bristol Siddeley had looked at a Pegasus-powered cargo lifter known as the 'flying pig'.

P.144 Six-seat, five-passenger flying vehicle using engine air to drive lift fans.

P.144

The P.144 'flying car' was not intended to be roadable.

P.144A

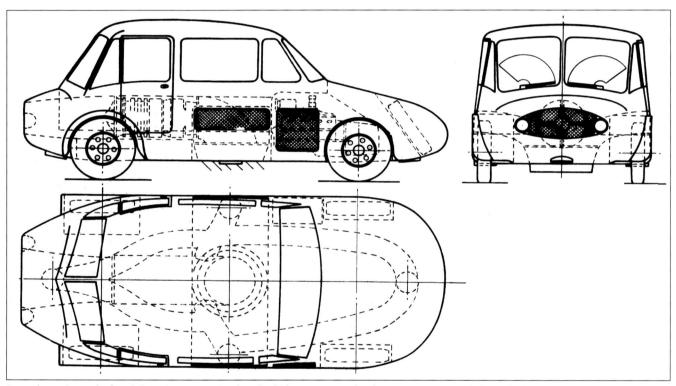

As an alternative to the futuristic P.144 a conventional road vehicle was proposed with a jet engine to provide limited airborne capability in the manner of the flying bedstead.

P.144A

As an alternative from the initial P.144, the company took on board Roxbee-Cox's comments and drew up the P.144A, which put forward the design for a road vehicle with airborne capability, again called a flying jeep or scout car. This design was nearing completion in June 1959 when BPA issued a paper addressing VTOL and transport problems. The new design was stressed to rely upon the 'ground cushion' provided under the vehicle by the underside outlet of the single horizontally installed jet engine and the peripheral control nozzles.

In this alternative the vehicle was a conventional car driven through its road wheels by a 3.6 litre petrol engine forward of the rear wheels, so the gearbox provided shaft drive to the rear wheels.

A single bypass RB155 engine sat on the centreline just aft of the front wheels and drove a central nozzle aft fan exhausting vertically under the vehicle through cascade doors. Four balancing nozzles for lift control ejected at the corners of the vehicle. With a wheelbase of 10ft and a track of 6ft, the design was 16.5ft long, 7ft wide and 7ft high. It could carry a payload of 1,100lb comprising five seated persons and two stretcher racks. The range was 300 miles on the ground at 12mpg and fifteen minutes flight time with the RB155 system. The intake for the jet engine had a conventional oval radiator grille but entrainment air for additional lifting fan came from side intakes and behind that were additional side intakes for the road engine cooling.

Both the P.144 and P.144A were considered discussion precursors to any formal specification that might be released.

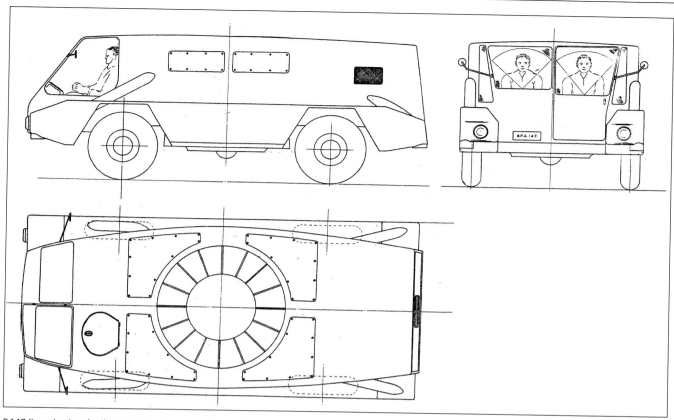

P.147 'jumping jeep' military reconnaissance vehicle with limited airborne capability.

P.147

In July 1959, as a result of the P.144 studies and discussions, the company produced a paper entitled 'The Application of Vertical Take-Off to Army Ground Transport Problems'. The Fig. 15 of that paper summarised a general picture of the design parameters for geared fans, RB144 air-driven fans and ducted fan engines, which later formed Fig. 1 of their P.147 study. The issue of the P.144A of September 1959 led directly to BPA being requested to tender to the Army for a 'Ground Borne Military Vehicle Having a Limited Airborne Capability'. BPA were at pains to point out that theirs was a feasibility study rather than a tender, as the whole of the aircraft industry currently had specialists in particular methods of producing vertical lift and these could exploit the full potential of their own system. BPA therefore chose to leave any alternatives and to concentrate only on the lift fan engine method.

The specification eventually released for this project was FVRDE 9258, dated March 1960, which called for a reconnaissance vehicle with all the normal road and cross-country capabilities (ie similar capabilities to the Ferret scout car) but also the controlled ability to fly a low-level limited distance over 10ft high, 30ft long obstacles, rivers and swamps. It was expected that the result would look like a good workmanlike army vehicle rather than the civilian-style car of the P.144A and could be carried in a Beverley transport. The code name was Project Prodigal but for virtually the whole of industry and certainly within BPA it was immediately dubbed the 'Jumping Jeep'. The design conference was held on 11 March 1960 attended by Folland, Vickers, Westlands, Shorts and BPA, with six months to formal submission.

The BPA P.147 outline certainly looked like a workmanlike military vehicle, having sloping front and rear and an overall boxed shape. With a length of 16ft and a wheelbase of 8ft 4in, the track was 6ft 4in with overall width 7ft 4in and height 6ft. For ground drive a Coventry climax engine was chosen after studying no fewer than six

variations of that manufacturer and engine, plus engines by Rover (Gas Turbine 15/90), McCulloch 6318, BMC Ado 9 and 10, Rootes Group 1.5 litre and even the Blackburn Cirrus-Minor aero engine. The Climax FBW engine was selected as being in production, with the better V-8 in development as a later alternative. It was appreciated, however, that these used 100 octane petrol and a diesel alternative might eventually be decided upon instead.

The transmission to the four wheels was to be hydrostatic for best four-wheel drive cross-country performance and systems were designed to prevent all power being sent to one wheel in a 'bogged-down' situation. Ground clearance was 1.33ft and the turning circle 38ft. Since the lift engine required 40–45% of the vehicle weight and 15% for the crew and kit then such a vehicle would not be viable unless the total framework and road engine came to 40–45% or less. Since the Ferret vehicle weight was 84% of its own total because of armour it was obviously necessary to follow aircraft structure techniques and lightweight materials if weights of half that of the Ferret were to be achieved. Conventional vehicle armour plate was impossible. At a calculated weight of 8,313lb, road speed was 45mph and cross-country 5 to 45mph depending upon terrain. Two crew including the driver/pilot had personal arms and a radio set only.

For lift engine selection a Bristol Siddeley BE59/7 engine was chosen as the prime design, but even increasing the diameter failed to give the correct bypass ratio. Help from BS revised the BE59/12 design by 1.14 to 1 scale up of the BE59/8. Happily, the revised exit velocity was deemed too low to explode ground mines. Starting of the lift engine (fifty starts) was to be by hydraulic drive from the wheel system; air or cartridge starting being impractical. The large engine had to be central and vertical and flight height was to be controlled by the throttle on the engine. Roll control had to be in the hands of the pilot to enable cross-wind landing and thrust control was via control

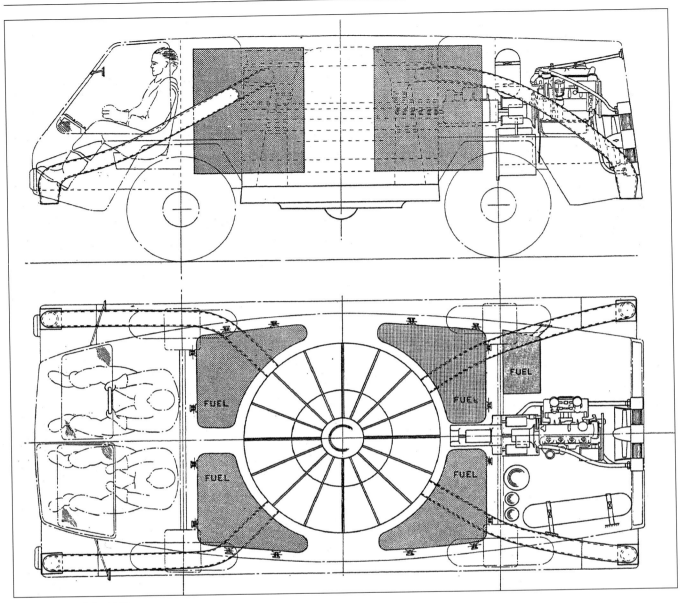

Interior layout of the P.147.

flaps because of the longer delay by engine throttle. For emergency decent a load of 15g was catered for, albeit with potential structural distortion damage similar to a helicopter auto-rotate impact. All normal operating modes could otherwise be controlled.

Results of Flying Bedstead and Short SC.1 testing were incorporated to design the control and autostab system, with air control at the four corners of the vehicle. For fifty missions a lift engine fuel capacity worked out at 250 gallons. New data on the BE59/12 just days before submission gave a range limitation of 35,000ft for fifty sorties or 43,000ft for forty-three sorties and a forward velocity of 72ft/sec in still air at a vehicle inclination of 10°. This range was less than hoped during brochure preparation and an addendum was bound into the document to correct the data.

For 10ft flight altitude, zero-height ejection seats would add too much weight. The suggestion was to have jettisonable side doors and static line parachutes so that a power climb above 250ft would allow safe bail-out by static line. Otherwise it was the 10ft emergency crash decent. Based upon size overall, it was commented that the vehicle would fit in an A.W.660 transport (Argosy) but not the Beverley requested.

A second engine type was considered as an appendix to the brochure. This was a Rolls-Royce engine with an aft bypass fan rather than a front fan, the RB162. The advantage was that the pitching moments, which are induced in all VTOL designs, would be reduced to a third in an aft fan and contra-rotation of fan and gas producer rotors was more easily achieved. By matching the thrust required, a modified RB162 would be shorter and match the roof line of the original P.147 engine design. The difference would be perhaps in the introduction of side intakes on the vehicle to feed the aft fan system. Suggestions for further development of key systems were also made and the full brochure was finally submitted on 11 October 1960. Even before this, John North had already advised his team that the project was unlikely to go ahead into production. A delay to any programme ensued when control of the study and any decisions was passed from the Fighting Vehicle Research and Development Establishment (FVRDE) to the Air Ministry. In the end it was BAC who were given a further study contract in around 1962 for their stored energy system with multiple fans. Eventually the whole idea was finally abandoned as pointless compared with AOP aircraft/helicopters.

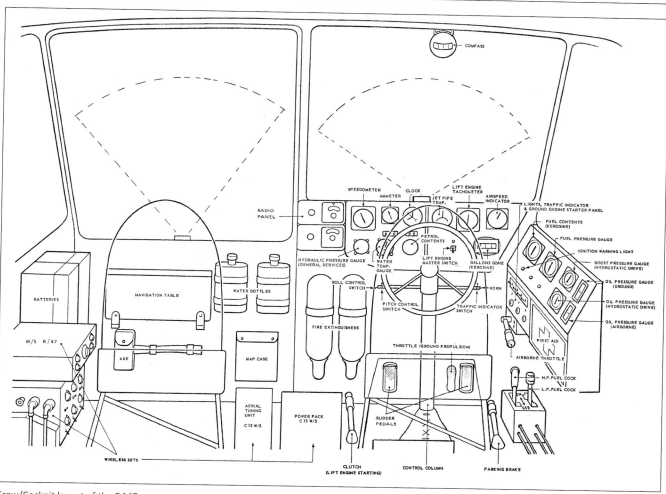

Crew/Cockpit layout of the P.147.

Model of the P.147 'Jumping Jeep'.

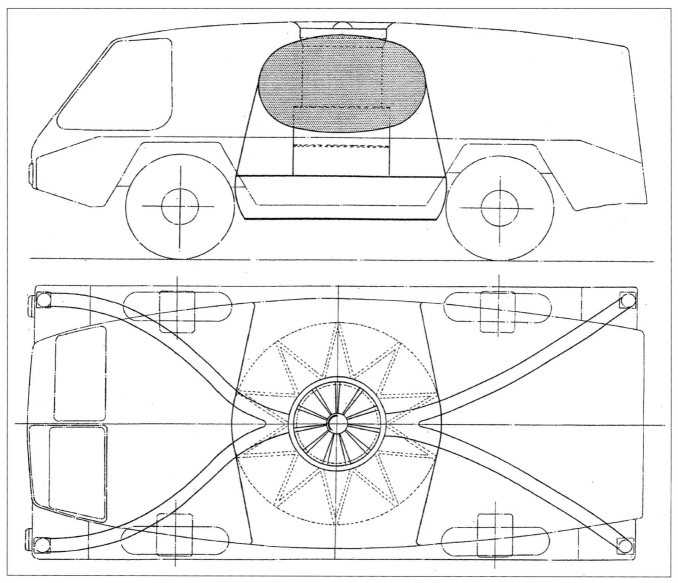

P.147 variant utilising a turbofan engine with the fan on the exhaust end.

The dual-purpose air transportable tanker carrying the final airframe design designation P.148.

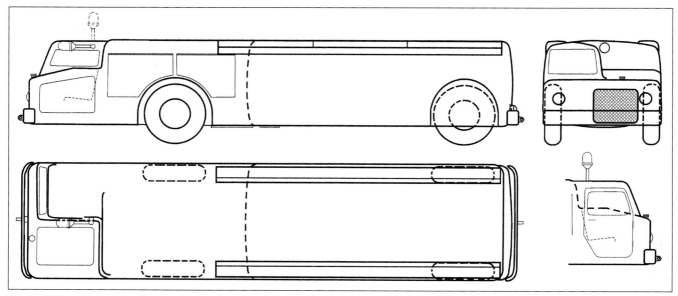

P.148

The last home design of the airframe division was an airborne vehicle but only in the sense that it would be air-transportable via aircraft such as the AW Argosy. The design data was submitted on 26 October 1960. The MoS requirement had called for a road-capable, dual-purpose refueller that could be transported anywhere around the world by RAF standard transport aircraft. The design looked very similar to modern low-profile aircraft tugs seen at civil airports today. On being asked during an internal meeting if BPA had solicited any assistance from the local experts, Thompson Tankers of Bilston, they confirmed that this had not been necessary and the design was solely a BPA effort.

The vehicle was a 48ft long, 6ft 8in wide, 6ft high (empty) four-wheel vehicle. The wheelbase was 16ft 3in and the track 5ft 7in. The ground clearance was 1ft empty and 0.9ft filled with fuel. Driver control was by front-steering, front-wheel drive. The 350cu in Vauxhall engine was offset to the left at the front and the driver sat in a cabin to the right. Between the two a pop-up folding warning light lay horizontally until required when transiting around vehicle and aircraft areas. Over the front wheels was the fuel pumping system, fuel tank for the engine and hose reels, filters, etc. The entire rear of the vehicle was an enclosed service fuel tank and when fully laden the centre of gravity of the vehicle was exactly between the four wheels. AUW laden was 30,180lb (6,865lb per front wheel, 8,225lb per rear wheel). Empty the weight was 9,800lb (3,820lb per front wheel, 1,080lb per rear wheel). The entire chassis structure was to be manufactured from ARC welded aluminium sheet, castings and extrusions. The design did not proceed past the submission.

By the end of January 1961 the study for the amalgamation of Boulton Paul Aircraft as part of the Dowty Group was under way and the dearth of in-house aircraft design work resulted in a move to continue in the subcontracting of structures and aircraft development work plus hydraulic flight control products – all areas that were to some extent overloaded with their own projects at the time. Any future airframe work was based upon military Canberra and Lightning development and Beagle 206 wing manufacture. The line of 'own-design' airframe projects ceased.

Artist's rendering of the P.148.

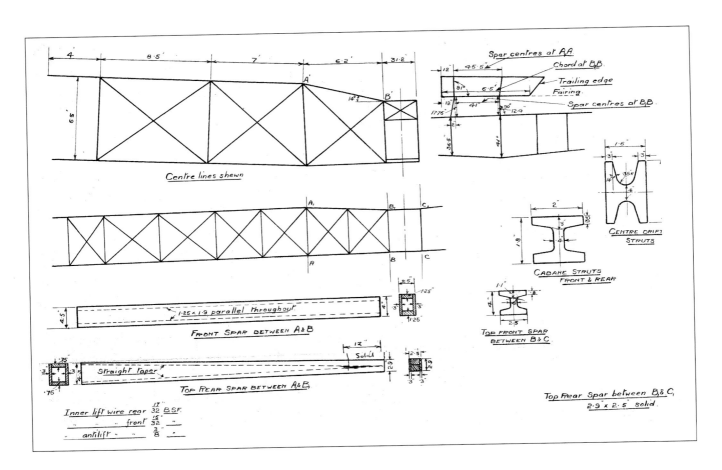

Appendix One

Dataset Accuracy

IN RESEARCHING or employing dimensional information on designs it is important to understand by what method the aircraft is dimensioned and important to recognise that information published in contemporary magazines and in modern literature is frequently very basic, randomly rounded, usually copied off older literature and therefore often inaccurate. That together with the small reproduction sizes of many illustrations makes it difficult for any researcher or model maker to be clear in generating a larger reproduction or a full-size replica of many historical designs.

During the First World War the designs were controlled by the War Department. The specifications set performance requirements, weight allowances to be used for internal equipment – including the pilot, ammunition and fuel (ie disposable load) – and varying standard safety factors to be used for sizing spars, etc. It was a requirement that drawings be supplied to the War Department 'Air Board' for the purposes of load and stress calculation. The tensile or compressive loads in each member of the fuselage and wing truss structure were to be tabled against the drawings provided. The Air Board team then carried out their own calculations (usually employing very efficient female mathematicians) and agreed or disagreed with the values provided by the company, making requests to change sections and applying the comment 'satisfactory' to others.

In the case of wing structure, the key dimensions for calculations were the interplane gap, spar centreline to spar centreline, in order to determine interplane strut length, and the true length of each spar

between and beyond jointing. Operating in this manner, the stated span of the B&P design described was often not the projected span we would know today, but the measured length along the top of the spar truss uncovered (which this author has termed 'structural span' or S-span, using P-span for the projected result). These distances ignored dihedral, providing total length of the connected spars if laid out flat on the bench. The data was used to draw up the bending moment diagrams to prove that the cross-sectional area of spars, etc., were adequate.

Drawing A384, a foolscap-size sketch on brown paper for a stressing data submission to the Department of Munitions, shows the 'B' wing layout but is dimensioned as the 'A' wing would be. It illustrates the method of measuring the usually published span of the machine. This measurement 'along the spars' of the 'A' wing gives the original stated span of 54ft, ignoring the loss of span due to the outer wing dihedral and showing the true strut length between any pinned joint centres.

Herein lies the first source of potential error in dimensioning or scaling GA drawings when looking at early three-views and stated 'span'. The P.7, for example, might have a stated span of 54ft. By then applying the design dihedral, the true span of the machine in plan and front elevation (the projected span or P-Span) was always a small but significant distance less than the quoted value. This S-Span also ignored the addition of varnished fabric covering outboard of the wood or metal tip material. The statement 'measured along the spars' was frequently used by B&P engineers of the period, but was ignored largely by publicists, who only wanted the simplest of figures in their magazines and articles.

The other difficult dimension is the fuselage length. In B&P's case this was always stated as 'approximate' in early aircraft rigging diagrams, the reason being that the cable-rigged fuselage structure could vary slightly depending on the tautness of the rigging and build tolerances including control cable tensions, making overall length a poor measure of rigging accuracy. Tail-down length/height was more important to consider stowage in hangars and the wing tip to nose and tail distances port and starboard were important to ensure the fuselage and wings were not twisted out of alignment by any over-enthusiastically tightened rigging cables. Adjustments of tension in control cables were frequently required to get a good balance of controls and prevent directional hunting or control surface flutter, etc, forming the origin of check or test flights.

It is important therefore to determine if we are talking about a structural span or a projected span when reviewing that time period. Unfortunately that is not always easy to decide. B&P in particular were very protective of data on government projects and would round

information or even significantly change information given to publishers such as *Flight* and *Jane's*. As we move into the 1930s there is an increasing use of projected span and the discrepancies disappear barring pure errors. From P.29 through to P.33, with some wings no longer a straight edge, this method slowly went out of fashion and projected span data was then employed on proposal three-views.

As we move into post-Second World War jet aircraft a different source of error appears. It is necessary to be clear on delta and swept aircraft if the quoted span is the basic planform span (ie the distance between the tip points of a basic triangle outline) or the true projected span after this has been truncated to form the shaped tip of the wing or in shorter spans extended to a tip fairing. These triangle or other outlines were used as calculation cases in the basic design and sometimes misquoted even in formal documentation. The P.111/111A/120 spans quoted herein are from the rigging diagrams.

The other item to remember when looking at projects is that they are merely a layout and size at a specific point in the early design process. They rarely represent the final appearance should a contract be obtained for a prototype. The built projects all differed in appearance/size from that first proposed by the time the iterative design process (and inevitable interference and changes dictated by Government officials) had run its course and their aerodynamic structures had been agreed and laid out in manufacture. Indeed, working from any GA drawing is fraught with potential errors since for speed, outlines were traced from other existing outlines when accuracy did not matter.

Even on component manufacturing drawings errors crop up to dumbfound the researcher, although thankfully they are less likely.

It should also be remembered that until the division became Boulton Paul Aircraft Ltd, the B&P group had the ability to design and make its own propellers. Here is the finished manufacture drawing for the Lion-engined P.15 propellers.

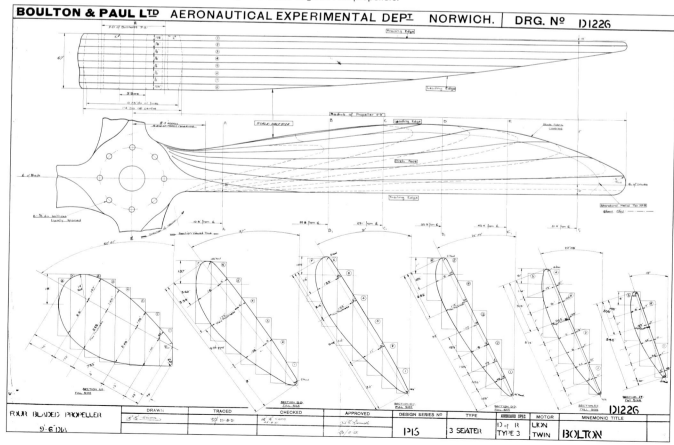

Regarding Publicist's Accuracy

Published information on early designs was heavily influenced by the secret nature of military contracts. B&P would avoid giving out any information on military aircraft and some published sketches of the time period are clearly very basic with dimensions added from study of the few pictures released. A new listing of built designs generated by the company in September 1954 has a number of errors in type, span and engine model because of the restricted size of the table itself and rounding of data, which relied heavily on copies of *Flight* and *Aeroplane* as a first source rather than the actual drawings and documents available.

In this volume, in contrast, the author has tried to use only original source data on the basis of stated dimensions cross-checked against original drawings or documents and measured dimensions compared with known or stated values on drawings checked for stretch or shrinkage.

Drawing Accuracy and Reproduction

Drawing techniques and scales varied considerably during the almost fifty years of the project list span. Ink on linen was the contractual delivery preference for three-quarters of the period, with ink on tracing paper the next choice. The accuracy of the three-view drawings varied as previously stated. These ranged from a quick pencil scheme on scrap paper for the decision to proceed, then to a 1/50th set of three-views in the 1930s by H. A. Hughes, which he or another draughtsman would ultimately draw to larger scale for his approval. One tenth scale was the most popular. The worst choice of materials was cost driven up to the Great Depression, when oiled tracing paper was used. This gathered dirt and discoloured, became brittle and ripped easily once it aged.

Three-view is something of a misnomer on many unbuilt projects because B&P preferred not to waste time on full three-views. Commonly they would produce a side elevation and a front elevation and only if the customer required it after first discussions, a plan or part of a plan with truncated wings. The front elevation was frequently incomplete, in that the tail unit, part hidden by the fuselage and wings to the foreground, was often ignored. All of these drawings were done initially in pencil with scribbled notes to save time. It was the job of the tracers (usually women whose lettering was better) to trace over the pencil in ink and stencil the titles.

With the installation of a Barco camera when at Wolverhampton from 1936 it was possible to reduce drawings of any scale to glass plates and the company obtained permission during the Second World War to send plate photographs for external reproduction requirements rather than actual full drawings. Immediately post-war, they also had one of the first Zerox hand photocopier systems adapted to the Barco camera. The exciting feature of this paper system was the ability to manually reduce the drawing to any scale required within about a minute.

Textual Accuracy

Again, as far as is possible, information has been gleaned from primary sources of originals and copies of formal proposal brochures and drawings, paper original or carbon copies of letter and memo correspondence, brief pencil notes made by the author from the remainder of J. D. North's security-vetted personal files prior to their destruction, formal test reports, production plans, maintenance logs and company notes of all forms. Vital also were the company photographic records, particularly the numbered and dated photographic logs maintained so copiously at Wolverhampton from 1937 to the period of the last photographer, Don Wilson, ending in 1987. Don had learned his trade well with the RAF on the Continent late in the Second World War.

Data Summary Table

BIPLANES

PROJECT REF	WING SECTION	PROJECTED SPAN	LENGTH	U-WING CHORD	L-WING CHORD	GAP	AREA	AUW	ENGINE(S)	MAX SPEED
P.3 Hawk	RAF 15	28ft 6.5in	19ft 10.875in	5ft 4.8in	4ft 1.5in	3ft 10.6in	262sq ft	1,807lb	ABC Wasp	
P.3 Hawk	RAF 15	28ft 11.58in	19ft 10.875in	5ft 4.8in	4ft 1.5in	3ft 10.6in	266sq ft	1,925lb	BR(a)	
P.3 Boblink	RAF 15	28ft 11.58in	19ft 10.875in	5ft 4.8in	4ft 1.5in	3ft 10.6in	266sq ft	1,992lb	BR.2	125mph @10,000ft
HN3	RAF 15	20ft	16ft 6in	4ft 6in	3ft	3ft	130sq ft	1,235lb	Clerget or BR.2	125mph estimated
P.6	RAF 15	25ft	19ft	5ft	5ft	5ft	235sq ft	1,725lb	RAF.1A	103mph@1,000ft
P.7 Bourges 1A/1B	RAF 15	57ft 2.56in	37ft	8ft	6ft 6in	6ft 6in	767sq ft	6,723lb	2 x ABC Dragonfly	124mph@10,000ft
P.7A Bourges II	RAF 15	53ft 11in	37ft	8ft	6ft 6in	6ft 6in	738sq ft	5,920lb	2 x BR.2	>120mph
P.7B Bourges III	RAF 15	61ft 2.56in	39ft 6in	8ft	6ft 6in	6ft 6in	830sq ft	7,600lb	2 x Napier Lion	130mph@10,000ft
P.7D Bourges VB	RAF 15	61ft 3in	38ft 8in	8ft	6ft 6in	6ft 6in	831sq ft	7292lb	2 x Liberty	
CSSP Mock-Up	RAF 15	40ft 3.2in	29ft 5in	7ft 3in	7ft 3in	6ft 6in	580sq ft	5,108lb	Napier Lion	110mph@SL
P.8 Atlantic	RAF 15	61ft 2.56in	39ft 6in	8ft	6ft 6in	6ft 6in	830sq ft	11,500lb	2 x Napier Lion	149mph@10,000ft
P.8 Civil	RAF 15	61ft 2.56in	39ft 6in	8ft	6ft 6in	6ft 6in	830sq ft	7,500lb	2 x Napier Lion	149mph@10,000ft
P.8 Production	RAF 15	60ft 2.7in	39ft 6in	8ft	6ft 6in	6ft 6in	816sq ft	7,880lb	2 x Napier Lion	149mph@10,000ft
P.9	RAF 15	27ft 6in	24ft 8in	5ft 6in	5ft 6in	5ft 6in	285sq ft	1,770lb	RAF.1A	104mph@1,000ft
P.10	RAF 15	30ft	26ft	5ft 6in	5ft 6in	5ft 6in	311sq ft	1,700lb	Lucifer	104mph@1,000ft
P.12 Bodmin	RAF 15	69ft 10.4in	53ft 4.5in	10ft	10ft	10ft	1,204sq ft	11,000lb	2 x Napier Lyon	116mph@ SL
P.15 Bolton	RAF 15	62ft 3.2in	49ft 8in	8ft 6in	7ft	7ft	955.4sq ft	9,500lb	2 x Napier Lion	130mph@10,000ft
P.25A Bugle J6984	RAF 15	65ft 5.6in	39ft 9in	8ft 6in	7ft	7ft	941.7sq ft	8,910lb	2 x Napier Lion	116mph@6,500ft
P.25 Bugle J6985	RAF 15	62ft 4.6in	39ft 9in	8ft 6in	7ft	7ft	924.7sq ft	8,110 (test)	2 x Bristol Jupiter	120mph@6,500ft
P.25 Bugle J7235	RAF 15	62ft 4.6in	39ft 9in	8ft 6in	7ft	7ft	924.7sq ft		2 x Bristol Jupiter	109mph@6,500ft
P.25A Bugle II J7266	RAF 15	67ft 0.5in	39ft 9in	8ft 6in	7ft	7ft	966sq ft	8,914 (test)	2 x Napier Lyon	118mph@6,500ft
P.15 Long Range	RAF 15	70ft 6in	44ft 8in	8ft 8in	7ft	7ft	1,092sq ft		2 x Napier Lyon	130mph@10,000ft
P.29 proposal	BP Flat Bottom	61ft 9.5in	39ft 10in	7ft	7ft	8ft 6in	980sq ft	9,220lb	2 x Napier Lyon	132mph@5,000ft
P.29 Sidestrand Mk.I	BP.10	71ft 11.3in	40ft 7.87in	7ft	7ft	7ft 6in	943.5sq ft	8,885lb	2 x Bristol Jupiter VI	130mph@5,000ft
P.29A Sidestrand Mk.II	BP.10	71ft 11.3in	46ft 2in	7ft	7ft	7ft 6in	979.5sq ft	9,232lb	2 x Bristol Jupiter VI	134mph@4,000ft
P.29B Sidestrand Mk.III	BP.10	71ft 11.3in	46ft 2in	7ft	7ft	7ft 6in	979.5sq ft	11,217lb	2 x Jupiter VIII & VIIIF	144mph@5,000ft

PROJECT REF	WING SECTION	PROJECTED SPAN	LENGTH	U-WING CHORD	L-WING CHORD	GAP	AREA	AUW	ENGINE(S)	MAX SPEED
P.29B bomb nose Mk.III	BP.10	71ft 11.3in	45ft 10.95in	7ft	7ft	7ft 6in	979.5sq ft	11,217lb	2 x Jupiter VIIIF	144mph@5,000ft
P.29B Coastal Torpedo	BP.10	71ft 11.3in	46ft 2in	7ft	7ft	7ft 6in	979.5sq ft	11,500lb	2 x Jupiter VIII	135mph@5,000ft
P.29B Survey	BP.10	71ft 11.3in	46ft 2in	7ft	7ft	7ft 6in	979.5sq ft	10,200lb	2 x Jupiter VIII	140mph@10,000ft
P.29B Seaplane	BP.10	71ft 11.3in	47ft	7ft	7ft	7ft 6in	979.5sq ft	11,500lb	2 x Jupiter IX	130mph@5,000ft
P.29B Export Mk.III	BP.10	71ft 11.3in	46ft 2in	7ft	7ft	7ft 6in	979.5sq ft	11,217lb	2 x Pegasus IM2	155mph@5,500ft
P.29B Export Mk.III	BP.10	71ft 11.3in	46ft 2in	7ft	7ft	7ft 6in	979.5sq ft	10,750lb	2 x Jupiter VIIIF	146mph@4,000ft
P.29B Export Floatplane	BP.10	71ft 11.3in	47ft	7ft	7ft	7ft 6in	979.5sq ft	12,836lb	2 x Pegasus IM2	144mph@5,500ft
P.29C Sidestrand IV	BP.10	71ft 11.3in	46ft 2in	7ft	7ft	7ft 6in	979.5sq ft	11,188lb	2 x Pegasus IM3	160mph@5,000ft
P.29D Sidestrand V	BP.10	71ft 11.3in	46ft 1.8in	7ft	7ft	7ft 6in	979.5sq ft	11,633lb	2 x Pegasus IM3	154mph@5,000ft
P.29D Sidestrand V offer	BP.10	71ft 11.3in	46ft 1.8in	7ft	7ft	7ft 6in	979.5sq ft	11,600lb	2 x Pegasus IIIM3	161mph@5,000ft
P.29 Sidestrand IIIS	BP.10	71ft 11.3in	45ft 7.35in	7ft	7ft	7ft 6in	979.5sq ft	11,217lb	2 x Pegasus	144mph@5,000ft
P.29 Test J9186 +bombs	BP.10	71ft 11.3in	46ft 3.6in	7ft	7ft	7ft 6in	979.5sq ft	9,967lb	2 x Jupiter VIII	141mph@5,000ft
P.29 Test J9186 Circ Ring	BP.10	71ft 11.3in	46ft 2in	7ft	7ft	7ft 6in	979.5sq ft	10,200lb	2 x Jupiter XF/XFB	167mph@11,000ft
P.29 Test J9186 Poly Ring	BP.10	71ft 11.3in	46ft 2in	7ft	7ft	7ft 6in	979.5sq ft	10,232lb	2 x Pegasus	146mph@6,000ft
P.32-Mk-II Proposal	BP.10	100ft	56ft 8in	10ft	10ft	11ft	2,000sq ft		3 x Jupiter VIII geared	130mph@10,000ft
P.32 Prototype	BP.10	100ft	69ft 1in	10ft 9in	10ft 9in	11ft	2,090sq ft	27,700lb	3 x Jupiter XF Exp	C >125mph
P.32 Prototype revision	BP.10	100ft	69ft 1in	10ft 9in	10ft 9in	11ft	2,090sq ft	27,600lb	3 x Jupiter XFBM Exp	C >125mph
P.33 Metal Gamecock	Semi-Symmetrical	30ft 2.5in	18ft 2.75in	4ft 8.875in	3ft 9in	varies	241.6sq ft		Jupiter VII	
P.33 Partridge	Semi-Symmetrical	35ft	23ft 1in	5ft 6in	4ft 6in	varies	311.3sq ft	3,097lb	Jupiter VII superch	167mph@10,000ft
P.34 Floatplane	Semi-Symmetrical	35ft	25ft 11.875in	5ft 6in	4ft 6in	varies	311.3sq ft	3,160lb	Jupiter VII superch	164mph@10,000ft
P.36 Passenger Machine	BP.10	100ft	63ft 11in	10ft 8in	10ft 8in	11ft	2,074sq ft		3 x Jupiter	
P.37 Streamline	BP.10	71ft 10.5in	54ft 8.25in	12ft	3ft	9ft	1,000sq ft		2 x RR 'H'	
P.40	BP.10	101ft 4in	66ft 3in	10ft 8.75in	10ft 8.75in	12ft 2in	2,262sq ft		3 x Mercury V geared	
P.40 with tail gunner	BP.10	101ft 4in	69ft 10.5in	10ft 8.75in	10ft 8.75in	12ft 2in	2,262sq ft		3 x Mercury V geared	
P.42 scheme	BP.10	72ft	49ft 4in	7ft	7ft	7ft 10in	1,000sq ft	9,185lb	2 x Lynx	
P.42 Final Proposal	BP.10	72ft 3.5in	49ft 3.25in	7ft	7ft	7ft 10in	1,000sq ft	9,185lb	2 x Lynx	
P.43 Survey	BP.10	42ft 3.8in	32ft 6in	5ft 6.25in	5ft 6.25in	varies	470sq ft		3 x Hermes	
P.45	BP.10	73ft 4in	49ft 2in	7ft	7ft	7ft 8in	1,038sq ft		Jupiter, Jaguar, Lion	
P.46	BP.10	51ft 11.75in	37ft 6in	5ft 10in	5ft 10in	6ft 2in	606sq ft		2 x Lynx Geared	
P.47 Streamline	BP.10	55ft 8.75in	42ft 7in	9ft 3in	3ft	7ft	615sq ft		2 x RR 'F'	
P.48	BP.10	140ft 1.5in	72ft 11in	11ft 11.75in	11ft 11.75in	varies	3,120sq ft		4 x Jupiter XF, Jaguar	
P.49 Streamline Racer	Semi-Symmetrical	32ft 2.25in	24ft 7in	5ft 4.375in	1ft 4.25in	7ft	704sq ft		2 x DH Gypsy	
P.52	BP.10	71ft 11.3in	41ft 8.6in approx.	7ft	7ft	7ft 6in	979.5sq ft		2 x AS Panther	
P.54	BP.10	73ft 4in	42ft 11in	7ft	7ft	7ft 8in	1,038sq ft		2 x AS Panther	
P.55	BP.10	50ft	38ft 4in	7ft	7ft	7ft 8in	700sq ft		AS Panther	
P.56 Streamline	BP.10	56ft 3in	42ft 8.5in	9ft 4.5in	3ft 1.5in	7ft 2in	646sq ft		2 x AS Panther	
Double-Deck Airliner	BP.10	104ft	69ft 10in	13ft 9in	11ft	varies	2,200sq ft	33,000lb	6 x Cyclone Geared	

PROJECT REF	WING SECTION	PROJECTED SPAN	LENGTH	U-WING CHORD	L-WING CHORD	GAP	AREA	AUW	ENGINE(S)	MAX SPEED
P.57	BP.10	71ft 11.3in	43ft 4in	7ft	7ft	7ft 6in	979.5sq ft		2 x Jaguar geared	
P.58	Semi-Symmetrical	45ft 2.5in	35ft 6.85in	6ft 3in	5ft 2.5in	6ft 6in	360sq ft		AS Panther MS	
P.58A	Semi-Symmetrical	45ft 2.5in	35ft 6.85in	6ft 3in	5ft 2.5in	6ft 6in	360sq ft		RR F12 MS	
P.58B	Semi-Symmetrical	45ft 2.5in	35ft 6.85in	7ft 6in	4ft	varies	370sq ft		Panther or F12	
P.59	BP.10	86ft 6in	59ft	10ft 6in	10ft 6in	7ft 6in	2,066sq ft		3 x Jaguar or Panther	
P.60	BP.10	72ft	46ft 4.8in	7ft 2in	7ft 2in	7ft 8.25in	1,030sq ft		2 x Jaguar geared	C >135mph
P.61	BP.10	50ft	41ft 6.75in	7ft	7ft	7ft 4in	350sq ft		2 x Jupiter XFB	
Single torpedo scheme	Munk M6	42ft 5in	34ft 7in	6ft	6ft	varies	500sq ft		Panther	
Twin torpedo scheme	Munk M6	50ft	38ft 6in	7ft	7ft	varies	570sq ft		2 x Panther	
P.62	Munk M6	52ft	41ft	7ft	7ft	varies	728sq ft	10,050lb	2 x Jupiter - Panther	186mph@10,000ft
P.62A	Munk M6	52ft	41ft	7ft	7ft	varies	728sq ft	10,050lb	2 x RR Kestrel	186mph@10,000ft
P.63	Munk M6	52ft	41ft	7ft	7ft	varies	728sq ft		2 x Panther	
P.64/P.65 Proposal	Semi-Symmetrical	32ft 3.5in	32ft 3.5in	6ft 6in	3ft 3in	varies	315sq ft		2 x Napier Rapier	
P.64 Mail Carrier	Munk M6	54ft	32ft 6in	7ft	7ft	7ft 3in	728sq ft	6,030lb	2 x Jupiter or Pegasus	195mph@5,000ft
P.69 Proposal	BP.10	89ft 6in	56ft	7ft	7ft	7ft 3in	756sq ft	10,500lb	2 x Pegasus IM2	195mph@5,000ft
P.69 Short Span	BP.10	80ft	56ft	7ft 6in	7ft 6in	7ft 7in	1,342sq ft	15,110lb	2 x Pegasus IM3	148mph@4,500ft
P.70 Bomber	Munk M6	54ft	40ft	8ft 5in	8ft 5in	7ft 7in	1,342sq ft	15,110lb	2 x Pegasus IM3	146mph@4,500ft
P.70 Bomber	Munk M6	54ft	40ft	7ft	7ft	varies	756sq ft	11,096lb	2 x Pegasus IS2	197mph@12,500ft
P.70 Bomber	Munk M6	54ft	40ft	7ft	7ft	varies	756sq ft	11,096lb	2 x Pegasus IIIM2	203mph@4,000ft
P.71	Munk M6	47ft 6in	36ft 10in	7ft	7ft	varies	756sq ft	11,096lb	2 x Pegasus IIIS2	210mph@11,500ft
P.71A Proposal	Munk M6	52ft 6in	40ft 6in	6ft 2in	6ft 2in	7ft 2in	585sq ft	7,000lb	2 x Dbl Mongoose	C175mph@4,500ft
P.71A Feeder Liner	Munk M6	54ft 1.5in	44ft 2in	6ft 10in	6ft 10in	6ft 2in	717sq ft	9,000lb	2 x Jaguar VIC	C150mph@5,000ft
P.72 Bomber Destroyer	Munk M6	54ft	40ft	6ft 10in	6ft 10in	6ft 10in	718.5sq ft	9,400lb	2 x Jaguar VIC	195mph@5,000ft
P.75 Prototype	BP.10	71ft 11.3in	46ft 1.8in	7ft	7ft	varies	756sq ft		2 x Pegasus	195mph@5,000ft
P.75 Overstrand	BP.10	71ft 11.3in	46ft 1.8in	7ft	7ft	varies	979.5sq ft	11,633lb	2 x Pegasus IM3	161mph@5,000ft
P.77 Overstrand GR	BP.10	71ft 11.3in	46ft 1.8in	7ft	7ft	7ft 6in	979.5sq ft	11,932lb	2 x Pegasus IIM3	153mph@6,500ft
P.80 Superstrand	Munk M6	71ft 11.3in	45ft 6in	7ft	7ft	7ft 6in	979.5sq ft	11,717lb	2 x Pegasus IIL	153mph@2,500ft
P.101 Ground Attack	Munk M6 Tapered	39ft 4in	33ft 6in	As P.82	As P.82	6ft 1in	410.8sq ft	15,200lb	Centaurus 12 mod	317mph@18,000ft
Composite Upper	Munk M6	63ft	45ft 6in estimated	7ft	7ft	7ft	980sq ft	15,004lb	2 x Pegasus IV	191mph@15,000ft
Composite Normal	Munk M6	63ft	46ft 8in estimated	7ft	7ft	Varies	880sq ft	5000lb	1 x Pegasus	40mph t/o
Composite Booms	Munk M6	63ft	45ft 10in estimated	Varies	Varies	Varies	1530sq ft	22000lb	3 x Pegasus	60mph t/o
Composite Booms	Munk M6	63ft		Varies	Varies	Varies	1530sq ft	22400lb	3 x Pegasus	60mph t/o

MONOPLANES

PROJECT REF	WING SECTION	PROJECTED SPAN	LENGTH	WING CHORD	ASPECT RATIO	WING AREA	AUW	ENGINE(S)	MAX SPEED
P.31A Bittern (First)	BP mod (RAF38)	45ft 6in	33ft 8.25in	8ft 4in outboard	5.59	370.5sq ft	4,500lb	2 x Lynx 210hp	145mph
P.31A Bittern (Second)	BP.10	50ft 6.5in	33ft 8.25in	8ft	7.9	395sq ft		2 x Lynx 210hp	
P.35	Semi-Symmetrical	40ft	32ft 2.5in	7ft	5.71	281.5sq ft		RR FII supercharged	
P.38	BP.10	50ft	33ft 9in	6ft 11in	7.23	347sq ft		3 x Gypsy	
P.39	BP.10	125ft	115ft 7.5in	25ft	5	3,125sq ft approx		6 x RR FII	70mph
P.41 proposal	BP.10	30ft	20ft 8in	4ft 3in	7.06	127.5sq ft	945lb	ABC Scorpion	80–85mph
P.41-1 Phoenix 1	BP.10	30ft	22ft 1.5in	4ft 6in	6.67	135sq ft	1,000lb	ABC Scorpion	92mph@SL
P.41-2 Phoenix II	BP.10	30ft	21ft 7in	4ft 6in	6.67	135sq ft	1,069lb	Salmson AD9	92mph@SL
P.41-3 Phoenix III	BP.10	33ft	21ft 7in	4ft 6in	7.33	148.5sq ft		Salmson AD9	
P.42A	BP.10	71ft 1in	55ft 3.44in	10ft 10in	6.56	760sq ft		3 x Lynx	
P.44	BP.10	53ft	33ft 10.25in	6ft 11.75in	7.59	370sq ft		Airsix (inverted)	
P.50	BP.10	42ft 1.5in	30ft	6ft 11.75in	6.04	294sq ft		AS Panther	
P.51	BP.10	50ft	35ft 7.5in	8ft	6.25	400sq ft		AS Panther	
P.53	BP.10	42ft 1.5in	33ft 1.5in	6ft 11.75in	6.04	294sq ft		AS Panther	
P.53	BP.10	55ft 6in	39ft 7in	9ft	6.16	499.5sq ft	5,730lb	Panther or Jupiter	144mph@5,000ft
P.66 Bomber	BP.10	55ft 6in	39ft 7in	9ft	6.16	499.5sq ft	7,300lb	Panther or Jupiter	142mph@5,000ft
P.66 Torpedo	BP.10	55ft 6in	39ft 7in	9ft	6.16	499.5sq ft	6,232lb	Panther or Jupiter	
P.66 Bomber Seaplane	Munk M6	40ft	29ft 4in	7ft 3in	5.52	290sq ft	4,650lb	2 x Napier Rapier	227mph@12,500ft
P.67	BP.10	53ft	41ft 6in	8ft 9in	6	463sq ft		4 x Popjoy	
P.68 Airliner	Munk M6 Tapered	60ft	43ft	Tapered	6.55	550sq ft	10,051lb	RR Griffin	203mph@13,000ft
P.73	Munk M6 Tapered	48ft	39ft 3in	Tapered	6.58	350sq ft	6,147lb	2 x Napier Rapier	195mph@15,000ft
P.74A Bomber Destroyer	Munk M6 Tapered	48ft	39ft 3in	Tapered	6.58	350sq ft	6,147lb	2 x Napier Rapier	203mph@15,000ft
P.74B Bomber Destroyer	Munk M6 Tapered	60ft	44ft 9in	Tapered	6.79	530sq ft	9,035lb	2 x Pegasus IV	226mph@15,000ft
P.74C Bomber Destroyer	Munk M6 Tapered	60ft	44ft 9in	Tapered	6.79	530sq ft	9,035lb	2 x Pegasus IV	232mph@15,000ft
P.74D Bomber Destroyer	Munk M6 Tapered	47ft 6in	39ft 3in	Tapered	6.64	340sq ft	5,797lb	2 x Napier Rapier	217mph@15,000ft
P.76A Bomber Destroyer	Munk M6 Tapered	58ft 6in	44ft 6in	Tapered	6.58	520sq ft	9,780lb	2 x Pegasus	250mph@15,000ft
P.76B Bomber Destroyer	Munk M6 Tapered	63ft estimated	45ft 7in estimated	Tapered	6.62	650sq ft	16500lb	2 x Pegasus	250mph
P.78	Munk M6 Tapered	87ft	61ft 3in	Tapered Outboard	7.93	954sq ft	23,500lb	2 x Taurus TE1S	247mph@15,000ft
P.79	Munk M6 Tapered	87ft	61ft 3in	Tapered Outboard	7.93	954sq ft	25,500lb	2 x Bristol HE1S	261mph@25,000ft
P.79	Munk M6 Tapered	87ft	61ft 3in	Tapered Outboard	7.93	954sq ft	24,250lb	2 x Pegasus 5SM	234mph@15,000ft
P.81	Munk M6 Tapered	42ft	36ft 3in	Tapered	6.42	275sq ft	5,009lb	Pegasus X	256mph@6,000ft
P.82 Proposal	Munk M6 Tapered	39ft	33ft	Tapered	6.34	240sq ft	5,774lb	RR Merlin F.5	323mph@15,000ft
P.82 Defiant Mk.I	Munk M6 Tapered	39ft 4in	35ft 3.9in	Double Taper	6.19	250sq ft	8,318lb	RR Merlin III	304mph@15,000ft
P.82 Defiant Mk.II	Munk M6 Tapered	39ft 4in	35ft 10.3in	Double Taper	6.19	250sq ft	8,424lb	RR Merlin XX	313mph@19,000ft
P.82 Defiant TT Mk.I	Munk M6 Tapered	39ft 4in	35ft 10.3in	Double Taper	6.19	250sq ft	8,191lb	RR Merlin XX	226mph@15,000ft
P.82 Defiant TT Mk.III	Munk M6 Tapered	39ft 4in	35ft 3.9in	Double Taper	6.19	250sq ft	7,758lb	RR Merlin III	232mph@15,000ft

PROJECT REF	WING SECTION	PROJECTED SPAN	LENGTH	WING CHORD	ASPECT RATIO	WING AREA	AUW	ENGINE(S)	MAX SPEED
P.83A Torpedo Bomber	Munk M6 Tapered	67ft	47ft 9in	Tapered Outboard	7.81	575sq ft	13,121lb	2 x RR Goshawk B MS	257mph@5,000ft
P.83B Torpedo Bomber	Munk M6 Tapered	60ft	47ft 9in	Tapered Outboard	6.26	575sq ft	13,165lb	2 x Pegasus	257mph@5,000ft
P.84A GR Bomber	Munk M6 Tapered	67ft	45ft 6in	Tapered Outboard	9.07	495sq ft	11,430lb	2 x Aquila AE-3M	239mph@5,000ft
P.84B GR Bomber	Munk M6 Tapered	67ft	47ft 9in	Tapered Outboard	7.81	575sq ft	12,915lb	2 x RR Goshawk	245mph@5,000ft
P.85 Carrier Fighter	Munk M6 Tapered	42ft 6in	37ft 8in	Tapered Outboard	5.68	318sq ft	6,852lb	Hercules HE1SM	318mph@12,500ft
P.85 Floatplane	Munk M6 Tapered	42ft 6in	39ft 9in	Tapered Outboard	5.68	318sq ft	7,237lb	Hercules HE1SM	267mph@12500ft
P.85 Carrier Fighter	Munk M6 Tapered	42ft 6in	38ft	Tapered Outboard	5.77	313sq ft	6,750lb	RR Merlin E	308mph@15,000ft
P.85 Floatplane	Munk M6 Tapered	42ft 6in	39ft 9in	Tapered Outboard	5.77	313sq ft	7,125lb	RR Merlin E	258mph@15,000ft
P.86 GR & TB	Munk M6 Tapered	60ft	Short nose	Tapered Outboard	7.27	495sq ft	12,700lb	2 x Aquila AE-3M	260mph@15,000ft
P.86 GR & TB	Munk M6 Tapered	60ft	Long nose	Tapered Outboard	7.27	495sq ft	12,820lb	2 x Aquila AE-3M	258mph@15,000ft
P.88A Cannon Fighter	Munk M6 Tapered	39ft 6in	32ft 8in	Tapered Outboard	6	260sq ft	6,573lb	Hercules HE1SM	337mph@15,000ft
P.88B Cannon Fighter	Munk M6 Tapered	44ft	36ft 3in	Tapered Outboard	6.05	320sq ft	8,100lb	RR Vulture	326mph@15,000ft
P.90 Heavy Bomber	Munk M6 Tapered	100ft	77ft 3in	Tapered Outboard	6.9	1,450sq ft	47,942lb	4 x RR Kestrel XXVI	267mph@15,000ft
P.91 Medium Bomber	Munk M6 Tapered	83ft	71ft 3in	Swept Outboard	7.25	950sq ft	35,734lb	2 x RR Vulture	297mph@15,000ft
P.92 Proposal	BP Special	62ft 6in	52ft 3in	Tapered	6	650sq ft	18,336lb	2 x RR Vulture	371mph@15,000ft
P.92 Prototypes	BP Special	66ft 3.3in	55ft	Tapered	6.7	650sq ft	22,000lb	2 x Vulture or Sabre	384mph@15,000ft
P.92/2 Scale Model	BP Special	33ft 1.5in	27ft 6in	Tapered	6.2	177sq ft	2,778lb	2 x Gypsy Major II	152mph@SL
P.93 Roc Carrier Fighter	NACA 2416	46ft	35ft 7in	Tapered	6.83	310sq ft	7,950lb	Perseus XII	223mph@10,000ft
P.94 Single Seat Fighter	Munk M6 Tapered	39ft 4in	35ft 10.3in	As P.82	6.19	250sq ft	7,855lb	RR Merlin XX	380mph@23,500ft
P.95 Light Bomber	Munk M6 Tapered	45ft	36ft 3in	Swept L/E Outer	5.7	355.4sq ft	12,440lb	Hercules VI	323mph@16,000ft
P.95 Light Bomber	Munk M6 Tapered	45ft	36ft 3in	Swept L/E Outer	5.7	355.4sq ft	12,500lb	RR Griffon	316mph@16,000ft
P.96A Night Fighter	Munk M6 Tapered	44ft	38ft	Swept L/E Outer	6	325sq ft	12,660lb	Napier Sabre CE6SM	410mph@34,000ft
P.96B (turreted)	Munk M6 Tapered	44ft	38ft	Swept L/E Outer	6	325sq ft	12,270lb	Napier Sabre CE6SM	400mph@34,000ft
P.96C (turreted)	Munk M6 Tapered	46ft	38ft	Swept L/E Outer	6.2	340sq ft	12,680lb	Napier Sabre CE6SM	400mph@34,000ft
P.96D (turreted)	Munk M6 Tapered	46ft	38ft	Taper Outer	6.2	340sq ft	12,326lb	Centaurus CE4SM	390mph@22,500ft
P.96D Night Fighter	Munk M6 Tapered	46ft	38ft	Taper Outer	6.2	340sq ft	12,306lb	Centaurus CE4SM	400mph@22,500ft
P.97A Night Fighter	Munk M6 Tapered	58ft 6in	45ft 6in	Taper Outer	6.5	525sq ft	19,586lb	2 x Napier Sabre	425mph@34,000ft
P.97B Night fighter	Munk M6 Tapered	58ft 6in	45ft 6in	Taper Outer	6.5	525sq ft	19,232lb	2 x Napier Sabre	418mph@34,000ft
P.98 Light fighter	Semi-Symmetrical	33ft	35ft	Swept Canard	4.84	225sq ft	8,861lb	RR Griffon II	440mph@20,000ft
P.98 Light Fighter	Semi-Symmetrical	34ft 6in	35ft	Swept Canard	4.82	247sq ft	9,892lb	Napier Sabre	446mph@20,000ft
P.99 Ground Attack	Semi-Symmetrical	44ft 8in	44ft 2in	Taper Outer	5.54	360sq ft	13,700lb	RR Griffon II	315mph@17,000ft
P.100 Ground Attack	Semi-Symmetrical	40ft 2in drg 41ft 2in	36ft 2in	Swept Canard	3.5	366.25sq ft	13,450lb	RR Griffon II	335mph@17,000ft
P.103A Carrier Fighter	NACA 66-2-216	38ft 8in	36ft 4in	Taper Outer	5.98	250sq ft	10,221lb	RR Griffon RGSSM	455mph@28,000ft
P.103B Carrier Fighter	NACA 66-2-216	38ft 8in	37ft	Taper Outer	5.75	260sq ft	11,180lb	Centaurus CE12SM	435mph@23,000ft
P.105 Torpedo	NACA 65	38ft	34ft 5in TD	Taper T/E	5.77	250sq ft	12,285lb	Centaurus CE12SM	463mph@20,000ft
P.105 Reconn	NACA 65	38ft	34ft 5in TD	Taper T/E	5.77	250sq ft	11,253lb	Centaurus CE12SM	435mph@12,000ft
P.105 Defended Reconn	NACA 65	38ft	34ft 5in TD	Taper T/E	5.77	250sq ft	11,713lb	Centaurus CE12SM	428mph@12,000ft
P.105 Fighter	NACA 65	38ft	34ft 5in TD	Taper T/E	5.77	250sq ft	12,500lb	Centaurus CE12SM	469mph@20,000ft

PROJECT REF	WING SECTION	PROJECTED SPAN	LENGTH	WING CHORD	ASPECT RATIO	WING AREA	AUW	ENGINE(S)	MAX SPEED
P.106A to C Trainer	BPA Special Section	34ft 6in	28ft	5ft 10in	5.9	200sq ft	2,647lb	Gypsy 6, Queen or III	145–158mph@SL
P.107 Escort Fighter	NACA65-3-218/316	38ft	34ft 8in tail down	Taper T/E	5.77	250sq ft	15,900lb	Centaurus CE12SM	470mph@24,000ft
P.108 Dart-Balliol		39ft 4in	38ft 0.5in	Double Taper	6.2	249.5sq ft		Dart (scheme only)	
P.108 Mercury-Balliol	NACA 65	39ft 4in	35ft 3in	Double Taper	6.2	249.5sq ft	7,595lb	Mercury 30 or 25	280mph@10,000ft
P.108 Balliol T.1	NACA 65	39ft 4in	36ft 6in	Double Taper	6.2	249.5sq ft	7,860lb	Mamba	307mph@20,000ft
P.108A Balliol T.2	NACA 65	39ft 4in	35ft 1.5in	Double Taper	6.2	249.5sq ft	8,175lb	Merlin 35	305mph@11,500ft
P.108B Balliol T.21	NACA 65	39ft 4in	35ft 1.5in	Double Taper	6.2	249.5sq ft	8,704lb	Merlin 35	305mph@11,500ft
P.108 Balliol T.2A scheme	NACA 65	39ft 4in	34ft 7in	Double Taper	6.2	249.5sq ft		P&W R1820	270mph@5,000ft
P.109 Trainer	NACA 65	41ft	33ft 9in	Double Taper	6	280sq ft	7,982lb	Bristol New Perseus	284mph@5,000ft
P.110 Light Aircraft	Semi-Symmetrical			Taper Wing				Cirrus / Lycoming	
P.111 Full Span Tip	Squires C	33ft 5.8in	26ft 0.8in	Delta 45°	3.8 (Design 4)	296sq ft		Nene 1	Mach 0.97 – 1.0
P.111 Middle Span Tip	Squires C	29ft 9in	26ft 0.8in	Delta 45°	3.05 (Design 3)	290sq ft	9,777lb	Nene 1	Mach 0.97 – 1.0
P.111 Small Span Tip	Squires C	25ft 11.54in	26ft 0.8in	Delta 45°	2.42 (Design 2.28)	278.2sq ft		Nene 1	Mach 0.97 – 1.0
P.111A Research	Squires C	Variable As P.111	31ft 6.1in	Delta 45°	As P.111	As P.111	10,994lb	Nene NR2	Mach 0.97 – 1.0
P.112 Trainer	NACA65	45ft 4in	35ft 2.4in	Double Taper	7.52	273.25sq ft	5,650lb	Alvis Leonides IVM	147 knots
P.112A Trainer	NACA65	45ft 8in	35ft 4in	Double Taper	7.43	280.5sq ft		P&W Wasp R1340	
P.113A Research	Squires C 0.55	26ft 2in	54ft 7in	Swept Taper	2.48	275sq ft	12,880lb	RR Avon	Mach 1.2 to 1.5
P.113S Research	Squires C 0.55	31ft 8in	54ft 7in	Swept Taper	3.47	290sq ft	13,480lb	AS Sapphire	Mach 1.2 to 1.5
P.114A Research/Fighter	Squires C 0.55	41ft	88ft	Swept Taper	2.48	670sq ft	28,728lb	RR Avon Reheat	Mach 1.5
P.114S Research/Fighter	Squires C 0.55	46ft 4in	88ft	Swept Taper	3.1	700sq ft	30,360lb	AS Sapphire Reheat	Mach 1.5
P.115 Trainer	NACA M6	38ft 10in	32ft 6in	Double Taper	7	215sq ft	4,106lb	Gypsy Queen 71	220 knot dive limit
P.116 Trainer	NACA M6	36ft 9in	30ft 8in	Double Taper	7	193sq ft	3,839lb	Gypsy Queen 51	C147mph@6,300 ft
P.117 Aerodyne	HS2 modified	100ft	100ft	Swing Wing	10	1,000sq ft	60,000lb	RR Avon	600mph@SL
P.119 & P.119N	Squires C	38ft 8.76in	42ft 6in	Swept Taper	5.03	298.5sq ft	9,696lb	RR Derwent 5	475mph@22,500ft
P.120 Research	Squires C	33ft 5.8in	29ft 7.5in	Tailed Delta 45°	3.8 (Design 4)	296sq ft	12,160lb	Nene NR2	Mach 0.97 – 1.0
P.121 Extended Wing	RAE101	60ft	72ft 8.9in	Swing Wing	5	650sq ft	34,100lb	2 x RR Avon RA8	Mach 1.34
P.121 Swept Wing	RAE101	37ft 9.96in	72ft 8.9in	Swing Wing	1.95	734sq ft	34,100lb	2 x RR Avon RA8	Mach 1.34
P.121 Fixed Wing	RAE101	42ft 5.4in	72ft 8.9in	Swept Wing	1.95	916sq ft	30,200lb	2 x RR Avon RA8	Mach 0.9
P.122 Rocket Interceptor	RAE102	21ft 2.04in	33ft 3in	Taper Wing	2.5	180sq ft	9,131lb	AS Screamer Rocket	800 knts dive
P.123 Pilotless Bomber	RAE102	21ft	34ft 3in	Swept Wing	4	110.25sq ft	9,297lb	RR RB93 Expendable	330 knots
P.124 Jet Trainer	RAE102	32ft	35ft	Swept Wing	4.36	235sq ft	6,033lb	2 x AS Viper ASV5	400 knots
P.125 Derwent-Balliol	NACA 65	39ft 4in	37ft 3.6in	Taper Wing	6.2	249.5sq ft	9,316lb	RR Derwent	400 knots
P.125 Sea Balliol	NACA 65	39ft 4in	37ft 3.6in	Taper Wing	6.2	249.5sq ft	9,476lb	RR Derwent	Mach 2
P.126 Thin Wing (Centre)	Bi-Convex	30ft		Taper Wing		300sq ft		2 x RR Avon	Mach 2
P.127 Thin Wing Fighter	Bi-Convex	30ft 4in	59ft 4in	Taper Wing	3.07	300sq ft		2 x RR Avon	Mach 2
P.128 Research/Fighter	Bi-Convex	28ft 3.4in	64ft	12ft 11.04in	1.92	312sq ft	26,493lb	2 x AS Sapphire SA7	Mach 2
P.129-1	Bi-Convex	32ft 6in	41ft 3in	8ft 4in	4.31	245sq ft	3,790lb	2 x Marboré	395 knots@SL
P.129-II	Bi-Convex	32ft 6in	41ft 3in	8ft 4in	4.56	232sq ft	3,750lb	2 x Marboré	

PROJECT REF	WING SECTION	PROJECTED SPAN	LENGTH	WING CHORD	ASPECT RATIO	WING AREA	AUW	ENGINE(S)	MAX SPEED
P.129-III	Bi-Convex	32ft 6in	41ft 3in	8ft 4in	4.56	232sq ft	3,900lb	2 x Marboré	
P.129-IV	Bi-Convex	18ft	41ft 3in	8ft 4in	2.16	150sq ft	3,650lb	2 x Marboré	395 knots
P.129 Revision	Bi-Convex	20ft 0.8in	41ft 3in	8ft 4in	2.47	164.4sq ft	7,185lb	2 x Marboré	Mach 0.8
P.129 Revision	Bi-Convex	28ft 9in	41ft 3in	8ft 4in	3.82	216sq ft	7,585lb	2 x Marboré	Mach 0.8
P.129 Revision	Bi-Convex	20ft 0.8in	41ft 3in	8ft 4in	2.5	167.1sq ft	8,632lb	2 x AS Viper + rocket	Mach 1.1
P.129 Revision	Bi-Convex	28ft 9in	41ft 3in	8ft 4in	3.82	216sq ft	9,032lb	2 x AS Viper + rocket	Mach 1.1
P.131 Jet Trainer	RAE102	32ft	36ft 1.3in	Swept wing	3.94	260sq ft	7,300lb	Bristol Orpheus	Mach 0.8

VTOL JET AIRCRAFT

PROJECT REF	WING SECTION	PROJECTED SPAN	LENGTH	WING CHORD	ASPECT RATIO	WING AREA	AUW	ENGINE(S)	MAX SPEED
P.130-S6 Study	Symmetrical	34ft 2in	41ft 3.5in	Delta 53° sweep	2.73	427sq ft		5 x RB108	
P.130-S8 Study	Symmetrical	34ft 2in	46ft 5in	Delta 53° sweep	2.61	446.7sq ft		2 x Bristol Orpheus	
P.132 Research	RAE104	38ft 7.2in	41ft 4in	Delta 58° sweep	2.68	556.5sq ft	17,250lb	4 x AS Viper 8	550 knots
P.133	Symmetrical	26ft 1in	71ft	Delta 79° sweep	0.69	981sq ft		2 x Gyr Junior/rocket	
P.133A	Symmetrical	17ft 10.5in	49ft 10in	Delta 80° sweep	0.67	475sq ft		2 x Gyr Junior/rocket	
P.133B Naval Strike	Symmetrical	28ft	57ft	Delta 76° sweep	0.95	828sq ft	40,120lb	2 x Gyron Junior	Mach 1.34
P.133C Naval Strike	Symmetrical	26ft 3in	63ft 6in	Delta 78° sweep	0.78	884 sq ft		2 x Gyron Junior	
P.134	Symmetrical	25ft	66ft 1.75in	Delta 76° sweep	0.93	676sq ft		2 x Orpheus BOR11	
P.135A Study	Symmetrical	33ft 4in	65ft	Delta dual sweep	1.69	868sq ft	21,314lb	2 x Orpheus BOR12	625 knots@SL
P.135B Study	Symmetrical	35ft	65ft	Delta 67.5°	1.42	865sq ft	21,314lb	2 x Orpheus BOR12	625 knots@SL
P.136 Study	Symmetrical	32ft 9.6in	62ft	Delta 67.5°	1.4	776sq ft	21,016lb	2 x Orpheus BOR12	631 knots@SL
P.137	Symmetrical	29ft	56ft	Delta 75° sweep	0.94	892sq ft	46,465lb	2 x Gyron Junior	822 knots@SL
P.138 Airliner				Swept Wing				4 x Orpheus BOR12	
P.139 Research	Semi-Symmetrical	58ft	67ft	Swept Wing	4	840sq ft	25,569lb	2 x Orpheus BOR12	542 knots
P.140 Airliner	Semi-Symmetrical	116ft	132ft	Swept Wing	3.97	3,393sq ft	134,225lb	8 x Orpheus BOR12	400 knots
P.141 Airliner	Semi-Symmetrical	92ft	117ft	Taper wing	5	1,690sq ft	4,8527lb	8 x RR RB108	
P.142 Research	Semi-Symmetrical	45ft	50ft 3.6in	Swept Wing	4.5	450sq ft	16,080lb	6 x or 8 x RR RB108	265 knots
P.143 Airliner	Semi-Symmetrical	85ft 6in	92ft	Taper Wing	8	916sq ft	64,100lb	10 x RB144	
P.145 Mixed Transport	Symmetrical	100ft	86ft 7.2in	Taper Wing	8	1,250sq ft	95,000lb	4 x RB153/12 x RB154	C385 knots
P.146 Airliner	Symmetrical	100ft	100ft	Swept Canard	6.05	1,650sq ft	128,000lb	3 x RB163/18 x RB155	C373 knots

AIRBORNE VEHICLES

PROJECT REF	WING SECTION	WIDTH	LENGTH	HEIGHT	No. WHEELS	ROAD ENGINE	AU WEIGHT	ENGINE(S)	MAX AIRSPEED
P.144	Symmetrical	17ft 6in	27ft 6in	13ft 6in	3	N/A	10,050lb	2 x RR RB144	160 knots
P.144A	None	7ft	16ft 6in	7ft	4	3.6 litre petrol		RR RB145	
P.147	None	7ft 4in	16ft	6ft	4	Coventry Climax FW3	8,313lb	BS BS59 or RR RB162	72fps (49mph)
P.148	None	6ft 8in	28ft	6ft	4	Vauxhall 350cu in	30,180lb	N/A	N/A

Notes

Project references in bold were as-built machines.

All data is in original English dimensions as employed at the time period of the designs.

Projected span quoted prior to Project P.29 is calculated from drawings. Prior to this all B&P quoted or published spans were a stressed span measured along the tops of the upper spars with the airframe uncovered.

Wing area generally includes the area projected inside the fuselage plan.

All-up weight and measured maximum speed are frequently mutually exclusive. Speed and climb tests or theoretical speed calculations were often carried out at lower weights than AUW. Weights also altered as equipment was changed. The AUW approved for the Defiant series in particular was progressively increased during its service life.

Exp after the engine name indicates a development variant with non-standard parts.

Prefix 'C' on speed shows cruising speed rather than maximum.

fps = feet per second.

Abbreviations

A&AEE	Aircraft and Armament Experimental Establishment, Martlesham Heath (1918–39)
A&AEE	Aircraft and Armament Experimental Establishment, Boscombe Down (1939 on)
AB	Air Board (a First World War-period office)
ACAS	Assistant to Chief of the Air Staff
ACAS(T)	Assistant to Chief of the Air Staff (Technical)
AD/ARD	Assistant Director/Assistant Research Director (at RAE)
ADGB	Air Defence Great Britain
ADRDA	Assistant Director Research and Development (Aircraft)
AD(Arm)	Assistant Director (Armament)
AE or Ae	Aircraft Experimental (Prefix of the internal order for booking works tasks or mods at company cost) – later numbers were prefixed Aes.
AI	Air Intelligence
AI	Air Interception (Radar)
AM	Air Ministry
AP	Air Publication – a series of manuals on aircraft, engines and components
ARI	Airborne Radar Instruments
AS	Armstrong Siddeley Motors Ltd
ASV	Air-to-surface vessel (radar)
AT	Anti-turbulence. B&P/North name for engine rings before Townsend patents
Avia	Prefix for historical records collated and stored at National Archives Kew
BEA	British European Airways
B&P	Boulton & Paul Ltd, Norwich
BPA	Boulton Paul Aircraft Ltd, Norwich and Wolverhampton
CAS	Chief of the Air Staff
CFE	Central Flying Establishment
c/c	Centre to centre (meaning centreline to centreline) the distance between two items
Cd	The coefficient of drag. A dimensionless ratio used to calculate load due to airflow over an object
COW	Coventry Ordinance Works
CoA	Certificate of Airworthiness
CoR	Certificate of Registration
CRD	Controller of Research and Development
C/W	Continuous Wave (radio)
DC (ARD)	Director in Charge (Aircraft Research and Development)
DCAS	Deputy Chief of Air Staff
DoR	Directorate of Requirements, Directorate of Research
D of R	A series of specifications to 1920 by the Directorate of Research, prefixed D of R.
DTD	Directorate of Technical Development
DDTD	Director of the Directorate of Technical Development
DDRD	Director of the Directorate of Research and Development, sometimes Deputy Director
FAA	Fleet Air Arm
HF	High Frequency (radio)
HS	High speed (aerofoil)
HAS	Hawker Siddeley Aviation
I/C	Intercommunication
IFF	Identification friend or foe
MAP	Ministry of Aircraft Production (a Second World War-period office 1940 to 1946)
MoM	Ministry of Munitions
MoS	Ministry of Supply (Responsible for aircraft and component purchase from 1946–59)
NA	Naval Air Staff Requirement (document)
NACA	National Advisory Committee for Aeronautics (America). Similar to NPL and RAE in the UK
NGTE	National Gas Turbine Establishment
NPL	National Physical Laboratory
OR	Operational Requirement (document)
PDSR(A)	Principal Director Scientific Research (Air)
PV	Private venture – a machine produced by the company at its own expense
RAE	Royal Aircraft Establishment – Farnborough
RAE	Royal Aircraft Establishment – Bedford (parallel site added from 1946)
RAF	Royal Aircraft Factory, Farnborough (First World War) – became RAE
RAF	Royal Air Force
RDA	Research and Development (Aircraft)
RD(Arm)	Research and Development (Armament)
RD(Arm).2	The sub-department in MAP and Armament for gun turret development
RDT	Research and Development (Technical)
RDT.1	The sub-department in technical responsible for reviewing performance proposals
RR	Rolls-Royce (engines and fans)
R/T	Radio Transmission
SAMM	Societe d'Applications des Machines Motrices, Issy-les-Moulineaux, Paris
SD	Siddeley Deasy engines
SD	Special Duties (for aircraft, equipment and personnel roles)
SD	Special Duties – documents like an Air Publication but much more restricted and usually secret. For example, those covering air intercept or air to surface vessel radar.
UHF	Ultra High Frequency (radio)
VHF	Very High Frequency (radio)
VTOL	Vertical Take-Off and Landing
V/STOL	Vertical or Short Take-Off and Landing
WD	War Department (a First World War-period office)
W/T	Wireless Transmitter-Receiver system

Dimensions

ft	feet (1ft = 304.896mm)
in	inches (1in = 25.408mm)
mph	miles per hour (1mph = 1.609km per hour)
knots	nautical miles per hour (1 knot = 1.852km per hour)
Mach	A velocity based upon a number fraction of the local speed of sound valued at 1.0
lb	pounds weight (1lb = 0.454kg)
sq ft	square feet (area) (1sq ft = 0.093sq m)

Appendix four

Glossary

People

Beaverbrook, Lord	William Maxwell Beaverbrook 1st Baron 1879–1964. Newspaper magnate, head of Ministry of Aircraft Production, appointed by Winston Churchill in May 1940. Favoured adding maximum output of Defiant aircraft to his other three fighters (Hurricane, Spitfire and Blenheim) because of good reports from air battles over Dunkirk. Needed maximum output of fighters until September 1940, as promised to Parliament.
Betz, Albert	Physicist 1885–1968. Designed an early wind turbine 1919 at Göttingen University.
Boudot, Edouard	Of French extraction. Designer at F. C. Nestler Ltd of Westminster, London, in 1916. The company had previously been importers of Sanchez-Beza aircraft from South America. Designed the HN.1 known as the Nestler Scout, the HN.2 and HN.3. Only the first design flew. Employed by North as chief draughtsman at B&P. Designed the P.3, P.6 and P.7 initial schemes. Moved to Graham-White Company in 1918.
de Boysson, Joseph Bernard Antoine	Inventor of gun turrets offered to the French Air Ministry. Prototype manufactured in Paris by SAMM.
Briggs, R. C.	Engineer at BPA involved in development of the P.126 slim wing and the use of lifting fans. Retired as head of Quality Assurance.
Bunkle, Slim	Mechanic and Fitter at BPA.
Clarke, H. V.	Chief Designer – Aircraft for Boulton Paul P.82 Defiant production.
Crocombe, Frederick Francis	Chief Engineer and Technical Director of BPA after Dr Redshaw. Designer of the General Aircraft Monospar, Hotspur, Hamilcar glider series and then resident at Blackburn Aircraft looking at variable sweep wings. Appointed on 1 January 1951, retired 1966.
Davies, E. D.	Officer at A&AEE who claimed in 1943 to have been instrumental in advising BPA not to install forward guns in the Defiant.
Fedden, Sir Alfred Hubert Roy	1885–1973. MBE FRAeS. Engine designer with Brazil-Strakker, Cosmos and then Bristol Engines. After knighthood moved to MAP during the war. Fundamental tutor at the University of Cranfield. Friends with Sir George Dowty and John North.
ffiske, G. M.	Director at B&P. Most of the family employed by the company as managers or directors.
ffiske, W. H.	Director at B&P. Nicknamed The Carpenter.
Flettner, Anton	1885–1961. German aircraft engineer who invented a style of servo control tab. Manufacturer of autogyros and helicopters in the Second World War.
Glauert, Herman	Extremely gifted engineer and Principal Scientific Officer at RAE Farnborough. Many papers on aeronautics and autogyros. Sadly killed 1934 when observing the dynamiting of tree trunks to clear Laffan's Plain when he was hit by flying debris. Brother of Otto.
Glauert, Otto	Schoolmaster and mathematician at Norwich. Assisted John North and B&P in the calculations necessary for aircraft design, but particularly with airfoil transforms and wings of optimum span.
Higley-Sayers (optional hyphen), Capt William	Designer at RNAS isle of Grain, First World War. Editor of the *Aeroplane* magazine. Recruited as a design engineer by North and developed the P.41 Phoenix. Stress department at BPA through into the Second World War.
Higgins, T. C. R.	Air Ministry officer who believed the bomber would 'always get through' and presented ideas for anti-bomber 'novel' fighters.
Howes, Stanley S.	Owner of Howes and Son Motors at Norwich. Joined with B&P during the First World War to build and deliver aeroplanes to the government.
Hughes, Henry Arthur	Chief Designer of aircraft at B&P 1920s onwards. Developed the gun turret used in the Overstrand and then became Chief Designer (Turrets) until 1941. Lost at sea 1941 when his ship was sunk by a U-boat while returning from the USA. All crew escaped to boats but none were ever rescued.
Joukowski, Nikolai	True name in Russian, Nikolai Zhukovsky. Originator of the Joukowski Transform (which see) used to calculate aerofoil shapes
Kármán von, Theodore	1881–1963. Hungarian mathematician who taught at Göttingen with Prandtl. Much later at the Jet Propulsion Laboratory USA.
Kenmir, Charles Vivian	Technical engineer responsible for the design and performance of the P.111 and P.120 delta aircraft and subsequent other studies.

Liptrot, R.N.	Responsible for assessment of performance of aircraft proposals and Head of Research and Development Department No. 1.
Lord, Leonard Percy	Austin manager appointed MAP representative at BPA by Beaverbrook for the period June 1940 to March 1941. Aimed to convert the factory over to full Defiant production. This was done at the expense of all gun turret manufacture, moved to Lucas, Cwmbran, where shadow factory entrepreneur Lord was short of work and machine tools. Large sections of the drawing office placed to assist other companies, such as the development of the Gloster Reaper. Later became Sir Leonard Lord, 1st Baron Lambury KBE.
Mayo, Maj. Robert Hobart	Patented a heavy aircraft used to lift a lighter one to altitude. Resulted in the Short-Mayo composite before the Second World War.
Maund, Grp Capt Arthur Clinton	Maund RFC/RAF commanding A&AEE 1933 to 1937. Later AVM. Sadly died 1942 aged only 51.
Munk, Michael Max	1890–1986. Scientist at NACA USA. Developed a series of aerofoil sections bearing his name. Previously a student of Prandtl.
North, John Dudley	Pupil at Bedford School. Marine apprentice and then aeronautical apprentice. The Aeronautical Syndicate 1911; Chief Designer and Chief Engineer of Claude Graham-White Company 1912–1915; Superintendent of the Aircraft Division of Austin 1915–1917; Department Manager and then Director of Boulton & Paul 1917 to 1934; Managing Director, Chairman, etc, of Boulton Paul Aircraft 1934 to 1968.
Prandtl, Ludwig	Mathematician who first performed rigorous analyses on aerodynamic and hydrodynamic flow. He was one of the first scientists to achieve sensible results by using model testing of fluid flow. The wind tunnel work of Prandtl and his protégées during the First World War was extensively published by the University of Göttingen.
Redshaw, Dr Seymour Cunningham	Chief Engineer of BPA. Appointed director of BPA 25 May 1948. Gave notice to leave before June 1951 as he had been appointed to the Chair of Civil Engineering at Birmingham University.
Riach, M. A. S.	Designer of propellers for Graham White Company. Joined North at B&P as technical engineer.
Roxbee-Cox, Sir Harold	Later Lord Kings Norton. Friend of North since the 1930s when he was Principal Scientific Officer at RAE. Appointed director of BPA on 11 April 1958.
Townend, Dr Hubert Charles Henry	Scientist at the National Physical Laboratory (NPL) when North was advisor to the director of airship design. The Townend patents pre-dated those on AT rings of North even though the North ideas were years earlier. B&P purchased the patents in order to control the business of engine rings and hence the North designs had to be called Townend Rings. Fees were paid to Townend and his widow until after the Second World War.
Trefftz, Erich	1888–1937. Mathematician. Pupil of Prandtl from 1908.
Wieselberger	Dr Engineer, Physicist at Göttingen.

Technical Terms

Anhedral	Wings where the tips are set lower than the centre, deliberately introducing instability to make the aircraft more manoeuvrable.
Amphibian	Although later used in industry as indicating a machine that could land on water or land, in early B&P design it was used in company records to indicate either a seaplane (ie on floats) or a flying boat having a main hull and outboard stabilising floats.
Autoslot	A slat that pops out of the wing leading edge automatically and channels airflow over the outer wing leading edge reducing the likelihood of a flow breakaway and stall. Handley Page developed and patented the idea first.
Cabane strut	French term for the struts from the fuselage to the upper wing.
Chord	Distance between leading and trailing edge of an airfoil surface or wing.
Coefficient (of)	A dimensionless ratio calculated as a result of model testing that can then be employed to work out full-size results. For example, Cl, the coefficient of lift (generated by an aerofoil) to lift the weight of the aeroplane into the air; Cd, the coefficient of drag as a result of passing through the air, used to estimate the power required to move the object.
Broad Arrow (engine)	An inline engine where there are three banks of cylinders each set radially to form an arrowhead shape from the front with the point at the propeller shaft. An example would be the Napier Lion.
Dihedral	The angle at which the wings are set at the tips above horizontal. In order to give better stability in the air. Often only the outer wings have dihedral.
Flapped (aileron)	Early B&P term for an aileron having a portion outboard of the wing tip and of reduced area but with a portion forward of the pivot points to provide balance to the assembly. Also for rudder and elevator.
Floating (aileron)	An aileron not built into or behind a wing but stood above or below the wing on struts.
Frise (aileron)	A superior nose-balanced design of aileron common from late 1920s.
Horned (aileron)	Same meaning but alternative term to flapped. Refers to the balance area ahead of the main shape as a 'balance horn'. Same for rudder and elevator.

Inset (aileron)	A horned aileron, B&P patented, where the aileron stopped at the wing tip for span and the horn was cut into the wing ahead of the aileron pivot on the outboard edge. It remained hidden behind the forward section of wing until control movement brought it outside of the wing's shadow. Could also be used on rudder and elevator.
Incidence	Angle of. For setting wing sections or tail sections past zero. Positive incidence increases lift from the section, while an angle that is variable on a tailplane allows the aircraft to be trimmed to fly level.
Inline (engine)	An engine where there may be anything from two to twelve cylinders aligned one behind the other. The cylinders may be air cooled by flying or water cooled through a radiator. Inline engines were usually four-stroke engines. See also vee and Broad Arrow inlines.
Joukowski Transform	A method of mathematically modifying a formulae (such as here the formula for a circle) to transform it into another shape useful in aerodynamics and then plotting that new shape from the calculated co-ordinates. Typically wing sections and fuselage shapes, such as the trailing edge at a straight line to the chord of the airfoil.
Kármán–Trefftz	A more general transform where the trailing edge of the airfoil does not end at zero in a straight line to the chord. If it does then it reduces to the Joukowski transform shape.
Longeron	French origin term for the long beams forming the main shape along the fuselage.
Nose balanced	Patented ailerons where the front portion tapered down to underside of the wing ahead of the pivot point. Similar to Frise ailerons.
Optimum lift wing	Since the lift of a wing increases as a square with area but the weight of the wing structure increases as a cube it was reasoned that there must be an optimum position where the best lift could be obtained for the best structural weight and cost. The solutions seem to lie in having a long span compared to chord (width), limited by the bending strength that could be designed into the spars.
P-Span	Author's term. The true span of a machine when viewed directly from above as if the shadow of its plan was projected on to the ground.
Pusher propeller	A propeller that was behind the engine normally and pushed the aircraft forward.
Radial (engine)	An engine having the cylinders radially disposed but the body is fixed and only the crankshaft, bolted to the propeller, turns.
Rib-tapes	Reinforcing tapes doped on to the wing fabric to reinforce areas where the ribs or other items might rub the overall covering fabric away. Also commonly applied under the main fabric at stress points and sharp corners.
Rotary (engine)	An engine having the cylinders radially disposed. The crankshaft is fixed and the propeller bolted to the engine. The entire engine therefore revolves about the shaft, allowing it to be cooled by the permanent rotation when running. Rotary engines were usually two-stroke engines.
Safety factors	as with all structural engineering, having calculated the load an item has to take, the load is increased by a safety factor to reach a value to which the same item must pass tests before it is judged to be safe to use. Safety factors might be increased or decreased based upon experience. Around 1917 the factors specified on spars were eight times for the front and six times for the rear spar. So if the front spar saw a load of 1,000lb then the spar design had to be designed and sometimes also tested to 8,000lb before it was considered acceptable.
Servo Tab	A small surface used to trim an aircraft inset into the larger surface. By moving the small surface in the opposite direction to the movement required of the main surface it helps the pilot overcome the air loads and pushes the large surface in the direction required. In the case of the P.29 Sidestrand and the P.75 Overstrand a Flettner servo tab was held away from the rudder on struts. The tab moved opposite to the way that the pilot required the rudder to move and gave a mechanical advantage in reducing the loads required by the pilot to move that surface.
Sesquiplane	A biplane having a short-chord lower wing and using the upper wing for main lift.
Slit	As in wing slits. A term used by BPA for fixed slots built into the wing leading edge to control the loss of lift near the stall. Same as wing slots. Insisted upon by RAE for the P.92 fighter, their incorporation and testing in the P.92-2 proved North's assertion that they were not required in wings with the taper of the P.92.
Spar	The main beams designed into the span of the aircraft to take and transfer all the wing loads seen by the structure.
S-Span	Author's term. The published rigged span of a machine measured by tape along the tops of the upper wing spars ignoring dihedral. This 'stressed span' was slightly longer than the P-Span and was used to calculate loads on the structure.
Stagger	The amount that one wing is set ahead of the other in a biplane. Stagger can be positive or negative on the upper wing compared to the lower. If negative it is said to have backward stagger.
Tractor propeller	A propeller that is normally ahead of the engine and pulls the aircraft forward.
Vee (engine)	An inline engine with two banks of cylinders forming a 'vee'. Typically one bank is offset slightly from the other in order to get all the connecting rods on to the crankshaft. An example would be the RAF 1A used on the P.6 and P.9.
Wing Section	The cross-section shape of an airfoil used to form a lifting surface on an aeroplane, hydrofoil etc. Each section will have particular characteristics in responding to fluid flow that are unique to its shape. Royal Aircraft Factory shape numbers 14 and 15 were most popular in the First World War.

Selected Bibliography

Since this book has employed mainly original documents, letters, company and government manuals, brochures and test reports not generally available to the reader, including the author's *An Engineering History of Boulton Paul 1916–1955*, which was written in 1970–71, the following selected references may be useful for anyone wishing to expand generally on the subjects covered. The list is, of course, not intended to be exhaustive.

Baughen, Greg, *Blueprint for Victory – Britain's first World War Blitzkrieg Air force* (Fonthill, 2014)

Baughen, Greg, *The Rise of the Bomber – RAF–Army Planning 1919 to Munich 1938* (Fonthill, 2016)

Baughen, Greg, *The RAF in the Battle of France and the Battle of Britain* (Fonthill, 2016)

Baughen, Greg, *The RAF on the Offensive 1940–41* (Frontline, 2018)

Brew, Alec, *Boulton Paul Aircraft since 1915* (Putnam, 1993)

Buttler, Tony, *British Secret Projects Jet Fighters since 1950* (Crécy, 2017)

Buttler, Tony, *British Secret Projects Jet Bombers since 1949* (Crécy, 2018)

Buttler, Tony, *British Secret Projects Fighters since 1935–50* (Crécy, 2017)

Buttler, Tony, *British Secret Projects Fighters and Bombers 1935–50* (Midland, 2004)

ffiske, W. H., *Boulton Paul Ltd and the Great War* (B&P, 1919)

Halley, James J., *Royal Air Force Aircraft K1000 to K9999* (Air Britain, 1976)

Kinsey, Gordon, *Boulton Paul Aircraft* (Terence Dalton, 1992)

Lumsden, Alec, *British Piston Engines and their Aircraft* (Airlife, 1994)

Meekoms, K. J. & Morgan, Eric B., *The British Aircraft Specifications File* (Air Britain, 1994)

Mason, Francis K., *The British Fighter since 1912* (Putnam, 1992)

Mason, Francis K., *The British Bomber since 1914* (Putnam, 1994)

Mason, Tim, *British Flight Testing Martlesham Heath* (Putnam, 1993)

Robertson, Bruce, *British Military Aircraft Serials 1878–1987* (Midland, 1987)

Sinnott, Colin S., *The Royal Air Force and Aircraft Design 1923–39* (Routledge, 2014)

Thompson, D. & Sturtivant, R., *RAF Aircraft J1 to J999 and Survivors* (Air Britain, 1987)

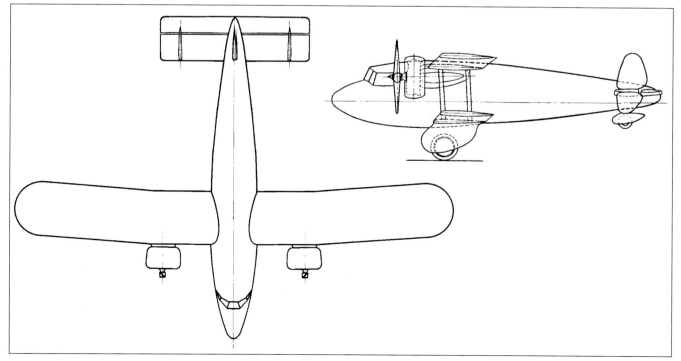

P.71A wind tunnel model tested by RAE Farnborough for the proposed modifications. The fins were of the same area but squared off like the tail-plane when built.

Index

SPECIFICATIONS
(Prefix letter omitted for Air Ministry specifications)